THE END OF
THE COLD WAR
1985-1991

Also by Robert Service

The Bolshevik Party in Revolution:
A Study in Organisational Change

Lenin: A Political Life
Volume One: The Strengths of Contradiction
Volume Two: Worlds in Collision
Volume Three: The Iron Ring

The Russian Revolution, 1900–1927

A History of Twentieth-Century Russia

Lenin: A Biography

Stalin: A Biography

Comrades: A History of World Communism

Trotsky: A Biography

Spies and Commissars: Soviet Russia and the West

THE END OF
THE COLD WAR
1985–1991

ROBERT SERVICE

PublicAffairs

New York

First published 2015 in the United Kingdom by Macmillan,
an imprint of Pan Macmillan,
a division of Macmillan Publishers Limited

Published in the United States by PublicAffairs™,
a Member of the Perseus Books Group

Printed in the United States of America.

PublicAffairs books are available at special discounts for bulk purchases in the U.S.
by corporations, institutions, and other organizations. For more information, please contact
the Special Markets Department at the Perseus Books Group, 2300 Chestnut Street, Suite
200, Philadelphia, PA 19103, call (800) 810-4145, ext. 5000,
or e-mail special.markets@perseusbooks.com.

Typeset by Ellipsis Digital Limited, Glasgow

Library of Congress Control Number: 2015942161
ISBN 978-1-61039-499-4 (HC)
ISBN 978-1-61039-500-7 (EB)

First Edition

10 9 8 7 6 5 4 3 2 1

For Oscar and Carla

CONTENTS

PART TWO

INTERMEZZO

PART THREE

List of Illustrations

Maps

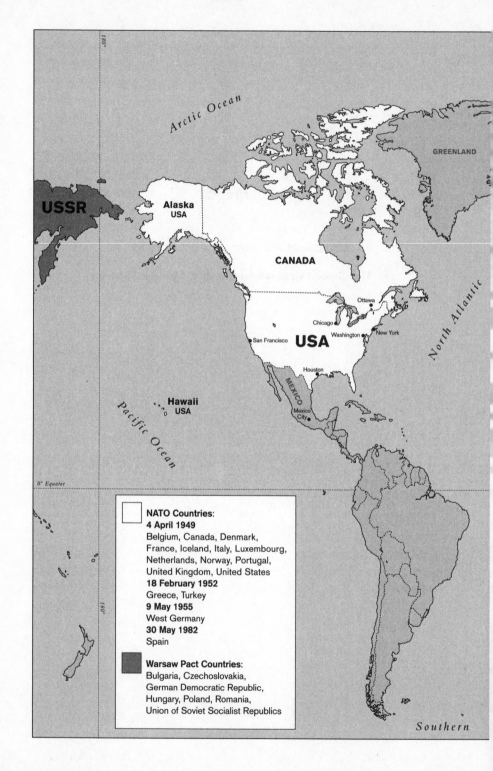

NATO Countries:
4 April 1949
Belgium, Canada, Denmark,
France, Iceland, Italy, Luxembourg,
Netherlands, Norway, Portugal,
United Kingdom, United States
18 February 1952
Greece, Turkey
9 May 1955
West Germany
30 May 1982
Spain

Warsaw Pact Countries:
Bulgaria, Czechoslovakia,
German Democratic Republic,
Hungary, Poland, Romania,
Union of Soviet Socialist Republics

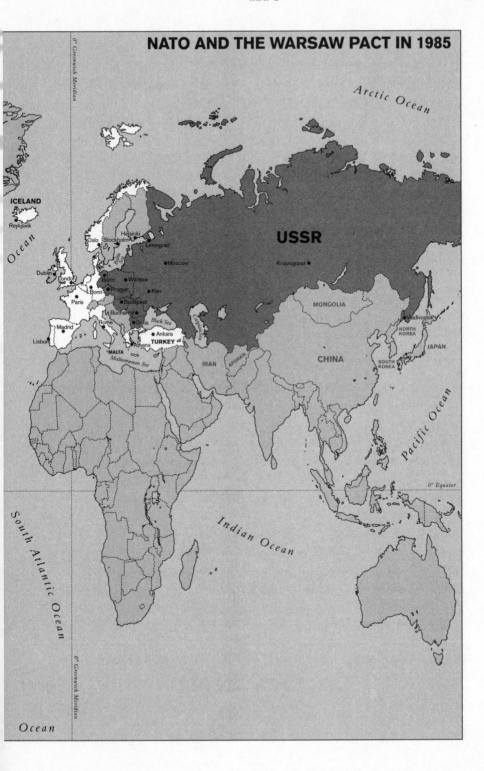

NATO AND THE WARSAW PACT IN 1985

THE SOVIET UNION AND EASTERN EUROPE 1985

500 miles

800 kilometres

SOVIET SOCIALIST REPUBLICS

Russian Soviet Federal Socialist Republic

•Sverdlovsk

Ural Mtns

•Moscow

Volga

Ural

Kazakhstan

Don

Aral
Sea

Uzbekistan

Azerbaijan

Caucasus Mtns

Caspian Sea

Sea

Sukhum•

Georgia

Tbilisi•

Azerbaijan

Baku•

Turkmenistan

Armenia

Yerevan•

Ashkhabad•

TURKEY

IRAN

IRAN

Preface

The end of the Cold War can now be explored in countless American personal papers, printed collections and online sources. Many are just beginning to be investigated. Soviet material from the Russian vaults is also plentiful even though a lot of it is accessible only in foreign libraries. Diaries and transcripts of meetings and conversations sharpen our picture of a momentous period in world politics. It has become possible, for instance, to trace exactly how Ronald Reagan's 1987 'Berlin Wall' speech underwent its successive revisions or how Soviet leaders amended their words before finalizing the Party Central Committee minutes.[1] The records have to be handled with some caution, not least because politicians filtered what they allowed to be recorded. But it is better to have more archives than fewer. The insights they afford are the foundation stone for this book.

For the Soviet side, Party Politburo minutes are found in the 'working notes' filed by the General Department of the Secretariat. Many of these notes are conserved at the Hoover Institution in its RGASPI Fond 89 and in the papers of Dmitri Volkogonov, who made copies from the Presidential Archive in the early 1990s. Furthermore, several of Gorbachëv's associates – Anatoli Chernyaev, Georgi Shakhnazarov and Vadim Medvedev – ignored the ban on keeping a record of what they witnessed. Their work has appeared in printed form, and in Chernyaev's case I have consulted his papers in the Russian Library at St Antony's College, Oxford. Also of importance is Stanford University's collection of the Party Central Committee minutes, which include successive drafts of the proceedings – and even speeches that were prepared but not delivered.

The Hoover Institution's collections on leading Soviet figures are among the most informative for the last years of the Cold War. Three are truly outstanding. Foreign Affairs Minister Eduard Shevardnadze asked his aide Teimuraz Stepanov-Mamaladze to take regular notes on his meetings and conversations. The result is an incomparable record of deliberations and decisions in Soviet foreign policy; it is a pleasure to bring them to attention for the first time.[2] Vitali Kataev of the Party Secretariat's Defence Department assiduously documented the discussions inside the Soviet leadership on arms reduction. This material is unusually helpful in elucidating the links between the politicians and the 'military-industrial complex'. Anatoli Adamishin, who headed the First European Department in the Foreign Affairs Ministry before his appointment as Deputy Foreign Affairs Minister, kept a diary through the 1980s and beyond. His observations offer an enthralling and largely unexamined source on the USSR's internal politics and international relations.

For the American side, I have consulted the holdings at the Ronald Reagan Presidential Library at Simi Valley, California. The Hoover Institution Archive also contains rich material from the Committee on the Present Danger and from the personal papers of CIA Director William J. Casey and National Security Adviser Richard V. Allen. Crucial for this account are the copious notes taken by Charles Hill during his work with Secretary of State George Shultz: I am grateful to them for allowing me to quote from this exceptional source. In addition, I found much in the National Security Archive at George Washington University, both on site and electronically. I also used the collections at the George H. W. Bush Presidential Library as well as online publications available via Freedom of Information Act requests. David Holloway at Stanford kindly shared his copies of CIA papers. Molly Worthen of the University of North Carolina at Chapel Hill did the same with some pages from Charles Hill's work diary; and I am indebted to Sir Rodric Braithwaite, UK Ambassador to the USSR and the Russian Federation in 1988–1991, for providing his diary of that period, and to Sir Roderic Lyne, who also served in the British embassy in the *perestroika* years and later became Ambassador to Russia, for his recollections of how things appeared at the time.

The Hoover Institution Archive staff have been unstinting in their assistance, and for this book I especially benefited from the advice I received from Lora Soroka, Carol Leadenham, David Jacobs and Linda Bernard. The staff in the Archives and Library have been a constant joy to work with. At the Reagan Library, Ray Wilson provided excellent guidance to its collections. At the National Security Archives, Tom Blanton and Svetlana Savranskaya pointed me in the direction of important documents in their collection. Richard Ramage at St Antony's has been helpful in looking out for books and articles in the Russian Library.

My thanks go to George Shultz for talking to me at length about his time at the State Department. I am also grateful to Charles Hill, Executive Assistant to Secretary Shultz in those years, for several informative conversations. Since it is part of my analysis that George Shultz – along with Eduard Shevardnadze – was one of the decisive enablers of the peace-making process, his oral testimony has been invaluable. I am indebted to Harry Rowen for explaining his memories and to Jack Matlock and Richard Pipes, who kindly answered queries by correspondence. On the Soviet side, I have enjoyed discussions in past years with Mikhail Gorbachëv's aides Anatoli Chernyaev and Andrei Grachëv, and former Deputy Foreign Affairs Minister Anatoli Adamishin has cheerfully answered queries about his diary and offered ideas about lines of research. Lord (Des) Browne, UK Defence Secretary in more recent years, and Steve Andreasan of the Nuclear Threat Initiative have sharpened my understanding on the lingering dangers of nuclear weapons in the world after the Cold War.

I have had frequent discussions at the Hoover Institution with Robert Conquest, Peter Robinson and Michael Bernstam. Each wrote influentially at the time of the events under scrutiny. I was helped by their willingness to explain the idiosyncrasies of the American politi-cal system and its dealings with the USSR. I would also like to thank Joerg Baberowski, Tim Garton Ash, Paul Gregory, Mark Harrison, Jonathan Haslam, Tom Hendriksen, David Holloway, Stephen Kotkin, Norman Naimark, Silvio Pons, Yuri Slezkine and Amir Weiner for discussions about the Cold War when we were together in the San Francisco Bay area. Hoover Institution Director John Raisian's support for this and other projects has been warm and consistent over many years and the financial sponsorship of the Sarah Scaife Foundation has been much appreciated.

Conversations with Roy Giles at the Russian Centre in St Antony's College have given me invaluable insights into Western military think-ing in the late 1980s. I also thank Laurien Crump for her advice on sources about the Warsaw Pact while she was a research fellow with us. I have benefited from bibliographical advice from Archie Brown, Julie Newton, Alex Pravda and Sir Adam Roberts. Richard Davy offered ideas on European security history. Over many years, Norman Davies's comments on Russia and Europe have enlivened our partnership in London and Oxford.

I have incorporated advice from colleagues who kindly agreed to read the entire final draft – David Holloway, Geoffrey Hosking, Bobo Lo and Silvio Pons. I owe them a large debt for many invaluable suggestions. The same is true of Anne Deighton, Paul Gregory, Andrew Hurrell, Sir Roderic Lyne, Melvyn Leffler and Hugo Service, who examined several chapters. My literary agent David Godwin discussed the idea for the book when I returned from California excited about the material in the Hoover Archives. His encouragement is much appreciated. At Pan Macmillan, Georgina Morley has offered constant help in sculpting the book into shape. By far and away my biggest debt is to my wife Adele, who has been through the draft twice and made innumerable suggestions for improvements. I can well imagine that some of my findings will prove controversial – it is unfeasible to write seriously on this subject without raising hackles. But the book has been a pleasure to research and write. The errors, misjudgements and infelicities that remain are my responsibility and mine alone.

Robert Service
London N16
June 2015

INTRODUCTION

Cold War was the state of neither war nor peace between America and the Soviet Union in the decades after the Second World War. Victory in 1945 over Germany and Japan had left them as the two global superpowers and their own subsequent stand-off could at any time have erupted into a 'hot' war with nuclear weapons that no one, anywhere on earth, would survive. On both sides, politicians and public alike quickly recognized the dangers of the situation. But although everyone wanted to prevent a Third World War, the US–Soviet struggle seemed interminable as ever more destructive atomic arsenals were built up.

In the contest of ideologies one corner was occupied by America, which stood for capitalism, while in the opposite corner the Soviet Union championed communism. After crushing the Third Reich, the USSR exported the Marxist-Leninist model of state and society to Eastern Europe. Revolutions quickly followed in China and elsewhere, and Joseph Stalin proclaimed that the global balance of power was tilting in favour of communism. America shored up governments in every continent that were willing to resist the spread of communist influence. The superpowers founded vast military coalitions, NATO and the Warsaw Pact. Washington denounced the Kremlin's abuse of human rights; Moscow condemned the American limits on welfare provision. They endlessly accused each other of being predatory imperialists. They financed coups and counter-coups, revolutions and counter-revolutions all over the world. They subsidized client states and sought to control them in their own interests. When forecasting the inevitable demise of the rival superpower, they predicted that all manner of evil would vanish from the earth on that joyous day.

At the same time they knew very well – and Stanley Kubrick's 1964 film *Dr Strangelove* made it vividly clear – that any small miscalculation could lead to the firing of nuclear missiles which would produce a planetary disaster. Despite every technological advance, mistakes could much too easily still occur along the chain of surveillance. The political leaders with responsibility for war and peace depended on their counter-espionage agencies and alarm systems for information about whether the other side was about to get their retaliation in first. The consequences of a false alert could be catastrophic.

America and the USSR constantly struggled with each other. In June 1950 the communists of northern Korea, with covert Soviet assistance, invaded the American-backed south of the country. America and its allies sent forces to halt their advance in a war that lasted three years. In October 1962 the superpowers teetered on the brink of world war when Soviet leader Nikita Khrushchëv began to install strategic ballistic missiles in Cuba as a challenge to American power. Khrushchëv backed down only after President John Kennedy threatened to use force to halt the process. The missile crisis shocked the rival leaderships into agreeing strategies to prevent the recurrence of such an emergency. They also negotiated about how limit the size of their nuclear weapon stockpiles. Under President Richard Nixon and General Secretary Leonid Brezhnev they moved towards a peaceful rivalry known as détente, at the same time vying for influence in what was known as the Third World. President Jimmy Carter suspended détente in December 1979 in response to the Soviet invasion of Afghanistan. After Ronald Reagan's victory in the presidential election in November 1981, the stand-off between the superpowers sharpened. In late 1983 Soviet leaders received intelligence reports that the Americans were planning a pre-emptive nuclear offensive under cover of NATO's Able Archer military exercise. The atmosphere cleared only when Washington provided assurances about its peaceful intent.

What held the two sides back from a 'hot' war, not just in the early 1980s but throughout the Cold War, was the certain knowledge that the enemy had the weapons to mount a devastating counteroffensive. Only a fool in the Kremlin or the White House could expect to emerge unscathed from any conflict involving nuclear ballistic missiles. Yet no serious attempt was made to end the Cold War. At best, the leaders strove to lessen the dangers. Their policies were conditioned by influential lobbies that promoted the interests of national defence. For decades the Soviet 'military-industrial complex' had imposed its priorities on state economic policy, and the Western economic recession that arose from the rise in the price of oil in 1973 encouraged American administrations to issue contracts for improved military technology to stimulate recovery.[1] The Cold War therefore seemed a permanent feature of global politics, and pacifists and anti-nuclear campaigners seemed entirely lacking in realism.

Things changed sharply in March 1985 when Mikhail Gorbachëv became Soviet General Secretary and formed a partnership for peace with Ronald Reagan. Not long before becoming President in January 1981, Reagan was shocked to hear that America had no defence against a nuclear attack. Wanting an end to the arms race, he called for a reduction in the stocks of atomic weapons held by both superpowers. Gorbachëv echoed his appeals to eliminate all nuclear weaponry, and the Chernobyl power station disaster of April 1986 heightened his awareness of the dangers of even civilian nuclear energy. A serious meeting of minds occurred as General Secretary and President directed their administrations towards cooperation in reducing the number of nuclear missiles held on land, at sea and in the air. As the rapprochement grew, Reagan and his successor George Bush watched with wonder as the USSR dismantled its totalitarian politics and communist ideology and permitted a growing measure of civil freedom and economic reform. As a result, in 1987–1990 alone, against every expectation, the superpowers signed agreements on intermediate-range and strategic nuclear weapons, on Afghanistan, on conventional forces and on German reunification. Anticommunist revolutions swept across Eastern Europe in 1989. Global politics would never be the same again and Bush felt safe in declaring the Cold War to be over.

How and why did the great change come about? The relationship between Moscow and Washington was acutely hazardous at the start of the 1980s, and yet by the end of the decade the USSR and America had achieved an historic reconciliation. That this happened so peacefully was a colossal achievement; the Cold War could easily have ended in catastrophe.

This is hardly a neglected topic, for the end of the Cold War has attracted a massive literature. Memoirs have poured from the pens of the leaders and their officials and there has been a flood of documentary collections, not to mention scholarly accounts. There have always been rival schools of explanation. In the eyes of Gorbachëv's admirers, a nimbus of acclaim hangs over him alone for reconciling the superpowers and giving peace a chance. This perception was widespread in East and West while he was in power and is an enduring article of belief even among some of his detractors. The General Secretary's determination and charisma are seen as the tools with which he realized his idealistic conception of politics in the USSR and around the world.[2] According to a rival school, however, it was really Reagan's anticommunist policies that dragged Gorbachëv to the negotiating table. The President is said to have achieved his purposes by the firm pursuit of American military modernization, and his Strategic Defense Initiative is regarded as the straw that broke the camel's back. He is praised for striking up a rapport with the Soviet leader without compromising his national objectives.[3]

Gorbachëv and Reagan were truly exceptional politicians working in cooperation in extraordinary times.[4] But even when Gorbachëv's contribution is recognized, the question arises as to whether he jumped or was pushed into reforming Soviet policy. And though Reagan is increasingly regarded as having achieved a decisive impact on the process, the need persists to assess the importance of his nuclear disarmament programme. In his handling of Gorbachëv, moreover, Bush by common consent was initially less nimble than his predecessor. In fairness to him, however, Bush rose to the highest office at a time of extraordinary change in Eastern Europe and else-where.[5] It makes sense to ask how it was that the leaders interacted and why they changed their minds about each other. This requires the sharing of attention equally between the superpowers. General Secretary and President in fact did nothing of importance in foreign policy without thinking about the likely response of the other, and the thread that holds together the events under scrutiny in this book is the desirability of a genuinely bilateral analysis.

American and Soviet leaders brought much pragmatism and improvisation to their dealings, and the stunning disintegration of communist order in the USSR and Eastern Europe required them to be hugely adaptive.[6] White House and Kremlin displayed this quality in abundance. Reagan, Gorbachëv and Bush coped skilfully with the unknown unknowns that arrived daily on their desks for rapid decision.

The importance of ideas also demands some fresh consideration. The Soviet reformers proclaimed their quest for a middle way between authoritarian socialism and advanced capitalism. They saw themselves as a vanguard on active service in a clash of value systems. The American administration displayed the same combative spirit when advocating principles of democratic choice and the market economy and defending what it regarded as the West's interest.[7] Crusaders fought on both sides, and Reagan and Gorbachëv were passionate about the righteousness of their campaigns. It soon became clear that

Reagan favoured a goal of denuclearization that failed to convince most of his leading officials. Gorbachëv, though, claimed to share Reagan's disarmament objectives and pressed for rapid signature of treaties. Whether or not Gorbachëv genuinely believed in the total elimination of nuclear weaponry, he acted as if he did; and as political and economic difficulties piled up in the USSR, the practical pressure on him to deepen the rapprochement with America intensified. The balance between pragmatic pressure and intellectual conviction is something that deserves examination.

It was never easy to build a durable confidence between Washington and Moscow. Such were Bush's suspicions that the first thing he did on becoming President in January 1989 was to order an exhaustive review of American foreign policy. The two leaderships continued to have much to learn about each other. The media of each superpower were consistently sceptical, if no longer aggressive, in depicting the other side. Gorbachëv has been said to have drawn his early analysis from the brighter products of Soviet research institutes.[8] But the influences on his subsequent thinking have to be examined in the light of his dismissive remarks about the briefings he received from both academics and the KGB. As regards Reagan and Bush, many of their own officials implored them to look on Gorbachëv as a trickster who was trying to coax undesirable concessions out of the Americans. Expert reports were heavy and frequent, and the task is now to establish what each President made of them and how much they relied on their personal instincts and face-to-face observations. Reagan's trust in Gorbachëv grew at the summits in Geneva, Reykjavik, Washington and Moscow in 1985–1988. Bush was Gorbachëv's friend from the Malta summit of 1989 onwards.

The leaders in Moscow and Washington had to find ways to carry their political establishments along with them. For years before the mid-1980s it had been argued that the American military-industrial complex had no interest in moves towards global peace. The heavy industry ministries and army high command in the USSR were similarly regarded as eternally attached to militarist objectives.[9]

Reagan and Bush were conscious of the scepticism among American conservatives about the agreements that they wanted to finalize with the Kremlin. Growing unease was also noticeable among Soviet communist conservatives about the concessions that Gorbachëv made to White House demands as he pursued rapprochement. Reagan succeeded in reassuring his political constituency; Gorbachëv did the same, at least until the end of the 1980s. Of the two, Gorbachëv had the tougher task, since he was all too obviously giving up to the Americans more than he appeared to gain; and whereas Reagan inherited a stable political and economic order, Gorbachëv was frantically trying to overturn decades of communist thought and practice. But why did the armaments lobbies in both countries prove to be the dogs that did not bark – or how did the leaders succeed in restoring calm when some barking took place? One part of the answer is that Reagan satisfied his military manufacturers and armed forces by boosting the contracts for research and production. But the same can scarcely be said about Gorbachëv and fellow reformers who switched the state budget away from the old priorities of defence. Leading officials in the party, KGB and Defence Ministry united against Gorbachëv in August 1991, but a question remains about why it took them so long to make their attempt.

Behind this lies another question that is seldom considered: to what extent did the Politburo understand the scale of its difficulties even before Gorbachëv became its General Secretary? Commentators have long recognized the economic pressures that were bearing down on the USSR's budget by the early 1980s.[10] Though the Politburo knew its allies in Eastern Europe to be mired in debt to Western banks, it was in no condition to bail them out or provide a path to technological regeneration. Poland was in chronic political crisis. The Soviet invasion of Afghanistan was expensive in lives and money. Moscow's support for Cuba, Vietnam, Ethiopia and guerrilla campaigns in southern Africa was a relentless drain on finances. Meanwhile the economic revolution inaugurated by the new information technology was leaving the USSR behind. Ever since the late 1940s America and its allies had imposed an embargo on selling advanced equipment with a potential for military use to the Soviet Union. They had interpreted this broadly to include many basic items of civilian industrial machinery, and the consequence was an ever wider gap in productivity. And the Politburo stayed vulnerable to international diplomatic pressure because of its human rights obligations under the terms of the Helsinki Final Act that Presidents Brezhnev and Ford had co-signed in 1975 with the leaders of Eastern Europe, Western Europe and Canada.

The USSR's difficulties by themselves do not amount to proof that the Soviet leadership recognized them for what they were. Fortunately, it is now possible to examine the Kremlin deliberations before 1985. Gorbachëv was to claim that the Politburo was unaware about the real situation in the country until he introduced his programme of reforms. Was his picture of Kremlin politics a credible one or merely a self-serving caricature? Much hangs on the answer. If he is to be believed, then he kicked down a barred door; if not, it was already half-ajar. This is an important field for enquiry, yet it does not exhaust the list of mysteries about Gorbachëv's contribution to change. The question also arises about how, once he started his reform of foreign policy, he succeeded in keeping the support of the rest of the Soviet leadership.

Of course, Gorbachëv and Reagan experienced many other demands on their time and energies. Though they are lauded for the results of their foreign policy, little attention has been paid to their management of the process. Gorbachëv's choice of Eduard Shevardnadze as his Foreign Affairs Minister has attracted inadequate attention. Shevardnadze pressed for radical options in foreign policy, and until 1989 their partnership was largely harmonious. Reagan's choice to head the State Department fell upon George Shultz, who was excited by the opportunities that presented themselves for arms reduction agreements. Whereas Shevardnadze initially enjoyed almost the entire Politburo's approval, Shultz had to struggle against several leading officials of the Reagan administration who opposed any conciliation with Moscow. Not until 1987 did Reagan definitively come down on Shultz's side against them. Shevardnadze and Shultz were imaginative planners who showed themselves indispensable as the strategic enablers of agreements on disarmament that their leaders could sign. This book will scrutinize how the statesmen whom I have called the big four – Reagan, Gorbachëv, Shultz and Shevardnadze – made their crucial collective contribution to rapprochement between America and the USSR.

It was the two superpowers that provided the crucial impetus for the process that brought the Cold War to a close. Both of them appreciated the need to carry their allies and friends along with them. In later years, West European presidents and premiers would line up to testify that they had worked consistently with the Americans to end hostilities with the USSR. Prime Minister Margaret Thatcher, President François Mitterrand, Chancellor Helmut Kohl and Foreign Affairs Minister Giulio Andreotti each claimed to have made a decisive useful contribution. (Their Canadian, Japanese and Australian counterparts showed greater modesty in their recollections.) This calls for an audit of the pile of evidence that America's NATO allies in the mid-1980s, with Thatcher to the fore, privately attacked Reagan for what they saw as his undue willingness to place his trust in the Kremlin.[11] Kohl and his Ten Points in favour of German reunification in November 1989 had a very obvious impact on events. The question arises about whether even he could have sustained his political campaign unless he knew he could count on American support. In addition, what influence is to be attributed to the pro-Gorbachëv campaigns of both the 'peace movement' and most communist and socialist parties in Western Europe?

Gorbachëv had an easier time with the Warsaw Pact than the American Presidents had with NATO. Though the East European party bosses felt disquiet about his attempt to reform the USSR, most of them endorsed his relaxation of the tension with America. They nevertheless became disorientated and confused as the communist order's difficulties grew in the 1980s.[12] But they did not leave power voluntarily, and the pivotal factor in their fall was the bravery of the activists and crowds who took to the streets. Gorbachëv refused to sanction armed intervention to save communism. Few would deny that his policy of encouraging people to stand up for their rights contributed to the revolutions that overwhelmed the old leaderships. But it is still left to ask why the events of the year 1989 caught him so much by surprise – and to examine the impact they had on the situation in Lithuania and other Baltic Soviet republics.[13] Indeed, his entire global strategy continues to raise questions. No one can doubt the importance of Soviet leaders' decision to abandon almost all the USSR's toeholds in the Third World despite their continuing objection to American global pretensions.[14] But they still call for further investigation. World politics changed at astonishing pace, and each big or little shift affected all the others. And almost without anyone noticing it, the Soviet Union lost its superpower status.

The Cold War's end was no pre-ordained process, but most accounts do at least agree that it was possible at any time for America and the USSR to relapse into their older postures of confrontation. Reagan, had he so decided, could have refused to deal constructively with the USSR. As an American conservative he had plenty of room for complaint about Soviet policies. Gorbachëv himself could have decided to halt or reverse his reforms. Many of those who had supported his appointment as General Secretary wanted him to do exactly this – and eventually his own leading appointees turned on him in the August 1991 coup. Enough of the communist system survived to have made this a practicable alternative. Gorbachëv, propped up by fellow reformers and prodded forward by Reagan and Bush, chose to travel in the opposite direction – and, step by step, the Cold War came to a peaceful end.

America won its struggle with the USSR, which fell into the ash-heap of history. Gorbachëv contended that the Soviet reformers were also victors since they had actively promoted conciliation between the superpowers and political democratization in the Soviet Union. Here a riddle awaits its answer. The American leadership made no attempt to disguise how it continued to pressurize the Kremlin. Reagan and Bush stipulated that if the USSR desired a rapprochement with America, it would not be enough to get out of Afghanistan and slacken the grip on Eastern Europe: Gorbachëv would also have to change the way that he treated his own people. The Americans made demands about radio jamming, exit visas, Baltic freedom, political prisoners and defamatory propaganda. The pressures were relentless before 1985 and lasted through all the years while Gorbachëv was in power.[15] But as the USSR's economic woes deepened from 1989, Gorbachëv found it ever harder to say no to Washington. What has yet to be established is how much of his willingness to compromise resulted from the stress applied by the Americans and how much from the Soviet economy's current and long-term troubles.

This agenda for enquiry encompasses one of the cardinal episodes of recent world history. Time was when accounts of the closing years of the Cold War depended overwhelmingly on reminiscences by leaders and officials. From the Washington and Moscow vaults there subsequently emerged documentary collections that threw light on decisions at the highest level. Now it is possible to go to the archives and examine the original records of what Reagan, Gorbachëv and Bush said and wrote at the time. Copious holdings exist, scattered across Russia, the rest of Europe and America as well as on the World Wide Web. These are extraordinary enough in themselves. But there are also exceptional sources in the unpublished diaries and papers of Soviet and Western officials who were close to the seats of supreme power – those of Anatoli Adamishin, Rodric Braithwaite, Anatoli Chernyaev, Charles Hill, Vitali Kataev, Jack Matlock and Teimuraz Stepanov-Mamaladze. The personal records that they kept at the time give an unmatched sense of the exciting, important events they were witnessing.

The final justification for yet another account of the end of the Cold War is the idea of giving equal attention to the Soviet Union and America and their interaction in a churning world of transformation, a transformation that encompassed politics, economics, individual choice, institutional opportunity, ideology, cognitive growth and geopolitical challenge. The Cold War could so easily have had a different outcome, with baleful consequences for all of us. But things turned out as they did, and overwhelmingly for the better. What follows is the story of how and why Washington and Moscow achieved their improbable peace.

PART ONE

1. RONALD REAGAN

The man who entered the White House as US President on 20 January 1981 inspired anxiety in many people around the world. Ronald Wilson Reagan had the reputation of a Red-baiter. Few people thought highly of his intellect, and many attributed his success against the incumbent Jimmy Carter in the election of the previous November more to unease about recent foreign policy than to any confidence in Reagan as a competent leader.

As a former Hollywood actor, he had the reputation of having been born in a lucky shirt in 1911. In fact he experienced an unsettling childhood in Illinois because his salesman father was an habitual drunk. His mother, a devout follower of the Disciples of Christ, steadied the family. At school Ronald was outstanding at acting, sport and storytelling and had a holiday job as a lifeguard. He went on to Eureka College, where he majored in economics and sociology before finding work as a radio announcer. After taking a screen test with Warner Brothers in California he became a movie actor, and though he never belonged to the handful of global stars, he did play alongside Humphrey Bogart and Errol Flynn. He married the film actor Jane Wyman in 1940 and they started a family. Conscripted into the armed forces in the Second World War, he continued to make films in the First Motion Picture Unit and in 1947 became President of the Screen Actors Guild. Jane Wyman divorced him in 1949 and three years later he married Nancy Davis, who was also a film actor. As his film roles became fewer, he worked for General Electric as the host of its weekly drama show. His second marriage became the rock of his personal life. Reagan hated being away from Nancy even for a short time and constantly discussed public affairs with her.

As a young man he had voted for F. D. Roosevelt and the Democratic Party, but steadily his politics shifted away from the Democrats and it was as a Republican that he won election as California's Governor in 1966. He unsuccessfully sought his new party's nomination as its presidential candidate in 1968. He lost again in 1976, to the incumbent Gerald Ford, but was an undeniable force on the American political right. He had no serious Republican rival in 1980 and proceeded to sweep aside the incumbent Jimmy Carter in the November election.

From Truman to Carter, the assumption since the end of the Second World War had been that the West should only try to contain the USSR; no US President had ever truly endeavoured to reverse the expansion of Soviet influence around the world. Ronald Wilson Reagan was determined to change things. He saw America as a country that had lost faith in itself after the debacle of the Vietnam war. He planned to increase the American military budget and put the USSR's finances under the strain of an arms race. He would challenge the Kremlin throughout the world. He intended to denounce communism in all its manifestations, and the Soviet invasion of Afghanistan in December 1979 appeared in every one of his speeches as proof that the USSR was an expansionist power. He wanted America to stand up for its values and protect its interests. As President he meant to pull NATO and other allies and friendly powers along with him. His values were those of an American conservative. A Christian believer, he sprinkled his speeches with references to God. He saw his religious faith as integral to his confidence in America, personal freedom and the market economy.

In Soviet official circles he was an object of instant fear and loathing. He was known as a Cold Warrior, and the central communist newspaper *Pravda* routinely denounced him as a warmonger. Moscow's commentators had been no gentler on Jimmy Carter. Stunned by Carter's reaction to the invasion of Afghanistan, they had professed indifference to the struggle for the presidency between Carter and Reagan. Soviet media routinely described both candidates as 'anti-Soviet'.

In Washington Soviet Ambassador Anatoli Dobrynin, who had headed the embassy since 1962, assured his Kremlin masters that he was doing everything to alert the Reagan administration to the current dangers to world peace. He drew attention to the propaganda of Gus Hall and the Communist Party of the USA.[1] He boasted about the embassy's celebration of the 110th anniversary of the birth of Lenin. Dobrynin in reality knew that Hall counted for little in American politics and that most Americans had negligible interest in Lenin. He was merely reporting what was expected of him. Realism had yet to enter the official reports to the Politburo. Politburo member Andrei Gromyko had been Soviet Ambassador in Washington and New York from 1943 to 1948, and with his long experience of America might have tried to break the cycle of Soviet official ignorance. He had no such desire. His outlook was shaped by the same ideological mould. Every leading politician in Moscow took it for granted that Reagan would follow a 'reactionary' and 'imperialist' line of policy. Soviet spokesmen suggested that an incompetent and reckless man was in occupation at the White House. The fact that US Democrats and even some Republicans agreed with this analysis strengthened this feeling in the Soviet Union.

Reagan disliked the idea of meeting any Soviet General Secretary until such time that he could be sure that a summit might produce results in line with his objectives. When Brezhnev died in November 1982, Reagan signed the book of condolences at the Soviet embassy in Washington. But he refused to go to the funeral. Reagan's Secretary of State George Shultz thought this a mistake, but the President held his ground.[2]

Close associates alone knew how genuinely he treasured the objective of making the threat of thermonuclear war a thing of the past.[3] He had begun to make this clear at a briefing session that Jimmy Carter had arranged for him in 1979. Whenever he spoke about the Cold War, Reagan brushed aside calls for arms limitation: he demanded arms reduction.[4] Indeed, he wanted to abolish all nuclear weapons. He wrote later about the awesome power of his office:

> As President, I carried no wallet, no money, no driver's license, no keys in my pocket – only secret codes that were capable of bringing about the annihilation of much of the world as we knew it.
>
> On inauguration day, after being briefed a few days earlier on what I was to do if ever it became necessary to unleash American nuclear weapons, I'd taken over the greatest responsibility of my life – of any human being's life.[5]

He wanted a stronger America. But while being determined to finance an expansion of American military power, he was committed to averting Armageddon.

When campaigning for the presidency, he paid a trip to the nuclear weapons bunker at Cheyenne Mountain in Colorado. Like most of his fellow citizens, he had assumed that the Americans had a reliable system against attack by Soviet missiles. His technical advisers

– Richard Allen, Fred Iklé and William Van Cleave – had always known otherwise. Their words failed to hit home until Reagan made his own enquiries.[6] He learned to his horror that America could not prevent a nuclear 'first strike'. The Americans could only retaliate – which would mean that they would blow Moscow to bits: this was the logic of 'mutually assured destruction'. The problem was that the entire planet would suffer from blast, fire, radiation and smoke that would kill hundreds of millions of people, perhaps billions. America too would be devastated, and Reagan found little consolation in the thought that the Russians would suffer an equal calamity. At the start of the First World War, British Foreign Secretary Earl Grey had commented that the lights were going out all over Europe. Reagan foresaw total global darkness if ever a Third World War broke out. He felt in his bones that he had to try to do something – something drastic – to make such a conflict impossible.

He had to prove his credentials as a competent leader. Already sixty-nine when he stepped into the White House as President, he needed to show that he was not too old for the job. Though he had a hearing aid, he was otherwise in good shape.[7] He loved the open air and enjoyed horse-riding and chopping and sawing the wood on his Californian estate. Once when White House staff were cutting timber on the South Lawn, he told Kenneth Adelman: 'Just wish I was doing what those fellows are doing instead of going to all these stupid meetings hours at a time.' Adelman noted that while many forest rangers had yearned to be President, Reagan was the only President who was dying to become a forest ranger.[8] His career as an actor had made him familiar to the public but also confirmed a prejudice that he lacked the mental rigour needed by a President. He himself had an aversion to being thought very intellectual – or indeed intellectual at all. He dispensed folksy charm and liked to appear an ordinary guy. If ever disagreements became intense, he dispelled them with one of his many Irish jokes. He spoke simply and avoided long words.

The people around him knew the reality to be different from the image. Milton Friedman, founder of the Chicago school of economics, enjoyed his company and conversation.[9] His spokesman Mike Deaver recalled that Reagan, when beyond the public gaze, was an eager reader of serious books on 'foreign policy, economics, social issues'.[10] Pete Hannaford, an adviser, was in no doubt about Reagan's studiousness before he became President after seeing him devour the *National Review*, the *American Spectator* and *Human Events*. As President he kept up his reading and grew to like the Cold War novels of Tom Clancy, whose *Hunt for Red October* he stayed up all night to finish. He also admired the poetry of dissident Soviet poet Irina Ratushinskaya, whose work he got to know when a British cleric sent him a copy; and he read the memoirs of the defecting Soviet Ambassador Arkadi Shevchenko.[11] But Reagan protected his image of bluff, ordinary man. Some associates felt that he found it easiest to understand complex matters by talking them over with experts rather than by private study.[12] Reagan retained a respect for Nixon after his resignation from the presidency in 1974 when the press exposed his lies about the break-in at the headquarters of the Democratic Party. As fellow right-wingers on the American political spectrum, they frequently corresponded whenever Reagan wanted to try out ideas before presenting them to his associates.[13]

Reagan talked to Arthur Hartman, the American Ambassador in Moscow, who confirmed his intuition that the Soviet economy was in a mess and that the Russian people were sceptical about the communist authorities and their ideas.[14] He corresponded with the British anticommunist campaigning journalist Brian Crozier.[15] Word spread that Reagan was ignoring the advice of informed Sovietologists. He was indeed cutting against the grain of American political science. A *Washington Post* editorial implied that this was proof of his wrong-headedness. Robert Conquest disagreed, quoting Gromyko on the 'world revolutionary process' and ridiculing those Western 'experts' who postulated that the USSR had a 'pluralist' political system.[16] National Security Adviser Richard Allen forwarded a copy of Conquest's letter to the *Post*.[17] Conquest had got to know Reagan in the Carter years and was impressed by his eagerness to ask questions about the USSR and listen to the answers.[18] Reagan was genuinely trying to understand the superpower across the Atlantic. Although he had his fixed general bias, he always wanted to know more.

He worked diligently on his prose. While conceding that his adviser Pete Hannaford had greater flair for newspaper articles, he could fairly claim that he could 'write the spoken word better'.[19] He drafted quickly and then spent hours on refining speeches that gave scope for his actor's skills in front of a microphone.[20] With his Hollywood experience, he required little time to decide how to deliver them.[21] He knew how to pace himself through the day but his penchant for afternoon naps caught the attention of comedians and satirists, who charged him with indolence. His hair colour also attracted comment as, unlike most other men in their seventies, he had gone neither bald nor grey, which led to speculation that he dyed his hair. Mike Beaver, his spokesman, claimed that it was Brylcreem that gave him the dark gloss.[22]

There was an underestimation of Reagan's ultimate purposes even at high levels in his own administration. National Security Adviser Richard Allen sought to rectify the situation by spreading the word that the President was serious about making nuclear war impossible.[23] Reagan had been talking about 'defensive concepts' since 1973. Hating the idea of mutually assured destruction, he searched for a way of protecting America from the threat of nuclear holocaust. Among those who knew his thoughts were theoretical physicist Edward Teller and President Nixon's Office of Management and Budget Director Caspar Weinberger, and after entering the White House he continued to talk about possibilities with them as well as with Ed Meese, Martin Anderson and Richard Allen.[24] Meese held some exploratory meetings, and Reagan in early 1982 instructed the National Security Council staff to explore ways of moving beyond traditional defence strategy. Teller encouraged this, as the President recounted in his diary: 'He's pushing an exciting idea that nuclear weapons can be used in connection with Lasers to be non-destructive except as used to intercept and destroy enemy missiles far above the earth.'[25] Support immediately followed from the Joint Chiefs of Staff.[26]

Reagan, however, continued to baffle his entourage even though no one yet doubted his conservative political credentials. He kept a psychological distance from other people; he always seemed to hold something back in his dealings with them. William F. Buckley Jr, who was close to him, still felt that 'the friendship was always 90% ideological'.[27]

If officials had difficulties in understanding Reagan, the confusion was still greater outside the administration. In his own eyes, he had a straightforward political approach and told George Shultz: 'I think I'm hard-line & will never appease but I do want to try and let them see there is a better world if they'll show *by deed* they want to get along with the free world.'[28] The problem was that he had jangled the tambourine of his anticommunism so noisily. Time and time again he declared that the Soviet Union had overtaken the Americans in military capacity. Allegedly, Brezhnev's claim to have merely achieved 'parity' was a smokescreen to disguise the massive build-up of the USSR's offensive capacity. The President used a language of hatred for everything about the USSR. He never missed a chance to stress his detestation of Leninist doctrines and practices. Coupled to this was a commitment to an increase in America's financial expenditure on the development and production of military equipment, and he urged the American Congress to support him in enabling America to gain a decisive superiority for its armed forces. He appointed people to his administration who were eager 'hawks' in the Western debate about the 'Soviet threat'. Most people saw and heard only this side of Reagan and were deaf to his genuine basic desire to make a Third World War impossible.

The President's early measures appeared to corroborate this analysis as he approved a sharp rise in US military expenditure. Believing that America had fallen behind in the arms race, he sanctioned an increase in the size of the nuclear arsenal. He allocated resources for research on new kinds of weaponry. He promoted 'strategic modernization'. He wanted the Americans to outmatch the Soviets in their lethal capacity. After the economic recession caused by the Saudi-led hike in the oil price on world markets in 1973, American administrations under Ford and Carter had approved programmes for the development of new weaponry for land, sea and air. They did this to a large extent out of a desire to assist industrial regeneration. Reagan in his electoral campaign had drawn on the support of manufacturing corporations that desired an expansion of contracts for development and production of what the armed forces were demanding. He needed no persuasion to fulfil his promise.[29]

His presidency nearly came to an abrupt end on March 1981, two months after inauguration, when John Hinckley shot and wounded him outside the Washington Hilton hotel. Rushed to hospital, he came dangerously close to death. He impressed everyone by his stoicism: as he was being wheeled into the operating theatre, he rang his wife Nancy and said: 'Honey, I forgot to duck.'[30] Though he had won the election by a massive majority, opinion polls revealed a large residual suspicion about him. The assassination attempt and his plucky reaction helped to improve his ratings. He himself reflected on how he wanted to handle things when he returned to the White House and fulfil his ambition to lessen the dangers of a world war. He in no way dropped his ambition for military modernization, but he intended to implement moves towards a diminution of tension with the USSR. The thought occurred to him that he had nearly died before seeing whether the Politburo was agreeable to serious talks. He wanted to make a definite overture in unambiguous language. He had no definite design, only a desire to make the attempt.

Writing a personal letter to Brezhnev from his sickbed, Reagan proposed a joint effort at making peace in the world. The draft was passed around officials in Moscow for comment, and everyone was struck by the emotional tone. But was it sincere? The Politburo decided that it was yet another move in Washington's propaganda game. When an aide advised Politburo deputy member Mikhail Solomentsev, he snapped: 'This is all nonsense. It's demagogy. Can you really not see that he's engaged in demagogy and just wants to deceive us?'[31] Reagan pleaded for the release of Anatoli Shcharanski from his labour camp. He promised that he would encourage no publicity about such an outcome; he also indicated that it would facilitate the possibility of resuming arms talks with the USSR.[32] Next day, he repealed the Carter embargo on grain sales. He was fulfilling an electoral pledge made to farmers in the American Midwest in order to secure their support in the 1980 presidential campaign. He argued the wheat export ban had never been an effective way to alter the behaviour of Kremlin politicians – he added that the recent easing of Soviet pressure on Poland had aided his decision. At the same time he warned the leadership in Moscow that he would 'react strongly to acts of aggression wherever they take place'. If Poland were invaded, the consequences would be dire.[33]

On 18 November 1981 Reagan sought to demonstrate his sincerity by announcing the objective of ridding the entire European continent of intermediate-range nuclear missiles. This became known as the 'zero option'. The President proposed to withdraw and destroy America's Pershing-2 ballistic missiles as well as the ground-launched cruise missiles in exchange for the USSR agreeing to do the same with its own intermediate-range arsenal.[34] Previously the two superpowers had relied on intercontinental (or 'strategic') weapons. The Americans installed the new rockets in reaction to the Soviet decision to put its SS-20 nuclear missiles in Eastern Europe. The result had been a drastic shortening of the time available for a decision on war in the event that one side suddenly started an offensive. European security, already perilous, was rendered still more so. Within a few minutes of being fired, a Soviet missile could hit any West European capital and an American one could strike Moscow.

He had little confidence that the Brezhnev administration would respond in a helpful spirit. The British and French weaponry was excluded from his proposal, and it was never likely that the Politburo would agree to a military settlement that left the USSR vulnerable to attack from Western Europe. No leader in the Kremlin was known to favour a drastic reduction in any category of armaments.[35] The so-called '1941 syndrome' had pervaded the thinking of politicians and commanders since Hitler's invasion of the Soviet Union had caught Stalin napping. Subsequent generations of leaders were determined to avoid any course of action that might expose the USSR to a sudden military onslaught. Priority was given to insuperable defence; it was impregnated into everyone's thinking. The Politburo and the General Staff were at one in assuming that a large stockpile of every category of up-to-date weaponry was essential to the USSR's security; indeed, nobody in the Kremlin trusted Reagan and everyone suspected that the 'zero option' was mere propaganda designed to hoodwink world opinion.

The coolness between Moscow and Washington turned to ice on 13 December 1981 when General Wojciech Jaruzelski, the Polish Prime Minister, announced the introduction of martial law. Poland's communist rule had been challenged since August 1980 by an unofficial trade union, Solidarity, led by the electrician Lech Wałęsa. Strikes and demonstrations started in the Lenin Shipyards in the northern port of Gdańsk. This working-class movement quickly gained national popularity and attracted cooperation from anticommunist intellectuals. For months there had seemed to be a possibility that Brezhnev would send in the Soviet Army as an occupation force. Jaruzelski's action spared him any such need. It also ruined any serious chance of movement towards conciliation between America and the USSR. Reagan held an emergency National Security Council meeting. The news was all bad, as he hurriedly recorded in his diary: 'Our intelligence is that it was engineered & ordered by the Soviet. If so, and I believe it is, the situation is really grave. One thing certain – they won't get that $100 mil. worth of corn.' The CIA did not yet know the exact influence that Brezhnev and his Politburo had exerted, but the whole administration was determined to make the Soviet leaders pay a heavy price for the events. Reagan liaised with Pope John Paul II and the Vatican Secretary of State Cardinal Casaroli; he concluded that Jaruzelski's moves must have been months in the planning.[36]

The President's ideas for dealing with the USSR gained some clarity in National Security Decision Directive no. 75, which he signed in January 1983. Decades of foreign policy were consigned to history.

Reagan would face down the USSR. He wanted 'to contain and over time reverse Soviet expansionism'. At the same time he intended to 'promote, within the narrow limits available to us, the process of change in the Soviet Union towards a more pluralistic political and economic system'. Though he wanted negotiations with Moscow, this would only occur on the basis of 'strict reciprocity and mutual interest'. He aimed to make it understood in Moscow that 'unacceptable behavior will incur costs that would outweigh any gains'.[37] America would modernize its armed forces. It was essential to sustain a growth in defence expenditure over a lengthy period. The American administration would avoid measures that might unduly ease the USSR's economic difficulties. Although Washington would lift the embargo on wheat exports, the list of prohibited industrial goods was to be lengthened. Reagan set his face against the transfer of any technology that had a potential for military use.[38]

American policy should be to seize the initiative: 'There are a number of important weaknesses and vulnerabilities within the Soviet Empire which the American should exploit.' The directive envisaged the 'empire' as involving Eastern Europe, Afghanistan and Cuba. America should discriminate in favour of any East European countries that rejected Moscow's control of their foreign policy or were undertaking some internal liberalization. On Afghanistan, the Americans should aim at maximizing the cost to the USSR and bringing about a military withdrawal. There should be assistance for efforts in Latin America, the Caribbean and southern Africa to remove the Cuban interventionist forces.[39] Communist China and Yugoslavia had spoken out against Soviet expansionism so America should continue to sell military equipment to China and increase financial credits to Yugoslavia.[40] No 'rapid breakthrough in bilateral relations with the Soviet Union' was likely as this could add to calls on the administration to adopt a less assertive posture: 'It is therefore essential that the American people understand and support US policy.' The West needed to reach a consensus on how to act together. Reagan wanted to show that he desired a 'stable and constructive long-term basis for US–Soviet relations' and not an 'open-ended, sterile confrontation with Moscow'.[41]

Reagan kept his options open. If Soviet international behaviour were to worsen, perhaps by an invasion of Poland, 'we would need to consider extreme measures'.[42] This was not exactly a grand strategy for the dismantling of communism in the USSR.[43] He set down guidelines that sometimes criss-crossed with each other. He wished to challenge the global power and pretension of the USSR; but he also sought peace in the world. He ignored the prospective difficulties. He wanted his presidency to make a decisive impact.

2. PLANS FOR ARMAGEDDON

Soviet military doctrine held that the USSR could win a nuclear war with America. There was no secret about this. Chief of the General Staff Nikolai Ogarkov, no less, wrote in one of his booklets:

> Soviet military strategy proceeds from the viewpoint that if the Soviet Union should be thrust into a nuclear war, the Soviet people and their armed forces need to be prepared for the most severe and protracted trial. The Soviet Union and the fraternal socialist states in this case, compared with the imperialist states, will be in possession of definite advantages: the established just goals of the war and the advanced character of their social and state systems. This creates for them the objective possibility of achieving victory.[1]

As leader of the Warsaw Pact, the USSR advocated communism and proclaimed its spread to be inevitable. It offered assistance to allied states which accepted its primacy in the 'world communist movement' and to forces and parties that were engaged in an 'anti-imperialist struggle'. It depicted America as militarist and imperialist in intention and practice. At the same time it professed a commitment to peace and suggested that the worldwide growth in Soviet armed power and political influence rendered world war less likely. But Ogarkov repeated that if such a war were to start, the USSR had the capacity to emerge as the victor.

Whereas in public he endorsed the idea of a winnable campaign and prepared for a 'limited' nuclear conflict, he privately rejected all this as gravely unrealistic. He concluded that the USSR had no choice but to ready itself for an all-out war with America. His deputy, Sergei Akhromeev, disagreed and wanted to prepare for a less than total conflict – he conducted a study of how Moscow might use its SS-20 missiles in an emergency. Politburo member and Defence Minister Dmitri Ustinov, who had served Stalin himself as People's Commissar of Armaments, had grown unaccustomed to people who disagreed with his opinions. He understandably preferred to discuss strategy with Akhromeev than with Ogarkov.[2] Although Akhromeev kept Ogarkov abreast of these conversations, acute tension prevailed between Ogarkov and Ustinov.[3]

Ogarkov and Akhromeev agreed that any kind of nuclear war would be disastrous. Throughout the 1970s, Cuban leader Fidel Castro had urged Soviet leaders to take a sterner approach to the Americans. He called on Moscow to prepare for a pre-emptive direct strike on America. The General Staff countered his arguments by highlighting the devastating ecological consequences of nuclear radiation for his small island. Castro reluctantly quietened down.[4] But relations between Ogarkov and Ustinov continued to deteriorate, and in September 1984 Ustinov got the Politburo to shunt Ogarkov into retirement and promote Akhromeev to Chief of the General Staff. Akhromeev immediately took a basic decision of exceptional importance. Soviet military technologists were designing the Dead Hand system, which would enable the automatic launching of Soviet intercontinental missiles if America were to start a war and kill the USSR's political and army leaders. The sensory detectors were designed to react to light, to seismic movement and to radiation. When Oleg Baklanov in the Party Defence Department endorsed the project, Akhromeev stepped in and overruled it: he felt horror at the idea of eliminating the subjective need for command and exposing the country and the world to the danger that a war might start because an electronic device had malfunctioned. The Dead Hand trigger mechanism 'was never fully realized'.[5]

NATO in the early 1980s planned on the basis that the Warsaw Pact 'could field at least ninety divisions' in Europe, including 13,000 tanks – mainly T-64s and T-62s.[6] This gave the USSR and its allies a vast quantitative superiority, and the Supreme Allied Commander Bernard Rogers admitted in confidence that his forces would be able to conduct a successful defence with conventional weapons for only a very brief period.[7] The NATO armies facing the Warsaw Pact had ammunition for only thirty days. To compensate for this, the idea was that new supplies would be ordered from a dozen big munitions factories in America, and Rogers was aware that production and transport would take time.[8] On both sides there were commanders who could see the implausibility of the schemes that were put in place. Little or no attention was given to the difficulties of moving across territory that had suffered devastation. Refugees would be streaming every-where. The weather could be snowy in the winter and wet and muddy in the autumn and spring. Rapid transportation would quickly become impossible.[9] What made things worse in any likely emergency was the time that would be needed for NATO to consult its member countries before going to war.

The caveat has to be entered that a lot of the Eastern equipment was of poorer quality than the Western. Quantity was not everything, and a confidential report by the West German Defence Ministry to this effect became public knowledge in 1983.[10] NATO technical intelli-gence was directed at assessing the designs and capabilities of arms, counting the number of troops and tracking their geographical move-ment. The high command understandably hoped to avoid being caught unawares. The concern was that the Soviet General Secretary might take it into his head – or be persuaded – to launch a sudden offensive. While much was discovered about the Warsaw Pact's dispo-sitions, even the West German report underestimated the weaknesses in the Soviet Army's readiness. Back in the USSR, as the General Staff was painfully aware, large parts of its garrisons lacked the basic neces-sary equipment. Despite the vast funds dedicated to the armed forces, they were never enough to satisfy the demands of contemporary con-ventional warfare. The commanders also revealed that they had an insufficient number of trained soldiers.[11]

In such circumstances it was almost certain that both sides would quickly resort to using their nuclear weapons. This was as true for NATO as for the Warsaw Pact. West German General Leopold Chalupa put it bluntly: the Western powers had an inferior quantity of conventional forces and no biological weapons; the military command would inevitably request the deployment of the missiles that were under American control.[12] The balance of military power was stabi-lized in a dangerous fashion in the mid-1970s when both sides installed intermediate-range rockets in Europe. The USSR had started the process by deploying its SS-20 missiles. Even when based on Soviet territory, they could reach Western Europe within minutes. The Amer-icans responded by persuading their allies to accept Pershing-2 missiles as a desirable deterrent. Britain and West Germany permitted their introduction on local American bases. The CIA's William Odom told National Security Adviser Brzezinski that it would make better sense to put them in more distant places such as Portugal or the Shet-land Islands.[13] There was some fatalism about the decisions in Moscow and Washington. It was as if the politicians found that once the weapons were being produced, it was hard to stop them from being deployed regardless of the probable reaction by the other side.[14]

Soviet political leaders had been numbed by the discovery of what their budgetary allocations were supporting. Brezhnev and government premier Alexei Kosygin attended a Soviet military exercise together in 1972 and learned about the probable consequences of an American nuclear first strike against the USSR. The General Staff's assumption was that the armed forces would have to operate at a thousandth of their peacetime strength. Eighty million citizens would have perished. The Soviet Union would retain only fifteen per cent of its industrial capacity. Its European territory would become contaminated by a devastating level of radiation. When the Soviet intercontinental missiles retaliated, the prediction was that America would suffer an attack of even greater proportions. The apparatus for launching these missiles was passed to Brezhnev as guest of honour. Although he knew that they had only dummy warheads, he blenched at the idea of pressing the button. His hands shook and he repeatedly sought Marshal Andrei Grechko's assurance that the procedure was entirely safe: 'Andrei Antonovich, are you sure this is just an exercise?'[15]

Brezhnev's reaction so worried the General Staff that it took to briefing Politburo leaders in soft language that would minimize any distress to them.[16] For their part, the politicians disliked to pry. They did not want to hear about anything too upsetting.

According to Colonel General Andrian Danilevich, the whole Politburo from Brezhnev to Gorbachëv left the General Staff to draw up its practical schemes without interference: 'They never really asked what we were doing.' The result was that politicians had little idea about the schemes available for activation in an emergency.[17] Even Defence Minister Ustinov had no better than a sketchy acquaintance with the likely level of destruction.[18] Apart from anything else, Soviet leaders wanted to avoid agitating their citizens about the ghastly consequences of war. The public debate was heavily controlled by the party leadership. It was confined to generalities about 'the destruction of civilization'. No comment appeared on the projections about casualty numbers or urban targets. Nothing was published or even written about post-war health care, food supply, agriculture or transport for the general population; but secret arrangements were put in hand to look after the country's elite. By the mid-1980s, according to confidential CIA reports, Soviet planning had established 1,500 shelter facilities for leaders at the central and regional levels. Underground facilities existed at Sharapovo and Chekhov for the supreme leadership.[19]

The USSR's General Staff and high command kept secret a report from the Main Intelligence Administration (GRU) that wartime contamination of the environment would be a planetary catastrophe. Warsaw Pact countries would suffer devastating damage regardless of the harm they wreaked upon America and Western Europe. The information was so disturbing that it was thought prudent to withhold it from most generals. The priority was to hold on to their confidence. The Pact's commander-in-chief, Marshal Kulikov, threatened to force the chief researcher, Lieutenant Colonel Vitali Tsygichko, into retirement unless he agreed to soften his findings. Although Tsygichko stood his ground, he had no authority to compel the dissemination of his work. He concluded that the high command recoiled from the challenge to revise conventional doctrine and shuddered at the possibility of a reduced budget for the armed forces. They imposed a rigid conservatism. In arranging military exercises, they insisted on the assumption that the Pact's armies would deftly circumvent balloon-shaped areas of nuclear radiation. This was pie-in-the-sky thinking as commanders trained the armed forces, from top to bottom, to be ready to 'attack to the thunder of nuclear strikes'.[20]

The Warsaw Pact's plans detailed only the initial operations in any war with NATO. According to Jaruzelski, the defence of East Germany received much attention. Allowance was made that if NATO started an offensive, their conventional forces might succeed in advancing forty miles. This might take three or four days, and Polish forces were expected to join the Soviet Army in halting the attack. It was not excluded that NATO might start simultaneous operations further south, perhaps starting from Greece or through the Caucasus. The Warsaw Pact counter-planned for its armies to fight their way to the Rhine. The campaign was expected to take ten to fifteen days. Resistance would crumble. The tanks of the Soviet Army and its allies would push back and defeat the invader. Jaruzelski saw that such a war would inevitably lead to the use of more than conventional weaponry. He was always sceptical about what he heard from the USSR's high command: 'When we thought about this, it occurred to us even at that time that this was not realistic! NATO would certainly use its nuclear weapons, and then we would use ours. The prediction was for several hundred nuclear explosions in this limited area. It was absurd!'[21]

General Tadeusz Pióro of the Polish army shared this assessment;

he described military preparations in the Warsaw Pact as 'science fiction'.[22] Every sensible commander could see that disaster was built into the war plans. But whereas Jaruzelski pushed these plans to the back of his mind while cooperating with the USSR, General Tadeusz Tuczapski felt that an alternative had to be found to preserve the Polish nation. He knew that even a small number of nuclear explosions would wipe out human life in Poland.

After much thought he proposed a demographic precaution that was nothing if not bizarre:

> One time at a training briefing in the General Staff, I was angry and could not hold back since there was money there that was returned to the government. I stood up and told Jaruzelski, 'General, more should be given to Civil Defence so that we could build a good, solid bunker. Lock up in that bunker a hundred Polish men – some really good fuckers – together with two hundred women so that we can rebuild the Polish nation. Give some money for that.' Of course, Jaruzelski took offence and said, 'What are you talking about?'
>
> We were viewing things realistically. We knew what was happening, what the threat was. We recognized what nuclear war meant for Poland. Well, we would not have existed after it all. Neither the Americans nor the Russians would have regretted that. We could have – I don't know – got something ready. And, really, one good bunker should have been prepared so that we could have eventually rebuilt the Polish nation.[23]

The reasons for Jaruzelski's anger with Tuczapski are unclear. Perhaps it was a matter of taste and decency for him; or maybe he thought that Tuczapski was being flippant.

Jaruzelski believed that geography and the sheer distribution of military power made it sensible for Polish leaders to seek an understanding with Great Russia. Confrontation with Moscow could lead to national suicide. After becoming Party General Secretary, he told President Mitterrand with brutal frankness: 'Either I condemn my people to live under the Soviet boot or else I try and gain what I can from the situation as it is. Are you in the West ready to make war for the sake of Poland? No. Well, there's no other course than the one I'm following.'[24]

A very different approach to the same problem came from Colonel Ryszard Kukliński. A Polish patriot, Kukliński had offered his services to the CIA when he saw the Warsaw Pact's plans for the kind of war it expected to fight in the event of military conflict between the USSR and the US. His temperament was ebullient and unrestrained, but his reasons were very clinical. He felt nothing but horror when he pondered the fact that, whatever happened in such a conflict, Poland would inevitably attract a blitz of American nuclear missiles. As a commander of high rank, he was privy to the Warsaw Pact's strategic assumptions. He knew and resented the fact that Poland could not even affect the original decision to go to war. The USSR monopolized all the big decisions. Kukliński soberly concluded that he could best help his country by keeping the Americans informed about what he learned about Soviet offensive plans. He reasoned that by enabling the American leadership to anticipate the USSR's actions, it could adopt preventive measures which would avert the outbreak of war – and Poland would be saved from nuclear holocaust.

The Soviet high command was divided about whether troops could really advance through irradiated territory to any practical advantage. According to Vitali Tsygichko, only a few hotheads thought this to be at all realistic.[25] Nevertheless, the basic assumption in the Warsaw Pact was that its land forces could move forward as many as sixty kilometres a day. Apparently a plan existed for the first thirty days – and a second one for the next thirty days.[26]

Both the Warsaw Pact and NATO had to think the unthinkable in anticipation of war. The West German commanders learned from General Nigel Bagnall, commander-in-chief of the British Army of the Rhine and commander of NATO's Northern Army Group, about a plan for the preventive destruction of a border town in West Germany that was a communications centre. Chalupa, commander-in-chief of Allied Forces Central Europe at the time, tackled Bagnall with a question about how he would have felt if he was fighting on this basis in an area between Newcastle and Carlisle.[27] The West Germans had an understandable preference for saving all their country from annihilation. Agreement was reached that there should be 'forward defence planning'. Supplies for NATO forces were warehoused close to frontiers with Warsaw Pact states to give West Germany the assurance that its allies did not regard it as an expendable asset.[28] The Americans and West Europeans, except for the French, held firmly to NATO's dispositions. Of course, there were national oddities. The Dutch had a tendency to expect war on five working days each week and allowed a lot of their troops home at weekends. The rest of NATO prayed that the Warsaw Pact was not keeping an eye on the calendar.[29]

Fred Iklé, the US Under Secretary of Defense, was not alone in the American administration in worrying about the conflicting interests inside the NATO alliance. He himself imagined a scenario where the Americans might feel the need for a pre-emptive strike on the USSR but would be thwarted by Western Europe. Britain, France and West Germany would for sure calculate that Soviet retaliation would lead to their total incineration. This in turn would expose Western Europe to the threat of 'nuclear blackmail'.[30]

In 1982 there was also an outbreak of controversy about the global physical consequences of a Third World War after the Swedish Academy of Sciences journal *Ambio* published an article on the likely consequences of fires on earth produced by the detonation of nuclear bombs. The authors were Paul J. Crutzen of the Max Planck Institute and John W. Birks of the University of Colorado. They took as their starting point a military conflict involving 14,700 warheads and 5,700 megatons of explosive power. They assumed that most cities with a population greater than 100,000 would be hit. According to their calculations, about 750 million people would instantly be killed by the bombing.[31] The focus of their contribution, though, was on the worldwide calamity that would ensue from the smoke, ashes and soot alone. Sunlight would be drastically reduced. All forms of animal and plant life would be threatened.[32] This hypothesis was quickly picked up by scientists in America. Some were sympathetic to the arguments, and on 31 October 1983 a conference was opened in Washington on the topic. Dr Carl Sagan published an article on 'Nuclear War and Climatic Catastrophe' in *Foreign Affairs* in the winter of 1983–1984. He suggested that any conflict involving nuclear weapons would wreak a planetary environmental disaster. It would make no difference if only a few such detonations took place. Sagan asked why, if Reagan genuinely wanted peace, he gave 10,000 times greater financial support to the Defense Department than to the Arms Control and Disarmament Agency.[33]

When Edward Teller poured scorn on him as a 'propagandizer' who did not know what he was talking about, Sagan wrote a letter deploring that Teller himself had written that 'nuclear winter' was the only possible outcome of a war involving nuclear ballistic missiles; he objected to Teller's readiness to engage in personalized polemics.[34]

Sagan's article was manna from heaven for Soviet leaders and propagandists. Already in March 1980 an appeal had gone from 654 American scientists to Presidents Carter and Brezhnev. The title was

'Danger – Nuclear War', the call was for a ban on all nuclear weapons. This was brought to the attention of Brezhnev, who expressed delight on behalf of the Politburo. He congratulated the signatories on their 'humane and noble activities' – and *Pravda* noted that Western news agencies reported on this in a constructive spirit.[35] Sagan had provided a scholarly basis for their standpoint. He himself was on good terms with Moscow scientists such as Yevgeni Velikhov – he thanked Velikhov for his and his colleagues' efforts in independently testing and confirming the hypothesis. Naive and enthusiastic, Sagan did not have anything like the knowledge of conditions in the USSR that was needed before he indicated that Velikhov was carrying out any such testing of his own. Minister of Health Yevgeni Chazov's booklet *Nuclear War: The Medical and Biological Consequences* was no franker than anything that Velikhov produced. Chazov relied heavily on Western sources and provided little in the way of Soviet empirical data.[36]

Velikhov continued to advocate the benefits of the civilian production of nuclear power but in private he held deep reservations, later telling Deputy Foreign Affairs Minister Anatoli Adamishin that the world would have been a safer place if the discovery could have been delayed for a further hundred years. No state was ready for it, least of all the USSR. Velikhov recalled that when the first Soviet nuclear power station had been built at Obninsk, the nearby collective farm was still using a wooden plough; and he lamented the condition of the USSR's computer industry.[37] No such thought was allowed in the media. The party leadership insisted on universal acceptance of the notion that the USSR pursued solely peaceful ends in foreign and security policy and enforced exemplary standards of safety at its civilian nuclear power stations. The reality was less than reassuring. In 1979, when still KGB Chairman, Yuri Andropov reported that crucial precautions had failed to be taken in the process of constructing the set of reactors at Chernobyl in central Ukraine.[38] The Ministry of Energy too had admitted that things were not entirely satisfactory; but it assured the Politburo that an on-site inspection had cleared up the difficulty.[39] Velikhov, of course, had military as well as industrial dangers in mind. He worried that the country's leadership might prove inadequate to supervising the vast power that nuclear energy put at its disposal; and there were many others who shared his concerns and were barred from expressing them in print.

A papal report came to Reagan in 1981 indicating that whatever else happened in a nuclear war, the facilities for tending to the wounded were utterly inadequate.[40] The President was a sympathetic reader: the Vatican's emphasis entirely corresponded to his own ideas on avoiding such a war at all costs. At a meeting with Cardinal Casaroli, Reagan emphasized his abhorrence of nuclear war.[41] The trouble was that he failed to convince most people of his sincerity. Around the world, he was still widely regarded as a warmonger.

3. THE REAGANAUTS

Everyone Reagan brought into his administration wanted to avoid undue concessions to the USSR. They scorned the idea of containment. They shared the President's contempt for détente and his resolve to overtake the other superpower in the arms race. The Reaganauts, as they were sometimes called, wanted America to show a new face to the world and challenge the Soviet leadership in every dimension of its activity. None of Reagan's appointees thought that Moscow would come to acceptable terms with Washington until American military power attained superiority. This dictum was fixed in the White House credo and was repeated time and time again by the President and his officials. It was scarcely surprising that when Reagan declared that he wanted to prevent world war and abolish all nuclear weapons, he failed to convince the Kremlin. The truth was that nearly every one of his appointees believed that the sheer frightfulness of atomic bombs had served to keep the peace since 1945. If nuclear weaponry were to be banned, there would immediately be global insecurity that could soon lead to world war. American arms control officials were distinctly unenthusiastic about his goal of abolishing all nuclear weapons. Not until Reagan was elected for a second presidential term did Secretary of State George Shultz hear any of them even discussing the topic.[1]

The Soviet leadership judged the President by his threats and actions as well as by the kind of people he promoted to high office. Reagan had campaigned for the presidency as someone who would take no nonsense from the USSR. Little wonder that the Politburo did not see him as a peacemaker.

In 1976, shortly before he stood for President against the Democratic challenger Jimmy Carter, Gerald Ford had allowed a review of policy towards the USSR. He and the then CIA Director George Bush did this in a most unusual way by commissioning two rival reports, one by Team A and the other by Team B. Team A consisted of CIA experts and people who agreed with their analysis; Team B, headed by

Harvard's professor of Russian history Richard Pipes, challenged the CIA's assumption that Soviet economic decline prevented Moscow from matching American military capacity.[2] Pipes himself thought it hardly worth the effort to talk to the Kremlin leadership. Any treaty on strategic weapons limitation, in his opinion, would simply enable Brezhnev and the Politburo to put off the day of final crisis. American policy should be centred upon 'the nature of the Soviet regime'. Until such time as the leaders of the USSR instituted a radical reform of the internal system of power, America could achieve nothing with them in international relations. Pipes warned that Soviet leaders might decide that war with America was preferable to the dismantling of communism. Reform was consequently far from being inevitable. Team B's argument's impressed Reagan, who put Pipes in charge of the Soviet and East European desk on his National Security Council. Pipes consented to work for the administration for only the first half of the presidential term since he was reluctant to forfeit his tenured Harvard post.[3] National Security Adviser Richard Allen admired his 'war-like proclivities' and welcomed him on these terms.[4]

When entering the White House, Reagan was drawing on the support of groups that sprang up to oppose any ill-considered concessions to the USSR in the arms talks. The best organized association was the Committee on the Present Danger. Among its leading figures were David Packard of the Hewlett-Packard Co. and Lane Kirkland of the American Federation of Labor and Congress of Industrial Organizations. Another was Reagan's foreign policy adviser Richard Allen. They highlighted what they saw as a military imbalance between America and the USSR. They claimed that America was being gulled by the Kremlin. Parallel to the Committee on the Present Danger were a number of organizations such as the Madison Group and the Heritage Foundation. Reagan drew his officials abundantly from such groups. No one he appointed was soft on communism. Just once, Paul Nitze – the chief American negotiator at the arms talks at Geneva – let out the idea that the Americans wanted to get to a situation where they could 'live and let live' with the USSR. This was too much for *Wall Street Journal* conservative commentator Irving Kristol, who asked what was going on inside the administration.[5]

The best-known of Reagan's appointees was Alexander Haig. Though Caspar Weinberger, William Casey and George Shultz were considered, it was Haig who became Secretary of State. Haig had been President Nixon's chief of staff who had gone on to head NATO forces.[6] Unlike several other leading officials, he was cautious about the way he approached the USSR. His sharp intellect ranged over many external and internal problems. Physically fit and military in bearing, he behaved like a commander in every office he held.

Reagan soon found him hot to handle. He admired Haig's capacity to analyse complex international situations, and Haig was quietly in favour of lessening the tensions with the USSR; but his rhetoric did not always convey this message. He was firmly anti-Soviet and left Moscow in no doubt that Soviet activity in Angola, Ethiopia, Cambodia, Afghanistan, Cuba and Libya was an impediment to an improved relationship with Washington.[7] But his imperious ill-temper damaged his effectiveness at the State Department. Reagan scratched his head about Haig's inability to get on with anyone in the administration – the frequent tirades struck the President as 'paranoid'.[8] Haig implicitly wanted to control all foreign policy. He underestimated Reagan, who was outwardly charming but had a titanium core. When Haig objected to his ideas, the President told him with firmness: 'Well, we're not going to do it some other way.' Haig was sent scurrying with the order: 'Well, you just go and work it out.'[9]

Matters climaxed over Haig's behaviour while Reagan was in hospital after the assassination attempt. On hearing of the shooting, Haig brashly claimed that he was in charge. He wanted Americans to know that a strong hand remained on the levers of power; speaking on national TV, he announced: 'I am in control here.' Others in the administration thought this crazed and power-hungry. Reagan, as he recovered, came to the same conclusion. His officials advised him to fire Haig before he could do any more damage. This was something that the President always found it hard to do. He hated personal conflict. But he ceased to show much enthusiasm for Haig, and this was enough to dent the Secretary of State's pride. He resigned office on 5 July 1982. Reagan was caustic: 'Actually the only disagreement was over whether I made policy or the Secretary of State did.'[10]

After his mistake with Haig, Reagan was circumspect in going about the recruitment of a successor. His choice fell upon George Shultz, who had served under Richard Nixon as Secretary of the Treasury. Shultz accepted the invitation. His friend Henry Kissinger was caustic: 'George has no knowledge of foreign policy, none at all; worse than that, he has no feel for it.'[11] He differed from Haig in recognizing that one man and one man only was President. The new Secretary of State could be gruff and blunt but his manner disguised the reality of a thoughtful intellectual who had taught economics at the University of Chicago Graduate School and had expertise both in business and in government. Shultz liked to test out his policies in government by asking: 'Could I defend it at a seminar at the University of Chicago?'[12] He was a public servant of distinction; he knew the corridors of power in Washington better than most of the Californians who had swarmed to the capital with Reagan. A former US Marine who had seen action in the Second World War, Shultz was tough-minded and determined. The secretaryship was offered to him at a stage in his career when he could handle the strains of the post. He had another advantage, one that Henry Kissinger and Alexander Haig lacked: he felt it would not be the worst thing to happen if ever he walked out of the State Department. He held to his values and knew his own value, and was in accord with most of the President's objectives.

He was almost alone in the Reagan administration in having any experience of negotiating with the Soviet leadership – as President Nixon's Treasury Secretary he had gone to Moscow for financial discussions in 1973.[13] He was confident about his ability to seize the available opportunities to pursue the President's stated objectives. He had a broad perspective on world politics and the global economy and counted Milton Friedman among his friends and correspondents.[14] Friedman tended to avoid discussions about the Cold War but from an economic angle he saw no point in indulging the USSR: he told Shultz that the world's big banks, notably those in West Germany, were reducing the world's 'capital pool' by lending money to the inefficient Soviet economy. There was only a finite quantity of capital around the globe. It was being wasted on the USSR.[15] Shultz shared the concern about the global economy and its current prospects of expansion.[16]

He also understood the need to perpetuate a degree of consensus on foreign policy inside the Reagan administration. Haig's State Department had been like a gas-filled room: no one could tell when the next explosion would occur. With this in mind, the new Secretary of State instituted a regular Saturday group to discuss current business; and he would invite Vice President George Bush and Ed Meese as well as leading officials of the National Security Council, Defense Department and CIA.[17] He had breakfast once a week with Weinberger, whom Reagan had made his Defense Secretary.[18] With Bush, he would have no difficulty. Reagan had selected him as his vice presidential running mate in 1980 because he straddled a middling position in

Republican party politics. Bush was content with proposals to open talks with the USSR. Others in the administration felt differently – and Shultz knew that he was going to have to surmount their resistance. He was also aware about the doggedness of people like Weinberger. The two of them had worked together in the Bechtel Corporation in San Francisco. They had never got on. Shultz found Weinberger impossibly inflexible in business; Weinberger thought Shultz too ready to concede to litigious complainants.[19]

The President trusted his Defense Secretary despite his lack of enthusiasm about eliminating nuclear weaponry.[20] They had been friends since Reagan's appearance on the Californian political stage, and Weinberger knew which ideas would best appeal to the President. He was also careful to avoid intruding unduly on his free time. Weinberger wanted the Soviet leadership to understand that a true warrior occupied the Department of Defense. He had indeed seen active service in the Second World War, but his experience in government under Nixon and Ford had been in the civilian sector as Director of the Office of Management and Budget and then as Secretary of Health, Education and Welfare. He was short, neat and dapper. He was courteous of manner but had a short temper and lacked much of a sense of humour.[21] He had little notion about how to win over people who did not already agree with him. He could handle a gentle interview on the TV evening news, but proved helpless at a news conference when asked a troublesome question.[22] Media professionals tended to dislike him as a warmonger. He gave an interview to the *New York Times* in an attempt to rectify this image: 'We aren't planning to fight any war, if we can avoid it. We're planning to deter war . . . We've said many times that we don't think nuclear war is winnable.'[23]

It was Weinberger's aim to achieve unconditional military superiority for America, and he reckoned that it might take the rest of the decade. American armed forces had to be modernized. Weinberger adopted an extravagant tone: 'When I left California . . . I expected to find some problems in Washington. But frankly, I was surprised to find conditions as bad as they are. The Defense Department reminded me of a business that had been neglected far too long.'[24] He had a brief to cut out financial waste from American armed forces and set about cost-saving exercises with gusto. He pursued this objective while stressing his determination that America should catch up with Soviet offensive capacity.[25] With this in mind he pushed hard for an increase in the Defense Department's yearly budget. Even the Republicans on the Senate Armed Services Committee commented on this, and Senator John W. Warner of Virginia by 1985 emerged as a leading objector to Weinberger's demands.[26] All through Reagan's first presidential term and beyond, there was a growing concern that the expenditure might be like pouring money down a drain.[27]

The Assistant Secretary in the Defense Department was Richard Perle. Henry Kissinger would later characterize Perle as 'a destructive son-of-a-bitch'.[28] Soviet diplomat Teimuraz Stepanov-Mamaladze thought that he looked like 'a Tiflis Armenian'. Coming from a half-Georgian, this was not exactly a compliment. Tiflis was the Russian pre-revolutionary name for Tbilisi and in those distant years the Georgian capital had been economically dominated by its large Armenian merchant class. Feelings between Georgians and Armenians were so bad that the Georgian communist leadership in the 1920s implemented a process of ethnic cleansing.[29] Perle had an almost unearthly calm, never shouting in order to get his way;[30] but his anti-Soviet ferocity earned him the soubriquet 'Prince of Darkness' in American liberal circles. He was careless of this reputation; if anything, he liked it.

Neither Weinberger nor Perle had time for anyone who sought to lower the tensions with the Politburo. Weinberger was furious with Robert McNamara, one of his predecessors as Defense Secretary, for demanding a fresh doctrine of war. McNamara and his friends argued for the need to renounce the 'first use' of nuclear weapons against the USSR and even what became known as 'hasty second use'. Weinberger denied that such a policy would enhance national security; he reasoned that if the Kremlin could cause trouble without risking rapid all-out retaliation, there would be no likely improvement in its behaviour. He endorsed the President's comment that the nuclear freeze movement in the NATO countries was being manipulated by people who sought to weaken America. Weinberger thought that American arms control specialists were a problem in themselves. He saw them as having an interest in prolonging talks; and if a definitive treaty were to be agreed between America and the USSR, their jobs would be put in jeopardy. They might not even be conscious of this bias.[31] Weinberger wanted Soviet leaders to know that if they started a war, America would fight as long as it took to defeat the enemy. He indicated that his Department had contingency schemes for a protracted conflict.[32]

Weinberger bristled whenever there was mention of the idea of selling advanced technology to the USSR. At a National Security Council he swept aside talk about the unease in NATO:

> We must consider our Allies' position, but we must consider whether we wish to aid the Soviets or not, and we must not adopt the attitude that if we don't sell to them someone else will. This is sometimes true, but our policy should be very restrictive. Almost everything aids their military and helps their economy. We know that they will only be satisfied by world domination, and we cannot satisfy them by appeasing them.[33]

When Commerce Secretary Baldrige spoke in favour of allowing the export of goods freely available in American retail stores, CIA Director Casey pitched in on Weinberger's side: 'It is a mistake to help the Soviets by exporting to them items they need.' He reminded everyone that America had sold scrap iron to Japan shortly before the Second World War.[34]

Casey was at one with Weinberger in believing that nothing good could come from negotiating with the USSR. He believed in putting the Kremlin under direct stress. Appointed CIA director at the start of Reagan's presidency, he was an intelligence agency veteran. In the Second World War he had served in the Office of Strategic Services under 'Wild Bill' Donovan and became head of its Secret Intelligence Branch in Europe. He was a rumbustious Cold Warrior in the postwar years. He was convinced that the Kremlin was the most fertile ground of evil in the world. His Catholic faith sustained his determination to stem the expansion of atheistic communism. As a law graduate, he became active in the Republican Party while working for large corporations. President Nixon appointed him Chairman of the Securities and Exchange Commission from 1971. Casey always hoped for a President who would confront the USSR; he was sceptical about the advantages of détente. He believed he'd found what he wanted in Reagan and offered his services as his presidential campaign manager in 1980. He saw the Soviet leadership as the centre of a global revolutionary conspiracy that was responsible for most of the terrorist outrages against America and its allies. He intended to turn the CIA into an organization fit and capable of undermining Moscow's purposes.[35] He kept Reagan informed about his efforts to 'revitalize the clandestine services' and introduce appointees whom he could trust.[36]

Not all NATO leaders treated contact and trade with the Soviet Union in the same way as Weinberger and Casey, who came together in objecting to the Siberian oil and gas pipeline under construction through to West Germany – they ignored Haig's argument that America's NATO allies in Western Europe would simply refuse to abandon the commercial deal. Haig gave this summary:

> We lifted the controls on three-fourths of our own trade with the Soviets when we lifted the grain embargo. It would be inconsistent to put pressure on them when we are loosening our own controls.[37]

Weinberger refused to give an inch:

> We are unequivocally in favor of stopping the pipeline. Leadership does not add up the columns on the opinions of our Allies, then conclude you are defeated. You decide what is needed and you do it. The Europeans should be clear on that. You decide what is needed and you do it.[38]

The meeting on 9 July 1981 petered out without a decision.[39]

Casey hinted that the President had missed a trick by lifting the grain embargo:

> A cartel of the US, Canada, Australia, and Argentina would control 78 per cent of all wheat in world trade, 87 per cent of all corn, and 90 per cent of all soybeans. By way of comparison, the thirteen OPEC nations control just 71 per cent of world oil. At current prices, for about $20 billion – less than one-tenth of the defense budget – the US could purchase every bushel of grain on the world market. It should take only a fraction of that to hold farmers in the American and Argentina harmless from the consequences of withholding their grain from the Soviet Union. That would be very powerful leverage indeed but it would be an extraordinary measure which cannot be taken lightly. It would not be justified in world opinion unless taken for a very specific and important purpose.[40]

Although Reagan rejected this particular idea, he apparently welcomed Casey to the National Security Council as 'a team player' – a somewhat eccentric description of a man who rocked any boat he thought was sailing in the wrong direction.[41]

Eugene Rostow, who was appointed as director of the Arms Control and Disarmament Agency, was equally pessimistic about making progress with the Soviet leadership. As a Yale law professor as well as a veteran official in Democrat administration, he was a talented disputant; and he told Ambassador Anatoli Dobrynin that America would sign no treaty until the USSR permitted the Americans to verify compliance. He stressed that the Americans had plenty of information about infringements of internationally agreed undertakings, including the Soviet programme to develop biological weaponry.[42] The man who represented the Joint Chiefs of Staff at the Geneva arms talks that Rostow headed was Lieutenant General Ed Rowny. He had resigned from the Carter administration rather than endorse the terms of the SALT-II treaty.[43]

The true Reaganauts in the White House, according to Weinberger, were very few. Apart from himself, he named them as Ed Meese, Jeane Kirkpatrick, Bill Casey, William Clark, Richard Allen and George Shultz. It is striking that he included his rival Shultz on the list. Weinberger claimed that Shultz started out with an undesirable readiness to accept 'the received wisdom' of the State Department. As Weinberger saw things, though, Shultz eventually came over to Reagan's standpoint in foreign policy. Late in life, Weinberger was willing to concede that they agreed on sixty to seventy per cent of public business; he also admitted that the State Department's professional staff would have been a handful for anyone. He accepted that Shultz gave constant support to the Strategic Defense Initiative.[44] It is undeniable that the American administration had deep divisions on policy. But about the need to confront and challenge the USSR, there was unanimity. The Reaganauts came to office with the express intention of putting an end to the idea of mere détente. The previous administration under Jimmy Carter had gone a long way in the same direction, and Reagan's officials were determined to proceed further. They were going to confront and challenge the Soviet leadership.

4. THE AMERICAN CHALLENGE

Reagan and his officials had no sharply chiselled ideas for overturning communism in Moscow or breaking up the USSR.[1] They knew that Soviet leaders remained a formidable force in the world. Jeane Kirkpatrick was to recall that Reagan hoped to 'spend them to death'.[2] This indeed was one of his main objectives, and reports from the CIA welcomed the results he was achieving. Its reports regularly highlighted the strains on the Kremlin's budget that stemmed from its foreign commitments. Afghanistan and Poland were new burdens for the Kremlin, which already subsidized Cuba, Vietnam and the African client states.[3]

Two years into his presidential term, Reagan gave two speeches that seized the world's attention. On 8 March 1983, at the National Association of Evangelicals in Orlando, he denounced the USSR as an 'empire of evil' and described totalitarianism as 'the focus of evil in the world'.[4] He explained:

> During my first press conference as President, in answer to a direct question, I pointed out that, as good Marxist-Leninists, the Soviet leaders have openly and publicly declared that the only morality they recognize is that which will further their cause, which is world revolution. I think I should point out I was only quoting Lenin, their guiding spirit, who said in 1920 that they repudiate all morality that proceeds from supernatural ideas – that's their name for religion – or ideas that are outside class conceptions. Morality is entirely subordinate to the interests of class war. And everything is moral that is necessary for the annihilation of the old, exploiting social order and for uniting the proletariat.
>
> Well, I think the refusal of many influential people to accept this elementary fact of Soviet doctrine illustrates an historical reluctance to see totalitarian powers for what they are. We saw this phenomenon in the 1930s. We see it too often today.[5]

He repeated his call for a fifty per cent cut in strategic nuclear missiles and for the entire elimination of intermediate-range weapons.[6]

The world's media ignored the thoughtful and theological ingredients of the speech. They preferred to highlight the militant implications of the President's anticommunism, and opponents of Reagan felt that their worst fears were being confirmed. He had spoken fiercely about the USSR before entering the White House. His Orlando speech was of a piece with his discourse over many years.

On 23 March 1983, after a fortnight of controversy, he delivered a televised address to the nation about his new project for an anti-missile defence system in outer space: a Strategic Defense Initiative that would enable the Americans to shoot down offensive missiles. Weinberger had alerted NATO defence ministers only a few days in advance.[7] Reagan had given next to no time for a discussion in his own administration. Perhaps he sensed that officials would object. When Deputy National Security Adviser Robert McFarlane got wind of the President's ideas, he cautioned his own boss William Clark: 'You've got to stop him. He can't make that speech yet. This hasn't even begun to be vetted.'[8] Shultz continued to feel doubts which failed to be alleviated by a briefing from General Abrahamson, who headed the programme. The Secretary of State concluded: 'I'm either being lied to, or there's nothing there!'[9] Reagan was at odds with 'the entire American defence intellectual establishment'.[10] But he stuck to his idea, and it stayed in the core of his foreign policy. He insisted that he had only peaceful intentions while making America impregnable. The Defense Initiative was meant to ensure that if the USSR started a war with nuclear missiles, the Americans would have the capacity to intercept and destroy them from outer space before they could do any damage.

Though Reagan emphasized his defensive intentions, he never erased suspicion that the project would bring technological advantage to America – and this was taken as proof that he was firing the pistol for yet another round of the arms race. The idea of a weapons system in outer space reminded people of the *Star Wars* movie series produced by George Lucas since 1977. Lucas's films were about the struggle between good and evil in deep space. The weapons included laser beam wands. Reagan's Strategic Defense Initiative quickly entered popular parlance as his Star Wars Initiative.

Once they got over their surprise, leading administration officials came round to seeing attractions in the Strategic Defense Initiative. Andropov and his Politburo immediately denounced America's militarism; they railed against a research programme that would add yet another stage to the arms race. Reagan's speech had obviously agitated them, and there was no Reaganaut who lamented their discomfort. Weinberger liked the Defense Initiative if only because, as he confided to his officials, it would increase the economic stress for the USSR while turning America into 'a nuclear sanctuary'. He called for parallel work to continue in building up the country's strategic offensive capacity.[11] Edward Teller was one of the leading scientists who had inspired Reagan to announce the research programme. He knew how to go about capturing the President's imagination. He kept up the campaign, writing to him on 23 July 1983 that urgent action was needed since the USSR might already be ahead in the field.[12] Reagan needed no persuading. The Defense Initiative provided him with the hope that he would achieve the protection of his country against attack by nuclear ballistic missiles. The fact that this caused distress in the Kremlin was a gratifying bonus.

Meanwhile the Soviet Union was engulfed in its war in Afghanistan on the side of the communist government. The American administration made arrangements to deliver military supplies to anticommunist forces – the mujahidin – which contained a high proportion of ultra-traditionalist irregulars fighting for Islam, national sovereignty and the expulsion of foreign infidels. The Americans overlooked the long-term international danger of fundamentalist jihadism. Their dominant thought was that aid should go to the enemies of the USSR. The jihadists were fighting to liberate their country from a communist despotism propped up by the Soviet Army. They were fighters who lacked for nothing in determination but were deficient in weaponry. Reagan wished to assist them. It was prudent to make this a covert operation. As early as 1981 there was a scheme to use a civilian cargo company registered in Canada. The destination would be Pakistan via Oman, and permission would be obtained from President Zia-ul-Haq in Islamabad. Twenty small Cessna aircraft would be bought to make the regular flights into Afghanistan. The mujahidin were not going to go down for want of firepower.[13] Weinberger went in person to Islamabad to discover how the war was proceeding. In October 1983 he met North-West Frontier Province Governor Fazl-e-Haq and discussed the huge influx of Afghan refugees.[14]

The Soviet leadership turned a calm face to the world about Afghanistan. But even inside the Ministry of Foreign Affairs, under Gromyko's iron rod, the dissenters made themselves felt. The diplomat

Anatoli Kovalëv refused to take over the Near and Middle East desks because he wanted nothing to do with the Afghan imbroglio. When Gromyko reasoned with him that the Americans were intent on setting up bases in Afghanistan, Kovalëv stood his ground.[15] Kovalëv survived in post but it was not always so easy for other officials to speak truth to power. Experts in the intelligence agency of the armed forces, the GRU, drafted a report pointing out the grave problems ahead. The Soviet Union seemed about to repeat the failure of the British in the nineteenth century. The GRU's boss received a reprimand from the Politburo and told his subordinates: 'You guys got me into trouble!'[16] In fact Gromyko himself quickly began to regret the invasion. In 1982 Yevgeni Primakov, Director of the Oriental Studies Institute, gave a talk to the Foreign Affairs Ministry in Moscow and exposed the futility of expecting success in bringing 'revolutionary changes' to Afghanistan. To everyone's surprise, Gromyko voiced agreement with Primakov's criticisms.[17]

On 18 August 1983 Andropov, at a reception in Moscow for visiting US senators, said he would end the USSR's moratorium on anti-satellite weapon testing if America went ahead with the Strategic Defense Initiative.[18] He was throwing down a gauntlet. At the same time he knew that Soviet experts were sceptical about the scientific chances of American success, and everyone could see that it was going to require 'astronomic amounts of money' from the USSR's budget.[19]

Reagan threw aside Carter's inhibitions and played the Chinese card for all it was worth. In July 1981 the Pentagon announced America's willingness to give consideration to China's requests to buy advanced armaments. Decisions would be taken on a case-by-case basis.[20] American corporations were eager to set up joint ventures without concern about technological transfer. The administration expressed a wish for cooperation in developing Chinese nuclear power for peaceful purposes. The calculation was that China's rise would help America to harass the USSR. The State Department wanted to see the Chinese spreading their influence around the world and thought that if they would intervene in Africa, the Soviet Union's capacity for mischief would be diminished.[21] Although the abuses of human rights in China were mentioned, they were seldom highlighted. The Americans saw the Chinese as a bulwark against the USSR's influence in South-East Asia; they also liked Beijing's ability to tie down dozens of Soviet army divisions along the long border between the two countries.[22] The American administration had few worries about selling advanced military technology to China – officials felt confident that the Chinese would never hand over secrets to their own enemies, the USSR and the Warsaw Pact. In June 1983 Reagan officially recognized the People's Republic of China as a 'friendly, non-allied country' and worked for the further relaxation of trade restrictions on commerce.[23]

He and his officials simultaneously strove to prevent sales of any equipment with a potential military use to the Soviet Union. America and its allies since 1949 had operated an embargo regime through their Coordinating Committee for Export Controls (or CoCom). Goods that used advanced technology were regularly monitored. American restrictions themselves were increased in 1975 when President Ford signed the so-called Jackson–Vanik amendment into law. Senator Henry 'Scoop' Jackson and Congressman Charles Vanik were seeking to penalize states which denied the right of free emigration to its citizens. The USSR, which was refusing to let Jews leave the country, was the prime target. US companies generally complied with the list of proscribed categories of products that CoCom drew up; but in 1980 Japan's Toshiba Corporation secretly agreed to sell propellers to Moscow that enabled submarines to move almost silently underwater. This was a blatant violation of the rules; it also conflicted with Japanese defence interests. Unsurprisingly, American politicians threatened to apply a comprehensive ban on Toshiba's freedom to trade in America.[24] Years of wrangling followed as the US Defense Department highlighted the damaging consequences. Not even America had the power to compel a foreign corporation to rip up a duly signed contract. But its allies learned the lesson that the White House under Reagan would not look gently upon further breaches of the embargo.

The American administration itself was inconsistent in its use of trade as a means of constraining the Kremlin. The lifting of the grain export embargo on 1 April 1981 relieved Soviet economic problems. A few weeks earlier, as the effects of yet another bad harvest were registered, the central party leadership had introduced a decree to remove the limits on the size of private plots on collective farms. Obstructions to the personal purchase of livestock had been eliminated – and the state bank was to make suitable credits available. There can be little doubt that Carter's agricultural embargo had made an impact here. When Reagan revoked it, the party decree was immediately withdrawn.[25]

An American trade delegation of 250 business executives visited Moscow in November 1982 despite the official state of mourning for

President Brezhnev. Commercial links were picking up – and forty Soviet trade officials were to pay a return visit to New York in May 1984. These were years when America's global balance-of-trade deficit gave rising concern. In 1983 it had risen to a record of $69.4 billion and the predictions were that it could be double that figure in the following year. Several big companies wanted the administration to assist them by lifting restrictions on trade with communist countries. The volume of commercial activity between America and the USSR tumbled from $4.5 billion in 1979 to $2.3 billion in 1983. American lobbyists pointed out that Western Europe was already taking the opportunities on offer from Moscow.[26] On 28 July 1983 permission was given for the USSR to increase its purchases of American grain by fifty per cent over the previous year and to prolong this volume of imports for another five years. Secretary of State Shultz and Commerce Secretary Baldrige saw this as a first step towards a repeal of the embargo on sales of gas and oil technology.[27]

Shultz and Baldrige followed a tradition in Republican Party in favour of free trade regardless of ideological disputes, even trade with a country whose government was regarded as totalitarian. Weinberger consistently opposed this idea: he wanted to pressurize the Kremlin by every means available short of war. If the Soviet Foreign Trade Ministry was pleading for advanced technology, it was not in the American national interest to supply it. Oil and gas were crucial exports for the USSR's economy. Without them, the Soviet budget would fall apart.[28]

Reagan overruled Weinberger's advice in December 1983.[29] Off-shore drilling equipment stayed off the CoCom list of banned exports. The State Department was worried about a regrowth of tensions with NATO allies that had occurred over the American sanctions against companies which helped the USSR to build its Siberian pipeline,[30] and the Commerce Department added that if the Americans did not sell the equipment, other countries would come to terms – and America would suffer economically. Shultz was simultaneously working to establish a less dangerous relationship with the USSR. William L. Armstrong of Colorado led a group of US senators who were unhappy with this turn of events. They spoke out against any attempt to increase the quantity of imports that could have been produced in the Soviet Gulag. They publicized three dozen products which were held to be the result of forced labour. When Treasury Secretary Donald T. Regan said he was open to persuasion about introducing an embargo, Shultz and Baldrige highlighted the danger of worsened relations with

Moscow. They pointed to the possibility that the USSR might retaliate by refusing to buy American farm produce.[31] Everyone knew that the President wanted to keep his electoral support in the agricultural states of the Midwest.

The USSR was constructing an enormous oil and gas pipeline from Siberia to Europe, and this had caused tremors in Washington. Mitterrand shared French intelligence reports about Soviet industrial espionage. American technology was being stolen by the cartful. The depth of the KGB's penetration of America's research programmes and illicit purchases of Canadian computer equipment was deeply disturbing, and the National Security Council decided to make the Soviet leadership pay a heavy price. Rather than expose the spies, the decision was taken to deposit faulty technology on them. The pipeline in Siberia was chosen as a prime target. As soon as the equipment was installed in Siberia, the turbines, pumps and valves registered excessive pressures and blew up the tubes. There was an explosion so large that the North American Aerospace Defense Command initially thought that Andropov had approved the launching of nuclear missiles from a secret site. Only Reagan and a few of his officials knew what had caused the disaster.[32] Once the damage was done, the CIA and FBI rolled in and arrested dozens of agents known to be operating on missions to steal technological secrets.[33]

Reagan was an unashamed enemy of communism, and sometimes his exuberance got the better of him. One incident stuck in the minds of many people. It occurred on 11 August 1983 as he was about to deliver his weekly radio broadcast. While doing the microphone check, he joked: 'My fellow Americans, I'm pleased to tell you that today I've signed legislation that will outlaw Russia forever. We begin bombing in five minutes.' The remark was relayed on the local sound system. When leaked to American media, it caused controversy. To Reagan's detractors it appeared that he had blurted out his administration's true purposes. The Politburo was outraged; the TASS news agency issued angry bulletins. US State Department officials worked overtime to allay American and foreign concern about what had come from the lips of the President.

Throughout the year there were clashes in diplomacy and the media between the USSR and America. None was more vituperative than about the shooting down of a South Korean passenger airliner over eastern Siberia. The plane had strayed into Soviet air space, and the regional defence commanders treated it as an espionage mission by the enemy. All 269 passengers and crew of KAL007 perished. Soviet spokesmen stuck to the spying allegation and exculpated the Siberian military action. Over subsequent days the furore mounted around the world. Reagan and Shultz condemned what they saw as nothing less than an act of state barbarism. Gradually the USSR's standpoint changed, and it was acknowledged that a mistake had occurred. This was not an apology, more an expression of political embarrassment. Things might perhaps have been different if Andropov had been fit and in attendance. He was angry with the Soviet military commanders who had shot down the KAL007 aircraft and undone his work to mend relations with the US.[34] First Deputy Foreign Affairs Minister Georgi Kornienko had forewarned him against lying that Soviet forces had no responsibility for the incident. Kornienko had rung Andropov in hospital to press the point. But the ailing Andropov was in no condition to take up the struggle; and although Kornienko was invited to put his case to the Politburo, Ustinov and Gromyko got their way.[35]

Pershing-2 missiles arrived in West Germany and cruise missiles reached Great Britain on 23 November 1983. The USSR had manifestly lost the struggle to prevent their installation and the consequences for the Politburo were bound to be dire as it moved to increase the military budget. *Pravda* rebuked the White House for starting a crusade against socialism.[36] The SS-20s could not reach the American mainland but had every European country well within their range. The Politburo failed to anticipate America's determined reaction. If the Soviet armed forces were going to have intermediate-range nuclear missiles, America would install cruise missiles in its bases in Western Europe. The abiding fear of West European leaders was that America might become decoupled from its commitment to NATO. They feared that a situation might arise when the Americans decided it was not worth launching strategic missiles from America in order to defend Bonn, Rome or London from attack by SS-20s. It was for this reason that countries began to accept the offer of cruise and Pershing-2 missiles. They wanted to keep America bound into an active alliance. Kovalëv told Gromyko that the introduction of SS-20s brought no gain and much insecurity for the USSR.[37]

Relations between the superpowers were worse than ever. Andropov felt edgy about Reagan's possible objectives: he thought him mad enough to order a nuclear Blitzkrieg against the USSR. In November 1983 there was a NATO command post exercise – Able Archer 83 – to deal with a potential 'escalation' of trouble between

America and its allies and the Warsaw Pact. It involved an attempt to experiment with new methods of silent communication, and the idea was to test out how the Western powers might eventually opt to attack the Soviet Union. As reports reached Moscow about what was afoot, the worry arose that the exercise might be a subterfuge disguising a build-up towards a real war. The series of American declarations and actions earlier in the year appeared to confirm the Politburo's worst fears.

Andropov ordered his successor as KGB Chairman, Viktor Chebrikov, to organize a campaign to gather any evidence that this was what the Americans were planning. Every Soviet intelligence official in America and Western Europe was told to prioritize 'Operation Ryan'. Ambassadors were informed by the resident KGB chiefs in each capital. Andropov did not want the country to be caught napping, as had happened in June 1941.[38] General Staff veterans would recall this period as the most worrisome since the Cuban missile crisis of 1962.[39] But not all of them felt that the world was truly on the brink of war. Colonel General Andrian Danilevich later explained 'that the KGB may have overstated the level of tension because they are generally incompetent in military affairs and exaggerate what they do not understand'.[40] In the Party Defence Department, if not in the General Staff, the possibility of war breaking out, was taken very seriously – and the work of officials was reorganized so that some of them stayed on site through the hours of night.[41] The USSR was put on a high level of alert. The slightest untoward accident could have induced Andropov to decide to strike before the Americans struck. The difference between this emergency and the Cuban crisis was that Moscow and Washington were barely communicating with each other in 1983 – and this was a difference that made for even greater danger.

Urgent messages passed between the two capitals before some kind of calm returned. Earlier in the year Reagan, agitated by the lack of progress in relations with the USSR, had tried to prevent things from spinning out of control by inviting Ambassador Dobrynin for a meeting at the White House. Shultz arranged for Dobrynin to be spirited into the building by the back entrance. Everything was done in strict secrecy because Reagan wished to preserve his reputation for standing up to the Soviet leadership. He talked to Dobrynin for a couple of hours. It was a productive meeting, as Reagan noted: 'I told him I wanted George [Shultz] to be a channel for direct contact with Andropov – no bureaucracy involved. George told me that after they left the Ambassador said "this could be an historic moment".[42] This was the first meeting between the President and anybody from the USSR since he took office. Though Dobrynin still felt perplexed about Reagan's true motives, he appreciated the overture as a step towards an unfreezing of relations.[43] But then Reagan gave his speeches on the 'evil empire' and the Strategic Defense Initiative and to sanction the Able Archer exercise; and Soviet forces downed the Korean airliner. Tensions were worse than before the President met the Ambassador.

Both sides could see the dangers of the situation. Andropov had lived through weeks of intense agitation; Reagan was horrified by the thought that his actions could have started a nuclear war. They understood that mutual reassurance was in the interests of everybody, but they failed to find a way to attain it.

5. SYMPTOMS RECOGNIZED, CURES REJECTED

As Party General Secretary, Andropov exercised unmatched personal power. There was a paradox in this. Although there was no higher post than the party general secretaryship, the holder was constrained by the whole framework of the Soviet order. The USSR was a one-party state and the communist party acted as its government in all but name. The ideology since the revolution of October 1917 was based on the ideas of Vladimir Lenin – Marxism-Leninism. The constitutional structure had been the same for decades. The economy rested on state ownership and gave precedence to heavy industrial output, and the military industrial sector was prioritized within it. The biggest ministries, the security police and the armed forces were directed and controlled by the territorially based hierarchy of party committees. Joseph Stalin had consolidated this system in the 1930s by brutal deployment of party and police rule. Nikita Khrushchëv introduced a modicum of reform and relaxation from the mid-1950s, but his policies offended the elites and he was replaced by Leonid Brezhnev in 1964. A long period of political and economic consolidation ensued, and the system of power acquired a force of inertia as elites worked to defend their interests. Andropov was conscious of the defects in the country's capacity to satisfy the demands of society as well as to compete with America; but he was timid about adopting measures to rectify the situation.

He was conscious of the need to carry the party leadership along with him. Every five years there was a party congress that elected a Central Committee whose membership included leading officials of the party, the government, the armed forces and the KGB. The Central Committee seldom met more than twice a year. Between its plenary sessions it delegated its powers to a small internal body known as the Politburo. The General Secretary could never afford to ignore the Politburo's collective opinion.

The Politburo gathered regularly at eleven o'clock in the morning for its Thursday meeting in the Walnut Room of the Great Kremlin Palace. Its dozen or so members gathered at the big round table and held a preliminary discussion before the proceedings began. The rituals of office were observed as the General Secretary led forward the full members, followed by those who had candidate (or deputy) status and then the Central Committee secretaries. The General Secretary took the presiding chair in the Walnut Room. Invited speakers gave their reports from a lectern to his right.[1] If a vote was taken, only the Politburo's full members could take part. Usually, a skilful General Secretary avoided anything so crude and tried to achieve a consensus by attempting to summarize the balance of opinion.[2] The men of the Politburo headed the institutions which governed the entire country. At the forefront of these institutions were the party, the KGB, the armed forces and the industrial ministries. The party dominated all of them. Although no clause in the USSR Constitution expressly enshrined the existence of a one-party state, this had been the political reality since within a year of the October Revolution. The party was the supreme agency of state in everything but name.

The status of Politburo member or Central Committee secretary involved perks that were hidden from the public. If one of them travelled abroad on an official trip, it had to be in a special plane.[3] He or she – it was almost always a he – automatically had use of a large dacha, maids, a chauffeur, a ZiL limousine with radio telephone and at least four regular bodyguards. The dachas typically had a sauna, a tennis court and a cinema as well as a greenhouse and orchard.[4] The 'Zarya' villa at Foros in Crimea was opulent by Soviet standards and was kept available for the General Secretary. Built in a period when general secretaries were incapable of the most moderate physical exercise, it had an escalator down to the beach. The villa's entire complex was rumoured to have cost an astronomical 189 million rubles.[5] There were just a few obstacles to the growth of official privilege. Office-holders could get into trouble if they built their own private apartments, for example, although usually it was possible to find ways round the prohibition.[6]

Brezhnev, Party General Secretary since 1964, had fallen into mental decline in the late 1970s as his health worsened and he spent months at a time in his dacha at Zavidovo, outside Moscow.[7] With its concentric series of guard posts and its panorama of fields – green in summer, snow-covered in the Russian winter – it provided peace and quiet for a sick old man. He had once gone there for its hunting. Now he repaired to Zavidovo to convalesce.

He had a group of Politburo members around him who quietly agreed the main lines of policy before submitting them to him. His personal aide Konstantin Chernenko, whom he promoted to the Politburo, was one of them. The others were KGB Chairman Yuri Andropov, Defence Minister Dmitri Ustinov and Foreign Affairs Minister Andrei Gromyko. Seeking to position himself well for the succession, Andropov gained Brezhnev's permission to leave the KGB in May 1982 and become a Central Committee secretary. He and Ustinov were on friendly terms, which had made for an axis of collaboration between the military-political and security-political sectors of the leadership. Ustinov and Andropov were close to Andrei Gromyko.[8] They settled policy among themselves on many occasions before turning to the rest of the Politburo. Although Gromyko tended to monopolize foreign policy, this was always on the understanding that he would do nothing to incur the disapproval of the others. Ustinov was known as a tremendously hard worker. This was just as well since, after the death of Marshal Grechko in 1976, he was both Defence Minister and Central Committee secretary.[9]

International relations were a peculiarity in the Soviet political setting. All other areas of official policy were held subject to robust, regular control by the Party Secretariat. The exception was the Secretariat's International Department, which had no authority over the Ministry of Foreign Affairs. The General Secretary and the Politburo alone could call Andrei Gromyko, the Foreign Affairs Minister, to account.[10] His ministry was on Smolensk Square, a few minutes from the Kremlin by car. The minister's office was no. 706, six floors above ground level.[11]

On 22 November 1982 Andropov gave a grim report to the Party Central Committee on the USSR's economic plight, so grim that his words were withheld from the press:

> Comrades, what we're talking about is the practice that has become a fixed one for us: the buying of grain and other products abroad.
>
> We went to this length several years ago in a dreadful period after a bad harvest. We went without hesitation. And the first person who for a long time didn't agree to this was our own dear Leonid Ilich: 'How can we, a grain-producing country, suddenly go to the Americans to buy grain!' But subsequently we became

accustomed to these purchases. It became an automatic sort of procedure: we started to buy grain abroad every year; and we got butter from somewhere or other, meat from somewhere else, milk from somewhere else again.[12]

Andropov attacked the policy:

Of course, you'll understand that they haven't given us all this because they thought we had beautiful eyes. Money is demanded. I don't want to scare anyone but I will say that over recent years we've wasted tens of billions of golden rubles on such an expensive thing.[13]

He offered no alternative to what had become normal policy, but made it clear that something had to change.

He entrusted the Party Agricultural Department with overseeing improvements. The department became famous inside the leadership for calling for additional massive extra investment in grain and dairy production. By 1981 the state budget included what has been called the 'highest food-and-agriculture subsidy known in human history' – it was $33 billion at the official exchange rate.[14]

Andropov called for action against the waste and humiliation that the degradation of the Soviet countryside involved:

How are we to look at this? It's said that we have the gold lying around. After all, it can never feed anyone. And so we bought up food supplies and we fed people. But this is untrue. It's untrue that there's gold just lying around. At the present time, comrades, gold is not simply lying around. Everyone who follows international life knows that gold is fighting a struggle at the present time and that the Americans are conducting a currency war against everybody and above all against the Soviet Union and the other socialist countries.[15]

He accused Washington of using finance as a weapon. The Americans in his view had deliberately brought Poland to its knees and had started to do the same to Hungary. Their success was encouraging them to try the same tactic against the USSR: 'Reagan has descended to such insolence as to say: yes, we'll sell grain to the Soviet Union, but we'll exhaust them by doing this. Isn't this correct? Yes, it's correct.'[16] Andropov would no longer tolerate this situation: 'We are the sort of power that really must wage a struggle against the Americans, including a currency struggle, at the necessary level.'[17] Again, he proffered no solution, only an indication that things could not continue in the same old way.

In contrast, Andropov remained somewhat optimistic about international relations, insisting that détente was not dead but only moribund. In another unreported comment he noted that Prime Minister Thatcher had called for both sides in the Cold War to reduce their stockpiles of nuclear weapons. He stated that the USSR was certainly not demanding unilateral disarmament by the West.[18] He gave the impression that the late General Secretary would have approved of his report. This was a diversion. He really wanted a break with the past.

When expounding policy to officials in the Ministry of Foreign Affairs, Gromyko spoke of a cult of the arms race in Washington. He called on them to believe in the justness of Soviet intentions and actions. He was repeating a catechism. No cardinal instructed his bishops with greater fervour. He passed over China quickly; the Chinese, he believed, were uninterested in 'normalization' of relations with the USSR and preferred to stand shoulder to shoulder with the US. There was therefore no prospect of better links between Moscow and Beijing.[19] Two days later, Gromyko repeated his sermon at a meeting of the ministry's party activists. Anatoli Adamishin, head of his First European Department, felt disturbed by the Minister's analysis. What was dispiriting was that Gromyko really seemed to believe his own words. Adamishin allowed for the fact that the Minister, like the other 'old men' in the Politburo, might be saying things to console himself and others. But if there was any insincerity, there was also self-deceit – and this was hardly the basis for a sound foreign policy.[20] Gromyko told the Party Central Committee, claiming that the Soviet Army was having a 'stabilizing impact on the situation' in Afghanistan. He reported that the Afghan army had kept control of operations even though there were grounds for concern about the intrusion of foreign armed units – Gromyko did not specify where they had come from. He mocked the 'hysterical campaign' mounted in the West against the Soviet military action as a sign that the USSR's strategy was proving effective.[21]

As early as February 1980, behind closed doors, the Politburo was starting to search for ways to extricate itself from Afghanistan.[22] But this was a fitful discussion and Soviet rulers generally thought it their duty and right to hold on to every gain made by the USSR since

1945. What they had, they intended to keep. They did not want to 'lose' Afghanistan, Eastern Europe or even Vietnam.[23] In June 1983 Gromyko again told the Central Committee plenum that all was well with the Soviet armed forces. By choreographed arrangement, Moldavian Communist Party First Secretary Ivan Bodyul stepped forward to emphasize how enthusiastic the Cubans were about the USSR and its political and economic system.[24] Alexander Chakovski, reporting on a congress of writers in Bulgaria, assured the Central Committee that all was well in Eastern Europe; he added that the American writers in attendance, Erskine Caldwell and John Cheever, were angry about their own country's bellicosity. He quoted British novelist C. P. Snow as having said: 'We mustn't allow atom bombs to fall into the hands of criminals and lunatics.'[25]

Soviet leaders were aware that economic reality was a different matter from the official rhetoric. On 18 January 1983 Nikolai Ryzhkov told a conference of Central Committee secretaries chaired by Andropov:

> We have now received the data from the Central Statistical Administration about the results for 1982. What's to be said about these data? Of course it's said there that the plan has been ful-filled. But that won't be the truth because it's the corrected plan that's been fulfilled whereas the plan envisaged by the nation-al-economic plan has not been fulfilled. This is how we get a situation here where we ourselves create disinformation.[26]

He was saying something that was general knowledge in the leadership. What was extraordinary was the fact that he brought it up for discussion. He would not have done this if he had not thought he had Andropov's blessing. Andropov had plucked Ryzhkov from the State Planning Commission and promoted him to the Party Secretariat as soon as he became General Secretary. Ryzhkov joined Vladimir Dolgikh and Mikhail Gorbachëv in a confidential research unit that Andropov created to ascertain the roots of the USSR's economic mal-aise – Dolgikh and Gorbachëv were Central Committee secretaries.[27]

Many Soviet officials saw that the USSR bore an excessive burden as a result of its military expenditure. What was less widely appreci-ated was the oddity of the arms industry within the economy. In the US, advances in military technology had often facilitated innovations in the production of mass consumer goods. The WD40 lubricant, Teflon non-stick coating, scratch-resistant lenses and robust computer keyboards were just a few examples among many. There was very little of this in the USSR, where the expenditure on armaments had resulted in few indirect benefits in material comfort or cultural facility. The 'military-industrial complex' was a law unto itself. Diplomat Anatoli Adamishin understood the true scale of the long-term economic damage.[28] Truly massive over-production of missiles took place. Stockpiles were increased for the contingency that a protracted sequence of nuclear strikes would occur if and when the Third World War began. There were officials in the Party Defence Department, Soviet patriots all, who knew that this made no military or economic sense.[29] But what the General Staff laid down, no politician was going to challenge.

Adamishin was shocked by what he learned on joining one of the policy-planning groups under Andropov in 1983. The economic prospects were grim and getting grimmer. By the 1990s, it was suggested, industrial output would grow annually by less than one per cent. The productive base had been neglected. The state budget had been wasted on defence, agriculture, housing and foreign aid. The leeway for dynamic initiatives within the current framework had vanished and it was only inflation that disguised the fall in average household incomes. Adamishin was horrified: 'The future's been eaten up!'[30]

The technological gap between the USSR and the West gave rise to frank discussion at a meeting of the Party Secretariat as early as 4 August 1979. Ivan Frolov, deputy department chief, reported that the country was sixty per cent less effective than capitalist societies in replacing manual labour. Nothing said on behalf of the ministries or the State Planning Commission contradicted this gloomy picture. Ministers struck back at Andrei Kirilenko when he rebuked them; they told him that ministries could hardly do better with their resources unless they were told how to go about it – and Kirilenko manifestly had no idea: he was merely handing out the usual threats and admonishments. The ministers made clear their resentment at being treated like naughty schoolboys.[31] The USSR was in an impasse. Its leaders knew that it faced economic competition that it stood no early chance of matching. Its institutional mechanisms of party rule and state industrial coordination were proving inadequate, and nobody was coming up with any ideas that would lead to basic improvement. There was plenty of criticism and too little thought about solutions. The Politburo was filled overwhelmingly with people who were habituated to an organizational and ideological order that had undergone scant change since the death of Stalin.

The USSR's usual way of easing its difficulties was to sell more oil and gas abroad. The growing problem was that the Soviet petroleum industry had outdated technology and was failing to achieve its targets. Although the State Planning Commission had a project to increase production to 650 million tons by 1984, the oil ministers reported that only a target of 625 million tons was realistic – and this would mean that hard-currency profits would almost disappear.[32]

The USSR would obviously have to rely on selling precious metals abroad; but it was no longer easy to find sufficient sources. The American trade embargo introduced by President Carter after the invasion of Afghanistan caused additional damage in 1980. Vodka distilleries were ordered to cut output in order to save cereal stocks for other purposes. Chemical industries also suffered from the cutting of US–Soviet commerce.[33] The Party Secretariat received further information of an unfavourable nature. None was more depressing than the fact that over two-thirds of collective farms were running at a loss. The State Planning Commission no longer had the funds to increase the subsidy to them. Even so, the farms themselves knew that the banks would never call in their loans. There was economic deadlock.[34] Things were made worse by the fall in the world prices for gold and diamonds. Reagan's squeeze on Western financial credits began to have an impact and the Politburo kept an eye on a situation that grew steadily less promising. The USSR was in a deteriorating condition that had dire implications for its capacity as a superpower as well as its ability to stave off popular discontent.[35]

Gorbachëv urged radical reform on Andropov. Each was aware that the annual budget disguised reality on a systematic basis. Retail prices were held fairly steady only by regular secret transfers from the state savings bank, where Soviet citizens kept vast sums of money mainly because there was a deficit of consumer goods to buy. Though Andropov withheld permission for Gorbachëv and Ryzhkov to gain unrestricted access to the budget, they could anyway see that the situation called out for fresh measures. They also recognized that it would never be enough to raise prices on food and clothing. The Politburo discussed the matter on a number of occasions and its members, being aware of the grumbles in society, were anxious about the predictable unpopularity of retail price reform. At the same time they wanted to accumulate the resources for industrial modernization. Andropov rejected Gorbachëv's advice. Instead he opted for 'a struggle for discipline' under the supervision of the party and the KGB.[36] Workers would be urged to carry out their duties conscientiously; officials would be threatened with penal sanctions for corrupt or lackadaisical activity. The Soviet state fell deeper into the clutches of the police.

While recognizing the growing difficulties, Andropov was determined to show that the USSR could match any American threat. He recruited a group led by Dmitri Ustinov to prepare policy on the Strategic Defense Initiative. Deputy Chairman of the Council of Ministers Yuri Maslyukov and Chief of the General Staff Sergei Akhromeev were appointed to it, and leading scientific institutes as well as the KGB were under orders to offer their services. Nominally the head of the group was Politburo member Ustinov but the person who coordinated activity was the world-renowned physicist Yevgeni Velikhov.[37] In subsequent years Velikhov became the human face of the USSR's critique of the Strategic Defense Initiative.[38]

This group – 'the Velikhov group' – operated in an increasingly frantic atmosphere. Soviet scientific and technological lobbies were eager to compete for funds to design and build a counterpart to the American programme. Later the Party Defence Department was to grouse that this was putting the cart before the horse. It would indeed have made sense for Velikhov and his colleagues to start by examining whether America's programme had a realistic chance of success or was just a President's thoughtless whim. There was a growing body of American scientific opinion – in Stanford University, Cornell University and the Academy of Arts and Sciences as well as at the IBM Corporation – that the initiative was unlikely to achieve its stated purpose. But the Velikhov group applied itself to the task that Andropov had handed it.[39] If the Americans were going to have a new weapons system, the USSR had to have one as well. 'The main enemy' must not be allowed to steal a march on the Soviet defence preparations.[40]

The budgetary imbalance built up like steam in a pressure-cooker. The Politburo did not ignore this and Andropov consented to price increases for gas, electricity and phone calls.[41] But he refused to remove the indirect subsidies that the USSR made to Eastern Europe. When the proposal was made to end financial support for Bulgaria, he came down firmly against anything that might weaken the togetherness of the 'world communist movement'. He quietly overrode the argument that the USSR received little benefit from Bulgarian agricultural supplies. His fear was that the Chinese would offer to plug the gap if the USSR ended its funding.[42] This had happened in Albania since the 1960s and Deng Xiaoping could well decide to make further mischief. While preserving the East European economic lifeline, Andropov was determined to avoid any indulgence to the Romanians. The Romanian President Nicolae Ceauşescu held up a Political Consultative Committee meeting with his objections to the draft summary communiqué, and no amount of persuasion made a difference. A Romanian official explained to the Soviet side that Ceauşescu would give way if the USSR guaranteed close to forty million extra barrels of oil. This infuriated Andropov, who absolutely refused to accept Ceauşescu's proposal. For once, Ceauşescu backed down and signed the communiqué.[43]

The atmosphere at Politburo meetings changed. Open discussion became normal and lively remarks could be made. But Andropov was the unchallenged leader, and it was he who summarized the decision and put it forward for acceptance.[44] This is not to say that the old rituals entirely disappeared. When Politburo members appeared on the platform at a Central Committee plenum, everyone still stood to applaud like schoolchildren.[45] But inside the Politburo and Secretariat there was a fresh practical urgency of purpose. Andropov liked to hear about the alternatives before settling his policy even if this meant hearing some uncomfortable ideas.[46] His Politburo protégé Mikhail Gorbachëv told him that the state budget was seriously unbalanced; he recommended the urgent need for a price rise in food and clothing. Andropov rejected the idea – evidently he thought it dangerous to annoy Soviet citizens who were less than satisfied with the goods on sale. There were limits on the kind of changes he found acceptable. Essentially he opted for the idea of making the current system work better. He put his emphasis on enforcing discipline in office and factory and on the farm.

The Politburo was ageing. Andropov and several other members of the Soviet leadership had health problems. As a result on 24 March 1983 the Politburo updated its orders about the personal routines of members of the Politburo and the Secretariat and deputy chairmen of the Council of Ministers. The working day should commence at 9 a.m. and end at 5 p.m. A break for lunch was obligatory. Any work outside these hours, including official receptions, should be reduced to a minimum. For leaders over sixty-five there were additional curbs: they should not start work until ten in the morning and should take two and a half months' vacation annually; they were also advised to work at home on one day every week.[47] Politburo veteran member Arvid

Pelshe commented that the man who most needed to look after himself was none other than the General Secretary.[48] Andropov's kidneys required regular dialysis, and he was frequently compelled to take periods of recuperation when he had to put public business aside. He was an ill man even before he assumed supreme power.

The confidential records of his period in office show that the Soviet leadership frequently discussed a wide spectrum of external and internal problems facing the USSR. Anxiety was not limited to the secret reformers who would reveal themselves in 1985. The entire Politburo under Andropov wrestled with the dilemmas of a growing emergency.

But it was one thing to have some awareness of the difficulties and entirely another to recognize the need for radical solutions. As ever, the leadership's instinct was to look for improvements by means of palliative measures. It held tight to Marxism-Leninism, the October Revolution and the one-party police state as the rock-hard foundation of stability. But Marxism-Leninism itself was in trouble. It was hopelessly inadequate in the struggle against Islam and Christianity. The Turkmenistan Central Committee First Secretary M. Gapurov reported that even civil weddings in his Soviet republic were always followed by a religious ceremony led by a mullah. Circumcision was a universal practice there. F. D. Bobkov, KGB Deputy Chairman, reported a growth of anti-Russian and anticommunist attitudes in Turkmenistani society; he also noted that eighty-five per cent of women of working age 'sit at home' just as their ancestors had done. Gorbachëv and the other secretaries expressed amazement that such a situation could prevail nearly seventy years after the October Revolution.[49] The obstacle to inculcating Marxism-Leninism was equally strong in Russia itself. Everywhere party propaganda departments were reporting attitudes ranging from apathy and cynicism to outright hostility. The discrepancy between official claims and the experience of reality was obvious, and the Politburo sensed a gathering crisis in popular consent to communist party rule.[50]

Though air was escaping from the tyres of Soviet ideology and society, Andropov remained essentially committed to tradition. In the late 1960s he had rejected advice from his aide Georgi Shakhnazarov, who advocated basic political and economic reforms and cast doubt on the sense of aiming at comprehensive military 'parity' with America. He had no intention of adopting a more modest foreign policy after Brezhnev's death; he also took pride in Stalin's collectivization of agriculture and rapid industrialization as well as the victory in the Second World War. His objective was to repair the Soviet order without destroying its foundations. He wished to start with measures affecting the Soviet economy, Eastern Europe and America.[51] But he had a petrified commitment to the system of power he had inherited from Brezhnev. As his health went into steep decline, he had no answer to the problems that he and the rest of the Politburo discerned.

6. CRACKS IN THE ICE:
EASTERN EUROPE

While the global rivalry with America intensified, Eastern Europe became more troublesome for the Soviet Politburo and its client rulers in the region. People said that the Polish situation was hopeless but not serious. The point about this joke, if it truly was a joke, lay in the feeling that although communism could do nothing to cure Poland of its ills, there was no prospect of the communists falling from power. The Polish People's Republic seemed locked forever in the cage that the USSR had fitted around it in 1945; and the same fate appeared to await most of the other East European countries.

Poles in their millions detested their Soviet oppressor. Even inside the ruling establishment there were many who shared this sentiment. The standard of living in Poland was higher than in the superpower on its eastern frontier; but the Polish people, with their large diaspora and access to global information, also knew how shabby their conditions were in comparison with the countries of advanced capitalism. They resented their nation's subjection to an alien power and its ideology. They yearned for genuine independence as well as cultural and religious freedom; and their history was full of episodes of revolt against foreign dominion. They had secured a degree of easing of their plight since the mid-1950s. The Catholic Church had permission to function, and even to welcome Pope John Paul II – Archbishop of Kraków until his election as Supreme Pontiff in 1979 – to the country so long as there was no direct threat to the political status quo. The communist leadership under Eduard Gierek had financed its ambitious industrial schemes through loans that it raised from West European banks. This had bought it time as subsidies were made to wages and food products; but by 1981, according to the American Senate Committee on Foreign Relations, Poland owed $27 billion in hard currency – half in private bank loans and half in governmental credits. The banks were calling time on the Warsaw communist authorities and refusing to ease the rescheduling.[1]

Reagan followed his predecessors in trying to improve relations with Eastern Europe. On 10 June 1981 Assistant Secretary of State Lawrence Eagleburger spelled out that America would do this only to the extent that these countries complied with the Helsinki Final Act and helped to lessen East–West tensions in Europe.[2] The American Senate Committee on Foreign Relations gave its assent.[3] The Polish authorities had not been the worst in the region; indeed, they had one of the better communist records in respect of human rights – but if America and Western Europe were to bail out Poland's economy yet again, it might well be money down the drain, and anyway many politicians in America objected to basing policy on the notion that there was a meaningful difference between one communist government and another.[4] Even if the Americans chose to boost their aid to Poland, it would be several years before the Polish economy recovered – and the financial strains on Western creditors would be huge. Unless the West did something to help, moreover, the USSR would be able to tell the Poles that the blandishments of the capitalist countries were mere rhetoric. On the other hand, there was the worry that in alleviating the Polish economic crisis, Western governments would be helping an oppressive communist administration at the expense of Poland's people.[5]

Brezhnev had unsettling meetings with East European communist leaders on their Crimean vacation. When Czechoslovakia's Gustáv Husák pushed for military intervention in Poland, Brezhnev offered no opinion of his own. Nicolae Ceauşescu of Romania demanded that the USSR should do something instead of just talking. Brezhnev snapped back: 'Why are you always repeating "do, do!"? We have headaches every day because of Poland. And all you can say is "Do something!"' The Bulgarian communist leader Todor Zhivkov sided with Brezhnev and said that Ceauşescu was just a bag of wind.[6]

It was a dire situation from the communist standpoint. But what was to be done? The Soviet leadership preferred it to be Poles who repressed Poles. Brezhnev's health was too poor for him to sustain constant supervision of the Warsaw situation. His regents – Suslov, Gromyko, Andropov, Ustinov and Chernenko – had intimidated the Polish leadership in the previous year when they ordered three tank divisions and a motorized rifle division to be made ready for a possible invasion of Poland. The Baltic, Belorussian and Carpathian military districts were put on permanent alert. If any of the Polish armed forces showed signs of disloyalty it would be necessary to heighten the scale of mobilization.[7] The Politburo wanted to keep the Poles on tenterhooks in order to help Jaruzelski go about his business of pacification. On 9 September 1981 it endorsed a proposal from Defence Minister Dmitri Ustinov and Marshal Sergei Sokolov to hold the next meeting of the Warsaw Pact's Military Council on Polish soil.[8] This would surely drive home the message that what had happened in Czechoslovakia in 1968 could be repeated.

On 16 November 1981 Suslov summarized the Soviet leadership's position at the Party Central Committee plenum. He condemned Gierek's 'voluntaristic economic policy' of using Western loans for a 'great leap forward'. The national debt had risen disastrously to $27 billion and yet the Poles still had to turn to the West for spare industrial parts. Poland had been drawn into the clutches of global capitalism. The Polish administration had been naive and irresponsible.[9]

According to Suslov, 'bourgeois ideology' had flooded into the country through its twelve million Polish emigrants. He did not spare Poland's communist leaders, who had increased the size of the party to three million members without sieving out unsuitable recruits. He objected to how Gierek had allowed peasant smallholders to join. Suslov no longer saw the Polish United Workers Party as a respectable communist party. Gierek could not claim that he had not been warned: Brezhnev personally had repeatedly expressed his concerns.[10] Suslov added that the West's 'subversive centres' had exploited the situation by infiltrating their cadres and spreading their ideas.[11] The Soviet Politburo had wanted General Jaruzelski to replace Gierek. But Jaruzelski had rejected the idea in favour of appointing Stanisław Kania. Whereas Jaruzelski might have stood up against the strike movement, Kania struck deals with them; and Suslov was pessimistic about future events.[12] The Politburo sent emissaries to compel Kania to comply with the USSR's demands. Kania objected to being told to get tougher with Solidarity. On 18 October the Central Committee of the Polish United Workers Party, supported by leaders of the army and the security forces, pushed him aside in favour of Jaruzelski. Suslov commended this as a 'positive phenomenon'.[13]

He reported that Brezhnev congratulated Jaruzelski the next day, offering comradely advice:

I think that the main thing you now need is to select for yourself some reliable assistants from the circle of dedicated, firm
communists, bind them together, bring the party into the movement, inspire it with the spirit of struggle. This is the key to
success in the literal sense of the word.[14]

The Cold War was not forgotten:

The aggressive forces of imperialism, especially the Reagan
administration, would love to warm their hands on [the Polish
crisis]. Prodding the Polish counter-revolution towards extremist
actions, they are at the same time openly provoking the socialist
countries, counting on us losing our nerve. They are provoking
direct intervention in Poland and simultaneously trying to find
grounds for accusing the Soviet Union and the socialist countries
of having such intentions.[15]

The Polish crisis had to be resolved by political methods. If the Soviet
Army moved into Poland, the West would make trouble in Cuba, Vietnam or Africa and probably enforce an economic blockade of Eastern
Europe. The USSR had to resist temptation.[16] The Central Committee
endorsed Suslov's report.[17]

Poland's central bank had foreign debts it could neither pay nor
reschedule. Polish communist leaders had approached the Politburo
for emergency assistance but the scope for a Soviet material subsidy
had narrowed as the USSR's own financial circumstances took a turn
for the worse; and indeed the economic planners in Moscow were
annoyed that East European countries – not just Poland – were failing
to supply the quantity of industrial goods specified in signed contracts
for Russian oil.[18]

At the Politburo on 10 December 1981, Andropov reported that
the KGB was as yet undecided about whether Jaruzelski had definitely
determined to make a move against Solidarity. He admitted to difficulty in increasing economic assistance but set his face against military
intervention. Jaruzelski had stated that Marshal Kulikov, the commander-in-chief of the Warsaw Pact, promised military help. No one
in the Politburo knew whether Kulikov had said any such thing; but its
members were of a single mind in turning down the idea.[19] The Politburo established its own Polish Commission to keep events under
review. Its first chairman was Suslov, who kept a brake on his instincts:
'We'll settle things peacefully even if Solidarity comes to power there.'[20]
Ponomarëv of the Party International Department pushed for some

signal from the Polish communist leadership that they remained committed to communism. He asked why the Poles, decades after the start of communist rule, had still not completed the collectivization of agriculture. Suslov hushed him by pointing out that Jaruzelski had more urgent tasks at a time when Solidarity posed a threat to communist rule.[21]

On 13 December 1981 Jaruzelski introduced martial law, threw Solidarity leaders and activists into prison and seized their printing presses. He was never to express regret for what he did. He reasoned that if he had not acted as he did, the USSR would have invaded. He claimed that Brezhnev had confirmed exactly this intention when they talked on 1 March 1981.[22]

Martial law did not settle the situation in Poland but merely delayed the moment of political explosion. The Western powers were faced with a dilemma in deciding what they could do about the situation. Richard T. Davies, former US Ambassador in Warsaw, urged Reagan to enable America to 'resume its leadership of the free world'.[23] Davies also wrote to Haig suggesting that financial credits to Poland should be made conditional upon the granting of reforms.[24] Reagan did not need to be prodded. He spoke with passion at the National Security Council: 'I took a stand that this may be the last chance in our lifetime to see a change in the Soviet Empire's colonial policy re Eastern Europe.' His preference was to place an embargo on trade and even communication with the USSR until martial law was lifted, political prisoners were released and talks were started with Lech Wałęsa and Solidarity. He banked on impressing on all NATO countries that they would risk estrangement from Washington if they failed to show the same toughness.[25] As he drafted his Christmas message to the American people, Poland remained close to his heart: 'We can't let this revolution against Communism fail without offering a hand.'[26] Thatcher expressed her support but other NATO leaders were more guarded in their statements.[27]

Even the Vatican took a cautious view. Cardinal Casaroli assured Reagan in December 1981 that 'the time was not yet ripe for major change in Eastern Europe'. Reagan explained his general strategy as moving beyond the constraints of mutually assured destruction towards big reductions in the number of weapons on both sides.[28] Casaroli in the same year was intervening with the Kremlin frequently on the Polish question.[29] Neither Pope nor General Secretary wished to see violent trouble in Warsaw. John Paul II made his second papal visit to Poland in August 1983. Having spent years combating communism as Archbishop of Kraków, he knew the tricks needed to undermine the communist order. He made regular pronouncements on spiritual values. He gave Poles a degree of confidence that things would eventually turn out well for them. Receiving Vice President Bush in the Vatican in December 1984, he called for the Americans to nudge Jaruzelski towards a less repressive policy. He reckoned that party rule left the Polish First Secretary with little room for manoeuvre. Only measures of cautious pressure on him stood any chance of proving effective and the Pope recommended that the West should lift the regime of economic sanctions.[30]

Back in Moscow, Gromyko was encouraging about Jaruzelski's chances. On 23 December 1981 he told his ministry officials that things were going better than he had thought conceivable. He was pleased about Poland's army and security forces. He accepted that problems would take years to solve even with the USSR's assistance; but he felt certain that Soviet people would understand that this was a price worth paying. Gromyko knew as much about Poland as he had known about Afghanistan. He declared that the counter-revolution had had its wings clipped in Warsaw and that Solidarity was defeated. Somewhat contradicting himself, he added that socialism could perish in Poland if Jaruzelski's martial law met with defeat; and he accepted that the process of 'normalization' might take many more years. He insisted that the Poles themselves were dealing with the situation without dictation by the Kremlin.[31] His performance did nothing to enhance confidence in the Politburo. Poland had been one of the touchstones of the USSR's status as a European power. It had been the same since the Russian Empire had helped to dismember the Polish lands at the end of the eighteenth century, and Russians prided themselves on their expertise in understanding and handling the Poles. Gromyko's tired exposition annoyed Ministry of Foreign Affairs officials who saw deep trouble ahead.[32]

The American administration had its own dilemmas about Eastern Europe, and the Defense Department clashed with the State Department. When the National Security Council met on 5 January 1982, Weinberger put the case for economic sanctions against the USSR. He wanted to prohibit the International Harvester Company from completing a deal to sell agricultural machinery to Moscow. Weinberger asked for the licences to be cancelled. While admitting the machines could not be turned into weapons, he declared: 'It helps them to harvest more efficiently – it improves their economic conditions.' Reagan disliked the idea of damaging the finances of an American company that had been having its own difficulties; he also worried that other Western countries would step into any void left by the kind of embargo that Weinberger wanted. Weinberger also called for a policy to call in the Polish loans. The communist leaderships in both Moscow and Warsaw, he declared, should be put under financial strain. Secretary of State Haig remonstrated: 'We must be careful. The United States has no interest in seeing a country like Romania go bust.' This failed to convince Weinberger, who contended: 'The Soviets can't take over all the tottering economies of Eastern Europe.' Reagan refused to take Weinberger's side. He continued to wrestle with the dilemmas about how to constrict the USSR's freedom of action without endangering the American economic interest or world peace.[33]

When Brezhnev met Jaruzelski in August 1982, he stressed the need to reinforce measures against 'antisocialist and counter-revolutionary elements' in Poland; at the same time he promised to send Soviet economic assistance.[34] The Soviet Union was paying dearly for its continued dominance. According to Gosplan's accounts in 1982, Moscow advanced credits to Warsaw to the value of $690 million in convertible hard currency to ease the burden of repayments to Western banks and to enable the purchase of grain, sugar and other foodstuffs. The USSR deferred the requirement for the Polish government to make the scheduled payment of the $1.8 billion it owed to Moscow. Soviet leaders got Hungary, Bulgaria, East Germany and Czechoslovakia to agree to a charge-free diversion of $465 million of Soviet oil supplies to Poland.[35]

The situation elsewhere in Eastern Europe was scarcely more inspiriting for the Kremlin. The point men for the Soviet leadership were the party general secretaries – according to Lev Shebarshin, the KGB did not possess an 'agentura' in Eastern Europe.[36] The Kremlin held discussions with them at meetings of the Warsaw Pact's Political Consultative Committee. Each member state took it in turns to host the meetings. The leaders were required to give reports on the situation in their countries. Open discussion was brief and the reports were long and tedious – the fact that the Soviet General Staff frequently supplied a speaker did little to enliven the proceedings. Critical comments by the Romanians could sometimes stir up the debate, but usually the boredom was intense, being broken on one occasion by the decision to divide the seating of member countries by the criterion of alcohol production! Czechoslovakia and the German Democratic Republic sat together as beer producers; Bulgaria, Hungary and Romania as specialists in viticulture; Poland and the USSR as distillers of vodka. Sometimes it was decided that a relaxed atmosphere would be facilitated by convening in some holiday resort in Crimea. This was the point: once they had delivered their compulsory reports they relaxed in each other's company and chatted 'heart to heart' on a confidential basis.[37]

When Brezhnev reported on his Crimean sojourn to the Politburo on 9 September 1982, he harped on familiar themes. The East Europeans had moaned about the under-delivery of Soviet products while acknowledging that they remained heavily in debt to the USSR as well as to Western creditors. Brezhnev argued that only greater regional integration of the economies would bring about improvement.[38]

When the USSR convoked a meeting with Central Committee secretaries from six Warsaw Pact countries, they frankly recognized that loans from the West were at the fulcrum of their difficulties. Soviet leaders wished to keep political and military dominion over Eastern Europe. They would have liked to have added economic control, but their own financial resources were stretched to the maximum. While warning about the dangers of indebtedness to Western banks, they could not step into the breach.[39] The alternative was too dreadful for them to contemplate. Romania's Nicolae Ceaușescu was the exception as he repaid his Western loans at the expense of his people's standard of living. At the June 1983 Party Central Committee plenum, Andropov yet again proposed greater economic integration inside the Warsaw Pact, arguing that this would benefit each economy.[40] As regards friendly countries in Asia, Africa and Latin America, he preferred to terminate subsidies and make them responsible for their own economic development. The USSR no longer had the resources to sustain its activities in Eastern Europe or more widely in the world. Not wishing to finish on a pessimistic note, he still managed to declare that world capitalism was undergoing a 'deepening of [its] general crisis'.[41]

When the topic had come up at a meeting of East European party secretaries in mid-1979, the Bulgarian Dmitri Stanishev abandoned the usual euphemisms and called things by their names:

What kind of coordination? . . . People need to be fed and dressed and to live as well as in the German Federal Republic, for example. In that eventuality there'd be no need for ideological coordination.

Here you are, for instance, grumbling that we're taking credits from the West and sliding into debt. But what can we do about it? You don't give them and can't give them. We produce this rubbish – [he tugged with his fingers on Zagladin's shirt front] – at a higher level of quality than you do, and then you sell such shirts in Moscow for foreign currency in the special 'Berëzka' store. So what are we to expect? And the people ask us: 'Why can't we live as well as or better than West Germans or Austrians or Danes who travel to our Golden Coast in their tens of thousands?' And it's not millionaires who travel to us but ordinary workers.[42]

He was blurting out a truth that usually nobody dared to express: that no economy in Europe east of the river Elbe, including East Germany, could meet the demands of its citizens with anything like the effectiveness of the countries of advanced capitalism.

The USSR had gripes about the East European communist administrations. For years Bulgaria had received a subsidy from USSR to improve its agricultural infrastructure. The idea was for the Bulgarians to use it to supply Soviet stores with fruit and vegetables of high quality. Bulgaria failed to fulfil its obligation. The deliveries were usually late and in poor condition – and Sofia still fixed the prices at higher than the world market rate.[43] The USSR was Bulgaria's milch cow; and Zhivkov, by reporting on the heavy effects of Bulgarian indebtedness to the West, was hoping that the USSR's leaders would find it desirable to save him from bankruptcy.[44]

Though Poland was communism's gaping wound in Eastern Europe, the situation in the other countries had a distinct potential to turn septic. The diplomat and party official Valentin Falin doubted that the German Democratic Republic could last much long when he became Ambassador to West Germany. He had issued an alert as early as 1971. Andropov was so worried that he withheld Falin's note from the Politburo; he told only Brezhnev. Falin persisted in his role as the Cassandra of Soviet foreign policy. In August 1980 he came to Andropov again and predicted that tanks would have to be used within the next five years if Erich Honecker stayed General Secretary. Andropov did not disagree, except that he thought that the trouble might happen sooner.[45] For Falin, the best option for the USSR was to aspire to the highest reward in return for agreeing to German reunification.[46] Although nobody thanked him for his frankness, he did not suffer demotion. The Soviet party leaders appreciated that Falin was drawing attention to a genuine problem even though they did not like his practical recommendation. Andropov's preference was to cross his fingers and hope for the best. He had no answer to the East German problem and made no effort to get Honecker removed from office.

Honecker disguised the East German economic malaise through secret loans raised through Bavarian conservative leader Franz-Josef Strauss. Gromyko had warned Honecker against this.[47] Honecker took no notice. In the absence of a subsidy by the USSR, he felt he had no choice.[48] Soviet leaders, fearing that East Germany was turning into a dependency of West Germany, aimed at least to prevent the deepening of trade and financial links between them.[49] Their suspicions about Honecker were fed by his political rival Willi Stoph, who thought that he had fallen under the influence of 'the evil genius' of his Secretary for the Economy, Günter Mittag.[50] Whereas Moscow thought nothing of finalizing agreements with Bonn without consulting East Berlin, it strenuously objected whenever East Berlin behaved publicly in the same way. The triangular relationship of the USSR and the two Germanies was in a deep tangle. Moscow expected East Berlin to castigate Bonn while Moscow itself, for its own reasons, avoided such polemics. Hermann Axen, one of the East German party secretaries, was too discreet to raise the matter in front of others; but he let his Soviet comrades know how he felt about the hypocrisy.[51]

Honecker pretended that he faced no difficulty. Apart from Ceaușescu, no Warsaw Pact leader was readier to tussle with the Kremlin. Moscow by the early 1980s was seeking to increase the amount of oil and gas it could sell on world markets. Honecker objected to any diminution in supplies to the German Democratic Republic. When Soviet officials proved intransigent, he insisted on receiving a written letter on the matter from Brezhnev himself.

Meanwhile Romania remained an irritant for the Politburo. It criticized the Warsaw Pact's invasion of Czechoslovakia in 1968 and opposed the USSR's pretensions to dominance in Eastern Europe. As a result it gained 'most favoured nation' status from America. Ceaușescu was feted on official visits to the NATO countries. He raised loans from Western banks. At the same time he imposed one of the most oppressive communist regimes through labour camps, police surveillance and a cult of his own greatness that blended nationalism and Marxism-Leninism. He depicted himself as the protector of Romanian independence.[52] Nevertheless a modicum of fraternal relations was kept with the USSR despite the harshness of Bucharest's rhetoric.

Brezhnev paid an official visit in 1975 with a view towards salvaging warmer links with Romania. Boris Ponomarëv, head of the Party International Department, appeared at a Politburo meeting and asked that official statements should become less indulgent to Ceauşescu. Brezhnev demurred and told him: 'Drop it, drop it! As regards theory and all theoretical matters, we've fallen behind him. We ought to try and catch up with him: he's an iron Stalinist!'[53] The Soviet leaders would have preferred Ceauşescu to stay quiet. But so long as he stayed inside the Warsaw Pact and promoted some form of the one-party communist state, they left him alone.

Enver Hoxha's Albania, on the other hand, had left the Pact in 1968 and sided with China in the Sino-Soviet dispute. The USSR accepted this as a fait accompli. Stalin had expelled Tito's Yugoslavia from the Soviet Bloc in 1948 even before the Warsaw Pact was created, calculating that this would soon bring the troublesome Tito to heel. The opposite occurred. While enforcing one-party communist rule, Tito thumbed his nose at Stalin and turned to the West for financial credits; he also introduced reforms that gave much freedom to Yugoslav workers to influence how their enterprises were managed. Yugoslavia was one of the founders of the global non-aligned movement which refused allegiance to either the USSR or America. Neither Stalin nor his successors could bring the country under control, and the same proved true with Albania. Moscow took a dispassionate view on this. The Albanian authorities remained committed to communism and were never likely to threaten Soviet geopolitical interests.

The USSR could never take East European approval for granted in the big questions of foreign policy – and not just on the part of the Romanians, Yugoslavs and Albanians. Minds were concentrated on the consequences for the region if nuclear war broke out. The Soviet leadership always had to prove its readiness to negotiate with the Americans. Even the USSR's 'peace policy' required regular defence. Gromyko found that he had to justify Soviet foreign policy even to the Czechoslovak communist leadership. Husák held power in Prague from 1969 only because the USSR had chosen him, and he never openly opposed its objectives in international relations. But the Kremlin wanted more than passive support from the client kingdoms of its 'outer empire'. For this to happen, Husák and his associates needed to become convinced. On 23 March 1982, for example, Gromyko tried to persuade Czechoslovak Foreign Affairs Minister Bohuslav Chňoupek that the Soviet Union had modernized its weaponry only after the Americans had done the same. The USSR's policy supposedly was defensive and reactive.[54]

The Hungarians hardly bothered to disguise their desire to move the pivot of their foreign trade away from the Comecon countries. They contacted Bryan Cartledge, UK Ambassador in Budapest, for advice about how to approach the European Community. They deliberately kept the USSR out of the picture. Hungary's independent interests, in the opinion of János Kádár and fellow leaders, were its own business.[55]

On 9 September 1982 Reagan signed a National Security Decision Directive about Eastern Europe. The idea was to supply systematic guidelines for the encouragement of more liberal and pro-Western tendencies across the region. The American administration hoped to loosen the ties between the USSR and the rest of the Warsaw Pact. American official measures would show economic and diplomatic favour to those countries that moved towards reform in internal and external policy. Applications for entry to the International Monetary Fund would be judged on this basis. Credit facilities would be withdrawn for failures to slacken repression.[56] There was an awareness in Washington that the peoples of Eastern Europe were discontented with their governments and resentful of Soviet domination. It was also known that the USSR lacked the economic capacity to increase its subsidies to the region. The President and his entire administration did not overlook the possibility that Moscow might decide to impose its will by military force just as Stalin, Khrushchëv and indeed Brezhnev had done – and nobody was willing to go to war over any such action. But Reagan was determined to increase the strain on Moscow. He knew that the Soviet Union faced difficulties, and he intended to aggravate them.

7. THE SOVIET QUARANTINE

The struggle between communism and capitalism was not restricted to economics. America and the USSR clashed over ways of organizing and thinking about politics and society. The mistrust on both sides was pervasive. Reagan and his officials felt they could have no confidence in Moscow until the Politburo lifted what Churchill had called the Iron Curtain. The Politburo based its thinking on the premise that seclusion was a guarantee of security. Walls and barbed wire were used to confine citizens to their Marxist-Leninist paradise. The less they knew about the outside world, the easier it would be to suppress the potential for resistance.

Soviet exit visas were a coveted privilege. Foreign reporters could work only under licence, and the authorities denied telephone and telegram facilities to any journalist who dared to write negatively about what he witnessed. A strict internal censorship was implemented through a central agency known as Glavlit. Novels, poems, symphonies and paintings had to obtain official validation before release to the public. All newspapers belonged to the party or the government and the general editorial line was centrally coordinated. A few foreign communist dailies were put on sale in a limited fashion, but solely on the understanding that their politics coincided with the Politburo's outlook. The purpose had been the same since Lenin's time. The party leadership wanted to impress on all citizens that its ideas were just, democratic and progressive. Communism was depicted as the exclusive repository of humanitarianism. Its spokesmen depicted capitalism as the gravest threat to peace in the world. People were taught to regard American power as reactionary and imperialist, and 'class struggle' was treated as underlying the conflict between the great coalitions led by the USSR and America.

Since Stalin's death in 1953 the Soviet leadership had relaxed the ban on foreign literature which anyway had never been universally applied. Glavlit and the party apparatus had always promoted classical authors such as Shakespeare, Byron and Dante. Indeed, the claim was made that the USSR was the only state where most people had easy access to such works of art. Under Khrushchëv and Brezhnev the scope of permitted translations was expanded. Readers could buy books by Rudyard Kipling, Arthur Conan Doyle and Agatha Christie. The novels of John Steinbeck and Ernest Hemingway were widely on sale. Apparently the authorities felt that Soviet citizens could be trusted to discern the critique of the system that such authors portrayed.[1]

Glavlit banned any works that eulogized the market economy, religion or the social hierarchy in capitalist countries. The security forces backed this up with a number of practical precautions. The KGB had long been alert to the way that dissenters could use typewriters and carbon paper to copy illicit material. Every typewriter in the country had to be registered with the authorities. Since every machine made its own peculiar imprint on the page, this would theoretically enable the security police to ascertain who was the source of the trouble. Photocopiers were regarded with even greater concern.[2] Only a few were obtained even for the highest level of state institutions – and everybody was strictly forbidden to run them for private purposes. Personal computers, which were becoming a standard item of domestic equipment in the advanced capitalist West, were almost unknown in the USSR. Libraries kept Western journals and magazines in rooms reserved for only the most trusted of readers. In the Leningrad Academy of Sciences library it was possible for senior physicists to consult monthlies such as the London-based *Nature*. But staff cut out advertisements which were thought likely to spread ideological contamination. The irritating result was that researchers could not read the scientific text on the obverse sides of such pages.[3]

It was reported that 70,000 lectures were delivered daily in the USSR to counteract 'alien influence' from abroad.[4] Marxism-Leninism was purveyed in schools, libraries and the media. The Politburo recognized that its doctrines were having less impact as people learned to ignore exaggeration and outright falsification. Whereas in the 1930s it had laid claim to supremacy in every branch of human knowledge, it steadily came to reduce its messages to a core of fundamental principles. Lenin was depicted as a secular saint who did no wrong; his embalmed corpse was kept on display in a mausoleum below the walls of the Kremlin on Red Square. The October Revolution of 1917 was interpreted as the pinnacle of human achievement. Communism was predicted to spread worldwide. The USSR was hymned for saving the world from the Third Reich in the Second World War; it was touted as the global bulwark against the reactionary, imperialist coalition led by the United States. Official propaganda no longer claimed that material conditions in the Soviet Union surpassed those in the advanced West. But pride and optimism were not abandoned. The Politburo under Brezhnev, Andropov and Chernenko insisted that the 'way of life' in the USSR was superior to anything encountered abroad. Employment, housing, education and health care were said to offer advantages to all rather than to a small, wealthy elite. The collectivist principle had supposedly proved its worth.[5]

This approach was applied in every country where communism was established after the Second World War. First it happened in Eastern Europe, then China, North Korea, North Vietnam and Cuba.

Nearly all large Soviet cities had facilities to carry out the jamming of Western radio broadcasts. The Russian-language programmes of Voice of America, the BBC, Radio Free Europe and Deutsche Welle were singled out for attention across the USSR. Broadcasts in Ukrainian on religious themes gave grounds for growing official concern, and the authorities started a campaign of counter-propaganda against Ukraine's Christian traditions. Vatican Radio was an irritant to the authorities in Catholic-inhabited Lithuania. Orders arrived from Moscow about what and when to jam. The work was never done with complete precision, and sometimes the employees – inadvertently or deliberately – interfered with Radio Moscow. The problem was also that Soviet radio sets had short-wave capacities that enabled determined citizens to switch around the dial and find some foreign 'capitalist' frequency. It was always easier to do this at country dachas than in the towns. The USSR's legislation meant that no one was banned from listening to whatever they wanted. Since Stalin's death in 1953 it was no longer a pretext for arrest. People could write to foreign radio stations so long as their letters did not contain 'knowingly false fabrications discrediting the Soviet political and social system'.[6]

The Soviet authorities systematically inhibited messages and packages passed to and from the USSR. Anyone wishing to phone an acquaintance abroad had to book the call a day in advance and use a special booth. This made it easy for the KGB to listen to what people were saying. The international traffic in letters and telegrams attracted the same kind of suspicion. The regulations were severe about the kind of goods that could enter the country. The American postal service had to inform customers that it was unable to convey several types of

parcel to the USSR. No photos at all, no photographic films or video-
tapes, no cameras. No images of a religious nature. No fashion
catalogues. No medicines, food or even underwear.[7]

The USSR never trusted Eastern Europe enough to allow free
passage to and from its allied countries: people, facilities, finance and
ideas were subject to severe restrictions. The border that stretched
along the eastern edges of Poland, Czechoslovakia, Hungary and
Bulgaria was heavily guarded. Affidavits from the authorities in
foreign communist states were required before permission was granted
to cross into the USSR. Moscow did not trust even its own Soviet
republics to issue visas. When technical specialists were needed for
work in Lithuania – such as three Czechoslovak radio experts in January 1983 – only the Lubyanka could give the go-ahead.[8] Everyone
from engineering specialists and academics to manual workers was
subject to the same vetting system. It was an exhaustive process. When
the Estonian Soviet Socialist Republic wanted a team of twenty build-
ers from Czechoslovakia in March 1983, the KGB leadership funnelled
a set of queries to its agencies in Estonia, Latvia, Lithuania, Belorussia
and the Russian city of Pskov near the Estonian border. Lack of vigilance was treated as an unforgiveable betrayal of the 'Motherland', as
the Soviet Union was described. The security forces tried to ensure
that the USSR would suffer no harm from the arrival of a score of
labourers from a friendly communist power.[9]

There was a comprehensive programme of surveillance and
arrests, and the KGB regularly advised the Politburo about additional
work that was needed to stamp out trouble.[10] Across the USSR there
was ceaseless pursuit of people who wrote anonymous written denunciations of the Soviet order. In 1979, for example, there were 2,020
authors – and the Soviet security agencies noted that this was 360
more than in the previous year.[11] Investigations were strengthened to
root out the problem. By 1983 the number had fallen to 1,325 and the
KGB took pride in its efficiency.[12] It also highlighted the activities of
foreign intelligence agencies. The CIA was thought to pose the greatest
subversive threat; the Chinese and the West Germans were thought
next in importance.[13] In Lithuania, the Vatican could not be overlooked. The KGB noted that Pope John Paul II and the Roman Curia
were exerting themselves, by methods legal or otherwise, to infiltrate
and undermine the USSR.[14] Catholic priests and nationalists reached
out to young Lithuanians ever more boldly in the early 1980s. Illegal
publications were on the increase. The anti-Soviet Lithuanian diaspora

was thought to be deeply involved in fostering such activity and to have received encouragement from the Reagan administration.[15]

The extreme nature of the USSR's concern about Western interference was revealed on 25 July 1980, when the Politburo resolved to treat Amnesty International as a subversive organization.[16] Hardly an organization existed abroad that might not prove pernicious to Soviet interests. The authorities were wary to the point of political paranoia.

The 'main enemy' – America – had supposedly made a practice of recruiting 'state criminals' as agents to send into Lithuania. The KGB was referring to individuals who had fled the country illegally and made themselves available to the CIA or other Western spy networks. One of the USSR's priorities had therefore been to secure the border with turbulent Poland. Anybody crossing from the USSR without the correct papers was guilty of 'treason to the Motherland'.[17] In 1981 the Lithuanian KGB tightened the regulations for permission for foreign travel. If anyone in possession of a 'state secret' applied for a foreign trip, the authorities should do everything to find a suitable alternative traveller who lacked access to such secrets.[18] Certain groups of Soviet citizens were regarded as particular targets for foreign attempts at subversion. In Lithuania, Jews attracted suspicion even though the Holocaust in the Second World War had left only 24,000 of them living in the republic by 1970. By 1981 the number had fallen to 14,000 as the consequence of emigration. The KGB still stayed on the alert in case the Jewish diaspora should seek contact and make mischief. The Israeli intelligence agency Mossad was thought to be at work in Vilnius and other cities.[19]

The authorities also placed limits on the number of foreigners legally visiting the USSR. Lithuania was a case in point. In 1984 as few as 58,566 non-Soviet citizens entered the republic. Only just over a quarter of them came from capitalist countries and businessmen were a distinct rarity: just 283 of them entered Lithuanian territory. American citizens formed the biggest contingent from the world of capitalism; next came the West Germans and the French.[20] Tourism from abroad could have become an impressive source of income for the USSR, but the dangers to the Soviet order appeared obvious: Western intelligence agencies would surely try to infiltrate agents among the holidaymakers. A schizophrenic policy was therefore adopted. The Inturist organization established offices in the world's capital cities and advertised schedules and prices for trips to the Soviet Union. Moscow and Leningrad were heavily promoted as venues. Cruise trips were advertised to the Baltic ports of Riga and Tallinn as well as for package holidays that took in Kiev, Vilnius or the cities of the south Caucasus. The other half of the policy was that the tourists were treated like sheep who could only move around in a carefully controlled herd. Guides delivered paeans to the wonders of the USSR's achievements. Each day was filled with a programme that would so occupy the visitors as to leave them no time to make a nuisance of themselves.

Lithuanian KGB officers could still see no end of problems. It was as if the sacred soil of the USSR would be defiled whenever people came into the country by land, sea or air.[21] Vilnius, despite being a jewel of European urban architecture and culture, attracted only 7,335 holidaymakers from capitalist countries in 1983. The KGB claimed to have discovered scores of troublemakers among them: eighty members of anti-Soviet émigré organizations, twenty representatives of Zionist bodies, ten Christian 'sectarians', twenty-one priests and eleven nuns.[22] The number of such holidaymakers rose to 15,449 in 1984, still a pathetically small number for a country twice the size of Belgium.[23] But this was how the policemen liked things: fewer foreigners meant less trouble. Even travellers from other communist states caused palpitations in the KGB, which reported that its efforts to prevent 'the uncontrolled crossing' of Poles into Lithuania were far from totally successful.[24] The ending of martial law in Warsaw in summer 1983 had made a bad situation worse by increasing the number of people travelling from Poland and opening a dangerous human 'canal' of subversion.[25] In Andropov's last years as KGB Chairman, he reported that more than seventy Solidarity activists had been deported for trying to stir up strikes. Thirty anti-Soviet groupings had been broken up in Ukraine, the Baltic and Armenia. Foreign-inspired strikes in Estonia had been crushed.[26]

The KGB liked Soviet people to move around as little as possible inside the USSR. The proposal for a car rally across the boundaries of Soviet republics caused trepidation. The counter-intelligence agencies were alert to the potential for trouble.[27] Quite what they suspected might happen, they did not explain.

As regards Soviet citizens travelling abroad, even scientific exchanges with the West were thought dangerous. While the USSR gained technological benefits, the entry of foreigners and the exit of Soviet citizens for lengthy periods could never be contemplated with equanimity.[28] The Party Secretariat drew up 'Basic Rules of Behaviour' for everyone about to make a trip across the border: politicians, diplomats and ordinary tourists. Permission for international travel was a privilege granted only to people who enjoyed the full confidence of the authorities. The worry was always that individuals might defect or might somehow be compromised by Western intelligence agencies. Vacations to Eastern Europe were regarded with much caution. The Politburo preferred its citizens to take their holidays at hotels and camping grounds inside the USSR's frontiers. Trips to 'capitalist and developing countries' were treated as vastly more dangerous, and the KGB tried to ensure that its citizens went in controllable groups with a designated leader. One or more of its officers would usually accompany them incognito. Travellers received strict lessons beforehand on the need to behave as their country's ambassadors.[29]

The 'Basic Rules' enjoined everybody to voice support for the Politburo's external and internal policies. There was to be vigilance against the devices of foreign intelligence agencies. Travellers were to minimize their vulnerability by confining their activity to the official purposes of their journey. They were forbidden to take documents of a personal nature out of the USSR. Once arrived at their foreign destination, they had to register their presence at the nearest Soviet embassy or consulate. They were to resist every temptation that could expose them to corruption. Paid private work was prohibited. Acceptance of expensive gifts was also put under ban. No one was to deviate from a planned itinerary without prior permission from the group leader. Under no circumstances was the traveller to incur any kind of debt. There was also a warning against taking an overnight railway journey in a compartment with a person of the opposite sex. (Since homosexuality was illegal in the USSR there was no need to issue an admonition against potential liaisons with anyone of the same sex.) Everybody was to appear well groomed and keep their hotel room clean and tidy. The rule was that a written report should be delivered to the authorities within a fortnight of returning from abroad.

If ever America and the USSR were going to improve their relationship, this quarantine had to stop. Communist leaders had introduced it so as to reinforce their control over their society and fend off foreign intrusion. The Soviet Union became a militarized police state. Official practices over decades led to a ruling mentality of suspicion about everything in the world beyond the state borders. Kremlin traditionalists and even advocates of moderate reform could not imagine life very differently; the American administration made it a requirement for any basic rapprochement.

8. NATO AND ITS FRIENDS

The Soviet Union was not the only superpower to experience trouble with its allies. America had constant difficulty inside the North Atlantic Treaty Organization (NATO), formed in 1949, which offered protection to Western Europe and Canada. The Americans also gave military guarantees to Japan, South Korea, Australia and New Zealand. All these countries had market economies and most of them practised democratic politics. The result was a continual internal flux that contrasted with the calcified systems of power in communist states. Despite America's continued primacy as a world economic power and its indispensable provision of military guarantees to its allies, Washington had to exercise sinewy skill to secure assent to its goals in foreign and security policy. No part of the globe was harder to handle than Western Europe with its communist parties, peace movements, proud nationalisms and recurrent doubts about American purposes. A British Foreign and Commonwealth Office memo put it starkly at the start of the 1980s: 'In the interests of solidarity with the Americans, which all recognize as an overriding interest, the Europeans have adopted policies in which they do not believe. The multiplication of "consultations" has hardly helped.'[1]

On 12 December 1979 the NATO Council had resolved to counteract the Soviet deployment of SS-20 missiles in Eastern Europe. This decision was taken even before Soviet forces swarmed into Kabul on Christmas Day. As usual, the NATO plan was formulated in Washington. President Carter proposed to send 108 Pershing-2 missiles and 464 Tomahawk land-based cruise missiles to member countries in Europe. Every Pershing-2 would have the capacity to strike Moscow within ten minutes of being fired, and the Tomahawks with their superior accuracy would be able to hit anything over a range of 1,500 miles.[2] The Politburo felt deeply alarmed even though it was its own reckless SS-20 initiative that had created the problem. The arms race was quickening, and the strains on the Soviet economy were bound to be enormous. Such gains as had been made in relaxing the tensions between the two military blocs in Central Europe were tossed away along with the benefits from the growing financial linkage with West Germany. Soviet leaders had misjudged President Carter. Far from lacking the stomach for confrontation, he aimed to make the USSR pay dearly for its latest military challenge. And the Kremlin's dispatch of air and ground forces to the Afghan war later in the same month only stiffened his determination.

Communist parties and groups had never thought well of Carter, and Reagan's reaffirmation of the plan to deploy Pershing-2s and Tomahawks increased their campaign against the American military bases on the continent. Other parties on the left had similar objections to NATO's policy, and the fact that a sizeable proportion of the electorates voted for them complicated the situation for Reagan. West European governments wanted the security of the American nuclear 'umbrella' but wanted to specify how the President should hold it over them.

Margaret Thatcher had swept to political victory in Britain in 1979 and was one of Reagan's few close European allies. When he entered the White House, the social-democrat Helmut Schmidt was Chancellor in Bonn; and in March 1981 the socialist François Mitterrand was elected French President. In Italy, the Christian Democrats had dominated cabinets since the Second World War but in August 1983 they were supplanted by the Socialist Party under Bettino Craxi. Reagan was pleasantly surprised when he and Craxi met: 'He's a different kind of Italian official. He's socialist but totally anticommunist.'[3] From Reagan's viewpoint, the situation improved somewhat when Helmut Kohl and the Christian Democratic Union, together with the liberal Free Democratic Party, won power in West Germany in October 1982. Schmidt as Chancellor had been a solid advocate of the NATO alliance (Reagan had recorded: 'Found ourselves in agreement on future course with regard to Russia'[4]), but Kohl was a conservative who sympathized with a broader range of objectives. Reagan had met him in October 1981, and there had been a meeting of minds: '[Kohl] said that the 250,000 demonstrators in Bonn against the US came from all over Europe and it was an affair orchestrated by the Soviet U[nion].'[5] Once Kohl became Chancellor, Reagan took pleasure in their encounter in Washington: 'We did hit it off and I believe we'll have a fine relationship.'[6]

Even Thatcher and Kohl, however, held reservations about

American policy. The earlier priority on both sides had been to build up stockpiles of strategic weapons that could be fired at each other across the Atlantic. As America and the USSR installed new intermediate types of ballistic missile just hundreds of miles from the Iron Curtain, there was discussion about the possibility of confining a nuclear war to the European continent. West European leaders feared that this could lead to a weakening of the American guarantee of all-out retaliation in the event of a Soviet offensive – and Reagan's passionate espousal of his Strategic Defense Initiative served to increase such an attitude.

France formed the core of West Europe's awkward squad. Trouble had occurred throughout the ten years from 1959 when Charles de Gaulle was President. In 1966 he went so far as to withdraw France from NATO's integrated command structure; he also expelled NATO from its headquarters at Fontainebleau. What lay behind his policy was a determination to retain French freedom of action. De Gaulle reasoned that his armed forces had their own nuclear weapons which could independently deter a Soviet attack. With military *sang froid*, he could see no national interest in defending West Germany against an East German assault. His dislike of France's subordination to any foreign power was shared by his successors regardless of party and ideology. They devised a hybrid approach to the other Western powers. They publicly emphasized French sovereignty while retaining membership of the alliance's political bodies and contributing to their deliberations. They also made overtures to the USSR independently of American wishes. De Gaulle had a vision of a 'Europe from the Atlantic to the Urals'. Implicitly he seemed to aspire to a warming of relations with the Soviet Union. But neither he nor any later French President did this at the expense of a rupture of ties with Washington. At root, Gaullism was more show than reality at acute moments of East–West tension.

West Germany, whose eastern border was shared with a line of communist states, never snubbed its nose at the Americans after the French fashion. The post-war arrangements left NATO bases in a large number of places, and it was obvious to most citizens that without them, Bonn would be helpless against a Soviet-led invasion. The threat of the SS-20s was bad enough. But there was also the danger represented by the huge size of Soviet and allied forces in Eastern Europe. Every NATO power in Western Europe felt trepidation since the Warsaw Pact held its forces in an essentially offensive disposition.

NATO AND ITS FRIENDS

The USSR denied that there was any need for concern. (Not until 1988 would any of its officials admit that there was even a grain of sense in the West's complaints.)[7] West Germans were all too aware that if war broke out, the first campaign would be fought on their territory. However much they resented occupation by the Americans, British and French, they appreciated the security they provided as they themselves built up their conventional troops and weapons. Membership of NATO permitted their businesses to flourish. The West German 'economic miracle', started in the 1950s, was sustained over ensuing decades, and there was no serious rival to the country's industrial might in the European Community.

The Bonn government tried to lessen the tensions between America and the USSR and saw intermediate-range weapons as a needless aggravation that, with goodwill on either side, could be eliminated. When Brezhnev met Schmidt in Bonn in May 1981, the West Germans made a drastic proposal for a reduction of intermediate-range nuclear missiles. If the USSR would remove its SS-20s, the Americans should take away their Pershing-2s. Taken by surprise, Brezhnev muttered something indefinite before Gromyko intervened to insist that the Soviet Union did not intend to halt its programme of deployment. When Schmidt refused to be put off, Brezhnev agreed to think about the proposal. Gromyko suggested a further conversation at the airport but he sent Deputy Minister Kornienko in his place. This failure to follow up Schmidt's idea was a profound error; it only gave succour to those in the American administration like Weinberger and Casey who argued that no compromise was feasible with the Soviet leadership.[8]

Schmidt nevertheless continued to seek closer and better ties with the USSR and Eastern Europe. With his approval, banks in Frankfurt and Munich provided Poland, Hungary, Romania and – above all – East Germany with financial credits that enabled them to give the impression of economic viability. He endorsed plans for Soviet natural gas to be piped to West Germany. The rise in the world market prices for petrochemicals in 1973 persuaded ministers to look outside the Middle East for their supplies. In the period of détente, moreover, Western powers got ready for opportunities for collaborative schemes that would rejuvenate the Soviet economy. The crises over Afghanistan and Poland undermined this as the Americans expanded the existing regime of embargos on trade with the USSR and Poland. They prohibited the sale of oil and gas equipment, and from June 1982 they claimed the right to compel compliance from foreign companies as well as American ones. This was bound to disrupt the deal recently signed between Schmidt and Brezhnev for a pipeline that would deliver gas to West Germany. Even Thatcher was annoyed with the American move. A Scottish firm was complaining that the White House was interfering with its contractual freedom, and the Prime Minister exclaimed in public: 'I feel I have been particularly wounded by a friend.'[9]

West Germany's natural gas came though increasingly from the USSR, and the Americans and other NATO governments trembled at the thought that this might weaken its resolve to stand by its treaty obligations. Bonn's reluctance to jettison the chance to help with the modernization of Soviet petrochemical facilities added to Washington's concerns. Both Schmidt and his successor Kohl, moreover, were known to be facilitating the provision of financial assistance to Honecker in return for concessions on exit visas from East Germany. Kohl at the same time paid the Romanian authorities for citizens of German ethnicity to gain permission to emigrate. The entanglement with Eastern Europe intensified. The worry for other NATO countries was that West Germany might fail to support American policy in moments of political emergency in Eastern Europe. Kohl understood this and showed a greater eagerness for the installation of Pershing-2s and cruise missiles than Schmidt had done. He evidently had no intention of becoming a pawn in the USSR's game if he could help it. But he was no puppet of the Americans either, and his known scepticism about the Strategic Defense Initiative added to the American administration's caution in the way it handled him.

Italy was another ally that gave some concern to the Americans. Its communist party was constantly a serious competitor at national elections and held power in several big northern cities. Its successive cabinets, usually headed by Christian Democrats, wavered about strategy. One of the Christian Democratic factions was led by Aldo Moro, who favoured some kind of political understanding with the communists. Moro was kidnapped and murdered in 1978 by the Red Brigades, the far-left terrorist group which accused the Italian Communist Party of betraying fundamental principles of Marxism. The death of Moro had the effect of weakening the trend among Christian Democrats to do any kind of electoral deal with communists, but the American administration continued to worry about the reliability of Italy as an ally. The automotive company Fiat had built a big car factory at Tolyatti, the new city on the banks of the Volga, in honour of the late Italian communist leader Palmiro Togliatti. Like the West Germans, the Italians relied heavily on the USSR for its supplies of natural gas. Giulio Andreotti, the former Prime Minister who served as Foreign Affairs Minister from 1983, was active in trying to secure a good working relationship with Gromyko. Not surprisingly, Reagan preferred Pope John Paul II to the Italian politicians of his acquaintance. The Vatican under the leadership of the Polish pontiff maintained staunch opposition to the USSR, atheism and Soviet domination of Eastern Europe.

While the Pope was close to the American President on many of the biggest questions about communism, Prime Minister Margaret Thatcher was still closer. They had bonded as political soulmates at their first meeting at the House of Commons in 1975.[10] Neither of them had been in power at the time, but they kept in touch and took pleasure in each other's subsequent ascent to national leadership. Thatcher regarded West European socialists such as Mitterrand in France and Schmidt in West Germany with distaste, and the unilateral nuclear disarmament leanings of a section of the British Labour Party simply horrified her. She welcomed Reagan's election to the White House as a sign that America was recovering its confidence after its humiliation in Vietnam. She stood out against all those in Western Europe who refused to accept the need for firmness in dealing with the USSR; and when *Pravda* branded her as the Iron Lady, she gloried in her achievement in annoying the Kremlin.

Even Thatcher's loyalty to Reagan was put under severe strain. In 1982 the Argentinian military junta annexed the Falkland Islands and for some days before the Royal Navy reached the South Atlantic, there was confusion about America's policy on the coming conflict. Unlike Secretary of State Haig, Caspar Weinberger at Defense wanted to assist the British. His intervention tipped the balance of opinion, for which Thatcher was forever grateful, and the Royal Navy received intelligence data that helped to achieve victory over the Argentinians. A much more serious contretemps with the American administration occurred in October 1983, when Reagan ordered the invasion of the tiny Caribbean island of Grenada to overthrow a new communist government. Grenada belonged to the Commonwealth and Thatcher felt that Reagan at the very least should have informed her of his plans in advance. He manfully endured the force of her fury by telephone. She already felt doubts about his Strategic Defense Initiative and warned the President of the risk of firing the starting pistol for yet another round of the arms race. She argued that the USSR might react by producing a fresh generation of nuclear weaponry. Reagan's programme, moreover, could turn out to be only ninety-five per cent effective. Sixty million people would die if even a few missiles penetrated the shield. Thatcher was a post-war traditionalist who reasoned that nuclear weapons had steadied a balance of power through the system of mutual deterrence. The result was forty years of peace in Europe. Reagan refused to budge. He stood by a basic position, as he explained: 'My ultimate goal is to eliminate nuclear weapons.'[11]

Yet he appreciated the fulsome support she offered on nearly every other question of world politics. He recorded in his diary: 'Margaret Thatcher is a tower of strength and a solid friend of the U.S.'[12] As she grew in confidence, she dispensed with her Foreign Secretary at meetings with him.[13] The Americans regularly consulted her about their initiatives in foreign policy – the unilateral decision to occupy Grenada was an exception. Steadily the Pershing-2s and cruise missiles began to reach Western Europe. They were installed at Greenham Common near Newbury in England and Mutlangen near Frankfurt in West Germany. Brezhnev and Andropov had thrown down a gauntlet which America and her allies proved willing to pick up.

NATO tried to face the world united despite the known disagreements. A secret system of inner consultation permitted the American administration to consult the United Kingdom, West Germany and France separately from the other allies. In European affairs, these were the powers that counted for most in Washington. Even de Gaulle's pull-out from the alliance's integrated military command failed to push the Americans into excluding the French from sensitive negotiations. The Quad, as the system was known, was implicitly aimed at keeping Italy and other NATO members out of discussions. It came into existence weeks after the Soviet invasion of Afghanistan and an early priority was to coordinate allied activity, including with Japan and 'the Australasians'. Arrangements were also made to involve Canada. The supreme objective was to restrict the USSR's global power and counteract its pretensions. Whereas Brezhnev's operations in sub-Saharan Africa were regretted but accepted as almost a natural feature of the Cold War, the Afghan war was treated as an intolerable extension of Soviet influence. From 1979 onwards, America's allies and friends around the world sought to 'roll back' Moscow's recent achievements.

British policy rested on the premise that 'destabilization of states in the Soviet orbit' was a desirable objective.[14] This was never stated openly, and indeed there were concerns about the economic damage that could occur if Poland or one of the other debtor countries in Eastern Europe went bankrupt. Violent national revolts against communist power could also have untoward consequences, at least in the short term. If this was a worry in London, it was felt still more keenly in Bonn where the financial implications of trouble in the East would be on a greater scale; and nobody could safely predict how the USSR would react to direct challenges to communist rule in its 'outer empire'. America and Western Europe had watched events in Poland in 1980–1981 with deep trepidation. There was never any confidence that Moscow would refrain from sending its forces into Warsaw. NATO had worked out no practical plan for such a contingency, and certainly no country in Western Europe aimed to make it a *casus belli*. In truth the Cold War was a contest of attrition and preparation, exhausting for both sides; and though West European leaders favoured the idea of a decommunized Eastern Europe, they trod cautiously in seeking its fulfilment and in some basic ways acted to prop up the communist administration they hated and feared.

Compared to Western Europe, Canada gave little trouble to the Americans. Pierre Trudeau as Prime Minister was often critical of Reagan's attitudes and doubtful about his competence, but offered only faint objections to US policy. The Canadians, like other allies, knew they benefited from the American nuclear guarantee. As one of the G7 countries, Canada was rich in natural resources which it profitably exported to American manufacturers. The main irritation to Washington came through its refusal to cut commercial ties with Cuba and strengthen the American economic blockade. There was a certain amount of hypocrisy here as Canadian companies worked with the Cubans to exploit nickel deposits on the island and sold on much of the metal to America, where it was used in coinage.

The Japanese gave greater grounds for concern to the American administration. Japan's economic progress in the 1970s had started to involve notable successes in advanced industrial technology. It made a global impact in the sectors that produced cars, cameras, TVs and radios, and its machine-tool factories were challenging the best that America could produce. Japanese companies began to manufacture military components that were used in ships for the American navy. This was not to the liking of a defence establishment that had a preference for NATO's leading power to maintain technological primacy. The Toshiba scandal of 1980, furthermore, seemed to demonstrate an undesirable looseness of ties among the allies. Japan benefited from the nuclear military 'umbrella' that America held over it against the Soviet threat; but there was a growth of nationalist resentment of the American armed presence in the post-war decades. Nevertheless the shooting down of the South Korean airliner in Siberian air space jolted Japanese public opinion back to an appreciation of the usefulness of the alliance; and the Americans for their part were regaining their industrial ebullience as the information technology revolution spread throughout California's 'Silicon Valley'.

America's network of alliances, including NATO, required dynamic management as military, political and economic problems arose. Even the most far-off countries could unsettle the situation. In Australasia there was little fuss until 1984, when New Zealand's newly elected Labour government under Prime Minister David Lange announce a ban on nuclear-powered or nuclear-armed vessels in its waters. This challenged the assumptions about American leadership of the world-wide resistance to the USSR and communism worldwide. Lange did something unparalleled by any West European, North American or Asian allied leader. There would have been an angrier reaction from Washington if those islands in the south-west Pacific had been a bigger power and Wellington half a globe away and outside the USSR's scope of pretensions. When all was said and done, the New Zealand case demonstrated the looseness and flexibility of the 'West' in dealing with the tasks of defence against the Soviet Union.

9. WORLD COMMUNISM AND THE PEACE MOVEMENT

The Kremlin used the world's communist parties in its efforts to try and achieve its global goals. This was a difficult process after the USSR's split with the People's Republic of China in 1960, when the Chinese offered themselves as a magnet attracting disaffected Marxist-Leninist parties and groups. Beijing in fact attracted only one communist state, Albania, to its side. Unable to match the USSR in economic resources and global military power, China was more an irritant than a threat. But its absence from the occasional world conferences held in Moscow made plain that the Kremlin was no longer unchallenged in the 'world communist movement'. Gromyko impugned the Chinese for showing no interest in the 'normalization' of relations with the USSR and preferring to stand allied with America. There seemed to be no prospect of improved links between Moscow and Beijing.[1] Brezhnev gave a speech in Tashkent in March 1982 which was characteristically polemical in tone; but it did at least recognize China as a socialist country and accept its right to sovereignty over Taiwan. The Chinese noted this with satisfaction. They concluded that the Soviet leadership was seeking to moderate its difficulties with Beijing when the Afghan war was going poorly for Moscow. Deng declined to reply either positively or negatively. He felt he could bide his time.[2]

Deng was angry about Reagan's support for Taiwan during the presidential campaign of 1980, and Reagan felt the need to dispatch his vice presidential running mate George Bush to allay Beijing's suspicion. This failed to reassure Deng, who spat into his spittoon whenever Bush mentioned Reagan by name. (Deng had obviously thought he had not made enough of a point by crumpling the letter that Bush handed over from Reagan.)[3] Despite his diminutive stature, Deng succeeded in demonstrating that he and his country expected to be treated as titans.[4] Reagan increasingly followed the line that

President Nixon had set on communist China since visiting Beijing in 1972. The American objective was to strengthen the Chinese capacity to act as a counterweight to Soviet power in Asia. On 21 April 1984 he approved a National Security Decision Directive to treat the People's Republic as a friendly, non-aligned power. The aim was to ensure China's disassociation from the USSR and foster a dual effort to 'liberalize its totalitarian system' and release market forces. Arms sales were to be continued. There would be a further easing of rules on sales of advanced technology.[5] The administration was agreed that Deng was reforming China in a desirable direction and should receive American help and encouragement.

On 26 April 1984 Reagan began an official visit to China. At his meeting with Prime Minister Zhao Ziyang, he emphasized that America did not want a formal alliance and was content for China to keep its non-aligned status in world politics.[6] Deng criticized American policy in the developing countries as well as the lack of progress towards nuclear arms reduction, and Reagan gave as good as he got. Both of them, however, avoided a dispute about Taiwan: they knew that this would have ruined the atmosphere irretrievably.[7] The general effect was positive for the two sides, and a protocol of agreement on American assistance with the Chinese nuclear power programme was signed before Reagan left for America.[8]

This heightened tensions in the Kremlin at a time when they were already under strain – nerves of Politburo members had been stretched to the extreme by the Able Archer emergency. The Americans were deliberately building up the economic and military strength of the USSR's rival power in Asia. Even in the years of détente, before the Soviet invasion of Afghanistan, US Presidents had made clear to Moscow that they were determined to keep warm ties with Beijing. Under Reagan, the linkage grew stronger. The Politburo was acutely aware of what was happening, and was apprehensive about the uses that his administration might make of the Chinese factor. Soviet propaganda against China's leadership was intensive. It was only slightly less fierce about communist Yugoslavia and communist Albania. The USSR had founded the Communist International in March 1919. It could no longer exercise authority over foreign communist parties as had happened in the time of Lenin and Stalin, but its leaders remained true to the idea that the Soviet Union was the leader of the 'world communist movement'. For them, it was an article of faith that Lenin's doctrines and the October Revolution were the foundation stones of all that was progressive, humane and desirable in the twentieth century.

The man with responsibility for the communist movement around the world was Boris Ponomarëv. He had headed the Party International Department since 1955. The party leadership had learned over the decades to trust his instincts and judgement. But Ponomarëv waited in vain for election to the Politburo, and it was widely suspected that his fellow veteran Gromyko liked it that way in order to sustain his primacy in decisions about international relations. Nevertheless, Ponomarëv was a party official of importance and the scope of his duties extended to the communist and other far-left revolutionary organizations throughout the world. The exception to this global prescription were the countries with ruling communist parties, which were handled by Konstantin Rusakov at the Department for Links with the Communist and Workers' Parties of the Socialist Countries.[9] Rusakov too wielded much influence even though the importance of Eastern Europe for the USSR's interests meant that the Politburo regularly intervened when emergencies occurred or were brewing. The Kremlin no longer actively promoted the outbreak of communist revolutions around the world. It welcoming them when they occurred, but its own daily preference was to use the parties as a means of spreading the USSR's influence.

A traditional way to keep the cooperation of communist parties was by way of subsidies. Even the Italian Communist Party, which criticized basic features of the USSR, received money from Moscow. This was done in complete secrecy. No foreign communist leader wanted his nation to know that the party depended on the favours of the USSR. The resultant publicity would have been too damaging. Gianni Cervetti secretly came to Moscow on behalf of the Italian Communist Party in October 1979.[10] Having spent some time in the USSR, he spoke Russian fluently. He subsequently claimed that the Soviet subsidy had ceased two years earlier.[11]

Ponomarëv held the purse strings through the Assistance Fund for Communist Parties and Movements of the Left. Most of the money was raised in Moscow, but the USSR did not fail to impose an obligation on 'our friends' in Eastern Europe to supplement this with regular contributions – apart from easing the problems of the Soviet state budget, this had the political advantage of binding the countries of the region to the Kremlin's global purposes.[12] Ponomarëv submitted his decisions to the Politburo for its approval.[13] He was not widely loved or respected abroad. The Communist Party of Great Britain, for instance, thought him too ready to issue advice without having much idea of realistic possibilities.[14] Though the USSR never disclosed the rationale for its distribution of largesse, the annual accounts in 1980 show that the Kremlin calculated on the basis of current foreign and security policy rather than on a desire to foster communist revolutions. The priority was to secure the Soviet Union's influence and prestige on all continents, and this necessarily involved competition with America. The Politburo wished to appear as the vanguard of the global 'anti-imperialist struggle'.[15]

The biggest grant that Ponomarëv made was the $2.5 million that he gave to Gus Hall and the Communist Party of the USA. American communist candidates, including Hall himself, had suffered defeat by voters at every presidential and state election since 1945.[16] This did not bother Ponomarëv. The USSR needed an agency of continuous propaganda for its cause, and Hall was the person whom Moscow regarded as the best at performing this task. (The fact that Hall was a dour, repetitive speaker with the charisma of a faulty metronome was overlooked by the International Department.) Hall had endorsed the invasions of Hungary in 1956 and Czechoslovakia in 1968. He rhapsodized on the virtues of life for people in the Soviet Union. He sang the praises of Brezhnev while lamenting the sequence of US Presidents who had held office since he had been elected General Secretary of the Communist Party of the USA. He passed every test in the Kremlin's book, even offering support of the Soviet Army's war in Afghanistan. He and his party were cheap at the price; and when in 1982 they asked for a remission of their debts, the Secretariat recommended approval.[17]

Next in the line of financial assistance were the French communists with $2 million; the position of their leader Georges Marchais in Western Europe as a spokesman for the 'peace-loving' intentions of the USSR in Western Europe was pre-eminent. They might not have won any national election, but they never did very badly and indeed they often received a substantial enough proportion of votes to be able to influence the composition of government coalitions. France was anyway the most awkward of the Western powers for the US to handle, not least because it had withdrawn from NATO's military command structure and several of its presidents had criticized American foreign policy. The Kremlin saw every reason to prop up the French Communist Party and get it to try and increase the tensions between Moscow and Paris.[18] Soviet leaders assumed that French comrades could not

cope without their assistance.[19] They felt the need for the same gener-
osity towards the Finnish communists, who received $1.35 million.[20]
The common border with the USSR made Finland a crucial zone
for the Soviet geopolitical interest. Then, lagging a long way behind,
came Portugal ($800,000), Greece ($700,000) and Chile ($500,000).
The South African Communist Party received a paltry $100,000.[21]
The Soviet leadership had no good opinion of Joe Slovo and fellow
communists and instead focused its assistance on the African National
Congress.[22]

The Kremlin had a low opinion of Europe's communist parties.
Though Marchais felt a personal loyalty to Moscow, the growing
public debate about the horrors of the Soviet Gulag made it impossible
to toss a blanket of approval over the USSR. By the late 1970s he had
started to criticize Soviet anti-democratic practices. French communist publishers produced literature that attacked many features of the
USSR's external and internal policies. This caused much annoyance in
the Party Secretariat of the Communist Party of the Soviet Union.[23]

The challenge to Moscow mounted by West European parties
came to be known as Eurocommunism, and Enrico Berlinguer and
the Italian Communist Party were at its epicentre. Coming to the
leadership in 1972, Berlinguer adopted a strategy of 'the historical
compromise', which involved making overtures to the Christian Democrats. He criticized the USSR's human rights record and lamented
the absence of democratic freedom. He denounced the invasions of
Czechoslovakia and Afghanistan. He licensed communists in Italy to
question the version of Soviet history given in Moscow's textbooks.
Soviet leaders resented the support he extended to the Solidarity
movement in Poland.[24] Their dislike of the Eurocommunists was fierce
and sincere. Anatoli Gromyko, son of the Soviet Foreign Affairs
Minister, pronounced that Berlinguer's ideas derived from his 'aristo-
cratic' origins; he also ventured a claim that the prominent Italian
communist Giorgio Napolitano was a CIA agent. This is no sign that
the entire Soviet leadership was equally crude, but the casual way
that Anatoli spoke in front of other officials suggests that he did not
think he was saying anything unusual.[25] Ponomarëv engaged in invol-
untary wit about the Italian communists: 'I'm not convinced: if war
breaks out, they'll take a position of neutrality against us.'[26]

Nevertheless the Eurocommunists remained of some use to
Moscow, mainly because they continued to campaign for nuclear disarmament in Europe, and the Soviet leadership continued to talk to

them despite the prickliness on both sides. Of growing importance to the Politburo was what was euphemistically known as 'military-technical collaboration' with fourteen non-communist countries. These included India, Syria, Afghanistan, North Yemen, South Yemen, Iraq, Algeria, Libya, Angola, Ethiopia, Mozambique, Nigeria, Guinea and Guinea-Bissau. Nicaragua had recently expanded the list to fifteen. Moscow sent arms and advisers to each of them. The Politburo's priority was the quest for global status and influence. Aid went forth without budgetary rigour. Over the years the Soviet leadership received only seventy per cent of the cost of its supplies. Several countries were entirely let off what they owed – or were asked for less than the total amount, usually in the form of locally produced goods. The Soviet government indulged Afghanistan, Angola and Ethiopia, Mozambique and Nicaragua in this way.[27] Behind the scenes, Soviet leaders referred to such countries as 'clients'.[28]

Though the military lobby had huge influence on Soviet politics, it was not completely united. In 1982 Defence Minister Ustinov supported Castro's assistance to Angola's President José Eduardo dos Santos in the struggle against South Africa. The General Staff disliked yet another extension of the USSR's military commitments around the world; its leaders were averse to the endless extension of the USSR's commitments that had taken place in the 1970s; and they avowed that the Angolans, whose training had been supervised by Soviet personnel, should be capable of conducting their own campaign. Varennikov, who assumed command of the USSR's forces in Afghanistan after Sergei Sokolov became Defence Minister, defended this position with some robustness. Dos Santos had success only when he appealed directly to the Politburo. Ustinov had trouble with Chief of Staff Ogarkov and Varennikov at the General Staff, who wanted no increase in the Soviet military commitment to southern Africa.[29] But it was Ustinov who was the Politburo member and had the authority and temperament to impose himself. He had served in the Brezhnev team that masterminded the policy of extending the USSR's global influence by providing military advice and financial credits. He could make or break a military commander's career, and Ogarkov was taking a risk in challenging Ustinov's favoured orientation.

Meanwhile the American plan to install Pershing-2 missiles in Western Europe agitated everyone in the Kremlin and induced efforts to seek help in preventing this from happening. The communist parties – even the troublesome Italians – could be relied on to do their best. But the countries that mattered most were America, the German Federal Republic and the United Kingdom, where communists had a negligible impact on national politics. The Politburo had an interest in encouraging and subsidizing groups that campaigned for 'peace' and against US policy.

In Sweden Prime Minister Olof Palme came up with an idea about declaring a demilitarized corridor between East and West Germany. Although this had no appeal to the Americans, some of the Soviet military-political negotiators thought that something like it might be of value. Vitali Kataev, deputy head of the Defence Department in the Party Secretariat, suggested that there should be a corridor 150 kilometres wide; he wanted all nuclear weapons, tanks and heavy artillery to be removed from it. Before taking the matter any further, he sought and obtained Gorbachëv's approval. Akhromeev spoke angrily to Kataev and asked him: 'And do you know how many tanks we'd need to withdraw from that zone?' When Kataev replied that he did, Akhromeev asked how many. The answer according to Kataev was two thousand tanks.[30] The Defence Ministry and the General Staff were at one in only considering proposals that would permit the USSR to keep all its missiles in place in Eastern Europe. People who thought otherwise either stayed silent or were ignored. The emphasis of practical policy lay on making difficulties for the Americans in completing their programme of installation. Soviet policymakers intended to restore the military imbalance that had existed since they had started to introduce the SS-20s.

This strengthened the importance of the Western 'peace movement' from Moscow's standpoint. The FBI reported to Congress on the subtlety of the Soviet efforts – rather than try to control the Western organizations, the KGB and the Party International Department covertly nudged them in a direction favourable to the USSR's foreign and security policies. As usual, the Communist Party of the USA involved itself in the process. Abundant funding was made available from Moscow. The Kremlin targeted the World Peace Council as an instrument of its purposes, and American communists filled posts in the leadership. Other organizations that were used to enhance the worldwide image of the Politburo's objectives included the National Council of American–Soviet Friendship and US–USSR Citizens' Dialogue.[31] The Kremlin had long taken an interest in the British Campaign for Nuclear Disarmament (CND) and covertly given it material help, so covertly that CND's leaders were unaware about where such funds came from. Funds were made lavishly available since it seemed possible that such organizations might win popularity and erect obstacles in the way of the NATO plan for Pershing-2s.

The British Labour Party was another potential point of access to political influence in Western Europe. On 10 October 1981 Michael Foot and Denis Healey met Brezhnev in Moscow. Foot was courteous, Healey so boisterous that he chipped in while Brezhnev was in mid-sentence.[32] There had been discussion among Soviet officials about how to address Foot, whether as 'Mr' or as 'comrade'. Foot resolved the problem for them by shaking Brezhnev's hand warmly and, while holding on to it, addressing him as 'comrade'. Neither Foot nor Healey mentioned Afghanistan.[33] The MP Stuart Holland went to Moscow three years later on behalf of British Labour Party leader Neil Kinnock, who wanted to know the official Soviet standpoint on nuclear disarmament before his own planned visit. The Kremlin had a strong interest in encouraging Kinnock. This was a man who might become Prime Minister and declare the United Kingdom a 'nuclear-free zone'.[34] By the time of Kinnock's visit the Politburo had come to a definite policy: Soviet leaders would offer to reduce their arsenal of warheads by the same number as the British agreed to remove; they would also cease to point any of the remainder at the United Kingdom. A fudge on the protection of human rights in the USSR was also agreed.[35]

The Soviet leadership looked out for chances of destabilizing the Western powers. This was handled with caution, for fear of aggravating relations with America and its allies, but the miners' strike in the United Kingdom in 1984 was an irresistible temptation. The Kremlin, operating through the Soviet trade union movement, shuffled funds to the National Union of Mineworkers through the Swiss Bank Corporation. Union president Arthur Scargill could see that the Thatcher cabinet might make a fuss. Nell Hyett was his political adviser at the time, and at a secret meeting with officials from the USSR's London embassy, Scargill asked for the money to be forwarded to Hyett's account at the Dublin branch of the First National Bank of Chicago. When Scargill also grumbled that the United Kingdom remained able to buy coal from abroad, Counsellor Parshin and First Secretary Mazur pointed out that the USSR had ceased to supply coal or any other fuel. Scargill denounced a large section of the British labour movement. In his eyes, Labour Party leaders Neil Kinnock and Roy Hattersley were purveyors of Tory propaganda, and Scargill declared a preference for the Communist Party of Great Britain and certain left-wing Labour militants.[36]

The Kremlin leaders pursued this policy without thought for the damage it caused to Anglo-Soviet relations. They felt that they had nothing to lose at that time. Détente was dead and America under Reagan had never been more combative. If the communist and social-ist left or the peace movement could do anything to undermine NATO's self-confidence, Moscow could only benefit. Soviet leaders ignored the evidence that Western governments had proved resilient in the face of domestic opposition. NATO was not going to buckle under pressure from industrial strikes or street protests. Nor would it call off the installation of new nuclear weaponry in Europe. The Kremlin's last available gambit had failed. The West's resolve had been tested and not found wanting. But Politburo members were jealous of the status of a superpower; it was unthinkable for them to make serious concessions to American demands. The question that the Politburo had yet to answer was whether its economy could afford its global pretensions. Its resources were overstretched in Eastern Europe, Afghanistan, Vietnam, Cuba and sub-Saharan Africa. Its tech-nology was losing ground to America. Its own people showed growing signs of disgruntlement.

As yet the Soviet leaders remained determined to confront and compete with the Americans. They were locked into a condition of collective denial.

10. IN THE SOVIET WAITING ROOM

Reagan was finding that all his pressure on the Soviet leadership under Andropov seemed only to make them dig their heels in. Nevertheless he resolved to maintain the pressure. In January 1984 he signed a directive about how to handle future talks with the USSR. He wanted a four-part agenda. His administration would insist that if the Soviet leaders wanted a deal on 'arms control', they would have to entirely change their behaviour on human rights, regional conflicts and bilateral exchanges. He had no intention of reverting to the practice of the détente years under Presidents Nixon, Ford and Carter, when the Kremlin had been rewarded for making concessions in any one area under discussion by America's willingness to moderate its demands in other areas. Such an approach, known as 'linkage', was anathema to Reagan's mind. He wanted to implement the most ambitious policy towards the USSR since the Second World War. At the same time he hoped to provide the USSR with 'incentives to bring the Cold War to an end'. He was firm but hopeful: 'If the Soviet government wants peace, then there will be peace.'[1]

When he opened the National Security Planning Group on 27 March 1984, there was a clash between Shultz and Weinberger. Shultz was worried about the dangerous lack of communication between Washington and Moscow. He proposed to resume arms control negotiations in Geneva. Weinberger had a visceral dislike of anything that implied compromise:

> We need to focus on the content of an agreement, not on agreement for agreement's sake. The Soviet Union has little interest in giving the President a victory. They would only give him an agreement for which he could not take credit. What are they interested in then? A SALT-II agreement that did not provide for reductions. To get an agreement, they will require us to make major concessions.[2]

Shultz retorted that it made no sense to refuse to negotiate: the sole result would be a free gift of propaganda to the USSR. Casey and Rowny were usually hostile to signs of indulgence towards Moscow, but on this occasion they held back from the fray. They knew that Reagan's mind was set on resuming talks in Geneva. Weinberger sat isolated, and Reagan pronounced himself in favour of Shultz undertaking his desired initiative.[3]

The American discussion took place at a time of uncertainty in Kremlin politics. General Secretary Andropov had been ailing even at the moment of his appointment, and on 9 February 1984 he died after his kidneys entirely gave out. Next day the Politburo endorsed Gromyko's proposal for Konstantin Chernenko to become the new General Secretary. Ustinov declared his support – Gorbachëv had asked him to put himself forward, but he declined.[4] He had an understanding with the ascendant group inside the Politburo and did not wish to disturb it. The Soviet leaders knew that Chernenko was in poor health and had never shown an imaginative understanding of the USSR's problems. For decades he had operated on the sidelines as Brezhnev's personal assistant. Indeed, it was his weaknesses that recommended him to most of the Politburo. The Politburo veterans had run affairs with little hindrance in Brezhnev's last years. They wanted to do the same again. They also aimed to put an end to the disturbances that Andropov had started to create. Chernenko fitted this requirement.

He nevertheless had a little surprise up his sleeve. As was the tradition, he kept an empty seat to his right for the man he wanted as his unofficial deputy. To the consternation of senior comrades, his choice fell upon Gorbachëv. As Andropov's protégé, he had attracted talk about being a future General Secretary. Andropov himself had implied that this role lay ahead for him; and Tatyana Andropova was to confide to Gorbachëv's wife Raisa that this was the late leader's dying wish.[5] Politburo veterans had conspired against him when Andropov wrote from his sickbed handing over the supervision of the Party Secretariat to Gorbachëv. The instruction was secretly struck from Andropov's letter.[6]

The vote for Chernenko was intended to block Gorbachëv's elevation. Now Chernenko designated him to head the Secretariat and run the Politburo's Polish Commission. Gorbachëv would also remain supreme curator of Soviet agriculture. He was never going to be a force of inertia; and whenever the sickly Chernenko was unable to function, it would be Gorbachëv who handled the levers of power. Tikhonov, Chairman of the Council of Ministers, spoke for the doubters when he said: 'Gorbachëv in the Politburo is occupied with agrarian questions, and this can express itself negatively in the activity of the Secretariat and engender an agrarian deviation in its work.' This was not a full statement of his case against Gorbachëv, whose very energy and imaginativeness gave cause for concern. When Ustinov spoke up in Gorbachëv's defence, Grishin – the Moscow City Party First Secretary – proposed to postpone the decision on Gorbachëv. To everyone's astonishment, Chernenko broke the deadlock by closing the discussion. He had made his choice and the rest of the Politburo had to get used to it.[7]

On 14 February 1984 the Central Committee assembled in the Kremlin's Sverdlov Hall to hear what the Politburo had decided. Everyone watched the door on the left of the platform to see who came through it first. Whoever it was would be the endorsed choice to become General Secretary. When Chernenko appeared leading the rest of the Politburo, the sense of collective disappointment was almost palpable. No one stood to clap.[8] This was the nearest thing to *lèse-majesté* that anyone could remember. Short of booing Chernenko, Central Committee members as a body could not have made it plainer that they deplored his appointment. Now they sat quietly and got ready to vote in his favour. Chernenko spoke in a shaky voice, holding his head low over his prepared text as he gave a brief eulogy of Brezhnev. Then Tikhonov announced the 'candidature' of Chernenko as General Secretary. A silence lasting several painful seconds followed before a perfunctory applause rippled forth as Chernenko was unanimously elected.[9] Gorbachëv closed the plenum expressing satisfaction that continuity of leadership had been assured.[10] Most of his listeners had been yearning for some kind of discontinuity; many had wanted him to become the Politburo's choice.

Chernenko chaired meetings in a limp fashion. He let people talk for as long as they liked at the Politburo, rarely venturing a comment of his own. When he sensed that the discussion was complete, he mumbled: 'Does it mean we're going to stop at this point?'[11] Ponomarëv informed his Party International Department officials that a weekly regime agreed for Chernenko gave him three full days off work and limited him to just a few hours of activity on the others.[12] No sooner had it elected him than the Politburo was treating him as a medical casualty. Each of its members got on with his duties liberated from the stresses that Andropov had introduced. The campaign against corrupt or inefficient officials ceased. Gorbachëv would remember the year 1984 with distaste, telling how Politburo members fought with each other to own the Lincoln Continental limousine that Nixon had given to Brezhnev: 'They almost killed each other.'[13] Urgency disappeared from governance. The leadership had thrown away its opportunity to set about the overdue reforms.

Gorbachëv did what little he could to counteract the trend. He was brusque and demanding with officials below the Politburo level. In August 1984 he led a discussion with provincial party secretaries on current difficulties with the harvest in Russia. He stamped on inaccuracy and evasiveness. His reaction to waffle was withering: 'Sit down, you haven't thought out your contribution!'[14] His self-belief was exceptional. He even told the Party Secretariat to end the growing cult of Chernenko in press, radio and TV. Though he had consulted Chernenko in advance, he took the risk of appearing to covet the general secretaryship.[15] The atmosphere was undergoing refreshment at the higher party levels. When the drafting group met to draw up the new Party Programme, people felt free to make jokes about Brezhnev and even about Chernenko and Gromyko.[16] At the Central Committee in October 1984 Gorbachëv played a gramophone record of a speech by Lenin. The sound engineers had done a good job in restoring aural quality. The effect was to sharpen the contrast between the masterly Lenin and the ailing Chernenko.[17]

At the Politburo's Afghan Commission, he supported the military commanders who argued that the sole way to finish the war was by political methods and wanted to aim at the Soviet Army's withdrawal. The high command sensed that there was at least one man in the political leadership who was willing to sort out the mess. Valentin Varennikov liked how Gorbachëv spoke at the commission: 'Well, what a fine fellow!'[18]

Gromyko was the main stumbling block to his further ascent. He and Ustinov acted as if they owned the Kremlin after Andropov's death. If Gorbachëv wished to impress himself on world affairs, he would have to deal with a Foreign Affairs Minister who had never been more powerful. Gromyko was a political mountaineer but he was no explorer: he had no interest in discovering about the foundation of Reagan's thinking. He thought in Marxist-Leninist clichés and sieved out all data that jarred against his ideas.[19] No ministry official dared to contradict his opinion.[20] But people knew where they stood with him.

He recruited talented people to work for him. He knew that several of them disagreed with the official line of policy.[21] Ustinov was equally dominant in the military-industrial sector; but although he was no friend of agricultural subsidies, he stayed on amicable terms with Gorbachëv. Unlike Gromyko, Ustinov defended him when others in the Politburo sought to trim his authority.[22] Gorbachëv was no mean political force in his own right. Yet he could never afford to forget that Ustinov and Gromyko were likely to have a decisive impact on his chances of succeeding Chernenko.

Ustinov never liked Ogarkov as Chief of the General Staff. Ogarkov was his own man and raised awkward questions about the USSR's military stance. He challenged the official Soviet doctrine that it was feasible to avoid total war after the first use of nuclear missiles by one side or another. He publicized his opinion in the Soviet military newspaper *Krasnaya Zvezda*:

> The calculation of strategists across the [Atlantic] ocean, based on the possibility of waging a so-called 'limited' nuclear war, now has no foundation. It is utopian. Any so-called limited use of nuclear forces will inevitably lead to the immediate use of the whole nuclear arsenals of both sides. This is the terrible logic of war.[23]

Ogarkov also wanted a complete reorganization of conventional forces. By halving the number of officers and troops, he hoped to make savings that would provide the resources to train the Soviet Army to a higher level of professional competence.[24] Ustinov was furious with him. As Politburo member and Defence Minister, he was determined to have a compliant General Staff. He got rid of Ogarkov in September 1984. Ogarkov was on vacation in Crimea, and Ustinov brusquely phoned him with the news.[25]

His deputy Akhromeev gained promotion as chief. Akhromeev had served on the Leningrad front in the Second World War. Such was his longevity of service that he liked to call himself 'the last of the Mohicans'. The UK's Ambassador Braithwaite was later to find him 'rather impressive – intelligent, with a twinkle in his eye, a long face, square skull, and not much hair'.[26] Ustinov hoped that with such a man, he could end the tensions with the high command and assert the supremacy of the political leadership.

This in itself was no solution to bigger problems. The entire Politburo knew that the USSR was in a mess. By controlling public discussion in its own country, it restricted the world's awareness of its crisis. Politburo members, though, were conscious of the many very disturbing symptoms. In their confidential deliberations they tried to make an assessment. They provided no realistic cure. They did somewhat better as diagnosticians even though they failed to deal with the entirety of the Soviet Union's malaise.

They knew that the countries of advanced capitalism were striding ahead in productivity and realizing their achievements in all sectors of their economies. The functionaries who were drafting a new Party Programme felt obliged to recognize that the West had a higher standard of living.[27] Western technological superiority was unmistakable – the Soviet timber industry was four times less productive than the American one.[28] There were only a few flickerings of optimism – one example was Comecon's agreement in June 1984 on a joint 'Complex Programme of Scientific-Technical Progress'. This was an attempt by the USSR and Eastern Europe to match American scientific progress.[29] The French were doing something similar with their Eureka programme as a rival to America's Strategic Defense Initiative.[30] Soviet ideology was adjusted in order to reflect an acknowledgement that the USSR would not overtake Western countries in material production in the foreseeable future. Marxism-Leninism had traditionally rested on comprehensive optimism. Spokesmen suggested that the country's claim to superiority lay in its 'style of life'. Whereas America gave priority to the rights of the individual, the USSR espoused collectivist principles and took pride in its guarantees of employment, free education and health care, affordable housing and cheap utilities.[31]

Even so, they recognized that Soviet agriculture was in a dreadful condition. Chernenko told the Party Central Committee in October 1984 that America might exploit Soviet dependency on cereal purchases to exert political pressure.[32] Forty-five million tons of grain and grain products would be imported that year along with half a million tons of meat.[33] Tikhonov prolonged the sombre mood. The latest harvest had yet again fallen far below expectations and drought affected wide regions. Costly irrigation schemes had failed to rectify the situation. Eleven million hectares of agricultural land had fallen into disuse in the past two decades. Budgetary plans would have to be rewritten, and Tikhonov wanted to make it compulsory for collective farms to find seventy per cent of the costs of necessary repairs from their own funds. He added that this showed the wisdom of the gigantic scheme to turn the USSR's north-flowing rivers to the south.[34] This scheme was so controversial among ecologists that Tikhonov's comment, like much else that he and Chernenko told the Central Committee, was withheld from the press. The party elite was left in no doubt that the economic situation was worsening. Without its exports of gas and oil, the USSR would never be able pay for the cereal imports it needed.[35]

Poland increased the grounds for concern as Jaruzelski's suppression of Solidarity failed to deliver economic benefit. This had woeful implications for the Soviet Politburo as much as for the Polish communist leadership. On 26 April 1984 Gromyko provided a depressing analysis. The leaders in Warsaw were obstructing an increase in trade with the USSR; they looked to the West for economic salvation. Gromyko, a believer in the benefits of collective farms, rebuked Jaruzelski for showing indulgence to rural smallholders and creating a kulak class. Jaruzelski rejected the accusation; he also claimed that the Catholic Church was more an ally than an enemy of communism. Gromyko concluded that Poland's leader had not 'matured' enough to manage his political responsibilities.[36] Ustinov said that Jaruzelski had misled the Soviet leadership and was much too complacent. Adding that the Polish United Workers Party was too passive, he expressed concern that '100 per cent of those serving in the Polish army are, if one can put it like this, the children of Solidarity'. Neither Gromyko nor Ustinov had a clue about how to solve the problems; but they agreed that Jaruzelski was the man who would have to shoulder the task.[37] When Ustinov proposed a stern conversation with him, Gorbachëv loyally hailed this as a 'far-sighted step'.[38]

The German Democratic Republic also caused anxiety in the Politburo. Articles appeared in *Pravda* in summer 1984 with implicit criticisms about Honecker's dalliance with Kohl.[39] Mutual confidence was breaking down between Moscow and East Berlin. Honecker received a summons to the USSR. Chernenko was too ill to attend and Gorbachëv presided and angrily tore into Honecker.[40] Gorbachëv was speaking for the entire Politburo, which recognized the grounds for concern not merely about East Germany and Poland but Eastern Europe as a whole. Ustinov told the Politburo that the behaviour of Kádár, Zhivkov and even Husák was just as suspect as Honecker. KGB Chairman Chebrikov sided with Ustinov. Gorbachëv too expressed his worries.[41]

The Politburo's worries about the arms race with America were intensifying, and on 29 June 1984 the Soviet leadership decided to propose talks about how to prevent the militarization of outer space. Moscow's hope was to bring the Strategic Defense Initiative to a halt by agreement.[42] The American administration welcomed the overture while staying determined that any negotiations should cover a wider range of aspects of arms control. This attitude, however, was challenged at the US National Security Council on 18 September, when Shultz and Weinberger fell into dispute.[43] Shultz wanted talks; Weinberger opposed the whole idea. Reagan refrained from arbitrating between them, but agreed to a Washington visit by Foreign Affairs Minister Gromyko. He did not want to end his term in office before giving world peace a chance. Shultz was hungry for more knowledge of Kremlin politics than American agencies were providing and hoped that Gromyko might give useful clues.[44] He commended Reagan for striking the right balance. Despite having condemned Soviet barbarity in shooting down the Korean airliner, the President wanted to send an arms control delegation back to Geneva for talks with the Soviets.[45]

When Gromyko arrived on 26 September 1984, a grand reception awaited him. At a cocktail party before lunch, the minister approached Nancy Reagan with unaccustomed charm. He was drinking cranberry juice, she soda water. He asked: 'Is your husband for peace or for war?' When peace was her answer, he enquired: 'Are you sure?' After she said yes, he asked: 'Why, then, does he not agree to our proposals?' As the guests took their seats at the table, Gromyko came across and said: 'So don't forget to whisper the word "peace" in the President's ear every night.' Mrs Reagan replied: 'Of course I will, and I'll also whisper it in yours too.'[46] The barriers to talks began to be dismantled over the following weeks. Reagan dedicated his energies to his campaign for re-election against Democratic Party candidate and former Vice President Walter Mondale. He achieved a stunning victory on 6 November by winning in forty-nine out of fifty states. Both he and the Soviet leadership saw the opportunity to resume negotiations about both nuclear weapons and outer space. On 17 November the Kremlin delivered its official acceptance, and Shultz and Gromyko were scheduled to meet in Geneva on 7 January 1985. The diplomatic frost had started – only started – to melt after years of glaciation.[47]

One of the obvious obstacles to progress was the state of Chernenko's health. The American side would find it difficult to come to an agreement with the USSR while an ailing leader remained in power. The fact that Chernenko appeared so seldom in public led to speculation in Western capitals about who was likely to succeed him. Gorbachëv's name was mentioned with rising expectancy, but nobody was predicting a political transformation if he were to become General

Secretary. Acquaintance with him and his potential remained rather faint. In 1983 he had headed a Soviet agricultural delegation to Canada and become acquainted with Prime Minister Pierre Trudeau, who laid aside time for unscheduled meetings and gained an early measure of the man's potential.[48] In June 1984 Gorbachëv led the Soviet mourners at Enrico Berlinguer's funeral. The crowds of two million supporters of the Italian Communist Party made an impact on him. He tacitly rejected Moscow's contempt for Eurocommunism, telling party official Anatoli Chernyaev: 'Such a party mustn't be tossed aside.'[49] Chants of 'Gorbachëv, Gorbachëv, Gorbachëv!' greeted him at the graveside. Italy's press treated him as Chernenko's crown prince.[50]

Even the British Prime Minister began to take an interest. While relishing her notoriety in Kremlin circles, Thatcher recognized the dangers of world politics and wanted to resume 'dialogue' with Soviet leaders.[51] She had held seminars about the USSR with specialists in the Foreign and Commonwealth Office and then with a group of academics including some leading 'Sovietologists'. These confidential sessions began to persuade her that the Soviet leadership was capable of undertaking reforms. She was even willing to test the waters with Chernenko. On the trip to Moscow for Andropov's funeral, her behaviour bordered on the flirtatious in conversation with the new General Secretary – one witness recorded that if a table had not separated them, she might have thrown herself into Chernenko's embrace.[52] She had been on ebullient form. She called for the generation of leaders who had lived through the Second World War to prevent another global war. She wanted more talks and more trade between the USSR and the West; she insisted that ideological differences should not be allowed to trump the need for an agreement on disarmament.[53]

It was not the British Prime Minister but France's President Mitterrand who took the next initiative, when he paid a state visit to Moscow in June 1984. He refused to hold back in his critique of the USSR but told Chernenko to his face – his pale and stricken face – that the Kremlin had only itself to blame for the arrival of Pershing-2s in Western Europe. While SS-20s remained in Eastern Europe, this perilous confrontation would persist. Mitterrand also protested about the treatment of dissenter Andrei Sakharov. At the official dinner Politburo member Geidar Aliev, in a loud stage whisper, exclaimed: 'It would be better if Giscard d'Estaing had been re-elected.' Gorbachëv arrived late for the occasion, pleading that he had had to attend a meeting on agriculture in Azerbaijan. Mitterrand tried flattery by expressing surprise that Gorbachëv had not as yet been included in the Franco-Soviet talks. Gorbachëv said the decision was not in his hands. When Chernenko made a mild enquiry about Azerbaijani farming, Gorbachëv abruptly replied: 'Everyone always says that everything's going well, but that's wrong. In fact agriculture is a disaster across the whole USSR.' Taken aback, Chernenko asked: 'Since when?' Gorbachëv, unabashed, responded: 'Since 1917.' The French had difficulty in suppressing their laughter at his frankness.[54] Mitterrand's delegation returned to Paris convinced that Gorbachëv was the coming man, and Soviet party official Vadim Zagladin in ensuing contacts confirmed that this was a distinct possibility.[55]

On 7 July 1984 Chernenko presented a dispiriting appearance to some British official visitors. Emphysema made him cough for a full ten seconds. He frequently broke off in mid-speech. He made no attempt to impress himself on those around him. When the topic for discussion was foreign policy, he turned abjectly to Gromyko for help. He apologized when he thought he had spoken too much. His logical capacity was negligible. When he paused, his aide Alexandrov spoke for him.[56]

Though Thatcher wanted to invite Soviet leaders to London, she drew the line at Chernenko. (She thought it premature to welcome him, an idea that was medically hard to justify.) She preferred to welcome someone from the coming generation. She had no preference for any particular individual.[57] Officials made enquiries in Canada, where Trudeau recommended Gorbachëv.[58] The British anyway did not want to bet exclusively on one man in Moscow. The Foreign Office proposed that Gorbachëv should be invited in 1984, followed by Aliev and Gromyko in the subsequent period. Thatcher agreed.[59] Gorbachëv jumped at the chance of a London visit. Since April 1984 he had served as Chairman of the Permanent Commission for Foreign Affairs in the Council of the Union.[60] This was an honorific body without authority. But it was a sign that Gorbachëv wanted to be known as more than an agricultural specialist. The new post was a help to his broader ambitions. He therefore had no hesitation in accepting Thatcher's invitation and arriving for an eight-day trip in mid-December 1984. Gromyko showed his jealousy by prohibiting his ministry officials from helping with the younger man's preparations.[61] But he had to release some of them to accompany him.[62] Gorbachëv also brought along the physicist Velikhov.[63]

On his London visit he impressed the entire Soviet delegation that he took with him.[64] When asked whether 'fresh approaches' in foreign policy were possible, he made no attempt at caution: 'Yes, of course.'[65] He also endorsed the call for an anti-alcohol campaign by Party Central Committee secretaries Yegor Ligachëv and Mikhail Solomentsev.[66] He was ignoring the etiquette of silence about matters on which the Politburo had yet to give its ruling.

The conversation between him and Thatcher at Chequers on 16 December 1984 went better than anyone had thought possible. The British interpreter saw a roguish twinkle in his eye.[67] She had Foreign Secretary Howe and her aide Charles Powell with her; Gorbachëv went along with the Party Secretariat's Leonid Zamyatin and the former Ottawa Ambassador Alexander Yakovlev.[68] The Prime Minister shook off her shoes beside the fireplace. Gorbachëv had come with a list of talking points but asked her: 'Could we do without such papers?' 'Gladly!' she replied. Putting her notes back into her handbag, she criticized Soviet curbs on Jewish emigration.[69] Gorbachëv questioned her knowledge of the USSR. He was incredulous about her idea that everything was centralized in the Soviet economy.[70] Thatcher objected to the money that Soviet trade unions were sending to the striking British coalminers. She threatened retaliation. When Gorbachëv replied that 'this has nothing to do with us', Thatcher exclaimed that such finance could not be reaching the National Union of Mineworkers without the Kremlin's knowledge.[71] Turning to Marxism-Leninism, she scoffed at what she described as the communist credo: 'Brothers: when you are free, you will do as you're told!'[72] Though Gorbachëv denied that the USSR was sending aid to the strikers, he carefully added 'as far as I am aware'.[73] He anyway promised that there would be no further subsidy. (He kept his word: when Soviet trade union leaders asked permission to send a million rubles to the strikers, the Politburo turned them down.)[74]

He adduced the *New York Times* to warn that any war with atomic bombs would create 'nuclear winter'.[75] He expressed alarm about people in Washington like Weinberger and Perle.[76] His *coup de théâtre* occurred when he took a top-secret General Staff map from his briefcase with coloured arrows marking the Soviet missile targets in the United Kingdom. Thatcher did not know whether to take him seriously. After a long pause, Gorbachëv said: 'Mrs Prime Minister, it's necessary to finish with all this, and the sooner the better.' Thatcher agreed.[77]

As she told the BBC that evening, her guest at Chequers impressed her:

> I am cautiously optimistic. I like Mr Gorbachev. We can do business together. We both believe in our own political systems. He firmly believes in his; I firmly believe in mine. We are never going to change one another. So that is not in doubt, but we have two great interests in common: that we should both do everything we can to see that war never starts again, and therefore we go into the disarmament talks determined to make them succeed. And secondly, I think we both believe that they are the more likely to succeed if we can build up confidence in one another and trust in one another about each other's approach, and therefore, we believe in cooperating on trade matters, on cultural matters, on quite a lot of contacts between politicians from the two sides of the divide.

But Gorbachëv showed a rougher side to Labour Party leaders. At lunch with Neil Kinnock, the two sides called each other 'comrades'; but when Kinnock read out a list of Soviet human rights cases, Gorbachëv turned red in the face and let forth a spate of expletives.[78] He warned that the British would get it 'right in the teeth' if they insisted on denouncing the USSR's record on human rights. He called dissenters like Anatoli Shcharanski 'turds'.[79]

Gorbachëv let nothing spoil his mood. On 19 December he felt carefree enough to stop his limousine and take an impromptu stroll along Downing Street.[80] This was hardly the conventional behaviour of a Politburo member, and the British media alerted the world to his novelty. But almost as soon as he appeared in England he was gone. Unexpected news arrived from Moscow that Politburo member Ustinov had died, and Gorbachëv had to cut short his visit in order to attend the funeral and ensure that nothing of importance was decided in his absence.

Thatcher wrote to Reagan about her impressions, stressing that he was intelligent, affable and 'relatively open'. She reported that Gorbachëv was definite about the USSR's intention to match the Strategic Defense Initiative if the Americans continued their research programme; but she added that he acknowledged that any Soviet rival programme would place a huge strain on the budget. She repeated that she could do business with him and commented: 'I actually rather liked him.'[81] Although American officials avidly read what she wrote, they exercised a degree of caution because they knew that she had her own concerns about the Strategic Defense Initiative.[82] They were sensitive to the possibility that this might have coloured her judgement of Gorbachëv. But Reagan was the President, and he trusted her instincts. She reinforced her message in person by flying to America and joining the President at Camp David on 22 December 1984. In their private meeting she repeated her excitement about the potential she saw in Gorbachëv. Unlike Gromyko, Gorbachëv had let her talk without interruption even when he disagreed with her – she liked this. He had been charming and unconstrained.

After Gromyko's trip, Reagan gave approval to a proposal to resume talks about arms control in Geneva. Weinberger, Casey and Kirkpatrick voiced disquiet – and Robert McFarlane, who had succeeded Clark as National Security Adviser in 1983, agreed with them. Their obstructiveness discommoded Shultz, who also resented the paucity of his information about the Strategic Defense Initiative. At a meeting with its programme chief, Lieutenant Colonel James Abrahamson, he felt that he received no better an account than Abrahamson might have passed to a *New York Times* reporter. Shultz showed him the door, vowing never to see him again.[83] On 14 November 1984 he told Reagan face to face about his disquietude. While Shultz carried out the President's instructions, Weinberger, Casey and Kirkpatrick treated him as an enemy and cut him out of their deliberations. They briefed journalists against him and made damaging leaks. They refused to follow up official decisions that conflicted with their preferences. Shultz objected that this made it impossible to construct a team that could achieve the kind of progress that Reagan wanted. He concluded: 'So put somebody else in at State who can get along with them. I can't – and you will see no results without a team.' The President was aghast at the idea that he might resign. Shultz appreciated the reassurance: 'I'm not ducking out. There's nothing I'd rather do. I have no hidden agenda.'[84]

Shultz wanted to bring a team to Geneva that enjoyed his confidence and was eager to bring Nitze with him. Rowny disliked what this implied. Nitze was a veteran negotiator accustomed to requirements of compromise, and Shultz turned to him for advice about how to handle Gromyko.[85] Rowny pleaded to be allowed to join the party to lend it better balance.[86] The Soviet delegation found Nitze congenial. One of them, Lieutenant General Nikolai Detinov, called him 'a man of culture and learning'. Detinov added: 'But Rowny, we don't like, can't establish a relationship with him personally.'[87] Shultz accepted the sense in having Rowny on board rather risk him causing trouble in Washington. He also brought Perle with him. Shultz's associates suspected that Perle supplied secret messages to Weinberger about the team's discussions – and Shultz expressed his annoyance: 'Richard Perle is not a nice man.'[88] He gave a pep talk to the delegation stressing that he and the President were reading from the same Bible.[89]

The plan was for Shultz and Gromyko to meet in Switzerland on 7 January 1985. The Politburo had welcomed the chance to explore possibilities for a relaxation of the tensions with America.[90] Gromyko was looking forward to having some days in the political sun. After Ustinov's death he felt free to act as if only his opinion mattered in questions of arms control.[91] He had no new ideas but assumed that the world was safer when negotiations were taking place than when the two sides refused to meet. Reagan and Shultz felt much the same. Neither of them was optimistic, and Shultz felt no warmth or trust towards Gromyko. They were calm to the point of coolness at their encounter. Gromyko was adamant about Reagan's favourite project: 'SDI is not defensive. If you develop a shield against [strategic] ballistic missiles, you could launch a first strike. We Soviets could do the same. But why do it at all? Why not just eliminate nuclear missiles themselves?' After two days of negotiation the two sides came to an agreement to meet again in mid-March. They declared it as their common purpose to halt the arms race on earth and to prevent one beginning in outer space. They committed their countries to the global liquidation of all nuclear weapons. They scheduled a resumption of arms control talks in mid-March.[92]

Shultz was pleased about the current progress but he also recognized the need to take account of the feelings of NATO allies. Nor did he forget about Eastern Europe. But Shultz was in a buoyant mood; he was confident that American could take proper advantage of the factors in play around the world.[93] At the Senate Foreign Relations Committee on 31 January 1985 Shultz justified the return to the negotiating table: 'We have reason to believe,' he said, 'that the "correlation of forces" is shifting back in our favour.' He assured everyone that the Reagan administration had no faith in the Politburo.[94] Reagan's readiness for talks annoyed many of his political supporters, and Senator Gordon Humphrey of New Hampshire confronted Shultz at the Senate Armed Services Committee on 26 February 1985: 'Do you think it is wise to put the security of the United States and the West in the hands of . . . a treaty whose co-signatory is a nation conducting criminal activities against a largely defenceless people?' Shultz replied: 'Come off it, Senator.' He added: 'We have rallied others, and we have done things that are completely consistent with our view of Soviet behaviour in Afghanistan. Not only that, Soviet behaviour in Cambodia. Not only that, Soviet behaviour in Nicaragua. Not only that, Soviet treatment of individuals in the Soviet Union.' But the important thing, Shultz stressed, was to go on working to achieve an arms reduction agreement and prevent a Third World War.[95]

The American administration was under assault for both softness and hardness, and Weinberger was attacked as often as Shultz. Leading veterans in the Senate queried whether the sums of money disbursed to the Defense Department were being well spent. Senator John W. Warner of Virginia proposed to cap the increase in appropriations at three per cent per annum after allowing for inflation. On 4 February, when Weinberger appeared before the Senate Armed Services Committee, Senator John C. Stennis, a Democrat from Mississippi, exclaimed: 'Tell us what we've gotten for that money. Why could you not try harder to make it go further?'[96] Weinberger asked the senators to remember that the USSR was still developing new weapons.[97] Unlike Shultz, he did not think it mattered much who Chernenko's eventual successor as General Secretary might be. He wanted to tighten the pressure rather than make overtures. The balance of influence in the American administration between Weinberger and Shultz continued to depend on which of them had the President's ear. The situation was not primed for easy conciliation with the USSR.

PART TWO

PART TWO

11. MIKHAIL GORBACHËV

Gorbachëv's chance to jemmy open the doors of Soviet and global politics came with the death of Chernenko on 10 March 1985. He called a Politburo meeting for the following day, at which Minister of Health Yevgeni Chazov reported a diagnosis of emphysema and acute hepatitis. Prime Minister Tikhonov delivered a statement of condolence. Gorbachëv turned to Gromyko, who had agreed to propose his name for the general secretaryship.[1]

The alliance with Gromyko was a recent creation. After Gorbachëv's British trip, Gromyko chided those ambassadors who reported warmly about the impact that the younger man made on Western public opinion;[2] and he may also have been responsible for the inattentiveness of the Soviet media to the visit.[3] But Gromyko, the Kremlin survivor, was soon plotting about how to be on the same side as the likely successor to Chernenko. His son Anatoli sounded out Yevgeni Primakov at the Institute of the World Economy and International Relations. The idea was to ask Primakov to approach Alexander Yakovlev, whom Gorbachëv had brought back from Canada to become the institute's director in mid-1983, for the purpose of discovering how Gorbachëv would respond to an overture from Gromyko senior.[4] Gorbachëv made an eager response. He had lost his patron Ustinov, but now with Gromyko on his side he became a virtual certainty as the next General Secretary. Upon hearing the news that Chernenko was no more, he called Gromyko and they had a conversation on a closed telephone line as Gromyko's limousine brought him into Moscow from Sheremetyevo airport. They met to lay their plans before the Politburo gathered. Gorbachëv told him: 'People expect changes.' Gromyko agreed. The pact was sealed.[5]

The Politburo gathered at 11 p.m. on the day of Chernenko's death. The meeting was of short duration and, surprisingly, Grishin proposed Gorbachëv as head of the funeral commission. Gorbachëv reckoned that his rival Grishin was attempting a last probe of the political line-up. He scheduled the next meeting, which was to decide who would succeed to the general secretaryship, for 2 p.m. on the following afternoon.[6] Gorbachëv stayed on at the office through the night. He arrived home at 4 a.m. Taking a walk in the garden with his wife, he rued the country's mess: 'We can't go on living like this.' The morning was filled with rumours, fears and expectancy. The other party secretaries besieged Yegor Ligachëv, Gorbachëv's cheerleader in the Secretariat, with demands for information.[7] Gorbachëv was not yet sure of victory. KGB Chairman Chebrikov had told him that Tikhonov had tried to persuade him against voting for Gorbachëv in the Politburo. Groups of provincial party leaders buttonholed Gorbachëv and urged him to hold his nerve; they told him that they were determined as Central Committee members to ensure that the Politburo took their opinions into account.[8] Gromyko was first speaker at the Politburo and put the case for Gorbachëv. He praised his creative energy, talent at handling people and political experience. He worded his eulogy as if the election was a foregone conclusion, and Tikhonov and Grishin endorsed the proposal despite their sceptical record – and Grishin abandoned his own ambition to take the post.[9]

The Central Committee had to confirm the decision before Gorbachëv could present himself as the USSR's new leader. Yegor Ligachëv canvassed for him till the very last moment.[10] Enthusiasm was high in the Central Committee, and it would have taken a political earthquake to overturn the Politburo's decision. Gorbachëv had lost out to Chernenko in the previous decision on the succession and few people in the Central Committee hoped to see him fail again. He spoke concisely about Chernenko and his achievements before calling for a minute's silence in his memory. He then handed over to his new ally Gromyko. Grishin appeared ill at ease, no doubt sensing that his career was nearing its closure. Gromyko improvised the speech of his life in praise of Gorbachëv. The Central Committee provided a heartfelt ovation and a unanimous vote of approval.[11] Gorbachëv declared his allegiance to the strategic line worked out at the 1981 Party Congress; he thanked the Central Committee for the confidence it had shown in him. With that, he closed one of the brightest short plenums in living memory.[12] He behaved with the aplomb of a man who knew that his time had arrived at last. Tactful on this sombre occasion, he nevertheless gave the impression of intending to seize his opportunities.

Gorbachëv had gained full membership of the Politburo as recently as 21 October 1980.[13] Born to a peasant household on a

Stavropol district collective farm in 1931, he grew up committed to Lenin and the October Revolution of 1917; but he was also aware that family members had suffered persecution at the hands of Stalin's security police. He worked hard in the fields and at school and gained a scholarship to study law at Moscow State University. On graduation, he married fellow student Raisa Titarenko and returned to Stavropol as a communist youth organizer. He agilely clambered up the local political ladder. He admired Nikita Khrushchëv's attack on Stalin in 1956 but let nothing get in the way of his promotion. He headed the Party City Committee from 1966 and the Regional Committee from 1970. Stavropol was a place where Politburo members landed en route to their summer vacations, which enabled him to make the acquaintance of Brezhnev and Andropov. His agricultural achievements won plaudits. In 1978 he was called to Moscow to head the Secretariat's Agricultural Department. Within a year he had become a Politburo deputy member. His rise was meteoric.

He had many qualities that made for a contrast with his three predecessors as General Secretary. He was in robust health; he talked easily with everyone he met and he was confident about himself and the country's potential. Aged fifty-four, he could reasonably look forward to many years in office. He was at work in his office at 9 a.m. and usually stayed for twelve hours. He often skipped lunch. When he finally got home, he went for a walk with Raisa. He would sit down again to his papers before turning in to bed. His resilience was extraordinary. Chernyaev thought that his stamina was the product of his tough peasant boyhood.[14] He could think fast and be decisive; he had an excellent memory.[15]

While he was charming and friendly, he kept a barrier between himself and most others, and people who worked with him tended to feel they did not really know him. He kept himself apart and felt no need for intellectual or moral guidance.[16] If there was one person who acted as his confidante, it was Raisa. Theirs was a strong marriage and he was solicitous towards her.[17] They talked about public affairs, and his political confidants were convinced that she advised on the content of his speeches.[18] Both came from southern Russia. Like Mikhail, Raisa came from a family that had suffered under Stalin's policy of agricultural collectivization but found ways to integrate itself with the Soviet order. When the Germans overran Ukraine and half of European Russia in 1941, the Stavropol region fell under occupation. In 1943, when they began to withdraw, they conducted mass executions of Jews and communists. Gorbachëv's mother spirited him off to a nearby village for fear that he might be shot.[19] He grew up a loyal Marxist-Leninist and both he and Raisa were proud of their cultural hinterland. When relaxing, he loved to recite from Lermontov's poem 'Mtsyri'.[20] His voice revealed him as a man from Stavropol, putting the stress in certain words in a southern fashion and he had several odd turns of phrase of his own.[21]

But Gorbachëv had greater experience of life abroad than anyone in the Politburo except Gromyko. In 1972 he had been with a Soviet delegation that visited Belgium.[22] He had taken his Raisa on road trips through France and Italy, each lasting twenty-one days – an exceptional privilege for Soviet citizens.[23]

Within minutes of the announcement of Chernenko's death, the news was conveyed to Washington, where staff roused President Reagan from his bed. The American embassy in Moscow welcomed what was happening. Later in the day, a car took Reagan over to the Soviet embassy and he signed the condolences book. This was the third time he had done this for a Soviet General Secretary.[24] He was surely pleased to learn that the next leader in the Kremlin was in sound health. As they looked for signs of change in the Politburo's foreign policy, Reagan and Shultz chose the path of 'quiet diplomacy'. When pressure was exerted upon the new General Secretary, it should be done on a 'one-on-one' basis without publicity, and the American media were to be kept out of things.[25] Reagan declined to attend the funeral; he wanted to see genuine signs of change in the USSR before going to Moscow. He asked Bush and Shultz to deputize for him, although he did write a letter for the Vice President to hand over to the new Soviet leader. The sentiments were inoffensive, the tone was friendly. He wrote encouragingly about the recent exchanges between the two sides in Geneva; he invited Gorbachëv to meet in America as soon as he felt it convenient.[26] Reagan watched and waited. The American media shared the administration's caution. The *New York Times* noted the generational turnover as well as Gorbachëv's impatience for change, but cautioned against high expectations.[27]

The Geneva arms talks projected by Shultz and Gromyko were set to restart on 12 March 1985. The Americans asked whether the Kremlin still wanted them to go ahead. Gorbachëv answered with a firm yes. The American delegation arrived in Switzerland under orders to concentrate on strategic nuclear weapons. The Soviet negotiators hoped for a more comprehensive agenda. They insisted on including intermediate-range missiles – American, British and French – in the discussion; they also registered objection to America's foreign bases for its nuclear forces as well as to the Strategic Defense Initiative. The Americans refused to give way and insisted that all categories of bombs, missiles and vehicles should be taken separately and in sequence.

Chernenko's funeral on 13 March 1985 gave an opportunity for foreign leaders to make the acquaintance of the new General Secretary. There was a rolling maul to get a seat in the front row at the committal – President François Mitterrand elbowed his way to a place between Margaret Thatcher and Morocco's Prime Minister Mohammed Lamrani.[28] Afterwards Gorbachëv, accompanied by Gromyko, talked with Babrak Karmal who was Afghanistan's General Secretary and chairman of its Revolutionary Council Presidium. While promising the USSR's continued support, he pointed out that the Soviet Army could not stay in Afghanistan for ever and urged Karmal to broaden the social basis of his support. Karmal could see that Soviet policy was undergoing deep change; he warned Gorbachëv that without assistance from Moscow, his government would fall.[29] Next day Gorbachëv talked with President Zia-ul-Haq of Pakistan. When Zia complained about the burden of sheltering three million Afghan refugees, Gorbachëv replied that Afghan rebel forces trained for their military operations in Pakistani bases – he later told the Politburo that he had taught Zia a lesson about regional politics.[30] Czechoslovakia's Husák was easier to handle. He told Gorbachëv that the Warsaw Pact should extend its existence for a further two decades beyond its current term.[31] Out of the scores of communist parties from the rest of the world which sent delegations to the funeral, Gorbachëv agreed to receive only one of them – the Italians: this was an early signal of his sympathy with their Eurocommunist commitment to democracy.[32]

Gorbachëv made a deep impression on Bush and Shultz, and they reported to Reagan that he was healthy and ebullient and could speak off the cuff without difficulty.[33] He did not return the compliment in his account to Party Central Committee secretaries. The Americans, he commented, had not brought 'a very serious team' with them – he said that Bush looked 'lost' when they touched on topics off the usual agenda. He had hoped for Reagan to make the trip instead of sending a letter of vague content.[34]

The West Europeans expressed hopefulness about the Geneva talks. Mitterrand expressed disapproval of the extension of the arms race into outer space. This pleased Gorbachëv. Less helpful was Kohl, who stood by the Americans. Prime Minister Nakasone of Japan raised the perennial question of the Soviet occupation of his country's northern islands in 1945. Thatcher emphasized her desire to resume a dialogue with the USSR and to increase confidence between NATO and the Warsaw Pact. She turned her charm on everyone – and it was noticed that she employed 'feminine' (po-zhenski) ways of enhancing her impact.[35] Chernyaev observed Thatcher with a fascinated eye and remarked: 'Beautiful, intelligent, extraordinary, feminine. It's untrue that she's a woman with balls or a man in a skirt. She's all woman and what a woman!'[36] He pinned up her pictures in his Moscow office.[37] Soviet officials suspected that she saw a chance of putting Kohl and Mitterrand in her political shadow.[38] Gorbachëv told her and the other West Europeans how frustrated he felt about the lack of progress in the arms talks. He emphasized that the USSR was trying to be 'more consistent and flexible'.[39]

He held a separate meeting with Warsaw Pact leaders and spelled out his policy for Eastern Europe. The USSR was no longer willing to use its armed forces to prop them up. This had been the reality since Brezhnev and Andropov had shrunk from military intervention in Poland earlier in the decade. Gorbachëv spelled out some new implications. His idea was that the East European communist rulers should take responsibility for affairs in their countries. Soviet interference was to be consigned to history. The so-called Brezhnev Doctrine was dead. As Gorbachëv noted, not everyone at the meeting believed what they were hearing. It was not unknown for a Kremlin ruler to mouth pieties and behave differently. Some were hoping that this was happening yet again. Gorbachëv was determined to prove them wrong.[40]

He left his own party leadership in no doubt that the times were changing and that he was the man to preside over them. When reporting to the Politburo, he often referred to himself in the third person as 'Gorbachëv'. This was his implicit way of stressing that he was someone special. From the start of his general secretaryship he imparted the sense that he had an important destiny in Soviet and world politics. He was a leader in a hurry. He was brash and impatient, and this side of his temperament was to the fore as he set about transforming the USSR. Gorbachëv overflowed with energy. Not for him the Hungarian system of meeting on a fortnightly basis.[41] The Politburo would meet every Thursday. He let others have their say and there was no censoring of opinion. Sessions started at eleven in the morning and, with a single break, sometimes did not end until nine at night. Gorbachëv soon came to recognize that this dragged things out too much and he carried a proposal to limit reports to ten minutes – with the maximum set at fifteen. Contributions to discussion should not last longer than five minutes.[42]

He insisted on a definite topography for the Politburo's movement towards big new decisions. The Walnut Room in the Kremlin lay between the Politburo venue and Gorbachëv's office, and it was there that he brought together five or six of the more influential members to agree on how to handle the agenda that he had drawn up.[43] He encouraged a corporate sense of responsibility. The crucial thing was for the Politburo to agree on a policy and stick to it. There was a break for lunch, which they ate together at a single long table. No alcohol was allowed, and everyone continued to discuss the same topics as in the formal meeting. Brisk efficiency was demanded.[43] The Party Secretariat too experienced the fresh atmosphere. Gorbachëv disliked its penchant for showy announcements and bureaucratic practices. He pointed out that economic growth had been nil in February 1985. He described this as an abysmal record, and called for instant improvement.[45] Likewise he accused government ministers of failing to understand the emergency in food supply because they themselves enjoyed the privilege of Granovski Street cafeteria near the Kremlin. He threatened to withdraw this facility and deprive their staff of their Chaika cars.[46] He organized urgent preparations for the next Central Committee plenum as well as for the Political Consultative Committee in Sofia. He wanted all-out action from every official.[47]

Gorbachëv favoured a drastic reform of the Soviet order. As yet he had no definite practical measures in mind. But his impatience was obvious. He told aides that farming cooperatives were superior to the existing system of collective agriculture.[48] Something drastic needed to be done. He resented how the leadership had been behaving for years: 'They strangled the countryside with rockets. Until recently, whenever the question arose about supporting the countryside, Ustinov would stand up and say: "Only over my dead body."'[49] Gorbachëv was later to claim that the general situation in the USSR had troubled him in Stavropol as early as 1975.[50] He and his friend Eduard Shevardnadze, the Georgian Communist Party First Secretary, met on holiday in the Abkhazian city Pitsunda in 1979 and shared their thoughts on the subject. Shevardnadze said: 'Everything's gone rotten – there's got to be change.'[51] Gorbachëv himself had taken risks in other private conversations. The painter Ivan Glazunov, a Russian nationalist, suggested that Gorbachëv would have been arrested if the KGB had bugged their conversations.[52]

Foreign and security policy was firmly on his agenda sheet for action. On 22 March 1985 he called for a halt to growth of the strategic nuclear arsenals of America and the USSR; he also called for the deployment of intermediate-range missiles in Europe to be suspended. On 25 March 1985 a letter arrived for Reagan from Gorbachëv via the chargé d'affaires at the Soviet embassy. The General Secretary expressed his hope that he and the President could interact in a constructive fashion. He asked for an end to the practice of saying one thing to each other in confidence and something different in public. Trust had to be cultivated between Moscow and Washington. Gorbachëv wrote of the urgent need for rapid progress. He welcomed Reagan's desire for a meeting face to face.[53] Shultz felt encouraged by the preview he received from Ambassador Dobrynin; he told the President how he liked the 'non-polemical tone'.[54] Gorbachëv was moving with impressive determination. On 7 April 1985 he announced that the USSR was dropping its scheme to deploy more SS-20 missiles in Europe. The relentless increase in Soviet offensive weaponry was to come to an end. Ten days later the Moscow media announced the proposal to introduce a global ban on nuclear explosion tests – the idea was for the ban to come into force on 6 August, which would be the fortieth anniversary of the dropping of nuclear bombs on Hiroshima at the end of the Second World War.[55]

On 10 April Gorbachëv received a US Congress delegation headed by Speaker Tip O'Neill, who handed over a letter from Reagan. He and O'Neill spoke for almost four hours. He expressed annoyance at the American administration's scepticism about his wish for peace; he described the Strategic Defense Initiative as essentially an offensive programme. O'Neill gave this report on him: 'He appeared to be the type of man who would be an excellent trial lawyer, an outstanding attorney in New York had he lived there. There is no question that he is a master of words and a master in the art of politics and diplomacy. Was he hard? Was he tough? Yes, he is hard, he is tough.'[56]

On 23 April 1985, at the next Central Committee plenum, Gorbachëv mixed Marxist-Leninist jargon and populist appeal: 'No people exists that would want a war . . . We are convinced that world war can be avoided. But as experience shows, the struggle for the preservation of peace and the attainment of general security is no easy matter, involving ever renewed efforts.'[57] He blamed America for the confrontation with the USSR. He accused the Americans of threatening the 'heroic people of Nicaragua' with the kind of military vengeance meted out to Grenada.[58] He castigated attempts by America to subvert the 'socialist countries'.[59] Yet he also adopted a more conciliatory tone. He made no mention of President Reagan. He praised the Helsinki Final Act and other agreements signed in the years of détente – and he called for a strengthening of economic and scientific-technical cooperation with the West.[60] He expressed regret that the Geneva talks were stalling because the Americans refused to concede on the Strategic Defense Initiative – he attributed this to the desire of 'certain circles' in the American administration to achieve world domination.[61] He pointed to his recent proposal for a moratorium on nuclear test explosions as proof of the Soviet leadership's pacific intentions. If the Americans wanted to reduce the potential for military conflict, they could now see that the Soviet leadership was willing to talk.[62] He expressed some hope that America's standpoint could be 'corrected' through his overtures.[63]

Among those who congratulated him was Eduard Shevardnadze. Noting the international clamour about Gorbachëv, Shevardnadze suggested that the West had a mortal fear of 'the bringing together of socialism with a strong leadership'.[64] Military commanders too were pleased about Gorbachëv's elevation. Defence Minister Sergei Sokolov commented to Chief of the General Staff Sergei Akhromeev: 'It seems as if we've got a leader at last!'[65] Foreign Affairs Ministry official Anatoli Adamishin called him a 'leader sent by God'.[66] But not everyone held a high opinion of him. Boris Ponomarëv, head of the Party International Department, thought he was an upstart with the talent of an Agricultural Secretary at best.[67] Gorbachëv intended to prove such people wrong. He had yet to work out a route or even a destination for his general secretaryship. He was someone who assumed that paths were made by walking. It was enough for him that he was going to end the Soviet 'stagnation' of the 1970s. He was sure that he would find the right policies as he moved along. This attitude would enable him to be decisive and imaginative, though it also laid him open to trying things out without a proper idea about what to expect. But all this lay in the future. In his first weeks as General Secretary, Gorbachëv was a man intent on big changes; and most people in the USSR and the rest of the world liked the direction he was taking.

12. THE MOSCOW REFORM TEAM

Every upward step on the slopes of reform required a tensing of Gorbachëv's leg muscles, and he knew that he could not complete the ascent without a reliable team of fellow climbers. In foreign policy no one would be closer to him than Eduard Shevardnadze, who became Foreign Affairs Minister. He was to take Anatoli Chernyaev and Georgi Shakhnazarov from the Party Secretariat as aides on a wide range of policy including foreign and security affairs. He had been consulting Alexander Yakovlev for a couple of years and was looking for the occasion to promote him to the Politburo – Yakovlev had unrivalled experience of North America. He was on the point of selecting Lev Zaikov of the Leningrad City Party Committee as another leading accomplice in promoting political and economic reforms that were becoming known as *perestroika* (or restructuring). Though Gorbachëv was aware that they were unlikely to agree about everything, he needed his experience in controlling the military-industrial complex. In any case, he would initially also have to rely upon people who had still greater reservations about some of his aspirations for reform: Viktor Chebrikov at the KGB, Sergei Akhromeev at the General Staff and Sergei Sokolov at the Defence Ministry. Each of these headed institutions of immense power. Gorbachëv knew that it would take time to obtain compliance with his objectives, and he had reason to think that Chebrikov, Akhromeev and Sokolov shared at least some of his thinking. He could prod, persuade and inspire; but he knew that he would get nowhere if he failed to lead a coalition of influential supporters.

He was also determined to transform internal policy but his choice of associates for this purpose was much more cautious. At the Central Committee plenum in April 1985 he raised Yegor Ligachëv, Nikolai Ryzhkov and Viktor Chebrikov to the Politburo. Ligachëv became his second-in-command in the Party Secretariat; Ryzhkov assumed general oversight of the economy and was made Prime Minister in

September 1985; and Chebrikov remained as KGB Chairman. All had helped him to gain selection as General Secretary, and this was among the reasons why he promoted them: he had to repay his political debt. He would soon discover that none of them shared the intensity of his commitment to radical change.

Though Ligachëv approved of reform, he hoped to hold it within limits not far beyond what Andropov might have imposed. As a former Siberian party secretary, he had the reputation for personal rectitude and indefatigability; and such was his self-confidence that he had once rejected Brezhnev's proposal to redeploy him as Soviet Ambassador to 'a prestigious European country'.[1] It would not be long before Ligachëv was trying to obstruct political innovation. Ryzhkov had similar misgivings about reforming the economy. As an ex-engineer of the Uralmash industrial complex, he believed in state owner-ship and central planning even though he had thought Andropov too timid about retail price reform.[2] Viktor Chebrikov had been a party secretary until his transfer to the KGB, where he became Andropov's deputy and his successor. He had the reputation of a professional policeman; he thought that leadership had 'rehabilitated' too many people whom Stalin had punished in the 1930s and 1940s.[3] Whereas he was willing to consider some new ways of thinking about security, his outlook was steeped in his agency's traditions. Gorbachëv would be frustrated by such individuals; but he was also to feel protected by their presence against criticisms from unconditional communist con-servatives that he was driving fast into a dangerous unknown.

In international politics, however, Gorbachëv took his foot off the brake within weeks of becoming General Secretary and terminated the alliance with Gromyko. His first step in this direction was to abolish the various Politburo commissions that Gromyko headed.[4] The old man's days of dominance drew to an end and a rumour spread around Old Square that Gorbachëv was plotting to move him into a different job. This really was the General Secretary's intention. On 29 June 1985 he asked the Politburo to approve Gromyko's promotion as Chair-man of the Supreme Soviet. Gromyko put up no resistance. He appeared to like the status that was about to accrue to him; he prob-ably also recognized that the demands of his work at the ministry were now beyond him. Politburo regulars noticed that he often seemed to run out of energy and although he still talked a lot at meetings, he was beginning to fumble his words.[5] The idea of becoming head of state acquired a distinct appeal for him, and Gorbachëv engineered the transition by showering the veteran with flattery: 'We're not going to find a second A. A. Gromyko.'[6]

Gorbachëv met with an initial refusal when asking Shevardnadze to become the Minister of Foreign Affairs. The whole proposal was too startling for Shevardnadze, who felt himself lacking in the necessary experience and worried that Russians might object to a Georgian taking decisions for the entire USSR.[7] He also spoke no foreign language unless Russian was included.[8] Gorbachëv refused to accept his demurral. Shevardnadze gave way, and Gorbachëv pressed his nomination at the Politburo. As he acknowledged, he was passing over distinguished diplomats such as Georgi Kornienko, Stepan Chervonenko and Anatoli Dobrynin.[9] Gromyko showed a degree of annoyance by mentioning Yuli Vorontsov as another potential candidate for promotion and expressing pride in the 'whole cohort of diplomats' that he had led. Gorbachëv ignored him.[10] At the Central Committee plenum on 1 July 1985, Shevardnadze was recommended as Foreign Affairs Minister and made up to full Politburo membership.

As Gorbachëv knew, he was picking a man who shared his passion for deep reform. Shevardnadze lived for years frustrated about the drift of communist conservatism. He aspired to play his part in transforming the USSR. Aged fifty-seven, he was of the same generation as Gorbachëv and they had been friends during their years in the Komsomol.[11] They kept in contact when Shevardnadze became Georgian Party First Secretary in 1972. After Gorbachëv moved to Moscow to head the Agricultural Department of the Central Committee, they talked about how to ensure economic improvement – and Shevardnadze arranged a tour of collective farms where he had introduced a wage system to reward farmers according to the size of the grain harvest.[12] His innovations had impressed Andropov.[13] Shevardnadze and Gorbachëv were holidaying together in Georgia when they read the news about the Soviet invasion of Afghanistan in December 1979.[14] In Shevardnadze's view, Brezhnev no longer functioned as someone who could make up his own mind but yielded to the opinions of others rather as Emperor Nicholas II had submitted to Grigori Rasputin's influence.[15] Shevardnadze and Gorbachëv agreed on the need to pull Soviet forces out as soon as possible. In the minds of both of them, the war had been a terrible mistake from the very start.[16]

Shevardnadze was committed to the Soviet multinational state despite the pain it had brought to both sides of his family. Shevardnadze's father had been arrested in 1937 and was lucky to obtain release some time later.[17] His own wife Nanuli had started by rejecting his proposal of marriage for fear that her father's execution as an enemy of the people would ruin Shevardnadze's career.[18] She did, however, eventually agree to the wedding and now had a busy life in Moscow as she looked after the family there while her own daughter went out to work.[19]

People found Shevardnadze charming and intelligent – not at all like a conventional Soviet Foreign Affairs Minister. (The only one they could remember was stony-faced Gromyko, who rationed his smiles and chilled every diplomatic conversation.) His curly silver hair lent a patrician appearance. Like Gorbachëv, he had literary interests. He also loved football and followed Tbilisi Dinamo. Unusually for a Georgian, he did not smoke.[20] As a seven-year-old, he had written a paean to Stalin that appeared in a children's journal.[21] His personal ambition remained with him in adulthood, and he undoubtedly had a ruthless side: for five years from 1967 he was Georgia's Minister of Internal Affairs and was not remembered for gentle policing methods. Among Georgians he was notorious for his obsequiousness to the General Secretary. He declared to the Party Congress in 1976 that whereas generations of scientists said that the sun rises in the east, he asserted that for Georgia's people it had risen in the north, in Moscow. In 1980 he assured a Party Central Committee plenum that people in Brazil had told him that no statesman in the world was more authoritative than Leonid Brezhnev.[22] Only political sophisticates understood that this was his way of getting Moscow to leave Georgia alone.[23]

Shevardnadze recognized that the new direction in foreign policy depended on Gorbachëv's survival in power.[24] He also understood that he owed his own elevation entirely to the General Secretary. Rather archly, he described himself as his 'feudal vassal'.[25] As he started to show extravagant admiration for Gorbachëv, he reasoned that a new 'cult of the individual' would benefit the cause of reform. On Gorbachëv's birthday, he delivered a eulogy so cloying that it earned a rebuke from the General Secretary.[26] This failed to discourage him from heaping praise on Gorbachëv's draft report for the Party Congress: 'Since Lenin, I can't remember such a document. We see here a new level of Marxist-Leninist thinking.'[27]

Alexander Yakovlev, who left the Institute of the World Economy and International Relations to become head of the Party Propaganda Department on 5 July 1985, squashed any idea about establishing a cult.[28] He and Gorbachëv believed that *perestroika* required a change in the entire style of Soviet politics. Cults were no longer appropriate. Yakovlev had enjoyed Gorbachëv's patronage since their Canadian encounter in May 1983, when they had found out how much they had in common. He had served as Ambassador to Ottawa for ten long years after the Party Secretariat disciplined him for publishing an article that condemned the growth of Russian nationalism – Brezhnev administered the reprimand in person. The embassy posting had been at his own request.[29] It seemed a good option at the time but soon felt to him like a kind of banishment.[30] He was never one of Andropov's protégés. Andropov, while he was KGB Chairman, criticized Yakovlev's interference with Soviet intelligence activities on Canadian soil.[31] Yakovlev thought seriously about what changes were needed to integrate the USSR into the world economy. He entered talks with the head of McDonald's Corporation in Canada to establish a branch in Moscow, and he persuaded the Soviet political leadership to discuss this seriously for a while.[32]

With Gorbachëv's approval, Yakovlev began to write to him with advice.[33] The two grew closer. But whereas Gorbachëv could contain his impatience, Yakovlev disliked having to help him to draft a new Party Programme on Chernenko's behalf; he also resented the fact that Alexander Alexandrov-Agentov, Chernenko's senior aide, rejected nearly all his suggestions.[34] Controversy began to dog him again. On a visit to West Germany he declared that German reunification was the business of the German people and no one else. Honecker protested to Moscow that there were two German peoples and never the twain should meet in a single state. Yakovlev was called into the Party Central Committee offices and told to be more cautious in his declarations.[35]

Yakovlev wore heavy horn-rimmed glasses and was pudgy and bald; British Ambassador Rodric Braithwaite was to compare him memorably to a 'dyspeptic frog'.[36] He often appeared grumpy even when he was in a good mood. Wounded as a young soldier in the Second World War, he had a bad limp and found stairs difficult. Holding on to the banister, he hauled up his lame leg step by step: he was nothing if not an independent personality.[37] His foreign experience was extraordinary for a Soviet public figure. As a youngster in the 1950s he took part in an academic exchange with America and spent a year studying at Columbia University, and he proceeded to publish works on American capitalism. The intellectual impact of his stay in New York endured. He learned to prefer the philosopher Immanuel

Kant to Marx the revolutionary.[38] He certainly had a cultural hinter-land. Less patient than Gorbachëv, he was willing to work under his aegis. Gorbachëv had rescued him from Canadian 'exile' and Yakovlev continued to need his patronage in order to realize the changes that he saw as being overdue. From Gorbachëv's point of view, Yakovlev was one of the few public radicals capable of handling a big political job. The two of them were men with a common mission.

Yakovlev's influence rose behind the scenes as soon as Gorbachëv ascended to power. For a while he avoided undue confrontation with the opponents of reform, but people who knew him attributed this to his cunning.[39] He was an advocate of drastic reform. By April 1985, as Gorbachëv and his entourage prepared for the month's Central Committee plenum, Yakovlev made a stunning proposal for the introduction of a multiparty political system, wider scope for private property and the loosening of controls over Eastern Europe.[40] In December 1985, in another memo, he called for a 'democratic society' and a 'market' economy. He compared the USSR under Stalin to the Egypt of the pharaohs.[41]

Gorbachëv set about changing personnel at the top. Gromyko stayed on in the Politburo and as President of the USSR. He might have tried to make serious trouble; but although he still spoke about foreign policy inside the leadership, he no longer had a trained team of informed assistants to help him.[42] For years he had dominated the deliberations about America in Moscow. Now he was just one con-tributor among many. He was not the only Politburo member whom Gorbachëv moved sideways or downwards – Grigori Romanov's agreement to step down from the Politburo on health grounds was quickly secured. Even the Party Defence Department had objected to Romanov. Obstructive and inefficient, he held up the work to such an extent that officials complained to Gorbachëv – and Gorbachëv anyhow wanted to eliminate a political rival.[43] He proposed that Lev Zaikov, the Leningrad Party First Secretary, should assume responsi-bility for the military-industrial complex. When Tikhonov queried whether Zaikov would be able to cope with the job, Gorbachëv cut short the discussion.[44] Tikhonov also expressed unease about the idea of promoting Boris Yeltsin, the Sverdlovsk Party First Secretary, to Moscow as Central Committee secretary for Construction, posing the query: 'And how will he perform in this new role?' Gorbachëv again took no notice: he had made up his mind.[45]

Zaikov was a formidable party administrator. In Brezhnev's last year he made a daring proposal to cut back the size of staff in the industrial sector and prevent regular overpayment.[46] He continued to call for a halving of ministerial personnel under Gorbachëv.[47] He understood that the USSR was oversupplied with nuclear weaponry, which was crippling the rest of its economy.[48] Soon after his promotion he consulted specialists in the Party Defence Department and concluded that the introduction of medium- and short-range missiles in Europe was a greater danger for the USSR than for America. He foresaw difficulty in getting the General Staff to accept a change in policy. But he was determined to achieve this.[49] He had formidable qualities. Although he was resolute in pursuing his ends, he was known as 'courteous and suave':[50] he was adept at lightening the atmosphere in moments of dispute. No one in the political elite had a bad word to say about him. When on 19 May 1985 Gorbachëv endorsed a new structure for military-political planning, he chose Zaikov to head a Politburo Arms Limitation Commission – the Big Five – which incorporated leaders of the institutions responsible for defence, foreign affairs, security and intelligence. People referred to it as the Zaikov Commission. It met in Zaikov's office, and Shevardnadze, Chebrikov, Sokolov and Yakovlev joined from the inception.[51]

The Big Five needed clear-cut advice rather that the complications of technical disagreements. Officials at lower levels conferred regularly about the details. Sometimes as many as fifty specialists attended. Usually they met in the general staff building. From May 1987 they were known as the Interdepartmental Working Group (or as the Little Five).[52] An affable atmosphere was fostered, even when Akhromeev attended and was in one of his grumpy moods, so that people could speak without fear of what their superiors might think. (Kataev's boss in the Party Defence Department, Oleg Belyakov, resented his inability to control him.) The aim was to produce recommendations that enjoyed a consensus among the experts. Party, army, industry and KGB cooperated with this in view – the Party Defence Department, for instance, was in daily receipt of up to ten secret intelligence coded messages. The system worked smoothly and the working group annually supplied over eighty draft decrees for use by the Big Five; and this environment nearly always enabled Zaikov to obtain agreement at the Big Five itself before drafts were submitted for ratification at the Politburo.[53]

This was what Gorbachëv needed from Zaikov. Unlike Brezhnev, he had no pretension to being regarded as a military expert and took little interest in new weapons or equipment. He wanted the country's genuine specialists – and not just the army commanders – to have an input.[54] Not once did Gorbachëv ask for a reworking of the drafts he received. He never imposed his personal preferences on either the Big Five or the working group. He only rarely addressed a personal query to the Party Defence Department – and that was only to get some detail or other clarified.[55] He accepted all proposals, big or small, that came up to him from the system he had sanctioned.[56]

His passivity was one of his conjuring tricks. The reality, as sceptics about reform ruefully appreciated, was that Zaikov and the Big Five were following Gorbachëv's instructions on the big questions of the day.[57] By remaining outside its membership, Gorbachëv could pretend to be impartial. He could also spare himself some time and energy. When the General Staff made a fuss, Zaikov spelled out the ground rules to Akhromeev: 'You know, Sergei Fëdorovich, the time has passed when you and Georgi Markovich [Kornienko] alone formulated the country's policy on disarmament questions. Now it's the state leadership that formulates it. You'd do well to take this into account.'[58] Kataev of the Party Defence Department admired how Zaikov insisted that the Ministry of Foreign Affairs should have as much influence as the Defence Ministry on questions of external security.[59] If Zaikov failed to secure what the reformers wanted, Shevardnadze would step in and say: 'Very well, let's put this aside and I'll talk it over with Mikhail Sergeevich.' People soon began to understand that Shevardnadze assumed that when he felt baulked, he could put his opinion to the General Secretary and compel the Big Five to comply with it.[60]

But Gorbachëv and his fellow reformers knew that they were only at the start of their campaign. Although they had the cooperation of Chebrikov and the KGB, they could expect difficulty with the high command despite all of Zaikov's successes in the Big Five. Akhromeev and Sokolov frequently behaved as if they would only support reform in the armed forces if they were the ones to initiate it. The wind of change gusting through party, government and Foreign Ministry was only a gentle breeze in the Soviet armed forces.[61]

For the transformation of Soviet foreign and security policy, Gorbachëv placed his trust in Shevardnadze. This allowed him to concentrate on internal political and economic reforms while Yakovlev oversaw the renovation of the media. The three of them set about their tasks with a furious intensity – and Shevardnadze began to suffer from insomnia.[62] He recognized the weaknesses in his grasp of international relations.[63] He told his aide Teimuraz Stepanov-Mamaladze: 'I'm caught in difficulty. In my previous work I always knew what I *could, wanted* and *had* to say. Here, I haven't found definition as yet.'[64] Initially he relied on Kornienko for arms talks advice.[65] He praised the record of his predecessor: 'Who am I compared to Gromyko, a battleship of world foreign policy? I'm just a rowing boat. But with a motor.'[66] Officials laughed at how they needed to spoon-feed him with rudimentary information.[67] Ponomarëv in the Party International Department was scathing: 'He completely lacks any understanding in [international relations].'[68] Gorbachëv shunted Ponomarëv into retirement. To take his place, he brought back Ambassador Dobrynin from Washington. This still left a lot of communist conservatives in post. Shevardnadze knew that several officials in the ministry operated an informal anti-reform intelligence network among themselves.[69] This did not daunt him. He told an aide: 'We need democratization like a valve for bringing a healthy social force into action.' He denied that this might have an explosive effect on society.[70]

It took until late August 1985 before Shevardnadze felt that he had made the right decision in accepting the ministry.[71] Fair-minded people admitted how quickly he was mastering his huge new brief. He had no model to follow since the ministry was created in Gromyko's image, and its personnel were trained in a conservative tradition.[72] Shevardnadze had a low opinion of many of his ambassadors, whom he thought were ignorant about their own country.[73]

Shevardnadze knew that he needed a lengthy tenure of office if he was to do what he wanted.[74] He believed passionately that the party had to lead the way in everything;[75] he felt an urgent need for action, saying: 'Now we've got to save socialism.' (He did not dare to say this in public, but only to his aide Stepanov–Mamaladze.) He accepted that the leadership would have to pay for past mistakes and introduced a fresh dictum: 'You m[ust] place peace above class interests.'[76] He urged his officials to raise any matter they liked or to ask about when it would truly be possible to drag the USSR out of 'the bog'.[77] He strove to root out idle chatter, nepotism and corruption. Too few Soviet diplomats, he thought, could write in a lively way or give an adequate public speech. There was far too little innovative thinking. He encouraged a spirit of democratic debate and deplored the ministry's failure to offer useful prognoses about the world situation; he indicated that he intended to recruit outsiders to help him remedy the situation.[78] On

1 December 1985 at a conference of party members in the ministry he issued a startling injunction: nobody was to think it acceptable any longer to steal or lie. Ritual references to Lenin were to cease. Indeed there should not even be eulogies of Gorbachëv, and Gromyko was to be treated as 'a monument', as history, as one of the set of problems that the Soviet leadership sought to solve.[79]

Gorbachëv and Shevardnadze, abetted by Yakovlev, were ready for the struggle. They had lived their adult years under the integument of an unimaginative gerontocracy. They resolved to turn the USSR upside down. In their favour was the recognition in the Politburo that things had to change if the USSR was going to deal with the challenges it faced. Gorbachëv was not to everybody's liking in the leadership, but once he became General Secretary he could take the opportunity to get rid of his outright opponents. He was showing a capacity to bring people along with him who did not share all his preferences for reform. His team of fellow radicals united around him. The way was clearing for a transformation of internal and external policy in Moscow.

13. ONE FOOT ON THE ACCELERATOR

Reagan's instincts told him that something extraordinary was happening in the Kremlin. Bush and Shultz felt the same after meeting the new General Secretary at Chernenko's funeral; and Shultz was eager to test out Gorbachëv's intentions in direct talks.[1] The news from Moscow was full of surprises, not least about the Afghan war. India's Prime Minister, Rajiv Gandhi, heard in person from the Soviet leaders in June 1985 that they were working on how to enable a military withdrawal. Gandhi passed this information on to the Americans. Big changes were in prospect.[2]

The American administration still needed the evidence that they were more than an ephemeral ploy. On 30 April 1985 the President wrote to Gorbachëv expressing disquiet about the recent shooting of Major Nicholson, a US military intelligence officer who had been on a perfectly legal mission north of Berlin. He lamented the Soviet military intervention in Afghanistan. He stressed that the Americans would base their judgement on what happened in practice rather than on promises. He expressed pleasure about the resumption of the Geneva talks but challenged the Soviet standpoint on his Strategic Defense Initiative. Gorbachëv had remarked to Speaker Tip O'Neill on his Moscow visit earlier in the month that the American programme was offensive in purpose. Reagan pointed out that Soviet scientists were carrying out research with the aim of matching the Defense Initiative. He offered his own assurance that American scientists needed years of further research; and he promised to consult with other governments before ordering any deployment. He drew attention to Moscow's infringements of the Anti-Ballistic Missile Treaty. He proclaimed the desirability of deep cuts in nuclear weapon stockpiles and looked forward to fostering a better atmosphere between the two sides.[3]

The ping-pong continued as Gorbachëv replied that responsible people in the American establishment knew full well that the Strategic

Defense Initiative had a disguised aggressive intent. (He failed to see that this was hardly a complimentary remark to make to the President.) He added that if the Americans could improve the chances of peace in Afghanistan if they ceased supplying the mujahidin.[4] He assured Reagan that the USSR would do whatever was necessary to preserve 'strategic parity'.[5]

Shultz guessed that Gorbachëv had not written the harsher bits of his correspondence; and Jack Matlock, who in 1983 had been brought into the National Security Council as its Russian-speaking expert and director of European and Soviet affairs, agreed with him.[6] But it was hard to persuade Casey that anything had changed in the Kremlin. The CIA forecast that the only difference that Gorbachëv would make in the arms control talks was in introducing a degree of political flair.[7] The USSR was constantly increasing its offensive capacity with more sophisticated weapon systems, and the Politburo was unlikely to allow its economic difficulties to affect this orientation. Although Soviet leaders might not want armed conflict with America, there existed potential scenarios when it would decide to order its forces into action. A Third World War remained a distinct possibility.[8] Casey and his officials repeatedly contended that the new General Secretary was a traditionalist who would continue to confront America, bully Eastern Europe and stay put in Afghanistan.[9] The CIA predicted that there would be only marginal adjustments in Soviet foreign policy. The USSR's economy might experience a temporary stimulus from Gorbachëv's efforts to change practices at the workplace; and he would probably pursue agreements in the arms control talks as a way of alleviating the strain on Soviet finances. But the general situation would remain the same.[10]

Defense Secretary Weinberger and Assistant Secretary Perle agreed with Casey; they could see no reason to change America's stance. Rowny did at least allow for the chance that Gorbachëv might astound them all, but he too thought it unlikely. The early signs as he saw them were that the new Soviet leader would opt for continuity.[11] This was also the line taken by influential conservative periodicals. William F. Buckley Jr, *National Review* editor and friend of Reagan, suggested that the very fact that Gorbachëv was 'humorous, well-traveled, well educated, articulate [and] intelligent' served only to make him 'a more dangerous man than he otherwise would be'.[12]

When Commerce Secretary Malcolm Baldrige mooted the idea of reviving trade talks with Moscow, Perle reacted with disapproval.

Baldrige was scheduled to open negotiations with USSR Trade Minister Nikolai Patolichev in Moscow on 20 May 1985. Perle, though, refused to relent. He had commissioned a report on the perils of allowing the Soviet economy to benefit from Western technological inventions. He obtained the results he wanted to pose against Baldrige's initiative. The writers recorded that the USSR was interested in buying automated production and control systems, computers, micro-electronics, fibre optics and telecommunications as well as products with an even more obvious military applicability. Their verdict was that if such technology had been transferred to the Soviet Union, Moscow would have saved up to $13.3 billion by avoiding the need to develop the products for itself – and it would also have spared itself between three and five years of research. Supposedly the USSR would make savings of $136 million on ball-bearings alone in 1986–1991 under the terms of its current tender. The report had a stark conclusion: it would cost the American economy $15 billion to match the gains for the Soviet military-industrial complex.[13]

Weinberger and Perle could see no point in budgeting to modernize strategic weaponry while actively enabling the enemy's modernization. But they could do little against Baldrige at a time when the State Department under Shultz was supporting the Moscow economic mission.[14] Perle nevertheless objected to the supposed premise that any arms agreement was better than none. He indicated that the USSR was flouting the agreements that it had signed. Soviet violations, he contended, ought to make everyone cautious – and he evidently had the President and the Secretary of State in mind.[15] He criticized British Foreign Secretary Geoffrey Howe for his recent voicing of concern about the Strategic Defense Initiative.[16] He also complained of the American administration's laxity about preventing the transfer of sensitive advanced technology to the Soviet Union. He described the CoCom framework of enforcement as weak and poorly funded; he advocated the case for toughening it up and reducing the categories of goods that were legally exportable.[17] Even Shultz had objections to current commercial policy. While seeking to lessen the tensions with the USSR, he opposed Reagan's approval of selling subsidized wheat to Moscow. He suggested that Soviet leaders 'must be chortling' about paying less for bread than American housewives.[18]

American frostiness annoyed Gorbachëv. When Italy's Prime Minister Bettino Craxi and Foreign Affairs Minister Giuliano Andreotti visited in late May 1985, he affirmed a wish to dispel the atmosphere of suspicion. Craxi urged him to permit greater flexibility at the Geneva talks. Gorbachëv gave him short shrift: 'If the Americans don't renounce SDI, the Supreme Pontiff in Rome will be able to celebrate the funeral of the negotiations.'[19]

The feeling was strong in the Politburo that Reagan was insincere in his proposal to eliminate all intermediate-range missiles.[20] Zaikov did not concur. Agitated about the stalling of the Geneva talks, he silenced the Party Defence Department's attempt to explain why the current obstacles were so hard to surmount: 'Stop, stop, stop! This is a very serious problem and we can't allow any delay in tackling it.'[21] He explained his concerns to Yuri Maslyukov, who headed the Military-Political Questions Commission for the Council of Ministers. Zaikov recognized that the USSR harmed its economy by producing far more weapons than were needed for security. It was the Politburo's fault, he said, that Pershing-2 missile sites now dotted the map of Western Europe – and these missiles needed only twelve minutes at most to hit Moscow.[22] If Soviet leaders wanted to get those missiles removed from Western Europe, they would have to agree to withdraw their SS-20s from Eastern Europe.[23] Maslyukov concurred and urged Zaikov to contact Ligachëv for his support. Ligachëv endorsed Zaikov's arguments and the two of them phoned Gorbachëv, who was on holiday in Crimea. Gorbachëv too was sympathetic despite knowing that trouble would ensure from the General Staff and the Defence Ministry. He did not flinch and gave the order: 'Go to it! I'll back you.'[24]

Zaikov looked around for a reliable team to help him draft a rationale. He turned to Kataev, deputy head of the Party Defence Department, to lead the work. Kataev agreed and in turn solicited additional assistance from Viktor Karpov in the Ministry of Foreign Affairs. Karpov was overjoyed: 'Wonderful! At last they've understood! But all intermediate-range missiles need to be liquidated. This means that we essentially have to accept Reagan's "zero option".' The team aimed to limit the discussions to Europe in the first instance and to keep the USSR's Asia-based weapons off the agenda. They hoped that Washington would appreciate the scale of the Soviet offer. Their chief worry was about the fuss that the USSR's military and industrial elites would probably make.[25]

The high command behaved exactly as predicted. When Kataev and Karpov expounded their ideas to Varennikov, First Deputy Chief of the General Staff, there was a furious dispute.[26] Reference was made to the awful precedent of Operation Barbarossa in June 1941. There was talk of treason and a 'fifth column'. Yet Kataev could not help noticing that Varennikov, unlike his fellow commanders, refrained from personal abuse. The KGB officers also held back. Kataev waited until the meeting finished before saying to Varennikov that emotional outbursts were unhelpful in settling matters of vital importance. The two men went on talking until after midnight. Theirs was a constructive conversation.[27] Varennikov seemed to recognize that the USSR could enhance its security by cooperating with the Americans in eliminating medium-range missiles from Europe. Chief of the General Staff Akhromeev and Defence Minister Sokolov were nowhere near as accommodating. They felt complete disgust with the proposals from Zaikov's group. Akhromeev had a short temper – on one occasion he pushed Kataev against a wall as he remonstrated with him. He shouted out that he would hand in his party card if Zaikov were ever to get his way.[28]

The Belgian government tried to ease international tensions by offering to stop the Americans installing Pershing-2 missiles on its territory if the USSR would withdraw the same number of intermediate-range missiles from Eastern Europe. Foreign Minister Leo Tindemans had repeated the idea to Gromyko when in Moscow for Chernenko's funeral. Gromyko gave him no encouragement.[29] There the matter rested throughout the spring and into the early weeks of Shevardnadze's tenure of the ministry.

The Americans took an initiative of their own when Shultz arranged to meet the new Soviet Foreign Affairs Minister at the American Ambassador's Residence in Helsinki on 31 July 1985. He arranged for his wife O'Bie to make the acquaintance of Shevardnadze's wife Nanuli. He also introduced his own personal security chief to Shevardnadze. The officer in question turned out to be a slim, young woman. Shevardnadze said: 'Now I can see that the fate of the USA is in safe hands.'[30] When they discussed politics, he remarked that if the Americans seriously desired a treaty on intermediate-range nuclear weapons, Britain and France had to be included in the deal – and America would need to abandon its space-based weapons programme. Shultz countered that the construction of a new early-warning station at Krasnoyarsk in mid-Siberia breached the Anti-Ballistic Missile Treaty; he called for a peace settlement in Afghanistan. He insisted that he hoped for agreements at the talks in Geneva and elsewhere in Europe. He said that both of them should set about 'kicking ass' whenever their delegations held up progress. Shevardnadze replied that the USSR truly sought a political resolution to the Afghan war. He denied that the radar station was illegal. He emphasized that America and the Soviet Union were militarily 'in a state of rough parity', which could now provide the basis for mutual conciliation.[31]

Gorbachëv and Shevardnadze knew that they would face internal difficulties before they could achieve any such aim. Getting Gromyko out of the Foreign Affairs Ministry was a definite help, but First Deputy Minister Kornienko behaved as if Gromyko was still the minister. When he did not like what the leadership suggested, he said that his 'party conscience did not permit' him to express approval.[32] His boldness drew strength from his work and friendship with Akhromeev in the General Staff. Speaking to the Dutch Ambassador, Kornienko claimed that nothing at all had changed in Soviet foreign policy. He said this despite Gorbachëv's orders for the ministry to give serious attention to Holland's follow-up to the Belgian overture on intermediate-range nuclear missiles.[33] The chance was lost to win over the Western Europeans by the kind of grand gesture that might have prevented the installation of cruise missiles in the Low Countries.[34] Shevardnadze decided to avoid a clash with Kornienko, whose expertise he continued to praise. He commented: 'In questions of security, the military have the last word.' Kornienko thought this gave him *carte blanche* to act as he wished.[35] Gorbachëv and Shevardnadze assumed that until they achieved something serious with America and its allies, it made little sense to ditch people like Kornienko.[36]

Gorbachëv did the rounds of the leadership and put the case for aiming at an arms reduction agreement. The General Staff was less than pleased, and Akhromeev got heated whenever Gorbachëv broached the topic. Akhromeev and Kornienko regularly conferred about how to hold the traditional line.[37]

Even Akhromeev, though, appreciated that the unremitting accumulation of nuclear weaponry was irrational.[38] But he wanted everything done on his terms. Gorbachëv had a degree of trouble at a consultation that he held for the delegation that was leaving for the Geneva arms talks. Primed by Kornienko, Akhromeev raged against the very idea of exploring the possibility of decreasing the nuclear missiles in Europe. Gorbachëv saw the need for support from the Politburo, and when he asked it directly to sanction an arms reduction policy, only Gromyko registered an objection.[39] On 18 September 1985 Gorbachëv called another meeting of military and diplomatic officials.

It lasted an hour and a half. Akhromeev and Lieutenant General Nikolai Chervov defended the policy of keeping all the SS-20s intact and in readiness. Kovalëv and Adamishin stood up to them. Such was Adamishin's enthusiasm for reform that Kornienko, his superior in the ministry, wanted to record a reprimand on his personal file. Gorbachëv handled the debate rather cautiously and Adamishin for a while wondered whether he himself had stepped too far out of line. But Gorbachëv won the debate. Adamishin was enraptured: 'The main thing is that he's as cunning as the Devil – or even better, as a peasant. A born politician, leader.'[40]

In August 1985 Gorbachëv took another initiative when he announced that the USSR would adjourn underground nuclear explosion tests through to the end of the year. He made no requirement for Reagan to copy him. The USSR was conducting a moratorium as a surety of its peaceful purposes. Gorbachëv signalled that if America were to do the same, he would aim to suspend the testing programme over a longer period.[41]

A bustle of exchanges between Moscow and Washington led to a decision for a summit meeting between General Secretary and President towards the end of the year. They chose Geneva as their venue. Reagan had never met any of Gorbachëv's predecessors or attended their funerals. Gorbachëv had already made a difference in global politics, and Reagan could not afford to ignore him. People all over the world were waiting for them to talk to each other. In this situation, he called together the National Security Council to arrange for the encounter in the light of the Soviet leader's growing impact. The debate was consensual in tone. Everyone agreed on the need to maximize support from 'three key audiences': America's allies, the American Congress and American public opinion. CIA Director Casey alerted him to the kind of traps that might lie ahead. He warned that Gorbachëv could try and push him into confining the Strategic Defense Initiative to research in laboratories and banning testing and deployment.[42] (Casey was making a guess that was soon proved to be prescient.)

Shultz asked for a brighter approach. He told National Security Adviser McFarlane that the President performed at his best when he felt 'confident and comfortable' – and too many people near to him were making him worried. He advised Reagan to stop listening to his advisers. Naturally this annoyed McFarlane; it was scarcely more appealing for Don Regan, the self-confident former CEO of Merrill

Lynch and Treasury Secretary who had served Reagan as chief of staff since February 1985.[43] Shultz refused to back down and enlisted Nitze's help in drafting ideas for Geneva. On 16 September 1985 he took them to the President. At the centre of Shultz's thinking was the need for serious negotiations. Whereas Weinberger treated the Strategic Defense Initiative as a way of making an arms deal unlikely, Shultz wanted to use it as a bargaining tool. Weinberger declared at every opportunity that the Americans wanted to move from research to deployment – and he sometimes added that the scientific laboratories were close to finishing their preparatory work. Shultz knew that the research was years away from completion. Funds and political sanction from Congress would continue to be necessary, and he had doubts about whether they would be available after Reagan left the White House. He persuaded the President to conduct a subtle manoeuvre. The idea was for Reagan to make an offer to Gorbachëv that he would delay a decision to deploy the initiative in return for drastic cuts in the stockpile of Soviet offensive nuclear weaponry.[44]

Shultz did not want to abjure the entire aim of deployment but rather to maximize concessions from the Kremlin. Such an approach, he suggested, was the best guarantee for the initiative's survival.[45] He had a further cause to be cheerful. On 23 September 1985 Soviet academic Georgi Arbatov asked Henry Kissinger how America and the USSR should try to get out of their impasse. Kissinger offered a personal opinion along the lines that Shultz had recently agreed with Reagan. Arbatov surprised him by saying that precisely such a compromise on the Strategic Defense Initiative might be 'possible' for the Politburo; he asked Kissinger to understand that Gorbachëv would be going as far as he could if he were to concede in this way. Arbatov also indicated that Gorbachëv might be able to come to an agreement with Reagan on Afghanistan. Kissinger assumed that no Moscow academic could talk in such a fashion without authorization. He phoned Shultz's executive assistant Charles Hill and passed on the exciting news.[46] Shultz was delighted. He felt that something was in the air in Moscow; and when he met again that month with Shevardnadze in New York, he guessed from his smiling composure that the Soviet leadership might be about to make some surprising moves in Geneva.[47]

The President, however, had one of his frequent changes of mind. On 17 September he suggested at a press conference that he might proceed to deployment even at the risk of breaching the Anti-Ballistic Missile Treaty. Shultz, Nitze and others hastened to counteract this impression after contact with politicians and journalists.[48] Casey and Weinberger by contrast liked what they had heard at the press conference. On 20 September 1985 at the National Security Council they put the case for no compromise with the USSR. McFarlane supported them by adding that many observers regarded Gorbachëv's pronouncements as 'old propaganda in new packaging'; he suggested the need for the President to shift the focus of attention from arms control topics to Afghanistan and human rights observance in the USSR. Shultz could do little more than say that the American side would get nowhere by insisting the Soviet leadership was merely engaged in a propaganda campaign.[49] He had to hope that the pendulum of the presidential mind would swing back in his direction before the summit.

Moscow newspapers endorsed the idea of 'nuclear winter'. Nay-sayers among Western scientists who challenged Carl Sagan's hypothesis were branded as 'obscurantists'. Moscow depicted itself as a fortress of science and humanity.[50] The Soviet leadership continued what it called its peace offensive in pursuit of convincing the world that all the warmongers were based in Washington.

Shevardnadze was cautious in preparing for his speech to the United Nations General Assembly in September 1985. He was in America for the first time. As yet he felt unable to strike a tone that differed from Gromyko's.[51] Events also pulled him up short. KGB officer Oleg Gordievski, under suspicion as a double agent, had disappeared in Moscow while out jogging in mid-July. His British controllers made arrangements to spirit him over the Finnish border and bring him to safety in the United Kingdom. Shevardnadze complained to British Foreign Secretary Geoffrey Howe in New York about the use of methods appropriate to a Conan Doyle story.[52] But he kept a smile on his face. His team were pleased with his willingness to think outside the traditional parameters.[53] Everyone commented on his charming demeanour. Having been unable to attend Shultz's speech, he offered gracious apologies.[54] The American press praised him as belonging to a new type of Soviet leader. When Shevardnadze met Reagan on 27 September 1985, he had a surprise in store. He brought with him a personal letter from Gorbachëv containing a proposal to halve strategic nuclear arsenals with immediate effect.[55]

Although Reagan stifled any obvious reaction, McFarlane was visibly disconcerted. The Americans had been talking about an initial reduction by thirty or thirty-five per cent. Now Gorbachëv was outmatching them.[56] Reagan and Shevardnadze spoke for three hours, and Shultz told the press that the President had generally welcomed what the Soviet Foreign Affairs Minister had put before him. But the Strategic Defense Initiative was a big sticking point since Gorbachëv had asked Reagan in his letter to halt work on it. Reagan told journalists: 'We are determined to go forward with the research.'[57]

Geopolitics were in flux, and American leaders looked for support from allies and friends. Some officials in Washington grew concerned about the possibility that Gorbachëv might initiate a rapprochement with Beijing. Deng had been repeating that America and the USSR were equal obstacles to world peace and security; he had also eased the tasks of Soviet diplomacy by criticizing America's Strategic Defense Initiative. Former President Nixon, on a private trip to China in autumn 1985, counselled the Chinese leader that this sort of talk was not going to make it easier for Reagan to continue the American policy on technological transfer. Deng replied that Beijing would reject every Soviet overture while the Kremlin occupied Afghanistan, interfered in Cambodia and kept large forces on the Sino-Soviet frontier; he strenuously denied that China would ever contemplate selling on US technology to Moscow. Nixon had hit a raw nerve – and Deng told him that the Chinese, regardless of their public statements, saw the USSR as their biggest difficulty. Deng could see no fundamental change in the Kremlin's policy on China since Gorbachëv had come to power.[58]

A month earlier, in October, he had in fact made an overture to the new Soviet leader through Nicolae Ceauşescu, who was paying a visit to China. He indicated that if the USSR helped in getting the Vietnamese to withdraw from Cambodia, there would be political room to consider a summit meeting with Gorbachëv. Deng was even willing to travel to Moscow.[59]

Nothing came of this very quickly, and neither China nor Japan gave much real cause for Reagan to worry. He could feel confident about Canada. His liveliest concerns were about Western Europe, where several states – France, Belgium, Holland and even the United Kingdom – kept a distance from American foreign and security policy on one feature or another. Gorbachëv was obviously going to do what he could to exert influence upon their governments. He predictably picked France for his first foreign trip as General Secretary. The French had withdrawn their forces from NATO's integrated military command in 1966. Soviet foreign policy was to widen the division between

Paris and Washington still further. President Mitterrand had been open about his unhappiness with the Strategic Defense Initiative. At Chernenko's funeral, he had issued an invitation to Gorbachëv to visit France, which Gorbachëv accepted a few days later.[60] The Americans, slightly disconcerted, passed on what they had learned from Shevardnadze about Gorbachëv's policy on arms reduction. They could not afford to let the new Soviet leader catch the French unawares. Mitterrand assured Robert McFarlane that he would not permit France's dissent about the Strategic Defense Initiative to become a 'weapon' in Gorbachëv's hands.[61]

The Paris visit lasted four days from 2 October 1985. The new General Secretary was at last on display to the outside world and the media interest was intense. As usual with a Soviet politician, crowds gathered to protest against the abuses of human rights in the USSR. A demonstration was organized at the Place du Trocadéro.[62] Gorbachëv dealt with all this calmly, and the French public liked his bonhomie and declarations of peaceful intent. He struck everyone as very 'Western' in appearance and demeanour. He dressed smartly. His suit and even his choice of hat attracted admiring comments. He scored high marks simply for refusing to look glum and calculating. With his ready smile and conversational style, he appeared a match in repartee for every Western politician he encountered. However formal or alien the nature of the occasion, he showed that he could adapt to its requirements. Nothing overawed him, not even the pomp of a weekend at Chequers with Mrs Thatcher the previous year, before he became General Secretary. His instinct had told him to avoid appearing too impressed. Likewise in Paris, he behaved as though he had taken in French politesse with his mother's milk.

He seized attention with his proposal for a fifty per cent reduction in all nuclear armaments. He called for a total ban on 'space-strike' weaponry. He was willing to keep the talks on intermediate-range missiles separate from all this. He also looked forward to negotiating independently with the British and French. He reported that the USSR had 243 SS-20s in its European zone – the number had not increased since the previous year. He promised to make no addition to these forces and called on America to do the same. National Security Council officials in Washington took note, and intelligence reports acknowledged that Gorbachëv's claims about his SS-20s could well be correct.[63] Gorbachëv was making his mark and the American administration needed to be ready to respond to any fresh overtures. Mitterrand pleased him to some extent by saying about the Strategic Defense Initiative: 'To my mind, this outer space question is very simple: I do no denouncing but I am hostile to it, and France will not associate with it.'[64] But Gorbachëv could no longer have any illusions about the prospect of splitting the Western powers. Mitterrand was a critical friend of the Americans but a friend none the less. If Gorbachëv wished to pull Reagan into a round of serious negotiations with the USSR, he could not base his tactics on lining up the Western European leaders on his side.

Where he could boast of unconditional success was in his impact on French public opinion. His flair for handling crowds and TV appearances had proven to be exceptional, and he began to think that this could be his most effective way of bringing the West to the negotiating table. Gorbachëv was willing to give everything a try.

14. TO GENEVA

After Paris, Gorbachëv focused on preparing the ground among Moscow's traditional allies and friends for the tactics he would use at the Geneva summit. Although none was likely to cause trouble, he hoped to enjoy their active cooperation. He was aware that his reforms were disturbing people in the 'fraternal' communist leadership. He had to convince them that what he wanted to say to Reagan conformed to their interests.

The Afghan communists would predictably be the ones who most disliked his ideas, so he invited Babrak Karmal back to Moscow for talks on 10 October 1985. It was a difficult conversation. Gorbachëv found fault with the Afghan army's inactivity while the Soviet Army was continuing to lose so many soldiers. He called on Karmal to re-introduce private trade, restore respect for Islam and share power with oppositionist elements.[1] Gorbachëv reported to the Politburo that he had given Karmal until summer 1986 to get ready to rely on his own forces. Although the USSR would continue its supplies of equipment, the Soviet armed forces would be planning their departure. At the Politburo, Gorbachëv read out letters from Soviet citizens who asked why Russians were still fighting in Afghanistan. While stopping short of calling the original invasion a blunder, he called for a speedy withdrawal regardless of the difficulty in predicting how Karmal would deal with the military consequences. Sokolov, Politburo member as well as Defence Minister, raised no objection. Nor did Gromyko, whom everyone knew was one of the perpetrators of the Afghan imbroglio, and his failure to oppose Gorbachëv was noteworthy. The new Politburo line was to remain confidential, but it was plain that big changes were under way in the Kremlin.[2]

Gorbachëv's next task was to brief the Warsaw Pact leaders about how he planned to handle the Americans at the Geneva summit. Flying to Sofia on 22 October 1985, he reported to the Political Consultative Committee. He wanted to work for an agreement to eliminate nuclear weapons of every type, by as much as a half in the first instance. He would offer to untie the question of intermediate-range nuclear weapons in Europe from questions about strategic and space weaponry; he also hoped to have direct negotiations with the French and the British in the near future. He meant to use the summit to break up the logjam in current negotiations.[3]

He knew how difficult this might prove: 'At the same time we don't nourish illusions that we'll meet with a new Reagan in Geneva or that he'll proceed to agreement of a serious and sufficiently concrete nature.' The campaign to stop the arms race had to go on even if the Americans were not yet ready to help.[4] Soviet diplomacy should make use of the movement of opposition to the 'Star Wars' project in Western Europe. He could see that he had to avoid seeming to aim at a split in the NATO alliance. There was some reason for optimism. Mitterrand had talked to him of his unease about American foreign policy.[5] Kohl had written to Moscow proposing closer ties between West Germany and Eastern Europe. Gorbachëv welcomed the overture while stipulating that if Kohl was serious, the West Germans had to forswear what he called their 'revanchist' pretensions against East Germany and end their compliance with the Americans.[6] His big worry was that Reagan and his administration lacked a genuine desire to negotiate an arms reduction agreement. He hoped that Shevardnadze, who was scheduled to leave for America after the Sofia meeting, could get the American side to take a more constructive approach before the two leaders met at the Swiss summit.[7]

The Strategic Defense Initiative, Gorbachëv repeated, was essentially 'militaristic'. He added that the French 'Eureka' project was equally warlike, and he discouraged the East European leaders from believing that Mitterrand was offering genuinely equal collaboration.[8] He called for faith in Comecon's own Complex Programme of Scientific-Technical Progress, agreed in June 1984 but not yet implemented; he lamented the lack of progress towards deeper economic integration between the USSR and Eastern Europe.[9] The East European leaders were accustomed to calls by the Kremlin to bring their economies closer together. Gorbachëv's latest appeal failed to cut much ice. On coming to power, he had signalled that Moscow would no longer feather-bed the region's budgets. One of his first steps had been to end the Soviet subsidy to Bulgarian vegetable production. Zhivkov reacted by almost doubling the prices charged for food exports to the USSR.[10] Gorbachëv refused to relent. When starting the Soviet temperance campaign, his government cancelled purchases of Bulgarian wine despite the predictable damage to Bulgaria's finances. When Gorbachëv asked Eastern Europe to integrate its economies with the Soviet one, he was whistling in the wind.

Fellow leaders listened more attentively when he turned to questions of foreign policy. East Germany's Honecker put in a good word for Chinese leaders who at last had dropped their doctrine of the inevitability of world war. Honecker evidently wanted to assert himself as the sagacious communist veteran. Gorbachëv graciously accepted the advice and indicated his desire for a rapprochement with Beijing.[11] Hungary's Kádár cautioned against any impatience since it would be some time before China could realign itself with other communist countries.[12] Ceaușescu, dispelling his usual scepticism, saluted Gorbachëv's focus on achieving a political settlement in Afghanistan and pulling out the Soviet Army.[13] Jaruzelski drew attention to his own problems. He grumbled that Reagan had recently welcomed a Solidarity leader at the White House – his only consolation came from a recent opinion poll that purported to suggest a growth in Polish popular antipathy towards America.[14] Gorbachëv thanked the leaders for their lively, comradely spirit. He hailed the display of unity and was optimistic about the communist order in Eastern Europe, declaring: 'It is important to get together and synchronize watches, and the watches are [in fact] running normally. Perhaps the second hands deviate somewhat, but not the hour or the minute hands.'[15]

Shevardnadze flew on to America and met Reagan at the Waldorf Astoria in New York on 24 October 1985. He deplored recent declarations by American officials, which he said were hardly conducive to success at the arms talks or at the summit. He asked for Shultz to fly over to Moscow so as to clear the political air. Reagan agreed to the request while emphasizing that there could be no treaty without a change in the Kremlin's attitude to human rights. Quite apart from his own opinions, he pointed out that the American Congress would not budge unless some improvement took place.[16] On the same day, accompanied by Shultz, he held a meeting with other G7 leaders. Everyone expressed the hope for a successful summit in Geneva. Thatcher called him 'our champion'. Kohl urged him to talk to Gorbachëv without a bevy of officials in attendance.[17]

Reagan wrote to Gorbachëv confirming agreement to the idea of reducing strategic nuclear weapons by fifty per cent; he added that ways should be found to eliminate intermediate-range weaponry – and he said that Shultz would visit Moscow to prepare the ground for the summit.[18] This in turn worried his own friends on the American political right. It would be the President's first encounter with a General Secretary, and Gorbachëv's performance in Paris had proved that he was a formidable politician with a panoply of skills. Senator Jesse Helms feared that Reagan might succumb to his charm and make undesirable concessions. On 29 October Helms and a group of senators signed a letter asking him to protest against violations of treaty obligations; they referred approvingly to Defense Secretary Weinberger's statements on the topic.[19] Reagan refused to be deflected. He used his next weekly radio address to inform Americans that he would pursue the proposal for a drastic cut in the number of nuclear weapons – he reminded everyone that he had been proposing roughly the same reduction in strategic missiles for more than three years. He said he felt 'encouraged because, after a long wait, legitimate negotiations are under way'.[20]

Shultz took National Security Adviser McFarlane with him to Moscow for his meetings of 4–5 November 1985. Gorbachëv readied himself for some tough talking. The Americans would almost certainly raise questions about regional conflicts, cultural and scientific exchanges and human rights.[21] If this was likely to be their approach, Gorbachëv decided to get his retaliation in first. No sooner had he shaken hands with Shultz than he delivered a tirade against the Strategic Defense Initiative. He described the American administration as operating on the basis of the thinking laid out in the Hoover Institution's publication *America in the Eighties*. He accused America of aiming at military superiority. He told Shultz that the Americans should cease to think that the USSR was in economic trouble and willing to yield to them in order to solve its internal problems. He warned that he would reject any kind of 'linkage' in the Soviet–American talks such as the Americans had practised in the Nixon years, and he voiced resentment about American objections to the abuse of human rights in the USSR.[22] He was brusque with Shultz to the point of unpleasantness.[23] He was obviously trying to drive home the message that he would be no soft touch in Switzerland.

Shultz weathered the storm and, once back in Washington, told Reagan about Gorbachëv's frantic comments about the Strategic Defense Initiative.[24] It was inept of the Soviet leader to reveal his sense of the USSR's vulnerability, and Shultz advised the President to spell out the need for the Politburo to revise its thinking about America. America was not an aggressive power; it was not run by its military-industrial complex. American leaders genuinely wished the super-powers to have stable forces at 'radically lower levels', but they would never abandon the Defense Initiative. The American people would always object to the USSR's human rights abuses and demand that the Kremlin should fulfil its international obligations. If Gorbachëv wanted an arms control agreement, he would have to adopt a less militaristic posture around the world.[25]

The Soviet leadership wanted to avoid yielding very much in Geneva. The Gorbachëv team prepared with what Shevardnadze called 'active, attacking work'. The Politburo as well as the Warsaw Pact's Political Consultative Committee gave their mandate for Gorbachëv to proceed as he wanted. The important thing for both of them was to bring an end to the confrontation between East and West. Gorbachëv was pleased about this support, and visits by leading communists from Vietnam, Laos, Mongolia and Ethiopia had cemented his resolve. He had also received encouragement from Rajiv Gandhi. On his Paris trip he had asked François Mitterrand for help and felt that he had made some progress with him. By the time that he left for Geneva, he felt hopeful that he could make an impact on Reagan.[26] His preparations included the unusual move of a wide-ranging interview with the American President in the pages of *Pravda*. The *New York Times* noted that the Soviet newspaper cut out Reagan's remarks about Afghanistan.[27] But the bigger fact was that the interview took place at all – and *Pravda* refrained from censoring his other broad points. The Soviet leadership no longer feared the ventilation of the American political breeze.

Gorbachëv took a wide spectrum of advisers to Geneva. The scientists Yevgeni Velikhov and Roald Sagdeev as well as arms control talks specialists joined his group along with academics Fëdor Burlatski and Yevgeni Primakov. Gorbachëv wanted all the help he could muster.[28] His team of political and diplomatic advisers also included Yakovlev, Kornienko, Dobrynin and Alexandrov-Agentov: a mixture of the contemporary and the antediluvian.[29]

They discerned weaknesses in America's standpoint. Shevardnadze commented to aides: 'Abroad [i.e. outside America], Reagan has often seemed like an ignorant old fool whose simplistic militarism was entirely capable of resulting in the world being blown to smithereens.'[30] He was largely right about the trends in West European opinion. But American surveys were more nuanced in their results. Americans recognized that the new General Secretary was different from his predecessors, but sixty-two per cent of them – according to a Harris poll – believed he could not be trusted. Reagan could depart for Switzerland in a calm frame of mind.[31] On 14 November 1985 he gave an address to the nation on television: 'This, then, is why I go to Geneva – to build a lasting peace.'[32] Behind the scenes, ex-President Nixon steadied Reagan's nerve in a friendly fashion.[33] The US delegation at Geneva, headed by Max Kampelman, shared the objective of an arms reduction agreement while cautioning against undue concessions. The British and French nuclear forces should be excluded from the talks. America's military modernization and the Strategic Defense Initiative should be continued; and Gorbachëv should be told to dismantle the Krasnoyarsk radar station.[34] If the Soviet delegation travelled with confidence, the Americans matched them in temper.

The Swiss authorities kept crowds of people waving anti-Soviet placards away from the Soviet delegation, but Gorbachëv was anyway adept at rolling with the tide. He knew that Western lobby groups would exploit his arrival for their own ends, and he refrained from overreacting to the placards and oral abuse. He fixed his mind on Reagan rather than on local protests.

Reagan's initial problem was not in Geneva but in Washington. Defense Secretary Weinberger thought the summit was a waste of time at best and at worst even dangerous. His concern was that the President, left to himself, might make undesirable compromises with the dynamic General Secretary. Weinberger was not part of the American delegation. He decided to make his mark on the proceedings by leaking his thoughts to the *New York Times* just days before Reagan left for Europe. This took the form of a memo he had written to Reagan against any idea of acceding to the resumption of the START talks or to the abandonment of the Strategic Defense Initiative. Weinberger underscored the USSR's attested violations of such treaties as existed. The American priority at the summit, he went on, should be to insist that any progress in fresh talks would depend on Moscow complying with its commitments and allowing a reliable system of verification.[35] Another President might have fired Weinberger for the embarrassment he was causing him, but Reagan was a reluctant disciplinarian – and he anyway shared Weinberger's commitment to American military modernization.

On 19 November 1985 Reagan welcomed Gorbachëv to the summit at the Maison de Saussure, which the Aga Khan had put at their disposal. This was an eighteenth-century chateau near the university in the old part of the city at the southern tip of Lake Geneva. The President had reconnoitred the venue two days earlier. The chateau was close to the lakeside, and he aimed to ask Gorbachëv to walk down to it and have a one-on-one conversation at the pool-house. He had read a pile of briefing papers and recorded in his diary: 'Lord, I hope I'm ready and not over-trained.'[36] He charmed everyone from the very start. Nobody in the Soviet leadership, apart from Ambassador Dobrynin, had expected the President to be quite so likeable. When Adamishin shook hands with him, he instantly decided he was 'a sympathetic old man'.[37] (This was not a retrospective judgement but what he recorded in his diary.) Reagan's affability overlaid his cunning. He stood on the steps of the building without benefit of overcoat on a cold winter's day. The intention was to emphasize that his age had no influence on his health and energy – and later when Gorbachëv hosted a Soviet reception for Reagan, he too dispensed with outdoor wear: he was a quick learner.[38] The tussle was not just about youthfulness and dress. Reagan and Gorbachëv were rivals for the image of the world's peacemaker.

Their first session was meant to last a quarter of an hour. In fact it continued for an hour.[39] Gorbachëv tried to persuade the President that, whatever he read in American publications, the Soviet economy was not facing collapse. The arms race was therefore not a way to force the USSR to its knees.[40] Reagan, when his turn came, stressed the desire for an arms reduction agreement. Limitation was not enough: there had to be a drastic decrease in the nuclear weapons on both sides. He insisted that his Strategic Defense Initiative had no offensive potential.[41] In the afternoon, Gorbachëv sprang a surprise by revealing his wish for a political settlement to the Afghan war. He asked for American cooperation in the process. He indicated a preference for Afghanistan to adopt a non-aligned status in world politics if he were to withdraw the Soviet Army.[42] Reagan was less pleased when Gorbachëv dismissed any idea that the Defense Initiative could ever prevent every single missile from getting through to its target. Gorbachëv was ratcheting up the pressure. He accused the President of starting a new stage in the arms race with the Initiative.[43] Reagan gave his word that his programme excluded the objective of launching a first strike on the USSR. He suggested that the focus of their conversations should be turned on how to reduce their nuclear weapons by fifty per cent.[44]

They adjourned before meeting up again at the pool-house unaccompanied by advisers. Reagan saw the point of playing the man rather than the ball, and sought to create a friendly atmosphere. In front of a roaring fire, they quickly agreed to get their negotiating teams to negotiate how to halve the stockpiles of strategic nuclear weaponry.[45] This was a big step forward. Reagan had also commented: 'If there were agreement that there would be no need for nuclear missiles, then one might agree that there would also be no need for defences against them.'[46] Gorbachëv wanted a lot more from the President and repeated his objections to the Strategic Defense Initiative; he added that the next US President might not share his peaceful intentions. Progress gave way to stalemate.[47]

Next day, Reagan proposed to cut back strategic nuclear weapons to 6,000 warheads for each side.[48] Gorbachëv assented; but he repeated his objection to Reagan's concept of space-based defence.[49] Reagan retorted: 'It's not an offensive system. I'm talking about a shield, not a spear.' This served to exasperate Gorbachëv: 'Why don't you believe me when I say that the Soviet Union will never attack?'[50] Gorbachëv repeated his question before allowing Reagan to reply. He interrupted for a second time when Reagan began his answer. Eventually Reagan stated that the assurance of a single Soviet leader would never be enough for the American people; this was why he was putting his efforts into 'sound defense'.[51] Gorbachëv took a grip on himself. Moving away from the Defense Initiative, he said he was willing to sign a separate agreement on deep cuts in intermediate-range nuclear missiles. He admitted to having spoken too heatedly. Moments later they were again going at it hammer and tongs about weapons in outer space. Reagan's patience snapped. Irked by Gorbachëv's claims about Soviet sincerity, he pointed to the Krasnoyarsk radar station as an infringement of the 1972 Anti-Ballistic Missile Treaty.[52] Gorbachëv hit back that Reagan's intransigence about the Defense Initiative was ruining their opportunity to halve the number of strategic nuclear weapons.[53]

That afternoon they went into plenary session at the Soviet mission. Reagan read out a statement calling for a fifty per cent reduction in offensive nuclear arms as well as for cuts in other categories of weaponry.[54] Gorbachëv readily agreed to this and was pleased about the resumption of dialogue between the USSR and the US; but he voiced his disappointment that they had not made greater progress.[55] The Reagans hosted the farewell dinner that evening, and the President struck an encouraging tone: 'We have started something.' This melted Gorbachëv's mood somewhat and moved him to say: 'If now we have laid the first bricks, we have made a new start – a new phase has begun.'[56]

Reagan returned to Washington delighted with how things had gone. He had made arrangements to address a joint session of the American Congress on 21 November 1985. He reported on how he and Gorbachëv had talked for fifteen hours – in five of them they had been on their own, except for interpreters. He emphasized the progress made during the fireside chat: 'I had called for a fresh start – and we made that start. I can't claim we had a meeting of minds on such fundamentals as ideology or national purpose – but we understand each other better. That's key to peace. I gained a better perspective, I feel he did, too. It was a constructive meeting.'[57] He hailed the agreement to move towards a halving of offensive nuclear weapons and to the complete elimination of intermediate-range nuclear missiles.[58] Senators and congressmen of both parties applauded his efforts. The reaction was the same in the press and on TV. The *New York Times* called it 'not a bad two days' work' and endorsed 'the spirit of Geneva'; and their conservative columnist William Safire wrote in congratulation: 'Mr Reagan took a long draught of heady wine and then wisely turned down an empty glass.'[59] Reagan savoured the shedding of his reputation as a warmonger.[60]

He took equal pleasure in the response of West European public opinion, which had begun with low expectations of him and was now supportive. The main sticking point was the undiminished disquiet in Europe's capitals about the Strategic Defense Initiative.[61] But the reaction to the summit around the entire world was immensely to the American advantage.[62] Even *Pravda* printed Reagan's speech to the Congress. There was also television coverage of the American and Soviet leaders standing together in Geneva. The American administration was delighted: 'The Soviet people saw on their own media for the first time in a long while a smiling, responsible American President rather than a cartoon ogre.'[63] Of course, as an American political conservative, he had to remember the sensitivities of his followers. He confided to his friend George Murphy, the former song-and-dance man who had preceded him as president of the Screen Actors Guild: 'Seriously, it was worthwhile but it would be foolish to believe the leopard will change its spots. He is a firm believer (so is she), and he believes in the propaganda they peddle about us. At the same time he is practical and knows that his economy is a basket case. I think our job is to show him he and they will be better off if we make some practical agreements, without attempting to convert him to our way of thinking.'[64]

Reagan sensed that the ice was cracking in global politics and wanted to strengthen his collaboration with Secretary Shultz. Together they were beginning to achieve an understanding with the USSR. Shultz was proving himself a brilliant enabler – the only worry for Reagan was that he might find the job too exhausting and quit.[65] Without the Secretary's persistence, the President knew he would find it hard to achieve his purposes. The summit had gone well. He saw reason to hope that it would be the first in a series of productive encounters.

Gorbachëv felt the same. From Geneva, Gorbachëv flew to Prague to report to the Warsaw Pact's Political Consultative Committee.[66] The absence of a definite agreement with Reagan failed to dampen his optimism. He had not gone to the summit expecting to sign a treaty. Although Reagan had refused to budge on the Strategic Defense Initiative, this had hardly come as a surprise. More work needed to be done. Foreign Affairs Ministry official Anatoli Adamishin prepared a statement for him announcing that a new stage in international politics had begun and that the lowest point in US–USSR relations was a thing of the past. This was too much for Georgi Kornienko, who scratched out what he saw as Adamishin's excess of enthusiasm.[67] The Political Consultative Committee was anyhow a triumph for Gorbachëv. Fellow leaders cheered his performance. Honecker spoke warmly about how Gorbachëv had awakened the conscience of the people he had spoken to; Husák commended his success in reaching out to broader circles of opinion than any Soviet leader had managed. Kádár welcomed what he called Gorbachëv's effective challenge to the anticommunist course of American foreign policy. Jaruzelski declared that the achievement at Geneva must never be lost. Even Ceaușescu squeezed out some approving comments.[68]

On 25 November 1985 Shevardnadze told his ministry that Reagan now knew that the USSR would never surrender. 'Positive dialogue' was on the horizon. But Shevardnadze also said that Kádár had been wrong to say that America's 'anticommunist course' had been broken.[69] An open discussion ensued in the ministry collegium. Looking for ways to crack Reagan's resolve, Kovalëv contended that the USSR could put Washington under political stress by seeking support from France, West Germany, Italy and Holland as well as from the non-aligned countries around the world.[70] This was wishful thinking. Gorbachëv's trip to Paris had demonstrated that even Mitterrand – the West European leader most ready with his criticisms of the American administration – was loath to rebuke Reagan for his foreign and security policy. Public opinion in Western Europe took a favourable view of the Soviet reformers, but it was far from clear that Gorbachëv could turn this into an instrument of constraint on the foreign policies of governments. The summit in Geneva created a friendly atmosphere without removing the practical impediments to rapprochement. Much needed to be done if progress was going to occur.

15. PRESENTING THE SOVIET PACKAGE

On 28 November 1985 Reagan sent a handwritten letter to Gorbachëv that offered grounds for hope of further progress. The President welcomed their shared ambition to halt the arms race and abandon work on new kinds of offensive nuclear weaponry. Reagan put the question: 'And can't our negotiators deal more frankly and openly with the question of how to eliminate a first-strike potential on both sides?' He admitted that the USSR had understandable concerns about the American negotiating position; he also gave a welcome to Gorbachëv's wish for military withdrawal from Afghanistan and offered help to achieve this outcome.[1] 'In Geneva,' he assured the General Secretary, 'I found our private sessions particularly useful. Both of us have advisers and assistants, but, you know, in the final analysis, the responsibility to preserve peace and increase cooperation is ours.'[2] Gorbachëv replied in a constructive spirit, accepting Reagan's sincerity in promising to keep the Strategic Defense Initiative clear of developing first-strike offensive weapons. He asked the President to accept that as General Secretary he had to assess the objective potential of the research. For this reason, he indicated, he would go on asking for the programme's abandonment as part of the process of rapprochement.[3]

The President and General Secretary agreed to deliver a New Year's television address to each other's people. The idea was Reagan's, and Gorbachëv greeted it with enthusiasm.[4] There had never been anything like it. Reagan assumed that his powers of delivery would win him friends with people in the USSR; Gorbachëv thought the same in reverse about America. They had no deficiency in self-confidence.

On 5 December 1985 Reagan groaned to Foreign Trade Minister Boris Aristov about the USSR's failure to honour its purchasing obligations under the Long-Term Grain Agreement. While wanting to expand trade between the two countries, he said, he could not afford to overlook the interests of American cereal farmers.[5] When Commerce Secretary Baldrige visited Moscow a few days later, he assured

Aristov that the Americans genuinely hoped to strengthen mutual economic links. Though the ban remained on exporting goods of 'strategic' importance, there was opportunity for the Soviet Union to bid for sales of medical, agricultural and mining equipment.[6] Moscow welcomed the idea. It was less happy about other measures that the Americans undertook after the summit. Secretary Shultz flew off on a tour of Europe's capitals and on 14 December, after reaching West Berlin, he stated bluntly that America did 'not accept incorporation of Eastern Europe, including East Germany and East Berlin, into a Soviet sphere of influence.'[7] He accentuated America's policy of favouring those East European leaders who kept their distance from the Kremlin. Next day in Bucharest he impressed on Ceaușescu that his repressive policies made it difficult to persuade the American Senate to assist economic cooperation.[8] He was gentler in Budapest, where, indeed, he praised General Secretary Kádár: 'I did a lot of listening, and I felt he had a great deal of wisdom.'[9]

Gorbachëv and Shevardnadze said nothing about Shultz's tour since they wanted to hold their focus on completing *perestroika* in the USSR and on achieving a relaxation with America.[10] If Eastern Europe started its own reform, that would be all to the good. But the time for orders from Moscow was at an end. Change had to happen through consent.[11] In March 1986, when appointing Vadim Medvedev as Central Committee secretary with responsibility for the 'socialist countries', Gorbachëv would remind him to avoid the temptation to meddle in their politics. Medvedev regularly contacted the East European party leaders and consulted Soviet ambassadors. His task was to free Shevardnadze to work on the rest of Soviet foreign policy.[12] Gorbachëv kept up the momentum achieved in Geneva. The concern for him and Shevardnadze was that Reagan might renounce the spirit of Geneva and become confrontational. They also worried about the resistance in the USSR to any programme of arms reduction. Shevardnadze contacted the leading diplomats at the talks with America in Geneva, Stockholm and Vienna – they were all in Moscow for the winter vacation. He instructed them to draft proposals to revive the prospect of bilateral agreements.[13]

The talks in the three European cities belonged to an interlocking process that was meant to make the world safer through mutual understandings. Those that took place in Geneva captured the greatest public attention because they centred on nuclear disarmament. The on-going negotiation in Stockholm dealt with 'security and co-operation in

Europe'; the idea was to find ways to boost mutual confidence and prevent dangerous operational misunderstanding. In Vienna the focus was on the attempt to find ways to reduce the size of the conventional forces of NATO and the Warsaw Pact. There were drawn-out discussions of quantities and categories of weaponry. This involved negotiations of fiendish complexity, and both the USSR and America assigned some of their finest diplomats to such talks.

On 30 December 1985 Gorbachëv invited five of them to his office at Old Square. Politburo members Shevardnadze and Zaikov were present as Gorbachëv explained his thoughts about arms reduction. He could achieve this, he reckoned, only by winning over American public opinion and bringing it to bear on the President. Gorbachëv looked forward to huge rewards for the USSR. According to his confidential figures, forty per cent of Soviet industry was devoted to military purposes. The Politburo had to cut this back so that the shops could begin to fill with the goods that consumers needed.[14] Viktor Karpov, leader of the Soviet talks delegation in Geneva, argued the need for boldness. He recommended acceptance of Reagan's 'zero option' as a starting point; he reasoned that even if Reagan rejected such a proposal, the USSR would gain credibility at America's expense in Western Europe. Gorbachëv liked the idea.[15] He was open to signing an arms reduction treaty even without insisting on the United Kingdom and France being co-signatories. A deal between the superpowers was of supreme importance. Oleg Grinevski, head of the Soviet delegation at the European security talks in Stockholm, persuaded him to tie this into a package to cut the number of strategic nuclear weapons by half; he forecast that this would help to bring the Swedish talks to completion.[16]

On 2 January 1986 Gorbachëv gained assent for these ideas at the Politburo.[17] Grinevski was witness to the atmosphere:

> The feeling of the meeting with Gorbachëv is very strong. With Brezhnev, Chernenko and even Andropov, I felt as if I was dealing with a being from another planet. They did not understand. And this is, at last, a normal person. He wins one's favour with his sincerity. Affable, well-wishing, and one can feel energy and firmness behind all this.[18]

Gorbachëv had not gone soft on the Americans but rather accused them of impudence. He fully expected Reagan to turn him down but aimed to draw him towards agreement by changing world public opinion; he predicted success with the West Germans and other Europeans. The American administration would find it difficult to stonewall him: 'This year is the year of peace.'[19]

Gorbachëv caused consternation in the General Staff.[20] Marshal Akhromeev did not mind pacific language as such: what he found shocking was Gorbachëv's apparent sincerity when using it. He had an accomplice in Kornienko at the Foreign Affairs Ministry. As the Deputy Minister, Kornienko cheekily slowed down the processing of documents which Shevardnadze had commissioned with an arms reduction agreement in mind.[21] Shevardnadze and Gorbachëv underestimated Kornienko's capacity for mischief. When they parted at Geneva airport, they took turns to embrace him and said 'thanks for everything.'[22] Akhromeev and Kornienko had no intention of letting Gorbachëv do as he pleased. As soon as they heard about his post-summit consultations, they plotted how to counteract the latest schemes that the Politburo had approved. Kornienko informed Akhromeev about the way things were going. Both could see that nothing could be achieved by means of a direct challenge to Gorbachëv and Shevardnadze. They opted instead for an approach that involved Akhromeev in offering his own programme for arms reduction on behalf of the General Staff. His real aim was to emasculate Gorbachëv's proposals through cunning and kindness.[23]

On 7 January 1986 Varennikov, Akhromeev's deputy, invited officials of the Ministry of Foreign Affairs and the Party Defence Department to a confidential meeting in his office.[24] He gave no advance signal. No one in the Politburo except Shevardnadze heard about it until after the event – and Shevardnadze himself received no invitation. The KGB and even the Defence Ministry was kept in the dark. Varennikov wanted to achieve a big impact, and surprise was his tool of choice.[25]

Varennikov read out a plan for disarmament that Akhromeev had drawn up. It would involve the elimination of absolutely every class of nuclear weapons. After explaining Akhromeev's computation of the destructive capacities of NATO and the Warsaw Pact, Varennikov described a programme for multilateral arms reduction in three stages through to the year 2000.[26] Akhromeev and Varennikov were being disingenuous, as Colonel General Andrian Danilevich of the General Staff later explained:

Gorbachëv talked about total reductions, but we in the General Staff did not think that this would really happen. We supposed that this could be some far-off prospect, but did not believe it. We [started] from the premise that an acceptable level compatible with mutual deterrence should be found. We still maintain that nuclear weapons should be preserved as an element of deterrence, given the real possibility of the appearance of nuclear arsenals among third countries.[27]

Years later Akhromeev confessed that he had never believed in the goal of eliminating all nuclear weapons.[28] But as Chief of the General Staff he knew what the General Secretary wanted. Akhromeev would obviously get nowhere if he simply opposed the orientation towards arms reduction. He pretended to support it by offering a scheme that he knew would be unacceptable to NATO. He absolutely did not want a world war and hoped to manage questions of international military rivalry in such a fashion as to avoid one. He assumed that the General Staff knew what was best for the USSR's security.

He had deliberately drafted a schedule that spanned fifteen years. As he was aware, there could be no guarantee that future political leaders would stick to it. He had also included British and French nuclear warheads in the first stage of arms reduction despite knowing that governments in London and Paris would guard their nuclear-power status.[29] Akhromeev had also purposefully restricted his scheme to nuclear arms. The Americans would inevitably grasp that, if they agreed to it, Soviet leaders would be able to threaten Western Europe with the numerical superiority of their conventional forces.

Silence descended on the entire room until Yuli Kvitsinski, a Soviet arms negotiator in Vienna, let out an ironic laugh. He was voicing what everyone in the room was feeling, that Akhromeev had pulled a fast one.[30] The diplomats pointed out that Western leaders would inevitably treat such a scheme with deep suspicion. Varennikov replied that the entire General Staff was against the slightest revision of it. Akhromeev in person strode into the office halfway through the meeting – Grinevski would later describe him as 'thin, nervous, ener-getic'. Varennikov ordered the military officers to stand to attention. Akhromeev acted like the master in the house. Refusing to sit down, he barked that the Politburo package of 2 January was obsolete. At that very moment a general – arms talks specialist Nikolai Chervov – was in a plane flying south to present the General Staff's ideas to Gorbachëv, who was taking a vacation in Pitsunda by the Black Sea.

Akhromeev claimed to have been working on his project for a year and a half. He said that the Politburo's recent discussions had served to bring forward the moment of presentation. Nobody challenged his story – and Akhromeev radiated confidence about gaining the General Secretary's seal of approval.[31]

Akhromeev ignored the convention for the Big Five to discuss drafts on arms reduction policy before they reached the General Secretary or the Politburo. Gorbachëv did not appear to mind. As Akhromeev had predicted, the General Secretary gave his instant approval to the General Staff's entire proposal. Gorbachëv never explained his motives in changing his negotiating tactics. In Geneva he had offered to bargain separately about each category of nuclear weapons. Now he put forward an all-inclusive package. Perhaps he reckoned his ideas as the best disarmament project that was acceptable to the high command. Or possibly it was the sheer scope of the three-stage programme that caught his fancy. The global liquidation of nuclear weaponry was just the kind of slogan that would gain the world's attention.

Shevardnadze recognized that the project might annoy the Americans; but once Gorbachëv had approved it, Shevardnadze could only give battle over the details. On 10 January 1986 he criticized Akhromeev's ideas at the Big Five. It was the first time that he spoke at variance with the General Secretary's known preferences. Either that or Gorbachëv had given his blessing for him to carry out what he chose not to do for himself. Two other Politburo members, Chebrikov and Zaikov, were at the meeting. The three of them came together in ridiculing Akhromeev's argument that his project would induce the Americans to agree to an arms reduction treaty. A brisk debate ensued, and Akhromeev could not pull rank as the troika from the Politburo insisted on drastic revision. Their main amendment demanded the complete removal of intermediate-range nuclear missiles from Europe in the very first scheduled stage of the programme. Shevardnadze was hoping to assure the White House that the USSR was not trying to postpone the most sensitive matters to the end of the century. After intensive discussion, Akhromeev saw that he had to give way. If ever he had imagined that the General Staff would completely dominate policy, he was beginning to learn his lesson.[32]

Nevertheless he had preserved his other main objectives, and his political opponents could get no further in amending the programme. There was lasting resentment in the Ministry of Foreign Affairs that the General Staff had bounced the Kremlin into a decision. The feeling was the same in the KGB, whose leaders were accustomed to being consulted about any big change of policy that involved state security.[33]

Akhromeev arranged for the production of a diagram that indicated the three stages in a visual format. He rushed the revised text to Gorbachëv in Pitsunda. Gorbachëv immediately signed it off and ordered *Pravda* to publish it as his own declaration.[34] Meanwhile on 11 January Gorbachëv finished a confidential letter to Reagan, objecting to American attempts to make the current talks on trade with the USSR conditional upon the satisfaction of demands about human rights. Gorbachëv warned that Washington's posture would 'bring no benefit'. But at the same time he stressed a desire for the 'normalization' of relations.[35] The letter gave no hint of the arms reduction proposals that he was on the point of making public. In Washington on 14 January, Ambassador Dobrynin alerted Shultz in vague terms while omitting to specify the contents. The same day in Moscow, Gorbachëv at last signed another letter to Reagan expounding the general rationale of his proposals for staged disarmament. He indicated a desire to move away from the 'extremely dangerous path' involving the development of space weapons. Instead he called for the total abolition of nuclear arms. According to Gorbachëv, this would remove any need for weaponry in outer space.[36]

He knew that his letter would reach the White House after his declaration was published. He intended it this way. The idea was to preserve the element of surprise and achieve the maximum of impact worldwide. He was reckless about the established etiquette of dealing with the other superpower.

Gorbachëv's declaration called for the global elimination of nuclear weapons by the year 2000. The first stage would last between five to eight years and involve a halving of stocks of strategic weaponry, leaving just 6,000 warheads on either side. Nuclear arms testing would undergo an immediate ban. Intermediate-range missiles of all types would disappear from Europe. The rationale was not to withdraw weapons but to destroy them. The Soviet Union and America were expected to lead by example. There would be an interdiction on passing strategic weapons to any third country; and 'England' and France were expected to guarantee that they would cease to develop such missiles. The second stage, starting in 1990 and lasting between five and seven years, would see the other nuclear powers joining the disarmament process. Soviet and American forces would continue to reduce their stockpiles and liquidate all their tactical nuclear arms (which were defined as having a range of up to 1,000 kilometres). The veto on offensive space weapons would become multilateral. The third and final stage would begin in 1995, when every remaining nuclear bomb of any kind whatsoever would be eliminated. The declaration also envisaged rapid progress in removing chemical weapons and a ban on the development of any form of non-nuclear weapons on new physical principles.[37]

On 16 January, when introducing his programme in *Pravda*, Gorbachëv announced an extension of his unilateral moratorium on nuclear arms testing and invited the American to follow his example. He announced the USSR's full commitment to the disarmament talks in Geneva and Stockholm. His proposals, he claimed, were preferable to an arms race in space weaponry. Instead of Reagan's 'Star Wars' project, he urged, efforts should be made to use the world's resources for peaceful purposes.[38]

He put his faith in winning over global public opinion and making it difficult for the American administration to reject his programme. Better than any Soviet leader since Lenin, he knew how to aim his appeal over the heads of political leaders. Shevardnadze rhapsodized about the prospect of a foreign policy based on the idea that America and the USSR were 'competitors' rather than enemies.[39] The Soviet internal reforms were changing the country's image abroad and helping to narrow the White House's choices in policy.[40] The Americans could no longer point to the USSR as the main obstacle to disarmament. The Kremlin was making a big offer, and the onus was now on Washington to decide how to respond.[41] Gorbachëv and Shevardnadze saw Weinberger, who did not hide his scepticism about arms reduction, as an easy target.[42] Radical officials in the ministry like Anatoli Adamishin were of like mind. While admitting that the January declaration contained elements of 'utopia', Adamishin was pleased that these were balanced by 'concretenesses'.[43]

Gorbachëv's diplomatic Blitzkrieg had started. Enthusiasm replaced calm judgement inside the Politburo. Soviet leaders were confident that they were thrusting the Americans on to the defensive.

16. AMERICAN REJECTION

The American administration received Gorbachëv's declaration very coolly. His smooth, pacific diction failed to divert attention from the corrugated implications of his new proposals. The proposed stages for disarmament were framed so as to give the edge to the USSR. Gorbachëv, if he had his way, would render America inferior in firepower in the next few years.

Washington talk was heavy with suspicion. At the Geneva summit, Gorbachëv had broached the possibility of agreements on various categories of weaponry. Now he was presenting an all-inclusive package, and nearly all of Reagan's subordinates concluded that the General Secretary was playing a cynical game to the world's gallery. They declined to take him seriously. Shultz was unusual in arguing for the merits of a more nuanced approach. In conversation with John Poindexter, the unobtrusive retired admiral who succeeded Robert McFarlane as National Security Adviser in December 1985, he argued that the declaration was far from being 'warmed-over Soviet propaganda'; and in discussion with his aide Hill, he described it as 'a big deal'.[1] He went to the White House to talk things over with the President. This was the first time, he stressed, that the Kremlin had put forward a staged schedule for the complete elimination of nuclear weapons. According to Shultz, something important was in the offing. He speculated that Gorbachëv had cracked; and he urged Reagan to take full advantage.[2] Reagan at first was more impatient than suspicious: 'Why wait until the turn of the century for a world without nuclear weapons?'[3] But since the idea of getting rid of all such weapons appealed to him, he listened attentively to Shultz's analysis.

Unfortunately Gorbachëv had been too clever for his own good. He had shown discourtesy to the Americans by releasing a copy of the declaration just a few hours before it became public knowledge. Ambassador Dobrynin forwarded the text of Gorbachëv's introductory speech on Soviet TV only after the broadcast.[4] Shultz vented his

anger when he next encountered Dobrynin.[5] He exclaimed that the
American administration did not take kindly to such tactics. The
sooner the Soviet leaders learned the lesson, the better.[6] The members
of the American delegation at the Geneva arms talks shared Shultz's
feeling of annoyance. Kampelman resented the fact that his Soviet
counterpart Viktor Karpov had not breathed a word about the news
over lunch on the very day when it would be released to the world's
media.[7] Nitze urged caution about the declaration since he doubted
that Gorbachëv had penned it: 'I wonder whose work of art on the
Soviet side this is.'[8] Reagan decided on a restrained response to
Moscow. A brief statement appeared in his name: 'I welcome the
Soviet's [sic] latest response and hope that it represents a hopeful
further step in the process. We, together with our allies, will give careful study to General Secretary Gorbachëv's suggestions.'[9]

TV and press commentators in the NATO countries exercised a
responsible caution. The New York Times, Wall Street Journal and
Washington Post gave a factual summary of Gorbachëv's declaration
with little editorial comment. They described the Strategic Defense
Initiative as the main obstacle to progress.[10] None of the three newspapers could see much chance of progress between the superpowers if
the Soviet leader insisted on the President abandoning his great project. Time Magazine summed up the viewpoint of sceptics some days
later: 'Gorbachëv's plan is an agonizing mixture of the old and the new,
uncertainty and concreteness, regular concessions and old demands.'[11]

Ambassador Hartman was unusual in accepting the sincerity of
Soviet concerns and asked for concessions on the Strategic Defense
Initiative in return for the USSR agreeing to cuts in nuclear stockpiles.[12] There was plainly a need to come to a settled analysis. On 22
January 1986 Shultz appealed to the President to set up a group outside the usual inter-agency structures to elaborate policy.[13] Reagan did
not wish to annoy his other leading officials, preferring to seek consensus in the traditional way through the National Security Planning
Group. The Defense Department and CIA offered harsh verdicts on
Gorbachëv.[14] Weinberger and Casey depicted him as remaining committed to modernizing his strategic nuclear forces and supporting
communist and anti-American insurgency, terrorism and subversion
around the world.[15] They could see no change in the Politburo's basic
strategy. Weinberger and Casey wanted Reagan to tread cautiously.
As senior officials, they kept quiet about their disapproval of his aim
to eliminate all atomic weapons from the face of the earth. Assistant

Defense Secretary Perle had never found it easy to stay silent. He told the American Senior Arms Control Group that Reagan's commitment to total nuclear disarmament was a disaster. Rowny too advocated a brisk scepticism. As an inveterate critic of Soviet policy and practice, he denied that there was anything good to say about *perestroika*. He suggested that if the Americans stayed calm and held their ground, the Soviet declaration would be seen for what it was and would 'fall of its own weight'.[16]

Nitze, who was usually on Shultz's side, put up a negative analysis. He slated Gorbachëv for having 'front-loaded' his declaration in such a way as to provide only the USSR with its requirements in the first stage. The West would have to wait for the later stages to obtain its objectives – and this would mean that America would need to rely on Soviet good faith over several years. What is more, Gorbachëv was demanding that France and Britain should eliminate their entire nuclear arsenal. He had also left Asia out of his declaration. Nitze worried that the Kremlin would keep nuclear missiles on its Asian territories and retain the instant capacity to transport them across the Urals and launch them from European Russia against Western Europe.[17]

By 3 February 1986, at the National Security Planning Group, the mood had moved perceptibly closer to Shultz. Even Weinberger was against portraying the January declaration as 'a publicity stunt'; he reasoned that any stark rejection of Gorbachëv's overture would serve to boost his image as a peacemaker. He was more like his usual self when he spoke against compromise on the Strategic Defense Initiative. He also opposed the idea of fixing a schedule for the total abolition of nuclear weapons.[18] Shultz favoured a more affirmative approach. The Americans in his opinion should concentrate on offering their own variant of a first stage of disarmament. By planning for a drastic reduction in nuclear weapons stockpiles, they would prevent Gorbachëv from monopolizing the image as a man of peace.[19] Casey intervened to insist that there could be no reduction without procedures of 'effective verification'.[20] Weinberger agreed about the insincerity of the Soviet leaders, arguing that this would help to 'smoke them out'. He bristled when Shultz teased him for moving over to the Department of State's position. Weinberger barked that although the administration's internal disagreements might be narrow, they were still very deep.[21]

The President declined to arbitrate between them. He preferred to emphasize his priority for exposing the insincerity of the USSR's recent pronouncements. He pledged his faith in the Strategic Defense Initiative, but this time he said he wanted to render it less worrisome to its adversaries. He had it in mind for America to hand the completed research over to the United Nations, which could then deploy it against any power that threatened to use nuclear weapons. This was heady stuff. It was also somewhat confusing because he simultaneously emphasized the need to go on pressurizing Gorbachëv. He stated that if the USSR intended to keep intermediate-range missiles in its Asian provinces, he would feel free to install equivalent weapons in Alaska.[22]

Next day, on 4 February 1986, the President signed National Security Decision Directive no. 210 setting out his considered objectives. He reaffirmed his personal commitment to the total abolition of nuclear missiles; but he rejected Gorbachëv's declaration and put forward his own standpoint at the Geneva summit as the best basis for discussions with the USSR. He called for a renewal of negotiations. In doing this, he signalled a preference for Shultz over Weinberger and Casey. Reagan wanted to aim at an immediate halving of the number of Soviet and American missiles, but only if the Americans could secure a fair underpinning for computation and a reliable system to verify compliance. This would open the way to scrapping the nuclear missiles of Britain, France and China. The President endorsed the goal of scrapping all intermediate-range nuclear warheads without delay.[23] His eagerness for total nuclear disarmament was genuine, and his directive was rather more hostile about Gorbachëv than he really felt. In private he was willing to say that he detected 'something of a chemistry' between the two of them, and he warmly remembered how the General Secretary had cited a verse from the Bible in their meetings in Geneva.[24]

On 16 February 1986 he sent an encouraging letter to Gorbachëv with some proposals to reduce the nuclear stockpiles. He promised to respond to his January declaration as soon as the American administration completed its examination. He indicated a continuing concern about regional conflicts, stressing that 'the Soviet Union is engaged in a war in another country and the United States is not'. He offered cooperation 'in every reasonable way' if Gorbachëv would withdraw his forces from Afghanistan. He commented that Moscow's support for Libyan dictator Gaddafi left him sceptical about the USSR's desire to put an end to terrorism.[25]

Indeed, the Americans had credible information that the USSR was deploying new mobile intercontinental missiles – the SS-25s.

Soviet authorities were also testing a range of cruise missiles and strategic bombers, as the CIA regularly brought to Reagan's attention.[26] The Moscow media were inadvertently assisting America's anti-Soviet crusaders. On 6 March 1986 Soviet TV aired a programme suggesting that America had procured the death of former Swedish Prime Minister Olof Palme. The killings of former Italian ex-Prime Minister Aldo Moro in 1978 and India's Prime Minister Indira Gandhi in 1984 were also attributed to American connivance.[27] Such allegations worsened the atmosphere between America and the USSR; and though Reagan leaned towards wanting a softening of relations with the Kremlin leadership, he had to keep account of the evidence of military build-up on the Soviet side. There existed the possibility that Gorbachëv's overtures were only a feint in the diplomatic game that he was playing. Reagan had always said that he would judge Moscow by its actions rather than its words – and anyway not all of its words were pointed in the direction of conciliation. As American President he was well aware that any administration could contain factions in conflict. He needed to feel sure that the advocates of peace genuinely held the upper hand in the Politburo.

Against this background, Shultz could not afford to appear too pliable in talks with Moscow. He told Ambassador Dobrynin and Prime Minister Ryzhkov that Gorbachëv's declaration was fundamentally unconstructive.[28] Gorbachëv wanted to finalize a deal exclusively about nuclear weapons; he had omitted conventional forces from his proposals. This was never going to be acceptable to Washington. Soviet leaders also needed to understand that the Americans would have little confidence in them until they respected human rights in their country, ceased to bully Eastern Europe and ended support for insurgency, subversion and terrorism around the world. If Gorbachëv wanted agreements on arms reduction, he had to alter his stance on the other matters of importance to the American administration.[29]

Shultz continued to prod the President into renewing the talks with the USSR: 'Although much of Gorbachëv's proposal is clearly designed for propaganda effect, we cannot dismiss out of hand the possibility that Gorbachëv is making an effort to maintain the dynamic of improving US–Soviet relations that you and he began at the summit.' He listed the signs of progress. Gorbachëv had taken steps forward in respect of human rights; he also accepted Reagan's ultimate goal of complete military denuclearization. The two sides concurred that the superpowers should start by moving towards having equal arsenals of intermediate-range nuclear weapons in Europe. Shultz admitted that the Soviet leadership still objected to American policy on British and French missiles and on the removal of all such missiles from Asia; but he urged that Reagan should seize the initiative by test-ing out Gorbachëv's sincerity in offering to negotiate.[30] This was also the opinion of Soviet specialists elsewhere in the administration. The National Security Council's Jack Matlock, while agreeing that Gor-bachëv had fumbled his move in January, wanted to raise the tempo.[31] Ambassador Hartman in Moscow was also eager for a resumption of talks.[32]

Reagan liked what he heard and signed a directive with the idea of exploring whether Soviet leaders would agree to reducing nuclear stockpiles on the basis of his own proposals.[33] On 22 February 1986 he wrote to Gorbachëv suggesting that the first stage of disarmament should involve a reduction of the strategic missiles of each superpower to 4,500. He proposed to get rid of all intermediate-range missiles by the end of 1989. He offered to keep research on strategic defence within the bounds of current treaty obligations. He called for 'concrete and meaningful confidence-building measures' and for a total ban on chemical weapons. While he was unspecific on the timing and sub-stance of subsequent stages, he expressed the hope that he and Gorbachëv could push things forward before meeting again.[34]

The White House and State Department needed consent inside NATO before conducting further negotiations with Gorbachëv. Reagan chose Nitze and Rowny as his emissaries. Nitze had a busy time in Western Europe, visiting London, Paris, Bonn, Rome, The Hague and Brussels – he reported that allied leaders remained suspi-cious about Soviet motives.[35] Nevertheless they were pleased that the President hoped to go on talking to the General Secretary, and they wanted him to keep squeezing concessions out of Moscow. Their fear was that if the January declaration were ever implemented, the Ameri-cans would fold away the nuclear umbrella that had protected them in the post-war decades. Such an outcome would expose Western Europe to the menace of the USSR's massive conventional forces. While Nitze was dealing with the NATO allies, Rowny set off on a tour of America's allied and friendly countries in the East; the trip covered Tokyo, Seoul, Beijing and Canberra. His summary report highlighted the suspicions about Gorbachëv. Leaders in that part of the world had not failed to notice that the Soviet proposals lacked the urgency about denuclearization in Asia that they showed about Europe.[36]

Mitterrand warned Gorbachëv by letter that he would get nowhere if he stuck to the idea of confining the talks to nuclear arms. He wrote in the same vein to Reagan while adding that the West ought to take account of the 'interesting elements' in the USSR's latest package.[37] Thatcher was even less positive. In her letter to Reagan she contended that Gorbachëv was still 'the same brand of Soviet Communist that we have known in the past'. His January declaration, she said, was nothing but propaganda that offered 'a spurious timetable of simple steps'. The problem was that he was encouraging 'unrealistic public expectations'. She advised the President to abide by his Strategic Defense Initiative and to make his willingness to decrease nuclear weapon stockpiles dependent on the achievement of progress in the development of a new defensive system.[38] Nitze found Foreign Secretary Howe and her other ministers to be, if anything, even more sceptical than she was about the January declaration. The British Conservatives continued to regard Gorbachëv as a traditional *apparatchik*.[39]

Although CIA officials preferred Thatcher to Mitterrand, they knew that Reagan wanted a disarmament agreement with the USSR; they also saw that it was no longer plausible to claim that Gorbachëv was offering nothing remarkable in the arms talks. If sceptics wanted to have influence, they needed to shift their ground of argument. Casey understood this clearly. In March 1986 he highlighted how the Kremlin was continuing to support programmes to modernize its weapon systems. The Soviet military threat would exist for the fore-seeable future. According to Casey, Gorbachëv was able and devious. By fostering the image of a peacemaker, he was trying to encourage America to reduce its defence expenditure; his other objective was to bring an end to the Western curbs on the transfer of technology.[40] Casey called for the administration to stay vigilant. He claimed that the Kremlin was regularly infringing its obligations under the Anti-Ballistic Missile Treaty – he pointed to the continuing work on the Krasnoyarsk radar station. In his opinion this absolved Washington of any concern about breaking the same treaty: Moscow should be taught that violations would be met with violations.[41]

Shultz disliked this way of thinking. He could see no gain for America if it was seen to rip up treaties. There had to be trust on both sides for Reagan to stand a chance of achieving a deal with Gorbachëv. Casey responded by bringing the CIA's economic intelligence into play and stressed that the USSR retained the capacity for a long-term military challenge to American power. A contest of analysis ensued.

All the American agencies agreed that the Soviet economy faced severe difficulties. The disagreement was about the scale of the problem. CIA researchers had been quick to recognize the consequences of falling prices of oil on the world market; but their settled opinion was that the USSR remained in a 'healthy financial position'.[42] Ambassador Hartman too judged that Gorbachëv's early economic measures were achieving a degree of success.[43] If this was the reality, it strengthened the case for America's need to keep up its financial allocations for military research and development.

But how reliable was the CIA's analysis? Harry Rowen, a former president of the RAND Corporation and recent chairman of the National Intelligence Council, challenged the idea that the economy in the USSR was achieving any growth at all. He circulated a paper to interested officials – Shultz, Weinberger, McFarlane and Casey – and got it published in the *National Interest*.[44] In April 1986 Rowen and four Soviet experts of like mind secured the opportunity through presidential aide Charles Fortier to brief Reagan and Shultz. The CIA assumed that economic output was growing in the USSR. Rowen contended that growth was at best negligible and that very possibly there was a yearly fall-off in output. He advised that the President was therefore in a strong position to face down Gorbachëv in any forthcoming talks.[45] Shultz, as both politician and business economist, welcomed this analysis.[46] He thought that Casey and Weinberger were talking up the USSR's industrial performance chiefly because they disliked the prospect of completing a disarmament treaty with Moscow. He asked for intelligence reports untainted by political bias. He surmised, in contrast to the CIA, that the Soviet reformers recognized that an economic emergency was imminent in the USSR. He sensed that their current overtures reflected their panic about the prospect.

Although Rowen's observations had much cogency, their implications were anything but clear-cut. If the USSR had an ailing economy, the time could be right to talk robustly to its leaders just as Shultz suggested. But it was equally possible for Weinberger to use the same data to argue that America should not rush into negotiations and agree to compromises. Weinberger and Casey failed to see their opportunity. They instead opted simply to keep a wary eye on the forays that Rowen made into the press.[47]

Not even the CIA was claiming that the USSR had no budgetary problems;[48] and Shultz, Weinberger and Casey did at least concur on the need to seize the initiative from Gorbachëv. On 5 March 1986

Shultz put forward some ideas on how to reduce Soviet meddling in regional trouble spots. Gorbachëv had indicated his wish to change policy on Afghanistan, and Shultz called for the preparation of a peace plan involving the withdrawal of the USSR's forces over a six-month period. But if Gorbachëv desired to stay on good terms with America, he would also have to impel his Vietnamese allies to pull out of Cambodia. America should be willing to assist with Cambodian economic reconstruction and to normalize its links with Vietnam. In regard to Angola, Shultz placed his emphasis on deterring the Soviet leadership from escalating its military intervention. He aimed to deal with the Nicaraguan question by offering to resume dialogue with the Sandinistas. He doubted that Gorbachëv wished to come to an understanding about Central America. But if Soviet supplies of armaments continued, the Americans should feel free to approach the American Congress for funds to assist the armed opposition to Nicaragua's Sandinista government.[49]

Shultz liked to ventilate these arguments whenever he met Shevardnadze and to ensure that the Politburo understood the intensity of America's determination.[50] He wished to test out the sincerity of Gorbachëv's peace offensive. The January declaration had proposed a three-stage process of total nuclear disarmament. Gorbachëv – or rather Akhromeev – had knowingly reserved several important measures for the third and last stage. The Americans concluded that the intention was to extract the maximum advantage for the USSR while delaying concessions that were on America's list of demands. Shultz intended to insist on bringing these measures forward to the first stage of the process. If Gorbachëv withheld his consent, Shultz could expose his disingenuousness before world public opinion. He told Assistant Defense Secretary Perle about his ideas with a view to building a coalition inside the administration. Perle warmed to what he heard, and he and Shultz decided that they could work together in discovering an answer to the question: was Gorbachëv truly willing to come to terms with America in the interests of global peace?[51] Things were changing on the American side. Shultz usually wanted to find a way to bring the Soviet leadership into serious talks. This was the first time that he had persuaded one of the sceptics. The hope glimmered in his mind that the chronic factionalism could be surmounted.

17. THE STALLED INTERACTION

Gorbachëv failed to anticipate the sheer suspicion that his January declaration would arouse in the West. Foreign trips in the previous year had provided him with impressions that no amount of advice from aides and research institutes could match as he tried to sharpen his foreign policy. Now he rested from his travels for several months. He assumed that he had made a splendid offer to America and the world. He expected a speedy constructive response. If he had made even a brief visit to any of the NATO countries, he would have seen things more clearly. He was dumbfounded by the coagulated reticence he witnessed in Western capitals.

In fairness to him, he had other urgent matters on his agenda sheet. He especially needed to work out how to present the programme of action to his party and people. His focus was on his report to the forthcoming Party Congress. It wearied him to receive the dreary drafts of his advisory groups. Yakovlev recruited people who might introduce some liveliness.[1] The Afghan question bothered everyone. Kovalëv, one of Shevardnadze's deputies, supplied a passage that described the war as a 'bloody wound' and made the case for a withdrawal of Soviet forces. Gorbachëv and Shevardnadze liked all this. When Gorbachëv circulated it to the Politburo, several leaders objected.[2] He judged it too risky to annoy them and decided to cross out the commitment to military withdrawal. When Shevardnadze found out, he was angry about Gorbachëv's failure to consult him and phoned to remonstrate. He threatened to raise the question in his own right at the Congress unless Gorbachëv reverted to their original understanding. Gorbachëv conceded. Leaving for the Congress on 25 February 1986, he picked up the phone and told Shevardnadze: 'Your instruction has been fulfilled.'[3]

They believed that they had important tasks to accomplish in tandem. Shevardnadze returned from Japan knowing that there was no prospect of breaking the CoCom restrictions on technological transfer. He and Gorbachëv badly wanted to achieve economic regeneration. They had tried to tempt the Japanese with the promise to buy their products, but this got them nowhere. The Tokyo government declined to annoy the Americans, and anyway the Soviet leadership refused to negotiate about the Japanese northern territories annexed by the USSR in 1945.[4] Shevardnadze drew up a list of other awkward questions that would soon require an answer. What was to be the USSR's relationship with other communist states? Where did the developing countries stand in Moscow's eyes? How did the answers affect how the Soviet leadership handled America? What was the official line about 'the problem about the democratization of international relations'? Shevardnadze, who had laboured as a boy in Georgian vineyards, liked to say that he was pouring new wine into new wineskins.[5]

The frustration for Gorbachëv was that Reagan appeared to prefer wine of an older vintage. Among his aides and advisers, Gorbachëv was frank about the need to rethink Soviet military doctrine: 'I bet there are as many definitions of strategic parity as we have people sitting in this room. I am ready to defend my own. Real strategic stability does not necessarily require that both sides follow each other, nostril to nostril.'[6]

The Congress was nevertheless a triumph for Gorbachëv. His keynote speech dwelt on an exciting agenda. While adumbrating a set of political and economic changes in the USSR, he emphasized his priority for ending the arms race in an 'interdependent world'. He expressed horror of the American 'Star Wars' programme and highlighted his January declaration as the basis for progress. Taking the Congress into his confidence, he noted that a 'right-wing grouping' held power in the Washington administration – throughout the speech he avoided mention of Reagan himself in pejorative terms. He admitted that the letter from the President, which had arrived only a day before the Congress, was less than clear about America's intentions. While some aspects gave grounds for optimism, others were dispiriting. To loud applause, Gorbachëv said he was unwilling to take no for an answer. He called for a deep change in global politics. He wanted an end to a wide range of regional conflicts. As agreed with Shevardnadze, he called the Afghan war 'a bloody wound'; he also announced the desire to pull out all the Soviet forces as soon as possible. No one listening to him was in any doubt that he was setting a broad new direction for the USSR at home and abroad.[7]

What he dared not publicly admit was that his country's economic plight had suddenly worsened in recent months, and not through his fault. The problem originated not in Moscow but in Riyadh. The OPEC organization relied upon Western governments to enforce prices of oil on global markets. But when Margaret Thatcher dismantled the British National Oil Company in spring 1985, the entire purchasing system was disrupted. Saudi Arabia dealt with the prospect of a fall in prices by hugely increasing production. This led to a sudden collapse in prices from $32 a barrel in November 1985 to a mere $10 in spring 1986.[8] The Soviet Politburo knew full well about the USSR's dependence on revenues from petrochemical sales to Western Europe. Suddenly the global price fell and a hole was blasted in Gorbachëv's budgetary planning.

Gorbachëv himself was indignant about Reagan at the Politburo on 20 March 1986: 'We have put forth realistic things. We really mean to disarm. Unfair play in such matters is impossible. No one will be able to deceive the other.' The American side, he claimed, had reacted with evasions and half-measures.[9] He told aides that whereas he had discharged his responsibility to his people and indeed to the Americans, Reagan was ducking his obligations. Mitterrand and Thatcher in his opinion were no better. The 'Europeans' had once pleaded with the USSR's leadership to rid the continent of intermediate-range rockets. But now the same people were requesting the delivery of more Pershing-2s. The Americans were making a bad situation worse. They were expelling Soviet UN diplomats and raising a hysterical campaign of propaganda about Nicaragua. They made threat after threat to Libya. They continued to subsidize Savimbi in Angola. They forwarded aid to the new anti-leftist government in South Yemen. US navy vessels had sailed into the Black Sea. He accused the American administration of trying to get him to 'slam the door' on negotiations. He vowed that their provocations would be in vain: he was determined to stick to the route he had mapped out in his January declaration.[10]

The US Defense Department and the CIA continued to feel suspicion about the USSR's real intentions in the light of information about Soviet nuclear force development and about Moscow's political and financial activities around the world.[11] Gorbachëv for the moment ignored Washington's concerns. But he was at least starting to understand that Soviet leaders had got themselves into a double bind about the Strategic Defense Initiative. By continually talking about the dangers it posed, they would appear weak not only to Reagan but also in the eyes of their own fellow citizens. If, on the other hand, they ignored the topic, they could easily give the impression of being unable to match America's military modernization. The General Secretary opted for a middle course. He spoke less often about the Initiative; and when he mentioned it, he avoided apocalyptic language.[12]

He assured the Politburo that he would make no undue compromise. Soviet scientists, he claimed, were confident about the situation. They had told him that 'a system can be created to annihilate the Strategic Defense Initiative stations'. But peace was infinitely preferable to war. He recognized that any conflict with America involving nuclear weapons could only end in the destruction of the defence systems of both sides – and, he added, the existence of 'our state' would be put into question.[13] He would not let Reagan bully him. He told aides that the same scientists reckoned that the USSR could build a counter-system at a tenth of the cost of America's Strategic Defense Initiative. He would do 'everything to avoid further wrecking the country through defence'.[14] He was pleased that his new course in foreign policy had dispelled a lot of the fear about the Soviet Union abroad. The impact was gratifyingly effective in the US, where public opinion gave him the benefit of the doubt and sidelined the political right.[15] At the Politburo on 3 April 1986 he displayed a cautious optimism: 'It's become more difficult for Reagan as a consequence of our policy. The USA wants to halt our peace offensive, to break it up. All their actions are aimed at provoking us. We can see what they want: to succeed by their steps to break up the process of growth of our authority.'[16]

He told the Politburo: 'We live on a single planet. We cannot keep the peace without America.'[17] Writing to the President on 2 April 1986, he grumbled about the American inaction. He asked why the White House had refused to do anything about his January declaration. Gorbachëv denied that he was merely making propaganda.[18] When talking in public, he avoided a severe public critique of the American administration. In the big speech he gave in Tolyatti on 9 April, he was curt but respectful. He could not afford to bait Reagan and Shultz while he worked to resume the 'Geneva process' and achieve a second summit meeting.[19]

His experiences abroad in 1984–1985 had pushed him towards some conclusions about Western Europe. Britain, he said, was likely to remain 'the key power in European affairs'. He did not explain why he thought so; but at a time when the British economy was hardly the continent's powerhouse, it may be that he was thinking about

Thatcher's links to the White House. British communist leader Gordon McLennan and several Labour Party politicians had urged him to try and prise her Conservative government free from its entanglement with the Americans. Gorbachëv limited himself to commenting that the Labour Party might return to power within a couple of years.[20] Meanwhile Thatcher entirely failed to follow up her congenial encounter with him before he became General Secretary. She was wary of becoming entangled with him. If Gorbachëv felt disappointed in her, he refrained from saying so. But he no more knew what to do about her than she did about him – and really it would have been easier for him than for her to break the ice. She bided her time and ignored the criticism of those who urged the case for an overture to Moscow.

Gorbachëv wanted to hold his choices open: 'We also mustn't forget Lenin's instructions about the importance of rapprochement between Germany and Russia.' Honecker remained difficult to control on the 'German–German question', and Gorbachëv wanted to keep watch over his contacts with West Germany. He recognized the need to take seriously the question of German reunification. Soviet interests lay in preventing the re-emergence of 'Bismarcks and Hitlers', and Gorbachëv meant to take academic advice on the subject.[21] By liaising with Chancellor Kohl, he hoped to prevent East Germany from falling under West German dominance. It would also do no harm if a rapprochement between Moscow and Bonn were to put the Americans somewhat on edge. Tokyo and Beijing could be treated in the same fashion. At the same time Gorbachëv plotted to keep Kohl on his toes by strengthening ties with Italy. The Kremlin had to manoeuvre deftly – and Gorbachëv asked the Party International Department to improve its practical advice. Although he knew that West European leaders were never going to break with Washington, he was aware of the support he enjoyed among socialist parties, the labour movement and 'other progressive forces', and he aimed to strengthen his appeal to Western businessmen, clerics, trade unionists and even soldiers: the idea was that if he could convince such people about his sincerity, governments everywhere would soon have to listen.[22]

As he pondered what to do about the Americans, he recognized his mistake in omitting the question of conventional weapons from his January declaration: 'We're ready to resolve this question too. We are for balance in all types of armaments, including conventional ones.'[23] He anticipated all manner of objections from the military leadership.

The Soviet talks delegation in Stockholm had complained about domineering interference by the General Staff.[24] Although Shevardnadze sympathized, only the General Secretary had the authority to face down Akhromeev. As the evidence mounted about how the General Staff had been flouting his orders, Gorbachëv angrily confronted Akhromeev at the Politburo on 24 April 1986: 'Once the political decision has been taken, there needs to be corresponding action. But there is inertia at the [Stockholm] talks. Nobody displays initiative.' He threatened to fire anyone found to be obstructing the negotiations in Stockholm, Vienna and Geneva.[25] He looked around the room and asked whether anyone objected to what he had said. Silence prevailed. Akhromeev had suffered a defeat, and everyone in the room knew it. Gorbachëv had started to show the General Staff who was boss.[26]

He did not feel strong enough to make changes in personnel at the top of the armed forces. Not yet. Shevardnadze had a freer hand at his ministry and sacked Kornienko for the 'treachery' of his collusion with Akhromeev.[27] Two new first deputy ministers, Anatoli Kovalëv and Yuri Vorontsov, were appointed. Both were known as reformers, and Shevardnadze hoped that they had the strength of purpose to run the ministry in Shevardnadze's absence. (As things turned out, he was to be disappointed in them.)[28] Kornienko was transferred to the Party International Department as second-in-command to Dobrynin, who was recalled from the Washington embassy.[29] Gorbachëv apparently hoped to turn the International Department into something like a National Security Council on the American model.[30] He was adept at counterbalancing his most energetic fellow reformers. Dobrynin was no unconditional enthusiast for radical change in foreign policy, and perhaps Gorbachëv wanted to keep a second team in readiness in case his first team ran into difficulty. It certainly made sense to have Dobrynin on tap for his knowledge of American high politics.[31] And several of the department's veterans were pleasantly surprised at his insistence that they should think for themselves and draft their proposals without fear of reprisals.[32]

Reagan's administration did not make it easy for Gorbachëv. At the end of March 1986 Washington demanded the expulsion of dozens of Soviet spies who worked under the cover of diplomats at the United Nations in New York. Such espionage was a long-standing genuine problem that US administrations had overlooked. Protests arrived from Moscow. Soviet official anger was of a confected nature; the leadership's real feeling was of worry that Reagan was abandoning the policy of rapprochement.

Events in the Mediterranean increased the tension. On 5 April 1986 a bomb killed three people and injured 229 others in West Berlin's La Belle discothèque – a venue known to be frequented by American servicemen. The White House, relying on CIA reports, held Libyan leader Muammar Gaddafi responsible. Libyan-supported terrorist groups had been targeting US citizens in Western Europe and the Middle East for a couple of years. Reagan had already issued a warning that the next time that Libya repeated its behaviour, he would order reprisals. In March 1986 he had sanctioned naval exercises in disputed waters in the Gulf of Sirte. Gaddafi ordered his forces to fire on American planes, and the Americans sank Libyan patrol boats in reply. After the discothèque explosion, Reagan decided that nothing less than an attack by F-111 aeroplanes over the Libyan mainland was appropriate. The French and Spanish governments withheld consent for flights over their air space, but Thatcher permitted the mission to start from a British airfield. The raid on Tripoli on 14 April 1986 was swift and devastating, despite the loss of one American plane. The Americans indicated that if Gaddafi continued to sponsor terrorist activity, the same thing would happen again.[33]

Libya was a client state of the USSR. Its armed forces used Soviet military equipment and received training from advisers sent by Moscow. Although the Tripoli air raid was not a direct challenge to Gorbachëv, it certainly raised a question about whether Reagan was the peacemonger he claimed to be. *Pravda* accused the American administration of imperialist aggression. As Shevardnadze noted, the problem was that Soviet leaders were vulnerable to the charge of hypocrisy when indicting America for imperialism: 'Eh, if only it weren't for Afghanistan!'[34] Gorbachëv and Shevardnadze quickly decided on a cautious reaction to the Libyan emergency. They were still hoping for a summit meeting later that year. With this in mind, they confined themselves to cancelling a scheduled meeting between Shultz and Shevardnadze. They also informed the Americans that Soviet flights to Libya were going to continue and that Moscow expected them to be unmolested.[35] But Gorbachëv refrained from issuing Reagan with a public rebuke. He did not even write a note of condolence to Gaddafi, who claimed to have lost an adoptive daughter in the raid.[36]

As Gorbachëv and Shevardnadze were pondering what to do next, a terrible disaster took place at a civil nuclear-power station in Chernobyl in Ukraine. The core of the nuclear reactor went into meltdown. At first the local authorities as well as the central ministries pretended that the problems were innocuous. But soon the catastrophe could no longer be disguised, and the Politburo became involved. The contamination, carried by rain clouds, reached far beyond Soviet borders into Western Europe; and foreign monitoring facilities raised an alarm. Gorbachëv initiated a thorough investigation of the disaster and the Soviet leadership put all thoughts of talks with the Americans on hold. Shevardnadze's aides asked him to explain the shambles and the misinformation. The Swedish media had been a better and quicker source than anything that had issued from TASS or appeared in *Pravda*. Shevardnadze was in bitter mood: 'I'm tired of all this. I'm tired of trying to show that one shouldn't keep quiet.'[37]

Gorbachëv, of course, was wrong in his claim that the Politburo had received no alert about the dangers at Chernobyl power station: the KGB had provided a damning report seven years earlier. But it was true that the Politburo had received assurances that the problems had been solved.[38] In fairness to Gorbachëv, moreover, he certainly arranged for the Soviet media to show greater openness and honesty in reporting on the disaster. Secretiveness only caused further damage to the USSR's reputation abroad. Scandinavian and other foreign monitoring facilities were registering horrifying data about the airborne spread of radiation. Gorbachëv publicly accepted that politicians and scientists at lower levels had been incompetent and mendacious. Ryzhkov flew to the district around Chernobyl to supervise the decommissioning of the power station. TV, radio and the press covered the topic in detail. Although criticism was kept to a minimum, no disaster in Soviet history had ever been treated with such frankness. Although no communist state allowed public censure to appear, politicians across Eastern Europe were no less agitated about the disaster than their peoples. Gorbachëv tried to calm popular opinion. But if anything, he was even more shaken than most Soviet citizens. An explosion at a single power station brought home to him what a catastrophe would ensue from any use of nuclear weapons.[39]

The accident at Chernobyl prodded the American administration into activity. Shultz told the President that Soviet leaders had become 'defensive and withdrawn' since the beginning of the year. Deadlock in US–Soviet relations was in nobody's interest; it also might damage the electoral prospects of friends like Thatcher and Kohl.[40] On 13 May

1986 Shultz went to the White House and persuaded Reagan to modify his stance on the Strategic Defense Initiative. Gorbachëv, he argued, was operating within heavy political constraints and needed America to show a spirit of compromise. Shultz's idea was to continue the research programme while reserving the ultimate right of deployment. In this way the Americans could continue to do what was in their interest while allaying the Soviet leadership's fears about military security. Shultz suggested a scheme to 'give them the sleeves from our own vest and make them think it's our overcoat'. Don Regan and John Poindexter liked what they heard. So too did the President after receiving the assurance that the Defense Initiative would be safeguarded.[41] They all agreed to proceed on this basis. Shultz asked Reagan to receive Dr Robert Gale, who had treated some of the Chernobyl disaster victims; he also recommended the sending of a personal letter to Gorbachëv.[42]

But the Americans had yet to come to a settled decision on Shultz's ideas. Gorbachëv and Shevardnadze in disappointment looked for other ways of breaking the deadlock in world affairs. At the Politburo on 29 May 1986 Gorbachëv accused Gaddafi of 'revolutionary primitivism'. The Libyan leader needed to be brought down to earth. The USSR was not going to start the Third World War on his behalf.[43] But what was to be done? Soviet leaders were coming to the conclusion that policy had been unduly occupied with America and that the Ministry of Foreign Affairs had almost ignored Europe. They worried too that Asia had been overlooked – it was essential to improve relations with China. They wished to surmount what they regarded as the disaster for the USSR in Afghanistan.[44]

A meeting of the Political Consultative Committee was arranged for 10 June 1986 in Budapest with a view towards briefing the Warsaw Pact allies on Moscow's latest thinking. Gorbachëv was on ebullient form as he rejected the old objective of achieving strategic parity with America in every military category. The USSR, he declared, now required only reasonable sufficiency. He said that Western politicians told him that America was trying to bring the communist countries to economic ruin by means of the arms race. Gorbachëv intended to prevent the Americans from developing offensive space weaponry. Accepting criticisms by the French and British, he aspired to a drastic bilateral reduction in conventional forces in Europe. He urged the need for sober analysis, recognizing that it was pointless to try to divide NATO: 'We cannot isolate the United States; we cannot split the

West; we cannot convert them to our faith.' He was somewhat more optimistic about China – and he announced the aim of making an overture to the Chinese leadership despite its long-standing objections to Soviet foreign policy.[45] Altogether it was a speech of importance. He was changing the line of the January declaration. He was admitting that Reagan was not going to budge and NATO's unity had proved unexpectedly solid. He had tried out Akhromeev's scheme and it had got him nowhere. Now he was adjusting the proposals on nuclear armaments and introducing new ones on conventional forces.

The trickier task for Gorbachëv came with the subject of Chernobyl. He revealed official data about radiation levels in concentric rings stretching out to Poland's eastern wetlands. He detailed the budget to deal with the emergency. His speech was sombre, factual and regretful. No Soviet General Secretary had addressed the Political Consultative Committee with words of such humility.[46]

Ceauşescu provided his own data on the radiation in Romanian territory; he called for cooperation among the Warsaw Pact countries to deal with the disaster.[47] Turning to Gorbachëv's ideas about talks with America, he said that USSR's foreign policy was its own business (which was his way of warning others to leave Romania alone).[48] Honecker praised Gorbachëv's peace initiative and suggested that both the Soviet Union and the German Democratic Republic could make progress by working with West Germany (which was his way of saying that Moscow should trust him in his dealings with Bonn).[49] Unease emerged when the meeting touched on trade among communist states. Gorbachëv groused about the Hungarians signing deals with foreign capitalist firms but not with the USSR.[50] Husák lamented the paltry results of Comecon's Complex Programme of Scientific-Technical Progress.[51] Zhivkov pulled the debate back to Chernobyl and asked whether it might be necessary to change the designs of the region's nuclear reactors. Gorbachëv replied that the Americans had not changed their technology after the accident at Three Mile Island in 1979.[52] The East European leaders were convinced by his willingness to engage in open debate; they also supported his renovated planning for the pursuit of an arms reduction agreement with the US.[53]

Five days later, back in Moscow, Gorbachëv boasted to the Party Central Committee about the support he had received. He stayed silent about his own change of approach to the US; he simply castigated 'the Star Wars programme' and vaunted his January declaration as a 'force-field' for good around the world.[54] As an afterthought, he made the implausible claim that the East European leaders had independently come up with exactly the same proposals about the quantitative reduction of nuclear weaponry.[55] Evidently he thought it prudent to limit the number of politicians who were privy to his innovation in Budapest; for he was less guarded when reporting to the Politburo. While continuing to hope for a rapprochement with America, he admitted that the entire 'world system of socialism' had become uncompetitive in technology. Whereas the European Economic Community was undergoing deeper economic integration, Comecon suffered from severe 'centrifugal' tendencies – and the reliance of Poland and other countries on Western credits was having heavy consequences. Romania, the German Democratic Republic and Hungary were pursuing their 'national ambitions' without thought for an agreed common foreign policy, and he noted that all Politburo members, when dealing with East European leaders, had experience of a decline in 'sincerity, frankness, trustworthiness'. Gorbachëv saw the solution as lying not in directives but rather in persuasion and example.[56] Behind the Politburo's closed doors he robustly condemned the 'methods that were applied to Czechoslovakia (in 1968) and Hungary (in 1956)'.[57]

While Gorbachëv quietly edged towards a new negotiating posture, the American administration took stock of the possibilities. At the National Security Planning Group on 6 June 1986 Shultz declared that the Kremlin leaders were at a fork in the road: either they could ignore the President's overtures and gamble on Congress cutting the American defence budget or else they might decide that 'Ronald Reagan is their best hope for selling an agreement to the American public'. Shultz favoured boxing Gorbachëv into submission by reversing Congress's recent cuts in the military budget. He urged the need to focus efforts on obtaining 'a good arms control agreement'. Reagan endorsed this line of thought. He felt sympathy with Gorbachëv in his struggle against the political resistance to reform. In his opinion, the American side had to frame their proposals in such a way as to avoid making the General Secretary 'look like he gave up everything'. The President at the same time repeated his commitment to the Strategic Defense Initiative and stated that if the current technological research proved successful, he would sanction practical tests. He hoped to induce Soviet leaders to accept this scenario by convincing them that the American anti-missile system would not be a threat to anyone but rather a 'defence against a madman'.[58]

Talking with Shultz on 11 June 1986, the President agreed that an encouraging message should be passed to Gorbachëv. Shultz assured Ambassador Dubinin that America was taking Soviet arms control statements seriously and recognized the steps of progress in respect of human rights in the USSR. Reagan, he said, welcomed the possibility of another summit in the near future.[59]

Weinberger disliked the direction that things were taking. On 12 June he struck back at Shultz in the follow-up meeting of the National Security Planning Group. He contended that Gorbachëv only wanted an arms treaty agreement because the USSR's defence budget had become unaffordable. In Weinberger's opinion, the Soviet leadership was thoroughly untrustworthy. He argued for a deployable space-based defence system as a crucial requirement for American security. Casey agreed with Weinberger, contending that America should demand changes to the Anti-Ballistic Missile Treaty. Shultz picked up the gauntlet. While continuing with the Strategic Defense Initiative and pursuing the 'zero option', he wanted to resume talks with Moscow. Reagan sided with him. He repeated his willingness to share the space-based defence technology with the entire world once all nuclear weaponry had been destroyed.[60] He reminded everyone that Gorbachëv was having to face down his 'hardliners'; he also accepted that Soviet leaders had genuine fear that 'we seek a first-strike advantage'. But he thought that Chernobyl had brought the General Secretary to appreciate the dangers of a nuclear war. Until then he had doubted Gorbachëv's sincerity about disarmament. Now he felt more confident: 'The time is right for something dramatic.'[61]

He was right about the impact of the Chernobyl disaster on Gorbachëv's thinking. A year later, Gorbachëv was to tell Bush about the danger facing both East and West:

> If nuclear power reactors were destroyed in France or some of these countries, it would be a kind of nuclear war. The elimination of the effects of Chernobyl cost us four billion roubles. And this was not even the most difficult situation. So the idea that one can do something when a nuclear war starts is a fantasy. Therefore if our foreign ministers cannot produce results in their arms control negotiations, they should be fired.[62]

Even the Soviet military newspaper *Krasnaya Zvezda* printed articles along these lines.[63] Gorbachëv hoped that everyone in the American leadership, then and now, shared the new understanding.

On 19 June 1986 Reagan delivered a speech at Glassboro High

School noting that the Soviet leadership had at last put forward a scheme that deserved America's attention.[64] The State Department, with the National Security Council's consent, cabled American embassies around the world with the latest information.[65] Shultz wrote to congratulate the President on the success of his policy in compelling the Kremlin to retreat from its earlier negotiating standpoint. Gorbachëv was no longer promoting his January declaration. He was now willing to separate decisions on strategic and intermediate-range nuclear weapons. He also accepted the idea of bilateral verification. The time was right to resume high-level talks between the two superpowers.[66] On the same day as Reagan was speaking at Glassboro High School, as things turned out, Gorbachëv was writing a letter calling on him to return to the tempo they had set at the Geneva summit. On 23 June 1986 Ambassador Dubinin delivered it at the Oval Office; he emphasized that Gorbachëv was willing to consider 'partial solutions' to some of the questions – including about intermediate-range nuclear missiles – that divided the two sides.[67] Not since the Geneva summit had the prospect seemed more encouraging to those in Moscow and Washington who strove after a fresh agreement. The months of diplomatic torpor appeared at an end.

18. THE STRATEGIC DEFENSE INITIATIVE

Moscow and Washington were silent in public about the biggest concession that Gorbachëv made that summer. The Strategic Defense Initiative remained an obstacle to his quest for an improved relationship with America, and he came to accept that Reagan would never abandon the project. Painful as it was for him, he had to offer a compromise if he wanted to break the deadlock. On 29 May 1986 he issued a momentous order to the Soviet talks delegation in Geneva. Until then he had demanded the total abandonment of the Defense Initiative. Now he was willing to let the Americans conduct the laboratory research so long as they renounced external testing and deployment. Shultz and Nitze recognized the importance of this shift in the USSR's standpoint: America was in receipt of an unprecedented opportunity.[1]

The American administration agreed that the Kremlin understood the difficulties which would ensue if it tried to finance another great stage of the arms race. The CIA claimed that the USSR still had the economic capacity to devote extra resources to military modernization, but agreed that budgetary exigencies had compelled the Politburo to engage in serious talks.[2] Whatever anyone thought about Reagan's Initiative, it did seem to be having a desirable effect on the Politburo. This was a customary analysis among American officials. The State Department's Directorate of Intelligence and Research had always maintained the USSR could not balance its finances unless it could induce the Americans to drop their programme.[3] Frank Carlucci, Poindexter's successor as National Security Adviser at the end of 1986, thought 'it became an obsession with Gorbachëv'.[4] Shultz, no enthusiast for Abrahamson's boasts about the research, later recalled: 'Well, it worked out beautifully from the standpoint of bargaining.' All American politicians and negotiators had the sense that the Initiative was shaking the Kremlin's self-confidence.[5] Even Henry Kissinger, who referred sniffily to the strategic ideas of the White House as 'the movie version', was willing to concede that 'pretty much all the Soviet [*sic*] I talked to were rattled by SDI'.[6]

There was debate in Washington, out of public earshot, about whether the Kremlin might have a rational basis for its fears. Reagan stressed that the research programme was geared exclusively by defensive objectives. Poindexter, however, understood Gorbachëv's worry that the Americans might be aiming to develop outer-space weapons that could hit targets on earth. He also sensed that once Gorbachëv had spoken against the programme, it would be politically embarrassing for him to back down.[7] The CIA's Robert Gates implicitly agreed. He knew, for example, that several current projects could have offensive applications at some time in the future.[8] But like every other official, he toed the public line that there was nothing in the programme to cause the other superpower to tremble.

With Gorbachëv as General Secretary, there was a danger that Soviet propaganda would exploit the White House's vagueness about the American ambition for the Strategic Defense Initiative. Nitze implored Reagan to bring clarity to the matter; he also asked for the administration to promise to stay within the framework of the Anti-Ballistic Missile Treaty. He asked him to abjure any ambition of military superiority and to aim for a dependable strategic balance. He also contended that offensive nuclear weapons would be necessary for mutual deterrence until such time as the two sides could agree on 'a transition to a more defense-reliant balance as a cooperative endeavor'.[9] Weinberger occupied the opposite end of the spectrum of analysis. To his way of thinking, America's interest lay in preserving a degree of vagueness about strategy. The more the USSR was kept guessing, the better – and Weinberger had no concerns about breaching the Anti-Ballistic Missile Treaty in order to save the Strategic Defense Initiative in all its intimidating potential. Only privately did he admit that extraordinary technological progress was still required. The new space-based system, he commented, would need to achieve the equivalent of 'hitting a bullet with a bullet'. But in public he avoided any hint about the scale of the task.[10]

While continuing to correspond with Edward Teller, Shultz had severe doubts about the claims that Lieutenant General Abrahamson made for the programme.[11] Scientists such as Thomas H. Johnson, director of the Science Research Laboratory, kept a close watch on progress. Johnson advised Jack Matlock, who oversaw Soviet affairs in the National Security Council, that it was far from clear that the President's objectives could be realized.[12] He emphasized that Abrahamson was exaggerating the facts about his achievements.[13] Johnson's worry was that the programme's organizers were misleading the politicians; he stressed that no segment of it would be ready for deployment for another ten years.[14] Subsequent enquiries confirmed that Abrahamson had arranged for 'tests' that were designed to fool Soviet analysts into believing that the programme was close to completion.[15]

Nevertheless the administration's sceptics did not want to make too much of their unease. It mattered little if Abrahamson unduly talked up the project so long as he and his research projects continued to worry the Soviet leaders. Everyone from Shultz downwards saw that this strengthened the Americans' bargaining hand in talks with the USSR.

There remained a lot of discomfort among the NATO allies. On 3 April 1985 NATO's Secretary General Lord Carrington talked to Reagan on his visit to Bonn; he dwelt on the fear that Western Europe would lie prone to a Soviet onslaught if America removed its nuclear weapons from the continent.[16] Canadian Prime Minister Brian Mulroney made open criticisms of the Strategic Defense Initiative and repeated them to Shevardnadze.[17] The State Department reacted by putting pressure on particular allies. Shultz told Kohl that Reagan would refuse to attend the scheduled commemoration of the Second World War at the Bitburg cemetery in May 1985 unless he spoke up for the project: 'No SDI, no Bitburg'. This had the intended effect, and Kohl issued this statement: 'We agree it is a prudent and necessary step.'[18] Hostility to Reagan's project remained among other governments – and when Mitterrand visited Moscow in late 1988, he was to reaffirm his sympathy with the Soviet standpoint on the Defense Initiative.[19] Thatcher had quietened her criticisms only after receiving that assurance that British companies could receive contracts for work on the American project. But the USSR's Foreign Affairs Ministry reckoned that the British were far from content with the kind of contracts they were obtaining.[20]

Few Western leaders thought the research teams would produce the results that the President was hoping for. Nearly everyone in Soviet public life shared this scepticism. Yevgeni Velikhov and fellow scientists Roald Sagdeev and Andrei Kokoshin wrote a book titled *Weaponry in Space* in which they pointed to the enormity of theoretical and practical difficulties. It was quickly translated and published abroad.[21] Velikhov, a scientist of global renown, genuinely thought it foolish for the USSR to emulate the Defense Initiative.[22] He had the guarantee of Soviet public approbation. The Western press ignored his book. Published by Soviet state outlets, it was treated as mere propaganda.

The Politburo did not rely on the judgement of scientists alone. Vitali Kataev in the Party Defence Department kept the programme under review using reports from the KGB and GRU about the publications of Abrahamson's research units.[23] America, in Kataev's opinion, would not be ready to deploy the results until the year 2000 at the earliest. There was therefore no immediate threat.[24] He also thought the American economy incapable of bearing the full costs of the programme. He questioned whether the Americans could really put six hundred 'objects' into permanent, reliable operation in outer space.[25] The technology would have to work perfectly if America was to be secure against attack. Kataev thought this wholly unrealistic, and he claimed that the Defense Initiative 'ideologists' understood this as well as he did.[26] Using American official sources, he estimated that even if the Initiative achieved a level of ninety-nine per cent effectiveness, any Soviet nuclear offensive attack would still result in twenty million American deaths. If the effectiveness reached only a level of ninety per cent, the death rate would reach between seventy-five and ninety million.[27]

Soviet leaders believed that the Americans were trying to draw the USSR into a new stage of the arms race and bankrupt the Soviet budget. This was what Shevardnadze told his people in the ministry, and most of them agreed with him.[28] KGB Chairman Kryuchkov later claimed that 'specialists' concurred that the Strategic Defense Initiative was 'the greatest deceit'.[29] The Party Defence Department's Oleg Baklanov considered it a gargantuan 'bluff' without chance of success.[30]

Gorbachëv was buffeted in two directions. While hearing in one ear that the Initiative was a mere pretence, he received messages in the other that the American research could end up being used for sinister purposes. Soviet politicians and their scientific advisers simply could never be sure that specific technologies lacked the potential to be used for attacking the USSR; and whatever Reagan said about the purposes of research, there was no surety that his successors would not refuse to sanction a bellicose adaptation of the programme. It would also be imprudent for Gorbachëv to discount the possibility that the American research teams were engaged in work at variance with public policy as Reagan had described it to the world. America's Defense Department and other agencies might be disguising the reality from the President. Gorbachëv commented that Reagan had an inadequate understanding of what the researchers were doing; and Velikhov expressed a suspicion that the Americans were working on weapons that could hit targets in the USSR. The 'bluff' might be that they were developing a new generation of offensive armaments.[31]

He and his colleagues were no more successful than the Soviet intelligence agencies in providing definitive guidance to their political masters. The KGB and GRU compiled copious reports about the programme. No military topic received quite as much attention. But the contents always proved to be weak on analysis.[32] Shevardnadze spoke for the whole Politburo when he said: 'People haven't been able to make complete sense of what the Strategic Defense Initiative really is.'[33]

Gorbachëv operated on the precautionary principle. If the Americans were building a new anti-missile system, the USSR would work to acquire the capacity to counteract it. While denouncing the warlike purposes behind Reagan's Initiative, Gorbachëv was secretly funding research for the construction of a rival system. Velikhov's dismissive book about the American project disguised the fact that he and other Soviet scientists and technologists were involved in efforts to match the US. Gorbachëv had approved a programme of 'asymmetrical response'. This would involve enhancing the capacity of Soviet military computers from 125 million to more than a billion operations per second. It was one of the largest defence programmes that the country had ever undertaken. The state budget was rewritten so as to include 117 new fundamental research projects: 86 would be devoted to scientific investigation and 165 to experimental construction. Between 40 and 50 billion rubles were to be allocated to the programme in the decade from 1986 – or according to another estimate, it was 40 billion in the Five-Year Plan for 1986–1990.[34]

This was kept top-secret as Gorbachëv licensed a robust campaign of propaganda against the American programme. Soviet publishers issued a stream of works denouncing Reagan and his purposes. 'The Star Wars programme' became a staple of the Moscow media. Efforts were made to translate the livelier pamphlets and secure their distribution abroad. When it proved that they were reaching few readers in the West, it became obvious that other methods were required. Gorbachëv encouraged contacts with leading foreign scientists who were known to oppose the American programme. In July 1986 the Soviet embassy in West Germany contacted the Max-Planck Institute of Physics and Astrophysics, whose executive director Hans-Peter Dürr had spoken against the militarization of outer space. Velikhov and his Committee of Soviet Scientists in Defence of Peace and Against Nuclear War received permission for further overtures to colleagues abroad – the idea was to send the physicist Sagdeev to West Germany with this in mind.[35]

Although the resultant publicity was helpful to Moscow's cause, the Politburo knew that it failed to dent the determination of the American administration to see the programme through to completion. It was in the light of this recognition that Gorbachëv had taken the big decision to offer a compromise to the White House whereby Reagan would agree to confine the Initiative to the research laboratories and abandon the schemes for testing and deployment. His calculations were both military and economic. He wanted to ensure that the Americans would not produce weapons that were superior to those which the USSR was developing. At the same time he aspired to an environment in international relations where his country would waste less treasure on its armed forces.

19. THE LOST SUMMER

The Americans exasperated Gorbachëv with their refusal to show some appreciation of the scale of concessions that he was making. His mood did not improve in the long, hot summer of 1986. Reagan's letter of condolence about Chernobyl made no mention of the arms talks. Gorbachëv thought ceaselessly about the disaster in Ukraine and was grateful for every expression of sorrow. But he deplored the President's refusal to move towards an agreement.

Shultz's victory over Weinberger and Casey in June 1986 was short lived because Reagan almost immediately had second thoughts. Despite his desire for a summit with Gorbachëv, he worried that talks might lead to the loss of his cherished Strategic Defense Initiative.[1] Reagan was always loath to disappoint his friend Weinberger, and Weinberger knew how to play on this feeling.[2] Shultz, like Sisyphus, had to push the boulder up the same old hill again. The arguments were what they always had been: Shultz thought it high time for a serious negotiation with Gorbachëv; Weinberger believed that Gorbachëv would exploit any American overture as proof of weakness. Weeks of wrangling between them delayed the White House reply to Gorbachëv. This vexed Shultz, who regarded Gorbachëv's latest ideas as 'substantive steps forward'. He described Weinberger as someone who would only accept 'wholesale Soviet capitulation to our most far-out positions'. If ever Weinberger were to prevail in foreign policy, according to Shultz, the effect would only be to prod the USSR into 'a massive offensive build-up'. The other consequence would be a fall-off of support for the Strategic Defense Initiative in the American Congress and in American public opinion.[3]

On 1 July 1986 at the National Security Council, Reagan laid emphasis on protecting his Strategic Defense Initiative. Everyone agreed with him. Weinberger reported worriedly on current attempts in the Congress to put restrictions on space-based research. Poindexter expressed his apprehension about Soviet moves to redefine what was allowable under the Anti-Ballistic Missile Treaty.[4] The Director of the Strategic Defense Initiative, Lieutenant General James A. Abrahamson, warned that the budgetary cuts of 1985 compelled him to reduce grants for some of his key laser projects.[5] Weinberger predicted that if Congress introduced further cutbacks, it would 'kill the programme and play into the Soviets' hands'. Meese called for a campaign of publicity to convince Congress that the Defense Initiative would lead to 'many potential commercial by-products'.[6] With all this support from the National Security Council, Reagan could stand firm by his basic objectives. He would continue to promote the Defense Initiative and modernize America's retaliatory capacity while pursuing opportunities for arms reduction.[7] Shultz was unusually quiet, perhaps seeing that the balance of opinion was unfavourable. The result was that nobody raised the matter of Gorbachëv's recent proposal to confine work on the space-based programme to the laboratories.

News about the stand-off in the American administration reached Gorbachëv through reports in the *New York Times*. As he saw it, Weinberger and other officials wished to prolong the confrontation of superpowers rather than take the path towards peace. Discommoded by the lack of response to his offers of compromise, the General Secretary passed a curt message to the President through Ambassador Hartman expressing doubts that Reagan truly desired to 'discipline [his] ranks'.[8]

He wished to put Washington into the dock of world opinion. Whereas Reagan had sent warplanes on a punitive raid over Tripoli, Gorbachëv ruled out any military action in pursuit of the ends of foreign policy: 'I would not "bomb" Pakistan.' The Asian factor should receive priority. He thought it might be worthwhile to make an overture towards China. Vadim Medvedev suggested building mutual trust by proposing that intermediate-range nuclear missiles should be removed from both sides of the Sino-Soviet frontier. Gorbachëv welcomed the idea as complementary to his January declaration; he called for work to be done on a properly staged plan for the removal of all nuclear weapons from Asian territories – and almost as an afterthought he suggested that the Indian Ocean should be declared a demilitarized zone. Although such an outcome would inevitably disconcert the Americans, Gorbachëv hoped to assure Reagan that the USSR was chiefly interested in peace across Asia and would stay clear of 'regional conflicts' and 'military groupings'.[9] Perhaps it was this consideration that ultimately dissuaded Gorbachëv from approaching

Beijing; or possibly he did not feel strong enough to face down Akhromeev on the question.

He declared to the Politburo that the USSR could not achieve its internal transformation without making progress in the disarmament talks. He admitted that he had no economic strategy: 'For the moment we have more questions than answers.' But he started from the premise that the Soviet Union lacked a highly developed economy. At best it had a 'weakly developed' one.[10] When talking to Central Committee secretaries and department chiefs, he underlined the productivity gap with the West. He had received a report that a Japanese sewing enterprise did with 600 workers what it took a Soviet work force of 900,000 to produce. The Politburo had to show the decisiveness of Lenin and Peter the Great: ineffective administrators needed to be fired. He said that Stalin had had the right idea in promoting young people to high office: 'The human potential is good. And we'll sweep away the rubbish.'[11] On the policy of official openness, Gorbachëv said: 'The people support this, and with the help of these ideas we will crush the resistance. And let there be no compromise on questions of *glasnost* on the grounds that we're stripping off in front of the world's eyes. Look, we're the ones who are doing the talking. We're actually neutralizing antiSovietism. This is where our strength is, not our weakness.'[12]

The Politburo heard repeatedly from him that the economy's plight was bad and getting worse. Ryzhkov laid the depressing data before it in the course of the summer. A fifth of the USSR's annual cereal consumption now depended on imported grain, at a cost of 26 billion rubles.[13] Gorbachëv momentarily considered terminating the purchases of grain from America.[14] The world oil price collapsed by seventy per cent between autumn 1985 and July 1986. A financial emergency was in the making. The Soviet state foreign debt climbed from $7 billion to $11 billion. Revenues were also diminished by the fall-off in sales of vodka since the introduction of the anti-alcohol campaign.[15] Ryzhkov said there would have to be a cut-back in investment in technological modernization. Gorbachëv gloomily concluded: 'The result is that we've been hitched to the work of slaves – getting raw materials and supplying them to other countries. Even Bulgaria makes us offers of its machinery in exchange for raw materials.'[16] The general discussion was no whit different from what the Politburo had heard before 1985. The novelty lay in the focus on vivid details. Ryzhkov and Gorbachëv felt no need to mince their words.

Everything depended on the American reaction to his foreign

policy. On 4 July 1986, when Mitterrand saw Reagan in Washington, he urged the need for a renewal of direct talks between America and the Soviet Union. He shared his doubts about the idea of completely abolishing nuclear weapons. He repeated his scepticism about the Strategic Defense Initiative. He warned Reagan to avoid including French weapons in any projected agreement with Gorbachëv. This was the standard French position, and Reagan listened calmly. He wished for a resumption of negotiations with Moscow. On this at least he could concur with Mitterrand.[17]

On 7 July 1986 Gorbachëv welcomed Mitterrand to Moscow and learned of France's objections to his recent proposals. Mitterrand stressed that although Reagan was committed to the Defense Initiative, he was genuinely working in the cause of world peace. The problem as Mitterrand saw things was that USSR and America were aiming past each other: 'In sum, the Americans want to negotiate without renouncing SDI. And you want to make them renounce SDI without negotiations. No progress is possible on this basis.'[18] He warned Gorbachëv that he would need to change his ideas if he wanted a deal. The January declaration was inadequate as a basis for talks. Gorbachëv could not have an agreement on nuclear armaments without including an understanding about conventional forces. He also had to take seriously the Western concerns about the SS-25s, about the Krasnoyarsk radar station and about future arrangements for verification.[19] Mitterrand was alerting Gorbachëv to what he had to resolve before meeting Reagan. Gorbachëv remarked that he was awaiting Reagan's reply to a recent letter; he stressed that the Soviet leadership was now willing to sign an arms agreement on condition that America limited the Defense Initiative to laboratory research.[20]

The President took until 21 July 1986 to draft a response to the General Secretary's messages in the previous month and show it to his administration for comment. He asked his officials to consult the American Congress and the NATO allies about the contents.[21] He signed off the letter on 25 July 1986. He made his usual point that there was no offensive purpose lurking behind the Strategic Defense Initiative. He claimed the right for America to go on with its research and testing for a further five years; he repeated the promise to share the technology once its feasibility was demonstrated. He called for a plan to reduce the stocks of all categories of offensive nuclear weapons. He wanted strategic arsenals to be halved.[22]

Soviet leaders undertook a review of Reagan's foreign policy. In late July 1986 they formed a working group from the main interested agencies – its members were Shevardnadze, Chebrikov, Sokolov, Dobrynin, Medvedev and Yakovlev. They produced a scathing analysis. Reagan was trying to 'exhaust' the USSR by both drawing it into regional conflicts and intensifying the arms race; his obvious aim was to disrupt the Politburo's course toward social and economic improvement.[23] He treated every non-socialist country and region as belonging to the sphere of America's 'vital interests'. He used a variety of methods. He was assisting counter-revolutionary insurgencies in Afghanistan, Nicaragua, Angola and Cambodia. He had deployed American forces against Grenada, Lebanon and Libya. He used economic levers to keep the rest of NATO and other allies in line. He was flexible in reaction to the changing situations around the world. When popular discontent grew in Salvador, Haiti and the Philippines, America gave its blessing for the removal of dictatorial right-wing governments. This combination of methods, according to the working party, proved that the Reagan administration was a practitioner of 'neoglobalism'.[24]

The group's advice was for the USSR and other socialist countries to continue their efforts in social and economic development while keeping their military power at 'the necessary level'. This was hardly controversial. The odd thing about the draft lay chiefly in its failure to mention any of the 'hotspots' around the world where Soviet forces or finances were involved. There was a reason for the omission. The group wished to emphasize the need to take proper account of 'our resources and possibilities' and to cut down aid to 'developing countries'.[25] Since China shared the anxiety about American neoglobalism, it recommended that Moscow should seek reconciliation with Beijing. Academic contacts might be a sensible first step. The Politburo, the memo continued, should 'use our work with the political circles in the West – including the United States itself – that are worried about the danger of a sharp deterioration of the international situation as the result of the adventurist actions of the Reagan administration'. Cooperation should be sought with all parties of the political left. The media should be used systematically to put a properly argued case.[26]

The Politburo endorsed the review.[27] This was a success for radicalism as Shevardnadze gained sanction for an attempt to halt both American and Soviet intervention in the wars in sub-Saharan Africa. He was already pressing the African National Congress to abandon the armed struggle.[28] Meanwhile Yakovlev persuaded Gorbachëv to make an appeal to anti-war opinion in America by renewing his unilateral moratorium on nuclear explosion tests. The idea was to make things difficult for the hawks in the American administration.[29] Gorbachëv needed little persuasion, and he could count on Ligachëv's eager support. Ligachëv ordered media editors to start an energetic campaign to make it difficult for Reagan to continue to permit the testing that had occurred through the spring in the Nevada desert. The USSR was to seize the chance to present itself as the true promoter of world peace.[30]

For some months Gorbachëv himself had been hoping to shift the Asian factor more towards the centre of his efforts in foreign policy.[31] On 28 July he used his trip to Vladivostok in the Soviet Far East to announce the desire for a transformation of the USSR's relations with countries of East Asia. He highlighted the need for peace and applauded the efforts of the Non-Aligned Movement in this part of the continent. He said it was time for America and the USSR to give the same intensity of attention to Asia as they had to Europe. Though he hardly praised the Americans, his speech was remarkably soft in its criticisms. He also stressed the wish for a cooperative relationship with China, suggesting that opportunities existed both in economic ties and in space exploration. As surety of his good intentions he emphasized that Moscow would keep only a minimal level of armed forces on its Asian territory; he promised that there would be no increase in the number of its intermediate-range nuclear missiles. He called for the demilitarization of the entire Indian Ocean. He declared that the Soviet leadership was 'ready to bring the Soviet armies home' from Afghanistan. His proviso was that those countries that were funding the rebellion against the Afghan government had to cease their interference. Gorbachëv was taking yet another sudden initiative. Speaking by the shores of the Pacific, he revealed his impatience with the pace of change in world politics.[32]

The State Department had its own reasons for irritation about the halt to progress. Whenever Shultz explained his difficulties with Weinberger to the President, there seemed to be a meeting of minds. The President never followed this up with action. By 5 August, the exasperated Shultz had had enough and handed over a letter of resignation. By chance Reagan had a medical check-up scheduled for that day. Chief of Staff Donald Regan rang Shultz at his home on the Stanford campus and pleaded with him to stay on. Shultz replied: 'It's a very frustrating environment to work in. I find it difficult to pull together a team in the security field. It's a debilitating situation. Constantly under attack. I get no sense of support. I feel I'm out there operating on my own. Maybe somebody else can do it better.' Regan impressed on Shultz that big 'games' were imminent in the international arena. The White House needed a united cabinet with 'no deviating, no undercutting, no sniping'. Regan added that the President would have to 'bang heads'. Shultz knew all this. Indeed it was because he doubted that Reagan would ever act with the necessary firmness that he had decided to resign. But he relented, agreeing to talk again in a few days; and on returning to Washington, he withdrew his letter and readied himself for the next phase in the struggle.[33]

On 16 August 1986 Reagan signed a directive to guide the American delegation when the scheduled talks reopened in Geneva. The negotiators were to emphasize America's right to carry out research, construction and testing of the Defense Initiative. Reagan was hoping to deploy the programme from 1991; he wanted to repeat the promise to share the technology with the Soviet Union.[34] In yet another directive, he stressed that his 'grand strategy' was to avoid nuclear war while preventing the expansion of Soviet global power. Deterrence was to stay at the centre of policy. It would remain in the American interest to thwart a rapprochement between China and the USSR. The modernization of its strategic nuclear forces should be a priority while intensive work continued on the Strategic Defense Initiative.[35]

Meanwhile Gorbachëv was squeezing fresh concessions out of his General Staff after Grinevski pointed to the weight that America gave to the need for an agreed process of notification and verification about large-scale troop movements in Europe. Gorbachëv gave his approval. He told Zaikov and Akhromeev to work out suitable guidelines. Akhromeev quietly declined to obey, and there was a fractious atmosphere at the following meeting of the Zaikov Commission on 21 June 1986. Shevardnadze, Politburo member and minister, heatedly argued that the American demands were harmless enough. Akhromeev's resistance collapsed that same day.[36] Yet the General Staff and KGB continued to dread the idea of America's inspectors snooping on the USSR's military facilities.[37] They accused Grinevski of straying outside the bounds of his instructions. Defence Minister Sokolov called for the Party Control Committee to investigate the matter. Grinevski admitted to Shevardnadze that in some technical respects he had overstepped directives. Shevardnadze himself had encouraged his ministry to be radical in revising foreign policy, and he disdained to let others suffer as the result of following his lead. Instead he went to Gorbachëv and repeated the arguments for new procedures of notification and verification. Gorbachëv rejected the charges against Grinevski.[38]

Akhromeev told Grinevski that many of the Soviet Army's divisions east of the Volga were under strength in troops and equipment: 'We cannot let foreigners see all that shame.' Grinevski retorted that he, as a patriot, welcomed inspections as a way of reducing the number of divisions and ensuring that the remainder were properly supplied.[39]

The Politburo met on 7 August 1986 to listen to their opposing submissions. When Grinevski said that inspections would enable the USSR to discover crucial information about American forces, Akhromeev turned red with anger and accused Grinevski of treason.[40] Gorbachëv had heard quite enough: 'Well, what have we here? You are Chief of the General Staff. Now go and take the measures to put the army in order so that there won't be any need to invite the Americans to bring about order in our army.'[41] He reminded Akhromeev that it was the political leaders and not the military commanders who took the ultimate decisions – and he told him to stick to his proper sphere of duties. The Politburo agreed and there was no need for a show of hands. As he left the meeting, Akhromeev shouted over at Grinevski: 'The armed forces will never, never, never forgive you for this!'[42] That evening Grinevski got his own back by persuading Shevardnadze to arrange for Akhromeev to go to Stockholm and speak in favour of a regime of inspections. The Americans would be impressed if a Soviet marshal expressed vocal support. The Politburo endorsed the idea.[43] Although Akhromeev travelled to Sweden in a foul temper, he performed his duties conscientiously and the American delegation reported warmly on him to Washington.[44]

The thread that still tied Akhromeev to Gorbachëv was the Politburo's commitment to the idea that there would be no nuclear arms agreement unless America assented to Soviet terms about the Strategic Defense Initiative.[45] Akhromeev, despite his authorship of the first variant of the January declaration, had always been sceptical about the chances of an arms reduction treaty. He probably calculated that the Americans were unlikely to accept the compromise that Gorbachëv was now proposing. He was willing to wait and see how Reagan would react.

A new difficulty arose between Washington and Moscow on 2 September 1986 when the Soviet authorities arrested Nicholas Daniloff, an American of Russian descent working as a Moscow correspondent. They charged him with being a CIA agent. The American administration denied that Daniloff had any such role and warned that there would be no summit between Reagan and Gorbachëv unless he was released. A blistering exchange of accusations took place. Though it was strictly true that Daniloff was not a spy, he had undoubtedly passed sensitive messages from a Soviet citizen to the American embassy. Unbeknownst to him, the CIA had become involved. Strombaugh, the CIA station chief in Moscow, had imprudently mentioned Daniloff's name when on the phone in the Soviet capital. The KGB concluded that Daniloff was an intelligence agent. Gorbachëv wrote a short letter to Reagan arguing that they should not permit the affair to disrupt negotiations on disarmament. The CIA's bungling appalled both Reagan and Shultz. But Reagan was also determined to secure an innocent American's liberation from captivity. On 12 September a compromise was agreed for Daniloff to be consigned to the American embassy while a Soviet spy, Gennadi Zakharov, was let out of prison and taken into the care of the USSR's diplomats in New York.

On 18 September Shevardnadze flew to America, where he was to give a speech to the UN General Assembly. He held discussions with Shultz in Washington over the next two days and delivered over Gorbachëv's letter to Reagan. Gorbachëv focused on the desirability of reinforcing the Anti-Ballistic Missile Treaty and confining the Strategic Defense Initiative programme to the research laboratories. He stressed how flexible he was being in excluding British and French nuclear missiles from his immediate proposals. He asked to meet Reagan in advance of their full summit later in the year – he suggested London or Reykjavik as a suitable venue.[46]

Shultz assured Shevardnadze that Reagan appreciated Soviet concerns about the Strategic Defense Initiative. He described how shocked the Americans were by the Chernobyl tragedy; he said that everybody understood that any kind of nuclear war would be a catastrophe. Shultz jested that there could be unanimity if only he could convince Perle – he added that he would break Perle's head if he caused any trouble.[47] When Perle joined the meeting, Shevardnadze quipped that the heavy artillery had arrived. True to form, Perle asked why the Kremlin was breaching the Anti-Ballistic Missile Treaty in building the Krasnoyarsk early-warning station. Shevardnadze said only that the Soviet Union would talk about this if the American would discuss its own station in Greenland.[48] He asked Perle to reconsider his hostility to Castro's Cuba.

(Perle, for once, chose not to reply.)[49] Regional disputes received attention; but only one of them, the Iran–Iraq war, brought Shevardnadze
and Shultz together – and even then they could not agree on a joint
declaration. The other regions produced dispute. Shevardnadze's people
felt annoyance at the American assumption that all would be well in
southern Africa if only Cuba withdrew its forces from Angola. The only
consolation for Shevardnadze was that Shultz made no mention of the
Afghan question.[50] Reagan said nothing about it either; but he did not
fail to accentuate his commitment to the Strategic Defense Initiative. A
gleam of light shone when the President assented to Gorbachëv's idea
about a pre-summit meeting.

There was a tussle over the venue. Shultz suspected that Reagan
would prefer London, where he could liaise with Thatcher. He lobbied
instead for Reykjavik.[51] Gorbachëv agreed to this idea. Reykjavik was
the capital of a neutral country lying roughly equidistant from the
American east coast and central Russia; and its very geographical
isolation would free the leaders from distractions.

Gorbachëv was not naive about his chances. On 26 September
1986 he told Shevardnadze and other leaders that many leading Americans wished to heighten international tensions and prevent the USSR
from enhancing its dynamism: 'And so, comrades, nobody's going to
help us.'[52] He resolved to be bold at Reykjavik and told his planning
group – Chebrikov, Zaikov, Kovalëv, Akhromeev and Chernyaev – to
draft such proposals as Reagan would be unable to reject out of hand.[53]
On 3 October 1986, on a short break in Crimea, Gorbachëv talked to
Chernyaev about what else he could do in advance of the encounter.
Chernyaev highlighted the benefits of boldness and simplicity; he
advised Gorbachëv to push Reagan on to the back foot by calling for
rapid big cuts in nuclear stockpiles. Gorbachëv, in his opinion, ought
to endorse Reagan's 'zero option' for intermediate-range nuclear
weapons and propose a fifty per cent reduction in strategic weaponry
in the very first stage of disarmament. Chernyaev said that the Defense
Initiative would cease to be a threat if Gorbachëv could persuade
Reagan to renounce the right to test the research results.[54]

On 4 October 1986, speaking to the planning group, Gorbachëv
focused on the links between internal and external policy: 'Our aim is
to break up the next stage of the arms race. If we don't do this, the
danger for us will go on growing. But not having conceded on concrete questions, even very important ones, we are losing hold on what
is really important. We're going to be dragged into an unsustainable

race and we'll be the losers since we're at the limit of our possibilities.'[55] He aimed to discover how much bluff there was in their Defense Initiative research, and he would warn that the USSR could develop an effective response. He would call for a halving of the number of strategic weapons – this would be a way of embarrassing the Americans, who favoured only a thirty per cent reduction.[56] On intermediate-range missiles, he wanted all of them to be removed from Europe since the Pershing-2s were like a pistol pointed at the USSR's head. He would postpone negotiations about French and British nuclear forces as well as about the Soviet missiles on Asian territory.[57] He asked for fresh drafts on regional conflicts, chemical weapons and human rights.[58] On human rights he intended to focus on American abuses. He wanted to present the USSR in a good light. He intended to relax the Soviet regulations on exit visas and to allow emigrants from the USSR to return freely on trips.[59] He told the planning group to go off and devise material suitable for a General Secretary, not just for a professional arms negotiator.[60]

He ordered the Soviet media to avoid raising hopes too high.[61] Canada's ex-Prime Minister Pierre Trudeau had advised him to remember about the constraints upon Reagan's freedom. 'Certain forces' had put him in the White House, and he could not afford to neglect them.[62] The American Sovietologist and Polish defector Professor Seweryn Bialer told Yakovlev that Gorbachëv would be wasting his time if he tried to cajole Reagan into abandoning the Strategic Defense Initiative.[63] (Gorbachëv, of course, was well aware of this.) Canadian Prime Minister Brian Mulroney assured Shevardnadze that Reagan had a serious commitment to peace and could be trusted. Disconcertingly he also remarked that he sometimes felt like a psychoanalyst when dealing with the Americans! Mulroney warned that Soviet human rights abuses remained a serious impediment to rapprochement between the superpowers. Reagan, according to Mulroney, sincerely believed that American military power had been fading before 1981. Shevardnadze promised that Gorbachëv would travel to Reykjavik in a spirit of flexibility and would arrive with a number of 'compromise variants.'[64]

The first item on the Politburo's agenda on 6 October 1986 was the news that one of the USSR's fleet of atomic submarines had disappeared in the Sargasso Sea. There was anxiety lest the Americans might reach the vessel and acquire technological secrets. Gromyko wanted to announce that no environmental damage had occurred.

After the Chernobyl catastrophe, this was not the advice that Gorbachëv wanted to hear. He aimed to say only that 'the specialists are studying the consequences'.[65]

The Politburo's planning group – now consisting of Zaikov, Chebrikov, Sokolov, Dobrynin, Yakovlev and Kovalëv – supplied the guidelines he had requested. They stressed that American public opinion was pressing for a deal with the USSR. The group advised him to link all aspects of disarmament.[66] Gorbachëv asked Politburo members to make any response before their next meeting.[67] When they reassembled on 8 October 1986, he admitted that a collapse in the talks was a possibility. But he leaned towards optimism. Reagan, he reckoned, understood that the advice from the American 'hawks' would do him no good in public opinion around the world. Gromyko commented that the decision to install SS-20s in Europe had been 'a crude mistake'. This was an impressive recantation by the former Foreign Affairs Minister. About negotiating tactics, Ligachëv endorsed Gorbachëv's proposal to put forward a package that brought together all the Soviet requirements. But he also recognized that Gorbachëv needed sanction for some flexibility at Reykjavik if Reagan should prove awkward; he suggested that the General Secretary should be permitted to agree to a partial bilateral reduction in nuclear weaponry. The point was to keep up the momentum for further progress.[68]

Shevardnadze continued to predict that the Americans would insist on unbundling the package as a condition of further progress. He had spoken to them more recently than Gorbachëv and understood that Reagan had invested his 'personal prestige' in the Defense Initiative.[69] He hoped to persuade Gorbachëv to drop the condition that the Americans should give up the Strategic Defense Initiative in return for a deal on nuclear arms reductions.[70] The General Secretary felt otherwise, aiming to negotiate on the basis of a single comprehensive package. He was counting on his ability to persuade the President to confine the research and testing of the Defense Initiative to 'laboratories'. Surely Reagan would want the prize of an immense bilateral reduction in nuclear weapons? He hoped to pull the President into the orbit of his project for arms reduction.

20. SUMMIT IN REYKJAVIK

Washington intensified its preparations as the date of the Reykjavik meeting approached. When Suzanne Massie asked Reagan what he wanted from the Russians, he needed no time before replying: 'I want to get rid of those atomic weapons, *every one!*'[1] On 2 October 1986 Reagan selected Regan and Poindexter to chair the final planning groups. He asked them to devise tactics for how he would present his arguments to Gorbachëv.[2] United Nations business kept Shultz in New York, so he wrote to the President advising him to restrict the size of the party he took into the sessions with Gorbachëv – he suggested that Reagan should limit his leading companions in Iceland to Poindexter, Regan and Shultz himself. Shultz urged Reagan to seize the initiative. He forecast that the meeting had the potential to lead to a resolution of the current difficulties about intermediate-range nuclear weapons and move on to questions of strategic weaponry. He warned Reagan to be ready for Gorbachëv to attack him for his announcement, on 27 May, that America might not renew its commitment to the SALT-II Treaty's limitations after it reached its term. He highlighted the reasons for optimism. Since the beginning of his presidency, Reagan had set his face against accommodating to Soviet demands. Now there was a chance of reaping a fine harvest from his efforts.[3]

Reagan's old pal Barney Oldfield wished him bon voyage. Oldfield recounted that the last time he flew to Keflavik airport had been in 1953, when his job had been to settle a royalties dispute which was stopping the local radio station from playing Bing Crosby's 'White Christmas' to the troops of the American military base. Reagan responded with an anticommunist joke and a recommendation of Tom Clancy's latest thriller, *Red Storm Rising*, which he had just finished reading.[4] Film actor and friend Charlton Heston sent a note advising: 'When you go to Iceland, don't blink.'[5] Though his tone was amicable and respectful, he implicitly shared the apprehension among the President's conservative followers that he might make undue concessions in

Iceland. Reagan took this to heart and called his spokesman Lyn Nofziger for a one-on-one meeting in the presidential living quarters. The normal procedure was for others to be present to guard against departures from the official line. Reagan wanted a frank, confidential chat with someone who would pull no punches. Nofziger, true to form, recounted that many Reaganites worried that he might fail to stand up to Gorbachëv – and that Gorbachëv 'might have his lunch'. Reagan told Nofziger that there was no cause for concern. He had learned how to deal with communists in his time at the Screen Actors Guild; he was confident that he could handle the General Secretary.[6]

Disquiet continued to be expressed by many politicians and supporters who had helped him get elected. The prospect of a summit encouraged Edward Teller and Congressman Jim Courter to urge him to increase funding for the Strategic Defense Initiative; and they explained their fear that the USSR alone would finance and develop such a programme.[7] The Lithuanian diaspora called on him to demand that Gorbachëv should renounce Stalin's annexation of their country in the 1940s.[8] Reagan paid little mind to the clamour until after an article by *Newsweek*'s conservative columnist George Will that ridiculed the 'headlong rush for a summit'. The President decided to invite him to the White House for a conversation. As they faced each other, he pointed out that no President of recent years matched his determination to face down the Soviet leadership. His self-composure reassured Will, and the fuss in the press died down.[9] Reagan also sought to allay the doubts of many in Congress. Following the custom before summits, he gave a personal briefing to a group headed by Speaker Tip O'Neill and Senator Robert Dole. He hoped to convince both sides of Congress that the President was firm and open about his purposes. Reagan stressed that he had always been frank about his vision of the American national interest. He promised to do nothing in Iceland that would take people by surprise.[10]

Of course, nobody in the American administration could predict how the Soviet leader would behave. The Kremlin kept its own counsel in the days before the Reykjavik talks. Gorbachëv played cautiously, restraining his usual flamboyance. What was he up to? The worry in Washington was that he liked to spring surprises and might try to do this in Reykjavik. On a trip to New York in late September 1986, one of Gorbachëv's advisers – the academic Georgi Arbatov – told Henry Kissinger that Shevardnadze would shortly arrive with Gorbachëv's new ideas to resolve the Strategic Defense Initiative question. Kissinger immediately phoned the State Department with the information.[11] Shevardnadze told the Canadians that Gorbachëv would bring some 'compromise variants' with him to Iceland.[12] This only served to persuade the Americans that the General Secretary was cooking up some mischief and that the President and his travelling party would need to stay very alert. Poindexter assumed that Gorbachëv would try to 'unravel the Western consensus on tougher policies towards the Soviet Union'. Gorbachëv had implied some willingness to drop the question of British and French nuclear stockpiles from talks with the Americans. Perhaps he would also change his stance still further on the Strategic Defense Initiative. Reagan's officials were divided whenever they discussed the possible outcomes.[13] Gorbachëv was gaining a psychological edge before the encounter in Iceland, and concern spread on the American side that he might get the better of the President.

The American agitation was understandable. The General Secretary infringed the etiquette of summits by which each side forewarned the other about its agenda. He thought he had a distinct chance of influencing Reagan through his own ideas and personality – the very thing that American right-wingers feared. As he saw it, Reagan in their confidential correspondence eschewed the kind of anticommunist rhetoric that he used in public.[14] Reagan himself was wary about possible criticism by his own conservative associates and supporters. He forbade officials to speak to the media without his consent – he planned to avoid any repetition of the mischief that Weinberger had wrought before the Geneva summit. On 7 October the President held a preparatory discussion at the National Security Planning Group with Weinberger and Casey in attendance.[15] Neither of them would be going to Iceland. Reagan intended to take charge with Shultz and only a small team at his side. He also wanted to strike a businesslike tone, and there would be only a minimum of social activities. Reagan doused any high hopes about the meeting. While hoping for a constructive dialogue, he did not expect to be signing an agreement in Iceland.[16]

On 9 October the Soviet and American delegations flew into Keflavik airport. The Icelandic navy prevented the Greenpeace vessel *Sirius* from entering Reykjavik harbour where, at Chebrikov's instigation, Gorbachëv and his people based themselves on two Soviet ships including passenger liner *Georgi Ots*. This was a precaution against being bugged.[17] Reagan stayed in the US Ambassador's residence while his officials stayed at the nearby Holt Hotel and set up offices in a neighbouring school building. The President met with his senior officials early next day.[18] He and Shultz talked at length in the 'bubble' – this was an anti-eavesdropping device made of translucent plastic five inches thick and capable of seating up to six people. Reagan quipped: 'My God, look at this, if we put a little cement statue there and fill it up with water, we could have goldfish here.' Space was tight and officials touched knees at they sat opposite each other.[19] Shultz went over the details of the agreed negotiating position, which was to stick to what the President had put forward at the Geneva summit.[20] Other government departments were jealous of Shultz's access to Reagan at such a distance from America. Shultz expected mischief. Sure enough, a CIA report was placed in front of the President implying that Soviet commanders were contemplating the possibility of assassinating Gorbachëv. This hardly brought peace and quiet to the American delegation. It was not meant to.[21]

The delegations spent the whole of the next day making preparations for the meeting between the two leaders. A vast pile of briefing papers was handed round on board the *Georgi Ots* and at the Holt Hotel.[22] Gorbachëv and Reagan made the last adjustments to their negotiating tactics. Reagan had dinner with Shultz, Poindexter and Regan. The excitement grew in the embassy residence and aboard ship. President and General Secretary felt the pressure of expectation even though it was not scheduled as an official 'summit'. Both of them liked to have their wives with them, but only Raisa made the trip. She spent her waking hours touring Iceland's geysers.[23] Nancy Reagan regretted that she missed out; she blamed Raisa for 'a bit of one-upmanship'.[24]

The President, by agreement, was to act as host for the first meeting on the ground floor of the Höfdi House on 11 October 1986, and he greeted the General Secretary at 10.40 a.m. They talked privately for an hour and agreed to make verification an important feature of any new treaty. It was a good start. Shultz and Shevardnadze then joined them. It was at this point that specific proposals were laid on the table, and Gorbachëv took the initiative in line with the recent discussion in the Politburo. He called for an immediate halving of stockpiles of strategic nuclear weapons as well as for the instant total elimination of intermediate-range missiles in Europe. He refrained from insisting that French and British weaponry should be included in the process; and in return he asked Reagan to drop the demand that the USSR should remove all its missiles from its Asian territory. He also wanted talks to begin on missiles with a range of less than 1,000 kilometres. He called for both sides to guarantee to abide by the obligations of the Anti-Ballistic Missile Treaty. At the same time he confirmed, face to face, his willingness to permit research and testing on outer-space anti-ballistic defence projects so long as the work was confined to laboratories.[25]

Shultz immediately grasped that Gorbachëv had made a 'sensational' proposal.[26] But, like a poker player, he hid his pleasure; and anyway it would be the President who dispensed the American cards. As it happened, the sweep of Gorbachëv's suggestions had made an impression on Reagan. But as a veteran union negotiator, he kept calm and inscrutable: he saw no point in relaxing his squeeze on the Soviet delegation.

Reagan raised several matters of his own. He pointed out that the Soviet leadership could exploit the situation by surreptitiously moving their Asia-based intermediate-range nuclear missiles westward to target them on Western Europe. He also called for the broadest interpretation of the Anti-Ballistic Missile Treaty. He repeated his solemn promise to share the Strategic Defense Initiative once it was completed; he saw this as a crucial contribution to world peace: 'The reason for this is that we can't guarantee in the future that someone – a madman like Hitler, for example – might not try to build nuclear weapons.'[27] Gorbachëv said he hoped that these were only preliminary remarks. He called for a constructive dialogue. Reagan assured Gorbachëv that he genuinely wanted to deploy the new strategic defence system only after all ballistic nuclear missiles had been eliminated. The USSR, he reasoned, should therefore have no fear of a first-strike attack.[28] Although Reagan saw this as a conciliatory gesture, Gorbachëv remained unpersuadable about the Defense Initiative and could not understand why Reagan lacked sensitivity to his concerns. As the dispute rumbled on, the Soviet compromise over laboratories faded from discussion.

The two teams broke for lunch, and the American delegation adjourned to their 'bubble' in the Höfdi House to consider the morning's proceedings. Shultz and the other Americans felt uplifted. Nitze called it the best Soviet offer in a quarter of a century. Even Perle admitted that Gorbachëv had made a noteworthy suggestion about missiles in Europe, even if the Americans continued to have concern that the Kremlin might suddenly move its weaponry from the Asian bases into the USSR's European zone.[29]

In the afternoon, Gorbachëv asked Reagan whether he accepted the proposal to reduce strategic nuclear missiles by fifty per cent. Reagan said he did, before making the proviso that any agreement should leave the two sides with equal military capacity – a simple halving would allow the USSR to keep far more warheads than America. He stood by his own call for the complete eradication of intermediate-range missiles in Europe and Asia.[30] Gorbachëv enquired whether Reagan would consider restricting his 'zero option' to European territories if the Soviet side could find a way of alleviating worries about the USSR's Asia-based rocketry. He also appealed to Reagan to appreciate his flexibility in offering to concede the laboratory testing of the Strategic Defense Initiative.[31] While recognizing America's superiority in financial resources, he predicted that the Soviet scientists would invent ways of counteracting the American programme. He refused to take Reagan seriously in his promise to share the products of the research. If the Americans prohibited the export of dairy-industry technology to Moscow, why should Soviet leaders believe that things would be different with anti-missile equipment? He contended that the President anyway failed to comprehend what his entire project for strategic defence truly involved. The same old topic continued to divide them.[32]

Shultz looked on the bright side. That evening, as his limousine carried him back to the Holt Hotel, he exclaimed to his aide Hill: 'Charlie, it was a *sensational* day! So much on the table!'[33] The arms reduction working group headed by Nitze and Akhromeev tried to narrow the divisions before the next day of talks. The discussion in the Höfdi House continued into the small hours. The two delegations occupied the first floor, above the rooms where the meetings between Reagan and Gorbachëv took place. At the top of the stairs, the Americans had rooms on the left and the Soviets on the right.[34] (The Icelanders had a good political sense of humour.) The American delegation's discussion 'bubble' was an impressive piece of kit but other features of their equipment were less so. Richard Perle had to improvise a desk by getting a door unscrewed and laid across a bathtub. He and his colleagues did not want to plug their electrical typewriters into the mains for fear that the KGB might somehow detect what they were typing. It was intense work. The Americans had only one professional secretary with them in the Höfdi House; they also quickly ran out of carbon paper and had to borrow some from the Soviet delegation.

Shultz heard Akhromeev joking: 'Well, once again Soviet technology comes to the rescue!'[35]

Akhromeev seldom let his colleagues get a word in edgewise.[36] But he worked tirelessly for a deal, and when tempers frayed, it was he who called for calm.[37] Perle noted how hard he was trying. Nitze had nothing like such pre-eminence over the American team. Indeed, the sceptical Rowny pushed him into producing drafts that took no account of Gorbachëv's summer concessions. There was a pause in the proceedings at 2 a.m., and the Americans repaired to Shultz's room in the Holt Hotel to gather their thoughts. Shultz felt annoyed when he heard from Nitze's lips: 'I was opposed by my own delegation.' The decision was taken not to rouse Reagan from slumber. Instead Shultz told Nitze to go back to the talks and get down to proper bargaining when the two sides came together again at 3 a.m.[38] Nitze and Akhromeev achieved progress towards an agreed method for assessing the size of each side's strategic nuclear forces – a task of fiendish complexity because so many diverse types and capacities of weapons were involved. The snags were of a predictable nature. Akhromeev objected to the Strategic Defense Initiative and Nitze to the USSR's nuclear missiles stationed in its Asian territory. Ten hours of debate ended without a solution to such questions.[39]

When Gorbachëv rose from his bed that morning, it was obvious to him that only he and Reagan could break the deadlock. He reopened the proceedings with the comment that just as the Bible said it took seven days to create the world, the talks were only entering their second day and there remained a lot of work for them to do. Reagan replied that since it was a Sunday, perhaps both of them should be resting from their labours.[40] After expressing regret about the impasse in the working group, Gorbachëv assured Reagan that he was wrong if he thought that the USSR had a greater need than America for arms reduction. The Soviet leadership was not going to capitulate – and the Reykjavik talks provided a chance that might not be on offer again.[41] After quickly consulting Shevardnadze, Gorbachëv announced that the USSR would agree to keep only a hundred warheads in Asia. He asked Reagan to match this concession with one of his own by committing America to adhere to the Anti-Ballistic Missile Treaty for a further ten years. He pointed out that he had shown goodwill by accepting the right of laboratory-based testing for the Strategic Defense Initiative.[42] Reagan responded that the Defense Initiative's whole purpose was to render the treaty redundant by making nuclear war entirely impossible. Neither would give way.[43]

The President told the General Secretary that America and the USSR could be 'friendly competitors' even though 'each side mistrusted the other'.[44] He welcomed the fact that Gorbachëv, unlike his predecessors, did not talk of a world communist state as his objective. These comments failed to soothe Gorbachëv, who noted reports in the media that Reagan still believed the USSR to be an evil empire. As tempers flared, Shultz moved the discussion on to formulating a joint statement on strategic and intermediate-range weapons. Gorbachëv and Reagan could at least agree on this.[45]

The two leaders felt sharp frustration, and Gorbachëv lamented the historic chance they had missed. Reagan changed the subject to human rights and economics. He asked why the USSR had failed to buy the minimum of American wheat that the Long-Term Grain Agreement required. Gorbachëv replied frankly that the collapse of the world oil price restricted Moscow's purchasing opportunities.[46]

The closing meeting between President and General Secretary took place that afternoon. Shultz had sat down with Shevardnadze in a last attempt to find consensus on the Strategic Defense Initiative. The two sides had narrowed the gap but ultimately failed to bridge it. Now only a change of stance by Reagan or Gorbachëv could bring about agreement. Gorbachëv wanted to try again. He read out a proposal to confine all research, development and testing within the Anti-Ballistic Missile Treaty framework for a further five years – and the USSR and America would halve the number of strategic offensive weapons in the same period. He called for the total elimination of such missiles after ten years. Reagan replied that he wanted America to be able to deploy its Strategic Defense Initiative at that future point. Gorbachëv refused any further compromise. There was stalemate.[47] Reagan could not see why the USSR would object to the deployment of an exclusively defensive system; Gorbachëv asked why the American would have need for such a system once the world was rid of offensive nuclear weapons. The two sides had come so close to sealing a deal that would have definitively eliminated a threat that had hung over the world since the late 1940s.

Turning again to the Defense Initiative, Gorbachëv pleaded with Reagan to recognize that the next American President might change any policy that he and Reagan agreed. The USSR needed to plan on the basis of reliable projections. Reagan replied that he needed to obviate the danger of 'someone who might come along and want to redevelop nuclear missiles'.[48] He also asked why the Soviet authorities were refusing to dismantle the Krasnoyarsk early-warning station; he indicated that American forces 'do not have a single defence against nuclear attack'. In ten years' time, he stressed, he himself would be a very old man. He looked forward to returning to Iceland with Gorbachëv when each of them would bring his country's last nuclear missile with him and 'they would give a tremendous party for the whole world'. He joked he would never live to a hundred if he had to worry every day about being hit by a Soviet missile.[49] An hour's break took place for each team to hold a final internal consultation. At the resumption, Reagan referred to 'the trouble Americans had getting along with each other'.[50] The two leaders began to look on the bright side. They were close to an understanding about strategic and intermediate-range missiles and felt confident that the two delegations in Geneva could work out the necessary details. Truly much had been accomplished in the Höfdi House.[51]

Gorbachëv, in a last effort, beseeched Reagan to concede on the Strategic Defense Initiative. Reagan said he could not go back on his word to the American people; he denied that America wanted to deploy weapons in space – and he affirmed the need to test the technology outside laboratories. Gorbachëv countered that the Initiative would clearly involve space weapons. Reagan refused to give way. When Gorbachëv asked whether this was his last word, Reagan said yes and heatedly asked Gorbachëv to take cognizance of the American political process. If Soviet citizens criticized the General Secretary, he commented, they went to jail. Gorbachëv replied that Reagan ought to look at some of the things now being written in the USSR's press. Reagan dismissed this as hyperbole and reminded Gorbachëv that America's political right, including its journalists, were 'kicking his brains out'. The Strategic Defense Initiative was anyway too dear to him. Gorbachëv remarked that Reagan was but a few steps away from becoming a great President who would not need to bother about right-wing critics when the peoples of America and the Soviet Union showered him with approval. Shevardnadze added that future generations would not forgive failure in Reykjavik. Still Reagan refused to yield. He wrote a note to the Secretary of State: 'George, am I right?' Shultz wrote 'Yes' and underlined the word.[52]

Their parting words had a poignant quality. According to the Soviet record, Reagan said: 'It's too bad that we have to part this way.

We were so close to an agreement. I think you didn't want to achieve an agreement anyway. I'm very sorry.' Gorbachëv, equally depressed, replied: 'I'm also sorry it's happened like this. I wanted an agreement, and did everything I could, if not more.' Reagan concluded: 'I don't know when we'll ever have another chance like this and whether we are going to meet soon.' Gorbachëv replied: 'I don't either.'[53] The American record was less specific and merely indicated that the President rose to his feet before the General Secretary asked him to pass on his regards to Mrs Reagan.[54] On the steps outside, they talked again. Reagan said, 'I still feel we can find a deal.' Gorbachëv was unimpressed: 'I don't think you want a deal. I don't know what more I could have done.' Quick as a whippet, Reagan remarked: 'You could have said yes.' Gorbachëv concluded: 'We won't be seeing each other again.'[55]

Reagan made straight for Air Force One, missing the opportunity to defend his performance in the talks. This was an unprecedented omission. The Great Communicator, as he was known, was remarkable for his ability to exploit chances to explain himself to the American public. He reassured himself in his diary: 'Well, the ball is in his court and I'm convinced that he'll come round when he sees how the world is reacting.'[56] He was genuinely disappointed. He was also exhausted. Though Gorbachëv felt the same he conquered his mood sufficiently to be able to host a press conference half an hour later. He spoke about his initial hopes as well as the process of the talks, constantly emphasizing how far the Soviet leadership had gone in pursuit of peace. While expressing no direct criticism, he stressed that Reagan had passed up the opportunity to realize his own zero option.[57] Shultz saw the damage that this was doing to the American cause around the world. He also arranged a meeting with reporters and declared that Reykjavik had been a success for America, its allies and global peace. In his press briefing later that day, he paid tribute to his President's 'magnificent' performance and hailed his commitment to the Strategic Defense Initiative. He avoided any criticism of Gorbachëv with the remark: 'I wouldn't say they came here not in good faith.' He refused to rule out the possibility that the American and Soviet leaders would eventually sign agreements.[58]

INTERMEZZO

21. THE MONTH OF MUFFLED DRUMS

The Reykjavik proceedings had started as a 'pre-summit' meeting. By the end, everyone was calling it a summit in recognition of the importance of what had occurred. Gorbachëv had systematically spelled out the Soviet negotiating position on nuclear arms for the first time. This had enabled him and Reagan to go over many of the matters that divided them. Indeed they had come close to a general agreement. But Gorbachëv played his hand too hard, and Reagan called his bluff. Each felt bitterly disappointed.

On the Aeroflot flight back to Moscow, Gorbachëv speculated on Reagan's conduct. He suggested that American conservative groups were making such a fuss that the President was not truly 'free in his decisions'. 'Certain circles in the West', he contended, displayed a fundamental misunderstanding: 'First: that the Russians are afraid of SDI and therefore will go to any concessions. And second: that we have a greater interest in disarmament than the United States.' Yet the summit had led to a lot of undeniable progress. But the Soviet and American sides had agreed in principle on a scheme for a drastic reduction in long-range and intermediate-range nuclear weapons. A further advance remained possible, and Gorbachëv thought this justified his decision to stick to an all-inclusive package of proposals. He had pushed Reagan on the Anti-Ballistic Missile Treaty and the Strategic Defense Initiative. He had forced the Americans to disclose the basis of their thinking. He thought that he had proved to the Europeans and the rest of the world that America and not the USSR was the main obstacle to a nuclear disarmament treaty.[1]

Reagan reached America tired and frustrated but equally sure that he had pursued the right track. Speaking next day on prime-time television, he held Gorbachëv responsible for wrecking the summit over the Strategic Defense Initiative. But he still felt able to add: 'I am still optimistic that a way will be found. The door is open and the opportunity to begin eliminating the nuclear threat is within reach.'[2] The

Kremlin, he said, had to take the first step. The White House would stand firm by its foreign policy: 'We prefer no agreement than to bring home a bad agreement to the United States.'[3]

Many on the political right had been ready to dispraise him. One of them, Norman Podhoretz, felt a shiver of relief that he had stood tall against the General Secretary: 'Well, God watches over the United States; but the truth is, Reagan actually did begin too much entranced by arms negotiations . . . and the build-down of nuclear weapons would have benefited the Soviets disproportionately. It was more of a strain to them as a proportion, so to speak, of their economy.'[4] George F. Will expressed thanks that Reagan had spurned the big deal on offer in Iceland. His piece for *Newsweek* played on an old theme of American conservatives: 'The formula for security is to keep your powder dry – and have lots of powder.'[5] William F. Buckley wrote a personal letter 'just to tell you that, by God, you lived up to our faith in you'; he also published an encomium in the *National Review*.[6] Inside the administration, mouths were sealed in loyalty to the President. But many felt the same way as Podhoretz and Will. Richard Perle hardly bothered to disguise his opinion when on a briefing mission to the Élysée Palace. He obviously regarded Reagan's commitment to the total elimination of nuclear missiles as disastrous; he was grateful that the President had laid down conditions that Gorbachëv had found unacceptable – and so catastrophe had been averted.[7]

Margaret Thatcher was less easily soothed. While on the phone to Reagan on 13 October 1986, she 'went through the roof' on hearing that the Americans had been discussing the total liquidation of nuclear missiles. She pointed out that this could leave Western Europe at the mercy of the USSR, which had massive superiority in conventional forces and chemical weapons. Thatcher was committed to Britain's retention of its independent nuclear force so that the Soviet leadership might never forget that 'some British missiles would always get through'. The only thing that consoled her was that Reagan had refused to give way on the Strategic Defense Initiative. According to Thatcher, this had averted an internal split in NATO. She left Reagan with no illusion that he could take his allies for granted. The talks in Iceland had shaken her confidence in him.[8]

Thatcher invited Mitterrand to London, where she directed a fusillade against Reykjavik. Reagan's behaviour dumbfounded her: 'I don't believe a word of it – he's out of touch with reality! New weapons will always get through the so-called SDI shield!' She accused him of going to Iceland completely ill-prepared. She feared that Gorbachëv might succeed in decoupling America from NATO. Would America risk the destruction of Chicago just to save Paris? Mitterrand shared her thinking. He scoffed at opinion poll findings that people thought that Reagan had stood firm in Iceland. He said that the truth was the exact opposite. He indicated that if ever the Reykjavik understandings came to fulfilment, he would sanction the production of chemical weapons – he would take every measure to keep France secure. All this pleased Thatcher. (It was an unusual episode of collaboration with the French.) Mitterrand tried to calm her down by affirming that the summit would have no practical results: 'Don't worry about it. The Russians can't walk past the SDI problem. There isn't going to be an agreement.' She spoke quite equably but then erupted again: 'Everything that took place in Reykjavik is a disaster!'[9]

An invitation arrived for her to visit Camp David for talks with Reagan. She had hoped to make the trip before any summit occurred, but the Reykjavik encounter forestalled her.[10] He was eager to welcome her despite what she had said to him by phone. He never objected to her fieriness. Indeed, he liked it, and he made arrangement to have a one-on-one session before their entourages joined them.[11] She and her advisers hoped to capitalize on the warmth of feelings that existed between President and Prime Minister. They set out to make him recognize the dangers in his negotiating standpoint in Iceland. Thatcher intended to be blunt. If his ideas for a drastic reduction in nuclear weapons came to fulfilment, there would be instability in Europe as the result of Moscow's numerical predominance in conventional and chemical weaponry. The NATO countries, as everyone knew, were unlikely to agree to finance the kind of reform of their armed forces that could countervail against Soviet superiority.[12] She and Reagan issued a joint statement reaffirming the principle of nuclear deterrence in defence policy and even pointing to the imbalance in conventional and chemical weaponry; and Reagan confidentially guaranteed that America would continue to supply Britain with Trident nuclear missiles.[13]

She returned to Europe somewhat calmer than when she left. She reported back to Mitterrand at the Élysée Palace. She now accepted that nothing catastrophic had occurred in Iceland. What had saved the day was the intransigence of 'the Russians' about the Strategic Defense Initiative. She thought this stupid of them because, in her view, Reagan's pet project would never achieve more than twenty per cent effectiveness. Gorbachëv had gone home empty-handed. She celebrated this outcome.[14] Mitterrand shared her determination to retain nuclear missiles so as to deter a Soviet military offensive. He told aides that 'we brushed with catastrophe' in Reykjavik.[15] The official concern that existed in London and Paris was quietly shared in Bonn. West European leaders feared that if the Americans were to rely exclusively on their Defense Initiative, they would move – albeit not by deliberate intention – towards an isolationist policy. Shultz had to listen to this argument when reporting to NATO allies in Brussels the day after the summit. He did what he could to reassure them; and, on the flight to Washington, he sent a cable to Reagan emphasizing those features of the Reykjavik talks that earned their applause.[16]

Shultz hoped to prevent the President from underplaying his achievement in Iceland. He wanted a display of pleasure. The understandings reached with the Soviet side about reductions in diverse categories of nuclear weaponry were unprecedented. Shultz sent yet another in-flight cable that stressed his 'conviction, especially after my session with our allies in Brussels today, that in fact you have an astonishing success on your hands'.[17] He considered that Reagan had smoked Gorbachëv out and extracted big concessions that the Soviet leader could not now abandon.[18] Reagan refused to focus his energies on the matter. So Shultz had to shoulder the load of defending the administration's corner.[19] He undertook a busy tour of TV studios and gave a speech at a National Press Club luncheon.[20] Constantly he underlined the progress that Reagan had made at the summit. He continued his efforts over the next few weeks as he crossed the country – on 31 October 1986 he spoke in San Francisco and Los Angeles on the same day.[21] His argument was that the USSR's willingness to negotiate was entirely attributable to the build-up of American military capacity and promotion of the Strategic Defense Initiative.[22]

TV anchors and newspaper columnists remained sceptical about this analysis and suspected that Shultz was holding something back from them. The *Wall Street Journal* declined to offer support. The *New York Times* editorial staff were equally discouraging. Few commentators outside the conservative ranks celebrated an Icelandic victory – and most conservatives were more pleased about Reagan's rebuff of Gorbachëv's demands than with anything of a positive nature.[23]

Gorbachëv took a dim view of Reagan's performance. When he first reported to the Politburo, he scowled about how the President had thrown away an opportunity to liquidate all nuclear weapons.

Reagan in his eyes was 'a class enemy' who had demonstrated his 'extraordinary primitivism, troglodytic profile and intellectual incapacity'. Gorbachëv saw the American administration as full of 'people without conscience, without morality'. He resented their assumption that he was pushing for an agreement only because of troubles in the Soviet economy. He aimed to teach them a lesson: 'They don't know what we'll do as a reply to SDI.' Nevertheless he remained 'an even bigger optimist' after Iceland. He clung to his tactic of requiring the Americans to accept a comprehensive 'package'. He drew confidence from how he had seized the initiative in the global media – and he looked forward to attracting support from Western Europe as well as from the anti-war movement and the neutral countries.[24] The Politburo liked what it heard. The only cautionary note was sounded when Zaikov asked Gorbachëv to announce the leadership's undiminished support for the defence industries. Gorbachëv welcomed Zaikov's request. Ligachëv applauded Gorbachëv's success in appealing over the heads of Western political leaders to entire peoples. Even Gromyko and Chebrikov approved as the Politburo endorsed Gorbachëv's general conclusions.[25]

Shevardnadze left for Bucharest to report to the Warsaw Pact's other foreign ministers. He divulged nothing of his personal reservations about Gorbachëv's tactics;[26] and when talking to his aides, he heaped the blame on to Akhromeev. He told them that the Chief of the General Staff had 'betrayed' the Soviet leadership by working with Perle to obstruct the pathway to the 'compromise'.[27] But really he understood all too well that the problems had arisen from Gorbachëv's insistence on bargaining for a single comprehensive package. He hated how the question of general disarmament had become 'hostage' to the Strategic Defense Initiative. But Gorbachëv was the General Secretary, and Shevardnadze knew he had to operate inside the framework that he imposed.[28] But how had Akhromeev come to exert such influence? Adamishin, who had his ear to the ground in the Foreign Affairs Ministry, argued that Gorbachëv had been reluctant to drive his military commanders too hard. He seemed to feel the need to carry them along with him. While appreciating the difficulty, Adamishin judged that the General Secretary had fumbled the chance that presented itself: 'His one defect is that he allows himself to be distracted. He was distracted in Reykjavik. He went after the big bird in the sky, forgetting the smaller one in his hands.'[29]

Gorbachëv and Shevardnadze could at least agree that they should not mark time after Reykjavik. Ambassador Dubinin talked to Shultz on 14 October 1986. He passed on greetings from Gorbachëv and Shevardnadze, to whom he had spoken after the close of the summit. Gorbachëv wanted Shultz to know that he was pleased about the 'good atmospherics' and 'real progress' in Iceland. Dubinin's instructions were to discover the reasons why Reagan had objected to the idea of confining testing to laboratories – he was to explain that Gorbachëv believed that this was a concession that would permit the Americans to conduct all the research they craved. Soviet and American leaders would then have years to work out an agreement that both sides would find acceptable. Gorbachëv was willing to expand the definition of laboratory so as to include test ranges. His one big proviso was that the Americans would be barred from carrying out tests in outer space. His message to Shultz was that he had shown a flexibility on this question that should have enabled an agreement in Iceland. He hoped that Reagan and his officials would now recognize the genuineness of his offer. Dubinin tried to kick-start the renewal of negotiations by asking when Shevardnadze could meet Shultz again.[30]

Gorbachëv wanted to continue to make it difficult for the White House to reject his overtures. He felt sharp frustration about how Reagan and his officials kept quiet about the Soviet offer to allow laboratory research on space defence.[31] He hoped to nudge the West Europeans into bearing down on Reagan. With this in mind, he contemplated making trips to London and Paris. Shevardnadze too ought to go on a European tour. Everything should be tried to render the Strategic Defense Initiative less of a threat for the USSR.[32] It turned out that Gorbachëv's work schedule made it impossible for him to leave Moscow that winter. But Shevardnadze was able to visit Vienna, where he held discussions with NATO leaders. On 4 November 1986 he implored British Foreign Secretary Geoffrey Howe to recognize how far Gorbachëv had moved towards compromise on the Defense Initiative.[33] Shevardnadze was loyally fulfilling official policy.[34] Privately he was urging Gorbachëv to change tactics. Something else had to be tried – and the sooner, the better.

One of the factors holding back Gorbachëv was his sense that he had to keep the general staff onside. He knew that Akhromeev had trouble of his own after Reykjavik. Whereas the Politburo found him a stern defender of military prerogatives, his fellow commanders felt that he made too many compromises. He was navigating a passage between Scylla and Charybdis. Matters came to a head when he gave a lecture to the General Staff Academy and proposed a new military doctrine for the USSR. He made the case for both superpowers to shift their emphasis towards defensive strategic planning. The priority should be to prevent war of any kind. Akhromeev stunned the Academy by renouncing the traditional notion of immediate, all-out retaliation to an American attack and advocating the case for defensive operations that might last for several weeks. Only if this failed would he approve a nuclear offensive against American cities.[35] Akhromeev was turning Soviet military doctrine upside down. There was total silence during the lecture. But as soon as he finished, he experienced a barrage of criticism for two long hours. Opinion in the officer corps was almost universally hostile. Akhromeev recognized that if he was going to remain an effective Chief of the General Staff, he had to bring Academy personnel into his drafting team.[36]

He had never been an untroubled reformer. But he recognized that times had changed and that the political leadership would no longer allow the freedom that the armed forces had enjoyed before 1985. He thought that he could get more for them by bargaining with Gorbachëv rather than treating him as an adversary.

This meant that the tension between Politburo and General Staff was going to continue. Each knew about the game that the other was playing. Strains were also growing inside the Politburo as its members digested the reports on Reykjavik. On 30 October 1986 Gromyko, veteran of countless summits, made his first criticism since departing from the Foreign Affairs Ministry. He had no objection to the goal of an arms reduction agreement but called for a clear definition of 'laboratory' research and testing for the Strategic Defense Initiative. Gromyko implied a fear the Americans might run rings around Gorbachëv. This stung Gorbachëv into replying: 'So what is to be done? Should we break off the talks?' Gromyko refused to back down and argued the need to cease negotiating on the basis of an all-or-nothing package. Gorbachëv clung single-mindedly to his tactics. He also saw his personal contribution as crucial: 'Nothing is going to be resolved in Geneva. That is garbage!'[37] Summits in his opinion were the sole key to progress. He desired to attract West European governments to a joint campaign against the Defense Initiative in the years before it became deployable. Meanwhile, he suggested, the USSR had to look as if it was negotiating from a position of strength.[38]

The problem, as the entire Politburo had known for a long time, was that the USSR's economy faced grave difficulties. Gorbachëv had

pretended the opposite to Reagan, but when talking to Soviet ministers, he admitted that the budget still relied excessively on oil and gas
exports and that technological progress and labour productivity were
chronically poor.[39] Drastic reform, he contended, was overdue. He
told them that no approval would now be given for big new projects.
There could also be no increase in wages. His only proviso was that
retail prices should be held steady at a time when society had yet to
receive material benefit from *perestroika*. And what if Eastern Europe
and other socialist countries pleaded for assistance? Gorbachëv was
emphatic: 'No promises to anyone, however much they ask.'[40]

Reagan could see no advantage in relaxing his stance. Poindexter
supported him, taking note of the hints dropped by Dubinin that there
might be some 'give' in the Soviet bargaining position.[41] The President
waited on events. He reckoned that if America were to offer concessions, the USSR would simply pocket them without giving anything
of importance in return. He felt that the Kremlin was at last beginning
to confront its problems – the Iceland talks had revealed that Soviet
leaders recognized their need to integrate the USSR into the world
economy. America, he sensed, had the upper hand. Reagan's idea was
to keep the initiative by modernizing the American forces and sustaining work on the Defense Initiative. Soviet politics were in enormous
flux. The White House had to be ready for the possibility that
Gorbachëv might suddenly crumble in the face of American demands.
Reagan ordered the Joint Chiefs of Staff to prepare a contingency
scheme under the direction of the Defense Department; he demanded
a progress report by December 1986. He also instructed the CIA to
keep a lookout for any new shifts in the Politburo's policies.[42] He
meant to prevent Gorbachëv from setting the negotiating framework.
If the Kremlin leaders wanted an arms reduction treaty with America,
they would have to meet his basic requirements. He confirmed the list
of the quotas and categories of weapons that the joint working groups
had agreed in Reykjavik. He was intent on holding the Soviet side to
the compromises they had made.[43]

As Reagan waited for his pressure to have its effect, his administration tumbled back into its internal disputes. Weinberger did not like
what he heard about the Iceland discussion and tried to toughen
America's stance in the weeks that followed. Weinberger objected to
any idea that the American delegation in the Geneva talks should
negotiate a definition of what was permitted under the Anti-Ballistic
Missile Treaty. He demanded complete freedom for work on the

Strategic Defense Initiative. Shultz could not see why the two sides could not at least start to discuss the subject.[44] Weinberger also urged that the President should highlight the requirement for reliable procedures of verification. If America were to agree on arms reduction, it had to secure firm safeguards. He warned against giving the impression that the American side was willing to makes compromises in order to attain an agreement. Weinberger advocated a policy of recalcitrance.[45] He had his usual ally in Casey, who disliked any unequivocal commitment to sweeping away all nuclear arms capacity. Casey pointed out that America and the USSR were not the only powers with such weaponry; he urged the desirability of moderating official optimism about how to achieve cooperation with all of them. The world would remain full of dangers in the years ahead.[46]

Shultz replied with a rationale for American optimism. He asserted that Reagan had succeeded in pushing Soviet leaders into assenting to drastic cuts in nuclear weaponry. They had also essentially accepted the four-part agenda that Reagan in 1984 had laid down for talks with Moscow. Gorbachëv now recognized that he could achieve no progress towards disarmament without giving way on human rights, regional conflicts and bilateral exchanges. The American administration ought to get ready to resume the negotiations.[47]

With this in mind, he drafted a 'notional plan' for Reagan to realize the American agenda. Strategic nuclear stockpiles should be halved and intermediate-range weaponry completely eliminated. This should be done in five years in the first of three stages to the accompaniment of agreed procedures for verification. If Gorbachëv would consent to detaching the Strategic Defense Initiative question from talks about offensive nuclear weapons, the American side should commit itself to adhering to the Anti-Ballistic Missile Treaty for the next ten years. International citizen-to-citizen contacts should be facilitated in stage one – and restrictions on foreign broadcasts and publications should be lifted. The USSR and America should cease to interfere in the world's regional conflicts. In stage two, which would also last five years, Shultz proposed to reduce each side's strategic weapons stockpiles from 6,000 warheads to a 'small residual strategic force'. Free movement of persons and information across national boundaries had to be introduced; there should also be guarantees of freedom of speech. The third and final stage would involve 'a legal enforcement regime for a world free of nuclear and mass destruction weapons'. All obstacles to international trade would be dismantled.[48]

Shultz's proposals were a delayed reaction to the three-stage scheme that Gorbachëv had announced in January 1986. There was little support for them in the White House – and not just on the part of Weinberger and Casey. Perhaps there was a recognition among those who wanted to renew the negotiating process that the Politburo would reject the proposals. At best, they would make good propaganda. The demand for freedom of information, expression and travel was entirely justifiable but unrealistic at that moment: it was tantamount to calling on the Soviet leaders to decommunize their country.

The changing political scene complicated the tasks of the American administration. On 4 November 1986, elections gave victory to the Democrats, and the Republicans lost control of the Senate. This was not quite the disaster it seemed for Reagan's prospects in foreign policy because the Republican Party contained the most acidic opponents of conciliation with the USSR. But Reagan had to continue to thwart Gorbachëv's efforts to appeal to the Democratic senators as the world's great peacemaker. Shultz made yet another attempt to restart the momentum of talks with Soviet leaders. He advised a campaign to highlight the Kremlin's abuse of human rights. At the same time he warned of the need to recognize the growing concerns about American foreign policy in NATO. London, Paris and Bonn may have declared support for how America was handling the USSR, but in private they expressed apprehension whenever Reagan talked to Gorbachëv about doing away with all nuclear missiles. Thatcher unremittingly drew attention to the dangers involved. The removal of nuclear missiles would leave Western Europe exposed to the USSR's enormous superiority in conventional forces. The military menace from the East would not disappear but increase. Shultz recognized the strength of these arguments. He told Reagan of the urgent need to work up proposals that would prevent Gorbachëv from driving a wedge into the middle of NATO.[49]

The West European leaders were not the only people who were disconcerted about the President's policies. Many of his own officials thought that he was risking too much. Weinberger and Casey agreed with the arguments that Thatcher was making. They were not alone. Poindexter had always believed it would be disastrous to eliminate nuclear weaponry; he believed in mutually assured destruction as the best way to keep world peace. Nitze was in favour of resuming talks with the USSR but feared that Gorbachëv wanted to get rid of nuclear weapons solely in order to put Western Europe at the mercy of Soviet tanks and troops. European experts in the State Department too saw that the Reykjavik proceedings would agitate America's allies – Rozanne Ridgway was only half-joking when she said: 'A lot of people are starting to love the bomb.'[50] Reagan received a warning that the Joint Chiefs of Staff were like to demand an increase in the military budget: if the President wanted to reduce the nuclear weapon stockpiles, the army would inevitably ask for extra divisions for its conventional forces.[51] Shultz agreed that a new military plan was essential after Iceland. He proposed a diminution of state welfare provision so as to meet the costs of his suggestions.[52]

Reagan made no reply, and the question about how to pay for the consequences of nuclear disarmament was left dangling in the air.[53] One thing was fixed in his mind: the desire to end reliance on mutually assured destruction. Global affairs had to rest on a different basis. On this, Reagan never wavered.

PART THREE

PART THREE

22. THE SOVIET PACKAGE UNTIED

The President experienced a political earthquake in early November 1986 after a Lebanese newspaper exposed illegal dealings between American administration officials and the Iranian government. The press soon discovered that Colonel Oliver North, a National Security Council staff official, had organized the secret sale of weapons to Iran despite the trade embargo that had been in place since 1979. As their part of the deal, the authorities in Tehran agreed to use their influence to obtain the release of US citizens who were being held hostage in Lebanon. North transferred the profits to the Contra rebels fighting Daniel Ortega's Sandinista government in Nicaragua. The American administration sought the overthrow of Ortega as a revolutionary who threatened its influence throughout Central America, and North assumed that he was acting in line with what the President wanted.

North's Iranian scheme circumvented the need to apply to the American Senate for funds to intervene in the Nicaraguan civil war. Reporters soon uncovered a trail of illegal arms transactions, and it became clear that a serious constitutional infringement had occurred. North, moreover, had liaised with Poindexter, who resigned as National Security Adviser on 24 November 1986. Their joint disgrace intensified discussion in the media. The White House was in turmoil. There was speculation that there was evidence implicating the President in the affair. Reagan saw the need to change the personnel around him and replaced Don Regan with Howard Baker as his chief of staff. Questions arose about whether the President had the right environment for the calm conduct of foreign policy. Reagan emphasized that he remained in charge and had not gone soft on communism. Speaking to White House senior staff on 26 November 1986, he said: 'And you know, after using those words before audiences across the country, I just can't help thinking that, for this administration, peace through strength is more than a policy. It's a promise – a promise we've made to the people – and a promise we intend to keep.' He declared it as his abiding priority to guarantee American military preparedness and pursue the Strategic Defense Initiative.[1]

On 28 November 1986 American critics felt justified in their concerns when Reagan sanctioned the deployment of an extra B-52 bomber equipped with cruise missiles. This was one more than the SALT-II treaty appeared to permit, and there was a risk of a breakdown of talks with the USSR. Deputy Foreign Affairs Minister Alexander Bessmertnykh prepared a diplomatic note to the effect that the Soviet Union no longer felt constrained by its treaty obligations. He received support from others in the ministry as well as from Kornienko and Akhromeev. Expert analysis, however, showed that the Americans had probably committed no infringement if Soviet submarines were taken into account. Kataev in the Party Defence Department suggested that Reagan was trying to wrong-foot the USSR by provoking a hostile reaction – he passed on his thinking to Shevardnadze and Zaikov in advance of a decision by the Politburo.[2]

Gorbachëv listened to both sides of the argument. Bessmertnykh was furious about the Americans: 'And so, do we have to look on this quietly? We'll show them! . . .' The General Staff was of the same opinion and signalled a desire to revert to expanding the Soviet nuclear arsenal if America should continue with its current approach.[3] But Kataev won the day. Gorbachëv wanted to avoid doing anything precipitate and claimed that a wild démarche was only to be expected from Reagan at a time when he needed to distract attention from the Iran-Contra scandal and restore his authority. Gorbachëv thought the President's decision was 'destructive' and out of keeping with the understandings achieved in Reykjavik. Gorbachëv thought the Americans might now undertake yet another military 'adventure', perhaps against Nicaragua or Syria. He reasoned that the Soviet leadership should make a sharp objection but continue to attend the Geneva talks. He hoped to use propaganda to shape American and European public opinion. (Endearingly, he commented that the Soviet Life magazine had an impact in America that worried the FBI. Who on earth was feeding him this nonsense?)[4] The Politburo endorsed his measured response to the B-52 deployment, and Shevardnadze undertook to persuade the Americans to adhere to the SALT-II treaty.[5]

One way to outflank Reagan, Gorbachëv said, was to hold an international conference on human rights in Moscow. Having freed Andrei Sakharov from administrative exile in Gorki, he wanted approval for a set of further steps. Gorbachëv asked why, when someone asked to go abroad for three months, permission was granted for only four weeks. Was it really a disaster if people decided not to return to the Soviet Union? He said it was better for the USSR to be rid of its 'riff raff'. The dissidents Orlov and Shcharanski had been freed from captivity in February 1986 and permitted to emigrate, and no damage ensued for Soviet state security.[6] Shevardnadze put Adamishin in charge of renewing policy on human rights and told him to ignore the predictable resistance of the KGB. At the same time he told Grinevski to conduct the talks in Stockholm without yielding to the demands of the military lobby. The General Staff and the Defence Ministry were no longer to determine the agenda. He asked Adamishin and Grinevski to act as battering rams in the cause of reform in foreign policy.[7]

On 19 December 1986 Gorbachëv met with Shevardnadze and his ministry's leading officials. Southern Africa, Lebanon and Nicaragua came up for discussion. Then Gorbachëv focused on the American factor: 'The present administration of the USA is the most reactionary as well as the most unpredictable. As such it is making a crude mistake.' He lamented America's weakness for military 'adventures', citing the recent examples of Libya and Grenada. While holding back from any overreaction, he hoped to exploit the situation politically. Shevardnadze agreed; he warned against any simplistic understanding of current foreign leaders. He stressed that Thatcher was in a strong political position after benefiting from 'a wave of chauvinism' in the United Kingdom. He stressed the need to keep an eye on Gary Hart, a leading contender to become the Democratic candidate in the 1988 US presidential election.[8] Gorbachëv had welcomed Hart to Moscow a few days earlier.[9] Nobody could say who was going to win the presidency, and the Soviet leadership had to keep itself ready for everything.[10] Nevertheless Gorbachëv remained in a quandary. While taking a certain pleasure from the signs of disarray in the American administration, he still could not answer the question for himself: 'What does America really want?'[11]

Analytical papers were prepared for the Big Five, and there was speculation that Reagan might find it difficult to hold on to his entrenched position as his pile of domestic political problems grew.[12] Soviet officials had orders to make enquiries, and yet clarity was difficult to obtain. Arthur Hartman, America's Ambassador to the USSR, explained that the 'zero option' proposal had always referred only to certain categories of nuclear weapons and not to all of them.[13] When the Soviet Foreign Trade Minister talked to former President Nixon in

December 1986, he asked how to kick-start the arms talks again with Reagan. Ambassador Dubinin repeated the enquiry after New Year. Nixon havered, advising that Gorbachëv should communicate directly with the President.[14]

Gorbachëv needed to sort out problems nearer to home as he prepared for the next Central Committee plenum. He had begun the work of forcing change on the General Staff and the Defence Ministry. Now he needed to impose himself on the military sector of Soviet industry. With this in mind he summoned leaders of big enterprises and their ministries to a meeting on 19 January 1987. He spoke bluntly about their failure to meet the country's needs in civilian goods. A drastic shift in priorities was going to be undertaken.[15] The plenum confirmed the need for reforms. Gorbachëv successfully recommended a range of drastic measures. Party posts were to become genuinely elective. Multi-candidate contests were to occur for seats in local soviets. A new law was to be passed on state enterprises which would enable workforces to choose their own managers and influence the organization of production. The party leadership would establish freedom to fill in the 'blank spots' in Soviet history, and Gorbachëv denounced the abuses of the Stalin period and the 'stagnation' that had happened under Brezhnev.[16] The focus was on internal change in the USSR and Gorbachëv said little new about foreign policy and nothing about the conversion of factories to non-military purposes. Nevertheless no plenum for decades had marked out such a prospect of transformation. Many details had yet to be agreed, but there was no doubt about the direction of movement.

The trouble was that Reagan was still no nearer to choosing between Shultz and Weinberger in their chronic dispute about foreign policy. Weinberger set out to rile the Kremlin. In mid-January he let the press know how he was coaxing Reagan to announce his choice of one of the competing options for the Strategic Defense Initiative.[17] When he championed a project to develop a new kinetic energy system to enhance America's military capacity, he knew that this would violate the Anti-Ballistic Missile Treaty.[18] He privately sought out the President and exploited his unease about anyone who was not fully behind the Initiative. This was a tactic that had served Weinberger in the past and drove Shultz and Nitze to distraction. As Nitze pointed out, Weinberger's strident advocacy of the Initiative could have the unintended consequence of turning the American Congress against it. Without adequate funding, it would wither away – and nobody but Gorbachëv would benefit from such an outcome. Shultz wearily concluded that 'the ultimate shoot-out with Weinberger was not far-off'.[19]

At the National Security Planning Group on 26 January Weinberger called for an interpretation of the Anti-Ballistic Missile Treaty that would permit deployment of the Defense Initiative. As everyone knew, this would wreck the talks with the USSR. It was decided to ask the lawyer Abe Sofaer to conduct an impartial review of what the treaty might or might not allow.[20] This failed to cool down Weinberger. At the President's meeting with his senior advisers on 3 February he repeated his call for the right to deploy. Shultz had to leave mid-discussion. Reagan in his absence mooted that America should proceed to deployment without making a public disclosure. It took National Security Adviser Carlucci to explain that this was unfeasible without a change to the National Security Decision Directive of October 1985, and that Congress would need notification. Reagan continued to push the matter until Nitze warned against constitutional impropriety.[21] Still Weinberger refused to accept defeat. The original schedule was to introduce the Defense Initiative at the turn of the millennium. On 4 February Weinberger advised the House Appropriations Subcommittee on Defense that he expected America to be able to deploy much earlier.[22] He also strove to toughen the CoCom restrictions by thwarting Soviet efforts to obtain products of biotechnology, communication systems and kinetic energy.[23]

Eventually Shultz put a hand on the steering wheel and wrote firmly to Reagan, reminding him that 'obviously, instantaneous deployment is not even conceptually possible'. He pointed out that ill-guarded statements could cause trouble in America and abroad. It was imperative, he said, to enable Sofaer to complete his review unimpeded. Shultz followed this up in conversation with the President, laboriously going over the arguments until he felt sure that his boss appreciated them.[24] He was forthright with the press about his scepticism about the prospect for early deployment. Everyone knew that he had Weinberger in his sights.[25]

Shultz could take comfort from events around the world. The Soviet leadership wanted to withdraw from its war in Afghanistan. Eastern Europe was no longer frozen in changelessness. He sensed that the Communist Bloc was beginning to crack up, and he asked the Deputy Secretary in the State Department, John Whitehead, to make a series of visits to the region. (Shultz had to surmount unease in the

State Department and the National Security Council about the possibility that Whitehead's tours might enhance the credibility of the
communist leaders.)[26] West European leaders shared Shultz's feeling
that opportunities existed to increase influence in Eastern Europe, but
the question was how to go about this. Mitterrand urged caution. As
regards Poland, he reckoned that Jaruzelski was preferable to any of
his likely successors. Kohl advised Mitterrand that Gorbachëv could
make it easier to liaise with Honecker. He was under the impression
– a false impression – that the East German leader enjoyed a high reputation in the Kremlin; he also suggested that Husák had an enhanced
scope for manoeuvre in his policies. On a practical level, Kohl wanted
to increase aid to Poland. Probably he and his intelligence agencies
were not as ill-informed as might now appear – his real game plan was
to persuade Mitterrand to accept what the West German government
wanted to do.[27]

Western initiatives on the USSR itself were in short supply as the
American administration remained in internal dispute and Reagan
failed to engineer approval for a clear plan of action. Insofar as the
President had a strategy, it was to wait for the Soviet leadership to
yield to the requirements he had set out in Geneva and Reykjavik. This
suited Weinberger, who on 11 January 1987 told the press that he
would not mind if the Moscow summer summit was called off.[28] He
suggested that the Strategic Defense Initiative should complement the
American nuclear arsenal and not replace it; he spoke as if Reagan was
wrong to aim at eliminating atomic warheads.[29] Weinberger warned
about the USSR's secret programmes to develop a ground-based anti-
missile system within the next three years.[30] Appearing before the
Senate Armed Services Committee on 17 February, he predicted that
America would soon be adopting the new broad interpretation of the
Anti-Ballistic Missile Treaty. He said nothing about the Sofaer review.
He gave the impression that his personal preferences were already official policy.[31] Speaking to the New York Times on 24 February, he said
he believed the Defense Initiative system could be brought into service
as early as the year 1994. He stressed: 'A lot of people think that we
have not decided to do this. The President wants to deploy.'[32]

Independent scientific advice quietly cast doubt on Weinberger's
prognosis. The Science Research Laboratory's Thomas H. Johnson,
sceptical as ever, advised Matlock in the National Security Council
that deployment was unlikely to be achieved any earlier than the turn
of the century. The problem was that Weinberger was relying on infor-

mation from Defense Initiative officials who overstated what could soon be achieved. Johnson remarked that America had never taken less than eight years to deploy a newly produced military system – and there was no reason to expect the Initiative to come into operation any sooner.[33]

But all this occurred behind the scenes. Nobody emerged from the American administration to contradict Weinberger. The result was panic in Moscow political circles. It seemed to Soviet leaders that America was hell-bent on intensifying the arms race – or at the very least that Weinberger might soon bring the President over to such a policy. Something had to be done to prevent this from happening. If Weinberger had his way, the USSR would have to drop its commitment to economic reform and dedicate increased expenditure on military technology. Shevardnadze had failed to persuade Gorbachëv that he would achieve nothing so long as he insisted on a single general package of proposals for arms reduction. The Americans, as Shevardnadze knew, were never going to yield to this demand. He had felt frustrated about Gorbachëv's negotiating tactics since the middle of the Reykjavik summit. Subsequent contact with the Americans convinced him that he was right and Gorbachëv wrong. But he could do nothing to change the policy until others in the Politburo shared his viewpoint and were willing to stand up and be counted inside the leadership.

As it turned out, Weinberger's campaign gave unintentional help to Shevardnadze's cause. As early as 20 January 1987, when the Big Five met to consider the latest news from America, there was unanimous approval for a challenge to Gorbachëv's tactics. His rigidity was not just dubious: it was downright dangerous, and a switch of direction was an urgent requirement. Zaikov and everyone else appended their signature. All the interested agencies were in agreement about the desirability of a fresh bargaining posture. Even Defence Minister Sokolov endorsed the suggestion to untie the negotiating package so as to enable a separate deal on medium-range nuclear weapons in Europe. The Reykjavik understandings about the other categories of weaponry, they agreed, should be adhered to. The Big Five's priority was to avert the possibility that Reagan's administration might break the Anti-Ballistic Missile Treaty. If Weinberger got his way, progress in the talks at Geneva would become impossible. The USSR badly needed to display an openness to compromise. It had to strengthen the hands of those in the American Congress who wanted success in Switzerland.[34]

Gorbachëv hardly knew what hit him at the next Politburo on 26 February. After itemizing the problems in Geneva, he could only propose to invite Shultz to Moscow to discuss the obstacles. This failed to impress Gromyko, who repeated the case for change in the Soviet negotiating posture. He advocated an unbundling of the USSR's negotiating package so as to enable the question of intermediate-range nuclear missiles to be dealt with separately. Gromyko made no apology for having once championed the installation of the SS-20s in Eastern Europe.[35] He failed to convince Gorbachëv, who described Reagan as only pretending to want world peace while threatening the USSR with the Strategic Defense Initiative.[36] Ligachëv supported Gromyko's side of the argument – something without precedent in the Politburo.[37] Yakovlev joined everyone else. While continuing to praise Gorbachëv's tactics at Reykjavik, he sent him a memo arguing that the situation had changed since Irangate. Now the best way to win over world opinion and make it difficult for Reagan and Weinberger to forestall a treaty with the USSR was to untie the package. If the Americans refused to negotiate, their intransigence would damage their reputation. Yakovlev scoffed at those Western Sovietologists who forecast material ruin and popular discontent: he predicted a great economic future for the USSR.[38]

The Politburo was asserting its supremacy, and it would have been unwise for the General Secretary ignore it when both conservatives and reformers were so united against him. After a lengthy discussion he gave in and adopted what Gromyko was recommending. Nothing like it had happened since 1985. The Politburo knew how much this was demanding of him: he was surrendering a position that he had fervently defended for over a year. But he had seen sense at last, and the Politburo had no hesitation in agreeing to the change of policy.[39] No public announcement was made. The leadership desired to preserve its image of imperturbable calm. But some kind of message had to reach the Americans if the changed stance was to have any impact. An arcane method was devised. Two days later, on 28 February, Gorbachëv issued a statement to the Western powers as Chairman of the USSR Defence Council. For the first time he spoke of the Strategic Defense Initiative without mentioning research and testing. Now his only gripe was against future deployment.[40] He had to hope that the White House would welcome his move and resume talks in a constructive spirit. Surely Reagan would see how much he had moved in the direction of compromise.

Although Gromyko had led the way in arguing the case at the Politburo, he was a declining force. What had occurred was a victory for the Shevardnadze line. Shevardnadze himself declined to celebrate. He understood the need to protect the General Secretary's prestige if *perestroika* was to succeed. Whenever his aides carped about the inconsistency in Soviet foreign policy, he shut them up and told them to accept the idea of 'not everything immediately'. He was willing to play the long game.[41]

Reagan proceeded with caution as he reflected in his diary on Gorbachëv's overture: 'It looks good but we mustn't get too carried away until we see how far they'll go on verification.'[42] He refused to be bounced into direct negotiations as had happened in Iceland. He anyway had his hands full with the aftershock of Irangate. When writing to friends, he hardly mentioned the USSR for several weeks while the American media's preoccupation was with the scandal about Colonel North, Tehran and the Nicaraguan Contras.[43] There was a growing public concern about his Soviet policy. Gorbachëv was pleased to hear in March that six former US defence secretaries had signed a letter to the President and Congress calling for adherence to the traditional interpretation of the Anti-Ballistic Missile Treaty. Senator Sam Nunn, Chairman of the Senate Armed Forces Committee, supported their initiative.[44] Reagan still declined to budge. But he did at least decide to send Shultz to Moscow to scout the opportunities. Not everyone in the administration was pleased about the trip, and some suspected that Shultz might offer undue concessions. Weinberger advised the President to limit the Secretary of State's negotiating licence in the Soviet capital.[45] Reagan agreed with this and on 9 April signed an order prescribing what Shultz could say and stipulating the need to stay within the bounds of earlier directives.[46]

Weinberger stuck to his opinion that patient toughness towards the USSR had proved its effectiveness. Gorbachëv had cracked once and should continue to receive the same treatment. Premature concessions were not in the American interest.[47]

Others in the administration were inclined to assume a more constructive stance. The decision was taken to expand trade with the USSR, and approval was given for the export of gas and oil industrial equipment.[48] Pressure had been applied by American manufacturers, who resented how the Japanese were signing contracts while they had to hold back.[49] But the administration remained annoyed that the Soviet state had failed to fulfil its obligation to buy a regular quota of

grain from Midwest farmers.[50] Fresh talks on the subject took place
from February 1987.[51] Since the moment that Reagan revoked the
cereal export embargo, the USSR had become the second biggest
market for American grain, and the White House was sensitive to the
domestic agricultural lobby.[52] Every American official was aware of
the reasons why Moscow had failed to honour its obligation. The
Saudis for their own internal reasons were flooding the world market
with their petrochemical exports, and the result was a prolonged
depression of the price paid for Soviet energy products. The Americans discerned the implications without drawing drastic conclusions.
Always the concern was that the Politburo might prove able to ignore
its budgetary malaise and rejoin the arms race with America. Washington was going to take no chances.

Shultz brought a personal letter from Reagan to Moscow, and
Gorbachëv was delighted about its conciliatory tone. Reagan still complained that 'much more needs to be done' about human rights and
that the dialogue on regional conflicts had been quite 'fruitless';[53] but
at the same time he was eager to make progress towards an arms
reduction agreement. The problem for Gorbachëv was that America
was increasing its stocks of short-range rocketry – including Lance
missiles – in advance of the time when both sides would eliminate all
such missiles. Although Shultz felt he could give way on this matter, he
made a fresh demand about 'sub-limits' for other categories of nuclear
weaponry. Gorbachëv immediately accused him of pulling back from
the Reykjavik understandings. Shultz made no attempt to contradict
him; he also refrained from answering a direct question about whether
America and the USSR in his opinion had attained 'strategic parity'. He
laid emphasis on the realistic possibilities of striking an important
deal.[54] Gorbachëv failed to mention his own recent offer to unbundle
his arms talks package. Instead he asked Shultz to appreciate how flexible he had been in Iceland in consenting to laboratory research for the
Strategic Defense Initiative. As if sensing that he was in danger of
spoiling the atmosphere, he assured Shultz that he was still 'willing to
look for compromise on the basis of such an approach'.[55]

Gorbachëv claimed to have chided the Americans by saying: 'And
what's happening? Nothing. Are you capable of anything or not? Your
behaviour is politically inexplicable. You insist that you are observing
important changes in the USSR, but you do not make any corrections
to your policies.' He had rebuked Shultz and the President for treating
the USSR's latest proposals like a bowl of porridge that was too hot to

consume. Gorbachëv had made light of America's objections about Soviet espionage: 'You know about us, and we know about you. And that's a good thing.' He concluded that even if a deal on intermediate-range nuclear missiles was possible, the chances of a further agreement were slim.[56] Shevardnadze reported that Shultz had stressed that everything depended on sanction from the American Congress. Gorbachëv joked that even if a treaty was signed, Zaikov would cause trouble by using the financial savings to build more rockets of other categories. He affirmed a confidence in the approach that the Soviet leaders had been taking: 'We are holding to the correct line. They will not get away from us, we will persist like this.'[57]

Shevardnadze issued clear guidelines to his ministry. On 2 May he told officials: 'Our power lies not in our number of rockets but in a stable and strong economy. It's not the missile launchers that guarantee the country's security so much as high labour productivity, the yield of cereal agriculture or the productivity of the young stud horse.' He itemized serious 'mistakes' that the leadership had made before 1985: the installation of the SS-20s in Europe, the production of chemical weapons, the invasion of Afghanistan and the policy on Cambodia. He lamented that the USSR was ten years late in taking human rights seriously after the Helsinki Final Act was signed in 1975. As regards the Strategic Defense Initiative, Shevardnadze groaned: 'Have we worked out what it is? Even from the military viewpoint it's not clear to us, even now. And such criticism as exists of that programme is not our own but the Western one that we've only picked up for hire.' He was mixing a fresh cocktail of foreign policy and asked his audience to speak out even if they disliked the taste. Nobody uttered any criticism. Shevardnadze knew better than to conclude that he had everyone on his side. He had yet to weed out all the traditionalists. But his confidence was high. He had Gorbachëv's support. The reform of foreign policy that the two of them had started was set to continue.[58]

They were adept at making the most of events, and luck had an influence. On 28 May a bizarre incident occurred in Soviet air space between the Baltic Sea and Moscow when Mathias Rust, a West German teenager, flew a Cessna aeroplane from Helsinki. It was an unauthorized flight. Rust moved into Soviet air space at a point a little east of Tallinn. He had a half-baked idea about delivering a manifesto directly to Gorbachëv about how to bring peace to the world. It was a cloudy day. Piloting very low to evade the Warsaw Pact's radar facilities, he succeeded in reaching Moscow and landed on Red Square. In earlier years he might have been intercepted and shot down; but when the higher defence authorities had received an alert about the aerial incursion, they were reluctant to attack the Cessna. Their minds turned back to the furore that had followed the destruction of South Korean airliner KAL007. Rust was apprehended on climbing out of his cockpit. As he eagerly explained his thinking to KGB interrogators, the initial Soviet suspicion was that he belonged to a vast international conspiracy. The world's news media poked fun at the entire communist order. The mighty USSR had never looked so foolish. While its arms talks officials had been discussing how to reduce the threat of a world war without diminishing the USSR's defensive capacity, the Soviet early-warning system had been exposed as ineffective.

Gorbachëv happened to be in East Berlin for a meeting of the Political Consultative Committee of the Warsaw Pact. While he was there, he talked about the need to recognize that there was an 'imbalance' of forces in Europe. The Warsaw Pact had a quantitative superiority that was unjustifiable if the USSR and its allies wished to conciliate NATO.[59] The news about the young West German came through by telegram and Gorbachëv immediately admitted to fellow leaders that it was a grave humiliation.[60] Although the East European leaders tried to express sympathy, their every word twisted a knife in the wound. Zhivkov remarked that if a sports plane could elude the USSR's radar network, so too could an enemy missile.[61] (Or was the Bulgarian leader deliberately teasing his Soviet counterpart?) But the embarrassment was only one side of the political coin. Rust's flight was an adventitious occurrence for the Kremlin reformers. Gorbachëv and Shevardnadze immediately spotted their long-sought opportunity to put the General Staff and Defence Ministry in their place. Shevardnadze celebrated by opening a bottle of brandy in his hotel room.[62]

When Gorbachëv convened the Politburo in Moscow on 30 May, he asked for a report from Defence Minister Sokolov about how the young German flyer had got so far before being spotted. Sokolov tried everyone's patience as he laboriously reproduced the various regional testimonies. Gorbachëv sat back while others expressed incredulity that no military personnel along the chain of command had seen fit to intervene. Sokolov began to flounder. Chebrikov explained that whereas the KGB shared responsibility for the country's security on land and in coastal waters, air security was entrusted to the armed forces alone; he wanted no taint of the Rust escapade to cling to his organization. Zaikov, as political overseer of the military industry, insisted that there was nothing wrong with the technical equipment available to the defence agencies. Shevardnadze commented that the Soviet armed forces had enjoyed too much freedom from control for far too long. Heads, he suggested, had to roll. Only then did Sokolov understand that the rest of the Politburo expected him to resign. He complied with deep reluctance. Having played no direct part in the butchery, Gorbachëv expressed thanks for Sokolov's work over many years and asked him to stay in post until a successor was appointed.[63]

Gorbachëv disbelieved Rust's story about his peace mission and ignored the foreign pleas for mercy. The young man had broken the law and deserved punishment.[64] At the same time Gorbachëv repeated the argument he had made in East Berlin that the USSR needed to accept America's case that the Warsaw Pact had numerical superiority in Europe.[65] Shevardnadze supported him. He could see no chance of completing a disarmament treaty until such time as the USSR openly acknowledged that it had more medium-range nuclear missiles in Europe than NATO.[66]

The General Staff and Defence Ministry had suddenly lost any right of resistance because of the Rust affair. A vast process of sackings took place in the armed forces. Gorbachëv was ruthless. He snarled to the Politburo that the bizarre episode showed why it was that the General Staff had objected to an agreement with America on arms inspections: 'It was so that we couldn't see the disorder there.'[67] His choice to replace Sokolov was Dmitri Yazov – apparently he had earned Raisa Gorbachëva's favour for expressing his admiration for the poet Pushkin. Hundreds of top commanders throughout the armed forces were pushed into retirement. The way was becoming clearer to deepen the rapprochement with America. This gave rise to pleasure on the other side of the Atlantic, where Shultz was able to inform Reagan that the Kremlin was at long last willing to negotiate a separate treaty on intermediate- and short-range nuclear forces. On 13 June the President signed a new national security directive that welcomed the Soviet climbdown as a victory for the line he had marked out in Reykjavik.[68]

Shevardnadze held a planning meeting in his ministry on the same day. Everyone agreed that the USSR obtained no true advantage from insisting on keeping a hundred missiles in its Asian territories. As things stood in the Geneva talks, Bessmertnykh said, the Americans could frighten the Chinese with the claim that the USSR had begun to concentrate on them as the enemy. Shevardnadze closed the meeting by telling his officials to 'prepare the question without worrying about the General Staff'.[69] He went straight to Gorbachëv and argued for the removal of all the missiles from Soviet Asia.[70] Having won his struggle to unbundle the Reykjavik package, he wanted to go further and win consent to making Asia free from the menace of nuclear weapons. Gorbachëv demurred. He had humbled the Defence Ministry, and this was not the time to annoy the armed forces unduly. While sharing Shevardnadze's goal of total denuclearization, he wanted to proceed with a degree of political prudence. As ever, he hoped to keep his doubters as well as his followers onside.

23. THE BIG FOUR

A remarkable quartet was powering the rapprochement in world politics. On the American side were Reagan and Shultz; their Soviet opposite numbers were Gorbachëv and Shevardnadze.[1] Reagan and Gorbachëv initiated the process of conciliation at Geneva and Reykjavik, and progress was rapid from 1986. Neither the President nor the General Secretary could not allow foreign policy to occupy their entire time, and it often fell to the Secretary of State and Foreign Affairs Minister to crowbar the general plans and assumptions on to each national agenda sheet. Shultz and Shevardnadze were always prodding their own leaders towards greater boldness in arms reduction talks with the other superpower.

Truth be told, Reagan and Gorbachëv had to take a broad range of factors into consideration and neither could afford to alienate the feelings of influential groups of supporters. They also had to feel that they could safely trust each other. The early summits convinced Reagan that if he wished to achieve the global elimination of nuclear weapons, he was unlikely to find a readier partner than Gorbachëv. He told President Mauno Koivisto of Finland in May 1987 that 'Gorbachëv is motivated less by his interest in developing a positive relationship with us than by the nature of his internal economic situation'. He added: 'He knows what we have long known, namely that his economy is a kind of basket case.'[2] Reagan did not mind if Gorbachëv was not as he liked to appear under public gaze. The point was that the Soviet leader was willing to make a lot of the changes that the Americans demanded. Steadily Reagan was choosing to favour Shultz over Weinberger and Casey. But he hated to fall into dispute with any member of his team. Once when Shultz gave him a draft copy of a speech he intended to make, the President offered no direct criticism. All he would say was: 'Oh yes, George. I looked it over. Not a bad speech. But I wouldn't give it.' This was the nearest he came to a presidential prohibition, and the two of them proceeded to rewrite the speech together.[3]

Reagan baffled people in his own administration, not to mention the Soviet leadership. Gorbachëv and Shevardnadze felt in the best position to take on the task of resolving the enigma since they were the ones who met him face to face.[4] The General Secretary was among the first to understand that Reagan's treatment in the Soviet media was a caricature.[5] The President's charisma was undeniable. Reagan had even won applause from Third World politicians at the United Nations General Assembly.[6] There was something special about him, and Gorbachëv had to get on with him. This was never going to be a smooth process. Gorbachëv said that the President sometimes behaved more like a film actor than a statesman.[7] He assured Warsaw Pact leaders that Reagan did not hold genuine power in the US. According to Gorbachëv, a handful of politicians – indeed principally Shultz – were in charge.[8] Shultz would have briskly disabused him of such an idea; but perhaps Gorbachëv was anyway just sounding off to an audience that wanted to hear him loosing off shots at the President.

Gorbachëv held his tongue when mentioning Reagan to the world's media. Whereas the President continued to make strident anti-Soviet speeches, the General Secretary found comfort in his observation that American officials declined to defend their President whenever Gorbachëv discussed Reagan's utterances.[9] Both Gorbachëv and Shevardnadze were alert to the Washington struggle over policy towards the USSR. The battling between Weinberger and Shultz was well understood, as Shevardnadze indicated: 'It's not just us who have departmental problems.'[10]

Reagan seldom put aside his polemical repertoire. At a meeting with Shevardnadze on 19 September 1986, he fulminated against Marx, the 'Empire of Evil' and the KGB.[11] A year later he provoked Gorbachëv into exclaiming: 'You're not the prosecutor and I'm not the accused. You're not the teacher, I'm not the pupil. And it's the same the other way round too. Otherwise we'll get nowhere.'[12] Reagan's criticism of the USSR's record on human rights grated on Shevardnadze, who expressed his annoyance.[13] He felt that the American attitude resulted in 'the impossibility of conducting a discussion'. He told his aides that the President was trying to spread the Gospel according to Reagan.[14] The Americans continued to raise objections about regional conflicts, human rights abuses and arms control – Reagan arrived at meetings with prepared statements that were akin to charge-sheets against the USSR.[15] Shultz was equally assertive; he refused to let Gorbachëv browbeat him as he had at their first encounter in November 1985. On one of his trips to Moscow, in April 1987, Shultz attended a Jewish seder. Gorbachëv barked at him: 'You live in America: govern America!' For good measure, he added: 'Send your Ambassador over to our Central Committee and get some suggestions for how to change *your* country. You meet with irritants. You ignore the masses of *happy* Jews!' Shultz stood his ground. The time had passed when the General Secretary could tell the Americans how to comport themselves.[16]

The atmosphere lightened once Reagan had decided that conciliation was in the national interest. Gorbachëv accepted that the President came from 'the most conservative part of American capitalism and bosses of the military-industrial complex'; but he also saw that he had a capacity to 'embody purely the human qualities, interests and hopes of ordinary people'.[17] Reagan confided to Shevardnadze that a unique chance existed if the President and General Secretary could stick together; he declared: 'And we're the only ones who can save the world.'[18] Kenneth Adelman later summarized what many in the White House and Kremlin thought about this: 'They were in fairyland.'[19] Reagan sent handwritten letters to Gorbachëv, striving to lessen the formality of their exchanges. He got to know him better by holding frequent conversations with only note-takers and interpreters in attendance.[20] Reagan knew almost no Russian except the mantra he memorized with help from Suzanne Massie: 'Trust but verify [*Doveryai, no proveryai*].'[21] The English language was unknown territory to Gorbachëv, but somehow they managed to communicate warmly, and Reagan commended the General Secretary to the American public as a leader worthy of respect.

Reagan was slower to hit it off with Shevardnadze. At their first encounter, on 28 September 1985, Reagan called for talks to commence at a level above the bureaucratic officialdom. Shevardnadze took offence: 'Neither I nor Mr Shultz is a bureaucrat.'[22] Reagan tried to relax things a few days later by telling some Irish jokes. Ambassador Dobrynin countered with his own anecdote about the Georgians. This was hardly soothing for Shevardnadze, himself from Georgia, who disliked humour based on national stereotypes and hated Russian condescension about the Georgian people. But he could see that he would never get on with the President unless he could join in the jovial atmosphere. He assured Reagan that he was no sourpuss and mentioned that one of Vice President Bush's anecdotes had very much amused him.[23] Gradually he got on easier terms with the President. At a difficult point in White House talks in March 1988, Reagan exclaimed:

'Perhaps I should have stayed in Hollywood.' Shevardnadze replied: 'But then there would be no treaty on intermediate- and short-range rockets.'[24]

The Americans pushed for signed agreements. In autumn 1987, when they thought Gorbachëv was dragging his feet, Shultz was brutally candid with Shevardnadze. If Gorbachëv failed to comply, he would have to deal with whoever next occupied the White House – the implication was that this would not be suit the USSR's interests.[25] On their side, Soviet leaders worried that Reagan's health might give out. One of Shevardnadze's aides noted on 15 September: 'Ronnie was exhausted. He lasted only fifteen minutes. His mouth gaped, his eyes lost their brightness and he looked piteously.'[26] Reagan grew visibly tired and inattentive if a meeting ran over three-quarters of an hour. His way of coping was to tell jokes or to hand over to Shultz.[27] In later years there was to be speculation about whether Alzheimer's disease had already begun to affect him. Weinberger believed him hale and hearty when in office.[28] Richard Allen could recall no signs of memory loss till 1991.[29] Martin Anderson suggested that a horse-riding fall in Mexico in 1989 could have caused the mental decline – the former President suffered a bang on his head and needed a cranial operation to relieve the swelling.[30]

Both sides wished to be on better terms. The friendliness between President and General Secretary was enhanced by the care that Reagan took never to crow over the concessions he extracted from Gorbachëv. Once he achieved a victory, he kept his pleasure to his diary. Results were what counted for him.[31]

Reagan peppered Shevardnadze with questions about Soviet history. This led to some interesting exchanges. When Shultz referred to Shevardnadze's remarks on American ignorance about the USSR, Reagan mentioned the American War of Independence and said: 'We too began with an armed uprising!'[32] Reagan quizzed Shevardnadze about the connection between Lenin and Stalin. Shevardnadze vaguely admitted that Lenin had not achieved everything he wanted. He acknowledged that agriculture in the USSR was 'ineffective', but then changed the subject by claiming to be a better wine-grower than any other foreign minister. Reagan recommended the introduction of private farming. Having read reports of internal opposition to Gorbachëv, Reagan asked whether this was akin to the situation that he himself confronted in the American Congress. Shevardnadze denied any similarity. He said that Gorbachëv faced a problem in changing mentalities more than with organized opposition; he ruefully added: 'It's more difficult to operate in conditions of democracy.' Shevardnadze came back to the agricultural question and asserted that nearly half of Georgia's farm output came from individual production.[33]

This was not something that he would have boasted about in Moscow. But the atmosphere eased, and Shevardnadze jovially requested Reagan to transfer Weinberger to the Ministry of Health. The fact that Reagan took no offence signalled the progress that was being made.[34]

Gromyko and his dourness was a butt of ribaldry for both Soviet and American leaders. Thatcher was another common target. Reagan told a gag about how when she paid a visit to Heaven, God asked her: 'How are things going, My daughter?' Thatcher answered: 'In the first place, I'm not Your daughter; in the second place, You're sitting in *my* place!'[35] (Shevardnadze claimed to have told the same gag at his first meeting with Reagan in September 1985.)[36] At the Moscow summit in summer 1988 Gorbachëv recounted the tale about an old man and woman who found a little basket with an egg inside. Their pleasure faded when suddenly a three-headed dragon emerged from the shell. Reagan responded with a story about how a man worked in a factory making carriages but found that the final products were machine guns.[37] The joshing between Reagan and Gorbachëv kept them both amused. Even so, Gorbachëv held back from using familiar forms of address; his instinct was still to keep some distance between them.[38] The initiative had to come from the older man, and it was not until this summit that Reagan at last asked Gorbachëv whether he could now regard him as a friend.[39]

Their spouses achieved at best only a stiff cordiality with each other. Nancy was not alone in finding Raisa difficult. UK Ambassador Rodric Braithwaite described her as 'teetering on amazingly high heels' and seeming 'artificial and doll-like, with a bird-like voice'. Her hauteur became notorious. When meeting her at a reception, Braithwaite tried to help start their conversation by reminding her who he was. This for some reason annoyed her, and she snapped at him: 'I'm not suffering from sclerosis.'[40] She seldom passed up a chance to compare America unfavourably with the Soviet Union. She exhibited total boredom when Shultz's wife O'Bie escorted her on a tour of Washington – she refused to get out of the limo and look at the Lincoln Memorial. Her edginess was notorious. When she had to shake hands with a line of people at a reception, she would reach for her packet of wet mini-wipes afterwards. The American side described this as her Pontius Pilate syndrome.[41] Americans were accustomed to their own First Lady buttoning her lip when on public display. They disliked Raisa's opinionated outbursts.[42] But Gorbachëv knew that there was much more to his wife than her image in Europe and North America and he was comforted by her presence.

Not everyone thought ill of her. On the trip to India in November 1986, she earned approval for her 'philosophical curiosity'.[43] Her problems arose when people had definite expectations about her. She bristled. She got bored very easily. She talked a lot. Underneath her brash exterior she was a pensive observer who wanted the best for her husband and their country.

In December 1988, when Gorbachëv drew together the Soviet team in New York before giving a big speech to the United Nations General Assembly, he felt no embarrassment in tenderly and respectfully asking for Raisa's opinion in front of the others.[44] She gradually learned to be less assertive. For instance, she deliberately moved to the side when Gorbachëv and Thatcher posed for photographers outside 10 Downing Street in April 1989.[45] She tried to avoid flamboyant clothes that might irritate the average Soviet TV viewer. At her husband's speech in the Guildhall on the same London trip, she decided not to wear a hat and gloves. (Mrs Thatcher, apparently wishing to make things easier for her, did the same.)[46] Soviet diplomat Anatoli Adamishin had not been among her sympathizers until he sat next to her at a performance by the Harlem Ballet in New York in May 1988. Her voice full of emotion, she exclaimed: '. . . But what difficult times we're living through!' From that moment Adamishin began to see her as the woman who had come to Moscow as a poor girl from the provinces and made a success of herself.[47] But ordinary Russians saw nothing of this vulnerability. They thought of her as pushy whereas Gorbachëv in reality badly needed her in the role of political confidante.

O'Bie Shultz and Nanuli Shevardnadze were content to stay out of the limelight, and they formed a friendly bond after meeting in 1985. The two couples got on well. Shevardnadze and his wife were people of emotional sensitivity – Nanuli looked after her autistic granddaughter during weekdays when their daughter was at work.[48] O'Bie, a former nurse, warmed to her. Their friendliness contrasted with the frostiness that separated Raisa and Nancy.

Shevardnadze enjoyed Shultz's company, sensing that he had a 'more realistic' viewpoint on international relations than Reagan's other leading officials.[49] In September 1985 he confided in him that he had bought a bottle of vodka in New York when such a purchase would have involved hours of queuing in Moscow.[50] He nursed 'good working contacts' with Shultz even after the disappointment at Reykjavik.[51] On more than one occasion he half-warned, half-implored: 'Don't try to mess around with the problems in the Caucasus.'[52] Shultz reciprocated Shevardnadze's warmth. In April 1987 he surprised him at a supper party in Moscow:

> And so some people gave me a toast, and I said, 'I'm not going to do that.' So I got the word—I got the sheet music of the song 'Georgia On My Mind' and I got the words translated into Russian. So came my time, I handed that to Shevardnadze . . . And then I had a recording of the Torch Singers singing it. Then I had three guys from our embassy who were Russian speakers sing it. Then I sang it. That was my toast. He loved it. He absolutely loved it . . . But then he said something very interesting. He said, 'Thank you, George. That shows respect.' I thought it was a really interesting reaction. And it tended to help in our negotiation. It kind of broke ice and changed the atmosphere.[53]

The other three singers were Jack Matlock, Tom Simons and the American official interpreter.[54] It was an experience that Shevardnadze found very touching.[55]

Shultz took pleasure in the joint progress they were making. Shevardnadze effusively agreed: 'One of my friends . . . asked me whether I'm ready to fly to Washington again to bring things to completion. I told him: I'd even travel to Mars with Shultz. On this occasion I've come to Washington, but Mars isn't off limits.'[56] Shultz could see that the Soviet leaders were groping for ways to handle the American political environment. Noting that the Politburo was hoping to invite the leaders of the American Congress to Moscow, he advised that a bigger group would help in getting the necessary support.[57] He referred to him openly as 'my friend Shevardnadze'.[58] As the partnership between Washington and Moscow deepened, Shultz ventured to counsel Gorbachëv about public relations. In December 1987 Gorbachëv was preening himself after a press conference in Washington. Shultz disabused him about his performance, which had been rambling and tendentious; he said he needed to change his style or risk losing his audience in America. Gorbachëv took the criticism in good part, laughing and pumping Shultz's hand.[59]

This reflected Gorbachëv's recognition of the importance of Shultz for the pursuit of agreements. He spoke appreciatively about him at the Politburo in April 1986, mentioning him as a 'special figure' who knew 'where politics begins – in the mud'. He and Shultz had plenty of difficult discussions. But Gorbachëv had learned that it was more effective to persuade him than browbeat him.[60]

Shultz bargained hard but he also engaged in fundamental intellectual debate. For one of his early meetings with Shevardnadze, he and Charles Hill prepared a statement of the arguments against closed societies as they flew across the Atlantic.[61] For talks with Gorbachëv in April 1987 he brought along charts illustrating how trends in the world economy were working against the USSR.[62] In March 1988 he explained to him how the economies of their two countries were projected to develop through to the end of the twentieth century. Pointing to his diagram, Shultz indicated that both America and the Soviet Union would soon have a decreased share of global production. The implications for the Kremlin were dire.[63] Shultz had been talking for many years about the Age of Information; he argued that communist rulers faced a choice between their fear of the subversive potential of information technology and their need to keep pace with economic change.[64] Apparently Gorbachëv made no attempt to dismiss this analysis. He recognized the need to keep abreast of what was happening around the world; and he apparently accepted that if Shultz was right in his forecasts, cooperation between the superpowers could be in their common interest.[65]

The Ministry of Foreign Affairs too studied what Shultz said about 'the information revolution'.[66] But practical change was minimal. Soviet leaders might nod approvingly in conversation, but they failed to follow up with action. Shultz refused to give up on them, as he was to recall:

> They were intrigued. We set up a little working group and I had a person—Dick [Sollen] was my policy-planning person—they had a separate person. So they tried to develop this kind of material and I think it had an impact in the end. For example, their attitude toward immigration, because I basically said, 'Here, in the information age, if you run a closed compartmental society, you're going to fall behind, because everybody else is interchanging ideas and it moves like lightning all the time. So you've got to open up.'[67]

In April 1988 Shultz tried again by telling Gorbachëv that the Americans had forty-eight times as many computers per head of the population than the USSR. Shultz – in one of his least diplomatic comments – said that only Moscow's nuclear weapons stopped America from handling the USSR like it did Panama.[68] Usually he was more tactful. He valued the environment of political and intellectual trust he shared with Gorbachëv and Shevardnadze.

The American and Soviet leaderships warmed to each other despite recurrent moments of irritation. Big interests of politics, economics and ideology were being contested, and each side felt that the other had much to learn about its counterpart. But it was surely of some significance that neither Gorbachëv nor Shevardnadze tried to give a sermon on the virtues of communism. They tended to focus on practical bargaining. The truth was that they were the ones who were yielding ground in the talks. The American administration laid down demands on a range of topics – not just about nuclear weaponry but also about human rights and regional conflicts. Reagan signalled that he and his officials felt no domestic pressure to sign agreements with Moscow. Gorbachëv persuaded the Politburo that he himself was not compromising the USSR's vital interests; and he and Shevardnadze made it their job to get on friendly terms with the Americans. Reagan and Shultz, appreciating that they had the Soviet leaders on the run, sensibly avoided humbling them in public. It was better to prevent the flow of concessions by the Soviet side from stagnating. And in any case they were beginning to find that they got on rather well with Gorbachëv and Shevardnadze. Together they formed the Big Four that was bringing the Cold War towards its close.

24. GETTING TO KNOW THE ENEMY

World politics were changing at an accelerating rate, and American officials saw the need to check its fancies against the facts. Unfortunately the Kremlin continued to put up barriers of mystery. In mid-June 1986, however, there seemed to be a breach in the wall when National Security Adviser John Poindexter received a startling memo in this connection from his subordinate Jack Matlock. Attached to it was a foreign policy briefing that Anatoli Chernyaev seemed to have written for Gorbachëv. Supposedly a Kremlin 'mole' had passed it on to the Americans. In fact it was a satirical spoof written by Matlock, who was having a bit of fun while describing the dilemmas that currently faced Gorbachëv.[1] Poindexter liked it enough to send a copy to the President, who asked for more briefings from the same 'secret' informant.[2]

The West's real intelligence agencies had performed their work efficiently for many years. In 1981 France's Directoire de la Surveillance Territoire (DST) recruited the KGB's Lieutenant Colonel Vladimir Vetrov, who supplied names of agents carrying out technological espionage in the NATO countries. Mitterrand told Reagan, and the Americans and their allies quickly closed down the spy networks.[3] The United Kingdom's MI6 was still more impressive, at least until July 1985 when its double agent Oleg Gordievski, a leading KGB officer, had to flee for his life to Britain.[4] Casey proudly reported that the CIA had enlisted thousands of individuals to help the cause: 'Some for money – some for freedom and power – some for patriotism.'[5] The Americans no longer had agents at the highest levels in Moscow: their best information came from outright defectors. The CIA's Aldrich Ames debriefed one of the most promising among these, Vitali Yurchenko, who was a leading KGB official, and Casey invited Yurchenko to dinner.[6] Soon Yurchenko abruptly chose to return to Moscow, where the KGB leadership was reluctant to trust him again.[7] In fact Ames had been secretly working for the KGB since April 1985; and even if he was not the primary influence on Yurchenko's decision to leave America, he and other Soviet double agents undoubtedly supplied information that compromised the CIA and FBI operations in the USSR. The KGB arrested at least ten Soviet citizens who worked for the American agencies. Although suspicions grew at Langley about Soviet penetration, neither Casey nor his successors gave due importance to the matter until the mid-1990s.[8]

The CIA's signals intelligence was always in better shape. The USSR presented formidable problems to outside observers since it was a closed society; but Casey claimed that America's superior technology gave the CIA an edge over Soviet countermeasures.[9] He expected the worst of the Soviet leadership and rarely felt disappointed. His chief specialist on the USSR was Fritz Ermath, who characterized Gorbachëv in mid-1986 as a 'neo-conservative, not a liberalizer' who would never make serious concessions in arms talks. Ermath saw his objective as being simply to get the West to slacken its defensive build-up.[10]

Throughout 1987 the CIA contended that if the USSR was to remain a world power, it had to make changes much more fundamental than those that Gorbachëv had introduced.[11] It entirely mistrusted his commitment to eliminating all his nuclear missiles.[12] It also cast doubt on him as an internal reformer and suggested that he would never run the risk of 'systemic ruin'. It forecast that the USSR would achieve only a marginal improvement in economic competitiveness but would continue to renovate its military arsenal and meddle throughout the Third World. Gorbachëv's personal position was a vulnerable one. He could be overthrown in a coup or might have to confront serious disorder in Eastern Europe.[13] On 24 November Casey's deputy Robert Gates summarized the CIA's advice in a briefing paper for the President. The USSR, he stressed, was still committing resources to 'exotic' new weaponry and stirring up trouble around the world. America needed to keep up its guard. Gates said that Soviet leaders wanted a more benign international environment only as a breathing space to enable them to modernize their economy. He dismissed Moscow's proposals on intermediate-range missiles as a cheap ploy to divide NATO and win friends in Western Europe; he flatly denied that the USSR had changed its underlying foreign objectives.[14]

Gorbachëv certainly took the matter of his global image very seriously. He had his book *Perestroika: New Thinking for Our Country and the World* speedily translated into the world's main languages and it became a bestseller. Its contents laid a stress on the commitment to democratization. He insisted that *perestroika* offered a fresh way of organizing societies; he wanted to chart a course between capitalism and Stalinist communism. Gorbachëv depicted his own reforms of the Soviet order as offering the best way of life for all humankind.[15]

While Gorbachëv's popularity soared around the world, dissatisfaction lingered in Washington about the CIA's performance. The Joint Economic Committee of Congress held hearings in April 1988 about concerns that the CIA had persistently overstated the USSR's economic performance. Douglas J. MacEachin, who headed the Office of Soviet Analysis, countered that his officials had constantly underscored Moscow's economic problems and pointed to the chronic failure to develop and absorb new civilian technology.[16] Soviet computing power was reported a mere tenth of America's.[17] The agency also estimated that military requirements constituted fifteen to seventeen per cent of the USSR's state budget. (At a dinner that Senator Edward Kennedy gave for him, Shevardnadze put it even higher at eighteen per cent!)[18] In the CIA's opinion, Gorbachëv had yet to make the necessary choice between economic reform and strategic weapons modernization – and all this time the Soviet external debt was on the increase.[19] MacEachin, writing to Deputy Director of Intelligence Richard Kerr, stressed his confidence that immense strains were growing in Soviet politics and society. He was frank about the limits to what was knowable about Kremlin discussions; he also revealed that CIA experts were divided about whether Gorbachëv could prevent a coup against himself and his reforms, perhaps led by Ligachëv or Chebrikov. Nevertheless, all officials agreed that there was a growing crisis in the USSR.[20]

Casey also had his agency behind him in sounding the alarm about Soviet industrial espionage in America. He attributed the USSR's technological progress largely to this source.[21] He was not the only one to emphasize Moscow's dependence on its spy network. The KGB did the same in its confidential reports to the Politburo, and its Chairman, Chebrikov, and his successor, Kryuchkov, boasted about their agency's prowess in stealing secrets from American factories and laboratories.[22]

Shultz had never believed in the impartiality of CIA reports on a wider front. He saw a chance to impose himself from mid-December 1986 when a brain tumour forced Casey's abstention from active work and Gates became acting director.[23] Shultz invited Gates for talks in the State Department soon after New Year. Forgoing any pleasantries, he accused the agency of contaminating its reports with political pre-judices.[24] He wanted information from espionage, not the opinion of spymasters, and he knew that not all the CIA's Soviet specialists agreed with the analysis that Casey been propounding.[25] He also charged the CIA leadership with saying things to the President that they with-held from the State Department.[26] Gates rejected all the criticism. He claimed that little or nothing was being held back from the foreign service; he added that the CIA was internally divided and not a mono-lithic agency. He asked Shultz to accept that the CIA and the State Department often had simply an honest disagreement about what was happening in the USSR. Gates and Shultz agreed to try to get on better in future. Shultz joked: 'I regard you as my psychiatrist and hope you'll help me be straight.'[27]

The American and Soviet sides worked intensively to produce agreements; but the struggle in public relations intensified and each side attacked hard through the channels of its agencies of propaganda. The Soviet priority was to denounce the Strategic Defense Initiative. Booklets were rushed into English. The style was usually less stilted than in earlier years, the appeal more emotional. *Whence the Threat to Peace* went through multiple editions. The tone was accusing: 'The threat to world peace comes from the American war machine, the militarist policy pursued by the American Administration and its efforts to conduct international affairs from the position of strength.' America's quest for military superiority had supposedly wrecked the Reykjavik summit. Thule and Fylingdales were said to be a breach of the Anti-Ballistic Missile Treaty. The booklet claimed that big Ameri-can corporations treated the Defense Initiative as the goose that lays the golden egg. The expansion of arms systems to outer space would disturb the global strategic equilibrium and make nuclear war more probable. Soviet military analysts denied that Warsaw Pact forces had numerical superiority over NATO.[28] The Committee of Soviet Scien-tists for Peace Against the Nuclear Threat took the same line – Roald Sagdeev and Andrei Kokoshin warned that the idea of a 'limited nuclear war' was a dangerous nonsense.[29]

The American political establishment accepted such tracts as unavoidable in a free society, and everyone in Washington recognized that it was impossible to insist upon publishing pro-Reagan booklets in Moscow. The Reagan administration did, however, take exception to the Kremlin's continuing campaigns of disinformation. 'Soviet active measures' were spreading downright lies about America's foreign policy. Republican Congressman Dan Lungren was emphatic that this activity had to stop if the Soviet leaders truly hoped for a rapprochement with America. The Party Secretariat and KGB made use of a range of outlets, including the Western peace movement, to undermine NATO's purposes.[30] CIA Director Casey pointed out that international friendship societies and various other 'front organizations' were favourite means for disseminating the contents of Politburo policies. Newspapers in Africa and elsewhere were another avenue whereby the KGB infiltrated misinformation into the world's media. Bribery of foreign editors and reporters was common. Forging American official documents was also a favourite technique.[31]

Reagan had appointed a Hollywood film director, Charles Wick, to the United States Information Agency. Wick's task was to carry the fight to the Soviet leadership. He received a budget that soon amounted to $820 million.[32] His agency and Radio Free Europe received $1 billion annually and the CIA's disinformation activity received $3.5 billion. Wick was an inspired choice. Despite admitting to a slender knowledge of international affairs, Wick had superb expertise in presenting America in the best possible light. He was equally effective in challenging Soviet misrepresentations – and this was where he laid emphasis in his work, if only because the Moscow media themselves were doing a superb job of exposing the abusive nature of communist rule past and present. Wick and his officials hardly needed to devote effort to denunciation.

He nevertheless felt the need to counteract the slurs about American official activity that continued to enter the public domain on a global basis. One such story was that it had been scientists at Fort Detrick, Maryland who had deliberately created the AIDS virus. *Pravda* printed a cartoon of a US general handing over cash for a test tube of the contagious virus. An additional ingredient of nastiness was suggested by depicting each germ as a swastika. Another slur was that America had developed an 'ethnic weapon' designed to be lethal for Africans and people of African descent and harmless for people of European ancestry. The charge of racist militarism received space in a number of newspapers around the world. (This was too outrageous an item for even *Pravda* to publish it.) A third was that America was violating the 1972 Bacteriological and Toxin Weapons Convention whereas the USSR dutifully abided by it. The Soviet media were awash with allegations in 1986–1987. They accused the CIA of having perpetrated the Jonestown massacre in Guyana in 1978 as well as of having assassinated Olaf Palme. American organizations were said to be engaged in shipping Guatemalan children to America for use in organ transplant surgery. It was made to seem that America was the active source of every evil around the globe.[33]

The US Information Agency relentlessly challenged Soviet official propaganda. Nothing pleased them more than to expose trickery. Herb Romerstein, with the anticommunist fervour of an ex-communist, put special markings on important American documents. This enabled him to ascertain quite a number of KGB forgeries. The accusation that the CIA planned to assassinate Rajiv Gandhi was disproved by this method.[34]

When it came to Romerstein's attention that a Soviet newspaper had printed a reader's letter that claimed that Reagan was using quotations from an old Nazi publication about the USSR, he went on to the attack at a meeting with *Novosti*'s director Valentin Falin. The phrase in question was: 'Promises are like pie crusts – they are meant to be broken.' *Novosti* went to town about the connections with the Third Reich. Romerstein told Falin: 'You insulted us last week, insulted our President.' Falin insisted that the phrase came from a pamphlet produced by Joseph Goebbels. 'You're wrong!' exclaimed Romerstein: 'Lenin made the remark, not Hitler.' He adduced the Soviet publication where Lenin wrote about pie crusts, and Falin had to back down.[35] Moscow's assault on Reagan had its origins in his reference to 'the Ten Commandments' of Lenin – and it was indeed the case that the Nazis had brought out a work with this title. It was also true that Reagan's comments wrenched Lenin's pie crust remark out of context. (This was noticed at the time by the *New York Times*.)[36] But Romerstein had shown that it paid to retaliate whenever the Soviet media or the KGB made indefensible claims – and if the USSR wanted conciliation with America, it had to change its ways.

The Soviet authorities grasped the opportunity for trusted individuals to speak to the American media about the USSR. The journalist Vladimir Pozner, affable and fluent in English, appeared on ABC News in February commenting on a speech by the President. Pozner had spent most of his early life in America, where he acquired a New York accent before his family returned to Moscow and he entered university. His activities on behalf of the Politburo caused some disquiet in the Reagan administration. Pat Buchanan, the White House Communications Director, suggested that the situation was as if the BBC in the 1930s had given airtime to a Third Reich functionary after one of

Winston Churchill's radio broadcasts.[37] American efforts to put across the administration's purposes were enlivened by the Worldnet TV channel that Wick masterminded.[38] Shultz and Carlucci agreed to put the Soviets on notice that if they wanted any kind of rapprochement, the lies had to cease.[39] Steadily the atmosphere cleared between the two sides as talks proceeded at the highest political levels; and the growing trend was for the Soviet media to expose real current and past abuses in the USSR rather than overdo the anti-American propaganda. Moscow newspapers and magazines started to criticize policies and practices under Stalin and Brezhnev. It was becoming open season on the unreformed communist order.

Soviet negotiators visiting America tried to ignore the jet lag; but they understandably always felt sleepy. The Americans worked through the night, on US Eastern Time, while they were in Moscow. The personnel of the USSR's General Staff stayed at their desks throughout summits in what they cheerfully called 'combat readiness'.[40] Who coped the better? There is no way of saying for certain, but Adamishin was in no doubt at the time: 'The Americans are more punctilious, more purposive; they know what they want and use toughness in trying to obtain it. It has seemed to me – and perhaps I may be wrong – that our side lacks the strictly applied intellect for the talks at hand.'[41]

Reagan failed to share this confidence in the quality of service available to him. He turned to Suzanne Massie for help with information about everyday life in the USSR – it was she who taught him the Russian saying 'trust but verify'. Massie was a freelance academic researcher on Russian history and culture, and she and her former husband had written a bestseller about Tsar Nicholas II and his wife Alexandra. Breezy and assertive, she made the acquaintance of National Security Adviser McFarlane and obtained an assignment to go to Moscow to test out Soviet official readiness to renew talks. Through McFarlane she met and entranced the President in January 1984.[42] Reagan liked her ability to impart a sense of what life was really like for Soviet citizens. He thought her 'the greatest student I know of the Russian people'.[43] She claimed direct experience of Russians high and low. (She even recounted having received a personal message from Gorbachëv.) While reserving judgement on Gorbachëv, she stressed that ordinary Russians could make up their own minds and would continue to reject the 'Big Lies'.[44] After a trip to the USSR in September 1985 she told the President about how often she had heard 'many expressions of goodwill for you'.[45] In March 1986 she confided that her reaction to Gorbachëv 'leans much more to the positive'.[46] Although Shultz disliked the idea of mavericks getting access to the President, he made an exception for Massie. He welcomed her reports on the signs of a Russian religious revival. He liked her emphasis on the reality of rapid change in Moscow as well as her help in countering the case against conciliation with the USSR.[47]

This was not everyone's attitude. Massie's influence worried National Security Adviser Carlucci enough for him to ask to sit in on their conversations. Reagan consented; he correctly foresaw that Carlucci would discover that she was not pumping the President's ears full of nonsense.[48] Basking in the presidential endorsement, however, she started to criticize the way that the administration was dealing with the USSR. She disapproved of the arrest of Gennadi Zakharov in retaliation for the imprisonment of Nicholas Daniloff. Carlucci replied that America could not 'let the KGB have the run of our country'.[49] Her technique was to flatter the President while finding fault with his officials. She always congratulated him on his handling of Gorbachëv;[50] but she tried even Shultz's patience with her gripes about the American embassy in Moscow. Massie criticized the diplomats for their poor Russian. Shultz commented that even when they spoke the language fluently, she would still insist that they lacked 'an understanding of the great Russian soul'. He doubted that the messages she brought back from Moscow really did come from Gorbachëv.[51] In late 1986 Reagan too concluded that she was getting a mite out of hand when she made a brash pitch to succeed Hartman as Moscow Ambassador. Reagan responded that while she remained his trusted adviser, he had already nominated Jack Matlock for the post.[52] Massie was disappointed, but had to accept the decision. She reasoned that the President should nevertheless meet her more often.[53]

No Soviet leader or agency knew about the President's curious tutorials with his favourite scholar in Russian studies. But Gorbachëv was definitely pleased about the progress that he himself was making in winning over Western opinion:

> In contacts with America in its diversity we've seen that our *perestroika* has reached even a society such as American society which has been carried to the extreme of anti-Sovietism. People were upset, for example, that we're backward in some aspects and have difficulties with our economy. What has interested them is the fact that [Soviet] society has moved forward, is revealing its

dynamism and is inspired by the idea of changing over to democratic principles. And strictly speaking, it's mainly this that has
interested everybody everywhere in our contacts with people.[54]

Gorbachëv was aware that America would try to squeeze further
concessions out of him. The Strategic Defense Initiative was not his
only cause for concern. He also worried about the USSR's reliance on
American grain imports and, like his predecessors, feared that the
White House could wield this as a political weapon. (Vice President
Bush remonstrated that no American administration had ever contemplated such behaviour.)[55] To Gorbachëv's mind, Soviet communism
was misunderstood abroad. He noted that the American political right
thought Soviet leaders were abandoning communist principles out of
recognition of the USSR's internal weaknesses. America's liberals, on
the other hand, envisaged Gorbachëv as trying to 'save socialism' just
as F. D. Roosevelt had saved capitalism in the 1930s. Though Gorbachëv rejected both ways of interpreting *perestroika*, he omitted to
explain where he thought the fault lines lay.[56] The Soviet leadership
continued to characterize America as a country pervaded by discrim-
ination based on class and race. Shevardnadze assured Shultz that the
USSR's workers were free to go on strike. Shultz replied that trade
unions in Moscow had to follow the dictates of the government's plan
for production – and this was not Shultz's idea of freedom. He also
denied that ethnic and racial obstacles were insurmountable in
America; he pointed out that Colin Powell, Reagan's National Security
Adviser from November 1987, was black.[57]

Gorbachëv and Shevardnadze remained loyal to Marxist-Leninist
doctrines in the first three years of *perestroika*. They aspired to
improving, not demolishing, the foundations of the Soviet order.
Gorbachëv's experience of foreign countries had failed to erode this
passionate commitment. On his Canadian trip in 1983 he had learned
that the farmers there relied on state subsidies, and this appeared to
leave him with a lasting scepticism about the merits of a market economy.[58] At the Politburo on 26 July 1986, Gorbachëv called on comrades
to stop being apologetic about the record of respect for human rights
in the USSR. The truth, he claimed, was that Soviet people enjoyed
protections that were unavailable under capitalism. He called for a
reaffirmation of the values of the October Revolution.[59]

The KGB, as Gorbachëv recognized, was a poor source for information and guidance about American politics. Although it had

penetrated the CIA through double agent Ames, it had no human 'assets' elsewhere at the top of the administration. It could disclose nothing important that Gorbachëv did not know. Whenever reports arrived from the Lubyanka on principal topics for talks with America, Gorbachëv passed them on to the central party apparatus for an assessment of their reliability.[60] He explained his attitude at the Politburo in February 1987 when grumbling about the quality of material that was being forwarded to him about the European Economic Community. The academic research institutes were falling short in their work and the KGB's assessments were no better. Gorbachëv, with characteristic frankness, said that Western open sources were more useful for the groundwork of policy.[61] It was only much later, when Gorbachëv's trusted associate Vadim Bakatin became KGB Chairman in the late summer of 1991, that the political leadership discovered the depths of chaos and incompetence in the way that the intelligence agency gathered and processed the files of its agents. Chebrikov and Kryuchkov received endless material from their 480,000 subordinates but failed to eliminate the prevalence of ideological clichés in the content.[62]

Gorbachëv realized that Marxism-Leninism distorted the leadership's perceptions of other countries. The air was leaving his ideological tyres:

> We've long ago been taught that a general crisis of capitalism is happening. So that if you take every opportunity to say the word 'crisis', you won't go far wrong! (Laughter). And here we are and now they're assuring us that a crisis in the [American] administration is taking place. Look how they're covering the President with unbelievable caricatures. And it's not realized that a different psychology – and a different political process – exists there. We need a short-term prognosis, but we also need a prognosis that extends for many years after Reagan.[63]

Soviet propaganda had always predicted the imminent dissolution of world capitalism. Yet the advanced market economy had reinvented itself in generation after generation despite intermittent crises. It was time for the Politburo to throw away old comfort blankets.

Gorbachëv paused for reflection in early 1987 when telling some bitter truths to the Politburo. If *perestroika* was going to succeed, the USSR needed to achieve technological collaboration with foreign countries.[64] He lamented how far the Soviet economy was lagging

behind – even Finland had retooled its industry with advanced technology: 'Our own laboratories are filthier than their factories for
livestock feed.'[65] He and Thatcher had talked about how the average
personal income in the USSR was half of the level in the United Kingdom: 'Where's it all going? The answer is in quality and wastage. The
planning order isn't reinforced by people's interests. It's a paper-based
bureaucratic methodology.'[66] He was soon to admit that the true figure
was not a half but a third. The Soviet Union seemed to do worse each
time he spoke at the Politburo.[67] Whereas the USSR claimed to have an
advanced economy with six million 'scientific workers', Gorbachëv
doubted that there were anything like as many in productive employment.[68] Japan had entered the first rank of the world's economic
powers and the Federal Republic of Germany had joined it there. Gorbachëv hoped to cement a partnership with Western Europe, which
had pulled far ahead in technology. Mitterrand had assured him that
the West Europeans intended to reduce their reliance on America.[69]

He and Shevardnadze still saw weaknesses in the American administration's posture. The White House could never take Congress for
granted, especially on the subject of the Strategic Defense Initiative.
Soviet leaders also doubted that America's economy was as buoyant as
Reagan assumed. Shevardnadze claimed that 'the Americans cannot
conduct the arms race on a permanent footing'.[70] The problem was that
the administration sailed intact through all its political storms; and
although the economic situation had its troubles, America undeniably
had new sectors of industry and technology which were restoring it to
the forefront of global competitiveness. Reagan, moreover, was doing
well in surveys of American public opinion. He was harder to knock
back than the Soviet leadership had hoped.

The President was heard to comment that if only Gorbachëv could
gain acquaintance with American everyday realities, the Cold War
would quickly be over. He once said this to Frank Carlucci while travelling by helicopter and looking down on a vista of shopping malls.[71]
He was not the only leader to think along these lines. American politicians, Democrats as well as Republicans, believed passionately in the
superiority of American values and the American style of life. They
nagged away about the abuses of power in Moscow. After they discovered much that was new to them about Soviet people, they continued
to reject the USSR's claim to legitimacy. But most of them did come to
drop the assumption that it was unsafe to trust any Kremlin ruler.
They started to like and admire the reformers. Some even loved

Gorbachëv. Reagan's right-wing critics thought that the President was revealing himself as a political fool or romantic. They contended that he had sold out his principles. But they missed the point. Reagan had not changed his standpoint on the USSR. What had happened was a sequence of basic changes at the apex of the Soviet leadership. Reagan was greeting the process with delight and understanding and trying to facilitate it from the American side.

As Gorbachëv contemplated radical reforms of the Soviet political system, he adduced America as an example to follow. Candidates for high office ought to be properly scrutinized: 'Just look at how in the American Congress they pick to pieces every minister that the President wants to appoint. What a contrast with us: who ever asks a question or coordinates with a Supreme Soviet Commission as to whom to appoint as a minister? We just read in the newspaper that so-and-so has been appointed to such-and-such a post; but who is it, where's he come from, why?'[72]

Shevardnadze admired how the Eurocommunists had revised their Marxism and tossed aside dogma about the working class and its leading political role.[73] He had his own second thoughts about the history of his native Georgia. Until 1921, when the Red Army invaded, the Georgians had been governed by Noi Zhordania and the Mensheviks. Although the Mensheviks were Marxists, their policies were less violent and impatient than those of Lenin and Trotsky in Moscow. Shevardnadze recognized 'healthy ideas' in Menshevism and grew sceptical about the tenets of Marxism-Leninism.[74] In the contemporary world he esteemed the political leaders of New Zealand and Denmark for their 'courage' and skill in keeping the support of their peoples.[75] This was an extraordinary attitude for a Soviet leader. Shunning the hauteur of a great-power statesman, he looked for inspiration to politicians of smaller countries who emphasized peace and reconciliation; and when speaking to Japanese Prime Minister Takeshita, he attributed Japan's post-war economic success to its abandonment of militarism. The USSR's establishment of a 'closed society', he concluded, had led to its failure.[76]

On a visit to Japan in January 1986, Shevardnadze felt envious of the products of their technology and was impressed by the consideration shown to the labour force.[77] Despite coming from the land of proletarian revolution, he acknowledged that the Nissan factory workers enjoyed better treatment than was available in the USSR; he was also impressed by their cooperativeness with the managers.[78]

Japanese industrial progress was unmistakable. By 1988 Gorbachëv, who together with the rest of the leadership had long recognized Soviet economic problems, believed that the USSR's entire development had been based on false principles: 'In the United States, services constitute fifty per cent of national income whereas with us it's eleven per cent. We forever drive after coal, oil, heavy machine construction.'[79]

Gorbachëv and his fellow leaders, moreover, would not have been human if they had not enjoyed the way that Western leaders treated them. The Daimler that took Shevardnadze from Heathrow airport enthralled him with its automotive grandeur.[80] The British Foreign Secretary's country residence at Chevening stunned the Soviet visitors with its Gainsborough paintings, parks and ancient furniture which captivated their imaginations: even the opulence of America's great houses seemed ascetic by comparison.[81] Luxury was not the only source of wonder. At the closure of the December 1987 Washington summit the leaders of the two sides – American and Soviet – came out on to the south lawn of the White House for a ceremony for the send-off in front of 5,000 spectators.[82] An evening shower of rain began and the American President opened an umbrella, holding it over his wife's head. This startled the Russians. They were accustomed to the woman acting as helpmate to the man; the idea was strange for them that a husband – and no ordinary person but a head of state – should trouble about his wife's comfort while appearing in public. This detail of everyday American life was a microcosm of bigger differences.[83]

A popular image of Soviet officials represented them as gauche, dogmatic and fond of the bottle. On foreign trips they sometimes conformed to stereotype. Those who travelled to Washington for the 1987 summit stayed at the Madison Hotel, where the guests had access to mini-bars stuffed with wines and spirits. The result was a binge of drinking that continued until Comrade Chaplin – head of logistics – told the hotel management to replace the alcohol with soft drinks.[84] As they sobered up, their lunches on Big Macs and Cola at McDonald's showed them a culinary world that contrasted with the cafeterias at home. They envied the fare available for 'extraordinary and plenipotentiary' US citizens.[85]

Gorbachëv hoped to prove that the USSR's leaders were essentially no different from those of the West. He meant to dispel prejudice through an interview that he gave to NBC's Tom Brokaw before going to Washington in late 1987. Though he appeared at ease before the cameras, he failed to achieve complete success mainly because he rambled in his answers and failed to stick to the point – and Brokaw inadvertently aggravated the problem by being unduly deferential. But Gorbachëv did at least put himself over as a reasonable, amiable fellow. This won him media headlines next day. He also caused a sensation through his off-the-cuff decision to order the chauffeur to halt the official limousine near Connecticut Avenue on the way to the White House. Gorbachëv wished to mingle with the crowd. When Shevardnadze in the following vehicle noticed the sudden standstill, he thought there had been an assassination attempt; he rushed from his limousine toward the one in front before catching sight of the General Secretary stretching out his hand to American well-wishers. Gorbachëv called on the crowd to encourage America's politicians to promote the cause of change. Security agents were scared that someone might pull out a gun on him. They shouted to everyone: 'Keep your hands out of your pockets!' This served to enhance the Soviet leader's reputation for scorning convention.[86]

Reagan arranged for Texan pianist Van Cliburn to give a recital on one of the summit evenings. Cliburn was well known in the USSR as the winner of the 1958 Tchaikovsky Piano Competition, and the Gorbachëvs were delighted to see his name on the programme. It was a spectacular occasion. After Cliburn's performance, which started with the 'Stars and Stripes', Raisa Gorbachëva asked him to play Tchaikovsky's Piano Concerto No. 1. It was a request from the heart that the pianist had to decline in the absence of an orchestra. Instead he played his version of the song 'Moscow Nights' and the Gorbachëvs sang along from the front row. Pianist and General Secretary embraced at the end.[87] Gorbachëv held his own reception at the Soviet embassy for 'the American intelligentsia' on another evening. Among the guests were hostile figures such as Henry Kissinger and William Fulbright. Also invited were actors, scientists, singers, artists and novelists who sympathized with his purposes: Robert De Niro, Paul Newman, Carl Sagan, John Denver, Yoko Ono, Norman Mailer and Joyce Carol Oates. Gorbachëv socialized with all of them, shaking hands and accepting hugs. Nobody needed to teach him how to work the room.[88]

American public figures became eager to win the trust of Soviet officials. Edward Teller, the veteran anti-Soviet scientist, made a proposal for research cooperation on 'controlled fusion' in nuclear physics. He wrote to Shultz that Andrei Sakharov was someone who could work productively on the topic (although he acknowledged that it might be unrealistic to invite him to America).[89] When Akhromeev as Chief of the USSR General Staff accepted the invitation of his opposite number Admiral William J. Crowe to visit Oklahoma City, he was visibly moved at receiving the present of a Native American feathered headdress.[90] The Americans continued to break down the traditions of restraint and mistrust. State Department official Richard Schifter asked Anatoli Adamishin to dinner at his home. Schifter gossiped about being pleased about his colleague Roz Ridgway's departure from office and her replacement by Raymond Seitz. He disclosed various titbits about the internal tensions inside the American administration. He made no objection when Adamishin described America's policy on Afghanistan as absurd. Adamishin's surprise was matched by his delight at the experience.[91]

Things also changed more widely in society in the USSR. Chebrikov had recognized that Gorbachëv's political reforms would disallow the KGB from following its old ways of handling society. Speaking to the Party Congress in February 1986, he emphasized how the American special services were exploiting the expanded channels of international communication to penetrate Soviet institutions and steal state secrets. He highlighted attempts to disseminate anticommunist ideas through Western radio broadcasts. He noted the campaign against the leadership's policy on human rights.[92]

Just a few months later, people could hardly believe their ears when they span the dials on their radio sets. The jamming of foreign broadcasts had become an embarrassment to Gorbachëv as the date of the Reykjavik summit drew near. The Secretariat's Ligachëv and the KGB's Chebrikov assented to allowing Voice of America, the BBC, Radio Peking and Radio Korea. Ligachëv and Chebrikov were not against jamming in principle but rather aimed to concentrate their facilities on operations against the radio services they most objected to – Radio Freedom, Radio Free Europe, Voice of Israel and Deutsche Welle.[93] By May 1987 the Soviet administration had permanently stopped jamming Voice of America.[94] The Politburo was also coming to the conclusion that the restrictions on foreign travel caused damage to the USSR's basic interests. Shevardnadze noted how many innovative ideas had entered the USSR through Soviet citizens who had travelled abroad. The USSR could only benefit from widening the channels of international contact.[95] At last in November 1988 the decision was made that every citizen had the right to emigrate so long as they were not in possession of state secrets.[96]

Another interesting phenomenon was the joint broadcasting of American and Soviet TV shows with live audience participation. These so-called 'telebridges' had started in 1982 in a patchy fashion – the Kremlin would not allow them to be aired on the Moscow channel. True reciprocity was at last introduced in 1986, and the American public could see and hear that Russians were not automatons but people like rather themselves with ordinary emotions and aspirations. Soviet audiences, as they watched the American adverts, discovered a world of consumer goods that entranced them.[97]

The USSR's connections with the outside world were expanded after 23 July 1987, when the Politburo approved a project to update the USSR's automatic telephone system.[98] The system of booking a time to phone from a special booth in the big cities was to be ended. The Ministry of Communications intended to extend automatic connectivity to 'the socialist countries' within a year and to enable Moscow residents to phone any country in the world before 1992. While acknowledging the 'whole complexity of the given problem', Shevardnadze predicted that international public opinion would welcome the news. Gromyko contended that foreign intelligence services would exploit the reform for their own nefarious purposes. Gorbachëv shrugged off his advice and the Politburo agreed with him.[99] An efficient 'hot line' had existed between President and General Secretary since the Cuban missile crisis of 1962. For the first time it would become possible for millions of private Soviet citizens to dial up Western countries on the spur of the moment.[100] The quarantine of communications started to be lifted. The process was far from complete, but nobody could deny that remarkable changes had occurred since 1985.

25. STICKING POINTS

The Strategic Defense Initiative continued to touch a raw nerve in the Soviet leadership. But even before Reykjavik, the Politburo recognized that Reagan would never give up his outer-space project. Moscow's priority changed towards finding a way to limit its potential to undermine the USSR's security. The possible options were obvious. The Politburo could cajole the White House. It could ventilate its objections before the court of world opinion. Or it could finance its own counterpart to the Initiative. Or it could simply hope that the programme would prove a waste of American time and finance.

The last option was not one that any Politburo member was minded to espouse. Zaikov, Shevardnadze and Chebrikov met on 13 January 1987 to discuss a letter to Gorbachëv from Dr Henry Kendall, Chairman of the Union of Concerned Scientists in America. Kendall stressed that, despite the President's promises, the Initiative had dangerous potential. His proposal was to divide the programme into two and allow the Americans to test one part in outer space while forgoing tests on the other part for the next ten years. Soviet leaders pointed out that America could experiment with search and tracking sensors in pursuit of 'strategic superiority'. The USSR needed to ascertain which of the Initiative's ingredients posed a cardinal threat and offer a deal on arms reduction in return for the Americans dropping them.[1] With this in mind, the Politburo reached out to all groups in the West that sought to stop or reduce Reagan's project. There was awareness in Moscow that there were opportunities even in Washington, where Democratic politicians frequently criticized the administration's efforts as either bellicose in nature or simply a waste of public money; and scientists like Kendall could possibly be nudged towards positions closer to the Politburo's claims about the intentions behind the American research programme.

Leading scientists in the USSR lobbied Gorbachëv to increase finance for a direct counterpart to the Defense Initiative. Acting on their advice, he boasted to Komsomol leaders in April 1987 that the USSR had succeeded in building its own supercomputer. Velikhov, who was present, was rendered speechless. Gorbachëv had swallowed a bowlful of nonsense. Sagdeev wrote to Gorbachëv pointing this out – and Arbatov delivered the letter in person. Other well-informed leading scientists made the same overture to Gorbachëv.[2] But Gorbachëv refused to intervene. Perhaps he preferred to believe the cheering fiction rather than face up to reality. Possibly Zaikov was culpable for encouraging the naivety. Gorbachëv liked to talk about the progress under way. He told Bush that December: 'Our scientists are now producing super-computers, personal and mini-computers and giant computers for industry.' He had Velikhov at his side and asked him to specify the projected quantity. Velikhov mumbled the figures, presumably deliberately.[3] Only at the end of 1988 did Gorbachëv come to his senses when the Politburo was discussing the computing industry: 'Wait, don't hurry with a claim. First verify if it is true. Computers are not tractors.'[4]

Gorbachëv felt cheered by a trip to the north-west of Moscow at Zelenograd, where the USSR's nascent information technology industry was based. He knew that the country lagged far behind America, but convinced himself that the Soviet economy had enough computers for its basic needs. The Zelenograd personnel's enthusiasm impressed him. He wanted to support their initiatives. It was Gorbachëv's opinion that the USSR would soon become a force in industrial electronics.[5] He soon recognized that conditions for research were far from being optimal – and the living conditions of the researchers also left a lot to be desired.[6]

On 17 May 1987 Defence Minister Sokolov alerted the Politburo to suggestions that the Americans might start testing components of their programme, involving X-ray lasers and nuclear explosions, as early as 1991–1995 – his people had read what Weinberger was telling the US media and drawn their own conclusions. Sokolov urged the need to accelerate work on the Soviet rival programme. The Politburo refused to let him stampede them.[7] Its main response was to put Maslyukov in charge of monitoring what was happening in America,[8] and on 10 July the State Commission on Military-Industrial Problems met to consider these questions. Shevardnadze stressed that 'the world community' had continuing worries about the Defense Initiative; he called for a strengthening of Soviet propaganda. Vitali Shabanov, Deputy Defence Minister for Armaments, doubted that a massed nuclear offensive could truly be prevented with non-nuclear weapons. He also said it was cheaper to base defensive plans on nuclear forces. The commission was divided about whether the Americans were capable of succeeding. Nikolai Chervov, who headed the General Staff's arms control section, made the point that it could never be safe to base Soviet policy on the assumption that Reagan's Initiative would fail.[9] Shevardnadze seemed to agree. On 19 August he said: 'If the Americans start to develop the Strategic Defense Initiative, our hands will be freed and we'll withdraw from a potential agreement on a fifty per cent reduction on strategic offensive weapons.'[10]

The Americans knew that the Politburo was secretly subsidizing its own parallel programme. This was pointed out to Soviet negotiators when they tried to claim that America was uniquely responsible for a new arms race. An American request to visit the USSR's laser experimental facilities at Sary Shagan in Kazakhstan was turned down.[11] Teller, one of those who had originally won Reagan over to the Strategic Defense Initiative, worried about the Soviet competition. In February 1987 he advised his colleague Frederick Seitz that too much information was publicly available about the direction that American research institutes were taking. Their Soviet rivals could pick up useful clues.[12] The programme that Velikhov headed was gathering pace. Velikhov had the ear of Gorbachëv; no other scientist matched him in influence on questions about which paths of investigation to follow. For all his brilliance, he let ambition get the better of judgement and fell for a claim by scientists at the Vernadski Geochemistry Institute to have invented a method to detect gamma rays from a distance of ten kilometres. His friend and co-author Sagdeev told him that the professed achievement was entirely spurious. Velikhov waved him aside and reported to Gorbachëv that the Vernadski group had made a certified discovery.[13]

In earlier years the temptation for Soviet political leaders might have been to emulate the American programme in all its aspects. Moscow politics had changed and the Politburo was ceasing to treat the Strategic Defense Initiative as reason to refuse to sign arms reduction agreements. There had always been scepticism in the USSR about America's chances of creating a reliable defence against nuclear attack, and at the Politburo on 8 May 1987 Gorbachëv repeated that the true purpose behind the Strategic Defense Initiative was to wreck the Soviet economy by compelling a competitive reaction.[14] He decided to stop letting the American programme bother him unduly. Certainly when writing to the President in September, he warned yet again against initiating a new arms race in outer space; but he omitted direct mention of the Strategic Defense Initiative.[15]

Shultz noticed this nuance and alerted Reagan to its meaning.[16] The French noticed that while Gorbachëv continued to protest about the American programme, he usually did this only in passing.[17] The Defense Initiative remained on the sidelines at the Washington summit in December 1987. Frank Carlucci, appointed as Defense Secretary a week earlier, welcomed Akhromeev to the Pentagon – an extraordinary occasion for the USSR's Chief of the General Staff. Akhromeev also made the acquaintance of General Abrahamson, the director of the Strategic Defense Initiative. Carlucci proposed a reciprocal programme of visits to research stations; he suggested that Soviet experts should look over the facilities at Stanford University and at the Livermore National Laboratory in California. Akhromeev did not deny that Soviet scientists were working on a rival research programme. When Carlucci described the Initiative as unstoppable, Akhromeev asked him to appreciate that the USSR would eventually – even if it took fifteen years or more – develop a system to counteract the American project. Velikhov was the only serious scientist taking part in the discussion, and he queried the potential of American laser technology to achieve its projected results; he voiced his doubts that the researchers were supplying the politicians in Washington with trustworthy information.[18]

The ripples of Gorbachëv's newly felt reluctance to make a bugaboo of the Defense Initiative had an immediate effect on public discourse. Politburo members, Akhromeev noted, gave up talking about the Initiative even among themselves.[19]

Soviet leaders made no announcement about their tactical shift. Perhaps they reasoned that there was no advantage in dropping a bargaining card without getting something in return. Possibly they also feared a loss of global prestige through a display of weakness. But though they never ceased to nag about the Defense Initiative, their change of stance was definite. Later when the Big Five met on 2 March 1988, Zaikov confirmed that it was no longer official policy to insist on a link between the Initiative and the other questions of military disarmament.[20] The problem was that nobody informed the Americans. Wanting progress in the talks about medium-range nuclear missiles, America's negotiators sketched out their ideas about a 'test range in space'. The intention was to prove a willingness to consider some restrictions on the Initiative. Gorbachëv had tried to tempt Reagan in Reykjavik with an elastic definition of 'laboratory' research. The Americans were now exploring whether the Kremlin might agree to stretch the permissible zone to the heavens. But when National Security Adviser Powell pressed Ambassador Dubinin for a response, he got nowhere. The Soviet leadership's approach was to express hostility to the Initiative while declining to seek any practical compromise or to enter a dispute.[21]

The Americans were pleased about the slackening of Soviet combativeness about Reagan's project. They remained implacable about the Krasnoyarsk radar station. The USSR's negotiators were slow to recognize how badly this was affecting talks. On 25 November 1986 CIA Deputy Director Robert Gates gave a blistering analysis. Belatedly the danger was appreciated in Moscow, where a background paper was prepared for the party leadership. The main finding was embarrassing for the Kremlin: namely that the station did indeed breach the Anti-Ballistic Missile Treaty signed in 1972.[22]

The Politburo's original idea had been to build the station at Norilsk in the Russian far north with the aim of closing the gap in the USSR's early-warning system against an American nuclear attack. But to construct a station in the frozen wastes was prohibitively expensive. It was also calculated that transport to the site would be restricted to the summer months and would have to be undertaken along the rivers, so Krasnoyarsk was chosen instead. According to Georgi Kornienko, the military commanders wanted Norilsk but the politicians overruled them.[23] This was not how Lieutenant Colonel Nikolai Detinov remembered things. Detinov claimed that Ustinov had presented the Krasnoyarsk project to the Politburo expressly on behalf of the Defence Ministry and the General Staff. Ustinov spoke with confidence that it would be feasible to deceive the world about the station's true functions. But as soon as Andropov denounced Reagan's Strategic Defense Initiative as a breach of the Anti-Ballistic Missile Treaty, the Americans made open objection to the Krasnoyarsk project.[24] The Soviet response was that the station was intended to deal with threats from outer space rather than to prevent a US missiles offensive. The Americans never believed this – and they were right.[25]

Shevardnadze knew how much the matter was undermining his efforts in talks with the Americans; he also recognized that Soviet leaders did themselves no favours by constantly denying that the Warsaw Pact had more troops in Europe than NATO.[26] His arguments took time to have an effect. In summer 1987 the Politburo tried to cool the dispute by inviting a group of American congressmen to inspect the Krasnoyarsk site. The idea of welcoming foreigners inside the perimeter of a military 'object' in the USSR was unprecedented. Gorbachëv was showing extraordinary flexibility. But the enterprise disappointed him because the visitors refused to abandon their opposition except insofar as they agreed that the Soviet authorities would not be in breach of the treaty until such time as they activated the station.[27]

On 15 September, on his trip to Washington, Shevardnadze faced further criticism at the White House from Reagan and his officials.[28] He suggested that the only way forward would be for each side to lean on its own defence establishment; he added that he had questioned Yazov about the disputed status of the radar station. He wanted to appear adaptable. But he offered no practical solution, and Reagan simply repeated his demand for the Soviet leadership to dismantle the facilities or else put the current round of arms reduction talks in jeopardy.[29] Shevardnadze's directives from Moscow did not allow him to reveal that the Politburo on 4 September had tentatively decided on a moratorium on the Krasnoyarsk building work; he was meant to use his trip only to gauge the strength of hostility.[30] Reagan and Weinberger left no room for ambiguity. That same October, on hearing Shevardnadze's report, Gorbachëv announced a one-year moratorium.[31] This took some heat out of the dispute for a while; and Reagan unusually said nothing about Krasnoyarsk at the December 1987 summit.

As Soviet leaders prepared for Shultz's Moscow visit in February 1988, the Big Five proposed that Shevardnadze should offer to put the station out of commission for the next ten years so long as the Americans agreed to dismantle their 'illegal' installations in Thule and Fylingdales.[32] This made no difference to Reagan. On 12 August 1988 he wrote to Gorbachëv explaining that America's entire political establishment saw the case for removing the Krasnoyarsk complex as non-negotiable. He and the Congress were in complete agreement. If Gorbachëv wanted a treaty on strategic nuclear weapons, he had to dismantle the facilities.[33] Gorbachëv went to Krasnoyarsk in September and floated the idea of handing over the station to the Academy of Sciences and establishing a centre for international cooperation for the peaceful use of outer space. He wrote to the White House to explain his scheme.[34] Reagan, Shultz and Bush briskly rejected it. (For once, the CIA wondered whether this was really fair on Gorbachëv.)[35] Shevardnadze tried to cajole Reagan and Shultz in the White House soon afterwards. Although he still could not reveal any specific Politburo decision, he asked them to understand that the Soviet leadership was truly probing for a solution.[36]

It took until autumn 1989, months after Reagan's departure, for a definitive transformation in the Soviet position when Shevardnadze, in his talks with President Bush's Secretary of State James Baker, divulged that the Kremlin had decided to close down the Krasnoyarsk facilities entirely.[37] By then, 530 million rubles had been spent and a whole new town of 30,000 inhabitants created. The Soviet authorities had abandoned the scheme for a research centre. They had dropped ideas of establishing some civilian kind of factory. When they plumped for a penal colony of some sort, it turned out that no ministry wanted to bid for the facilities.[38] In December 1989 there was an announcement that the station would be fully dismantled at some point in 1991.[39]

The White House had been raising parallel objections to the USSR's secretiveness about its military expenditure. The Kremlin continued to lie about the size of its armed forces and their weaponry. If Gorbachëv and Shevardnadze genuinely wanted some kind of partnership with America, this situation had to change. The Foreign Affairs Ministry was raising the question in autumn 1986, and on 22 October a decree issued from the Central Committee ordering the Defence Ministry to supply proposals for a scheme and schedule for what kind of details could be published.[40] When on 5 March 1987 Akhromeev came back to the Politburo, he moved Gorbachëv to anger: 'The whole world is laughing. The United States is spending three hundred billion whereas we spend [only] seventeen billion. And we ensure parity.'[41] The Politburo would no longer tolerate evasion by the Soviet military lobby. Gorbachëv wished to be able to talk to the Americans with a straight face.

The Party Defence Department asked for permission to go on publishing an inaccurate budget while it carried out some research.[42] Gorbachëv was annoyed about the attempted subterfuge, and called for a shift in attitudes. On 8 May he told the Politburo that the USSR had always lied about the number of its troops stationed in Central Europe. NATO had far fewer and knew it. No progress with America was feasible until the Soviet side showed some honesty.[43] When Gromyko tried to resist, Shevardnadze and Yakovlev sided with

Gorbachëv.[44] Akhromeev could see that it was futile to object. Gorbachëv referred everyone to Thatcher's remark that the West had a genuine fear of the USSR after its invasions of Hungary, Czechoslovakia and Afghanistan. He reasoned that Soviet policy had to take this seriously into account. Calling loftily for the 'humanization' of international relations, he demanded a change in military doctrine from parity to sufficiency – and he wanted to reduce armaments to 'the lowest level'. If the arms race continued, the Soviet Union would have to be 'a military camp'. Disarmament was the only realistic alternative. Gorbachëv talked of decreasing the USSR's military strength in Eastern Europe to 170,000 soldiers and inducing America to withdraw its forces back across the Atlantic.[45]

In July Shevardnadze added that if he was expected to represent the country effectively abroad, the leadership had to be less secretive. Government, military-industrial agencies, army and KGB were invited to give an opinion on this demand.[46] Although Ryzhkov voiced no objection, he doubted the feasibility of satisfying Shevardnadze's demands before the tax-year 1989–1990.[47] On 6 August the Politburo accepted this schedule.[48]

Meanwhile it remained the official claim that military expenditure was only 4.6 per cent of total state expenditure.[49] Yakovlev recalled a remarkable conversation on the subject:

> There was once, I remember, when Zaikov phoned me: 'Listen, Alexander, have you any idea how many warheads we have?' I say: 'Well, I suppose it's about thirty-nine thousand.' 'No,' he says, 'it's really forty-three.' I say: 'Where did you get that from? We have thirty-nine in all our documents.' He says: 'But I've been searching for one of the bosses in the Defence Ministry and there was nobody to be found. In the end we got hold of one, a boss from the rear armed forces. I asked him how many warheads we have there. He says: "Forty-three thousand."' This is how we've been deceived on other types of weaponry as well. Well, to hell with them.[50]

Even Akhromeev, no enthusiast for the ending of secrecy, admitted that something was wrong: 'Well, you understand that any Supreme Soviet deputy can ask our General Secretary how we with so small a military budget can stand up to the USA with so huge a military budget. And here's us saying that we do everything on the basis of parity [with the Americans]. Who's going to believe us?'[51] The KGB's

Chebrikov commented that if Soviet analysts could learn so much from open sources about what went on at California's Los Alamos and Livermore nuclear test bases, the Americans should be allowed to inspect Semipalatinsk in Kazakhstan.[52]

Years of obfuscation had to be surmounted. It transpired that the traditional budget specified only expenditure on military personnel. Research and production were hidden under misleading headings. Vadim Medvedev was to recall that four or five individuals alone received data on the true costs. As the reform of account-keeping proceeded, it emerged the armed forces cost not five but at least sixteen per cent of the state's financial burden – and Medvedev guessed that the real figure was around twenty-five per cent.[53]

Arms talks with the Americans were hindered by spurious official claims about Soviet nuclear stockpiles. The truth, as Shevardnadze explained to his inner circle on 9 November 1987, was that the USSR had more intermediate-range rockets than America: 'An imbalance exists, that's something we know. But it's not something we publicly acknowledge.'[54] Akhromeev could no longer resist the force of such arguments. When negotiations were resumed in Washington on 24 November, Shultz and Shevardnadze felt able to leave it to Nitze and Akhromeev to resolve some important particulars. Akhromeev yielded on inspections once Nitze agreed to limit them to six a year. But he objected to the American reluctance to let his inspectors into a Utah weapons factory. When he called for an examination of the Martin Marietta factory in Orlando, Florida, Shultz exclaimed: 'That's Disneyland!' Nitze added that Martin Marietta no longer produced armaments. Colin Powell intervened and contradicted Nitze.[55] For the agreement to work, both sides needed to sharpen their efforts. The preparations intensified. By February 1988 the Soviet side was getting ready for the arrival of American inspectors at the Votkinsk installation in the southern Urals.[56] In May Shevardnadze gave a detailed report to Shultz on the number of Soviet strategic nuclear weapons. Since it was in Russian, it was incomprehensible to Shultz; but he showed his appreciation of the signs of progress.[57]

Gorbachëv and Reagan had concentrated on long- and medium-range weapons at their Reykjavik summit and left short-range missiles for their working groups to handle. Much remained to be done, and the leaders knew they would have to deal with the matter sooner or later. Short range was defined as any distance up to 500 kilometres. The American and Soviet sides were acutely aware that a single so-called operational-tactical nuclear missile fired from just over the line between NATO and the Warsaw Pact would start a world war. On 2 February 1987 Gorbachëv proposed to add such missiles to the intermediate-range ones for removal from Europe.[58] His priority was to remove all barriers to agreement with the Americans.

While the American negotiators agreed on this as an objective, they worried about the time that it might take to attain it. Indeed, they called Soviet sincerity into question. Their grounds for suspicion were the USSR's installation of its new SS-23 ('Oka') missiles in the German Democratic Republic and Czechoslovakia. According to the designers, these missiles could cover a maximum distance of 400 kilometres and was therefore a short-range nuclear weapon. The American side expressed their concern that a way could be found to increase the range and secretly get round the projected agreement on medium-range missiles. In fact it was technically unfeasible to extend the range; but the USSR's negotiating team was forbidden from divulging this information for fear of revealing the secrets of the research. Everyone could see that the Americans had some justification in the light of the publicly available information. Shevardnadze was for simply stopping production and deployment whereas Akhromeev suggested modifying the SS-23s in such a way as to shorten their range. Akhromeev was being helpful after a fashion. But Zaikov realized that Akhromeev's proposal would still fail to satisfy the Americans. Shultz would be soon arriving in Moscow and would certainly create trouble unless the Soviet leadership gave way.[59]

Gorbachëv gave his word to Shultz that the USSR would eliminate the SS-23s – he agreed with Zaikov on the need for a quick resolution in order to secure the signature of the Intermediate-Range Nuclear Forces Treaty. He claimed to have had Akhromeev with him at the time. Akhromeev later denied having been present at the precise moment when Gorbachëv made his concession.[60] What is more, gossip spread round Moscow that Shevardnadze had pushed Gorbachëv into making a concession that damaged the USSR's interests. There was disquiet in the Ministry of Defence and the Military-Political Commission. When Varennikov arrived on a trip from Kabul, he made straight for Akhromeev's office. Akhromeev did not even say hello but immediately stated: 'Valentin Ivanovich, it's not me who's at fault. What happened was that the order was given "up there".' Varennikov had not had time to mention the SS-23s, but Akhromeev could easily guess what was on his mind.[61] Gorbachëv stuck by his promise and threatened leading commanders with disciplinary sanctions if ever they tried to voice their objections at communist party gatherings.[62]

Soviet technical specialists anyway lent no support to the criticism; they felt sure that Gorbachëv had done the right thing. The fewer nuclear missiles on the European continent, the better.[63] Even Akhromeev, when he applied his mind rationally to the question, accepted the need for a drastic numerical reduction. Kataev in the Party Defence Department shivered at the thought of a field commander who might start the Third World War by deciding to fire a short-range nuclear missile in support of forces under threat near the lines of East–West confrontation.[64] He and arms talks specialist Nikolai Detinov had a further reason to oppose the critics. Both of them appreciated the dilemma that had faced Gorbachëv: if he had refused to withdraw the SS-23s, the Americans would have felt free to deploy their new Lance-2 missiles with a range of 450 kilometres – and the result would have been a sharpening of military insecurity in Europe. Detinov was an army man with a record of falling out with the diplomats in the Soviet talks delegation in Geneva; he was not someone who automatically believed in the wisdom of Gorbachëv. But on this vital occasion he believed that the General Secretary had no other sensible option.[65]

Gorbachëv, with the approval of the Big Five and the Politburo, made concession after concession in pursuit of bilateral agreements to reduce the stockpiles of nuclear weapons. All concurred that it was a price worth paying. Reagan wanted a deal as badly as they did. But Gorbachëv and his colleagues needed it more than he did – and Reagan knew this.

26. GRINDING OUT THE TREATY

On 8 September 1987 America's National Security Planning Group gathered to prepare for the next of Shevardnadze's visits to Washington. Excitement mounted about opportunities to achieve agreement on strategic as well as intermediate-range nuclear weapons before the end of Reagan's presidential term.[1] Shultz, usually an optimist, deemed this premature at a time when the two sides had yet to sign any kind of fundamental agreement, but he applauded the progress that the American delegation was making in Geneva: 'We need to make decisions and get the treaty on the table before Shevardnadze gets here.'[2] His comments agitated Weinberger, who warned against 'reaching quick decisions under the pressure of a meeting'. Shultz declined to contest the point, explaining that he had information to the effect that the Planning Group had been leaking like a sieve. If the day's proceedings were to become public knowledge, he contended, complications could arise in negotiations with the USSR.[3] Weinberger bridled at the comment. He also objected to Shultz's request to authorize a degree of flexibility for American negotiators in the talks on strategic forces. In Weinberger's opinion, the Secretary of State was prescribing a rationale for nothing less than surrender to the Kremlin.[4]

Reagan did what came naturally to him by staying out of the dispute between State and Defence. But he none the less revealed where his sympathies lay:

> You've got to remember that the whole thing [about the negotiations] was born of the idea that the world needs to get rid of nuclear weapons. We've got to remember that we can't win a nuclear war and we can't fight one. The Soviets don't want to win by war but by threat of war. They want to issue ultimatums to which we have to give in. If we could just talk about the basic steps we need to take to break the log jam and avoid the possibility of war. I mean, just think about it. Where would the survivors of the war live? Major areas of the world would be uninhabitable. We

need to keep it in mind that that's what we're about. We're about bringing together steps to bring us closer to the recognition that we need to do away with nuclear weapons.[5]

As if sensing that this sounded like the call of a political dove, he added: 'I have a friend who tells me that in the Soviet Union their right-wingers are starting to call Gorbachëv "Mr Yes" because he agrees with everything I propose.'[6]

Weinberger, sensing that the President was anaesthetizing his own old ideas, sought to revive suspicion of the USSR's policies past and present. He spoke like a schoolmaster correcting a disappointing pupil:

We have to be very careful on this area, Mr President, because what we want to do is get rid of nuclear weapons and if we handle this badly, we will not be able to get rid of them. We can't live with nuclear weapons if they are used. We can't get rid of them because there are no defences against them. We must do nothing to inhibit our ability to defend against nuclear weapons. We need to defend early; we need to defend our continent, not just a few sites.[7]

According to the latest information, the Strategic Defense Initiative was not going to be ready for deployment until 1995. There was a danger in accepting the demands that Soviet negotiators were making. Weinberger did not mind if arms talks were suspended for two years or more. America had to demonstrate firmness.[8]

Although Reagan mouthed yes to Weinberger, the punctilious minutes-taker recorded that he was 'basically shaking his head'. He badly wanted to make a success of the talks. He made one short move to placate Weinberger by promising that if America were to share the Strategic Defense Initiative technology with the USSR, he would insist on getting the same access to the new Soviet defence system. Weinberger remained unmoved: 'I don't believe we could ever do that.' General Robert Herres, Vice-Chairman of the Joint Chiefs of Staff, agreed: 'Mr President, there is a great risk in exchanging technical data. Much of our technology is easily convertible into other purposes and into an offensive area.' Adelman added: 'Mr President, that would be the most massive technical transfer that the Western world has ever known. We would make the Toshiba incident look piddling. If they understood our system that well, it would be easy for them to move to countermeasures.'[9]

Kampelman said that people were missing the point. He said that the American delegation in Geneva, after thirty months of intensive bargaining, had secured assent to 'a fantastic agreement' on intermediate-range missiles. He asked for further compromise in order to move towards signature. Kampelman desired to confine the Strategic Defense Initiative to being a research programme only. He was talking without his normal precision. He knew that not even Gorbachëv was demanding so restrictive a set of conditions. He angered Weinberger, who contended that America should never forgo the right to deploy the results of research.[10] The President came down yet again in favour of facilitating progress at the negotiating table: 'I've been reading my Bible and the description of Armageddon talks about destruction, I believe, of many cities and we absolutely need to avoid that. We absolutely need to avoid that.' Carlucci willingly conceded: 'We certainly need to avoid Armageddon.' Weinberger sensed a slackening of the presidential will and bluntly asserted: 'The answer is SDI.'[11] These were the last words recorded at the meeting, and victory lay with Shultz and those who wanted a treaty. Weinberger never recovered from his reverse. Within a few weeks he was to decide to step down from office.

Shevardnadze flew to America for talks with Reagan and Shultz. He was in a confident humour. He told aides that the differences between the two sides were merely a matter of 'cosmetics'.[12] His mood changed at the White House on 15 September 1987 when Reagan sharply objected to the Soviet Army's continued presence in Afghanistan: 'If you want to withdraw [your] armies, withdraw them!' Shevardnadze took umbrage at the tirades about Soviet policy on human rights and on Eastern Europe. He bluntly posed the question to Reagan: 'Do we or don't we want an agreement?'[13] When Shevardnadze proposed to put Weinberger in touch with Soviet Defence Minister Yazov, Weinberger bridled: 'If they invite me to Red Square to make a public admission of breaking the INF Treaty, I'll come!' But even Weinberger calmed down, remarking that as Secretary of State for Health under Nixon he had got on rather well with his opposite number, Minister of Health Petrovski. Shevardnadze expressed regret that Petrovski had not taken over the Defence Ministry. Reagan grew philosophical: 'If suddenly the earth's civilizations are threatened by other worlds, the USA and the Soviet Union will unite. Isn't that so?' Everyone wondered how to deal with such a question. Bush did it with one of his jokes: 'An interplanetary spacecraft entered our galaxy. The CIA conducted surveillance on it and picked up the following conversation: "Four heads are anyway better than two."'[14]

Shevardnadze and Shultz got together later that day and agreed about how to organize the working groups to draft the final details of the Intermediate-Range Nuclear Forces Treaty.[15] This pleased Shevardnadze, who thought it possible to proceed to a fifty per cent reduction in strategic weapons. The USSR still had some good cards to play. Shevardnadze reckoned that if Gorbachëv did not like what the White House offered, he could still turn down the invitation to a Washington summit meeting without loss of face.[16]

On 17 September 1987 Shultz handed over a list of demands running to sixty pages. He pushed for rapid signature of the treaty. Shevardnadze, who was suffering from insomnia, declined to be rushed. Far too many questions remained unresolved. The pace needed to slacken.[17] Shultz replied that if there was any delay, Soviet leaders might have to negotiate with whoever became President after Reagan. Better to finish things off quickly between the Soviet Union and America. Big arms reduction agreements were in reach. Shultz showed annoyance when Shevardnadze continued to demur. Both agreed that important details needed clarifying before the summit, but the Americans worried that there was a lack of a sense of urgency in Moscow.[18] Shevardnadze for his part sought assurances that the conflict inside the American establishment would quickly be resolved. The USSR did not want to hold a signing ceremony in Washington, only to hear that the American Congress refused to ratify the treaty. The Soviet leadership was not going to put the reputation of its General Secretary in jeopardy.[19] Shevardnadze wanted Shultz to appreciate that Gorbachëv and the reformers faced a difficult situation at home. They simply could not afford to appear as being too ready to yield on every matter of difficulty in international relations.

The military lobby in the USSR continued to harp on the dangers. The General Staff agreed with the official priority for a bilateral reduction in nuclear arms. The Americans and their allies worried that the consequence could be to leave Soviet conventional forces in a position to pose an insurmountable threat to Western Europe. (This was why Akhromeev had left these forces out of his proposals in January 1986.) Reagan lent urgency to military modernization. There was no let-up in the process, and voices on the Soviet side expressed concern that NATO would soon take a leap forward in its non-nuclear equipment. The USSR was being outstripped.[20]

On 14 October 1987 the US National Security Planning Group drew pleasure from the fact that Soviet leaders no longer treated the

Strategic Defense Initiative as a barrier to a treaty. According to Kampelman, they had learned 'that they have to live with it'. Carlucci explained: 'That's what Shevardnadze said to me during his visit'.[21] Reagan referred everyone to a film screened at Camp David that 'really refutes the scientific groupies that have it all wrong'. This boosted his confidence about winning over the American public.[22] Weinberger warned against undue compromise:

> I want no restrictions. Any restriction on testing is too restrictive. It's just a scientific matter; you're asking me not to think about something. If we would have taken this attitude, we would never have had the auto or the cinema industry. For example, Mr President, you'll notice that on their list, the electromagnetic masked accelerator is restricted to 1.2 grams per fathom. That's certainly too restrictive.[23]

His pernicketiness gave rise to some amusement.[24] He was evidently a spent political force, as he increasingly recognized. The impetus from the White House was in the direction of agreeing a treaty. Reagan wanted the talks to succeed.

The President agreed for Shultz to fly to Moscow for discussions about the remaining obstacles to a treaty. On 23 October Shultz met with Gorbachëv to reaffirm that the Strategic Defense Initiative was untouchable. Gorbachëv replied that if this was going to be the American attitude, there was no point in his crossing the Atlantic. Instead of a Washington summit, he suggested an encounter with Reagan somewhere halfway between the two capitals.[25] He was obviously hoping that a display of obduracy would force the Americans to give ground.[26]

Gorbachëv had to think again when Shultz made clear that he was not going to budge. His difficulty, as he knew that Shultz was aware, was that he wanted a treaty as badly as did Reagan. This removed high cards from his bargaining hand. Without further fuss he dropped the objection to Washington as a summit venue and moved on to practical matters. The two sides tried to formulate a common basis for evaluating their capacities in intermediate- and short-range weapons; they also edged towards agreement on procedures of verification. As Gorbachëv pointed out, this still left the big question of strategic nuclear weaponry and the Anti-Ballistic Missile Treaty unresolved. He accused Washington of intransigence and called on the Americans to stick to the Anti-Ballistic Missile Treaty for another ten years; he offered to negotiate about exactly what kinds of device were to be permissible for deployment in outer space. As a token of good intent, he said he would consider suspending work on the Krasnoyarsk radar station; but he rejected Kampelman's argument in Geneva in favour of keeping separate the talks on strategic weapons and those on the Strategic Defense Initiative.[27]

Gorbachëv and Shultz concurred that they had the basis at least for a treaty on intermediate-range nuclear missiles, and the Soviet side called for Gorbachëv's trip to receive the highest status in Washington. After the autumn of political trouble in Moscow, Gorbachëv sought to boost his image through the medium of international acclaim. His aides asked for him to receive an invitation to address a joint session of the American Congress. This was an accolade too many for an American conservative administration.[28] The working parties had yet to resolve several problems that stood in the way of the treaty, and Reagan trod carefully in his preparations for the talks. People around Gorbachëv were equally cautious. On the flight to America, one of his team quipped: 'If any general discovers who's on this aircraft, he'll brandish a rocket and that'll be the end of *perestroika*.'[29] The joke referred to what the Soviet high command might get up to. Everyone laughed while hoping against hope that Gorbachëv would keep command of the situation. To put it mildly, a lot was at stake on both sides of the Atlantic and Gorbachëv and Reagan were wise to approach the summit with prudence.

The summit started on 8 December 1987 before everything was settled. The Soviet delegation arrived in Washington refusing to hand over a technical photo of their SS-20 missile. The draft treaty required the destruction of all such missiles. Soviet negotiators explained that SS-20s were assembled inside a kind of canister that made them impossible to photograph. Powell was minded to overlook the difficulty; but others on the American side wanted to hang tough, and Shultz agreed with them. Soviet negotiators learned that if they wanted a treaty, they would have to give way.[30]

This they duly did, and the way was clear for a signing ceremony in the White House. It was an occasion of importance. The superpowers were not just limiting but rather eliminating a whole category of nuclear weaponry from their forces. Reagan and Gorbachëv appended their signatures in the East Room of the White House – only the process of ratification lay ahead. Next day, on 9 December, Reagan went into talks with Gorbachëv accompanied by Shultz and Carlucci. He confirmed acceptance of the objective of halving the number of strategic ballistic missiles. Although Gorbachëv complained about the Strategic Defense Initiative, he did so in a somewhat perfunctory fashion; he entirely ceased trying to make any further progress in arms reduction conditional upon Reagan agreeing to scrap his favourite project. Instead he merely suggested that if the Americans went ahead with deployment, the Kremlin would order the development and construction of more powerful new missiles that could overwhelm any defence system. He also repeated his intention to pull Soviet forces out of Afghanistan. While declining to set a date for the withdrawal, he promised that it would happen soon. He asked in return for America to refrain from assisting the mujahidin. Reagan turned down the request: he could see no reason why the Americans should withhold help from those who were rebelling against an illegitimate government installed by the USSR.[31]

The exchanges were robust but friendly even though Shultz thought it insensitive of the President to tell a favourite joke about the USSR while Gorbachëv was trying to explain his hopes to reconstruct Soviet society. Shultz said bluntly: 'Mr President, stop. Gorbachëv makes an impassioned and positive statement and then you tell a joke that insults him.' Reagan refused to curb himself: he used humour to impress his ideas about the need for the Soviet authorities to acknowledge the rights of the individual, and he did not mind if he offended them – and Shultz came to appreciate his President's attitude.[32]

Reagan thought it 'the best summit we'd ever had with the Soviet Union.'[33] This was how he briefed Democrat and Republican leaders at breakfast on 11 December. Surveys of American public opinion indicated a rise in his rating. On all sides he was receiving plaudits. The world appeared safer after he and Gorbachëv announced their accord about intermediate-range nuclear forces. Reagan phoned leaders in Tokyo, Paris and London with his news.[34] He and Shultz were elated about the prospect of further progress towards arms reduction. A serious compromise had been mooted at the summit when Shultz had indicated that the Americans might be willing to adhere to the Anti-Ballistic Missile Treaty for several years ahead and abandon their freedom to carry out tests of the Strategic Defense Initiative. Gorbachëv liked any idea of delaying deployment. He in turn signalled that the USSR would not object to America deploying its system at the end of the agreed period. This opened a possible route towards a new treaty on strategic nuclear weapons. On 13 December Shultz made a jubilant announcement to the world's media. If only the two talks delegations in Geneva could speed up their work, he said, it might prove feasible to get a draft treaty ready for signature at the next summit in Moscow.[35]

As Shultz headed off for a meeting of NATO foreign ministers in Brussels, he cautioned against undue optimism: 'It is too soon to tell whether this prefigures a profound change in the nature of the Soviet Union and how it deals with the world.'[36] Yet there had been unquestionable progress at the summit, and Shultz took pride in it. A unanimous decision emerged from the meeting to urge the American Senate to ratify the Intermediate-Range Nuclear Forces Treaty without delay.[37] He told the Senate's Foreign Relations Committee that Reagan's toughness had proved that America would never give way in matters of vital interest. He expected no difficulty for the White House with the NATO allies.[38] He wrote to Senate Democrat leader Robert Byrd promising to provide senators with confidential information to assure them that the administration was keeping nothing back. He was willing to release the entire record of the American–Soviet negotiations.[39] When Senators Byrd and Nunn wrote back in a friendly spirit, Shultz promised that the administration would stick to its publicly announced understanding of the clauses. There would be no sudden deviation that might cause unease in the Senate.[40]

Shultz worked for that further agreement on strategic weapons before Reagan left office.[41] There was agreement about holding the next summit in Moscow in summer. On 9 February 1988 the American National Security Planning Group met to map out strategy. The President gave his word: 'I *will not* rush to an agreement for agreement's sake.'[42] Powell predicted difficulties.[43] When even Shultz expressed unease, Reagan exclaimed:

> From my past experiences as a labor negotiator, maybe we need to do this; we need to go for the gold. You need to put down what the ideal agreement would be. After you've done that, you can decide among yourselves what our bottom lines should be – what we can and what [we] can't give up beyond; also where there's no bargaining – those items on which we can't bargain.[44]

He encouraged his officials to play a harder game for victory. Defense Secretary Carlucci tried to douse the enthusiasm. He reported that he and William Crowe, Chairman of the Joint Chiefs of Staffs, heard at the Congress about a growing worry that the President might rush into a treaty.[45] Chief of Staff Baker said that the administration had to stay united.[46] Shultz stressed that 'the Soviets also want to ratify these treaties'; he asked for approval from everyone around the table. Powell said he could count on this.[47]

Gorbachëv was eager to keep up the momentum, as he explained to the Politburo on 25 February:

> Yes, we've obtained military-strategic parity with the United States. Nobody considered how much this cost us. But we really should count it up. It's now clear that without a significant reduction in military expenditure we can't resolve the problems of *perestroika*. Parity is parity, and we must preserve it. But it's also necessary to disarm. And now such an opportunity exists.[48]

He called for a proper scientific analysis of the Strategic Defense Initiative: was it 'a bluff or a reality'? Only when this question was authoritatively answered would it be possible to establish 'the sole correct policy'. He added that it was essential to create a peace that was genuinely dependable: 'The people remember the year 1941!'[49]

But the American Senate stalled about ratifying the Intermediate-Range Nuclear Forces Treaty. Former Secretary of State Kissinger scowled about it even though he saw no alternative to signing it.[50] Not all conservatives were as accommodating. Dan Quale, a young Senator on the Armed Forces Committee, denounced the terms as damaging to the national interest.[51] Trouble also came from Senator Jesse Helms, the veteran Republican known for his hostility to conciliatory moves toward the USSR. When Shultz appeared at the Senate Foreign Relations Committee, Helms accused the administration of 'confusion, misstatements and . . . even mispresentation' in its public presentation of the treaty. Shultz had heard enough. He asked Helms directly whether he was accusing him of deliberately distorting the facts. Although Helms backed down, Shultz's anger was not yet spent: 'I don't know what I'm doing here.' This comment induced Helms to jab back: 'You'll have to decide why you're here.' Senior Senators from the Democratic Party intervened to help Shultz out. The Democrats were not entirely helpful since they wanted to deny the President any right to reinterpret the treaty after ratification; but they certainly endorsed the need for ratification.[52]

US Senators Nunn, Cohen, Levin and Warner met Gorbachëv in Moscow in March with a view towards facilitating the process. When Gorbachëv talked airily about creating a European 'corridor' free from nuclear and chemical weapons, Nunn explained that the Americans would have no interest in enabling this unless the USSR also removed the tanks. Gorbachëv switched direction. Calling for compliance with the Anti-Ballistic Missile Treaty, he implausibly tried to deny that his scientists were working on a response to America's Strategic Defense Initiative.[53] It was not the quietest meeting. But it did at least enmesh the two political systems more deeply into mutual contact and understanding.

Shevardnadze arrived in Washington nine days later. The two delegations met in the State Department and split up into small groups for talks on human rights, regional disputes, disarmament and US–USSR bilateral relations.[54] Shevardnadze asked Shultz to recognize the progress being made in the USSR: 'Everywhere smells of newly ploughed earth.' He took pride in the reforms of Soviet psychiatric hospitals while castigating American record on racism. He criticized American attempts to widen the interpretation of the Anti-Ballistic Missile Treaty. Shultz refused to give ground.[55] But a worrying uncertainty remained about strategic nuclear weapons, and Shultz decided to go to Moscow for talks in late April. He took Powell and a large team with him and came upon a Soviet leadership that resisted compromise on contentious matters. Shultz observed: 'People have gone slack on their oars.' He and his team speculated that the Kremlin was distracted by internal political tensions. Shevardnadze reasoned that the USSR could not afford to help America to bring an end to the Iran–Iraq war for fear of inducing the Iranians to make mischief as the Soviet Army withdrew from Afghanistan. But as Nitze noted, this did not account for the halt to progress in the nuclear arms talks. Shultz concluded that it was unfeasible to draft a strategic weapons treaty before the Moscow summit. He and Shevardnadze agreed to continue to work on it through the summer and beyond.[56]

Their collaboration was about to undergo a further complication. On the day of Shultz's arrival in Moscow, Reagan spoke to the World Affairs Council of Western Massachusetts in Springfield and delivered some blunt thoughts on the USSR: 'We said freedom was better than totalitarianism. We said communism was bad.'[57] This had always been his opinion, and his words reassured his conservative political base. They hardly made things easier for Gorbachëv in the USSR.

Unfortunately the White House had omitted to liaise with Shultz about the Springfield speech. On 23 April he found Gorbachëv in an angry frame of mind. Gorbachëv demanded to know whether Reagan had changed his Soviet policy. Shultz was in the embarrassing situation of not having received a copy of the text. The presidential speechwriters, he thought, had overlooked the sensitivities of the diplomatic moment.[58] Shultz had no option but to sit back and let Gorbachëv's rage blow itself out before impressing on him that Reagan really had benevolent intentions. He also pointed to the vote in the House of Representatives, by a majority of 393 to 7, in favour of the Intermediate-Range Nuclear Forces Treaty. The atmosphere steadily cleared.[59] Shultz reported to Reagan: 'Today Gorbachëv was peppy, reflective and humorous by turns.'[60] But he wished to focus attention on the requirements for the forthcoming summit. Another Springfield speech would hinder this. Having spelled out his concern, Shultz recalled that when he first became Secretary of State, Reagan had given him a glass tablet inscribed with the quotation: 'There is no limit to what you can do or how far you can go as long as you don't care who gets the credit.'[61]

Unfortunately the American Senate had yet to complete its deliberations. At talks in Geneva on 10 May, Shultz told Shevardnadze of his annoyance about the delay. Shevardnadze replied: 'For us this has been unexpected to the highest degree.' The news that the Chinese were selling ballistic missiles to Saudi Arabia was also agitating him. Shultz and Shevardnadze agreed to consult about the problem.[62]

On 23 May Reagan told the National Security Planning Committee: 'I want to leave as a legacy as complete and coherent an arms reduction position as I can.'[63] Shultz admitted: 'The only thing we can do right now is listen and keep our options open and look for the right opening.'[64] He swore to be firm about the Strategic Defense Initiative and to stipulate the need to dismantle the Krasnoyarsk radar station in return for America. He argued that America's interest continued to lie with adhering to the Anti-Ballistic Missile Treaty.[65] Defense Secretary Carlucci was in no doubt: 'I'm here to tell you, George, that if you come out of the review with the K-radar not down, and you don't declare a material breach, you'll never see a [strategic nuclear weapons reduction] treaty!' National Security Adviser Powell warned about the criticism that Senator Helms would level against any display of softness towards the USSR. Rowny, as the President's Special Adviser on Arms Control, recommended telling Gorbachëv that America's position on Krasnoyarsk was closed to negotiation. Shultz replied: 'How can you claim a material breach and still retain the Anti-Ballistic Missile Treaty? And by the way, when we call material breach for that, they'll call a tit-for-tat at Fylingdales.' Carlucci nagged away until

Shultz proved willing to say that all 'agreed that there would be no START treaty until the K-radar is down'.[66]

Neither the American nor the Soviet leaders expected to take definitive decisions on strategic nuclear weapons at the Moscow summit. As the Big Five set about drafting advice for Gorbachëv, they offered few guidelines beyond advising him to keep account of the political pressure that the American political right was exerting upon Reagan.[67] This vagueness lent Gorbachëv some latitude for personal initiative. He intended to accord the kind of freedom that he himself had received in Washington. Reagan would deliver a speech on live, uncensored TV to Moscow State University students. Gorbachëv also had the idea for the two of them to take a public stroll on Red Square. He trusted ordinary Russians to behave with suitable dignity.[68] The Americans could invite whomever they liked to their embassy gatherings: Gorbachëv wanted to demonstrate that things had really changed fundamentally in the USSR. Moscow was clean but dowdy, and Gorbachëv gave orders to brighten the appearance of the buildings. The police cleared the prostitutes from the tourist hotels in the central zone. The authorities were determined that the President's party of 800 officials and the press corps of 3,300 should gain no glimpse of Soviet lives lived outside the law.[69]

At last on 27 May the Senate voted its approval of the treaty by 93 votes to 5. The USSR Supreme Soviet ratified it by unanimous acclamation. This confirmed the rationale for the summit and the President and First Lady flew immediately to Moscow, arriving in Air Force One at Vnukovo airport on 29 May.

Shevardnadze welcomed Shultz on the same evening. When Shultz expressed regret about the failure to produce a draft on strategic weapons, Shevardnadze replied that at least they had laid the foundations. He added that the General Staff shared this attitude – and Akhromeev backed him up. Work would begin immediately.[70] Nobody expected it to reach completion before the year was out – and by then Reagan would be reaching the end of his presidential term. Moving on to other matters, Shevardnadze mentioned what he called abuses of power in America. He said he had heard that there were 11,000 political prisoners. But as he acknowledged, he had no list of names and could not cite a source for his allegation.[71] He was more confident when talking about Afghanistan. He bemoaned Pakistan's infringement of the Geneva Accords; he commented that Gorbachëv saw the Afghan question as 'the touchstone' of the superpowers' capacity to settle regional conflicts. Moscow's compliance with the Accords would depend on Islamabad's behaviour.[72] Shultz declined to react to this implicit threat and simply repeated his demand for the dismantling of the Krasnoyarsk early-warning station. Shevardnadze had given a private commitment to this outcome, but Shultz asked for action. There was a sticky moment before Shevardnadze deftly passed the topic over to Akhromeev for elaboration.[73]

In the working group on regional conflicts, there was an exchange of information about southern Africa – and Adamishin stressed that there could be no peace in the region until apartheid was ended.[74] Soviet officials stressed that foreign forces should nevertheless pull out of Angola; and they included the Cubans in this.[75] As regards Kampuchea, both sides opposed a return to power by Pol Pot's genocidal administration. The Americans pointed out that a complete withdrawal of Vietnamese forces alone would satisfy China.[76] The Americans were 'still looking for the beef'.[77] In truth, many conflicts were beyond direct control of either superpower. On North Korea, nobody had any idea about how to induce Kim Il-sung to lessen the tension. There was even more gloom about events in the Middle East.[78] The Americans took exception to the continued military supplies to Nicaragua.[79] Soviet officials countered that Pakistan was systematically violating the Geneva Accords by shipping arms over the Afghan border. The Americans gave them short shrift. If the USSR had agreed to cease supplying Afghanistan's communist government, they might have listened more sympathetically.[80] They added that the mujahidin were fighting with arms they captured from the Afghan communists that Moscow persisted in delivering. America's preferred solution was for the USSR to cease transferring weaponry to their Afghan clients.[81]

Disagreements took place without polemics. One of the smoothest encounters was between Defence Minister Yazov and Defense Secretary Carlucci. According to Carlucci, the Warsaw Pact's forces had a structural bias towards invading Western Europe. Yazov replied that Soviet military doctrine was preponderantly defensive; he cited official statements to this effect and asked why American leaders did not believe in them. Akhromeev unfurled a map showing all the American military bases around the USSR's borders. If America felt threatened, so too did the USSR. Carlucci asked Yazov to appreciate the logistical needs of an 'island nation' like America. Yazov forbore to ask what Canadians and Mexicans might think about this geographical conception. Carlucci's main point was that American forces were designed to deter an attack, not to start one. To everyone's surprise, Akhromeev acknowledged that the Soviet force structure had features of an offensive nature. He asked Carlucci to accept the genuineness of the USSR's commitment to military reform. This, he remarked, would inevitably take time. He teased Carlucci by saying that the CIA must surely have reported on Soviet military moves towards a defensive posture. Yazov pointed out that the latest military exercise in East Germany was entirely premised upon defence.[82]

While this was happening at the side of the summit, the spotlight remained on Reagan. His charm and affability conquered nearly everyone who saw him in Moscow. He was cheered everywhere he went, and the only annoyance for him was the way that the Soviet security agencies manhandled some people in the crowd that gathered on the street when the Reagans made a surprise appearance.[83] He had to submit to the usual counter-intelligence precautions at the American embassy, where he and Nancy were staying. As he had done in Reykjavik, he went into the 'bubble' to agree tactics with his travelling team.[84] There was little new that had to be decided. The Intermediate-Range Nuclear Forces Treaty text had been agreed at the Washington summit: it remained only for it to be signed into definitive operation.

At their first private meeting, Reagan spoke to Gorbachëv as a friend and pleaded for the liberalization of rules on religion beyond the Russian Orthodox Church. Gorbachëv rejected the request. But they went on talking amicably and agreed to call each other Mikhail and Ron.[85] At their second one-on-one meeting on 31 May, Gorbachëv went to his desk drawer and took out letters from Soviet citizens who had written to congratulate them on the advance towards peace in the world. Some had named their children Ronald in the President's honour. Reagan was touched and offered to write to them personally. He then gently recommended the benefits of free enterprise and competition. Gorbachëv agreed that traditional state monopolies had not worked well for the USSR. The single combine-harvester factory in Krasnoyarsk had produced shoddy machinery until the government refused to bail it out. Now, he claimed, the standard of output had reached a satisfactory level. His entire purpose, he told the President, was to introduce a new form of socialism. He was sure that the people would support it. He revelled in the way things were going, and said the Soviet Union 'was now the number one country in the world when it came to debate'. He denied wanting to level society out like a wooden board – and he pounded the coffee table with the flat of his hand to reinforce the point.[86]

On 31 May Reagan gave his speech at Moscow State University. He had drafted it in an avuncular style. His themes were freedom, peace and cooperation. He memorably recounted the scene in the *Butch Cassidy and the Sundance Kid* movie when the two outlaws are poised on the edge of a cliff overlooking a river. Butch urges Sundance to jump. Sundance replies that he cannot swim. But they both jump and survive. Reagan likened the episode to '*perestroika* and what its goals are'. He wished the Soviet reforms well.

Gorbachëv was his equal as a showman. When they took their scheduled stroll that day in Red Square, Gorbachëv picked up a young boy and told him to shake hands with *Dedushka Reigan* ('Grandad Reagan'). The President reacted with characteristic gracefulness. As they turned into the Kremlin at the Spasski Gate, a crowd of reporters shouted for their attention. One of the questions was: 'Do you still think you're in an evil empire, Mr President?' Reagan simply replied: 'No, I was talking about another time and another era.'[87] That single word 'No' was relayed in TV and press bulletins around the world. It was indeed a statement of importance. A president who had once denounced the USSR in blistering terms was walking with a general secretary as if nothing was more normal. American conservatives worried that their President might have fallen for the charm of the Soviet leader. They were also apprehensive that, even if Reagan's judgement of Gorbachëv's sincerity was well founded, there was no guarantee that he could survive for long in power. On 31 May Shultz took a question on the topic from Tom Brokaw of NBC News. Without commenting on the General Secretary's future tenure of office, he assured American viewers that the President was right to persist in seeking further agreements with the USSR as soon as possible.[88]

On 1 June Gorbachëv and Reagan came together in the Kremlin's Vladimir Hall to sign the treaty. Dignitaries from both countries were in attendance. Senators Doyle and Byrd had flown over, and Reagan was surrounded by Shultz, Carlucci and Powell while Gorbachëv brought along his entire Politburo. Nancy Reagan gave Shultz a kiss before taking her seat next to Raisa Gorbachëva. The moment of signature happened on schedule at midday. Politics were not forgotten on the American side as Reagan gave thanks to the American Senate for its support.[89] The unimaginable had suddenly happened. America and the Soviet Union had not just agreed to limit the number of nuclear weapons they held, they were going to eliminate an entire category of ballistic missiles. World politics had been in crisis since Moscow had installed SS-20s and Washington had reacted with Pershing-2s. The Intermediate-Range Nuclear Forces Treaty at a stroke removed the threat that such weapons would bring the day of Armageddon to Europe. Both sides saw this great advance as only the first stage in progress towards general nuclear disarmament.

27. CALLS TO WESTERN EUROPE

To a man and woman, the West European leaders joined the chorus of approval of the results of the Moscow summit. But their minds retained twitching filaments of scepticism. Mitterrand frankly warned Reagan that the Intermediate-Range Nuclear Forces Treaty provided no safeguard against the USSR's superiority in conventional forces. The French, British and West Germans recognized the ultimate desirability of progress toward an agreement on strategic missiles but asked Reagan to move beyond his preoccupation with nuclear missiles.[1] Mitterrand put words into practice and secretly ordered an expansion of France's chemical weapons programme.[2] The closer that Reagan drew to Gorbachëv, the deeper the anxiety in NATO capitals that Western Europe might end up vulnerable to Soviet bullying or even invasion. East–West conciliation was involved definite perils.

The American President knew there were few European leaders whom he could entirely trust. While Mitterrand was firm in his desire to resist the Soviet threat to Western security and to retain the American military presence in Europe, he disliked the Strategic Defense Initiative and the attempt to bankrupt the USSR. His country resolutely stayed outside NATO. He also led the Socialist Party – hardly a political organization that appealed to Reagan. West Germany's Helmut Kohl, a Christian Democrat, was a likelier partner for the American administration, and he certainly had a keen awareness of the menace from the Warsaw Pact on his country's borders. His sole consolation, as he told Mitterrand, was his belief that the Soviet economy's condition was beyond the possibility of any serious improvement.[3] But he was really no more sympathetic than Mitterrand to the Strategic Defense Initiative, and had expressed public support for it only under pressure from Shultz.[4] Kohl also took a longer time than Reagan to feel he could usefully bargain with Gorbachëv, whom he dismissed as an 'an orthodox communist' heavily under the influence of Kádár and Jaruzelski.[5] He shared Mitterrand's priority for avoiding friction with Moscow. He took time to put his faith in Reagan.

Margaret Thatcher and Pope John Paul II had been the President's foremost supporters since he first entered the White House. America and the Vatican joined together in opposition to communism in the USSR and Eastern Europe, but their coordination was of a loose kind. John Paul II communicated his thinking through the Papal Nuncio in Washington.[6] The Pope, a Pole by birth, justifiably assumed that he knew the east of Europe better than any politician across the Atlantic, and took his own initiatives whenever he thought he could undermine atheism and dictatorship. His plan in 1987 was to make a summer visit to his homeland. This would obviously require permission from Poland's communist authorities. Jaruzelski consented so as to avoid opprobrium for denying a visa to the Polish Pope and gain credit among Poles for strengthening a workable relationship with the national Church. The remaining question for John Paul II was whether to fly on from Poland to Vilnius to celebrate the 600th anniversary of Christianity in Lithuania.[7] Such a possibility alarmed the KGB, which feared that religious celebrations could lead to nationalist disturbances – with baleful consequences across the USSR. In the end, the Pope confined his trip to Poland. He seems to have thought it prudent to avoid destabilizing a Soviet leadership that was handling Eastern Europe with unprecedented gentleness.

He began his trip on 8 June 1987 after intense negotiations between Warsaw and the Vatican. Jaruzelski knew that if he prevented the Pope from coming, the ban would have annoyed millions of citizens. He also calculated that he himself might gain a degree of respectability with fellow Poles by sanctioning a pastoral visit. The communist authorities were aware of John Paul II's capacity to stir up strong antipathy towards them even while speaking with diplomatic correctness. He gauged his statements with a wily sense of political undercurrents. Jaruzelski and his ministers felt that he behaved 'more aggressively than we expected'.[8] The Pope went to Gdańsk, one of the centres of the protest movement, as well as Warsaw. His homilies about human rights, dignity and justice raised people's spirits; and by holding a private meeting with Lech Wałęsa, he gave ecclesiastical benediction to Solidarity. His appeal to Poles to live their live in accordance with their Christian beliefs was a challenge to atheistic communism's claims to political legitimacy. The enthusiastic crowds left no doubt about national pride in his dignified, principled words of defiance.[9]

Margaret Thatcher communicated more frequently and directly with Reagan than the Pope did. She and the President were soulmates in politics. Letters passed frequently to and fro, and they phoned each other when rapid decisions of importance were necessary.[10] While recognizing that America outmatched Britain in global power, Thatcher hoped to use her influence with Reagan for the good of their common cause. She sought at the same time to promote the British national interest; and when Reagan failed to support her before the Falklands war in 1982 or alert her about his invasion of Grenada in 1983, she gave vent to her annoyance. She was also eager to communicate her enthusiasms. In 1984 she had told the President that Gorbachëv was a new kind of Soviet leader in the making.

But as soon as Gorbachëv became general secretary, she went off the boil. Far from acting as an intermediary between East and West, she sniped from the sidelines at the moves towards conciliation. Her fear was that Reagan might yield too much in discussions with Moscow, and she assured French Prime Minister Laurent Fabius that Gorbachëv was only a 'charming communist'.[11] Her hostility to Reagan's idea of abolishing nuclear weapons never left her. The only adjustment to her position after Reykjavik came with her advice to the President to provide Gorbachëv with a clearer idea about the projected stages for introducing the Strategic Defense Initiative; she also advised Reagan to promise that the Americans would refrain for a fixed period from deploying the results of their research.[12] Percy Cradock, her Foreign Policy Adviser, thought she was overly occupied with questions of American policy. He nagged her in 1986 – in the nicest possible way, no doubt – to seek an invitation to visit Moscow. She consistently refused, arguing that there 'might be too little to show'.[13] What she apparently meant was that Gorbachëv was unlikely to make concessions to the British national interest. Chernyaev astutely reckoned that she instinctively valued him predominantly because he was likely to bring about 'the self-liquidation' of a political and social order that was alien to human nature.[14] But foreign policy was a different matter. Thatcher was not going to provide Gorbachëv with undue publicity by appearing to cooperate with him. She could see no purpose in making it easy for Gorbachëv and Reagan to liaise.

Her inactivity perplexed even some of her friends in the United Kingdom. Her critics went on to the attack. Labour Party leader Neil Kinnock sympathized with Gorbachëv's efforts to lessen international tensions and spoke disrespectfully about her when meeting Soviet officials.[15] Thatcher took no notice. The worry for her remained that the Soviet leadership might be fooling everyone. In the American spectrum of analysis, she was nearer to Weinberger than to Shultz. She was jealous of her reputation as the Iron Lady.

If Soviet leaders were going to soften her metal, they had to light a furnace in Moscow. Gorbachëv appreciated Thatcher's communion with Reagan. The convention for America and Britain was that if one of them had contact with Gorbachëv, a report would be made to the other.[16] Gorbachëv wished to use Thatcher as a way of exerting influence on the White House. By late 1986 he had abandoned any illusion about playing the West Europeans against the Americans. He no longer imagined that he could persuade France to act separately from NATO. In May 1987 he advised the Politburo that the French Prime Minister Jacques Chirac felt a political need to appear tough-minded in any negotiations with the Kremlin. Chirac was at one with Thatcher on questions of military security.[17] Gorbachëv had no greater confidence about Chancellor Kohl, who in October 1986 had compared him to Joseph Goebbels in public relations technique.[18] Kohl had half-apologized for the gaffe but Soviet resentment still simmered even though Gorbachëv recognized the need for better ties with West Germany.[19] Gorbachëv's planning stayed focused on Thatcher, and an invitation went out to her to visit Moscow – which, to the delight of her advisers, she immediately accepted. There was excitement in British political circles about the projected trip.[20]

The Politburo had little presentiment about her likely impact in Moscow. Mannered in diction and laboured in rhetoric, she had always been at her best in front of people who were already on her side. Her ability to win over the unconverted was open to doubt. The Soviet authorities assumed that it was they who possessed the more communicative leader. Only Reagan matched Gorbachëv's stellar appeal. Surely the General Secretary would be more than a match for the Iron Lady! They overlooked her combative side. Gorbachëv had experienced it at Chequers in December 1984. He was about to discover that she could deploy it just as readily on Soviet soil. As was her wont, she prepared intensively. She took advice from the KGB defector Oleg Gordievski about how to behave and what to say.[21] Gordievski knew better than anyone about the vulnerable points for a Westerner to probe. In the Prime Minister, he found a listener and learner.

On 29 March 1987 Prime Minister Ryzhkov welcomed her at Vnukovo airport. Ahead lay five days of meetings and appearances.

She started with panache. She dressed glamorously in fur hat and coat. She visited the Russian Orthodox Church monastery at Zagorsk outside the capital. She joined an ordinary Russian family in their apartment – the British embassy took care to ensure that the family were not KGB operatives. Her chance to make a public impact came when she gave a live TV interview to three senior journalists. Their professional experience counted for nothing as she tossed their questions back at them and expounded the virtues of an open society and a market economy. She, not they, set the agenda. They were accustomed to compliance from the female sex. They had never encountered such an Amazon. The TV audience loved how she punctured the balloon of official Soviet complacency. Nobody had ever been allowed to use the Soviet media to issue so direct a challenge to the credo of Marxism-Leninism. Her forthrightness and charm won friends for the West in the USSR. She expressed her thoughts 'beautifully', purring like a cat as it approaches a huddle of rabbits.[22]

She behaved no differently in her private sessions with Gorbachëv, as Ambassador Cartledge recalled:

There can never have been a case where two heads of government so radiated a kind of chemistry between them. You could see the sparks flying off. They both liked talking. They both liked the sound of their own voices. They were both very difficult to interrupt. But they both managed to interrupt each other, and they had met their match.[23]

Knowledge of their personal rapport somehow filtered through to the Soviet public, and there was a profusion of risqué jokes about it.[24]

Gorbachëv looked on the bright side. As he admitted to his political confidants, the Prime Minister was hard to categorize: 'Madame is more cunning, Mitterrand is dirtier.' He had said that Britain's insistence on keeping its nuclear weapons merely discredited her around the world and indirectly encouraged other states to develop them. She replied that once invented, such weaponry could not be got rid of. They were talking at cross purposes, as when Gorbachëv asked her what she had done to help the process of nuclear disarmament. On 1 April she flew on to Georgia, where she spent a day in Tbilisi. Deputy Foreign Affairs Minister Kovalëv reported that when she mingled with the crowds, people began to shout: 'Peace, peace!' Gorbachëv acknowledged that her performance in the USSR had gained many admirers, especially among Soviet women. But he felt confident that she was going home talking well of the Soviet leadership and *perestroika*. The word was that this had annoyed the Americans. There was in fact no evidence for this; but he was justified in saying that her visit had turned into a success for the Soviet cause in international relations.[25]

Next day at the Politburo, on 2 April, Gorbachëv offered a brisk assessment of Western leaders. He claimed that Thatcher's epiphany had proved the validity of a new formula: 'He who doesn't have relations with us loses authority at home. Look at Kohl for an example.' He noted that the West German Chancellor had been compelled to admit his mistake in comparing him to Nazi propaganda chief Joseph Goebbels. Gorbachëv was proud of his own diplomatic record.[26]

He told the Politburo that Thatcher at one stage had seemed on the point of walking out of their talks. He was scathing about her tirades and said he had conceded nothing to a 'feisty old woman' who 'behaved like she does in her own parliament'. Having shown off his communist – and somewhat male-chauvinist – credentials, he asked the Politburo to recognize her good side: 'Unlike Mitterrand, she doesn't know how to disguise her real thoughts and plans.' Gorbachëv believed that she was impressed by what she saw in the USSR and genuinely desired to foster mutual trust. When she raised the question of the 1944 military occupation of the Baltic states, he had responded that they had belonged 'to us' since Peter the Great. He had disconcerted her by telling *Pravda* to publish her speeches in full. He thought that her rating in the United Kingdom was of some concern to her party: she could not afford to appear to obstruct a deal with the USSR if she wished to win the electoral struggle with the Labour Party – and, according to Gorbachëv, she recognized that 'Reagan was becoming decrepit'. Gorbachëv concluded that her bargaining position was weaker than it once had seemed.[27]

Her aide Charles Powell saw things differently: he reckoned that her performance had assured her of victory in the next general election.[28] Less parochially, her British critics wanted to see signs of her ceasing to obstruct America's rapprochement with the USSR. At the House of Commons on 26 June the Labour Party Shadow Foreign Secretary Denis Healey called on the government to appreciate 'the biggest change in Russia's approach to the world since 1917'. If President Reagan was working for a global reduction in nuclear weaponry, why were British ministers not cooperating? Foreign Secretary Sir Geoffrey Howe's inertia appeared paradoxical in the light of his past criticism of the Strategic Defense Initiative. Healey received no enlightenment from Howe, who confined himself to expressing doubt that the dogmas of communist policy had disappeared even under Gorbachëv.[29]

Thatcher was displeased when she heard that Gorbachëv was going to America in December 1987 to sign the Intermediate-Range Nuclear Forces Treaty. Nobody had consulted her for the duration of the negotiations between America and the USSR. Having recently dropped her frostiness towards Gorbachëv, she wanted to become involved. Summoning Ambassador Zamyatin, she exclaimed: 'Please, tell Gorbachëv that I am prepared to receive him on his way to Washington for two to three hours at our Brize Norton base where no Russian aircraft has ever been.'[30] Chernyaev counselled that it was in the Soviet interest to make her 'the big present' of enhancing her global prominence by granting the request. This was something she was eager for. In return the USSR would obtain her support for *perestroika*.[31] Gorbachëv agreed. Thatcher boasted to the press of their spirited exchanges:

> The atmosphere today has been very, very good indeed. It usually is when Mr Gorbachev and I get talking, because we talk certainly in quite animated debate as always. He is a powerful personality and I do not think I am anything other than that too! So, it is quite animated, but that way you get to grips with the issues very quickly. The atmosphere was good. Of course, I am not a go-between. I am quite an important part of the NATO alliance, and I am a very reliable ally, and no one has any doubt where I stand.[32]

She omitted to mention that she was no longer trying to impede the conciliation between Gorbachëv and Reagan. Gorbachëv conceded nothing to her at Brize Norton and flew on to America having achieved her promise of support.[33] The reasons for her cooperativeness can only be guessed at. Perhaps Chernyaev, her secret admirer, was right about her need for the oxygen of prestige. Or possibly she at last decided that if she could not beat them, she was going to join them. Was there also a personal factor? Her warmth towards Gorbachëv had been quietly evident to her advisers since the visit to Moscow. They began to find it hard to 'talk objectively' with her about him.[34] There was abundant evidence that the USSR had a huge stock of chemical weapons. Thatcher deplored this to Ryzhkov. When Gorbachëv gave his word that no such stocks existed, Thatcher refused to believe that he was lying. She believed that 'the facts had been kept from him'.[35]

She in truth had a thing about him. They began to get on 'like a house on fire', and had intense and enjoyable disputes whenever they met.[36] Foreign ministers Howe and Shevardnadze also warmed to each other but their transactions had no international impact.[37] This was because Thatcher monopolized her government's handling of the Soviet question. She made a point of excluding her Foreign Secretary from her meetings with Reagan and Bush. Shultz noticed that she did not bother to bring him with her to Washington.[38] Increasingly she valued Gorbachëv as someone who was changing the direction of history in the USSR. Recognizing the difficulties he faced, she saw a parallel with what she was trying to do in the United Kingdom.[39] It is true that she never abandoned her suspiciousness about his relationship with her other friend, Ron. Gorbachëv liked and respected her but felt he needed to treat her with caution. On 10 March 1988 he told the Politburo that she continued to head those Western politicians who accused the Kremlin of demagogy and insincerity.[40] As he saw it, he needed to keep himself informed about her dealings with the White House as the American and Soviet leaderships moved towards ratifying the treaty on intermediate-range nuclear weapons. Britain and France still refused to give up their nuclear weapons. Thatcher and Gorbachëv charmed each other without either dropping their basic reservations.

While she spared this one communist leader from criticism, her anticommunism was unrelenting. On her visit to Poland in November 1988 she reserved space in her programme to meet Lech Wałęsa and place flowers on the grave of the murdered Father Jerzy Popiełuszko. Jaruzelski felt he had to permit this. Communist administrations in Eastern Europe no longer believed they could prescribe the perambulations of a foreign leader on their territory. Jaruzelski's priority was to ensure that she arrived and departed without disturbance. He reasoned that her very presence would show Polish people that the West regarded communist Poland as a normal country.[41] She took her chance to indicate the opposite. Her floral tribute to the late Popiełuszko meant more to most Poles than her formal encounter with Jaruzelski. Her impact in Poland was almost as deep as that which she had achieved in Moscow a year earlier. But she worried that as Reagan's second term drew to a close, the sun might set on her international influence. She had imposed herself to a large extent by triangulating between the Kremlin and the White House from her base in Downing Street. She had never got on with Mitterrand or

Kohl, and had rarely bothered herself with Andreotti. Rodric Braithwaite talked to her before taking up his appointment as UK Ambassador to Moscow: 'She sees a parallel between herself and Gorbachëv. The relationship, she thinks, is close. "If Dukakis wins the election, Gorbachëv will be my only friend left."'[42]

Gorbachëv's diplomatic moves hardly lifted her gloom. The pivot of international relations in Western Europe was moving from London to Bonn. Shevardnadze undertook an exploratory visit in January 1988. He and the West German Foreign Minister Hans-Dietrich Genscher quickly agreed that Moscow and Bonn should increase their cooperation. Shevardnadze stressed that he was not seeking to prise the West Germans away from America; he claimed that Soviet foreign policy was now founded on 'general human interests'. He was frank in acknowledging that the USSR was facing economic difficulties. Boldness, he said, was required in international relations. While hoping for an improvement in diplomacy and trade with West Germany, he lamented the continuation of the CoCom embargo system on technological transfer – he commented even shoemaking machinery came under a ban. He called on the West Germans to recognize the benefits that would accrue from increased commerce with Moscow. Genscher countered that the USSR itself should show greater flexibility. He had said the same to Gorbachëv without getting a reply after lamenting about how the Kremlin operated its own version of CoCom through Comecon and restricted the transfer of its own technology. He urged Shevardnadze to consider collaboration between the European Economic Community and Comecon over space exploration.[43]

Whereas Genscher was fairly open-minded about Gorbachëv, Kohl still regarded him with what he called sceptical sympathy. He wanted more action and less blether – he saw Gorbachëv as simply aiming at a more efficient form of communism.[44]

But he began to see the sense in cutting Gorbachëv some slack. When telling Shevardnadze that the USSR was 'our most important neighbour to the east', he offered the opinion: 'The experience of history teaches that when Russia and Germany collaborate, peace reigns in Europe.' This irked Shevardnadze, who reminded him of the consequences of collaboration between Stalin and Hitler. But Shevardnadze did not want to spoil the occasion and added: 'Hitlers come and go but the German people remains.' Kohl explained a little about himself: 'We Germans can't talk about disarmament theoretically. Do you know that I'm a refugee? My brother and I are refugees. He was seventeen and I was fifteen.' Kohl and Shevardnadze discovered that each of them had a brother killed in the Second World War. Shevardnadze liked Kohl's comment that he felt guided by the words of his mother: 'Do as you would be done by.' He thought this a sound precept for world politics and invited him to visit Moscow. Kohl unexpectedly stood on his national dignity. Gorbachëv had visited London and Paris and was about to go to Belgrade. The German people, said the Chancellor, would not like him to go to the USSR without the General Secretary first coming to Bonn. He asked for Gorbachëv to alter his calendared schedule: this would be an important signal.[45]

The diplomatic minuet between Moscow and Bonn got livelier as Shevardnadze talked to Kohl confidentially about how NATO and the Warsaw Pact might resolve their disagreements about conventional weapons. He felt free to describe Mitterrand as 'a cunning one' – no doubt this was a way of indicating the importance that Moscow was now attaching to Kohl.[46] Kohl himself continued to exercise some caution. The Soviet Army retained a menacing presence close to West Germany's eastern border, and Kohl appreciated the need to hold close to Reagan. He appreciated the American President's political intuition: 'He was one of the few visiting statesmen and politicians who sensed physically what it is to divide a nation. When we were here in Berlin and we stood on the Berlin Wall, and he saw this, he compared it to one dividing the human body.'[47] A kind of friendship grew between them: 'It was such a personal relationship. It's that simple. We had no problems with protocol. We would call each other up from time to time and whenever we would see each other again, it wasn't a big "to do".'[48]

Gorbachëv bided his time about West Germany and welcomed Mitterrand to Moscow in late November 1988. Mitterrand was the only foreign leader whom Gorbachëv addressed with the familiar form of the Russian 'you.'[49] (Gorbachëv and Thatcher were to remain 'Mr President' and 'Mrs Prime Minister' to each other even after more than a dozen meetings.)[50] When Mitterrand called Gorbachëv a political romantic to his face, Gorbachëv did not deny the description while adding that he was also a realist.[51] Mitterrand with his wide historical sweep entranced Gorbachëv in conversation. Another point of attraction was the French President's willingness to express concern about the Strategic Defense Initiative. Mitterrand sought Gorbachëv's trust. He said he knew how hard America was trying to 'pour salt' on the USSR's sores in Eastern Europe. He gave encouragement to ideas for scientific and technical cooperation between Paris and Moscow; and Gorbachëv reported to the Politburo that Mitterrand promised to campaign to lift the CoCom restrictions on sales of advanced technology.[52] Gorbachëv's was an over-optimistic report. Really he had only persuaded Mitterrand to ask his ministers to supply him with their lists of banned goods. This was a long way short of a commitment to changing policy.

Mitterrand anyway had a habit of saying one thing and doing another, and Gorbachëv was aware of this. When talking to the Politburo, the General Secretary was giving things a spin that suited his current political designs. He had an interest in conserving the consensus among Soviet leaders on foreign policy. A bit of exaggeration was an instrument in his toolbox.

Western Europe presented problems. While Mitterrand was unreliable and Kohl stand-offish, it was prudent to stay on good terms with Thatcher. Having accepted her invitation to visit London in April 1989, he found her on combative form. She flailed at the British establishment. She attacked the other Western leaders, including President Bush. She tore into the USSR and predicted doom for the Soviet revolutionary syndrome. In her opinion, Gorbachëv had no choice but to take the same road as the rest of the world. She said that when this happened, the whole world would become a different place.[53] This reasserted her belief in mutually assured destruction: 'Both our countries [USSR and UK] know from bitter experience that conventional weapons do not deter war in Europe, whereas nuclear weapons *have* done so for over forty years. As a deterrent, there is no substitute for them.'[54] Her ease with him was remarkable as they tumbled about in dispute. She even disclosed that she expected to step down at the next general election. She saw similarities between his reforms and hers, saying that the British '*perestroika*' had already lasted nearly seven years. She chuckled: 'Look, we have Thatcherism and you have Gorbachëvism.' She said he should have prioritized measures to raise the Soviet standard of living. For once, she sensed that she sounded too brusque. Confiding that the situation in Northern Ireland gave her a headache, she admitted: 'I know that you too have a headache about the future USSR.'[55]

Whenever they appeared together in public, by then, Thatcher no longer voiced reservations about his policies. She appeared Gorbachëv's amicable follower more than his rival and critic. Interpreter Igor Korchilov recalled:

I had noticed, like probably everyone else in the room, that when Gorbachev was giving a speech, she'd looked at him with such intense adoration in her eyes that this could only be interpreted as a manifestation of that 'special personal chemistry' that was said to exist between these two extraordinary leaders. Later, when we returned to the Embassy after dinner, Yakovlev would attempt to tease Gorbachev about this, but Raisa Maximovna discouraged the insinuation by gripping him firmly by the arm and leading him away upstairs, saying, 'Good night, everybody.'[56]

Yakovlev was not the only one to notice Mrs Thatcher's strange comportment. Perhaps she had picked up an idea or two from Nancy Reagan's way of supporting her husband. She had decided to identify herself with the Soviet leader and his bid to transform the Soviet Union. Her tendency was always to follow a line unflinchingly once she had made up her mind. She was determined to demonstrate the bond that she felt with Gorbachëv.

Gorbachëv sat down with Raisa, Yakovlev, Shevardnadze and Chernyaev to mull over his London experience. The Prime Minister had her ideas, he concluded, and 'we' had ours.[57] He told the Politburo: 'I like Thatcher's independence. One can talk to her about anything one likes. And she understands everything. She's a dependable person. Every time we argue very sharply about nuclear arms. She has the need to fight her corner. She senses the flaws in her position.'[58]

This was a long way short of adulation. Indeed, Gorbachëv said she had conceived a foolish ambition to become 'the leader of the West' after Reagan's departure from the White House. He claimed to notice that Bush and Kohl regarded her 'rather ironically'. But Gorbachëv urged that it remained useful to keep talking to her: 'Contact with her is important.'[59] She warmly reciprocated despite authorizing the expulsion of eight Soviet officials and three journalists from the United Kingdom a month later. She sent a confidential letter explaining to Gorbachëv that this would not change her friendly attitude to him and *perestroika*. She was also going to minimize publicity for what she was doing.[60]

Thatcher, Kohl and Mitterrand had steadily grown less worried about him as he showed a readiness to appreciate the reasons why they continued to worry about the Soviet military threat. The Americans had become used to warnings from their NATO allies about the need to avoid undue concessions to Moscow. The Kremlin's eagerness to dispel foreign suspicions improved the diplomatic prospect – and Gorbachëv's popularity in West European capitals soared to new heights.

28. EASTERN EUROPE:
PERPLEXITY AND PROTEST

Gorbachëv could not afford to court Western European governments at the expense of Soviet interests in Eastern Europe. Events in the region had always impinged on Moscow politics. The USSR was the dominant regional power. The Politburo had sent in its tanks and fighter aircraft when the communist order appeared under threat in Hungary in 1956 and Czechoslovakia in 1968. But increasingly the Politburo consulted with the East European rulers about both economic relations and military preparations. There was constant discussion of budgetary dilemmas. Usually it was East Europeans who pushed for reforms. Under Gorbachëv it was the Soviet leadership which campaigned for radical change.

The Party General Secretaries of the Warsaw Pact countries met four times in 1985, first in Moscow and then in Warsaw, Sofia and Bucharest, to discuss a common strategy. As the gnarled veterans gained acquaintance with the USSR's new ruler, he changed little in his thinking about Eastern Europe in his early years of power. He hoped that the region's rulers would take the Soviet path to reform. He wanted them to act of their own volition, but did not expect this to happen very quickly since he knew that all of them were conservative in their communism. He calculated that he had no choice but to work with them. He needed time and calm to conduct *perestroika* in the USSR and feared that any outbreak of political instability in the region could have the consequence of blowing him off course. At the same time he issued a warning to the East European rulers that they could no longer count on Soviet forces to rescue them from internal political trouble. They had to cope on their own in ruling their countries. Gorbachëv saw this as a useful incentive for them to phase out their traditional policies. The USSR, he maintained, had to establish a fresh relationship with the region. He hoped to drain the waters of national resentment by forswearing the Muscovite imperiousness of his predecessors, and he committed himself to engaging in more frequent consultation.

Deals were signed inside Comecon to enhance economic cooperation across the region. The Soviet leaders were proud of an agreement to form an 'Interrobot' company.[1] Their naivety shone out of their declarations. They underestimated the seismic effects of informational technology in the West. They really had no strategy for Eastern Europe, only a hope that its rulers would somehow find a way to integrate their industrial and technological efforts.

The Politburo – not Gorbachëv alone – hardly bothered itself with the East Europeans except when they were causing trouble. Of course, the Warsaw Pact allies had to be kept informed about plans for talks with the Americans. Fellow communist rulers were suspicious of Gorbachëv's reforms in the USSR. Moscow's foreign policy was a different matter. All of them sought a relaxation of tension in Europe, and Gorbachëv provided the hope of an end to military confrontation; and if he proved successful, Eastern Europe would be able to divert expenditure to the needs of consumers. When Shevardnadze went to the gathering of foreign ministers in Poland in mid-March 1986, he heard little but praise for Gorbachëv. Ilie Văduva, the Romanian Foreign Affairs Minister, was unusual in striking a sour note – Văduva called for the disbandment of NATO and the Warsaw Pact and for the removal of foreign garrisons. The Romanians had always wanted to get the Soviet armed forces out of the region, and Gorbachëv's promises about national sovereignty provided a chance to raise the matter. They knew that the others would frown on Văduva's contribution. The East Germans predictably rallied to the Soviet side and thanked Shevardnadze for sharing his news about how things were going with the Americans.[2] Shevardnadze felt pleased. At least about the USSR's global strategy, nearly the entire alliance had offered warm support.

Gorbachëv thought Reagan might make a fuss about Eastern Europe at their talks, and went over policy towards the two Germanies in preparation.[3] He visited Warsaw to see things for himself in late June 1986. Communist leaders received him with applause and swore abiding friendship with the USSR. Gorbachëv acknowledged the damage done to Poland by the Chernobyl nuclear explosion – this earned him an ovation. He felt that he had learned about how divided Poles were about their government.[4] If anything, he still failed to recognize that the people's hatred of Jaruzelski's administration was nigh universal. What he and the rest of the Soviet leadership did recognize was the scale of the economic emergency. On 23 October 1986 Ryzhkov gave a report to the Politburo. Poland was deep in debt, Hungary perched on the edge of ruin. Soviet credits were saving Bulgaria from disaster. But none of them genuinely wanted to integrate their economies with the Soviet Union. They looked exclusively to Western banks for their salvation. Foreign loans were really a trap for them, but they still hoped to buy valuable electronic technology if they sold enough natural resources. Ryzhkov was in despair: 'We don't have a concept that is genuinely political-economic.' Having got that off his chest, he assured the Politburo that Soviet financial aid was producing a warmth among Poles about the USSR. Gorbachëv liked what he heard.[5]

As Soviet leaders sleepwalked towards a crisis in Eastern Europe, Valentin Falin forwarded a paper by the analyst Rem Belousov who predicted that the countries of the Warsaw Pact would enter economic collapse by around 1989–1990.[6] The Politburo treated the problems as containable. On 10 November 1986, a month after Reykjavik, Gorbachëv called the East European leaders to Moscow, where he admitted the past mistakes in the region. He stressed that the era of Soviet military intervention was definitively over. Every communist state had to render itself accountable to its citizens.[7] Bulgaria's General Secretary Todor Zhivkov exclaimed: 'This is the first time that the [Communist Party of the Soviet Union] has spoken about itself like this.' Ceaușescu was less generous. He found nothing good to say about the Soviet *perestroika* and claimed that Romania had undertaken its own successful reforms. (In reporting this to the Politburo, Gorbachëv scoffed at Ceaușescu's 'dynastic socialism'.) The Vietnamese and Cubans were also present at the gathering, and Castro pleaded for the return of General Kurochkin as military adviser to the Cuban contingent in Angola. Jaruzelski exuded a confidence that he would win out in Poland. Kádár spoke with noticeably less panache, but Gorbachëv kept faith in him as he did even in Husák. He looked forward to success for communism in the USSR and in Eastern Europe.[8]

Gorbachëv gave a rousing account to the Politburo about the eagerness of East European leaders to start a *perestroika* in their own countries. The reality was that none of them was keen. Ceaușescu continued to run Romania despotically and Honecker, Husák and Zhivkov never intended to conduct a serious reform.[9]

East Germany gave mounting concern to Moscow. Honecker

was a double irritation. He had racked up an unpayable debt to West German banks; at the same time he refused to contemplate the slightest reform to communism in his country. The Soviet leaders had for years thought he was taking an exceptional risk with his budget through his secret dealings with Bonn. This, of course, was exactly why Kohl liked him: nothing pleased him more than to deal with a beholden, cooperative East German leader. By 1986 Kohl could celebrate the fact that three million East Germans had received visas for trips to West Germany – five years earlier the figure had barely reached 400,000. He recognized that the very success of his policy might worry his friends in Western Europe, and he offered a promise to the French that he would do nothing that might harm their interests. His priority was to seize the opportunities that were opening in the East. He wished to exert influence over Poland and Hungary as well as East Germany. As for Romania, Kohl expected to go on paying annually for 5,000 ethnic Germans to join West Germany at a cost of DM25,000 each; he knew that Ceaușescu was never going to sanction political and economic reform.[10]

In January 1987 a Warsaw Pact meeting of Central Committee secretaries took place in the Polish capital. Yakovlev, Dobrynin and Medvedev represented the USSR and had to listen to a chorus of disquiet. The East German leaders reported that the Soviet *perestroika* was causing 'political discomfitures' to communist administrations.[11] Honecker accused the USSR of a Yugoslav-style break with Marxist-Leninism. He called the latest play about Lenin by Mikhail Shatrov a betrayal of the October Revolution; he objected to Andrei Sakharov's release from administrative exile in Gorki.[12] When Gorbachëv learned about the proceedings, he lost his temper. He had never respected Honecker, whom he likened to the fictional Soviet con-man Ostap Bender,[13] and regarded Honecker's outburst in Warsaw as insufferable. If he continued to cause trouble, Gorbachëv told the Politburo, Moscow could apply the ultimate sanction of stopping his supplies of gas and oil or insisting on payment in hard currency. Both measures would be disastrous for East Germany. What held Gorbachëv back was the knowledge that such a policy would hardly benefit the USSR. He insisted that it was 'necessary to remain friends' with all the sceptical leaders in Eastern Europe. He knew that Honecker was not the only East European leader to have doubts about *perestroika*. Husák agreed with Honecker that it was unwise to regard the Soviet reform process as irreversible; and Zhivkov kept in mind how Khrushchëv's reforms had resulted in national revolt in Hungary. The solution, according to Gorbachëv, was to turn *perestroika* into a success and make it worthwhile to imitate it.[14]

Gorbachëv, Shevardnadze and Yakovlev crossed their fingers and hoped for the best. Shevardnadze valued Jaruzelski's speeches for their maturity. He wanted him to rally support from 'the advanced part' of society, including ex-members of Solidarity. He considered that 'the basic difficulties have been overcome' and he was pleased that Gorbachëv and Jaruzelski had 'a complete mutual understanding'.[15] Gorbachëv was no less optimistic. The main thing bothering him about the Comecon countries was that their standard of living was higher than that which the Soviet people enjoyed. (Can he really have meant to include Romania in his analysis?)[16]

Gorbachëv should have known better. He had heard from Markus Wolf, head of the Main Intelligence Administration in East Germany, that Honecker was obtaining secret loans from West Germany to stave off economic ruin. Gorbachëv admitted to the Politburo that he had yet to work out a practical policy to deal with East Germany. Prime Minister Ryzhkov expressed annoyance at the attitude struck by Honecker and his entourage. As the result of exporting oil and gas to the Comecon countries at knock-down prices, the Soviet Union found itself in debt to them by 14 billion rubles. Yet East Germany's Prime Minister Willi Stoph demanded payment strictly on schedule. Ryzhkov said that East Germany's only interest in trade with the USSR was in pursuit of raw materials; he was dismayed by the way that Honecker and Stoph were 'orientated upon China'. Gorbachëv could only suggest the need for a fresh effort to bind East Germany close again to Moscow.[17] Wolf told his Soviet contacts that Honecker's policies had brought the country to the brink of unavoidable collapse. By autumn 1987 Valentin Falin – the USSR's former Ambassador to West Germany – was counselling Gorbachëv to drop his idea of declaring that two Germanies would exist for another fifty or a hundred years. Gorbachëv ignored the advice.[18] Falin continued to warn him that East Germany could suddenly experience destabilization at any time.[19]

Hungary was another country that caused Moscow some concern. In March 1987 the Hungarian communist leadership warned the USSR Ministry of Foreign Affairs: 'It would be right for you to consider the question of the further presence of your forces in our country and generally in Eastern and Central Europe. For events in the future can take an undesirable turn. If this question is raised from below, we'll suffer a whole sequence of undesirable consequences.'[20] Shevard-nadze shrugged this off. He continued to regard Soviet armed might as the guarantor of regional stability. He pointed to the tensions between the Hungarians and the Romanians. The Poles and Germans too had underlying difficulties. Shevardnadze thought 'our friends' were ill prepared to shoulder additional burdens of military expenditure.[21]

Gorbachëv began a three-day visit to Czechoslovakia on 9 April 1987. Big crowds turned out for him. People shouted to him to stay longer in the country; they wanted him to bring about communist self-reform in Prague. By cheering Gorbachëv, they were demonstrat-ing against Husák. Everyone understood what was going on. But true to his policy in Eastern Europe, Gorbachëv avoided saying anything in public that might undermine the ruling communist leadership. He even expressed appreciation for how Husák had handled the situation after Brezhnev's military intervention. Gorbachëv had not changed his mind about the overthrow of Dubček, but though he was starting to dismantle authoritarian rule in the USSR, he saw himself as a realist and retained a definite sympathy for authoritarian leaders whose sur-vival appeared to strengthen stability in the region. He felt this about Husák: 'He's decent.' He left it to Husák to decide whether to start a Czechoslovak *perestroika* and how to handle the question of 1968. His only advice was that things could not stay as they were.[22] Gorbachëv's feelings were conflicted. He later told his aides that he could see that the aged Husák's powers were on the wane. He added from the heart: 'When I was in Czechoslovakia, everything inside me was crying out. The main thing I saw was that the mood in society was overtaking the mood in the leadership.'[23]

He was equally pessimistic about the prospects of reform in Bucharest, where he went in late May 1987 on his way to East Berlin for the next meeting of the Political Consultative Committee. He reck-oned that the crowds who cheered Ceaușescu had been specially brought to the capital for the purpose. He heard that, after his own departure, people pillaged a market which had an artificial supply of desirable products for the duration of his visit. Ceaușescu had been a disgruntled host. He scorned Gorbachëv's proposal to change the Warsaw Pact's military doctrine to one of mere 'sufficiency'. He bridled at Gorbachëv's speeches about *perestroika* in the USSR. He saw this as a hostile action on Romanian soil and accused Gorbachëv of trying to punish him for his strategy of economic independence.

Gorbachëv retorted that Ceauşescu had courted a financial linkage with the West and now, through no fault of the USSR, was suffering the consequences. While inviting him to mend the old ties with Moscow, he had no illusions about the chances of success with a leader of Ceauşescu's vanity and arrogance.[24]

At the Political Consultative Committee, in the heart of East Berlin, Gorbachëv contended that the Berlin Wall required discussion among communist leaderships. Honecker took this badly. He regarded any hint about easing the strict division between the two Germanies with horror.[25] Apparently Gorbachëv desired agreement on how to deal with Reagan's scheduled visit to West Berlin in June 1987. The White House was aspiring to make a big impact: the West Germans had told the French as early as March that the President would give a big speech in front of the Brandenburg Gates and call for the free passage of people and ideas between the two halves of Europe.[26] Whether Gorbachëv's suggestion came from Soviet intelligence or his own intuition is not known. What is certain is that he was raising a fundamental question about Soviet and East German strategic policy.

The Political Consultative Committee took no decision, and indeed it was unclear what exactly Gorbachëv had it in mind to do. East Germany was a source of growing concern to the Politburo. As worries spread, the KGB took soundings about popular opinion there.[27] Gorbachëv decided to do nothing. Much as he would have liked the East Germans – and the rest of Eastern Europe – to take up the model of *perestroika*, he foresaw trouble if he helped to remove Honecker. The same considerations troubled Shevardnadze, but he came to a different conclusion. It would seem that he had been reconciled to German reunification for at least a year; but perhaps he recognized that his Georgian national sensibility enabled him to see this more clearly than Gorbachëv and other Russian politicians.[28] On 30 May he brought up the question of the two Germanys in one of the discussions he held at his ministry. Like Gorbachëv, he wanted a clear policy on how to deal with the potential fallout from the American President's visit to West Germany in the following month. Shevardnadze asked his officials to help him plan for the future: 'Reagan can propose the idea of the unification of Germany. Sharp reaction of our friends [in East Germany] to this idea. Think up long-term programme of work in this direction.'[29]

Reagan's speechwriter Peter Robinson was drafting a speech exactly along the lines that Soviet leaders feared. Robinson wanted the

President to say: 'Mr Gorbachëv, tear down this wall!' Although the phrase was not a summons to rebellion, it implicitly personalized responsibility for the changes that America wished to see in Eastern Europe. Gorbachëv might well take offence. The question engaged Shultz and Powell as well as the speech-writing team.[30] Powell came down in favour of toning down the rhetoric.[31] But Reagan overruled him. He liked the idea of challenging Gorbachëv and had an intuitive sense that a firm political push was now appropriate. He passed on his personal thanks to Robinson.[32]

On 11 June Reagan spoke at the Brandenburg Gate. No American President had spoken quite like him. Even President Kennedy, when calling himself a 'Berliner' in the same city in 1963, had stopped short of nailing personal blame to Party First Secretary Khrushchëv. Reagan hailed West Germany's achievements in political freedom and economic advance since 1945. 'Even today,' he declared, 'the Soviet Union still cannot feed itself.' He welcomed the limited reforms that were occurring in the USSR, but he called for more to be done.

He made no direct mention of the German Democratic Republic. Insisting that the source of the trouble lay in Moscow, he issued the following injunction: 'General Secretary Gorbachev, if you seek peace, if you seek prosperity for the Soviet Union and Eastern Europe, if you seek liberalization: Come here to this gate. Mr Gorbachev, open this gate. Mr Gorbachev, Mr Gorbachev, tear down this wall!' He gave a consummate performance. Every phrase, pause and repetition in the speech was managed for the greatest impact. He remarked that the Soviet leadership had entered serious talks because NATO had increased its military strength. He expressed the hope that one day the two halves of Berlin could jointly host the Olympic games.[33]

Pravda, in a break with precedent, avoided an expression of anger.[34] Calm was the order of the day in Moscow, if not in East Berlin where Honecker went on TV to release his splenetic fury. Gorbachëv himself stayed silent. Though it had been he and not Honecker whom Reagan had named in his speech, the Soviet General Secretary could see no point in uttering words of displeasure. He would only look weak and ineffective. He anyhow still wanted to complete agreements with the Americans. He avoided a spat with the President.

He had other concerns in Eastern Europe in those weeks as the news from Poland grew ever more unsettling. Jaruzelski admitted that Western creditors had Poland by the throat – his latest idea was to escape their grasp by signing deals with Japan to build a car factory in

Poland. The Papacy sharpened Jaruzelski's difficulties. John Paul II's pastoral visit by coincidence took place at the same time as Reagan was in West Germany, and Solidarity's confidence was on the rise throughout Poland.[35] Vice President Bush visited Poland for four days at the end of September 1987. He spoke with both Jaruzelski and Wałęsa.[36] He visited the grave of the murdered priest Jerzy Popiełuszko. He stressed to Jaruzelski that human rights had to be better respected for America to sanction financial credits to Poland. Next month Bush announced his candidature for the presidential election of the following year. He had achieved a balance between appearing calm and statesmanlike and asserting firm demands. He later told Gorbachëv of his Polish impressions, expressing admiration for Jaruzelski as a national leader in a difficult situation. He had also spoken with Lech Wałęsa. He also suggested that a growth in economic links with Poland was possible – and Gorbachëv did not fail to propose that America should take the same line with the USSR.[37]

He had his own internal difficulty after 27 October, when Yeltsin criticized him at the Central Committee. Yeltsin called for a faster pace of reform and accused Gorbachëv of allowing his wife too much influence over him. He surprised everyone by resigning from the Politburo. There had been nothing like it in Soviet political history, and Gorbachëv lost one of the committed radical reformers from the leadership. Yeltsin felt so demoralized that he made an ineffectual attempt to kill himself with a pair of kitchen scissors. Subsequently he was to be dragged before the Moscow City Party Committee and fired as its secretary. After this ordeal he received mercy from Gorbachëv, who made him Deputy Head of the State Construction Committee.

Eastern European leaders arrived in Moscow in these chaotic days to commemorate the October Revolution anniversary. The fate of *perestroika* hung in the balance, and there was speculation that Gorbachëv would soon be replaced by Ligachëv. When Gorbachëv addressed the East Europeans on 10 November, he offered no political prognosis but focused on economics. He wanted a 'Complex Programme of Scientific-Technical Progress of Comecon member-countries'. He reminded East European leaders that it cost the USSR dear to supply them with oil, gas and military security. There was nothing new in this. Where he did break fresh ground was in his proposal to found multinational companies that could meet consumer demands in automobiles, video technology and personal computers. Though he hoped to involve Western corporations in this project, he was aware that such corporations preferred to establish their operations in Western Europe.[38] He had no ideas about how to end the CoCom embargo on technological transfer. He was implicitly abandoning any claim that the USSR could lead Eastern Europe's economic regeneration. He was acknowledging that communism somehow had to find a way to piggy-back on capitalism.

On 19 November Ryzhkov told the Politburo that the Czechoslo-vak leadership was at last moving towards reform. Prime Minister Lubomír Štrougal had told him that Czechoslovakia was 'pregnant' with a *perestroika* that was long overdue. Gorbachëv welcomed the report while stressing the need to leave the Czechoslovaks to work things out for themselves. He doubted that Štrougal could unite the leadership if ever he were to become Party General Secretary.[39] But the East European 'friends', he continued to insist, had to act as they wished. The hope remained that they would find their own path towards reform. According to Gorbachëv, Kádár sensed that his polit-ical career was coming to an end and had told him that he wanted to retire from the Hungarian leadership. Gorbachëv demurred and advised Kádár to give further thought to the matter.[40] This became his general policy: he wanted rid of the veterans but refused to raise his hand against them – and his desire remained to avoid dangerous instability across the region.[41] He left even Romania to its own devices. General Nicolae Militaru took the risk of approaching the Soviet con-sulate in Constanta with a request for help with a coup d'état against Ceauşescu. Gorbachëv would have nothing to do with this: 'We're not interfering in their affairs.'[42]

On 11 December he flew to East Berlin to report to Warsaw Pact leaders about the Washington summit – only Ceauşescu absented himself. Gorbachëv spoke without notes, boasting that American well-wishers had hung out of windows to make him welcome as if he had been in Prague rather than Washington; and he emphasized that the enthusiasm was not artificially organized.[43] His listeners knew that, outside on the Alexanderplatz, were ranks of youths in identical uniforms waiting to give exactly the pre-arranged greeting that he was criticizing.[44] He was in ebullient mood. He claimed that Reagan had at last admitted that the USSR was no longer bent on world domina-tion.[45] (Reagan had said no such thing, but Gorbachëv wanted to impress.) Kádár congratulated Gorbachëv and Shevardnadze on what he called the first success for *perestroika* in international relations. Even Romanian Foreign Affairs Minister Ioan Totu seemed pleased.

Husák confined himself to 'cloudy' generalities, prompting one of his listeners to whisper to his neighbour that the Czechoslovak leader was applying for his retirement pension. Only Zhivkov spoke grudgingly. He asked for greater attention to be paid to Eastern Europe and denounced Soviet commentators who were writing about 'socialism' remaining at a 'feudal stage of its development'.[46]

On 11 January 1988 Gorbachëv told the new First Secretary of the Czechoslovak Communist Party Miklos Jakes that the Italian comrades had urged him to ask for a re-evaluation of Alexander Dubček. They denied the idea that he was an enemy of the people. Jakes replied that rehabilitations had already taken place, but the case of Dubček was a step too far for him. Gorbachëv lamely agreed; he declined to propose the Prague Spring leaders as his own predecessors as reformers.[47] On 18 April 1989 he underlined this attitude when telling Jakes that the Czechoslovak situation had moved towards counter-revolution by summer 1968.[48] This was not the way he spoke to friends, and it was a sign of his willingness to forswear his opinions in pursuit of geopolitical objectives.

Gorbachëv's focus in Eastern Europe remained on preserving 'the political stability of the socialist countries'.[49] Soviet economic interests were another priority. He explained his dilemma to the Politburo in March 1988: 'We've got to think out the integration process in Comecon. This is politics on the biggest scale, not to mention economics; 80 billion rubles in commodity exchange. It's not just that they can't manage without us: we can't manage without them.'[50] Whereas the USSR could produce special ball-bearings for 60 rubles and sell them for 400 rubles on the world market, its 'friends' were too poor to pay such a price. Poland and Hungary depended on Western financial credits and cheap raw materials from the USSR. So what should be the Politburo's strategy? The snag was that the current economic situation in Eastern Europe could not last indefinitely: 'It needs to be said directly in Comecon: are we going to integrate or not? And they have to decide, because we can't endlessly be a fount of cheap resources for them. If they say no, our hands will be freed. We need to say: you've got a straight choice. And let's quit putting out triumphal information about mutual relations in Comecon. Everyone knows what the real situation is.'[51]

Gorbachëv visited Yugoslavia soon afterwards and experienced the enthusiasm of crowds in Belgrade. Whereas Stalin had tried to bully Tito into subjection, Gorbachëv pledged his commitment to 'principles of equality and non-interference'. He stressed that the USSR expected all the socialist countries to 'define for themselves the path of their own development'.[52] But when Yakovlev went to Ulan Bator for a meeting of 'fraternal parties' in the same month, the East Germans denied any need for a 'renewal' of socialism.[53] The German question came up in a different guise a few days later at the gathering of Warsaw Pact foreign ministers in Bulgaria when Poland's Marian Orzechowski expressed concern about West Germany's perennial refusal to recognize the European borders imposed in 1945. East Germany's Oscar Fischer warned that West Germany's growing liaison with France presented the danger that Bonn would gain access to nuclear weaponry.[54]

The East European leaders answered the call to reduce the conventional forces of NATO and the Warsaw Pact. It anyway mattered little to Shevardnadze if the Political Consultative gave trouble: 'It won't be a tragedy if one or other socialist country doesn't vote for us on some question.'[55] He and Gorbachëv contemplated the withdrawal of Soviet forces from Eastern Europe. They had no notion about whether it would be of a partial or total kind. Foreign Affairs Ministry officials warned that the process would take time and that the social consequences required close attention. They foresaw difficulty in resettling so large a contingent of troops in the USSR. This did not discourage Shevardnadze, who reasoned that Soviet leaders had no choice: if they failed to take the initiative by removing the troops, the peoples of the region would sooner or later turn upon them. He spoke about the terrible consequences of using force to resolve political crises – he mentioned the enduring anger among Georgians about the Tbilisi protest demonstrations of 1956. World history was strewn with precedents of mass resentment leading to all-out revolt. Pre-emptive measures were preferable. The military pull-out that he proposed would be entirely voluntary. No foreign power, not even America or China, would be responsible for bringing this about; and 'anti-Sovietism' would be drastically reduced around the world.[56]

Soviet spokesmen denied that a change in policy was at hand, but the Hungarians leaked the information to the Americans. The CIA kept the process under review. If Moscow did any such thing, the debate would be intense throughout NATO. The USSR would appear to some of America's allies as an entirely peaceful superpower. This could complicate American efforts to hold NATO to the agreed objective of military modernization.[57]

Events in Poland had a momentum of their own. Jaruzelski's suppression of Solidarity failed to prevent a series of strikes and political protests in March 1988. The authorities carried out further arrests but by April there was paralysis in factories, mines and shipyards. Calm returned after yet another round of police activity. When Gorbachëv visited Warsaw in mid-July, he coaxed the Polish communist leadership to undertake political and economic reforms – he felt he could no longer sit quietly on the sidelines.[58] He enjoyed the reception he had from ordinary Poles; and he convinced himself that they favoured deepened collaboration with the USSR.[59] He mistook friendliness towards himself for acquiescence in Poland's communist administration. Bigger strikes broke out practically everywhere in August. As the economy juddered to a halt, opinion was divided in the Polish Party Politburo. Some members called for a redoubling of military repression until Internal Affairs Minister Mieczysław Rakowski pointed to the damaging consequences.[60] Jaruzelski decided to form a new cabinet that would include ministers who had no association with communism. His guideline was be 'compromise, yes, capitulation, no'.[61] He applauded the policies of Gorbachëv in the USSR and expressed appreciation of the Soviet 'hands-off' approach to the Polish crisis.[62]

Moscow continued to push the Polish communist leadership towards internal reform. In September 1988 Nikolai Shishlin of the Party International Department gave an interview to Le Monde expressing a lack of fear about the open re-establishment of Solidarity. Negotiations ensued in Moscow with Poland's sluggish authorities.[63]

Georgi Shakhnazarov was impatient with how things were being handled. He had worked for years in the Party International Department before becoming one of Gorbachëv's personal assistants. In his view, the Politburo had been muddling its way without a distinct policy on Eastern Europe. He could see at close quarters that Gorbachëv, laden with so many other items on his agenda, was failing to appreciate the dangers of the situation. On 6 October he sent him a stiff memo laying out his concerns. Shakhnazarov lamented the refusal of Honecker and Ceaușescu to take the path of reform; he wrote that their conservatism could only deepen the crisis within socialism around the world. Soviet leaders had to face up to the likelihood that Poland, Hungary, Bulgaria, the German Democratic Republic and even Czechoslovakia were about to go bankrupt. Popular discontent was easy to predict. Shakhnazarov called for the Politburo to decide on a policy for the probable contingencies. What would Moscow do if

Western financial aid became available to Eastern Europe? Should the Politburo encourage or put up with such an outcome? Was the continued basing of Soviet troops in Eastern Europe in the USSR's interest?[64]

Shakhnazarov urged the Soviet leadership to concentrate on the region and produce a policy for active implementation before disaster ensued. Yakovlev and Shevardnadze were sympathetic to this analysis. Shevardnadze learned from fellow foreign ministers of the Warsaw Pact in late October 1988 that Eastern Europe was on the brink of bankruptcy because of its debts to Western banks.[65] When Yakovlev met with the Czechoslovak leaders, they warned him about the threat to communist rule if the Soviet press continued to hint that Soviet policy on the 1968 Prague Spring was about to be reversed.[66] Yakovlev was well-known for favouring the ventilation of such matters. Shevardnadze meanwhile heard about difficulties in Hungary, where the new communist leader Károly Grósz admitted to him that the country's financial credits had gone exclusively on consumption at the expense of capital investment and industrial modernization. The Hungarian leadership obviously had no solution in mind; and when asked whether the Soviet military presence in the country was causing problems, Grósz suggested that popular disturbances might be in the offing.[67]

The Soviet movement towards military withdrawal gathered speed. On 10 November there was a meeting of leaders from the military and industrial leaderships in Belyakov's office. The main item was the reduction of Soviet troops in the region. There was talk about establishing a smaller and more mobile kind of army, and Yazov and the Defence Ministry made less fuss about change than they would have done in earlier years. The constraints on the USSR's power were appreciated. Maslyukov reinforced the case for a reduced presence. Ryzhkov as government premier told the blunt truth: unless the Soviet Army was cut back, there could be no hope for the campaign to reform the economy.[68] Outer empire and internal reform were contradictory objectives.

America's State Department kept its focus on Moscow and held back from interference in Eastern Europe. So long as Gorbachëv gave preference for the peaceful resolution of problems, it was thought best to avoid interfering. Republican Senator Jim Sasser criticized this conduct of policy as too passive; he urged that Western banks should cease to lend to the communist governments. Defense Secretary Carlucci agreed with him. Both of them reasoned that if the banks continued to bail out communism, the NATO countries would only have to foot an increased bill for their defence – and this seemed at best a quixotic way of proceeding.[69] The CIA sided with the State Department. Intelligence reports stressed that Romania was in a very volatile condition, but Gates and his officials stressed that America could have only a marginal influence on events in Eastern Europe. It appeared better to wait on developments.[70] Despite the signs of big changes on the horizon, the CIA leadership in May 1988 was confident that there would be no 'unravelling of Moscow's East European empire'.[71] That November the agency asserted that the USSR would never engage in a unilateral withdrawal from the region.[72]

Old assumptions and analyses were trumping open-minded speculation. This was equally true in the capitals of America and the Soviet Union. Everyone felt the ground of politics was shaking. The American administration sensed that trends were favourable to its wishes and interests, but nobody in Washington was yet forecasting an earthquake.

29. THE LEAVING OF AFGHANISTAN

Strange as it may seem, questions about East Germany, Hungary and even Poland cropped up little in the talks between America and the Soviet Union. Afghanistan by contrast attracted ceaseless attention. The Americans since 1984 had included 'regional conflicts' on their agenda for talks with the USSR. For them, the Afghan question was a litmus test of Gorbachëv's sincerity in changing his entire foreign policy. Reagan and Shultz made a constant demand for the pull-out of Soviet forces. Gorbachëv had indicated at the Geneva summit of November 1985, albeit in general terms, that he already had this in mind. His commitment increased in the years that followed, and he regularly read out searing letters to the Politburo from mothers who wished to know what was happening to their boys.

Most governments were pleased with the signs of incipient change in Moscow's policy, but this was not true of all of them. Rajiv Gandhi and other Indians counselled Gorbachëv and Shevardnadze to tread with caution about how they left Afghanistan. They themselves sought to make trouble for the Pakistanis. They warned Kremlin leaders that Pakistan, an American ally, had the potential to move into any power vacuum in Kabul – a source of worry for both New Delhi and Moscow.[1] Some African politicians visiting Moscow showed a similar caution about the projected military withdrawal of the Soviet Army; they warned that the USSR's influence around the world would fade as 'imperialism' took its opportunity to go on the offensive.[2] These were not the usual reactions to Gorbachëv's initiative. Although Fidel Castro was no admirer of the Soviet *perestroika*, he gave warm approval to the retreat from Afghanistan. His grouse to Shevardnadze was that the invasion had always been a terrible mistake and had put the Cubans into 'a completely impossible situation'.[3] Gorbachëv had grounds for thinking that Castro was more in line with world opinion than Gandhi. He anyway saw no point in prolonging the army's travails on Afghan soil.

Reagan could see no advantage for America in easing the USSR's difficulties since he had no guarantee that the Politburo would not change its policy back to occupation. Soviet leaders had exploited American difficulties at the end of the Vietnam war, and now they were going to discover how that had felt. In March 1986 the President sanctioned measures to supply the mujahidin with Stinger missiles. The first such missiles soon arrived in Pakistan for onward dispatch to Afghanistan.[4] Within months, the American intelligence agencies reported that the USSR had lost two transport planes and a helicopter to the new weapon.[5] Weinberger received a roar of welcome on his visit to the Afghan refugee camps.[6]

The Politburo ignored these complications and stuck to the goal of withdrawal. On 11 June 1986, as a first step, it ordered the pulling out of six whole regiments. Defence Minister Sokolov spoke in favour. Gorbachëv commented that the return of the 8,000 troops stationed there would prove that the USSR had no pretensions to 'the warm waters' of the Indian Ocean. The Afghan communist leadership should be told to prepare for life without the Soviet military guarantee.[7] Gorbachëv laid down that 'the result must not look like a shameful defeat' for the USSR. Of all people, Gromyko commented: 'It's not our war.' Gorbachëv must have wondered why, then, Gromyko had pushed for the invasion; but he said nothing.[8] At the Politburo on 14 August 1986 he called for Soviet advisers to cease attending meetings of the Afghan communist leadership: 'We,' he declared, 'are not the Americans.' (The peoples of Eastern Europe would have been interested in the idea that the USSR was not in the habit of taking command in a foreign country.)[9] On 25 September 1986 the Politburo sent the diplomat Yuli Vorontsov as Gorbachëv's special representative in Kabul. Vorontsov was to arrange for Karmal's replacement by Mohammad Najibullah and to set up a meeting between Gorbachëv and Mohammad Najibullah, whom the Soviet leadership thought amenable to bringing the Afghan political opposition into a governmental coalition. His other task was to undertake a confidential overture to the Pakistan government.[10]

It took until 13 November 1986 before the Politburo took its momentous decision to pull all its troops out of Afghanistan. Even Gromyko admitted that the intervention had been undertaken on faulty premises. Gorbachëv wished to complete the withdrawal inside two years. Chebrikov and Shevardnadze agreed, and Gorbachëv proposed that the Politburo should enable Afghanistan to become simply 'a friendly, neutral country'. He wanted to repatriate half of the Soviet forces in 1987 and the rest a year later. With this in mind, he hoped to begin talks with Pakistan. His main concern was that the Americans might 'creep into Afghanistan'. Akhromeev assured him that this was very unlikely; he called on everyone to recognize a basic truth: 'We have lost the struggle. The Afghan people is now in its majority following the counter-revolutionaries.'[11]

The Politburo appointed Shevardnadze to 'curate' the Afghan question. He worked well in this capacity with the General Staff and Defence Ministry, which sided entirely with the new policy. Wanting to acquaint himself with Afghanistan, he went with Dobrynin on an exploratory visit to Kabul and they attended a Central Committee plenum of the National Democratic Party on 5 January 1987. Party General Secretary Najibullah itemized the problems that his administration faced in town and village. He highlighted the hostile interference that Pakistan and Iran were conducting. Taking advantage of Shevardnadze's presence, he stressed that communist rule would collapse unless the USSR continued to render assistance. Shevardnadze wanted it to be understood that the days of Moscow ordering the Afghan comrades around were finished. The hammer blow for Najibullah was the news that the Soviet Party Politburo was entirely behind Gorbachëv in prioritizing the pull-out of military forces. He added that 'we have reserves for cooperation': he had started to feel an emotional attachment to Najibullah and did not want to demoralize the Afghan communist leaders as they faced up to the tasks of fighting without an army of external intervention.[12]

On 8 January Shevardnadze reported to the Politburo's Afghan Commission. He asked for recognition of the complexity of the withdrawal process. He wanted work done on a plan to retain Soviet military bases in the country – evidently he expected to keep some kind of toehold for the USSR.[13] He also asked for serious thinking about the political consequences. In his estimation, the pull-out would weaken Soviet prestige around the globe among 'socialist countries'. (He can hardly have been thinking about ordinary Czechs or Vietnamese but more likely about some of their leaders.) The commission had to draft its ideas for the Politburo's consideration. What alarmed him more than anything else was that withdrawal would leave a vacuum of power in Afghanistan that would foster the scale of ethnic and religious bloodbath that had occurred in Lebanon. Bitter civil war was in prospect.[14]

The Politburo listened to what Shevardnadze had to say on 21 January. He spoke of the 'good impression' that Najibullah had made on him despite how badly he had let down the peasantry. The annual cost of the war to the USSR was at least a billion rubles – the Americans thought it could be double that total while the Japanese put it at triple: 'We must do everything we can to get out.' No amount of assistance from Moscow would improve things in Kabul. The Soviet Union had an interest in starting up confidential talks with the Americans and dissuading them from meddling.[15] Shevardnadze questioned whether Soviet leaders had known what they were doing when ordering the invasion. This was an affront to Gromyko. Gorbachëv intervened to prevent a dispute because he needed consensus in the Politburo on the current agenda. Ryzhkov praised Shevardnadze for his 'realistic picture'; he called for the Soviet Army to leave a 'neutral, friendly government' behind in Afghanistan. Ligachëv spoke in support. The Politburo hoped to withdraw its army without detriment to the interests of the Afghan 'progressive forces'. Sokolov warned that this was unachievable by military means. Political action was required in Afghanistan and abroad.[16]

According to Gorbachëv, the Soviet leadership had been under the spell of ideology when invading Afghanistan. Reality proved the impossibility of moving from feudalism to socialism in one big leap. The military intervention had to be brought to a close. Approaches should be made to the United Nations, Pakistan and America. (He had no confidence that he could persuade Iran to help.) He wanted to bring the process to completion inside two years.[17]

Shevardnadze presented his proposals to the Politburo in February. He said it was crucial to equip the Najibullah administration with the capacity to survive. If the withdrawal happened in too hurried a fashion, the Kabul government would fall apart. Najibullah's people were already panicking.[18] Gorbachëv liked what he heard and professed a willingness to come to terms with Pakistan's Zia-ul-Haq: in return for his cooperation he would override Najibullah's objections.[19] Even Gromyko came round to supporting the pull-out. He recalled that the Afghan communists had appealed eleven times to Moscow for military intervention before the Politburo gave its consent; but he admitted that the leadership had entertained a simplistic idea about the likely consequences. With hindsight, he doubted that any amount of Soviet assistance could have established an effective Afghan army. The old man's semi-apology exasperated Gorbachëv, who offered the sarcastic remark that the Politburo still had the option of sending another 200,000 troops into the war. Gromyko took the hint and fell silent. Gorbachëv drew this conclusion: 'So that the withdrawal of forces is the only correct decision.'[20]

In May 1987, as the military and political situation worsened for Najibullah, the Politburo gathered for an emergency discussion. Varennikov ridiculed the notion that the Afghan people had any interest in socialism or democracy. Kryuchkov talked of his worry that Afghanistan might be 'lost' to the USSR. The priority had to be to keep it as a 'friendly' country. Kornienko and Akhromeev spoke of the weaknesses that had been revealed in Najibullah and his entire party. Gorbachëv contemplated the future. The mujahidin would not forget that the Soviet armed forces had killed so many of their fighters. The Afghan communists would resent the USSR for having let them down. The outcome was unlikely to be an Afghanistan on friendly terms with Moscow.[21] He asked for guidelines from the Afghan Commission, and suggested that Shevardnadze ought to make yet another trip to Kabul. Big changes were needed since Gorbachëv opposed the idea of the next Afghan government being subject to communist domination. Work had to be done on Najibullah. In Gorbachëv's opinion, he was unsuitable as President and at most should be Prime Minister. Gorbachëv wanted to finish with Afghanistan inside the next eighteen months. He was shortening the schedule.[22]

Shevardnadze witnessed the depressing situation in Kabul. On 11 June he reported to the Politburo that the Afghan Communist Party was on the edge of collapse and that the Soviet military intervention had damaged almost every family and settlement: 'Anti-Sovietism is going to last a long time in Afghanistan.'[23]

The Politburo had yet to decide how to deal with the consequences of withdrawal for Kabul and Moscow, and a heated discussion continued inside the Kremlin leadership. Shevardnadze meanwhile told the world that the Soviet intervention was ending. On 15 July he informed Foreign Secretary Howe, at Lancaster House in London, that the USSR's decision on withdrawal was irreversible. Howe promised to pass on the encouraging news to Thatcher.[24] In September Shevardnadze delivered the same message to Shultz at a private meeting that he had specially requested.[25] After the Washington summit in December 1987, Shultz reported to the North Atlantic Council that Gorbachëv had promised Reagan to terminate the military intervention so long as Soviet leaders could secure a process of Afghan 'national reconciliation'.

Shultz thought this unrealistic after all that had happened in the country.[26] But he and the rest of the American administration were pleased about the way that things were going. Afghanistan, since the Soviet invasion, had become one of the testing grounds of Soviet intentions in external policy. The Americans sometimes talked about how they would like to help the process of withdrawal. In reality they continued to aggravate problems by aiding the mujahidin. The USSR, as they saw it, needed to accept the consequences of its military failure. There was going to be no direct alleviation of the pain of withdrawal.

The Afghan communist leadership had removed Karmal from power in November 1986 and sent him into retirement in Moscow. But Najibullah, who made himself President in September 1987, proved to be no better at the task of national reconciliation than Karmal had been. It fell to Shevardnadze in January 1988 to fly to Afghanistan and press the case.[27] He explained to Soviet officials in Kabul that the Politburo wished to push for agreement on a coalition government. When Najibullah objected, it was their job to strip him of his illusions.[28] Varennikov reported that conditions varied from city to city – he thought they were best in the east of the country. Shevardnadze and his team knew that Najibullah's people had no plan for what to do after the Soviet pull-out. Najibullah, according to Varennikov, believed that he would not long survive and nobody in Kabul contradicted this prognosis. Shevardnadze had no solution for the Afghan comrades. The point for him was that the Soviet leadership had contrived a dreadful situation and had to withdraw from the country and its war.[29]

The Americans prolonged their pressure in the Geneva talks and demanded the departure of forces before Reagan arrived in Moscow for his summer summit with Gorbachëv. The Politburo's Afghan Commission was always unlikely to approve of such acceleration, and at its meeting on 11 March Kornienko and Akhromeev were furious about the idea.[30] Days later, on 23 March, Shultz and Shevardnadze clashed. Shultz called for 'symmetry' in policy on American and Soviet arms shipments: he offered to recommend an end to US military supplies to Afghanistan in return for the USSR ceasing to arm its Afghan communist clients. Shevardnadze exclaimed: 'In no circumstances whatever! That idea won't pass!' Shultz and Shevardnadze also failed to agree on which kind of fighters should be allowed to receive assistance. The Americans wanted to ban allocations to 'hired' men while exempting the mujahidin on the grounds that they were volunteers. Shevardnadze rejected this suggestion but failed to provide an alternative that Shultz would accept.[31] There was no way through the impasse. Soviet leaders had to accept this reality or forfeit the chance to sign the rest of the agreement.

On 2 April the Politburo considered the draft accords to be signed by the governments of Afghanistan, Pakistan, America and the USSR. Shevardnadze had tried yet again to get the Americans to cut off supplies to the mujahidin. Shultz replied by letter that if Soviet leaders really wanted a deal, they had to drop any such stipulation.[32] They saw that Reagan was not going to yield on the matter; they anyway reckoned that even if he signed his assent, it would not be worth the paper it was written on. Gorbachëv decided to get the Politburo to approve the deal as it stood. He was keen to have matters resolved before the Moscow summit so as to avoid giving the impression of acting under American duress. He wanted the entire Politburo to take responsibility for the decision and asked for the vote of each of its members to be recorded.[33] His proposal received unanimous approval. The General Staff had prepared an operational plan for withdrawal, and Akhromeev had been invited to the meeting to explain it. Akhromeev was just as keen as Gorbachëv to bring the Soviet Army home. Unrolling a map of Afghanistan, he indicated how he intended to do this. The Politburo agreed to implement his plan from 15 May regardless of what happened in the Geneva talks.[34]

Gorbachëv and Shevardnadze shared the political load. Shevardnadze flew to Kabul to confer with Soviet military and civilian personnel about how to accomplish the final retreat. He informed Najibullah about the Politburo's intentions. It was a depressing experience for Shevardnadze, who lamented that the presence of Soviet troops had served to unify the Afghan resistance.[35] Najibullah was naturally displeased, and Gorbachëv invited him to a meeting on Soviet soil – in Tashkent – on 7 April. Gorbachëv took Kryuchkov with him so as to have someone who had personal experience of Afghan conditions. He explained the change in Moscow's policy and urged the desirability of concessions to political pluralism, peasant demands and Islam.[36] When reporting later to the Politburo, Gorbachëv admitted that he could not be sure that Najibullah had the capacity or desire to follow the advice.[37]

But the way was clear for treaty signature on 14 April. Shevardnadze, seated alongside Shultz and the foreign ministers of Afghanistan and Pakistan, carried out the task in Geneva. United Nations Secretary

General Javier Pérez de Cuéllar attended. Soviet military disengagement was finally agreed. On 18 April Shevardnadze put on a brave face at the Politburo, claiming that the USSR's withdrawal would bear no resemblance to the way that the Americans had scuttled out of South Vietnam. He added that the Americans were at last disbarred from supplying arms through Pakistan. He was fantasizing. The Geneva Accords did nothing to terminate the Afghan civil war. Fighting would inevitably intensify, and the Soviet Army would trudge out of Afghanistan while America remained committed to assisting the mujahidin. Shevardnadze was franker when he offered his bleak assessment of condition of governance and economy throughout the country. He made no attempt to suggest that things were likely to improve. One day, Shevardnadze stated, the Politburo would have to admit in public that the 1979 invasion had been a grievous mistake.[38]

Gorbachëv and Shevardnadze unexpectedly came into conflict on how to complete the withdrawal. For years there seemed nothing that divided them on Afghan questions. But Shevardnadze was the only Politburo member who was a frequent visitor to Kabul, and he had come to like Najibullah. He hated the idea of abandoning the USSR's ally to his fate. This at least is what he told the Politburo. A few months later he hinted about a different motive when he told an aide that he feared for the cause of *perestroika* unless something was done to help the Afghan government to survive.[39] He worried that the reformers could soon pay a heavy political price for doing the right thing about Afghanistan. He desired to make it impossible for the Soviet generals to moan that the political leadership had let them down. This was something that could easily happen if ever the mujahidin should succeed in overthrowing the Najibullah administration. An official enquiry might well place the blame on the Politburo's ascendant leadership. Shevardnadze hoped to obviate this possibility by leaving a military contingent behind when the bulk of Soviet forces marched out.[40]

Gorbachëv advocated a different approach and faced Shevardnadze down at the Politburo on 18 April. Since the beginning of 1987 he had warned against the possibility of what he called the 'Vietnamization' of the Afghan imbroglio.[41] The Americans had kept their forces for too long in South Vietnam and had suffered humiliation as a result. He was determined to avoid such an outcome for the Soviet Army. Now, when Shevardnadze urged the Politburo to keep 10–15,000 troops in Afghanistan, his patience evaporated and he criticized the 'hawk's shriek' of his political partner. A noisy debate ensued. Kryuchkov stood up for Shevardnadze whereas Chebrikov sided with Gorbachëv in demanding complete withdrawal. Gorbachëv carried the day.[42]

The General Staff proceeded efficiently with the logistics. When Shevardnadze next visited Kabul, in August 1988, the Soviet Army was close to withdrawing fifty per cent of its occupying forces. The lingering worry was about the fate of the POWs in the hands of the mujahidin. The Ministry of Foreign Affairs asked the Americans to intercede.[43] Memories of the American exodus from Vietnam were stirred. At the fall of Saigon in 1975, the Vietnamese communists had used American prisoners – including their remains – as bargaining tools. Now the USSR was discovering how hard such a situation could be.[44] General Varennikov assured Shevardnadze that Soviet forces would at least be leaving a stable Afghan government behind. General Gromov, based in the south, provided a gloomier picture.[45] It was Gromov's report that convinced Shevardnadze, and he repeated his own appeal for increased help for Najibullah's administration. Varennikov and others proposed to carry out a bombing offensive against the mujahidin. The anticommunist leader Ahmed-Shah Masud was on the point of cutting the main road from Kabul through to the USSR. The supply line to Najibullah would soon be broken. Chernyaev objected that bombing raids would achieve nothing unless accompanied by troops on the ground – and nobody in the Soviet leadership wanted to re-invade (although Gorbachëv was in two minds for a while).[46]

The mujahidin were relentless. Najibullah's prospects worsened daily as the rebellion spread and the Afghan forces at his disposal showed signs of demoralization. The Soviet General Staff concentrated on the tasks of retreat. The priority was to leave with as few casualties and as much dignity as possible. The schedule was set. By mid-February 1989 no army or air force unit was to be left in Afghanistan.

Shevardnadze took yet another trip to Kabul in mid-January 1989 and witnessed the economic siege of the capital.[47] On his return to Moscow he called again for the maintenance of a Soviet military contingent. Najibullah had pleaded for a brigade to break the blockade of Kandahar. On 23 January the Politburo's Afghan Commission met to hear from Shevardnadze. Others present included Yakovlev, Chebrikov, Kryuchkov and Yazov.[48] Yakovlev asked for a ban on bombers flying over Afghanistan from Soviet bases; he wanted to keep public opinion around the world on the Kremlin's side. Shevardnadze retorted that the Najibullah administration was not doomed; he added that the USSR would lose sympathy around the world if Soviet actions led to that result.[49] Yakovlev rang Chernyaev begging him to intercede with Gorbachëv, who proved to be worried about the growing rift with Shevardnadze. A three-way phone call was arranged among Shevardnadze, Yakovlev and Chernyaev with Gorbachëv listening in to the contending arguments. Chernyaev accused Shevardnadze of upsetting the plan for withdrawal. Shevardnadze replied that Najibullah had assured him that if he could last out the next year, he might survive indefinitely. Gorbachëv consulted Kryuchkov, the KGB's chief officer for Afghanistan. Kryuchkov had recently spoken up for Shevardnadze. Now he gave a grimmer account. What Gorbachëv heard quickly removed any thought of sending a brigade.[50]

On 15 February 1989 the last soldier of the USSR walked across the bridge into Soviet Tajikistan. The war has lasted a few months short of an entire decade. The attempt at communist revolution had been accompanied by economic and educational reforms. There had been a constant assault on local social traditions and Islam. The USSR's intervention had served to strengthen the resistance to the Afghan communists. The experiment had been a lamentable failure.

Najibullah's plight worsened as the mujahidin forces laid siege to Jalalabad near the Pakistani border. If the city fell, the road would be open for an assault on Kabul. On 9 March Najibullah pleaded for an airborne bombing campaign undertaken from Soviet territory. When the Politburo met next day, it turned down the request. Shevardnadze expressed his distress on the grounds that it was a matter of honour for him to stand by Najibullah.[51] (He did not mention his more acute concern about the possibility of a future official enquiry.) At an emergency session of the Politburo on 11 March, he repeated his arguments against abandoning the USSR's 'friends' in Afghanistan. Kryuchkov gave him some support whereas Chebrikov hedged his bets; but Yakovlev attacked any suggestion of sending Soviet troops back to help Najibullah. Ligachëv was on a trip to Prague at that time and Ryzhkov was visiting Siberia. Nevertheless the outcome was never in serious doubt after Gorbachëv rebutted Shevardnadze. He denied that anyone had ever assumed that Najibullah would be able to hold out. He insisted on respect for the Geneva accords so long as he remained General Secretary.[52] With this, the terrible Soviet military adventure reached its conclusion. The Politburo had gone into Afghanistan reluctantly but with confidence; it came out humbled.

30. SPOKES IN THE WHEEL

American public opinion was losing its hostility to the Kremlin like snow off a dyke. People saluted what Gorbachëv had done for peace in the world. Surveys also confirmed that most of the electorate also looked favourably upon Reagan's moves to conciliation with the USSR. There was enthusiasm for a President and General Secretary who appeared on the brink of making the Cold War a thing of the past.

Those among Reagan's officials who were nervous about this found their influence on the wane. Ill health forced Casey's retirement as head of the CIA in November 1986 after he collapsed at his home on the very day he was scheduled to testify before Congress about the Iran-Contra affair; he died of a brain tumour the following May. Acting Director Robert Gates changed little in the agency's analysis. The CIA estimated that Soviet debts to foreign countries in real terms were only sixteen per cent above their level in 1985 since the Kremlin wanted to avoid the trap that had caught countries in Eastern Europe. But the consequence was a fall in the volume of those imports so badly needed for industrial re-equipment and consumer satisfaction. The Politburo hoped to encourage joint ventures with capitalist firms. The idea was that such firms would have an interest in making their investment work for them, which would help to revive the Soviet economy.[1] Discussion in the CIA allowed for the possibility that the Kremlin might give Eastern Europe the freedom to sign deals with West European businesses. Gorbachëv at the same time pursued a newly pragmatic policy in the Third World. The CIA thought it unwise to apply further pressure for fear of driving him off the path of reform in foreign policy. His continuation in office seemed to suit American national interests.[2]

Weinberger in April 1987 nevertheless accused the KGB of 'massive espionage' at the American embassy in Moscow. With an extravagant flourish, he likened such penetration to the violent occupation of the Tehran embassy by the National Revolutionary Guard.[3] In August he wrote in the New York Times attacking those organizations like the

Common Cause and the American Physical Society which denied the possibility of constructing a perfect defensive system. Weinberger said that this would scarcely matter if the system itself acted as an effective deterrent. The other benefit would come from the ruinous costs imposed on the Kremlin: 'Without incentives to reduce armaments, the Soviets will continue their build-up.'[4] He scoffed at the idea that the Politburo had 'a very deep commitment to democracy or freedom or revulsion at communism'; he could hardly believe how Gorbachëv continued to appoint dreadful people to high office in the USSR.[5]

His report to the American Congress in early 1987 rebuked those senators and congressmen who gave priority to reducing the nation's financial deficit. Reneging on a lifelong commitment to fiscal rectitude, he contended that the greatest fraction of the current debt – forty-two per cent – was held by American corporations which would use their dividends to America's economic benefit. The drive to modernize the armed forces, including offensive weaponry, ought to proceed with presidential approval.[6] He depicted the USSR as being committed to 'expansionism' and world revolution.[7] He applauded the Strategic Defense Initiative for having pulled the Soviet leadership back into negotiations.[8] Weinberger implicitly denied that the programme had exclusively pacific purposes. He wanted to turn America into the dominant power over Europe. He criticized the Krasnoyarsk radar station as an infringement of the Anti-Ballistic Missile Treaty; he praised the upgrading work at America's early-warning stations in Thule and Fylingdales.[9] Weinberger distanced himself from the Reykjavik understandings about medium-range nuclear missiles. Under questioning, he certainly affirmed his allegiance to Reagan's objective of their total elimination, but he did this in a way that left no doubt about his private opinion.[10]

The year 1987 brought discomfort to Weinberger as his efforts to thwart Shultz and the State Department ran into the sand. Reagan had made his definitive choice in policy, and Weinberger had lost his place of preferment and had no realistic chance of regaining it. Proud and exhausted, he tendered his resignation. He left his post on 23 November. The rumour went the rounds that he was leaving his post because his wife had cancer. (This understandably upset Jane Weinberger, who issued a public denial that this was the reason for his departure.)[11] Reagan gave a warm speech of thanks at the White House and Weinberger went into retirement. The relief felt in the State Department was shared by the Politburo – Shevardnadze's entourage celebrated the

departure of a man who had baulked every attempt at rapprochement.[12] Weinberger stayed true to himself and told a reporter: 'I think
it's awfully early to conclude that [Gorbachëv] is a warm, caring, trusting man who's not going to do anything wrong. He's got claws and
every once in a while those claws come out.'[13] In February 1988 he
appeared before the Senate Foreign Relations Committee and called
for vigilance against Soviet cheating and for protection of the American military budget and the Strategic Defense Initiative.[14]

Weinberger was not the only leading official who stepped down.
Assistant Secretary Perle had left the Defense Department in June
1987; he had formed the opinion that he could influence foreign
policy more effectively outside the administration. He disliked the
concessions that were being mooted with the USSR. He hated the
spirit of compromise. In Perle's opinion, it made no sense to hurry
towards signing a strategic arms treaty.[15] Whereas Weinberger continued to see little purpose and much danger in summit meetings, Perle
came to accept that they could at least be useful in grinding the Soviet
Union 'into the ground'.[16] But Perle still insisted that the American
side had to bargain toughly; and as officials got ready to sign an Intermediate-Range Nuclear Forces Treaty towards the end of that year,
he warned them not to count on his automatic support. He aimed to
keep his options open in the American media.[17] Nevertheless when
he examined the draft treaty, he proved willing to recommend it for
ratification.[18] This was also the position taken by former UN Ambassador Jeane Kirkpatrick. The proposed treaty, she asserted, would
weaken Western Europe's defences while making the USSR 'somewhat
less vulnerable'; but she ended by endorsing its acceptance.[19]

This still left people inside the administration who looked askance
at the rapprochement with the USSR. The CIA's Fritz Ermath wrote to
Colin Powell: 'The new Soviet leadership believes that it has a good
chance of getting its main goal with us, Détente Two, without fundamentally altering its policies in the Third World.'[20] Defense Secretary
Carlucci, speaking confidentially to leaders of American Jewish
organizations, declared: 'Gorbachëv has bamboozled Europe. Image
of peace, compassion, but arms double talk.'[21] Fred Iklé, co-chair of
Reagan's advisory commission on long-term defence strategy, asserted
that verification would remain impossible.[22]

Conservative commentators ventilated their concerns. Among
them was Kissinger, who questioned whether the USSR had provided
reliable promises regarding American national security. He implied

that if he had been involved in the talks, he would not have settled for as little as Reagan. Shultz did not conceal his irritation on ABC News.[23] Reagan's old friend William F. Buckley shared Kissinger's doubts. In January 1987 he wrote that Reagan's words sounded as if they had come out of *Pravda* and *Izvestiya*: 'What Mr Reagan refuses to dwell on is that men and women who by no means believe war is inevitable, believe that the INF treaty weakens the West's deterrent posture.'[24] On 5 May, when Buckley's *National Review* raised an alarm about national security, Reagan remonstrated that he had definitely not gone soft on the USSR. He wrote that he still regarded it as an evil empire; he also made the less than accurate claim that he had told Gorbachëv at Reykjavik that if Soviet leaders failed to agree on reducing stockpiles of nuclear weaponry, they would restart an arms race they could not win. He made clear his commitment to 'a redressing of the conventional-weapon imbalance'.[25]

This did not deflect Buckley from publishing a critical article by Nixon and Kissinger in the same month.[26] It was months before he accepted the President's assurances, and he continued to accentuate the probability that Congress would remove adequate funding for the Strategic Defense Initiative after Reagan had left office. He sympathized with those West European powers which looked on American ballistic missiles as the crucial deterrent against Soviet military blackmail; and he noted that he had plenty of American conservative friends on his side of the argument.[27]

Reagan took note of the unease that was made manifest after the December 1987 Washington summit. Buckley raised objections about Cuba, Nicaragua, Vietnam, Mozambique and Angola: 'If Gorbachev is indeed going to turn his back on the faith of his fathers, God bless him. The point is that it has not happened.'[28] George Will went as far as comparing Reagan to Neville Chamberlain: 'There was similar disagreement – majority euphoria, minority dismay – in Britain when a summit, at Munich, supposedly domesticated Hitler.'[29] Reagan could see that if he wished to continue his search with Gorbachëv for peace, he had to dispel the doubts that were being expressed. He also had to promote more people to office who would help Shultz and the State Department. He could not afford to let anyone rampage around as Weinberger had done. They had served their purpose in intimidating the Politburo. Without Weinberger, Gorbachëv might have refused to alter his bargaining posture as he eventually did in March 1987. But now Reagan needed to quieten the angry bulls. Ill-tempered exchanges between Washington and Moscow would be counterproductive.

The President did not yet look on things in quite this way when he asked Carlucci, his National Security Adviser from December 1986, to take the place that Weinberger was vacating at the Defense Department. Carlucci had a jaundiced opinion about the proceedings in Reykjavik.[30] Furthermore, he and Shultz had not always found it easy to work with each other. Shultz took precautions. In the wake of the 'Irangate' affair he wanted no more backstairs diplomacy to which he was not privy. He forbade US ambassadors to communicate with Carlucci unless they had either obtained his sanction or at least informed him in advance.[31] But Shultz also wanted to mend fences with Carlucci and invited him to spend a couple of days at his Stanford home, where they talked over breakfast about how they would work together. Shultz included Colin Powell, newly appointed as National Security Adviser in Carlucci's place, in the house party. Powell was unusual not only as the first African-American to hold this post but also in his diplomatic skills – he was known as a 'people person', good at preventing conflict. Shultz thought him incomparably better than any of his predecessors. At last there was a chance of some harmony in Washington when the arms talks were under discussion.[32]

When appearing before the Senate Armed Services Committee on 12 November 1987, Carlucci offered to reduce the number of programmes of research and production with a view towards making at least some of them operational. The defence budget had been frozen in real terms for two years. Carlucci was hoping to improve the relationship with Congress. He admitted that he had yet to be convinced that the Strategic Defense Initiative would ever prove cost-effective. Committee Chairman and Democrat Sam Nunn welcomed the contrast with Weinberger's stridency and lack of candour.[33] Carlucci at the same time wanted the President to talk to people outside the administration with experience of negotiating with Soviet leaders. (Was he quietly trying to dilute Shultz's influence? So much for the Stanford breakfast accord.) Reagan disliked the idea of consulting Perle or former National Security Adviser Brzezinski, perhaps because he thought that anti-Sovietism was too ingrained in them. He preferred to meet former President Nixon, despite their past and current disagreements. The historical legacy of Watergate meant that Nixon had to be smuggled into the White House so that no reporter knew what was going on. A helicopter landed on the south lawn with him on board.[34]

Gorbachëv, of course, had no concerns about the kind of publicity that Reagan wished to avoid. On the inside of the USSR's institutions, however, it was becoming a different matter. The armed forces were an epicentre of discontent – Shevardnadze quipped that the difficulties in the arms talks were not with the Americans but with the lobbies on the Soviet side.[35] Gorbachëv had always been sensitive to this. When preparing for a Politburo meeting on 28 September 1987, he drew comfort from the army leadership's acceptance of the new military doctrine and was delighted about his conversations with Defence Minister Yazov. He appreciated the Ministry of Foreign Affairs' adaptiveness under Shevardnadze. He was aware that the KGB was conducting its own internal debate about *perestroika*; but Gorbachëv liked the fact that the agency contained 'intellectual people': he trusted it to remain helpful and dutiful. He claimed to enjoy his discussions with Chairman Chebrikov.[36]

The Law on the State Enterprise came into effect in January 1988. Its main intent was to liberate the planned economy by loosening the central shackles on industrial and commercial operations. Factory directors were empowered to set their own prices for the goods being produced. Their workers acquired the right to elect them – Gorbachëv aspired to establishing conditions of labour democracy. His aim was to re-energize the USSR's industrial performance just as he had done to change the political environment through the reforms he had intro-duced at the January 1987 Central Committee plenum. He believed that he was liberating the vast potential of the Marxist-Leninist social order. He and fellow reformers concentrated on changing conditions in the Soviet Union, and many of them expected the country to narrow the technological gaps between the USSR and the West. As yet the emphasis was on internal transformation and the external compli-cations about the grain purchase agreement, CoCom and industrial espionage were ignored. The reason for the neglect was mainly politi-cal: Gorbachëv wanted to focus on what was quickly practical. In the longer term, he knew he could count on Prime Minister Ryzhkov's support in altering economic links with Western capitalist countries. Ryzhkov was telling foreigners that two of his ultimate ambitions were to reduce the Soviet defence budget and obtain the USSR's entry into the International Monetary Fund.[37] This could only be a long way ahead. For the foreseeable future, the USSR had to cope on its own.

Gorbachëv pushed forward with his foreign policy despite some disturbing signals from Washington. In January 1988 a commission appointed by the Defense Secretary and the National Security Adviser published a report titled *Discriminate Deterrence*. This was clearly an attempt to obviate Reagan's purposes once he had left office. The co-chairmen were Fred Iklé and Albert Wohlstetter. Their fellow signatories included other sceptics about total denuclearization such as Henry Kissinger and Zbigniew Brzezinski. The report recommended the need to budget for modernized conventional forces that could strike deep into enemy territory. It also called for greater attention to preventing attacks from outer space and for the boosting of America's capacity to make 'discriminate nuclear strikes'. The American military budget had to be increased. Foreign policy based on long-term benign relations with Moscow would be unwarranted; and the rising economic power of Beijing, Tokyo and even New Delhi made for uncertainty in global strategic planning. America had to remain flexible about its choices. The Warsaw Pact continued to pose an acute threat and could mount a surprise attack. The USSR might undertake one without help from its allies.[38]

The historian Paul Kennedy criticized *Discriminate Deterrence* on several grounds. As the author of a best-selling book on 'imperial overstretch', he worried that the report underestimated the dangers of America's global strategy. Under Reagan, America had become a massive debtor nation. *Discriminate Deterrence* assumed that American technological brilliance would compensate for every difficulty. Kennedy thought this unduly optimistic. He queried the report's statistical accuracy and lamented its inattention to the low quality of general educational standards. For Kennedy, *Discriminate Deterrence* fell short of being an integrated agenda for future success.[39]

He could have added that it totally rejected Reagan's objective of abolishing all nuclear weapons, which could bode ill for continuity in policy when his successor came into office. Even so, Gorbachëv made no change in his foreign and security policy. Ligachëv confined his grumbles to internal political conditions. He detested the growing depreciation of communism's historical achievements. When Gorbachëv went off on a trip to Czechoslovakia in March 1988, Ligachëv licensed the *Sovetskaya Rossiya* newspaper to publish a letter by an obscure Leningrad chemistry teacher, Nina Andreeva, objecting to the critical campaign against the achievements of the 1930s. She showed a distinct trace of anti-Semitism and pro-Stalinism. Not until Gorbachëv returned from abroad did the media dare again to advocate reform. Ligachëv disingenuously denied complicity in the affair. When

Gorbachëv made further enquiries, *Pravda* editor Ivan Frolov dropped a strong hint about Ligachëv; but Gorbachëv refrained from asking Frolov to be explicit. He judged that he could not yet afford to fall out with Ligachëv.[40] He had reason to be cautious. Gromyko, Solomentsev and Vorotnikov agreed with Ligachëv that Andreeva had written a good letter; and Gorbachëv had to go to the Politburo to secure the rejection of any such piece again. Yakovlev, Ryzhkov and Shevard-nadze took Gorbachëv's side; even Chebrikov and Yazov did.[41]

Gorbachëv went on appointing reformers to leading posts in foreign policy. In spring 1988 he removed Dobrynin from the Party International Department and appointed Yakovlev to oversee it. Dobrynin had failed to turn the department into a dynamic alternative 'think tank' on global problems – he always appeared preoccupied with America, where he had served as Ambassador.[42] Gorbachëv wanted a practical radical, and Yakovlev fitted this requirement.[43] Having poached Chernyaev and Shakhnazarov from the International Department as his advisers, Gorbachëv also continued to rely on them for ideas on foreign policy.[44] Chernyaev said they provided him with only 'a semi-manufactured product': Gorbachëv alone took responsibility for the finished article.[45]

For technical advice about nuclear arms reduction, he continued to look to Zaikov and the Big Five and relied heavily on their recommended guidelines for each round of high-level talks.[46] Such was his confidence in Zaikov that he made him Moscow City Party secretary after Yeltsin's removal in November 1987. Zaikov was renowned as someone who put out political fires, and Gorbachëv asked him to put them out throughout the party hierarchy of the capital. Gorbachëv underestimated the effect of the additional burden he was placing upon Zaikov.[47] Running Moscow was an enormous job and Zaikov already had his hands full with his duties in the Politburo and the Big Five. His problems with the General Staff had always existed and compromise was reached with difficulty. Zaikov, never the greatest enthusiast for *perestroika*, was made daily aware that the reformers could not take their ascendancy for granted. He pointed to the obstacles that people from the Soviet military-industrial complex were laying in his path. He called for the party leadership and government to help him out – and at the same time he was being expected to oversee public affairs in the Soviet metropolis.[48]

Gorbachëv made things worse by appointing Valeri Boldin, his own personal assistant, to take over the Party General Department.

Boldin proved strangely lethargic in facilitating international communication. The result was that Soviet delegations sometimes had to conduct talks without having received the usual guidelines.[49] Probably Boldin was being deliberately unhelpful out of dislike for the concessions being made to the Americans. Gorbachëv also failed to reform the Party Defence Department. Its head, Oleg Belyakov, was regularly obstructive to Zaikov.[50] Belyakov had a protector in Oleg Baklanov, who was the Central Committee secretary with responsibility for military industry. Baklanov, with his courteous manners and the slight Ukrainian burr in his accent, treated his staff with consideration; he was well known for an aversion to drinking parties.[51] He applied a personal sternness to the projects of disarmament. Gorbachëv remonstrated with him at the Politburo on 3 March 1988: 'And you, what kind of money are you gobbling up? Level one of your rocket: how much does it cost? You only need to spit into outer space and it costs billions . . .' Baklanov refused to give way. The days were gone when a subordinate had to hold his tongue.[52]

Grumbles about Gorbachëv's foreign policy were heard at a Central Committee plenum in May 1988 when Kornienko urged the desirability of reverting to the objective of strategic parity.[53] He was obviously attacking Gorbachëv's idea that 'sufficiency' should be the goal. As Deputy Head of the Party International Department he was showing unprecedented truculence. Shevardnadze was angry at the speech, and it took Yakovlev to restrain him from rebutting Kornienko on the spot.[54] This proved wise. No one supported Kornienko and the commotion faded. Shevardnadze tried to raise the pace of change. At the Politburo on 20 June he demanded a reduction in military budget in favour of projects devoted to 'the well-being of the peoples'. Gorbachëv ignored him on this occasion even though he agreed with the case that he was making.[55] Shevardnadze was rampant. He told an open colloquium at his ministry in July that the confrontation of communism and capitalism was no longer the vector of global politics. Ligachëv disliked what he heard. Ambassador Matlock was also present – itself a sign of changed times – and declared his delight, pausing only to ask whether he had understood Shevardnadze correctly to the effect that America and the USSR should become partners rather than enemies.[56]

On 30 September Gorbachëv made further progress by easing Gromyko out of the Politburo. It was over a year since 'Gloomy Grom' had produced a paper criticizing recent changes in the philosophy of foreign policy;[57] and when he later tried to insert traditional slogans into official theses, Gorbachëv merely retorted that 'it's only when we need to make the people go without food that we make mention of class struggle'.[58] It was high time to remove the seventy-nine-year-old veteran. When shunting Gromyko into retirement, Gorbachëv ostentatiously thanked him on behalf of party and country. Gromyko responded by confirming his belief that *perestroika* was the only correct policy for the USSR.[59]

Gorbachëv transformed the highest level of the party's constitutional structure. He abolished the Central Committee departments and replaced them with a set of commissions. One of them would be dedicated to international politics, and Yakovlev was to chair it.[60] It was not entirely good news for the radical cause since Akhromeev and Kryuchkov were nominated to Yakovlev's commission.[61] Neither man was genuinely enthusiastic about talk of the need for further concessions in external policy, but Gorbachëv thought he could trust and control them. He liked to give the impression that he sympathized with communist traditionalists even while he was marching firmly towards a destination of reform. Obfuscation was in his blood. He hoped to drag the sceptics along with him until such time as it was too late for them to reverse his policies. The Rust affair had enabled him to get rid of doubters like Sokolov from the Defence Ministry. Now he also replaced Chebrikov with Kryuchkov as KGB Chairman. Chebrikov was put in charge of the new Central Committee Rights Commission. Although he was hardly a sympathizer with the human rights goals that Gorbachëv espoused, the advantage was that he was no longer running the KGB, and Gorbachëv felt that Kryuchkov would be more malleable.[62]

Chebrikov had given a disturbing report on the KGB's work in the year 1987. It claimed that America and its NATO allies were 'exercising a definite influence over the formation of terrorist and extremist objectives among persons of an anti-Soviet disposition and other hostile elements'. Foreign Muslim organizations were sending secret emissaries into the USSR. Ukrainian nationalists were active from abroad. Afghan counter-revolutionaries had their agents on Soviet soil. A serious nationalist plot had been uncovered in Georgia. Violent activity was rare: there had been only five cases of criminal explosions across the USSR as a whole. The KGB was more concerned to highlight the increasingly overt nature of anti-Soviet militancy. Demonstrations had even occurred on Red Square and outside the

Central Committee building. The KGB was working with the Ministry of Internal Affairs to suppress trouble.[63]

There was nothing unusual in the KGB sounding an alarm in its annual reports, and Gorbachëv reacted with equanimity. He was equally calm about the armed forces. Shevardnadze felt less comfortable in the light of continual criticisms by the military lobby. On 9 November 1988 he told Gorbachëv that the high command was playing fast and loose with the Politburo and its policies. Shevardnadze said that the armed forces were trying to provoke NATO by intelligence operations and new weapons locations.[64]

Heart problems pushed Akhromeev into retiring as Chief of the General Staff in November 1988. Gorbachëv invited him to stay on as his military adviser.[65] He had always made a point of taking him along to talks with the Americans;[66] and he noticeably ignored Defence Minister Yazov whenever Akhromeev was present.[67] It is true that he was never a pushover. Indeed Shevardnadze regarded him as a terrible reactionary whose memoranda could have 'brought the entire negotiating system to collapse'.[68] Akhromeev held to his earlier opinion that a 'limited' nuclear war was feasible without the consequence of global destruction. Through to 1987 he was still exploring the possibilities for the SS-20s.[69] He did accept the new concept of strategic 'sufficiency'. Or at least he did not find it politic to object. He admitted that *perestroika* was personally difficult for him. He disliked how he was having to rethink the answers to so many questions.[70] Nina Andreev's letter delighted him. He rang up the *Sovetskaya Rossiya* editor Chikin to offer congratulations and support. The Main Political Administration of the Soviet Army received the order from him to publicize the article among all military units: 'Well, at long last a true word has appeared!'[71]

Gorbachëv saw advantage in holding on to Akhromeev if he wanted to dispel fears in the Soviet Army that he was selling out the state's vital interests. Akhromeev had his own reasons for accepting the invitation. By working with the General Secretary, he aimed to extract compromises from him and obtain a degree of autonomous influence on decisions.[72] Many of his fellow commanders saw him as a traitor who had ceased to expose the dangers in current proposals for disarmament; they thought his behaviour wholly inappropriate for someone whom they expected to represent the armed forces.[73] Gorbachëv seemed to be getting too much his own way. When he substituted Yazov for Sokolov in the Defence Ministry, there was less of the customary obstructiveness. Yazov displayed a gratifying appreciation of recent changes in the international situation; he understood that world politics were changing irreversibly and worked in a cooperative fashion with Gorbachëv and Zaikov.[74]

Not that Gorbachëv could feel comfortable. Mikhail Moiseev, Akhromeev's successor as Chief of the General Staff, was quickly under pressure from the rest of the military leadership to oppose further proposals for reform.[75] Morale was dropping in the high command. General staff personnel said that whereas once they had pursued a strategy of overwhelming destruction, now they had one of capitulation.[76] The high command thought Gorbachëv 'incompetent and perfunctory' on military questions in comparison with previous general secretaries: 'We had one exercise in Minsk when he arrived, gave a prepared speech, without seeing the exercise itself and left.'[77] He declined to inspect armaments factories or talk to inventors and engineers as Brezhnev had done.[78] He liked to keep his distance from military commanders. According to naval chief Vladimir Chernavin, he lacked any feeling for their importance for the country.[79] The fight for political supremacy was only just beginning in the USSR. Reagan had won the struggle against his grumblers. It remained to be seen whether Gorbachëv's leadership was equally secure.

31. REAGAN'S WINDOW OF DEPARTURE

On 1 June 1988 Gorbachëv bade farewell to the Reagans at Vnukovo airport. At the Politburo's next session he declared:

> Our forecast has been fully realized; once again it's been proved that a principled and constructive policy based on realism is the only correct one. This alone can bring results. And the President showed himself a realist here. He managed to see the processes that we have happening on the political plane. While he was in Washington he announced that it was necessary to study the culture of the people. At that time, however, he was looking at us through an artificially wrought conception of the rights of man. The Americans in the days of his visit spent whole days looking on their [TV] screens at our life, at ordinary Soviet people.[1]

His colleagues liked what they heard. He himself had always voiced the hope that the USSR might gain a breathing space for its necessary self-modernization. The signing of his first big treaty appeared to validate the advantages of his *perestroika*.

Later in the month Gorbachëv addressed a special Party Conference where he took pride in what had been achieved with Reagan. His main purpose, though, was to further the cause of internal political reform. He had it in mind to break the shackles of the one-party state by compelling party officials to submit themselves to the disciplines of election. Nobody was to hold on to his post without the possibility of challenge. Gorbachëv's other big reform was a proposal to change the entire Soviet constitution. At its core would be a parliament known as the Congress of People's Deputies. Out of 2,250 seats, only 400 would be reserved for communist party and other public organizations. The rest would be available for anyone to contest, and Gorbachëv let it be known that party officials would have to take part in them in a free and fair fashion. Yeltsin made an appearance and pleaded for readmission to party life. Gorbachëv, wanting to have a counterweight against his own communist-conservative opponents, allowed the request. The plan was to hold elections in March 1989 and for the Congress of People's Deputies – as well as its inner body, the USSR Supreme Soviet – to remain in almost permanent session. The days of mere ceremonialism and quasi-parliamentarianism were coming to a close. This would be a constitutional revolution, astonishing as it was unprecedented in Soviet history. Gorbachëv had the bit between his teeth and was racing to the line.

On 15 July he was full of confidence when addressing a meeting of the Warsaw Pact's political leaders. He announced a new stage in world politics. The Soviet promise to withdraw from Afghanistan, he claimed, was serving to unblock the resolution of other regional conflicts. Links with America had never been closer.[2] He admitted that the American political right continued to advocate a policy of armed force and technological embargo. But their denunciations of the USSR, in his estimation, were evidence of the strength of *perestroika*. Right-wing politicians and columnists feared that 'socialism' might succeed in reforming itself in the East. According to Gorbachëv, they could see that Western capitalism would eventually face serious competition, even if this might require another couple of decades before it came to fulfilment. He anyway doubted that the American political right would be able to change opinion in the White House. He forecast that the rapprochement with America would outlast Reagan's departure from office. He stated this baldly, without explaining his reasoning. He asked the East European leaders to take his word for it that whoever won the presidential election would want friendly relations with the USSR.[3]

He spoke robustly about the irreversibility of Europe's division into two political halves; but at the same time he laid stress on the need to change the way that the Warsaw Pact operated. He told the East European leaders that he would have no worries if they strengthened their links with the European Economic Community.[4] Gorbachëv told them that things had changed since 1985. As far as he was concerned, they now had the freedom to negotiate as independent states. He expressly denied that West Germany was any kind of threat – indeed, he depicted Kohl as having an approach to foreign policy close to his own. Eastern European communist leaders were used to saying and hearing that Kohl was a danger to stability across the continent. Ever since he became Chancellor in Bonn, the Warsaw Pact's press had denounced him for advocating German reunification, loading East Germany with debt and playing one Warsaw Pact member country against another. Gorbachëv was ending the chorus of rebuke. The one thing that he insisted upon was that if Kohl wanted to enhance West Germany's situation, he would have to respect the 'legacy of Yalta'. Eastern Europe's separate status was sacrosanct for him.[5]

The Politburo sought to keep up the momentum of rapprochement with Washington. On 28 August 1988 the Soviet authorities gave American officials a demonstration of their agreed process of 'liquidating' intermediate nuclear missiles.[6] They also arranged visits to the Krasnoyarsk radar station. Gorbachëv wanted to use this as a way of enabling further treaties with the Americans before Reagan left the White House. He wrote a letter for Shevardnadze to deliver in person to the President, lamenting that there was still no agreement about how to obtain a fifty per cent reduction in strategic nuclear weapons and commenting that 'it takes two to tango'.[7]

On 23 September Shevardnadze met Reagan and his officials in the Oval Office and remonstrated about the American refusal to take reciprocal steps after the USSR's recent moves. He asked permission for Soviet experts to inspect the American radar stations in Thule and Fylingdales. Carlucci smiled while signalling a refusal. Shultz lightened the mood by describing Shevardnadze as his 'friend' and focusing on the projected agreements about nuclear explosion tests, regional conflicts and human rights. When Shevardnadze continued to object to the American radar stations, Shultz repeated that America would never sign a treaty on strategic nuclear weapons while the Krasnoyarsk station remained.[8] Reagan added his demand for the Berlin Wall to be pulled down, stressing that he had never accepted the legitimacy of the German Democratic Republic. But then he recognized that the conversation was becoming unproductive. This was not at all what he had intended. Abruptly he changed direction by proposing that the Olympic Games should be awarded to Berlin. Shultz picked up the idea and recounted how Hitler had refused to shake the hand of the black athlete Jesse Owens at the last Olympics held there in 1936. This encouraged Reagan to say how much pleasure he took in what the two superpowers had achieved during his second term in office. He expressed regret that his time in the White House would be soon be over.[9]

Nothing came of the Olympics idea, and new practical initiatives were few and far between. George Bush, now the Republican Party candidate in the presidential campaign, asked to see Shevardnadze. (The Democratic Party candidate Michael Dukakis inexplicably made no such request.) The advice that Bush gave was for Soviet leaders to transact as much business as they could before the end of the year. Arms agreements ought to be completed with all speed. Although he expected to win the election, Bush pointed out that he would begin with a lower standing with the American Congress than Reagan. When Shultz heard about this, he thought it a 'dumb' way to talk to Shevardnadze and revealed a poverty of expectation.[10] A visionary presidency was coming to an end. The White House was about to yield occupancy to a man with doubts where once there had been a leader of clarity and hope.

Shultz worked to guarantee at least a smooth finale to Reagan's time in the White House. Tensions with the Kremlin were to be minimized. CIA Deputy Director Robert Gates annoyed Shultz, not for the first time, with a speech he made on 14 October 1988. Addressing the American Association for the Advancement of Science, he spoke of his uncertainty about Gorbachëv's capacity to carry out a basic economic reform and added that his hold on power could soon become precarious.[11] Shultz felt it necessary to announce that there was no change of direction in the White House. He had not finished with Gates. Three days later he tore into him in person, accusing him yet again of trying to make policy when his real job was to collect and process information. It was not the intelligence agency's proper function to take part in public politics. Gates had omitted to seek clearance for the speech, and Shultz took him to task him for contending that Gorbachëv had only three supporters in the Politburo. He reminded Gates about how late the CIA had been in coming to recognize that Gorbachëv was different from previous Soviet leaders. As if unsure that his message had not hit home, he concluded: 'So you have as you know for a long time a very dissatisfied client.'[12]

Gorbachëv hoped to make it impossible for the next American President, whether it was Bush or Dukakis, to change the current line of foreign policy. On 31 October he held a planning session about his upcoming visit to New York, where he was scheduled to address the United Nations General Assembly. He wanted his speech to be a sort of 'anti-Fulton'.[13] Whereas Churchill in at Fulton, Missouri in 1946 had described an Iron Curtain as dividing the two halves of Europe, Gorbachëv intended to proclaim the need to remake the continent without any such barrier. He dreamed of creating a sensation. He would take the American political establishment by storm. Having presented his thoughts to the USSR Defence Council, he went to the Politburo and said: 'It's a serious matter. The Americans are scared that we might do something as in the spirit of Reykjavik . . . We'll push forward our internal and external politics – and there'll be nowhere for Bush to turn.'[14] He enjoined strict secrecy on everybody: 'We'll get rid of anyone who leaks and deprive them of their posts and privileges.' He was plotting to surprise the General Assembly by announcing a unilateral reduction of Soviet troops by 500,000. He would deny that such concessions derived from the pursuit of Western economic assistance. The dazzling occasion would be an opportunity for him to avow his confidence in the Soviet future.[15]

Shevardnadze urged Gorbachëv to be even more radical by withdrawing all Soviet forces from Hungary. This was too much for Gorbachëv, who agreed on the desirability of reducing the military presence but rejected immediate total withdrawal.[16] Shevardnadze had also been nagging him to put questions of human rights at the top of the Politburo's agenda: 'It's a great cause!' He wanted the Soviet leadership to endorse the United Nations as a 'universal organization', seemingly with authority over the USSR and the USA.[17] Gorbachëv demurred. His own ideas were a massive break with the USSR's traditions; he felt he was going as far and as fast as he safely could. He did, though, accept Shevardnadze's proposal to commit the USSR to what he called the 'zero option' in political prisoners and refuseniks. He agreed that the country should no longer have any of them. Shevardnadze had also called for the complete removal of restrictions on leaving or entering the Soviet Union. Once Gorbachëv had shown it to the rest of the leadership, he received strong objections from the security agencies. He thought it unwise to annoy the KGB unduly and trimmed back the proposal. Even so, he retained an advocacy of the right of any citizen to emigrate so long as they were not in possession of state secrets.[18]

He discussed the draft with the Soviet delegation that accompanied him to New York. It was a motley group including Shevardnadze, Yakovlev and other members of the foreign-policy establishment. Raisa was among them. The Soviet creative intelligentsia was also represented – film directors Tengiz Abuladze and Mark Zakharov were with him. The atmosphere was entirely positive. Ambassador Dubinin was the most fawning as he told Gorbachëv: 'You're bearing a new conception of the world.'[19]

On 7 December 1988 Shevardnadze and Shultz hurried to the assigned boxes, where Raisa and O'Bie were happily seated together. (Shevardnadze's aide Stepanov-Mamaladze recorded the 'vain' Kissinger as having drawn attention to himself in the vicinity.) The hall was packed out and noisy. Expectations were at a peak.[20] Gorbachëv did not disappoint either in style or in content. He committed himself and his fellow leaders to 'the principle of freedom of choice'. While praising the French Revolution of 1789 and the Russian Revolution of 1917 for their contributions to human progress, he declared the need for a 'de-ideologization of interstate relations' as the world tackled the problems of 'hunger, disease, illiteracy and other mass ills'. His asserted 'the primacy of the universal human idea'. Turning to the USSR, he indicated his desire for democracy and the rule of law. He heralded the end to radio jamming. On questions of disarmament he said that he would reduce Soviet forces by half a million troops. He heralded the conversion of military factories to the production of civilian goods. He called for a fifty per cent reduction in strategic nuclear missiles. He expressed gratitude to Reagan and Shultz and looked forward warmly to cooperation with Bush.[21]

The entire hall joined in an ovation. Arbatov tugged back Stepanov-Mamaladze when he stood to applaud: 'It's not customary to get to your feet here.' Stepanov-Mamaladze replied that if the Americans stood up to clap their President, he would do the same for the General Secretary.[22]

Gorbachëv gave the speech in the morning and was looking forward to the other scheduled events of the trip; but on his way to a meeting with Reagan and Bush on Governors Island, he received a telephone call from Ryzhkov. The news was terrible. An earthquake had struck Armenia and killed 25,000 people. It was obviously impossible to stay in America. He talked briefly to Reagan and Bush on Governors Island. The conversation was light and nostalgic. Reagan allowed himself a joke when a journalist asked whether there was opposition to Gorbachëv's military cuts in the USSR. Gorbachëv said no, and Reagan said that Gorbachëv's Russian *nyet* sounded a little like yes.[23] He also retold President Lyndon Johnson's humorous grouse about the press – Johnson had said that if ever he walked on top of the water across the River Potomac, the reports would say that he could not swim. Bush assured Gorbachëv that he would continue to build on

what had been accomplished by Gorbachëv and Reagan; he also intimated his wish to promote James Baker and Brent Scowcroft to high
posts in his administration. The meeting ended after Reagan recalled
fondly how he had told Gorbachëv at the Geneva summit that the two
of them had the capacity to start the next world war or bring peace to
the world. He was pleased that it was peace that they had chosen.[24]

Bush talked by phone with Gorbachëv next morning, shortly
before the Russians left for Moscow. While looking forward to working constructively together, he issued an alert that he would take his
time about this.[25] Shultz had told Shevardnadze the same thing; he
had also warned him that the Soviet leaders had to do much more
about human rights if they wanted further agreements with America
– Shevardnadze continued to hope that he was wrong.[26]

Shultz did what he could to finish off his current business with the
USSR. The sudden departure of the Soviet delegation for Moscow had
left him unable to agree progress on the Vienna talks about European
security and cooperation. If Gorbachëv cooperated, it might just be
possible to secure an agreement before he and Reagan stepped down.
He asked Ambassador Matlock to explain this to Shevardnadze, who
welcomed the approach.[27] A few details remained for elaboration.
Human rights in particular continued to divide the two sides, despite
everything that Gorbachëv had promised in his New York speech.
Shevardnadze delegated the negotiating role to Anatoli Adamishin
while Shultz appointed Richard Schifter to represent the State Department. These two officials gave impetus to the search for common
ground, and Shultz judged that the USSR had moved close enough to
satisfying American demands for him to recommend the adoption of
the 'concluding document' of the Conference on Security and Cooperation in Europe. He crossed the Atlantic to witness the act of signature
on 17 January 1989.[28] Among the outcomes of this agreement was a
commitment by America and the Soviet Union to start discussions
about conventional forces in Europe within the next seven weeks. The
idea was to effect a drastic reduction of such forces in the countries of
NATO and the Warsaw Pact.[29]

At the Politburo sessions to review the recent events, starting on
27 December 1988, Gorbachëv put his New York visit above the
Armenian earthquake on the agenda. He was proud of the impact he
had made and declared: 'We want and propose to build a new world,
new relations.'[30] He denied that an eagerness to end the Cold War
signified a desire to move away from socialist objectives, and he

noticeably failed to refer to the de-ideologizing of international relations or of universal human values. He claimed that American liberals
welcomed his programme of socialist renewal whereas the Heritage
Foundation and other organizations on the American political right
called for the maintenance of direct pressure on the USSR.[31] There was
uncertainty about how Bush would turn out as President, and Gorbachëv emphasized that Bush had a deserved reputation for 'natural
caution'. Bush had also defined himself as 'a centrist'. Unfortunately
this meant that he could not act as freely as Reagan, who had enjoyed
the advantage of being trusted by the American political right. But
Gorbachëv was optimistic about being able to come to terms with
Bush; he indicated that Shevardnadze should arrange to meet the new
Secretary of State James Baker as soon as possible.[32]

Prime Minister Ryzhkov disliked the press coverage around the
world about the New York speech. He asked for the media to explain
that the Politburo was not retreating from socialism but rather from a
distorted version of it; he also warned that the process of integration
with the world economy contained possible pitfalls.[33] Gorbachëv
changed the subject and regaled the Politburo with an account of his
ecstatic reception by New Yorkers – he evidently felt that Ryzhkov had
stinted the praise that was due to him.[34]

Shevardnadze was more expansive in his congratulations. American popular opinion, he predicted, would compel the Bush administration to continue with Reagan's policy of conciliation with the USSR.
He asked the Politburo to sanction initiatives on strategic nuclear missiles, on chemical weapons and on human rights. He noted that he
himself had come under criticism for having failed to liaise with the
Defence Ministry about the latest variant of the policy to withdraw
Soviet armed forces from Eastern Europe. Shevardnadze rejected the
accusation as groundless. He also objected to Yazov's attempt to restrict
the information about the Defence Ministry's practical plan; he said
that Moscow had to show to the world that it was serious about changing the Soviet military posture to defensive requirements alone.[35] In the
same combative fashion he put the case for deepening the USSR's
cooperation with America. He rebuked the Leningrad Party secretary
Yuri Solovëv for inspiring a local radio broadcast about the subversive
activities of 'imperialist spy agencies'. He said that such behaviour
played into the hands of people like Kissinger. If the Politburo wished
to make progress in its talks with Washington, care had to be taken to
avoid giving unnecessary offence.[36]

Yakovlev spoke in a similar vein. While expecting the political right to make difficulties for Bush, he reported US Ambassador Matlock as regarding the incoming President as more professional and better informed than his predecessor. Yakovlev asked the Politburo to appreciate the advance that had been achieved. He reasoned that America no longer dominated the agenda. There was a growth in concern among American leaders about Europe and the Pacific as zones where Soviet foreign policy might get the better of them. Yakovlev expressed his delight: '[The Americans] have not wanted to jump on to a train already in motion, far less on to one that is moving into the distance. They are used to being the drivers. The activation of our foreign policy in other regions very much worries them.'[37] He commended Gorbachëv for doing so much to rid the country of its 'enemy image' around the world. He ridiculed the Marxist-Leninist tenet that 'capitalists care less about people's needs'. He spoke angrily about the inaccuracies in the press about the Soviet economy; he expressed his exasperation about the ineptitude of the USSR's trade officials. Yakovlev insisted that the only way forward was to deepen the process of reform. Much had been done, but more was still needed.[38]

All this made Yazov feel somewhat uncomfortable. He reported on unease in the armed forces about the potential damage to the USSR's security. He admitted to refusing to supply the Supreme Soviet with his plan of withdrawal from Eastern Europe; but he promised to release it to the Defence Council.[39] Gorbachëv could see that Yazov was trying to compromise. He eased the situation by commenting that if the Americans kept secrets, why shouldn't the USSR. Yazov immediately calmed down and announced that three entire divisions were scheduled to leave Eastern Europe in 1989.[40] Gorbachëv expressed sympathy for the difficulties involved in having to reduce the officer corps by 100,000. Shevardnadze, Zaikov, Yakovlev, Yazov and Chairman of the State Foreign Economic Commission Vladimir Kamentsev were asked to draft a suitable policy for the Politburo.[41] Ligachëv proved harder to placate than Yazov. He insisted that the 'class character' of international relations should not be relegated to oblivion. Essentially he was warning against straying away from Marxism-Leninism.[42] It is true that he praised the emphasis on disarmament. But he also noted that provincial party leaders were querying the path of current internal policy. He claimed that the new economic freedom for cooperatives had led to instances of greedy speculation. Though he finished by complimenting Gorbachëv on his performance in New York, he left an impression of some degree of discontent – and as Gorbachëv's deputy in the Party Secretariat he had opportunities to make things difficult for him.[43]

A hero abroad, Gorbachëv came back to a Politburo that distinctly refrained from offering uniform endorsement. But at least he avoided censure, and he took his chance to stress the economic benefit rationale for military withdrawal. Military expenditure, he remarked, had recently doubled as a proportion of the USSR's state budget. This was not a sustainable situation. Cutbacks were inevitable. At the same time, he affirmed, there was nothing in his policy that posed a threat to the country's capacity to defend itself.[44] It was only then that he moved on to the Armenian earthquake. Ryzhkov reported on the measures he had undertaken.[45] Gorbachëv was receiving an early warning of political trouble ahead. He tried to smother it inside the party by refusing the advice of his radical associates to lead them off into a separate organization of fundamental reform. He stuck to his favoured tactic of keeping all public agencies together under his aegis. The abiding horror for him was that a coalition might emerge against his radicalism. However much he disliked communist conservatism or even moderate reformism, he felt he had to cohabit with their leaders until such time as he made transformation irreversible.

PART FOUR

1. Ronald Reagan at his inauguration in January 1981.

2. George Shultz in 1985. After three years at the State Department, he felt frustrated by the lack of progress in arms reduction talks.

3. Standard official photograph of General Secretary Yuri Andropov. He was much more poorly than this air-brushed image suggested.

4. Konstantin Chernenko standing between Ethiopian leader Haile Mariam Mengistu and Party International Department head Boris Ponomarëv in December 1984. Chernenko's arched shoulders give a sign of his breathing difficulties. By common agreement – including his own – he was someone who was physically and mentally unfit for the supreme party office.

5. Mikhail Gorbachëv,
General Secretary and,
from 1990, President
of the USSR.

6. Eduard Shevardnadze,
Soviet Foreign Affairs
Minister from 1985 till
his dramatic resignation
in 1990.

7. Erich Honecker on one of his staged walkabouts in East Germany. He was at last to be removed by his own Politburo in October 1989.

8. Polish communist leader and cautious, unpredictable reformer Wojciech Jaruzelski.

9. Nicolae Ceauşescu,
Romanian communist
dictator till his overthrow and
execution in December 1989.

10. The multinational line of Warsaw Pact commanders in the years before the
Soviet perestroika. Note Jaruzelski wearing his sunglasses – his eyesight had been
permanently impaired by the snow glare in Siberian exile.

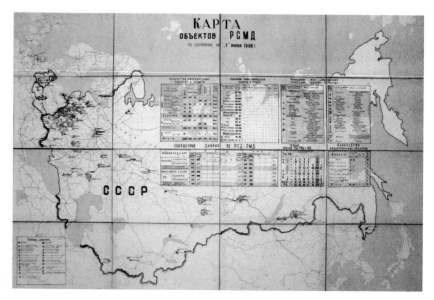

11. Secret Soviet map of the USSR's medium- and short-range nuclear-missile firing and production sites. This map was drawn up in 1988, when the treaty on the total elimination of such missiles was ratified at the Moscow summit.

12. Key to the 1988 map of Soviet medium- and short-range nuclear missiles and their support facilities. It shows the sites for production, repair, training, storage, testing, liquidation and development. The medium-range listing is in the left-hand column, the short-range listing in the right-hand one.

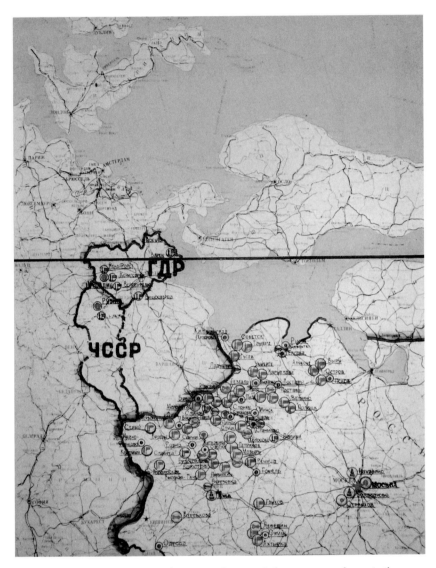

13. Detail of the 1988 map of Soviet medium- and short-range nuclear missiles, showing their geographical concentration in the German Democratic Republic and the western regions of the USSR.

THE WHITE HOUSE
WASHINGTON

March 11, 1985

Dear Mr. General Secretary:

As you assume your new responsibilities, I
would like to take this opportunity to
underscore my hope that we can in the months
and years ahead develop a more stable and
constructive relationship between our two
countries. Our differences are many, and we
will need to proceed in a way that takes both
differences and common interests into account
in seeking to resolve problems and build a
new measure of trust and confidence. But
history places on us a very heavy responsibility for maintaining and strengthening
peace, and I am convinced we have before us
new opportunities to do so. Therefore I have
requested the Vice President to deliver this
letter to you.

I believe our differences can and must be
resolved through discussion and negotiation.
The international situation demands that we
redouble our efforts to find political
solutions to the problems we face. I valued
my correspondence with Chairman Chernenko,
and believe my meetings with First Deputy
Prime Minister Gromyko and Mr. Shcherbitsky
here in Washington were useful in clarifying
views and issues and making it possible to
move forward to deal with them in a practical
and realistic fashion.

In recent months we have demonstrated that it
is possible to resolve problems to mutual
benefit. We have had useful exchanges on
certain regional issues, and I am sure you

RELEASED

14. Reagan's letter to Gorbachëv of
11 March 1985, congratulating him on
his accession to high office and calling
for help in changing the climate of
bilateral relations.

15. Gorbachëv's letter to
Reagan of 10 June 1985,
calling for a 'normalization
of our relations'.

Уважаемый господин Президент,

Я отметил выраженное в Вашем письме от 30 апреля намерение делиться
мыслями в нашей переписке с полной откровенностью. Таков и мой настрой.
Только так мы можем донести друг до друга существо наших подходов к проб-
лемам мировой политики и двусторонних отношений. При этом я исхожу из
того, что мы с Вами будем ориентироваться в обмене мнениями на необходи-
мость продвижения вперед по вопросам принципиального порядка, без чего
нельзя рассчитывать на поворот к лучшему в советско-американских отноше-
ниях. С необходимостью такого поворота, как я понимаю, Вы тоже согласны.

Настраиваться на что-то меньшее, скажем, на то, чтобы просто удержи-
вать напряженность в каких-то рамках и пытаться как-то перебиваться от
кризиса к кризису, – это, на мой взгляд, не перспектива, достойная наших
двух держав.

Мы обратили внимание на то, что Вы разделяете мнение о необходимости
дать импульс процессу нормализации наших отношений. Это уже немало. Но
скажу прямо: вызвали недоумение и озабоченность ряд положений Вашего
письма, на которых, притом, делается особый акцент.

Я имею в виду те обобщения в отношении советской политики, которые со-
держатся в Вашем письме в связи с прискорбным инцидентом с американским
военнослужащим. Что касается самого инцидента, то хотелось бы надеяться,
что разъяснения, сделанные нами, были правильно поняты Американской Сто-
роной.

Теперь о проблемах широкого плана. Я также считаю, что одного лишь
согласия об общих принципах недостаточно. Важно, чтобы такое согласие нахо-
дило отражение и в практических действиях каждой из Сторон. Подчеркивая,
именно каждой из Сторон, поскольку из Вашего письма определенно следует,
что Вы усматриваете расхождения между принципами и практикой в действиях
Советского Союза.

Это очень далеко от действительности. Ни в чем не соответствует фактам
утверждение, будто СССР в своей политике не желает вести дела с США на
основе равенства и взаимности. Какую бы область наших взаимоотношений ни
взять, при действительно объективной оценке оказывается, что именно Совет-
ский Союз последовательно выступает за равенство и взаимность, не ищет для
себя преимущества за счет законных интересов США. И как раз тогда, когда
аналогичный подход проявлялся и с Американской Стороны, удавалось приходить
к существенным договоренностям.

Его Превосходительству
Рональду У. Рейгану,
Президенту Соединенных Штатов Америки
г.Вашингтон

16. The fireside conversation between Reagan and Gorbachëv at the Geneva summit of November 1985. They got on better than anyone had expected but not as well as they would soon need to do.

17. The poster that Chief of the General Staff Sergei Akhromeev produced for the Soviet political leadership in January 1986, offering his plan for the stage-by-stage global elimination of all nuclear weapons by the year 2000. The General Staff's proposals became the basis for Gorbachëv's own unilateral declaration that month.

18. A tense moment in the tête-à-tête discussion between Gorbachëv and Reagan in Reykjavik's Höfdi House on 11 October 1986.

19. General session at the Reykjavik summit on 11 October 1986. Gorbachëv, Shevardnadze and Shultz appear pensive while Reagan manages to smile.

20. 15 November 1986, Camp David: Margaret Thatcher gives Reagan a piece of her mind after hearing about what had passed between the two sides at the Reykjavik summit that October.

21. Yasuhiro Nakasone, Margaret Thatcher, Ronald Reagan, Amintore Fanfani, François Mitterrand and Helmut Kohl at the G7 meeting in Venice in June 1987.

22. Reagan speaking at the Brandenburg Gate in June 1987: 'Mr Gorbachëv, tear down this wall!'

23. Helmut Kohl and François Mitterrand at their joint press conference in 1985. Kohl was to change from stealthy subverter of East German economic independence into boisterous promoter of German reunification; Mitterrand would feel disconcerted by this transformation but, unlike Thatcher, refrained from overt criticism.

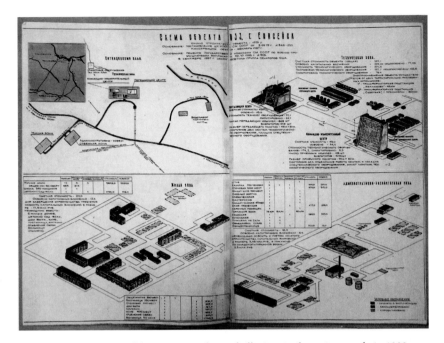

24. Soviet diagram of the Krasnoyarsk anti-ballistic missile station, made in 1988. The top right quadrant indicates the military technical facilities; the bottom quadrants indicate living quarters and a building for a 456-strong garrison.

25. Secret 1980s Soviet map of US medium- and short-range nuclear missile operational bases and facilities sites in the continental US and Western Europe. Much-thumbed through use in the Party Defence Department, it highlights the Kremlin's fear of an American-led NATO attack with nuclear weapons.

26. Vice President Bush escorting an ebullient Gorbachëv on a Washington street in December 1987.

27. Reagan and Gorbachëv sign the Intermediate-Range Nuclear Forces Treaty at the December 1987 summit in Washington. After subsequent ratification by the Senate and the USSR Supreme Soviet it would be ratified at the Moscow summit in June 1988.

28. Reagan gives a speech at Moscow State University in June 1988 beneath the incongruous image of Vladimir Lenin, founder of the USSR.

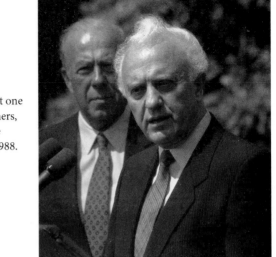

29. Shultz and Shevardnadze at one of their last official get-togethers, in the Rose Garden of the White House in September 1988.

30. President George Bush and General Secretary Mikhail Gorbachëv in expansive mood at the Malta summit of December 1989. James Baker and Eduard Shevardnadze stand expectantly to Bush's left; Alexander Yakovlev looks benignly over Gorbachëv's shoulder.

31. Western leaders at their G7 summit in Houston in June 1990: Jacques Delors, Giulio Andreotti, Toshiki Kaifu, Margaret Thatcher, Helmut Kohl, François Mitterrand, George Bush and Brian Mulroney. Only Kohl spoke up for economic assistance for Gorbachëv and the USSR.

32. THE FIFTH MAN

On 20 January 1989 George Bush was sworn in as President on the West Front of the Capitol. As one of his first measures he nominated Brent Scowcroft as his National Security Adviser and James Baker as Secretary of State. Scowcroft was Bush's alter ego and was cautious and self-effacing.[1] The *New York Times* wittily described him as 'the White House buddy system's odd-man-in'.[2] Nearly as important to Bush was Secretary Baker, who was the only truly prominent figure to survive the new President's cull of the Reagan administration. Stolid and cautious, Baker was no keener on the limelight than Scowcroft. Bush, Baker and Scowcroft had been friends for a long time, and throughout the time that Bush was in office they had no serious disagreement about how they should handle the USSR.

The new President was better qualified for the highest office than anyone in living memory. Born in Massachusetts in 1924, he won a place at Yale University but chose to volunteer for active military service at the age of eighteen. He was a lanky young fellow with a liking for sport. He trained as an aviator and fought in the Battle of the Philippines. He was shot down in 1944 – he bailed out just in time and was rescued from an inflated raft. His time in the armed forces left an imprint on his sense of humour as well as his patriotism, and he always liked to tell jokes – often of a risqué nature if women were not present – to lighten the atmosphere. After the war he married Barbara Pierce and started a family. They had six children. He also took up his Yale scholarship and captained its baseball team. After graduation he entered the oil industry, mainly in Texas, and made a substantial fortune. He always intended to tread in the political footsteps of his father, Senator Prescott Bush, and gained election to Congress in 1966. He was the first Republican to represent Houston. He quickly came to the attention of President Nixon, who persuaded him to stand for the Senate in 1970. Despite this support, he lost the election. Nixon appreciated his potential and, as consolation, nominated him as Ambassador to the United Nations in 1971.

In 1973 he became Chairman of the Republican National Committee. A sequence of stellar postings followed. President Ford made him envoy to the People's Republic of China: this was an ambassadorship in all but name at a time when America formally preferred to base its Chinese diplomatic relations in Taiwan. His competence in handling complex matters of high politics induced Ford in 1976 to bring him back to America as CIA Director. He put himself up for adoption as Republican candidate in the 1980 presidential election, but settled for becoming Reagan's running mate. He was chosen as someone who was known as a 'centrist' in the party and would bring balance to its campaign. When appearing in public, he was often dour and inexpressive. As such he appeared a useful electoral counterpart to the charismatic Reagan. He served two vice-presidential terms, sat in the National Security Council and talked frequently to Gorbachëv and Shevardnadze.

Bush acknowledged that, in contrast to his predecessor, he would not be offering 'the vision thing' to the American public. He made a virtue of being cautious and pragmatic, and had written to Gorbachëv to confirm his desire for a pause while the new administration reflected on foreign policy.[3] He gave the letter to Henry Kissinger to deliver while in Moscow with Giscard d'Estaing and Yasuhiro Nakasone, among others, as part of a delegation of the Trilateral Commission – a body founded in 1973 by businessman and philanthropist David Rockefeller as a forum for retired public figures to report on problems of world politics. (Bush had wanted to demonstrate to the Soviet leaders that he had not forgotten about them, but this was hardly a brilliant move. The new President was to confide to Gorbachëv a few days later that he would ask Scowcroft to assess Kissinger's report but would not necessarily believe everything he said 'because this was, after all, Henry Kissinger'.)[4] Outgoing Secretary of State Shultz had been hoping for more action. On 8 January he and his wife took their leave of the Shevardnadzes. The two couples were on amicable terms and O'Bie came along despite her frail health.[5] Shultz confided that he personally favoured an easing of the trade restrictions as a reward for the USSR's promise to withdraw its armed forces from Afghanistan.[6]

Bush had no clear political line. By using Kissinger as an emissary while indicating that he had no serious confidence in him, he was giving a mixed signal to the Kremlin. At the same time he asked

Gorbachëv to wait until he established whether continuity in policy was truly in the national interest. Shultz with typical thoroughness had devised a series of briefings to enable a smooth transition between administrations; but Bush declined even to give him a call.[7] He also weakened the ties with Thatcher. The French and West Germans celebrated the ending of Britain's privileged entrée to the White House. Mitterrand commented that, whereas she spoke forcefully to her European partners, she had behaved like an eight-year-old girl when talking to Reagan. (Mitterrand had forgotten about Thatcher's bruising conversations with Reagan after the Reykjavik summit.) Bush was not going to fall for her charms.[8] He had always shown an analytical cast of mind. Whereas Reagan had learned to forget about his lifetime's suspicion of the Soviet leadership, Bush wanted to prevent the onset of national amnesia. He aimed to feel totally sure that Gorbachëv had not fooled his predecessor as President.

Scowcroft was on record as advocating the prudence of holding on to a variety of nuclear weapons. He never shared Reagan's objective of total denuclearization.[9] He had publicly criticized the Intermediate-Range Nuclear Forces Treaty draft – and Bush had been lukewarm about it when he was Vice President. They now had the freedom to ask whether it was prudent to resume the line that Reagan and Shultz had marked out. On 9 February Bush declared to a joint session of Congress: 'Prudence and common sense dictate that we try to understand the full meaning of the change going on there, review our policies, and then proceed with caution. But I've personally assured General Secretary Gorbachev that at the conclusion of such a review we will be ready to move forward.'[10]

Not everybody in the NATO leadership was happy about the American slowdown. West European governments had never felt comfortable with Reagan's diplomacy, especially after Reykjavik; but they did at least appreciate that, in his own mind, he was trawling for a catch that would benefit the entire world. Bush seemed to be content to sail across a barren sea without purpose or destination. His performance was dispiriting to Western powers, who wanted a proper captain in the White House wheelhouse.

Genscher felt this very keenly. Still excited about Gorbachëv's United Nations speech, the West German Foreign Minister yearned for Washington to reciprocate. When this failed to occur, Genscher buttonholed Shevardnadze and insisted that the Soviet leadership instead should seize the initiative. Gorbachëv had promised to cut the size of Soviet conventional forces in Europe. In Genscher's opinion, he should also immediately conduct a unilateral reduction in tactical nuclear missiles. The Bush administration saw his intervention as some sort of challenge to America's dominance of policy-making. Thatcher aligned herself with the Americans; she wrote in abrupt terms to Kohl that he should apply some restraint to Genscher. She and Bush at least agreed that NATO had to present a common face to the Warsaw Pact. Bush started from a simple premise: if Western Europe wanted America to continue to guarantee its security, it had to accept the retention of nuclear missiles. When word went round the allied capitals about all this, Mitterrand commented: 'The new [American] administration will be even more brutal than the previous one.'[11]

On 10 January Gorbachëv strove to assure the Party Central Committee plenum that Reagan's departure would make no difference to world politics. He declared the Cold War on the wane. He looked forward to working for agreement on strategic offensive and chemical weapons.[12] As usual it fell to the Big Five to make the preparations. On 16 January they discussed the technicalities of calculating the military balance in diverse arms categories. According to Shevardnadze, the USSR had more land-based nuclear weapons but fewer sea-launched missiles. He hoped that America, like the USSR, would give up its programme to upgrade tactical nuclear weaponry.[13]

He found time in his own schedule for talks with Kissinger, who called for the two superpowers to focus on the fundamental questions of world politics and avoid a preoccupation with the details of disarmament. He assured Gorbachëv that Bush did not share Reagan's intense commitment to the Strategic Defense Initiative.[14] The rest of his message was blunt, even crude. He asked Gorbachëv why he had taken 'idealism' as his compass and based his policies on concepts of good and evil.[15] He was still thinking as he always had done. He hinted that the USSR and the Americans should agree on a 'condominium' over Europe. He said that this would ensure that 'the Europeans did not play up'.[16] Giscard was more tactful but no less disturbing. He enquired how Moscow would react if the East Europeans applied for membership of the European Economic Community.[17] Kissinger told Yakovlev of his concern about any idea for the withdrawal of Soviet forces from Eastern Europe; he warned about 'the adventurism of the Europeans themselves' and said it would be 'politically harder for us of necessity to return [our forces] there than for the Soviet Union'.[18] Gorbachëv refused to be drawn into any such discussion. He intended to preserve the 'socialist basis' of the East European states, but not in the dominating fashion that Kissinger was hinting at.[19]

Maybe Kissinger was just trying to entice Gorbachëv into showing his hand. Perhaps. But later he claimed to have meant what he said – and he added that he had only been trying to help Gorbachëv.[20] He failed to understand that *perestroika* derived from a fresh understanding of global politics.[21] Gorbachëv told his officials: 'Kissinger absolutely can't rid himself of his reactionary ideas. He's stuck in the past.'[22]

As he explained to the Politburo on 24 January, he was loath to waste the political credit that he had accumulated in Western Europe.[23] Soviet foreign policy had to be demonstrably void of menace. Eastern Europe remained problematic. He asked the Central Committee's newly formed commission on the region to formulate a policy based on the maintenance of a 'socialist basis'. His conversation with Kissinger highlighted the need to plan for 'how we'll act if the Hungarian People's Republic moves off into the European Union'.[24] This was astonishingly new ground for debate. Gorbachëv was facing up to the reality that 'our friends' wished to enter the European Economic Community. In Hungary, communist radicals under Miklós Németh were rising in strength and appeal in contrast with the elderly Kádár. Gorbachëv described them, exaggeratedly, as 'an oppositionist party' and wanted to encourage them.[25] This was an extraordinary idea in the light of the USSR's invasion in 1956. Gorbachëv knew that difficult decisions lay ahead: 'We, comrades, stand before some very serious things. We simply can't give them more than we're now giving. And they need new technology. If we don't sort this out, there'll be a split and they'll run off.' Gorbachëv rejected the idea of reducing energy supplies to Eastern Europe: 'This would be betrayal.'[26]

The Soviet economy still awaited transformation, and Gorbachëv prodded the Defence Ministry to arrange to make military technology available to the civilian sector. He wanted Yazov to complete a full plan inside two months.[27] He recognized that the implementation might disrupt production and cause 'social tensions'. In the initial projected stage, merely three out of a possible 1,700 factories would undergo demilitarization.[28] The budget was rewritten to pay for the expected costs of transformation.[29] The year 1989 was the first since the 1920s when the financial outlay for the armed forces failed to increase.[30]

Leaders of military industry such as Oleg Baklanov were usually obstructive about reforms, but this was one that had their approval.

Baklanov and Ivan Belousov, working with data from the KGB and the International Labour Organization, analysed what advantages might result from an ending of the arms race. They predicted that the Inter-mediate-Range Nuclear Forces Treaty could save $8 billion for the American budget even though it would cost $2.5 billion to destroy stockpiles and carry out inspections. They predicted a net gain of 8.2 billion rubles from the parallel process in the USSR, and this did not even include the savings that would accrue from the rundown of strategic offensive weapons.[31] They suggested that the West's big cor-porations would suffer from the diminution of governmental contracts for military research and output. There would also be mass unemploy-ment. They forecast that the USSR would avoid any such outcome for the basic reason that its economy, as they mildly put it, did not have 'an oversaturation of the market' in consumer goods. This was Marxist jargon for something that had bothered Soviet leaders for decades. The deficits in civilian output were a chronic problem. Baklanov and Bel-ousov prophesied a bright future for the country's industrial capacity.[32]

The sooner there was a comprehensive arms agreement, the easier it would be for the USSR to realize the benefit for Soviet people. This in turn would boost the appeal of *perestroika*. Gorbachëv badly needed Bush to confirm that he would stick to the line that Reagan had marked out. One positive trend, from the USSR's standpoint, was the President's disinclination to give priority to the Strategic Defense Ini-tiative. Lieutenant General Abrahamson saw the way that the wind was blowing and resigned his post. On 9 February 1989 he delivered his 'end of tour' report, convinced as ever that some of the basic research – he picked out the so-called Brilliant Pebbles project as an example – could be completed and ready for deployment by 1994.[33] But the reality was that the American Congress wanted to reduce funding for the programme. Bush sympathized with this desire even though he left it to people to work this out for themselves – he did not dare imply criticism of his popular predecessor.

The other signals from Washington steadily depressed Gorbachëv's hopes. The nadir was plumbed on 3 March when Bush ordered the CIA to carry out a comprehensive review of American policy on the USSR. He had seen every important paper that reached Reagan's desk. Yet now he dithered. He gave neither approval nor disapproval of the foreign policy of his predecessor – the only point of distinction lay in his omission of the Strategic Defense Initiative from the terms of reference of the proposed review.[34] Bush instructed officials under the CIA's Fritz Ermath to examine the following question: 'How can we make [inter-continental ballistic missiles] survivable?'[35] This was hardly a question that encouraged a constructive approach to Gorbachëv and Shevardnadze, and Ermath had anyway always been sceptical about the Kremlin's intentions. When Bush said that he wanted the review to be as thorough as possible, he was not just indicating his reluctance to be hasty. He also seemed open to the idea of changing the entire direction of American foreign policy.

Shevardnadze encountered the new attitude when meeting Baker on 7 March at the Conventional Forces in Europe talks in Vienna. Baker demanded freedom for all the peoples of Europe and called on Soviet leaders to undertake an explicit rejection of the Brezhnev Doctrine. He slated the USSR's lack of respect for human rights. He deprecated its military supplies to Nicaragua. He objected to what he saw as Shevardnadze's efforts to cosy up to Iran's Islamist leadership by visiting Ayatollah Khomeini. Shevardnadze replied as best he could that the priority for America and the USSR ought to be to resume their collaboration on nuclear arms reduction. Baker was implacable, explaining that the Americans had begun their policy review and could not say how long it would take. Shevardnadze warned: 'If you begin to modernize your tactical missiles, we'll be obliged to react.' He pushed for arms talks to recommence after Baker's scheduled trip to Moscow in April. This only made Baker more annoyed. The Bush administration, he insisted, would return to the talks only when it felt properly ready.[36] What made things worse for Shevardnadze was that the West Europeans were no more encouraging in Vienna. Scepticism was growing among their leaders about 'what was happening in the Soviet Union'. There were even doubts about whether Gorbachëv's *perestroika* could last much longer.[37]

As he flew back from Austria, Shevardnadze took stock. Baker at one point had at least promised to build on the foundations left behind by Shultz; he had also affirmed that the entire administration wished *perestroika* to be a success. But the trip had been a dispiriting experience: 'Baker is harsher.'[38] Earlier, Shevardnadze had overheard Howe saying: 'Shevardnadze isn't a Gromyko.' Shevardnadze had interjected: 'Well, and Baker's no Shultz.'[39] He kept his thoughts to himself when reporters were present. Any mention of the frost between America and the USSR could have unwelcome consequences.[40] There was anyway little that he or Gorbachëv could do about the situation until the American 'pause' finished. US Congressman George Brown suggested that their best option would be to invite leading members of the Congress to Moscow. He pointed to the important changes that were quietly occurring. Among other things, the Strategic Defense Initiative, which Brown had always opposed, was being scaled back. He urged the Soviet leadership to widen its spectrum of contacts and reach out to sympathetic politicians in Washington.[41]

While Bush probed the old question about Moscow's reliability, Soviet leaders were asking a new one about themselves: could the USSR resolve its gathering economic emergency and put an end to its political volatility?

The long-awaited elections to the Congress of People's Deputies took place in March 1989 after some hustings that were frequently uproarious. Although no opposition parties were allowed to stand, plenty of dissenters found their way on to the ballot sheets and won seats. Thirty-eight province-level party secretaries were defeated. The party bosses in Kiev, Minsk and Alma-Ata suffered the same fate. Gorbachëv refused to overturn the results. The communist political establishment experienced a momentous humiliation. Nevertheless, the Congress was going to contain many deputies who resented the course of the reforms. Eighty-eight per cent of them were communist party members and a sizeable section of them wanted a complete change of official policy.[42] A faction calling itself Soyuz (or Union) was to gather around military commanders such as Nikolai Petrushenko and demanded a more assertive approach in international relations than Gorbachëv and Shevardnadze had adopted. At the same time, on the other side of the political spectrum, were deputies who demanded a faster pace of reform. These were about to establish the so-called Inter-Regional Group in the Congress – and Yeltsin, who gained a crushing victory in his Moscow constituency, associated himself with them. Gorbachëv had brought a noisy, divided parliament into existence. Politics would never be the same again as he made himself Chairman of the Congress's Supreme Soviet.

Political volatility spread throughout the USSR as Moscow's authority shrank. National assertiveness was on the rise, and demonstrations laid down a challenge to the Georgian communist leadership under Dzhumber Patiashvili. Reverting to old Soviet ways, Patiashvili called in the troops. The army commander ordered them to use force in breaking up a protest in Tbilisi on 9 April 1989. Twenty demonstrators were killed, hundreds were wounded. This cleared the streets but led to commotion throughout Georgia. The Soviet republic was becoming ungovernable. Shevardnadze was the only Politburo member who had the knowledge and experience to calm the situation. He happened to have been en route to Berlin as matters came to their fatal climax; as he admitted to an aide, he had tried for some time to avoid being identified with decisions unpopular with the Georgian people.[43] The Tbilisi massacre came as a terrible shock. He immediately changed his plans and hastened to Georgia, where he cleared the armed forces from the city and restored a degree of calm.[44] He concluded that he had been wrong to steer clear of 'the national question' since coming to work in the ministry in Moscow.[45]

Soviet leaders saw the need to show greater frankness about their problems in talks with foreign leaders. Gorbachëv and Shevardnadze were known as open in their negotiating style. Now other Politburo members began to talk with some frankness. The stereotype of the unforthcoming Kremlin politician was being eroded.

On 18 April Prime Minister Ryzhkov met other European heads of government in Luxemburg.[46] Thatcher spoke warmly about Gorbachëv's reforms but urged Ryzhkov to focus on the demands of consumers.[47] Ryzhkov himself wanted to increase trade between Comecon and the European Economic Community. He acknowledged the USSR's deficits in meat and grain at a time when the armed forces continued to gobble up excessive resources. The budget was unsustainable. Ryzhkov said he was aiming to carry out a basic 'price reform' even though people would be furious about paying more for everything in the state stores.[48] Kohl asked him about the prospects of agrarian reform. Ryzhkov was candid about the plight of the countryside and proposed economic cooperation with West Germany as a way of alleviating the problems.[49] Reporting on the earthquake in Armenia, he compared it to four or five nuclear bombs being dropped on an area the size of Luxemburg.[50] Ryzhkov only showed any poise when discussing the Austrian desire to join the European Economic Community. The USSR, as one of the Big Three in 1945, could still put obstacles in Austria's path. But Ryzhkov said that the Soviet leadership had no objection so long as the Austrians did not join NATO. The sole request he made in return was for the West European leaders to nudge the Americans towards reviving the arms talks.[51]

The Washington policy review was still no nearer to delivery. Really there was no need for fresh research on matters that had occupied Ermath and his CIA colleagues for years. In fact they had finished their first draft by mid-March. Their main conclusion –

hardly unpredicted – was that 'our strategic success is incomplete, inconclusive and reversible'. They accepted that the Soviet leaders were arranging to reduce expenditure on their armed forces; they also reckoned that Gorbachëv would remain in power for another half-decade. They warned against idealizing him, pointing out that the USSR still aimed to modernize its strategic weapons arsenal.[52] As the redrafting continued through April 1989, they asked themselves whether America's priority should now be to reduce risk or to save money. Ermath's team was divided in its suggestions.[53] Some put their trust in a parallel effort to modernize the American nuclear forces; others judged it safe to cut back the military budget. There was no consensus about whether the national interest lay in making things easier for Gorbachëv.[54] By handing over the duties of analysis to the specialists, Bush had simply shifted controversy down from the White House to the CIA; and it was clear that he would never receive a set of unequivocal recommendations.

Debate broke surface around this time when Bush's Defense Secretary Dick Cheney talked publicly about the danger of tying American strategic decisions to 'Mr Gorbachëv's tenure'.[55] The President's spokesman, Marlin Fitzwater, dismissed this as 'personal observations' that did not reflect opinion in the White House.[56] Bush, like the rest of his administration, had private doubts about the durability of *perestroika*. But he liked people to keep quiet about such thinking. Cheney's candour forced him to speak out in Gorbachëv's favour and dissociate himself from what his Defense Secretary had said.[57]

Concerns about how to handle the USSR were not an American monopoly. On 25 April 1989 Ambassador Braithwaite went to Viktor Karpov in the Foreign Affairs Ministry and explained that the British disbelieved the official claim that the USSR had only 50,000 tons of poison gas.[58] The United Kingdom also raised an alarm about information about an illegal biological weapons programme that came through the defection of Vladimir Pasechnik, who had worked at one of the secret facilities.[59] This discomfited Gorbachëv at a time when his priority was to bring Bush back into talks. The Politburo considered a memo that its experts had prepared about the germ warfare facility in Sverdlovsk. Supposedly the Soviet scientists restricted their research to defensive purposes.[60] This was never going to be the end of the matter because the British learned everything they needed to know from Pasechnik. The Big Five met on 27 July 1989 to draft a policy for the Politburo using data supplied by the Ministry of Medicinal Industry.

The truth was obvious. The USSR had been caught in breach of its obligations, and the potential for international embarrassment was boundless. Such was the matter's sensitivity that the Big Five recommended that the Politburo should meet in a 'closed session' to settle the matter.[61]

Gorbachëv's preference was to hold on to the biological weapons but to convert them, somehow or other, to defensive purposes. A Central Committee decree was signed on 2 October 1989. It was three years since the authorities had decided on a 'liquidation' of the stocks at its various facilities – a party decree of 19 November 1986 had started the ball rolling and a similar decree confirmed the move eleven months later by ordering preparations for international inspections of facilities for the production of biological weapons.[62] The more recent intervention by the British and Americans shook up the pace. Gorbachëv had to decide where he stood on the matter.

Baker went to Moscow and talked to Gorbachëv and others on 11 May 1989. After decrying the Soviet lack of cooperation over Central America, he emphasized that the American administration wished *perestroika* well. He admitted that not every American official was optimistic. Baker called for a constructive relationship. He also tried to get Gorbachëv to hasten the reform of retail prices, saying it was wise to proceed quickly while the economic difficulties could still be blamed on the political leaders in power before 1985. There was a desultory exchange of opinions on the progress of nuclear arms reduction. As officials on both sides entered the deliberations, Akhromeev demanded respect for the principle of reciprocity. Shevardnadze, with Gorbachëv's endorsement, highlighted the Soviet leadership's difficulties now that it faced criticism by military commanders for conceding to the Americans on the SS-23 question. Baker sensed the need to provide a general statement of American intentions and announced that 'a minimal number of nuclear devices is absolutely necessary for our strategy of flexible response which assures the preservation of peace in Europe'. He announced the intention to modernize the Lance nuclear missile.[63]

The American administration reasoned that the Lances were allowed by the Intermediate-Range Nuclear Forces Treaty. His arguments failed to enthuse Gorbachëv, who had shown goodwill by getting rid of the Soviet SS-23s in order to get agreement with Reagan. Bush and Baker were breaking with the spirit of compromise. Gorbachëv gloomily commented that cooperation was a two-way street.[64]

It was in this atmosphere that the review of American foreign policy in its final variant arrived on Bush's desk on 13 May. Divisions about the future of Soviet 'strategic behavior' persisted. The only point of agreement was about the need for a cautious approach while the USSR remained 'the principal adversary of the United States and its allies through the 1990s'. America would nevertheless find opportunities to change its policy if the USSR genuinely stayed on the path of demilitarization. The American administration needed to be flexible but vigilant. Ermath had ceased to give unidirectional advice. The review presented the choice starkly before the President, and he alone could make it. He could either lessen the degree of insecurity in world politics or else decrease the military component of the budget. The first option would involve prolonged competition with the Soviet leadership; the second would take Gorbachëv at face value and run down expenditure on the armed forces. Ermath described the arguments as finely poised.[65] The review recommended the modernization of America's strategic offensive forces; but it also advised a decrease in the national 'defense efforts' and underlined the fact that the USSR had 'significant disadvantages' in military technology.[66]

At long last Bush accepted that he would have to make up his own mind. No one could be President but the President. For four months he had havered. On 29 May he called an end to his 'pause' and sent Gorbachëv a letter on arms reduction. He put forward a proposed schedule for cutting back conventional forces in Europe. He mentioned that he was about to explain his ideas to the North Atlantic Council on the same day.[67]

This was not yet a commitment to serious negotiations across the entire spectrum. On 13 June, while on a trip to London, Reagan broke his silence and encouraged a renewal of the momentum: 'I believe Mikhail Gorbachëv is the Soviets' best hope to turn things round. It is true that the West could stand pat while this is happening. We are not the ones who must change. It is not our people who're isolated from the information that allows them to be creative and productive. But it is exactly when you are strong and comfortable that you should take risks.'[68] Gorbachëv, visiting Paris, lamented to Mitterrand that the American President lacked any 'original thinking altogether' and that Baker lacked imagination.[69] As it happened, Bush was coming round to understanding the need for action. In July he wrote again to Gorbachëv proposing that they should hold their first summit. He offered Camp David as the venue, perhaps in September. He suggested that Gorbachëv might use the trip to give a second big speech to the

United Nations General Assembly. Bush suggested that, for the talks between them, they should meet on an informal basis, 'with neckties off' and without a large team of associates.[70]

Gorbachëv welcomed the overture but held out for a different geographical location. He baulked at Camp David or elsewhere in America.[71] Without much trouble the two sides agreed on Malta. Or rather they agreed to anchor in the Mediterranean off the Maltese coast in two ships, one Soviet and the other American. It would be the first marine summit between the superpowers.

One of the problems for Gorbachëv was that the American 'pause' had encouraged the grumblers in Moscow. He was alert to the danger. On 28 May 1989 he rebuked Karpov at a Central Committee plenum for denigrating the high command. He was proud of having succeeded in getting the General Staff to accept a drastic decrease in the number of generals, and tact was essential while the politicians applied pressure upon the armed forces.[72] The military-industrial lobby was becoming more difficult to placate. On 6 June Belyakov wrote to Baklanov that Bush was hoping to push the Soviet leadership into a corner. How, asked Belyakov, could it be realistic for the USSR to agree to destroy 40,000 tanks within the next two years? He feared that the Politburo would give way just because it had a fear of adverse international propaganda. He had the same presentiment about Bush's proposal for a drastic reduction in the number of military aircraft. Belyakov was not completely intransigent. He was willing for Soviet forces in Eastern Europe to drop to 275,000 men.[73] But he wanted Gorbachëv to stand his ground more firmly. Four years of indulgence were ending. Gorbachëv had reason to worry as he began to face fundamental opposition to his foreign and security policy.

Baker wanted to freshen the atmosphere and in July invited Shevardnadze to pay a trip to Wyoming, where he had recently bought a ranch, for one-on-one talks in a relaxed atmosphere. As they got down to business, Shevardnadze complained about the way that things were going in Afghanistan. Baker as usual indicated that progress would depend on Najibullah's departure; he denied that America wanted to see an Islamist fundamentalist government in power in Kabul.[74] At the same time he insisted: 'I want to repeat that we are strongly committed to the success of *perestroika*, recognizing that this very much depends on what you do and how you respond to the challenges you face.'[75]

Shevardnadze flew to Washington to explore the possibilities of new agreements with Bush and Baker on 21 September. Bush insisted that nobody in Washington wanted 'your reform' to fail; he denied trying to cause complications in the USSR.[76] He added: 'We have no interest in a Kabul regime that is hostile to the Soviet Union.'[77] He expressed pleasure about the USSR's refusal to interfere in Eastern Europe, and added: 'We think the Soviet leadership has handled the Polish situation admirably.'[78] He claimed, inaccurately, that more Poles lived in Chicago than in Poland; he commented that they shared his pleasure in Poland's recent political settlement. On Latin America, Baker recognized that the Kremlin was no longer supplying Nicaragua with arms. For once, the two sides skipped over the problems posed by Cuba.[79] Baker and Shevardnadze met next day to prepare an agenda for the next summit. They planned how to resolve questions about nuclear, chemical and conventional weapons as well as about regional hotspots such as Cambodia, Vietnam and Israel. In a flush of bon-homie, Shevardnadze suggested a joint US–USSR mission to Kabul to settle current problems. Baker brought him down to earth by handing over a list of people still being refused exit visas from the USSR. Shevardnadze had brought along his own list of alleged political pris-oners in US prisons.[80]

He and Baker knew that he was holding few big cards in his hand. He had brought the leading Soviet economist Nikolai Shmelëv with him; and Shmelëv, ignoring protocol, predicted a Soviet economic catastrophe. Baker replied that the CIA was nowhere near as pessi-mistic in its projections.[81] But he did know that the USSR was in more urgent need of treaties than America was. He spelled out the Ameri-can terms. Shevardnadze had to understand that the chances of repealing the Jackson–Vanik amendment, which restricted trade with the Soviet Union, intimately depended on how well the Kremlin dealt with abuses of human rights.[82]

Baker accompanied him to Wyoming, where, in the peace of the countryside, they had informal conversations. Shevardnadze admitted that the Soviet leadership had badly underestimated the dangers of the 'national question' in the early years of *perestroika*. This frankness attracted Baker, who replied with equal openness. Baker repeated that American support for the independence movement in the Baltic region of the USSR was sincere and permanent – he asked Shevard-nadze to recognize the public demands being made upon Bush: 'I don't raise this to pressure you or to hector you.' Shevardnadze answered that the Soviet leadership was averse to the use of force. He called for the disbandment of NATO and the Warsaw Pact: 'Let's release your allies and ours. While NATO exists, the Warsaw Pact also exists.' Baker suggested that it was high time for East Germany to undertake its own *perestroika*. Shevardnadze stuck firmly to the idea that this was the business of the East Germans alone; but then he spoke with total candour: 'If I were in their shoes, I'd let everyone go, leave. Of course, it is true that if as many as one million people leave, that would be a serious problem for Eastern Europe, but I would let them go.'[83] There had never been an exchange like it between a Secretary of State and a Soviet Foreign Affairs Minister. From that moment onwards, Baker felt certain that Shevardnadze was a man he could deal with.

Though the President and Secretary of State had made up their minds in Gorbachëv's favour, others in the administration remained sceptical. Lawrence Eagleburger, Baker's Deputy Secretary, caused an upset in October by talking about how Soviet policies might give rise to instability in Europe. Democratic Party leaders expressed horror at what they interpreted as a State Department preference for continued confrontation. Baker stepped in smartly to reaffirm the official line and to contend that, regardless of whether Gorbachëv's could achieve his objectives, *perestroika* held out the promise of aiding American interests. The priority, he maintained, should be to lock the USSR into treaties on arms reduction and other such matters. Baker at the same time barred Deputy National Security Adviser Robert Gates from addressing the National Collegiate Security College about Gorbachëv's current difficulties. In a speech in San Francisco, he made a call for optimism: 'If the Soviets have already destroyed weapons, it will be difficult, costly and time-consuming for any future Kremlin leadership to reverse the process and to assert military priority.'[84] From a pause to a leap, Bush and Baker found themselves on the path that Reagan and Shultz had laid out.

33. THE OTHER CONTINENT: ASIA

The Soviet preoccupation in international affairs remained with policy towards America and Western Europe, and talks with the American President trumped everything. Not until the winter of 1988–1989 did Gorbachëv and Shevardnadze widen their angle of attention in Asia beyond troubled Afghanistan. Though Gorbachëv had given a big speech in Vladivostok about the Pacific region in July 1986, he also told the Politburo that December: 'Civilization in the twenty-first century will move to the East.'[1] He wanted to be on friendly terms with Asian countries which in the past had been enemies of Moscow. Confrontation merely squandered resources and peace was anyway his priority. Gorbachëv wanted to renew the USSR's status as a Eurasian power. Shevardnadze agreed with all this but felt that too little progress was being achieved, and he tried to push him to do more than issue formal declarations of intent. In July 1987 he urged the need to offer to withdraw a hundred nuclear missiles from the USSR's Asian territory.[2] In his opinion, Soviet leaders had to give definite proof to China and Japan that their plans for disarmament were not restricted to America and Europe. A unilateral initiative could help towards this end.

Gorbachëv refused to be rushed, for the Chinese question was fraught with dilemmas. Deng Xiaoping made no secret of his scepticism about the Soviet *perestroika*; and Gorbachëv in any case was wary about jeopardizing his ties with Washington by becoming over-friendly with Beijing.[3] He also worried about the USSR's security. While agreeing on the complete removal of medium-range nuclear missiles from Europe, he kept a hundred of them on its Asian territory. Until the Soviet Union and China began to cooperate, he and the Politburo wanted to keep a nuclear deterrent force near the long and contested border.[4] The Chinese remained proud, suspicious and implacable. It was therefore up to the Soviet leadership to make the first move. In early December 1988 Shevardnadze welcomed China's

Foreign Affairs Minister Qian Qichen to Moscow and assured him of Gorbachëv's desire for a rapprochement. Qian in turn assured him that Beijing wanted an improved relationship. While repeating the Chinese demand for equality of treatment, he conveyed his appreciation of Shevardnadze's offer to help in prising the Vietnamese forces out of Cambodia.[5] For a long time Gorbachëv had quietly taken a dim view of Vietnam and its economy with what he claimed were ten million unemployed.[6] It was no trouble for him to weaken Moscow's ties with Ho Chi Minh City. Reconciliation with China was becoming a distinct possibility.

He and Shevardnadze wanted to assure Asia's other governments that Moscow had no bellicose intentions towards them either. Shevardnadze scheduled a tour of hotspots starting with Japan in late December 1988. He had visited Tokyo three years earlier and gained acquaintance with Japanese territorial grievances and economic power. The Japanese had been in dispute with Moscow since 1945 when the USSR seized their northern islands, known to the Russians as the southern Kuriles, and defeated Japan always refused to sign a peace treaty with the USSR. Shevardnadze registered the strength of feeling on the matter. But he ceased to engage in diplomatic overtures in autumn 1986 when the Tokyo government sanctioned Japanese companies joining the Strategic Defense Initiative programme.[7] On the same trip he had gone to North Korea and Mongolia. But although he had learned a lot, he had achieved next to nothing. And he and Gorbachëv shifted their attention to other regions of the world.

Gorbachëv returned to Japanese matters at a meeting with figures from Soviet journalism and the arts in May 1988: 'Look, Khrushchëv promised to give Soviet territories [i.e. the South Kuriles] back to the Japanese. Yet we to this very day fight over those stones and bare rock out there. And how much soil, truly productive soil in our own country is left untended and falls into neglect.'[8]

When Shevardnadze met with Foreign Minister Sōsuke Uno in December 1988, there was the old difficulty about the annexed islands. Shevardnadze called for a strengthening of trade links. Uno was implacable; he could see no chance of progress while the ruble remained a non-convertible currency.[9] Prime Minister Takeshita emphasized the abiding importance of the islands for Japan.[10] In a further conversation with Shevardnadze in America on 8 January 1989, Uno refused to receive Gorbachëv in Japan until such time as Moscow addressed 'the territorial question'. He indicated that once the USSR satisfied this condition, the Japanese would look favourably upon Soviet overtures for economic assistance. To Shevardnadze, this sounded too much like an ultimatum. But he refrained from discounting the possibility of giving up the South Kuriles and was pleased that Soviet leaders could again talk to the Japanese.[11]

As Gorbachëv had guessed, the Americans felt some concern about the USSR's moves in Asia, and Bush quickly organized a presidential visit to China. This contrasted with his drawn-out indecision about the Soviet Union. Bush knew his own mind about the Chinese question and resolved to pre-empt Gorbachëv's overture to Beijing. His three-day visit started on 23 February. The Americans put on a show of military power. USS *Blue Ridge*, the command ship of the Seventh Fleet, arrived at Shanghai – and the agreement was for it to stay at anchor throughout the presidential trip.[12]

Gorbachëv knew that the Chinese would be tough negotiators. When Prime Minister Li Peng attended Chernenko's funeral, he had spurned Gorbachëv's attempt at graciousness and warned that China would never accept subordinate status to the USSR; but he did not rule out a thaw in contacts.[13] He returned to Moscow in June 1985 to sign a pact on economic and technological cooperation – at that time the Chinese remained interested in acquiring Soviet help in modernizing China's industrial sector. When Li visited the USSR again that December, Gorbachëv made a pitch for the normalization of relations. He said that the two countries shared an interest in opposing the Strategic Defense Initiative. He queried the rationale for Chinese support of America's Afghan policy; he disowned any desire by the USSR to use Vietnam as a way of causing trouble for China.[14] Li simply repeated that China wanted to guard its independence and avoid the role of 'little brother' to the Soviet Union. He told Gorbachëv that there could be no normalization until the Kremlin altered its policies towards Afghanistan and Cambodia – Li sharply objected to Moscow's endorsement of the Vietnamese military presence on Cambodian territory.[15]

If Soviet leaders wanted a rapprochement with China, they had to give way on this. Shevardnadze and his ministry well understood that the Chinese objected to Vietnam's status as a client state of the USSR. The Kremlin had supported the North Vietnamese in their war against the Americans through to 1975, and this assistance had continued after Vietnam's reunification. Shevardnadze could see that Moscow would eventually have to choose between Vietnam and China.[16] The

USSR's alliance with Vietnam was anyway becoming a troubled one. The Vietnamese leaders objected when Shevardnadze mooted the possibility of visiting Cambodia; they disliked any hint of an idea that they alone were not going to dominate the settlement of the Cambodian question.[17] Gorbachëv resolved upon an entente with China, albeit without giving the impression of desiring it at all costs.[18] This would involve concessions by the USSR. Gorbachëv told the Politburo on 8 May 1987 about the difficulties as he saw them. He stressed that nothing could be achieved until the Chinese leadership felt ready. Moscow had made the first conciliatory approach: it was up to Beijing to respond. In the meantime he wanted to do nothing that would 'frighten' America.[19]

The Kremlin's steady protestations of goodwill eventually secured an invitation for Shevardnadze to visit Beijing and Shanghai. On 3 February 1989 Shevardnadze met Prime Minister Li in the Chinese capital and tried to draw a line under past troubles. Li agreed on the goal of 'normalization' and expressed appreciation for what Gorbachëv had done for peace around the world. There was agreement that Gorbachëv too should come to China, but Li stipulated that this should take place without the kind of excitement that greeted him elsewhere. The Chinese leadership warned against any kind of political disturbance. Li baulked at the idea of issuing a joint communiqué since Shevardnadze had failed to quieten his doubts about Vietnam's sincere intention to withdraw all its forces from Cambodia by September – the Chinese, he said, knew the Vietnamese better than the Soviets did. China was putting the Soviet leaders on notice that much needed to be done before they could count on its compliance.[20]

Shevardnadze flew south to Shanghai in a Chinese Boeing-737 to hold talks with Deng Xiaoping at his guesthouse. Old and wizened though he was, the tiny Deng had a firm handshake and left no doubt about his mental vigour. He entered the conversation without preliminary flim-flam and eschewed small talk. Deng called in very broad terms for a fresh start to be made in the Sino-Soviet relationship. Shevardnadze was delighted. He tried to push things further along by means of flattery: 'Very wise!' Deng spoke about their shared belief in communism and expressed the hope that it would not take another two millennia to realize the dream; he added that he was simultaneously committed to extending the Chinese market economy. Shevardnadze interjected: 'There's a truth which runs as follows: it's better to take ash than fire from the past.'[21] Touching on Afghanistan, he stressed that the USSR's military intervention was really at an end. He added that the Afghans were conducting their own civil war and there were no Soviet troops serving in false uniforms.[22] Deng smoked frantically as he gave his account of China's recent diplomatic history. He noted that President Nixon's trip to Beijing in 1972 had enabled America to appreciate the importance of Taiwan to the Chinese administration. He added that China and Japan had resolved several matters of dispute in 1978. He emphasized that Hong Kong, whose lease to the United Kingdom would come to its term in 1997, was high on his agenda.[23]

Deng's tone sharpened when he discussed the USSR. Distrustful of the Vietnamese, he said there would be no peace in Cambodia until they had truly withdrawn to their own country. He picked up the comment about fake uniforms and accused Vietnam's forces of exactly this subterfuge.[24] Shevardnadze offered to do what he could, adding that the USSR's slogan of 'international assistance' to the Vietnamese had lost its currency: the Kremlin was open to the idea of ending its support for Vietnam in the conflicts of South-East Asia.[25] This failed to calm Deng, who exclaimed that nobody knew the leadership of Vietnam better than he did. If the USSR wanted conciliation with China, Soviet leaders would have to give direct support to the Chinese cause. His hands shook with anger as he spoke. Deng railed against the Vietnamese for aiming at a South-East Asian Federation under their aegis. If he hadn't already known, Shevardnadze was learning that China looked on Vietnam and Cambodia as a litmus test of the USSR's sincerity in seeking a mending of relations.[26] He was later to recall that Deng also dwelt on the Chinese territories lost to Russia in the nineteenth century. Deng warned: 'There'll come a time when China will perhaps restore them to itself.'[27]

No foreign leader had talked so ferociously to Soviet politicians. Deng was using rudeness to show that China's future friendship would not come automatically or cost-free. Shevardnadze could see for himself why the Chinese leadership felt such self-confidence. The economic reforms that Deng had introduced since the late 1970s had released entrepreneurial energy in the coastal periphery and, with America's permission, attracted a huge amount of direct foreign investment. The contrast with the USSR was unmistakable. Shanghai impressed the visitors from drab Moscow with its 'modern culture' and its 'business relations'. The skyscrapers and the shop windows demonstrated the material progress in the 'special economic regions'.[28] As Shevardnadze got ready to fly back to Moscow, the Chinese were slow about agreeing a communiqué – indeed, he had reached the next stage of his Asian tour, Pakistan, before receiving Beijing's draft: they acted as if they were the rising masters of the continent.[29] The trip to China had been a revelation. He had imbibed basic lessons about Chinese grievances, and on 16 February even asked the Politburo to consider giving up territory around Khabarovsk in the Soviet Far East.[30]

Whereas USSR's old enemies in Asia continued to query the sincerity of Gorbachëv's new foreign policy, its Asian client states were agitated about the implications of his rapprochement with America. It was one of Shevardnadze's tasks on his Asian trip to persuade old friends that Moscow would stick by them. This was probably why he failed to visit Vietnam, for the Soviet leadership had made a basic choice in favour of improved ties with the Chinese.

But the Politburo had no wish to lose its collaborators in the Middle East and, after a brief stopover in Islamabad, Shevardnadze flew on to Syria for talks with President Hafez al-Assad. Two years earlier Gorbachëv had assured the Syrian dictator of the USSR's continued support for states that stood up to 'American imperialism'.[31] After a formal exchange of greetings, Assad expressed doubts that the Soviet leadership was fulfilling its promise. Shevardnadze faced an uncompromising negotiator. Despite the visible signs of age and a shrillness of voice, Assad knew how to impose himself on everyone around him. He established an ascetic atmosphere. There were no portraits of him on the walls of his official residence, only a picture of one of Saladin's battles against the Crusaders. He kept Circassians as his bodyguard. (For a man from the multi-ethnic south Caucasus like Shevardnadze, this was more than a little fascinating.) Assad was blunt about his concerns. Recalling that he himself had been a student in the USSR in the 1950s, he remarked that people were claiming that the Soviet order was on the verge of collapse and could no longer support friends like Syria. Assad tore into Israel's attempt to appear as a force for peace in the Middle East. He decried the recent shift in the Kremlin's policy away from promoting the Arab cause and lamented the abandonment of allies in Afghanistan, Cuba, North Korea, Vietnam and even Eastern Europe to dire fates. Assad was an angry man; he did not disguise his feelings about the turn in Soviet foreign policy.[32]

Shevardnadze then travelled to Baghdad, where he aimed to alert Saddam Hussein to the Kremlin's hope for a rapprochement with Tehran. Until then, Soviet policy had favoured Iraq over Iran. Now the

USSR wanted amicable links with every Asian country. Saddam took the news stoically. He said he understood why Gorbachëv might want to resolve his differences with the Iranian government even though he detested what the Ayatollah Khomeini stood for. The Iraqi dictator made a joke of it all: 'May Allah help you. Only let it be our Allah and not the Iranian one!'[33]

On to Iran, where Shevardnadze hoped to mend fences. But if Deng and Assad had been bad-tempered hosts, Khomeini was even more difficult in his own peculiar way. The Ayatollah refused to see him in Tehran. Shevardnadze had to fly down to Qom, where Khomeini received him in his modest little house: power had not made him materialistic. It was the strangest of diplomatic encounters since the old man proved interested only in questions of spiritual belief and practice. He would talk about nothing else. To Shevardnadze he gave the impression of an impoverished widower. Khomeini rejected every attempt at dialogue about foreign policy despite knowing that this was the sole purpose of Shevardnadze's trip. There was no exchange of practical options, and Khomeini gave no sign even about whether he wanted better relations with Moscow.[34] The USSR was no nearer to achieving a process of conciliation. It was a futile trip, except insofar as the Politburo acquired a better idea about what it was dealing with on its southern frontier; and at least the Americans were made aware that the Soviet leadership remained capable of at least trying to establish relations independently of them. Indeed, when Gorbachëv heard Shevardnadze's report, he gave thought to how the USSR might sell arms to Tehran.[35]

Shevardnadze's Asian tour prepared the ground for Gorbachëv's own trip to China. He was scheduled to arrive on 15 May. American nerves were on edge at the project, and the Beijing embassy advised the State Department to remind the world that 'Sino-American relations generally continue on the upswing in political, military and economic areas'.[36] The State Department worried that China might exploit a rapprochement with the USSR so as to induce America to moderate its policy on Taiwan. The Americans noted the growth of political demonstrations led by Chinese students. They sympathized with the democratic demands of the protesters, but were wary of being seen to interfere. The State Department gave advice to voice a 'preference for dialogue'.[37]

The Chinese agreed to receive Gorbachëv on condition that he caused no trouble for them. They had seen how crowds gathered round him in foreign countries, and wanted to avoid disorder. Gorbachëv gave his consent. Deng for his part looked askance on the Soviet *perestroika* and had irked Gorbachëv by counselling him not to hurry with it.[38] Gorbachëv himself was no less disrespectful about the Chinese reforms. On 29 September 1986 he had confided to his aides:

> The Chinese have developed agriculture on a private basis. They have achieved stunning successes. But there should not be euphoria as if China had resolved everything. But what next? They don't have fertilizers, technology or intensive methods. We have all of that. But we have to unite that with personal interest. This is our problem. This is where we can ensure a burst forward. Ilich [Lenin] tormented himself with how to unite the personal interest with socialism, and this is what we have to think and think about.[39]

In August 1988 he told Chernyaev:

> I don't understand all the fuss as regards China. People come back from there saying that there's everything on the shelves in the shops. The same thing about Yugoslavia. I'm happy that China is on the rise materially. This is ultimately a support for us as well, just as we are a support for them. Fine But why such euphoria? One has to look into the essence of the matter: yes, there's everything on the shelves in the shops but there's nobody buying. It's a capitalist market. And the law of that market operates in such a fashion that prices are inflated to the point that everything lies around on shelves and when the goods go stale they sell them off cheap.[40]

This was at best a nonsensical exaggeration. Somehow he had convinced himself that nobody was buying the goods on sale in China's urban stores.[41]

Deng insisted that there should be no hugging but only a handshake when they met; he wanted to keep the discussion businesslike. Gorbachëv took the hint and decided to treat him with due concern for his age.[42] Even so, their exchanges started scratchily on 16 May 1989. When Gorbachëv asked for a 'normalization of relations', Deng lectured him on the territorial depredations that the Russian Empire had perpetrated.[43] He declared Russia and Japan to have been historically the worst threats to China. The Russians had stolen 1.5 million square kilometres, and this was not forgotten. He also remarked that it was hopeless to expect more from the classics of Marxism-Leninism than they could give; and he saw no point in forcing the pace of restoring links between the Soviet and Chinese communist parties.[44]

This was hardly the reception that Gorbachëv had anticipated, and he hoped to get down to a more constructive discussion with Li Peng.[45] Disappointment awaited him. Showing no interest in an expansion of trade, Li focused entirely on the matters of concern to the Chinese leadership. He denied that capitalism had taken out a 'patent' on human rights. He mentioned that China was experiencing difficulty with America about Taiwan and Tibet, but was delighted that Indian Prime Minister Rajiv Gandhi had offered to end India's support for the Dalai Lama. He talked about the damage that the Japanese had wreaked in China in the Second World War, adding that he recognized the pragmatic need to collaborate with Japan as a powerful industrial country.[46] Gorbachëv commented that the USSR's shortage of capital investment was one of its basic problems. This failed to divert Li, who insisted that China and the Soviet Union should give priority to an agreed demarcation of the Sino-Soviet frontier. Gorbachëv at last lost patience, complaining that the Chinese were ignoring his proposals for cooperation in energy, transport and metallurgy. He badly wanted some signs of progress before departing from China. He told Li that Moscow would dearly like to achieve the demilitarization of the frontier zone between the two countries.[47]

Gorbachëv and his travelling party behaved with the propriety demanded by his hosts. This did not stop students in Beijing from massing on the streets and chanting his name. Slogans were unfurled asking for political reforms. The Gorbachëv effect was evident even though the man himself stayed away from the crowds. Shevardnadze had to conquer an impulse to go and talk to the students on Tiananmen Square.[48]

The one opportunity for Gorbachëv to make a stirring speech came at the Great Hall of the People on 17 May. While acknowledging the historical problems that had divided the USSR and the People's Republic of China, he contended that it was in the interests of both countries to resolve them. He highlighted that his agreement with the Americans entailed the destruction of 436 medium- and short-range missiles from the Soviet eastern territories. He suggested that the USSR's railway network could become a new Silk Road for the Chinese to export their goods to Europe. When explaining his own ideas for economic reform, he stressed the need for workers to have an influence over the process. He also emphasized his commitment to political 'democratism'. He admitted that the process had led to unforeseen complications. He ridiculed those Western commentators who hoped that the reforms in China and the USSR would lead to the restoration of capitalism; he insisted that the path of economic and political democracy would in fact strengthen the foundations of socialism. He explained his ideas to bring settlement to Asian trouble spots.[49]

Shevardnadze held talks on the same day with Jiang Zemin, Politburo member and Shanghai party leader, who said that the Chinese aspired to the role of intermediaries in the conflicts of south Asia. He added that the Nepalese wanted the USSR to help them to improve relations with India; and Pakistan's Prime Minister Benazir Bhutto had asked for the Soviet authorities to regularize the situation in Afghanistan. Shevardnadze exclaimed that Bhutto herself ought to start to act with the same objective in mind.[50] Nevertheless the Chinese desire to mediate was something new. This pleased Shevardnadze, who concluded: 'In fact the normalization of relations with China is an historic event.'[51]

The trip was different from any that Gorbachëv made. When he visited foreign countries, be they capitalist or communist, he exercised fascination for their politicians. China's supreme elite was uniquely aloof. The USSR was patently not a priority for Deng and Li, and they certainly felt they had nothing to learn from Moscow. Deng did not offer China as a model for any other state in the world. He was transforming his own country and had only its needs in mind when talking to foreigners. Gorbachëv had received a signal about this when the Soviet visitors were taken on a tour of Shanghai factories and shown the production of Nike trainers, some Teflon kitchenware and various up-to-date toys and medicines.[52] If the Chinese could modernize and expand their economy by attracting Western capitalist corporations into their country, they would hardly want to saddle themselves with a close relationship with the USSR's ailing manufacturing sector. While the CoCom restrictions stayed in place, moreover, there remained little chance that the USSR would make its own burst forward towards industrial renovation. The same facts pointed to why Gorbachëv would have found it difficult to imitate communist China. Without foreign direct investment, Deng could never have made his great economic leap since the mid-1970s. CoCom precluded that option for Gorbachëv, and he would probably have discounted such a route even if it had been open to him.

But the evidence of the trip failed to cure Gorbachëv of his blindness about China's economic achievements. Having seen inside those thriving industrial enterprises, he acted as if they were an industrial sham put on for gullible foreigners. He would never change his mind while he was in power. When talking to James Baker later in May 1989, he assured him Chinese technical and scientific capacity was hitting the buffers.[53]

This crude misjudgement that had multiple roots. He took it for granted that the modernization of the USSR and any other country required a process of democratization. He had come to power with this in mind and never questioned it – and no foreign leader apart from Deng and Honecker ever tried to raise doubts. He also simply assumed that time and morality were on the side of the Chinese students – and it was far from unreasonable to think that Deng would find it difficult to sustain the political autocracy in Beijing. He sympathized with the student protesters, who carried posters demanding some kind of *perestroika* such as he had introduced in his country; but the terms of his visit disallowed him from talking to them. The tensions between protesters and government intensified after he departed. His sojourn in the Chinese capital had served to increase the intransigence of the students. Placards were held extolling his advocacy of democratization. They remained visible in subsequent days. State authority was under direct challenge. The Chinese leadership split on how to tackle it. In the ensuing controversy, Deng and Li purged those like Zhao Ziyang who favoured concessions to student opinion. On 3–4 June repressive measures were undertaken. Tanks trundled across Tiananmen Square and troops fired on protesters. China was going to continue its economic reform without conceding political and civil rights – and Deng did not care if this required violent measures.

The Beijing massacre appalled leaderships in Moscow and Washington. The USSR's Congress of People's Deputies called for a peaceful resolution of difficulties. But Gorbachëv told the Warsaw Pact's Political Consultative Committee in July that he would firmly resist the temptation to interfere in Chinese affairs.[54] This was his credo in world affairs. His priority was to complete the transformation of his own country while strengthening the rapprochement with America.

The Americans, of course, had a deeper stake than the USSR in China's internal transformation. Without their investments and military assistance, Deng would scarcely have made much economic progress. The current question for the American administration was about what steps might alleviate the trouble in Beijing while protecting America's national interest. Baker's first instinct was to move cautiously regardless of feelings of outrage at the Tiananmen massacre. He warned Bush that Gorbachëv was likely to try and reinforce ties with China. Baker sought to prevent Moscow from taking advantage of any rift between Washington and Beijing.[55] Nevertheless the dominant opinion in the administration was that the Americans had to give some sign of displeasure at the massacre. On 5 June Bush halted arms deals with China that were worth $600 million to American corporations. He did this with some regret: 'Down the road we have enormous commonality of interests with China, but it will not be the same under a brutal and repressive regime.'[56] For some weeks he had been under criticism from Senator Goldwater after approving the sale of jet fighters to Beijing. Goldwater had feared that such planes could be used against Taiwan.[57] The Tiananmen bloodshed made it impossible to brush his words aside.

Gorbachëv saw his chance to make at least a little progress with the Chinese. The two sides met in November 1989 to find ways of decreasing the forces near each other's borders and enhancing mutual confidence. Sessions were held in Beijing and Moscow and continued in the next year.[58] Normalization was becoming a reality at the state level. The Chinese economic reforms stalled as Deng continued the repression and stabilized the political order. He also judged it prudent to remove some of the leading proponents of market economics from their posts. This probably reinforced Gorbachëv's dismissive attitude to the road that Deng had been taking. When Gorbachëv met Giulio Andreotti in July 1990, he assured him that China's reformed economy was vulnerable to its enemies.[59] He mistook a temporary interruption for permanent abolition, and he overlooked how much change remained in place. While coming to diplomatic terms with Beijing, he continued to underestimate its achievements and to overplay Moscow's industrial and agricultural potential under the aegis of his own favoured policies.

34. EPITAPH FOR WORLD COMMUNISM

While repairing the links with the People's Republic of China, the Soviet leadership also gave thought to those communist states that had long been associated with Moscow. The transformation in the USSR's foreign policy was causing obvious trepidation among allies and friends abroad. When Gorbachëv made his moves towards giving up Afghanistan, they wondered whether could they put faith in any of his professions of support.[1] It made sense for the Kremlin to call them together and explain the rationale for its initiatives. A meeting of 'fraternal parties' was called in Mongolia on 16–17 March 1988. Yakovlev attended on the Politburo's behalf. Not only the East Europeans but also the Vietnamese, Laotians, Cubans and Mongolians attended. Most of those present hailed what Gorbachëv was doing in the USSR and in his foreign policy. Even the Romanians behaved cooperatively, if only because they were looking for support in their current dispute with the Hungarians. A slight difficulty arose when the East Germans denied the need for any 'renewal' of socialism – not exactly music to the ears of Soviet reformers. Then the Cubans objected to any idea about *perestroika* being up for export; they also partnered the Vietnamese in their concern about the USSR's rapprochement with America.[2]

Yakovlev had never had high hopes about the proceedings and endured the implicit criticism without embarrassment. He knew that the 'world communist movement' had suffered an irreversible wreckage of meaning and practice. Both he and Gorbachëv drew similar conclusions. Neither of them saw any point in marking out a line that the other parties had to follow. Gorbachëv felt no temptation to convene a global conference in Moscow as Brezhnev had done in June 1969. The experience had been deeply discouraging for Brezhnev and his Politburo. The Chinese, Albanians, Thais and Burmese openly refused to attend – and the North Koreans and even the Vietnamese quietly declined the invitation for fear of annoying Beijing. Dispute marred the conference itself. The Italians objected to political repression in the USSR and denounced the invasion of Czechoslovakia. Several of the West European parties spoke on the Italian communist side. There was difficulty in getting others to sign any common declaration as the discussions reached their term. The final statement on the 'Tasks of the Anti-Imperialist Struggle' appeared with notable abstentions.[3] Gorbachëv had no intention of getting embroiled in any such nonsense. When he talked about communism, he took the precaution of confining himself to the theme of *perestroika* in the Soviet Union.

This did not mean that the Soviet leadership lacked a concern for the fate of foreign communist and left-wing parties. The Politburo still felt obliged to help those organizations that were struggling for power. This was a traditional sentiment for the USSR's political elite. It was also a useful way of enhancing prestige and influence around the globe and showing the Americans that they were not the only superpower.[4] Requests continued to arrive for money, equipment and training. The SWAPO forces fighting for Namibia's independence from South Africa appealed for arms, asking for delivery without need for payment.[5] The Party Central Committee secretariat in May 1987 approved a request to subsidize the British communist *Morning Star*. Moscow officials liked the newspaper's opposition to Eurocommunism.[6] (Gorbachëv at that point had not yet openly shifted Soviet doctrine in the direction of the Italian Communist Party's ideas.) Money was not the only facility offered to fraternal parties. On 18 January 1988 the Secretariat granted fourteen training places for the Communist Party of Chile for 'conspiratorial work'.[7] The Chilean comrades were to learn techniques of communication, sabotage and subversion for use against General Pinochet's dictatorship.

Moscow had for decades provided this kind of schooling. Soviet leaders now worried that they might stray over the boundary of what America and other NATO countries found tolerable. When in January 1989 a request arrived from Sean Garland of the Workers' Party of Ireland to train five of its activists, Karen Brutents in the Party International Department recommended refusal. This was not a question of principle for him. He simply thought that the danger of a leak was too strong, with consequent damage to Anglo-Soviet negotiations.[8]

On 11 December 1989 the Politburo approved a budget of $22 million for the work of the International Fund of Assistance to leftist workers' organizations in the coming year. The state bank was to deliver the money to Valentin Falin in the Party International

Department. The outbreak of East European revolutions meant that communist parties in that whole half of the continent stopped contributing to the fund. (By then, of course, it was they who needed financial support from Moscow.) Falin reported that seventy-three 'communist, workers' and revolutionary-democratic parties and organizations' around the world remained in receipt of Soviet beneficence.[9] Direct grants were not the only way of subsidizing the world's communist parties. The USSR agreed to buy large quantities of their newspapers: forty-two countries benefited from this kind of subvention. The problem was that the Soviet authorities could no longer afford a regular annual outlay of 4.5 million rubles in foreign currency. The Party Secretariat pointed out that readers in the *perestroika* years had little need for such newspapers now that *Pravda* was cheaper, more informative and available on the date of publication. Censure was expected from communist parties that were dependent on the Moscow subsidy. But savings had to be made.[10]

Whenever geopolitical dilemmas arose, party officials passed them on to the highest level for decision. Reagan and Shultz regularly indicated their concerns about Soviet political and economic intervention in southern Africa, Cuba, Ethiopia, Nicaragua and Libya. Since the 1970s the Soviet Union had been providing them with credits, weaponry and advisers. The American administration treated this as an intolerable effort to expand the Kremlin's global power. The USSR's budgetary difficulties worsened because of its external commitments. Something had to give.

The Ministry of Foreign Affairs led the way in revising official thinking. Adamishin had long believed in the need for a change in policy towards southern Africa. He was an acknowledged expert in African affairs, and the freedom of thought under Shevardnadze emboldened him to speak his mind. During the long years of Brezhnev's general secretaryship it was a tenet of Soviet foreign policy that the USSR's duty lay in devoting financial resources to the various armed struggles against apartheid in South Africa and against the governments in the neighbouring regions that were backed by Pretoria. Adamishin thought this intolerably expensive as well as damaging to the interests of rapprochement with America. The fact that Castro, with a Moscow subsidy, had installed thousands of Cuban troops in Angola confused the situation. Gorbachëv sympathized with Adamishin's ideas, which fitted with his own about global affairs. On 27 November 1987 he discussed them with Zambia's Kenneth Kaunda. The Soviet leadership, he indicated, would continue to work for the liberation of the region's peoples. But his emphasis was going to move from military conflict to economic aid. On 21 February 1988 Adamishin delivered a final draft on policy to Shevardnadze, who passed it on to Yazov, Chebrikov and Dobrynin to consider, and on 14 March it was ratified as official policy.[11]

Shevardnadze encouraged Adamishin to apply the same policy to the rest of sub-Saharan Africa. When Adamishin explained how bad the situation had become for Mengistu in Ethiopia, the minister told him to talk frankly at the Politburo's Ethiopian Commission without any worry about giving offence. On 15 April, at the commission meeting that Yakovlev was chairing, Adamishin dismissed the Ethiopian revolution as a lost cause that was costing millions of rubles and was completely unjustifiable. The army commanders, with Kornienko in their support, attacked his reasoning. But they failed to dismantle his case, and Yakovlev phoned later to congratulate him on his courage and analytical freshness.[12] Both Shevardnadze and Yakovlev appreciated the importance of the African question for a settlement with America. Shultz protested about the Cuban military intervention at his next meeting with Shevardnadze on 10 May; he stressed how much it discommoded the Americans. If Gromyko had still been minister, he would have replied that it was none of America's business. Shevardnadze made no attempt to dispute the point.[13] He had accepted that change on Africa was necessary. The last thing he wanted, when the Intermediate-Range Nuclear Forces Treaty was about to reach the occasion of signature, was to fall out with Shultz.

The strange thing was that Gorbachëv suddenly became reluctant to say anything about Africa; and Adamishin guessed that the General Secretary had become worried about laying himself open to the charge of betraying Mengistu's revolution. Gorbachëv hardly needed to take on an additional burden.[14] Shevardnadze had a personal preference to continue to favour states and organizations on the political left. With this in mind he and the new KGB Chairman Kryuchkov argued for the USSR to assist countries of 'socialist orientation' in economically developing parts of the world. Adamishin disagreed, contending that the USSR needed to make a more drastic break with tradition.[15]

Chernyaev concurred with Adamishin and told Gorbachëv that it was high time to change direction. When Gorbachëv rebuffed his arguments, Chernyaev on 10 October 1988 enlisted Yakovlev's help in placing the matter on the Politburo agenda. Chernyaev was aware that the people of Ethiopia faced utter destitution; his solution was for a joint effort by the Soviet and American leaderships to achieve 'a regulation of the Ethiopian regional problem'.[16] Gorbachëv was at first averse to changing policy – quite possibly he did not want to incur criticism by communist conservatives for surrendering yet another traditional position in foreign policy to the Americans. But the logic of Chernyaev's standpoint gradually convinced Gorbachëv. The USSR was wasting finance in propping up a brutal regime that was bringing it into global political discredit. On 19 September 1989 the Politburo approved a letter for General Varennikov, Deputy Defence Minister after his return from Afghanistan, to take in person to Mengistu. The Soviet leaders supported the peace initiative of the Popular Front for the Liberation of Eritrea; they asked Mengistu to accept the desirability of opening talks with his enemies.[17] By 20 December the Politburo had lost its stomach for military intervention in conflicts anywhere outside the USSR's frontiers. The Cuban forces were at last being withdrawn from Ethiopia and, on Ryzhkov's suggestion, no longer allowed to receive Soviet material assistance.[18]

Chernyaev and fellow aide Shakhnazarov called for a systematic exposition of the new line. They wanted the USSR to abandon 'the ideological principle' in dealing with the Third World; and they put their case directly to Gorbachëv. They said that the USSR incurred global opprobrium for aiding 'the totalitarian regime of M. Gaddafi', fostering the 'militaristic adventurism of H. Mengistu' and taking sides in the 'endless tribally-based strife of South Yemen's leaders'. They called for Shevardnadze and Yakovlev to be asked to draft fresh guidelines for submission to the Politburo – and Gorbachëv passed on their message to them.[19]

The Libyan connection had been under review for more than a year. On 8 February 1988 a decree was passed prohibiting the sales of armaments to Gaddafi's government. The motive was a wish not only for improved ties with America but also to make budgetary savings. The Soviet leadership was also reluctant to hand over weaponry and equipment that the Libyans lacked the expertise to handle.[20] Shevardnadze gave a further signal of change on 8 January 1989, in one of his last discussions with Shultz. They were talking about Muammar Gaddafi. The American side claimed that the Libyans were developing chemical weapons at a secret chemical factory. Shevardnadze asked how Washington expected to react; he added that the USSR had provided Libya with many advisers, who had given no indication that anything illegal was under production. Basically he preferred a proper investigation to take place before drastic measures were instigated. But he made little attempt to restrain Shultz.[21] The reality was that Gaddafi had become an embarrassment to the Soviet leaders, who were no longer willing to expend their political capital in trying to save his neck.

They found it harder to let go of Cuba. The island had nearly brought the world into a catastrophic war between the superpowers in 1962 when Party First Secretary Khrushchëv tried to set up missile bases there. His climbdown had preserved the peace, but at the price of humiliation for the Soviet Union. America agreed to the secret removal of its missile batteries in Turkey; it also offered a confidential promise not to invade Cuba. Moscow in subsequent years propped up the Cuban revolution with subsidies and political support.

Cuba was an awkward and expensive ally, and the Soviet leadership always found Castro a handful. His fighting record and charisma were impressive; his refusal to wilt under America's pressure added lustre to his reputation. Kremlin leaders were in awe of him. When Shevardnadze visited Havana in October 1985, he asked for his autograph and told a crowd: 'You're lucky that you live in a socialist country and have a leader like comrade Fidel!'[22] Castro pulled no punches about foreign policy, telling Shevardnadze that Brezhnev's Politburo had failed to think out the consequences of their invasion of Afghanistan.[23] On his second trip to the island in October 1987 Shevardnadze found Castro unhappy about the Soviet reforms under Gorbachëv and critical of the rewriting of Soviet history. Shevardnadze replied that Gorbachëv's forthcoming book on *perestroika* was a necessary corrective for the wrongs of the past. Stalin's victims, including Nikolai Bukharin, had to receive political rehabilitation. Criticism of this nature, he reasoned, was a healthy phenomenon. This failed to convince Castro, who admitted that if he engaged in the same policy it would have to involve criticism of himself and Cuba's other communist veterans.[24] He had no intention of emulating Gorbachëv. Castro expressed the hope that he would not forget to underline the USSR's great achievements in times gone by.[25]

Deputy Foreign Affairs Minister Adamishin visited Castro on 30 March 1988. He scarcely got a word in edgeways in a conversation that stretched over five hours. Adamishin learned that the Angolan military intervention and the struggle against apartheid and its influence in sub-Saharan Africa were the supreme cause in Castro's life. Castro had a grasp of the details of the war in Angola; he supervised current operations, holding strategic discussions on a daily basis. He scoffed at those Soviet and Cuban academics who did not understand that South Africa's forces were in trouble. He himself was willing to risk everything for victory. He violently gesticulated; he leapt from his chair and paced around the room. But when Adamishin stood up, the Cuban leader told him to sit back down: there was room for only one emotional person in the room. Castro became so heated that he forgot to offer a cup of coffee to his visitor. Of course, he had spent half a lifetime dazzling Soviet leaders with his revolutionary élan, and Adamishin recognized Castro's guile in the way he built up to a request for Moscow to continue its assistance for the Angolan war effort. Castro brushed aside Adamishin's account of the growing difficulties in Angola: he had made a definitive assessment and expected his visitor to accept it.[26]

Gorbachëv wanted to keep up the Cuban alliance despite Castro's mutterings about his *perestroika*. He had intended to visit the island at the end of his visit to New York before the Armenian earthquake had stopped him.[27] The trip was rescheduled for April. At the discussion in the Politburo, Gorbachëv drew attention to Cuba's demands on the USSR's budget. Castro received 20 billion rubles' worth of oil annually without having to pay in hard currency at a time when the Soviet authorities could not afford to buy the amount of foreign products it needed.[28]

In Cuba, Gorbachëv witnessed how little could be bought in the shops under the rationing system. Cuban people appeared at the limits of endurance. He recognized Castro as a person of huge talent and knowledge of world affairs, but there was a distinct coolness in their first conversation. Gorbachëv saw through Castro's exploitation of his charm. He thought that the decades of American blockade had fostered a definite 'sectarianism' in his manner of thinking. Gradually, though, the atmosphere lightened and they started to speak usefully with each other. As was his habit with the leaders of foreign communist states, Gorbachëv declined to put direct pressure on Castro – he subsequently told his Politburo: 'We've got to take Cuba as it is.' He was anyhow at one with Castro about the need to prevent interference by the West in the island's affairs. He promised to continue to provide a military shield for Havana; he also gave an assurance that the USSR regarded Cuba's revolution as its own business. Castro for his part agreed to recall Cuban military advisers from Nicaragua. This was important for Gorbachëv in his search for improved relations with the Americans.[29]

The Nicaraguan question remained irksome for Washington. Soviet leaders pondered how to handle the results of the forthcoming election in that war-torn Central American country. On 13 February 1990 Shevardnadze and Yakovlev prepared a paper for the Politburo about it, at a time when Secretary Baker was on a visit to Moscow. They urged that the Sandinistas should be told to do nothing to provide the Americans with an excuse to deny recognition to the new government; they recommended that if Daniel Ortega achieved his expected victory, he should govern in a spirit of national reconciliation. The USSR ought to adopt a 'pragmatic, de-ideologized' policy towards Ortega and his future ministers and prolong its suspension of military supplies. Shevardnadze and Yakovlev suggested that Castro should be told, tactfully but firmly, to give priority to reducing international tensions in the region. The Politburo accepted their ideas.[30] This was recognition that the Soviet Union had to accept a diminished role for itself around the world. Apart from German reunification, Soviet internal political and economic problems consumed almost all the leadership's time. It was time to discard the commitment to Central America – or, indeed, to liberation movements elsewhere in the world.

The USSR halted its military supplies to Angola, Mozambique and Ethiopia. It also ceased shipments to Iraq, Libya and Yugoslavia despite the potential loss of $7 billion a year. Communist governments that failed to pay for their arms received the same treatment – Vietnam, Cambodia, North Korea, Cuba and Mongolia fell into this category. The USSR also terminated its financial credits to other states.[31] On 15 March 1990, when Najibullah pleaded for the maintenance of assistance, Zaikov passed on the request to the Defence Ministry, which replied that items to the value of 1.8 billion rubles could be spared. This included twenty-three MiG fighters. The ministry promised to send six highly qualified military specialists who could help with the necessary training. But First Deputy Minister Mikhail Moiseev pointed out that the military budget for 1990 had already been cut back. If the political leadership required the ministry to bolster the Afghan government, additional funds would have to be released.[32] Gorbachëv tried to persuade Najibullah that the Americans were starting to recognize the dangers of the spread of Islamic fundamentalism and Najibullah spoke confidently about completing 'normalization' within two or three years, despite the growing interference of neighbouring Muslim countries.[33] Their alliance was fraying. The Afghan communist administration stood at the edge of a precipice.

Yet the Soviet leadership stuck to its established line in geopolitics. On 13 April 1990 the Politburo approved a memo from Shevardnadze, Yakovlev and Kryuchkov welcoming the recent moderation of Sandinista policy and advising the need to put pressure on Castro to be more 'constructive' about resolving conflicts in Central America.[34] In June the Soviet leadership told the Americans that it was willing to drop its support for Cuba. It suggested a deal could be struck on the basis that Moscow would withdraw its military commission from Havana if Washington would dismantle its Guantanamo Bay base and confirm its guarantee never to invade.[35] Bush and Baker were in no mood to compromise. They demanded nothing less than an end to the USSR's influence in the region.

Gorbachëv was disinclined to yield without getting something in return. Being under attack by Soviet critics of his reforms, he could not afford to appear to surrender. Better by far to conduct his retreat in a quiet fashion. Hardly anyone noticed the relinquishment of the USSR's hegemonic pretensions in what had been known as the 'world communist movement'. When the Italian Communist Party reconstituted itself as the Democratic Party of the Left, a faction of radical leftists established the Communist Refoundation Party. The Soviet Politburo had to decide what, if anything, to do about this. It was ceasing to prioritize the links with communist parties and reaching out to the world's conservative, liberal and socialist parties. Nevertheless the Party International Department opted to keep in touch with the Communist Refoundation Party.[36]

Gorbachëv was too distracted by other matters to unscramble this component of his foreign policy. Maybe, indeed, he saw advantage in allowing a degree of uncertainty that made it difficult for his opponents to say that he was treading on the neck of international communist solidarity. The same thought perhaps supplied the incentive to issue his usual invitation for leaders of friendly socialist countries to spend their summer vacations in the USSR. By May 1990 few such countries existed. Gorbachëv instead invited a clutch of communist party leaders from Eastern Europe, and a sorry lot they were by that time. Romania's Ion Iliescu was the only one among them who held power – and he no longer called himself a communist. Old favourites like Fidel Castro, Heng Samrin and Kim Il-sung received their usual invitations; but the likelihood of any one of these three accepting the invitation to spend days of leisure with the man who was steadily throwing aside the legacy of the October Revolution was low. Kim anyway had a pathological fear of international travel.[37] Gorbachëv was probably pleased that the North Korean leader was unlikely to leave his peninsula. He had a cluster of urgent international dilemmas to resolve, and a shared vacation with the Far East's aged dogmatist would hardly sharpen his reflections.

35. REVOLUTION IN EASTERN EUROPE

Eastern Europe had always troubled the Soviet leadership, and Poland was a constant complication. On 6 February 1989 the Polish communist leadership and Solidarity gathered at a 'round table'. Although Jaruzelski did this by choice, he also had encouragement from Moscow. He wanted to ensure industrial peace at a time of economic emergency and hoped to co-opt Lech Wałęsa into the governing circle. Hardened by his spells in prison and buoyed by his Catholic faith, Wałęsa was not minded to yield unduly. Jaruzelski was going to make no headway unless he made ample concessions in politics. Weeks of strenuous negotiations ensued.

A bleak memo arrived on Yakovlev's desk from the Party International Department which sounded an alarm about the USSR's neglect of the region. Things were getting dire, and a 'new type' of relationship had yet to be created with the Soviet Union. Poland, Hungary and Czechoslovakia were suffering from internal trouble which their communist administrations were failing to contain. The Bulgarian communist leadership's commitment to reform was mere pretence and all Bulgarians knew this. The German Democratic Republic had secretly incurred a huge external debt. Romania was conducting harsh repression to impose a regime of austerity so as to pay off the loans from Western banks – a policy that could soon end in an eruption of popular discontent. The only constructive aspect of the situation, from the Soviet viewpoint, was the fact that Moscow's economy was at last running a surplus in its balance of trade with Eastern Europe. There was little prospect of deepening the industrial and commercial integration with the East European states, which were seeking ties only with Western Europe. The International Department advised that the USSR had no option but to encourage this tendency in the hope that the Soviet Union might piggyback on any progress that the East Europeans succeeded in making.[1]

As the outlook for communism in the region worsened, Ligachëv began to question the foundations of Gorbachëv's foreign policy. On 12 March 1989, after returning from a trip to Prague, he told the Politburo that 'the Czechs' were upset about Soviet publications that implied a wish to take 'the capitalist road'. Gorbachëv brushed aside any such idea: 'A total dog's dinner. It would only make sense if we were raising the question of private farmers. But that would be unrealizable and devastating.'[2] Whereas he disliked the most radical economic options, he had bolder thoughts about politics. In early April, when Gorbachëv met Hungarian General Secretary Károly Grósz, they had a conversation which would have been inconceivable only months earlier. Grósz indicated the intention of disbanding his Politburo and allowing the party to elect a new leadership for the country's benefit. Shakhnazarov joked that this was something worth trying in the USSR. Gorbachëv quipped that his own Central Committee would never come up with the necessary Politburo.[3] It was in the same month that Jaruzelski in Poland arrived at a grand bargain to accord legal status to Solidarity. The Soviet leadership immediately offered approval.[4] Despite what he said to Grósz about the Central Committee, Gorbachëv could still rely on his Politburo.

On 20 May 1989 Shevardnadze and Honecker had a discussion on economic questions. Honecker thanked the USSR effusively for normalizing relations with the People's Republic of China, but Eastern Europe acutely worried him. The Hungarian communist authorities were wandering into the dangerous territory of the unknown, and Honecker urged that 'Poland mustn't be lost'.[5] On the other side of the Iron Curtain there were equally extraordinary conversations. Thoughts that had once seemed utopian were quietly being voiced. Mitterrand told Bush in May 1989 that he was not opposed to German reunification: he just wanted it to happen – if at all – over a ten-year period.[6]

The Polish elections of 4 June, which by chance took place on the same day as tanks rolled over the bodies of protesters on Tiananmen Square, resulted in a massive victory for Solidarity. There was joy and shock across Poland as the Polish communists went down to a humiliating defeat. When the full results became available, Solidarity had won all but one of the hundred seats in the Senate. It also took 173 out of 460 seats in the lower house – the Sejm; this was an equally remarkable achievement because Jaruzelski had drawn up an electoral law that prevented Solidarity from contesting sixty-five per cent of Sejm seats. Even the Solidarity leadership failed to anticipate the scale of its triumph. Jaruzelski decided to brazen it out and, with his still-guaranteed majority in the Sejm, secured his own re-election as President, albeit by only one vote. He then nominated Minister of Internal Affairs General Czesław Kiszczak as Prime Minister. Kiszczak was notorious among Poles as a practitioner of repression, and he and Jaruzelski aimed to seek a way out of the political emergency by offering minor concessions to Solidarity in return for the continuation of communist rule. This was not an outcome that Solidarity felt inclined to accept.[7]

Soviet leaders recognized that they had for too long failed to focus their gaze on Eastern Europe. Gorbachëv had a pile of preoccupations in internal and external policy and Shevardnadze sped around the world on ministerial business. According to the records of their aides, neither of them had anticipated the final anticommunist crisis in Poland during those long, hot months.[8] The Polish electoral result had taken the party leadership in the Kremlin entirely by surprise – and the same seems to have been true of the KGB and the Foreign Affairs Ministry. But Gorbachëv refused to interfere; he made clear that he would never endorse a reproduction of the Chinese methods in Warsaw or sanction military intervention from abroad. Poland's communists had lost and had to cope with the consequences.[9]

When Shevardnadze met Honecker on 9 June 1989, he concentrated on the 'crisis' in the USSR rather than the extraordinary situation in Poland. He focused on the idea of the necessity of *perestroika*. However difficult it was to conduct the Soviet reforms, he wanted the East German leader to understand that the Politburo had no option but to bring them to completion. He told of how millions of people, including pensioners, were living below the poverty line. He remarked on the dire situation in housing. He added that the old party leadership had made a primitive error in declaring the national question solved once and for all. He admitted that 'demagogic' criticisms were on the rise, but he expressed faith in the party's ability to retain control of the situation. Honecker as usual omitted to criticize Gorbachëv's record, preferring to boast about East Germany's industrial achievements. His concerns lay with the movement of events throughout Eastern Europe. He said that if things were called by their real name, the Polish Communist Party had suffered defeat at the hands of Solidarity. In Hungary, things were moving in the same direction. Honecker was adamant that Poland should not be 'lost'; he also urged the need to prevent a split in the Hungarian Communist Party.[10]

On 7 July Gorbachëv reinforced this analysis when addressing the

Political Consultative Committee of the Warsaw Pact in Bucharest. It was an astonishing occasion. The Romanian capital was a bastion of reactionary communism. Its leadership was being constrained to give a respectful welcome to the arch-reformer Gorbachëv. Ceauşescu's annoyance was balanced by a sense of relief that he was not having to deal with anything like the situation that faced Jaruzelski. The Polish leader was the first communist leader since the late 1940s to undergo the indignity of electoral defeat. Communists were notorious for fixing such processes by whatever means were necessary. Jaruzelski created a precedent.

There was to be no doubt, as Gorbachëv saw it, that the Warsaw Pact had to demonstrate its acceptance of Poland's popular verdict. He took pleasure in the recent statements by Bush and Thatcher to the effect that the Cold War was over. A new international order was in the making, and Gorbachëv wanted the alliance to enhance the process.[11] He noted that Western leaders thought they had achieved a triumph over socialism as they noted the growing technological gap with the West as well as the rise in Eastern Europe's debts. Gorbachëv intended to stay calm and ignore the display of bourgeois self-satisfaction. He denied that the socialist future was any cause for concern. He declared that it was better to prove this by their deeds rather than to bluster about it.[12] He informed his fellow leaders about Soviet plans to withdraw a large number of troops in line with agreements for the reduction of conventional forces throughout Europe.[13] He spoke warmly about the opportunities for scientific and technological co-operation with France. He and Mitterrand had agreed on this, and Gorbachëv no longer talked disparagingly about the French Eureka research programme.[14] (Indeed, he now told Mitterrand of his wish for the USSR to join programme.)[15] On human rights, he insisted that his own reforms in the USSR were not a concession to the West but a 'deep internal necessity' that was integrally connected with the process of *perestroika*.[16]

Jaruzelski, as Poland's President and commander-in-chief, stressed that as the rapprochement between the superpowers proceeded, his country needed West Germany to recognize Poland's western frontier. The Poles dreaded the rebirth of ideas of a Greater Germany and the possibility that Kohl would lay claim to the territory that Poland had gained in 1945.[17]

The American administration could hardly believe that a communist leadership in Eastern Europe had peacefully accepted rejection in a free national election. Every cliché about worldwide communism was being dispelled. The Americans adapted themselves eagerly to events, and Bush flew to Poland and had talks with Jaruzelski on 10 July. They agreed on the need to prepare for German reunification – neither of them liked the idea, and Bush stressed that he wanted to prevent anything happening that could jeopardize understandings with the USSR. Jaruzelski welcomed his promise to eschew interference in Polish affairs; he added that he expected to be able to appoint a communist as the next Prime Minister in a coalition government.[18] Bush emphasized that America had difficulties with its own balance of payments and could not plug the hole in Poland's budget. Speaking to the current Prime Minister, Mieczysław Rakowski, he indicated that any American help would be tied to further progress towards democracy and a market economy.[19] Travelling on to Hungary, Bush spoke to Prime Minister Miklós Németh, a communist who wanted to form a coalition ministry and introduce a programme of economic privatization.[20] While he was in Budapest, Bush emphatically endorsed the commitment to steady, peaceful reform; and he added his wish to do nothing that might undermine Gorbachëv in Moscow.[21]

Bush was straddling two lines of action. After months of indecision, he was keen to make progress in deals with the Soviet leadership; at the same time he wanted to encourage the East European communist reformers to continue along the path they had chosen. Outwardly the Americans wished to show confidence in Gorbachëv's durability – and at a meeting of ambassadors in Moscow on 12 July 1989, Matlock denied that he was at any risk. He could see no danger coming from Kryuchkov. (UK Ambassador Braithwaite was more sceptical and thought that 'we wouldn't get advance warning of a move against Gorbachëv'.)[22] When Matlock saw Yakovlev on 20 July 1989, he assured him that America had no desire to exploit the situation to the USSR's disadvantage. Bush and his administration saw the continuation of *perestroika* as being in the American interest. Yakovlev nevertheless blamed the President for causing mischief with his comments about the Baltic region. When the conversation turned to arms talks, Matlock commented that Bush had rejected Reagan's dream of completely liquidating nuclear weapons but still wanted to bring the stockpiles down to a minimum.[23]

Vadim Zagladin, who had joined Gorbachëv as a foreign policy adviser, promised that the USSR would cooperate with whatever kind of government emerged in Warsaw: 'This is purely an internal Polish affair.' Yakovlev sought assurances that Poland would remain inside the Warsaw Pact. On receiving them, he declared that the choice of a new government was a matter for the Poles alone.[24] General Secretary Rakowski made a last effort at stopping Solidarity's Tadeusz Mazowiecki from becoming Prime Minister. Gorbachëv would have none of this, and in late August 1989 phoned Rakowski and urged him to be more conciliatory.[25] The Kremlin expected the Polish comrades to accept defeat. On vacation outside Gagra in the mountains by the Abkhazian coast, Shevardnadze confided: 'One thing is certain: we're not going to get sucked into Polish affairs.'[26] It was for the Poles to settle the crisis in Poland. The Soviet leadership had plenty of difficulties of its own to resolve.

Ceauşescu called from Bucharest for a meeting of the Warsaw Pact's Political Consultative Committee. The Pact's 'last Stalinist', as Shevardnadze called him, could see that the Polish example might become contagious in Eastern Europe. Ceauşescu had opposed the invasion of Czechoslovakia in 1968. Now he worried about his own administration's survival and told the Soviet leadership that drastic action was needed to conserve communist rule in Poland.[27] On 19 August 1989 he wrote to all the Warsaw Pact countries calling expressly for military action to prevent Solidarity from forming a government. Belatedly adopting the Brezhnev Doctrine as his credo, he professed that Poland's politics could not be an exclusively Polish matter.[28] Even Honecker could see that Ceauşescu's proposal, if acted upon, had the potential to play into Solidarity's hands.[29] Ceauşescu in fact had unwisely copied the Polish Party General Secretary, Rakowski, into the correspondence. His comradely courtesy came back to bite him. Rakowski had by then resolved that he had to seek an accommodation with Solidarity, and he divulged Ceauşescu's message to the press.[30] The Soviet leadership rebuked the Romanian leader;[31] and KGB Chairman Kryuchkov flew to Warsaw to wish the new Polish cabinet well.[32]

Solidarity's confidence strengthened as it gained support from the small parties that were allied to the communists, who suddenly found themselves in a minority in the Sejm. On 24 August, after Kiszczak resigned as Prime Minister, Jaruzelski felt compelled to offer the post to Solidarity's Tadeusz Mazowiecki.[33] Solidarity played a deft game and accepted Kiszczak's reappointment as Minister of Internal Affairs; and Polish armed forces stayed inside the Warsaw Pact. It was obviously going to be an unstable symbiosis, and Mazowiecki remorselessly undermined the bastions of the communist state. A quiet revolution with near-universal popular support was proceeding.

The foundations of Poland's post-war state order disintegrated and the rumble of change was heard elsewhere in Eastern Europe. The KGB's Lev Shebarshin returned from East Germany with a depressing account of his experience.[34] He later wrote that Gorbachëv ignored what he and other intelligence leaders reported. Shebarshin claimed that whenever the Soviet leaders took an interest in the KGB's activity, they only wanted to know about what Yeltsin was getting up to.[35] Politburo member Vadim Medvedev, who visited the country in the summer, was another who warned about the simmering discontent.[36] Germany, even more than Poland, was the arena of the US–Soviet contest in Europe. On both sides of the Iron Curtain there was concern that if ever West and East Germany were reunited, the security of neighbouring states could be put in jeopardy. The division of Germany after 1945 suited the wishes of many governments. But if East Germany were to collapse after the Polish fashion, all bets would be off, and Gorbachëv started to consider whether the contagion could spread. Margaret Thatcher felt a pang of sympathy with his plight. On 13 September, talking to UK Ambassador Braithwaite, she blurted out: 'The poor man's in trouble!'[37]

Defence Minister Dmitri Yazov adjured the Central Committee on 19 September that 'we don't have the right to forget 1941'. He was clearing his throat before making an indirect criticism of official policy. Whereas Gorbachëv talked only of 'sufficient' defensive capacity, Yazov insisted that the USSR had to be sure of 'absolutely reliable defence'. The Defence Ministry evidently lacked confidence that the country would be defensible if its forces went down to the minimum that Gorbachëv demanded.[38] Yazov highlighted how the American administration continued with the 'modernization of its strategic offensive forces and the realization of the Strategic Defense Initiative' while making demands about bilateral arms reduction. Even Gorbachëv acknowledged America intended to maintain the deterrent capacity of its nuclear weaponry – Bush had made this clear in a speech he gave in Baltimore on 7 September.[39]

The American President and his administration were surprised and delighted about Solidarity's advance on power, and the Soviet leadership proved to be much less agitated about Poland than outsiders had forecast. A working group of Shevardnadze, Yakovlev, Yazov and Kryuchkov designed a practical policy. What they agreed on 20 September was unprecedented – and for this reason it was important that the Defence Minister and the KGB Chairman were involved in the discussion. They noted that Mazowiecki was signalling the new government's desire for friendly links with the USSR. The group welcomed this overture and suggested the need for of direct talks with the Vatican. They urged Gorbachëv to raise Polish affairs at his projected meeting with Pope John Paul II. They said that if Soviet diplomacy was managed with care, the Warsaw Pact could survive as the instrument of regional security coordination – and this was in the USSR's interest. The group regarded the Political Consultative Committee and even Comecon as having lasting usefulness.[40] On 28 September the Politburo passed the submission as guidance for official policy.[41]

Political disaffection became manifest in East Germany. The two superpowers and their allies pondered the growth in unrest. Dissenters were becoming bolder. Church activists, youth rebels and political dissidents united in producing anticommunist leaflets and petitioning for change. Honecker's instinct was to rely on his security forces; he knew that he could not count on assistance from the Soviet military garrisons. Speculation mounted that the emergency could culminate in German reunification under Kohl's aegis.

Thatcher set her face against this outcome. She distrusted the West German leadership and its pretensions, telling Mitterrand: 'Kohl lies the whole time.' What made a bad situation worse was that her friend Gorbachëv was proving 'feeble'. Mitterrand soothed her with the comment that Gorbachëv would never accept a new Germany belonging to NATO; he added that France and the United Kingdom could rely on the USSR and America to stand up to Kohl.[42] Mitterrand's aide Jacques Attali, talking to Gorbachëv's adviser Vadim Zagladin, floated the idea of a Franco-Soviet alliance, including even military 'integration':[43] this extraordinary idea came to nothing – more than anything else, it was a symptom of panic in French ruling circles at the idea that the Paris–Bonn axis in Western Europe was crumbling. Thatcher too foresaw that communism could soon collapse in East Germany. On 22 September she bluntly told Gorbachëv:

> Britain and Western Europe are not interested in the unification of Germany. The words written in the NATO communiqué may sound different, but disregard them. We do not want the unification of Germany. It would lead to changes in the post-war borders, and we cannot allow that because such a development would

undermine the stability of the entire international situation and could lead to threats to our security.[44]

Thatcher opposed 'the destabilization of Eastern Europe or the dissolution of the Warsaw Pact', and claimed that this was also Bush's opinion.[45] When she spoke again to the Soviet leader a few days later, she railed against the idea of a greater Germany. Chernyaev recorded: 'Thatcher, when she asked for her conversation with M. S. [Gorbachëv] "not to be minuted", was resolutely against "the unification of Germany". She wanted to tell him things that she could not say in public.'[46]

Gorbachëv flew to East Berlin to celebrate the German Democratic Republic's fortieth anniversary in early October. Though he was reluctant to appear alongside Honecker, he could not afford to provoke trouble by absenting himself. Joyous crowds greeted him. Placards proclaimed in Russian: 'Gorbachëv, you are our hope'. Hardly anybody waved messages in favour of Honecker.[47] Gorbachëv played the role of loyal comrade. Honecker refused to acknowledge any basic problems, and Gorbachëv had to bite his tongue when Honecker ribbed him about the empty shelves in Soviet stores.[48] Attending the East German Politburo, Gorbachëv continued the charade and spoke as if Honecker enjoyed his confidence.[49] Meanwhile out on the streets there was agitation. Demonstrations were organized in Dresden. A rumour spread that people would use the occasion of Gorbachëv's visit to storm the Berlin Wall. Such stories reached East Germans from West German TV news programmes.[50] Honecker was helpless to take repressive action without Gorbachëv's approval. He could only warn Gorbachëv that Hungary would soon be lost to the socialist fold as a result of Kohl bribing the Hungarians to open their border with Austria.[51] Gorbachëv returned to Moscow on 7 October.[52] Leaving Honecker to his fate, he told Shakhnazarov and Chernyaev that the East German leader was 'an arsehole'.[53]

The communist leadership in East Germany flew into a frenzy. Something had to be done about Honecker, and fast. Politburo members Egon Krenz, Günther Schabowski and Harry Tisch secretly arranged for Tisch to consult Gorbachëv about how to remove Honecker from office. Tisch's report on public opinion contained no secret revelations. Gorbachëv was restrained in his reply: 'That is nothing new to me. The trip to the fortieth anniversary of the GDR was very embarrassing. I only went out of a sense of duty and to help.' He indicated his support for what Honecker's fellow communist leaders had in mind.[54] On 18 October the East German Politburo took decisive action by firing Honecker and making Krenz the General Secretary, and the ground was at last clear for reforms.

Gorbachëv recognized that the presence of his own armed forces added to the agitation in Eastern Europe, but he also saw the danger in annoying the Soviet high command. On 18 October the USSR's Main Military Council met to review the situation. This was a body that brought together the leaderships of the General Staff, Defence Ministry, KGB and Ministry of Internal Affairs. It was a fiery session as military commanders explained the difficulties for the Soviet armed forces in pulling out of the East European countries. Withdrawal would be a costly process that would wreck their annual budget.[55] Shevardnadze decided to quash any incipient attempt to reverse official policy. He gave one of the speeches of his life at the Supreme Soviet, where he stressed that the USSR should have been quicker in deciding how to deal with the whirlwind of changes in the region. He wanted to see further progress in arms reduction; he denounced the whole Afghan debacle since 1979. He stressed the need to base policy on moral principles and demanded help from the Supreme Soviet in passing laws on human rights. He reserved his own right to stand down if pushed to pursue objectives at variance with his understanding of politics and morality.[56] Gorbachëv and Shevardnadze were adamant about keeping to the line they had established in the summer. The Kremlin's political apparatus had once intimidated and controlled the entire region. Now its officials were like everyone else in the USSR, simply watching events in Warsaw, East Berlin and Prague on television – and the Politburo was not much better informed than anyone else.[57]

Gorbachëv talked scathingly about East European leaders. Meeting with Poland's ex-Prime Minister Rakowski in mid-October, he blamed him and the rest of the Polish communist leadership for the incompetent way that they had confronted Solidarity. Rakowski still saw Gorbachëv as his political protector. He thought that the Solidarity-led government could soon be in trouble because Poles had no bread on their plates. He warned that a dictator on the model of Poland's pre-war leader Józef Piłsudski might come to power.[58] Rakowski had not adapted his thinking to a Europe where Moscow was no longer willing to come to the assistance of Polish comrades. Or perhaps he was just in shock. His leading comrades in government elsewhere in Eastern Europe were hardly in better shape. In Hungary, Grósz was floundering as public protests intensified in Budapest. Even Ceauşescu

faced disturbances. They took place under the severe eyes of the Securitate in northern Romania and involved the national and religious
grievances of the Hungarian minority there.

As old problems resurfaced, the Soviet leadership sensed that it
could play a role as mediator. There was friction between the Poles and
the East Germans as Jaruzelski sought guarantees about post-war
Poland's western frontier. Romania had acquired territory from Hungary in 1919, and this was giving rise to tension between Budapest and
Bucharest. Several countries in Eastern Europe, moreover, prevented
travel across their borders. Economic links in the region were on the
decline.[59] On 26 October Shevardnadze spoke to the Warsaw Pact's
Foreign Ministers in the Polish capital. He said nothing about the
growth of the anticommunist resistance in the region. The priority
in his judgement was to strengthen international security, and he
reported that the Americans understood Soviet official thinking. He
saw the Warsaw Pact with this in mind; he recounted his recent conversations with Prime Minister Tadeusz Mazowiecki and Foreign
Affairs Minister Krzysztof Skubiszewski as if it was the most normal
thing in the world for a Soviet leader to parley with Polish Catholic
liberals and conservatives who had prised power from the grasp of
Poland's communists.[60]

Western public figures gave reassuring signals about the German
Democratic Republic. Ex-Chancellor Willi Brandt told Gorbachëv
that the question of German reunification was not at the top of his
agenda.[61] Zbigniew Brzezinski arrived from America for talks with
Yakovlev. Born Polish, Brzezinski feared the consequence of a reunified Germany. He worried about German revanchism, and for this
reason he counselled the Soviet leadership to hold the Warsaw Pact
together – as political rather than a military alliance.[62]

On 1 November Gorbachëv and Krenz spoke by phone about the
current troubles. Both tried to put a brave face on a situation that was
running out of control. Street demonstrations took place in East
German cities. Dissenters sensed that they had the administration on
the run, but Gorbachëv assured Krenz:

> You need to know that all serious politicians – Thatcher, Mitter-
> rand, Andreotti, not to mention Jaruzelski and the Americans – might
> now be showing different nuances in their position but they have a
> guarded attitude to the idea of Germany's unification . . . All these
> politicians start from the premise of preserving the post-war
> realities, including the existence of two German states.[63]

He insisted that they wished to preserve the separate alliances of NATO and the Warsaw Pact.[64] But what about East Germany? Gorbachëv said that the way forward was to encourage cooperation among East Germany, West Germany and the USSR. He was caustic about Eastern Europe. Poland and Hungary were bankrupt and had no choice but to turn to the West for assistance. The Soviet Union could not bail their astronomical debts.[65]

On 3 November the Politburo dealt with questions of fiendish complexity. One was about the need for flexible tactics to buy grain on foreign markets. (Soviet leaders were reminded that Soviet agricultural productivity was a long way below the American norm.) The next topic on the agenda was interethnic conflicts across the USSR. The Politburo then discussed how to handle a scheduled meeting with the Papal Nuncio Angelo Sodano. As the date of Gorbachëv's encounter with the Pope drew near, it was crucial to prepare the ground for talks. Only then did the Politburo get round to the momentous events in the heart of Europe – a sign of Moscow's fading influence over the situation as Krenz sought to impose his authority. Kryuchkov reported that the KGB had information to the effect that half a million might take to the streets of East Berlin and other German cities next day. Gorbachëv asked simply whether Krenz stood any chance of survival. Shevardnadze, advocate of support for Afghan communist leaders, did not feel the same about the German Democratic Republic: 'The best thing would be if we ourselves took down the "Wall".' Kryuchkov muttered: 'If it's taken down, things will be difficult for the East Germans.'[66] But not even the KGB leadership recommended measures of repression. The entire Politburo had an acute sense of its impotence.

Gorbachëv again emphasized that 'the West' had no interest in German reunification; he reported that foreign leaders were trying to provoke him into preventing reunification, and he refused to do their dirty work for them. He himself favoured open negotiation with the two Germanies, and suggested that this way of proceeding was in the USSR's basic interest.[67] Shevardnadze lamented the poor quality of information that had reached Moscow about Poland and East Germany.[68] But the main need was for the Politburo to deal with what was already known. East Germans were taking to the streets in the cities. If the Wall fell, the entire military and political settlement in Europe since 1945 would be undermined. Gorbachëv had come to the point of decision. He indicated to the Politburo that Krenz was not worth saving. He did not intend to save the Wall. His aim was to manage the East German crisis quietly.

Krenz's Politburo were beginning to panic when news reached them on 9 November that groups of East Germans might be about to try and breach the Wall. Kohl and Wałęsa talked on the same day about the crisis in East Berlin, but Wałęsa's chief concern at the time was about how to keep Poland at the centre of the world's attention.[69] This was also Shevardnadze's preoccupation in discussions inside his ministry.[70] Krenz telegrammed Moscow for guidance on the situation. His own officials were in a quandary and one of them gave a TV interview implying that the authorities were resigned to the idea of free passage between the two halves of Berlin. Krenz had made no such decision, but took no practical precautions. East Berliners in their thousands took this as permission to take matters into their own hands. By the evening they had massed at the Wall and begun to chip away at the concrete. Its guards had no orders to stop them and it was not long before they had made breaches and started to walk through to the West. Joyous celebrations occurred on both sides of a city that popular action was starting to reunify.

Kohl's joy knew no bounds and he called Bush next day to say: 'I've just arrived from Berlin. It is like witnessing an enormous fair. It has the atmosphere of a festival.'[71] Gorbachëv wanted everybody to be clear about the USSR's policy. He wrote immediately to Bush, Kohl, Thatcher and Mitterrand emphasizing his commitment to the existence of two German states. On 11 November he phoned Kohl and called for the USSR, West Germany and East Germany to keep in contact.[72] Three days later he rang Mitterrand to say that Kohl had claimed to be opposing those in West Germany calling for reunification.[73]

Although the Soviet leaders were shaken by revolutions that they had failed to anticipate, they searched for reasons to be confident. Critics had been buffeting Gorbachëv about his tactics in the arms reduction talks. The danger for him now was that they would make the additional objection that he had needlessly lost Eastern Europe – or at least was in the process of losing it. On 18 November Shevardnadze held an overdue discussion with his aides on the German question. If East Germany could keep going, he contended, the entire 'commonwealth' – by which he meant the Warsaw Pact – could endure. The reunification of Germany in his view would enable the economic integration of Europe as a whole; and he could not see how the Americans would think this to be in their interest. As he saw it, the Kremlin lacked accurate information about Poland, Hungary and East Germany. German nationalism had been underestimated. He noted that the French were thinking along the same lines. The USSR needed to improve its analytical readiness. On Shevardnadze's recommendation the Soviet leadership established an internal working group whose task was to keep watch on Eastern Europe and make recommendations on policy.[74]

Falin in the Party International Department felt that Gorbachëv and Shevardnadze were too passive towards the Western powers.[75] He saw the need to open a channel of communication with Bonn. Chernyaev agreed, and he and Falin sent an emissary to West Germany for talks with Kohl's personal assistant Horst Teltschik. Falin was brilliant, quirky and headstrong. He took an initiative which would have been unimaginable in earlier Soviet times by instructing the emissary to raise the possibility of forming a German confederation. His idea was to protect East Germany against being gobbled up by West Germany.[76] This had the unexpected effect of prodding Kohl and Teltschik towards formulating a scheme for reunification. Kohl feared that if he failed to intervene, events might overtake him.[77]

His solution, as he told the Bundestag on 28 November, was a ten-point plan for German unity that involved democratizing East Germany and setting up a confederation with West Germany. He made this on the strict understanding that a political and economic transformation was set in motion that would be irreversible. The communists had to give up their monopoly on power, negotiate with opposition parties and groups and do the groundwork for speedy, fair elections. He insisted that he was not laying down preconditions or aiming to exercise tutelage; but it was hard to interpret his words in any other way. Kohl noted that Hungary and Poland had accepted help according to Bonn's requirements. He could see no reason for East Germany to reject this model. He omitted to mention that while the Hungarians and Poles retained their national independence, he intended nothing of the kind for the East Germans. Having spoken to Hans Modrow, the communist reformer who had become East German Prime Minister a few days earlier, he was willing to provide assistance so long as the government conducted the radical change that Kohl demanded. He tied all this to a concern for security throughout Europe.[78]

Kohl's failure to give advance warning of his Ten Points caused fear in both Moscow and the Western capitals that West Germany was bulldozing the architecture of post-war Europe without bothering to consult the rest of the world. Bush alone was gentle, telling Kohl: 'I appreciate your Ten Points and your exposition on the future of Germany.'[79] The NATO allies were furious. Thatcher's nightmare was becoming reality and Mitterrand, who had enjoyed his collaboration with Kohl, felt traduced by having to learn about the Ten Points from news agency dispatches. Trust between Paris and Bonn collapsed. The consolation for French leaders was their thought that Moscow would surely reject Kohl's pretensions. And anyway would the East Germans, being Prussians, wish to fall under the control of West Germany?[80] Mitterrand and Thatcher despaired after learning that Bush, who shared their annoyance at Kohl's abandonment of political etiquette, endorsed the idea of a German confederation. The only remaining hope for the French and British governments was that Gorbachëv should veto the Kohl plan. Gorbachëv certainly wanted Kohl to know how angry he was. Falin, the person whose actions had nudged Kohl into formulating the Ten Points, urged Gorbachëv to exact the maximum of financial compensation from Bonn and teach him a lesson about future behaviour.[81]

Soviet leaders remained annoyed with Kohl, but none of them thought it feasible to tear up his proposals. They had let the Poles deal with the Polish question. Now they held back from unilateral intervention in East Germany. It was the same story elsewhere in Eastern Europe. Multiparty elections were being scheduled in Hungary as the communist reformers sought to win popular legitimacy. On 10 November the Bulgarian Politburo removed Zhivkov from power and replaced him with the communist reformer Petar Mladenov. Czechoslovakia seethed with demonstrations against communism. On 28 November the communist leadership in Prague promised to dismantle the one-party state structure. Gorbachëv heard the news with trepidation but stuck consistently to the principle of self-determination. He lacked the resources to turn back the tide of national revolutions. He could not afford to fall out with the Americans. He anyway believed that peoples should have freedom of choice. His solace was the absence of serious dissent inside the Soviet elites about his policy of non-interference. Only the Poles had yet come near to completing their revolution, but others were following them. The communist order was collapsing across Eastern Europe and not a Soviet bullet was fired in anger. It was a result that nobody could have safely predicted just a few months earlier.

36. THE MALTA SUMMIT

Bush resisted the temptation to go to Eastern Europe to celebrate the revolutionary upsurge. Senator George Mitchell, the Democratic Party's staid voice on foreign policy, found this regrettable.[1] But Bush judged that it would serve no good for the national interest if the American President danced amidst the rubble of the Berlin Wall. He had a point. Gorbachëv was shunning the idea of Soviet military intervention, and Bush wanted to keep things that way. Bush still needed Gorbachëv's cooperation in reducing arms and troops in Europe and reunifying the continent. With a summit meeting about to occur off the Maltese coast in early December, there was nothing to gain by crowing over the USSR's discomfiture.

The Americans had to assess Gorbachëv's chances of surviving in power after everything that had been happening in his country and Eastern Europe. Everybody in the American administration recognized that the revolutions against communist power in Warsaw and other capitals could undermine the cause of the Kremlin reformers. Gates and his USSR specialists at the CIA pointed out that *perestroika* had not brought material improvement for Soviet citizens. The possibility of popular unrest was growing. The authorities might use force to suppress it and the Baltic protest movement could be a target. Political democratization was disrupting the working of the administration and obstructing the path of economic reform. Nevertheless the CIA was divided about the future. The alternative internal opinion was that Gorbachëv would continue to advance towards a pluralist system but that the consequence would be an increasing loss of control from the centre.[2] Both opinions nevertheless suggested that trouble was in store for Gorbachëv. Arms reduction adviser Ed Rowny concluded that in these circumstances there were 'potential risks and few gains' in starting talks on reducing strategic nuclear weapons.[3] Rowny was hoping to pull Bush back to his earlier scepticism about Gorbachëv and arms treaties with the USSR; he was proposing a policy of inactivity as being the best for the American administration.

Others in the administration rejected this as being too passive a way to deal with the situation. Scowcroft advised the President to campaign at the National Security Council to repeal the Jackson–Vanik amendment to the National Security Council. He discouraged anything more than this at the next summit, emphasizing that the time had not arrived for the USSR to gain entrance to GATT, the IMF or the World Bank.[4] Matlock, cabling from the Moscow embassy, recommended the President at least to signal his support for *perestroika*. But he opposed any offer of financial assistance. In his opinion, the Kremlin needed to absorb the economic facts of life whereas a new Marshall Plan would only slow down the learning process. If Soviet leaders wanted to attract American private companies, they had to transform the entire commercial and legal environment in the USSR – and Gorbachëv needed to be told about this prerequisite.[5]

Bush had a quite different approach in mind. He certainly knew that the Kremlin's negotiating strength was steeply on the wane. He told Kohl:

> We recognize the Soviet Union as a sovereign nation that has great pride. Shevardnadze said recently that he didn't want America to 'bail us out'. I will be sensitive, but will want to see what I can do to help. We want him to succeed. In the briefings I have had, it is apparent that the Soviet economy is much worse than I realized before in-depth study. I will help, but in a sensitive way.[6]

Quite what he meant by sensitivity is not clear. He certainly had no intention of emptying his own treasury.

His main ambition, after a year of applied caution, was to keep his personal freedom to improvise at the summit. Something told him that this was the wisest way to extract the best results from the talks at a time when world politics were unstable. He asked Gorbachëv to agree to an open agenda; he himself promised not to spring any surprise on him.[7] When Baker heard of this, he warned Bush that Gorbachëv might do something disconcerting. He might, for example, make proposals for the dismantling of the Warsaw Pact and NATO. He would surely demand the end of restrictions on the USSR's integration in the world economy. He would oppose German reunification. Baker counselled against making any economic concessions until Gorbachëv had introduced an acceptable law on freedom of emigration. America's interest, in his opinion, lay in achieving stability, security and democracy in Eastern Europe after its revolutionary upsurge. Baker advised Bush to assure Gorbachëv that he would do nothing to undermine Gorbachëv's authority in Estonia, Latvia and Lithuania; but the President should at the same time reaffirm America's non-recognition of those Soviet Baltic republics. Bush should also draw attention to the discrepancy between Gorbachëv's rhetoric and the Kremlin's subversive practices in the Third World.[8]

Most leading officials in the American administration were pushing in the same direction: the summit ought not to become an occasion for undesirable concessions. Chernyaev heard that the CIA gave Gorbachëv six more months in power.[9] He noted that most Western commentators wrote approvingly about *perestroika*'s potential to transform the economy – the most prominent exceptions were Richard Pipes and Zbigniew Brzezinski. According to Chernyaev, the most impressive pieces were those which accepted that a reformed USSR was not going to turn into 'a Western society' or produce 'a Soviet economic miracle'. He noted that they usually suggested the need for Gorbachëv to achieve further breakthroughs in policy. Chernyaev thought they underestimated the scale of difficulties that faced the reformers. Direct resistance impeded progress less than the weak momentum supplied by Soviet society for its own transformation. Gorbachëv could not do everything alone.[10]

The usual group of advisers prepared guidelines on arms talks strategy for him in advance of his departure for America. The Big Five recommended a set of firm demands. Zaikov called for an agreement to renounce 'the creation of weaponry on new physical principles' – whether this was yet another attempt to undermine the Strategic Defense Initiative, he did not make clear. He also argued for obtaining agreement on how the two superpowers would manage industrial demilitarization; but again he was writing in unspecific terms. Baklanov added a request for a ban on anti-satellite weapons. He wanted Gorbachëv to warn the Americans that, now that the Politburo was dismantling the Krasnoyarsk radar station, the American installations at Thule and Fylingdales threatened progress.[11] Zaikov could handle Baklanov without undue difficulty at the Big Five. The difficulty was that Baklanov was saying things that everyone knew reflected feelings to be found widely in the military-industrial complex. Gorbachëv and Zaikov had quietened the critics since 1985, but both were conscious that things could crumble. At times it was prudent to agree to sterner guidelines than they thought that Gorbachëv would be able to impose on the Americans at the talks.

Soviet leaders were beginning to panic as the internal and external difficulties grew. Gorbachëv focused on the economic crisis. For weeks he and Ryzhkov had been trying to quicken the conversion of industry to the needs of consumers. Ryzhkov intended to remove 250 billion rubles from the budget for defence by the year 2005. Gorbachëv strongly backed him. With people from the military-industrial complex present, he stressed: 'You understand that we're shifting you so that you're face to face with the needs of the people. And all without any loss in security.'[12] The problem was that financial reallocations alone were not going to stave off ruin. The economy went from bad to worse. On 29 November, after reaching Rome, Gorbachëv held a discussion with his aides and leading figures from the arts. It was put to him that nothing good could happen until he rented out the collective farms. He rejected the advice: 'I don't want us to get yet another variant of collectivization. What? Should we cut society at the knee yet again? If society isn't yet mature and if initiative can't be awakened in it, we won't achieve anything.' His feelings were poignant and from the heart. Admitting that he lacked academic qualifications, he regretted that none of the prominent scholars in the room could tell him how to rescue the USSR.[13]

He was disallowing the proposal for a faster and deeper introduction of the market economy. If Ambassador Matlock had been privy to the debate, he would have felt vindicated. Gorbachev in the same breath appeared to want change and no change. He also had other things that were bothering him, and the Italian trip gave him a chance to see what he could do about them.

On 1 December he met Pope John Paul II in the Vatican. He had prepared the ground through talks in Moscow with Cardinal Casaroli in the summer. There had been a common emphasis on the wish for world peace, and Gorbachëv had assured the Vatican of the official tolerance that would always be shown to the Catholic Church.[14] The Pope, wearing a white soutane, now gave him an audience of an hour and twenty minutes and made no fuss about speaking in Russian. Casaroli, the overseer of policy in Eastern Europe, sat by the Pope's side. It was a warm conversation that left Gorbachëv thinking that their ideas overlapped. The Pope laid emphasis on peace in the world and thanked Gorbachëv for his recent efforts; he expressed gratitude for his draft law on freedom of conscience in the USSR. Gorbachëv said he hoped that his country and Poland would remain friends. The Pope thanked him 'in the name of my Motherland'. He also promised to do nothing to destabilize *perestroika*. This was important for Gorbachëv. If the Roman Catholic Church were to join the resistance to the Kremlin, Lithuania would surely go up in a fire of revolt. Gorbachëv made a brave effort to thank him in Polish for his hospitality and good wishes. This was a bridge too far for the patriotic Pole, who corrected the Russian's mistakes. They still managed to talk by themselves for ten minutes before inviting the help of interpreters again. The occasion ended on a bright note with Gorbachëv inviting John Paul to Moscow, where no Pope had set foot.[15]

The planning staff omitted to seek advice from meteorologists. The records of decades showed that the sea around Malta could be very rough in midwinter. As the Soviet and American cruisers dropped anchor near Valletta, the worst possibilities were realized. A storm blew up that was going to last for several days.

Gorbachëv and Bush flew into Valletta with large complements of officials. The Soviet team included Eduard Shevardnadze, Alexander Yakovlev, Sergei Akhromeev, Alexander Bessmertnykh, Anatoli Dobrynin and Anatoli Chernyaev. Bush brought James Baker, Brent Scowcroft, John Sununu, Denis Ross, Bob Blackwill and Jack Matlock. The first session was scheduled for 2 December 1989 on the Soviet passenger liner *Maxim Gorki*. Bush suggested that he and Gorbachev should meet with only their interpreters and aides in attendance – the Americans hoped to reinforce the movement towards agreement on contentious matters. This was how Gorbachëv had proceeded at summits. Now it was Bush who was hurrying things along. Gorbachëv did not mind: he wanted to get to know Bush better and attain the atmosphere of confidence he had enjoyed with Reagan. He agreed to sit down with Bush in the neighbouring room for their initial discussion.[16] Gorbachëv started with a remark on growing disquiet in the USSR to American armed activity in the Philippines, Panama and Colombia. When Bush tried to brush this aside, Gorbachëv interjected that people were talking of the replacement of the Brezhnev Doctrine with the Bush Doctrine; he expressed a preference for the peaceful resolution of difficulties. He mentioned that many people in the Soviet Union felt that the Politburo had renounced ideas about the 'export of revolution', only to experience 'the export of American values'.[17]

When they returned to the general room for a plenary session,

Gorbachëv offered praise for Bush. The President responded warmly and recounted that, on the flight to Valletta, he had reflected on how he had changed his standpoint on the USSR by 180 degrees. His administration and the American Congress, he said, believed that success for *perestroika* would bring benefits for world peace. His administration would do what it could to get the Jackson–Vanik amendment repealed. Credits could then become available, and this would enable the Soviet economy to import the foreign technology it needed for modernization.[18] At the same time he called for an improved official respect for human rights in the USSR. He also asked for Castro to be discouraged from exporting revolution. Gorbachëv answered that Havana and Washington should seek a normalization of their relations. Bush warned that Soviet indulgence of Castro would undermine the broader process of ending international tensions. It would anyway be better for the USSR if it ceased to waste its money on Cuba. Gorbachëv asked Bush to accept that Cuba and Nicaragua were independent countries; he repeated the USSR's objection to the American military action in Panama that had ended in the arrest of President Noriega.[19]

Gorbachëv objected to how Kohl was exploiting the theme of German reunification. Gorbachëv called for a pause before any decision about whether the new Germany could join NATO. Bush denied seeking to embarrass the Soviet Union in Eastern Europe. Gorbachëv interjected: 'We see and appreciate this.' Bush mentioned that several NATO countries spoke up for German reunification while quietly feeling concern about the practical potential; he himself promised to act with due caution.[20] The two leaders agreed on a scheme and schedule for disarmament in several categories: nuclear missiles, chemical weapons and subterranean test explosions. They promised to look at global ecological questions. They agreed on increasing cultural exchange between the USSR and the US, including student scholarships. Gorbachëv said: 'The United States and the USSR are simply fated to have dialogue, interaction, collaboration. There's no other way. But for this to happen we have to stop looking at each other as enemies.' At that moment, without any planning, Bush stretched a hand across the table to Gorbachëv. This physical gesture, by an American President who often fumbled his words, moved all those present.[21]

At lunch on 2 December Gorbachëv raised the question of financial credits. Baker, as Reagan's former Treasury Secretary, offered the opinion that Soviet leaders were imperilling *perestroika* by their slowness in undertaking price reform. Why wasn't Gorbachëv using Soviet gold reserves? This touched a raw nerve. To Gorbachëv and his team it seemed that the Americans wanted to be their teachers. Gorbachëv confined himself to saying that the priority was to reduce the budgetary deficit by half. He boasted that the government intended to rent out small and middle-sized enterprises in the near future.[22]

The next day's session, on 3 December, was meant to take place on the USS *Belknap* but was moved to the *Maxim Gorki* liner because Gorbachëv felt nervous about the stormy weather. Gorbachëv joked that nevertheless he was now Bush's guest; Bush said he liked his new ship.[23] The pleasantries over, Gorbachëv said: 'Above all, the new US President has to know that the Soviet Union won't start a war in any circumstances. This is so important that I wanted personally to repeat this announcement to you. Moreover, the USSR is ready to stop regarding the USA any longer as its adversary and to announce this openly.'[24] He repeated that the Americans for trying to impose 'Western values' on Eastern Europe at just the time when the Soviet leadership had abandoned the idea of exporting revolution.[25] His own behaviour over Poland and East Germany, he implied, demonstrated his trustworthiness. He said that he stood for 'freedom of choice', and he and Yakovlev insisted that there was nothing specifically 'Western' about their thinking. Shevardnadze rejected the idea that *perestroika* in the USSR was the product of Western policies applied from a position of strength.[26]

Gorbachëv received Bush's assurance that America was no longer giving Israel its unconditional support in the Middle East – he wanted Baker and Shevardnadze to confer about how to achieve peace with the Arabs. Shevardnadze faulted the Americans and Pakistanis for supplying the Afghan mujahidin.[27]

Bush havered before making a defence of what he said were the principles of 'glasnost'. He advocated pluralism, openness and fiery debates. He spoke up for the free market.[28] He denied that he presented them as specifically Western values. Gorbachëv's rejoinder was that every country ought to have the right to choose its own way of life. Here Bush could conclude: 'I don't think that we disagree here.' Gorbachëv added: 'I'm in favour on constructive cooperation.' He claimed that 'world civilization' depended on this. Bush expressed pleasure at the content and outcome of their conversation.[29] At their closing one-on-one session on 3 December Bush intimated some concern about the possibility of a tightening of the screws in the Baltic region.[30] But he and Gorbachëv wanted their summit to be recognized as historic. They were completing a process that began when Reagan and Gorbachëv had started to talk about world peace. The Cold War was over, completely finished. As the stormy weather died down over the northern Mediterranean, the two delegations could fly from Valletta with the confidence that their countries no longer confronted each other as enemy powers. Shevardnadze told aides: 'This is a much more significant breakthrough than in Reykjavik. Reykjavik was bloated whereas here the entire content corresponds to the scale of the meeting.'[31]

The next step was to inform the allies – a vital task at a time of tumultuous change in Eastern Europe. Bush sent Scowcroft and Deputy Secretary of State Eagleburger to Tokyo and Beijing to deliver briefings.[32] He himself met Kohl on 3 December and told him that Gorbachëv thought Kohl was in too much of a hurry. Kohl replied that things were happening altogether too fast in East Germany; he did not intend to let them get out of hand, and said he had already assured Gorbachëv about this. He admitted that Andreotti and other leaders in Western Europe felt some concern about his Ten Points. He denied being reckless. He said that when people like Kissinger called for a two-year delay before unification, they showed no comprehension of the depths of the East German economic crisis. Postponement of action, Kohl said, could result in a disaster. He asserted that Poland and Hungary would have collapsed but for the assistance that West Germany and America were rendering. He rejected Thatcher's attitude, saying: 'She thinks history is not just. Germany is so rich and Great Britain is struggling. They won a war but lost an empire and their economy. She does the wrong thing. She should try to bind the Germans into the European Community.'[33]

Flying back to Washington, Bush gave his account of the Malta discussions to the National Security Council on 5 December. Scowcroft advised him to stress the need for urgent work to prepare arms reduction plans for the next summit with the Soviet leader.[34] The Americans were pleased with what they had achieved at the summit. The main thing was that Gorbachëv had made no difficult demands. There was a firm possibility of stabilizing an Eastern Europe free from any Soviet military menace, and Gorbachëv and Bush could begin to add to the arms reduction understandings that were Reagan's legacy.

On 4 December Gorbachëv reported to the Warsaw Pact leaders in Moscow. He was speaking in circumstances that nobody present would have found imaginable a few months earlier. Around the table from Poland sat the communist President Jaruzelski and his liberal and Catholic Prime Minister Mazowiecki. Gone was Honecker. In his place sat Egon Krenz along with Hans Modrow representing a German Democratic Republic that few expected to last much longer. Ceauşescu, furious and nervous in equal measure, was the only communist veteran still in power.[35] Gorbachëv decided to act as if all this was a perfectly normal congregation for the celebration of an extraordinary event: the end of the Cold War.[36] He gave a garbled version of his talks with the Americans. Purportedly Bush had agreed that the Warsaw Pact and NATO should provide the foundation of stability and security in Europe. Changes were to happen but slowly.[37] He claimed that Bush had admitted: 'We were wrong about Najibullah's government.' The American President had even criticized Israel. Gorbachëv said that when Bush brought up the Baltic and south Caucasus republics, he had pointed out that Moscow had refrained from undermining the American Constitution or supporting breakaway movements in Quebec and Ulster.[38] On the German question, he claimed that Bush had acknowledged that the West European leaderships were now closer to the USSR than to America.[39]

Gorbachëv presented his vision for a universal settlement of world affairs: 'Now, when the changes in our countries have attained such a scale, we must definitely speak out. We are for the elimination of blocks, but we get approaches even from the West with the request not to ask to stay on the road that we have taken.'[40] A tea interval was called, and Gorbachëv repeated his case while chatting to the delegations. He turned his charm on everyone except Ceauşescu, who held himself rigid and apart as he waited for someone to come over and talk to him. No one did.[41]

After refreshments, Bulgaria's Petar Mladenov thanked Gorbachëv for his report – ever the little Bulgarian brother of the Russian leader. Hungary's Resző Nyers was less compliant and urged Gorbachëv to recognize that Comecon's day was over. Hans Modrow of East Germany revealed what he knew about Kohl's latest moves towards uniting the two Germanies in a confederation. Jaruzelski praised Gorbachëv for his encounter with Pope John Paul. (Bizarrely, he also called for the strengthening of Comecon.) What agitated Jaruzelski was the recent talk about a new German confederation. Ceauşescu could contain himself no longer. He exclaimed that Bush was boasting about the Malta summit as a moral and political victory for NATO; in flat contradiction of Gorbachëv, he said that world politics had become more dangerous than at any time in the Cold War. His remedy was to strengthen economic linkages in Eastern Europe and to hold an international conference of communist parties. He hit the tablecloth with the palms of his hands and, after a dramatic pause, commented: 'We simply can't understand why it's necessary to discredit several former leaders of fraternal parties and states.'[42]

When Gorbachëv proposed a joint denunciation of the 1968 invasion of Czechoslovakia, Ceauşescu interjected that he had done this very thing at the time; he now urged Gorbachëv to withdraw Soviet forces from Czechoslovak territory. Arguments broke out as a draft communiqué was passed from hand to hand – Mazowiecki versus Ryzhkov, Modrow versus Mazowiecki, Krenz versus Ceauşescu, even Jaruzelski versus Gorbachëv. The Hungarians were not against a Soviet pull-out from the region as a whole but were wary about picking out just one country such as Czechoslovakia. Ceauşescu objected to the time that all this was taking. Quick as a flash, Gorbachëv said: 'Pluralism, comrade Ceauşescu! For us this has long been the norm!'[43] The meeting ended with less applause for Gorbachëv than had been customary. This was of little surprise. Apart from Mladenov, nobody wanted to appear a Moscow stooge. And everyone understood the need to take Gorbachëv's optimism with a pinch of salt. Politics were in a condition of intense volatility. Lurking in the minds of East Europeans was the feeling that the future of the region was going to be dominated by a greater Germany. The Cold War was ending. New fears were growing as old fears faded.

Gorbachëv had a trickier task when reporting to his own Central Committee on 9 December. He again struck an optimistic note: Bush had given way on a lot, having promised to try to get the Jackson–Vanik amendment repealed so as to allow the USSR to buy American technology without restriction. America, Gorbachëv claimed, was likely to supply financial credits and make big investments in the Soviet economy – an exaggeration, not to say fabrication.[44] Alexander Melnikov, First Secretary of the Kemerovo Party Provincial Committee, criticized the handling of foreign policy. He charged that not even the entire Politburo was taking the big decisions. He wanted the Central Committee to have a greater influence. He noted that 'the entire bourgeois world' plus the Pope and every past and present adversary of the party pronounced approval of the leadership's course in reforms. Melnikov argued that this at the very least should give pause for thought – and the sooner, the better.[45] Gorbachëv lost patience as never before. He offered to step down and enable the Central Committee to elect a new Politburo. He was defiant: 'What I'm doing – I'm convinced – is what's necessary for the country!' Ligachëv, who was chairing the session, calmed the tempest by denying that Melnikov wanted rid of Gorbachëv. Melnikov in fact wanted exactly that result, but the dust settled and Gorbachëv prevailed.[46]

Gorbachëv felt chastened enough to reject a call to add 'the current political situation' to the agenda.[47] He even avoided the subject of the summit. Far from glorying in his performance off the Maltese coast, he gave no account of the proceedings. Leonid Zamyatin, Soviet Ambassador to the United Kingdom, stepped forward on his behalf. Although Zamyatin worried that the street demonstrations in Eastern Europe could spread to Moscow, he applauded Gorbachëv's foreign policy since 1985 and claimed that there were grounds for cautious optimism. He noted the hostility of the British, French and Italians to Kohl's Ten Points. This provided the USSR with a genuine opportunity to mould the process as the Warsaw Pact and NATO brought about the necessary stabilization.[48] Gorbachëv must have wished that Zamyatin had not been the sole Central Committee member to speak out in this way. At the summit, Bush had made him feel like a hero. The Western press offered psalms of praise. When the Soviet party leadership withheld its appreciation, he knew that danger was bearing down on him.

37. REDRAWING THE MAP OF EUROPE

The weeks after the Malta summit witnessed the fastest and least predictable mutation in East European politics since the late 1940s. America and the USSR were agreed on the need to avoid violence and ensure stability. They concurred that the Cold War was coming to a close. But problems could arise as the newly free states of the continent's eastern half gave consideration to the borders established in 1945. Reagan and Gorbachëv had begun their rapprochement by focusing on nuclear arms reduction, and the process was continuing under Bush. The chances of success suddenly depended on what happened to the map of Europe – and nowhere was cartographically more sensitive than East Germany.

On 5 December Gorbachëv and Shevardnadze held talks with Genscher in Moscow. They insisted that the German Democratic Republic was still 'the partner and ally' of the USSR. Genscher reported that Bush had told Kohl that he favoured the idea of a new confederation across German territory. This inflamed Gorbachëv, who felt that the NATO powers were doing things behind his back. He accused Kohl of trying to lord it over the East Germans.[1] Kohl had promised to do nothing to destabilize East Germany but then proceeded to announce his Ten Points. Gorbachëv called this a cardinal error; he said that if West Germany valued cooperation with the Soviet Union, this way of doing things had to stop.[2] He spoke more calmly next day on the phone to Mitterrand, who expressed alarm about Kohl's failure to recognize the Polish western frontier. Gorbachëv repeated his concerns about the idea of a confederation, the members of which usually had a single foreign and security policy; such an outcome, he said, would undermine the Warsaw Pact.[3] Although Mitterrand had no desire to see Germany reunited, he could see no way of halting the process; and he was hardly eager to intervene after hearing from Gorbachëv that he did not intend to act against Kohl.[4]

The carousel of talks continued on 8 December when Thatcher flew to Paris for consultations with Mitterrand. She had come armed with two continental maps. Pulling them from her handbag, she accused Kohl of intending to grab East Prussia and even Czechoslovakia. She charged him with inflaming a combustible situation.[5]

Mitterrand shared her concerns but noted that neither Bush nor Gorbachëv was willing to stop Kohl by force. He agreed that Eastern Europe was in a dangerously unpredictable condition, and he shuddered at what might happen if the USSR experienced a coup and mutated into a state ruled by militaristic nationalists. His sole proposal was that France and the United Kingdom should stick together.[6] This failed to soothe Thatcher, who called for action against Kohl. The trouble was that she herself refused to commit Britain to preventing the surge towards German unity. That evening she lost her temper face to face with Kohl when he declined to sign a joint communiqué confirming Europe's existing frontiers. Mitterrand thought Kohl was playing a perilous game. But Mitterrand did nothing, and Thatcher felt let down.[7] On returning to London, she called Ambassador Zamyatin at the Soviet embassy and urged that Gorbachëv should act on behalf of the common European good.[8] Zamyatin reported her as panicking about 'events in "our" Europe'; he speculated that she was desperate to demonstrate her remaining ability to influence current events.[9] Britain counted for less and less in the European situation. On 4 November Rodric Braithwaite commented in his diary about international politics: 'It's clear how little the UK counts, apart from the personal relationship with Mrs T.'[10]

Decommunized Eastern Europe had become a reality everywhere except for Romania and Albania, and Gorbachëv and Bush at their Malta summit had agreed on efforts to seek a peaceful resolution of problems of European security. Soviet leaders were aware that the Poles, Czechoslovaks and others were nervous about the territorial claims that Kohl might present. They saw the chance, in the debris of communism across the region, to step forward as the guarantors of East European borders. When Shevardnadze visited NATO headquarters in Brussels on 17 December, he put the Soviet official case to Secretary-General Manfred Wörner. The seed fell on stony ground. Wörner contended that NATO and the Warsaw Pact should focus on bringing the Vienna disarmament talks to completion.[11]

The USSR's leaders had long thought that Romania was on the brink of a political eruption. General Nicolae Militaru, an opponent of

Ceauşescu, approached the Soviet Ambassador in Bucharest and handed over a letter with a proposal to overthrow the dictator. The consistent policy in Moscow was to encourage the East European reformers to conduct the necessary changes through their own efforts. Gorbachëv endorsed the embassy's reaction: 'Correct: no reaction. We're not interfering in their affairs.'[12] Gorbachëv could see for himself at the Political Consultative Committee meeting on 4 December 1989 that the Romanian President was alarmed about the possibility of sharing the fate of Honecker and Zhivkov.[13] The disturbances in Timisoara intensified, and Shevardnadze feared the worst. He told Enrique Barón Crespo, president of the European Parliament and a leader of Spain's Socialist Workers Party, that if Ceauşescu chose to act 'against his people', there would be a tragedy like the Tbilisi butchery earlier in the year.[14]

So it very nearly proved to be. But on 21 December, when Ceauşescu appeared on the balcony of the Central Committee building in Bucharest, the crowd forgot its fear of the Securitate. Instead of applauding, they booed. Ceauşescu sensed mortal danger and fled by helicopter. The administration fell apart, and the party and army leaders crossed over into rebellion. Demonstrations filled the streets of all Romanian cities. Ceauşescu and his wife were captured. A summary trial was held on 25 December before they were led out to be shot.

The Politburo in Moscow had given recognition to the National Salvation Front two days earlier. It wanted the Romanians to sort out their own revolution. It approved measures to prevent Romanian-speaking Moldavians from crossing the Soviet border and joining in the protests. Priority was given to maintaining stability in the USSR.[15] But if the Warsaw Pact was to have a future, the Kremlin leadership had to find willing partners in Eastern Europe. On 3 January 1990, less than two weeks after the collapse of the Romanian communist administration, Shevardnadze visited Bucharest. Some in his entourage queried whether this made sense. Shevardnadze cut them short. Only by going in person to Romania, he insisted, could he work out how to restore Soviet influence.[16] He found it an encouraging experience. President Ion Iliescu appeared sympathetic to his rationale for the avoidance of strategic instability.[17] Somehow, Shevardnadze told himself on the flight back to Moscow, the Warsaw Pact would survive. However changeable the conditions might be, the Soviet Union could still succeed in discovering a path to its own 'salvation' in a Europe that was no longer divided between East and West.[18]

The German question mattered more than any speculation about the prospects for the Warsaw Pact. East Germany was in turmoil, and Kohl dropped the idea of a confederation and advocated a rapid merger that would prevent economic disaster.[19] On 26 January Gorbachëv held an informal gathering on Old Square, where he said: 'It is now already clear that unification is inevitable, and we don't have the moral right to oppose it.'[20] Kryuchkov agreed: 'Modrow is a transitory figure; [he] behaves on the basis of concessions but soon there'll be nothing for him to concede.' In Kryuchkov's opinion, it was crucial for the Soviet media to prepare popular opinion for what was about to occur.[21] Gorbachëv declared: 'In these conditions we have to defend the interests of our country to the utmost, secure a recognition of borders, a peace treaty together with the departure of the Federal Republic of Germany from NATO – or at least with the withdrawal of foreign troops and the demilitarization of all Germany.'[22]

On 29 January the Warsaw Pact held a discussion about the size of conventional forces adequate to preserve peace and stability.[23] The Kremlin's cooperation was a requirement for the withdrawal of Soviet forces. It was important that nothing took place near the garrisons that might provoke trouble. Soviet officials explained to Czechoslovakia's President Havel that the USSR did not yet have enough housing in the USSR for the returning troops. For them, this was no trivial matter. Havel retorted that the Soviet leadership had received plenty of time to make its preparations. Surely, he said, its intelligence agencies had been telling them for a long while about what people were thinking in Eastern Europe.[24] But he soon calmed down. Like the other new rulers, he was wary of annoying the USSR at a time when nobody could yet be sure about whether the new Germany would recognize Europe's post-war frontiers. He avoided making political trouble for the Soviet leadership. If Gorbachëv were to fall from power in Moscow, nobody could say what kind of government might emerge in its place. The leaders of the anticommunist revolutions sympathized with the secessionist movements in the USSR; but apart from a few official visits by Polish politicians to Kiev and Vilnius, it was noticeable that they withheld active assistance to the popular fronts of the Soviet republics.

Chief of the General Staff Moiseev objected to how Havel had spoken: 'We're not some second-class power for anyone to talk to us like that.' This time it was Shevardnadze who expressed exasperation: 'You were told four years ago about the mood in Hungary, Czechoslovakia, Poland. What, did the intelligence people really not keep you informed? And was there no awareness that sooner or later we'd have to leave? So why didn't you prepare for departure?'[25] Gorbachëv sensed danger and took the precaution of involving the rest of the political leadership in the process of withdrawal. The vote of each Politburo member was recorded.[26] In February 1990 the Soviet authorities agreed to withdraw their forces from Hungary and Czechoslovakia by July 1991.[27]

On 5 February, at the Central Committee plenum, there was a barrage of criticism. Akhromeev made an angry speech.[28] Other leading grumblers about official policy – Baklanov, Zaikov and Moiseev – were denied the floor. Baklanov had intended to deplore the absence of criticism of US military intervention in Panama. He lamented the treatment of Honecker, who seemed likely to be summonsed to court in the new Germany.[29] Zaikov had hoped to tell the Central Committee: 'Our sacred duty is to strengthen the Armed Forces, show care for the Army and Navy and for the people who had dedicated their lives to the Motherland's defence.' He wanted to call it a crime to discredit the men on active military service.[30] Moiseev had intended to be trenchant about the inattentiveness to the armed forces.[31] It was no accident that people from the military-industrial complex were the first to make an assault on Gorbachëv's position. Soviet troops were scurrying back home under a hail of obloquy in the countries where they had been garrisoned. A sense of affront was spreading in the USSR. Many political and military leaders shared these feelings. They had gone along with Gorbachëv and began to regret the consequences. As yet, they lacked a leader for their dissent, but there was no surety that they would always be quiet and inactive.[32]

Bush and Gorbachëv had intended to hold another summit in February 1990, and Baker wrote to Shevardnadze about the need to give practical shape to the understandings reached at Malta.[33] Arms control was at the forefront of American concerns. The Americans soon recognized that the growing uncertainties in Eastern Europe had to rise to the top of their agenda. The German question towered over everything. Baker flew to Moscow for preparatory discussions.

On 9 February he told Shevardnadze why America disliked the Soviet demand for the new Germany to withdraw from both NATO and the Warsaw Pact and adopt a neutral status. The Germans, he emphasized, had to be deflected from acquiring their own nuclear weapons.[34] He pushed for agreements on nuclear and conventional forces. He repeated the case for Najibullah to step down in Afghani-stan if ever there was to be a prospect of peace there. He promised that Washington would recognize a Nicaraguan government under Sandi-nista leader Daniel Ortega so long as the elections were fairly conducted, but he expressed unhappiness about the USSR's failure to withdraw support for Cuba.[35] Shevardnadze rejected the demand about Najibullah and deprecated American actions in Panama.[36] When Baker put the arguments to Gorbachëv, he sensed that he was making some progress and thought Gorbachëv was showing greater flexibility than Shevardnadze. Kohl too had the feeling that the Soviet leadership was beginning to budge.[37] But the discussions were incon-clusive.[38] Baker had tried hard to reassure Gorbachëv by offering a 'guarantee that Germany's unification will not lead to the eastward spread of the NATO military organization'.[39] He failed to convince him. On that crucial point there was no meeting of minds.[40]

On 10 February Baker addressed the Foreign Relations Committee of the USSR Supreme Soviet. Expressing thanks for the honour of speaking to 'the Founding Fathers of a new Soviet Union', he referred warmly to 'my friend, Foreign Minister Shevardnadze' and claimed that he and his President 'very much want *perestroika* to succeed'. According to Baker, they desired this for the sake of 'the Soviet people' and because the USSR's foreign and defence policies had become 'fundamentally less threatening to the American people than the hostile Stalinist approaches of the past'. He talked of the Cold War in the past tense.

He undertook to help in securing the release of Soviet POWs in Afghanistan and in getting the Jackson–Vanik amendment repealed. At the same time he emphasized that America had never recognized the USSR's annexation of the Baltic states in the Second World War. He claimed a legal basis for American military action against Presi-dent Noriega in Panama. He made the case for the new Germany to belong to NATO. He suggested that the USSR could do better things with its finances than make grants to Cuba, Angola, Nicaragua and Cambodia – he jibed that if there was one politician whom Castro criticized more than Bush, it was Gorbachëv.[41] He insisted that the Bush administration wanted Gorbachëv's reforms to succeed; but as a former Treasury Secretary he believed that Soviet leaders had to make the choice between a command economy and a market economy: 'But you can't have something in between.' Although he wanted to help, he had difficulty with American conservatives who opposed his proposal to relax the CoCom restrictions on trade with the USSR.[42]

His listeners brought up their grumbles about the mujahidin, the Jackson–Vanik amendment and America's armed intervention in Panama; they also asked him to explain American policy on the Soviet republics of the Baltic. Akhromeev pushed him to accept a moratorium on nuclear bomb test explosions. Baker made no concessions other than promising to consider measures to reduce the CoCom technological restrictions. He refused to give a commitment to permitting the purchase of computer licences. He advocated the new Germany's membership of NATO.[43]

Gorbachëv received Kohl in Moscow on the same day. They agreed that Germany should be unified in a calm fashion, and Kohl reported on the growing problems that faced the East German leadership in advance of the forthcoming elections. The currency was volatile. There was a continual exodus of people to West Germany. Political groupings were engaged in furious attacks on each other. The whole situation was dangerously febrile. He stressed that although he wanted to recognize the existing frontier with Poland and Czechoslovakia, he still needed to assure himself of support in German public opinion. He tried to assure the USSR that nothing would take place against the interests of Soviet security: 'We consider that NATO mustn't expand the sphere of its activity.' He indicated that he understood the task that Gorbachëv was shouldering in explaining this to the Soviet people. It was a pleasant exchange of opinions and Gorbachëv thanked Kohl for that.[44]

Next day, on 11 February, Baker and Shevardnadze sped from Moscow to the Open Skies Conference which was about to start in Ottawa. The agenda included the removal of restrictions on East–West travel. Shevardnadze also wanted to discuss the German question, and he and Baker held six negotiating sessions in the course of one and a half days.[45] When Baker talked about the timing of German reunification, Shevardnadze said he would have to consult the Politburo.[46] He told Genscher that even a reunified country was far from a settled common objective. Genscher pointed out that Gorbachëv and Kohl had already recognized the principle in a joint communiqué; but Shevardnadze and his team insisted on moving slowly on German affairs, and the statement agreed with Baker contained no mention of the word 'reunification'.[47] Shevardnadze was pleased with his performance, calling it 'the beautiful harvest of Ottawa'.[48] On his return to

Moscow, Shevardnadze held a discussion with his ministry collegium. His opinion was that Germany ought to attain its unity in the course of a lengthy process that avoided sudden improvisation; and he wanted to ensure the introduction of reliable security structures for Europe as a whole.[49]

Kryuchkov resented the way that things were going on a broader front. In the KGB's annual report to Gorbachëv as Chairman of the Supreme Soviet, he claimed that the priority had been to discover the 'military-strategic plans of the enemy'. Despite the recent warmth of US–USSR diplomacy, it remained the KGB's task to look for 'signs of preparations for a possible sudden unleashing of a nuclear-missile war'.[50] Surveillance continued on 'nationalist, anti-socialist, extremist forces' in the USSR; but Kryuchkov added that his agency had helped with the rehabilitation of 838,630 Soviet citizens subjected to repression in the 1930s and 1940s.[51] Other activities were more traditional for the KGB. It continued to conduct scientific and industrial espionage on behalf of the USSR's military needs. (Evidently Kryuchkov felt that such needs took precedence over those of ill-provided Soviet consumers.) As regards the inspections of Soviet forces that were prescribed under the Intermediate-Range Nuclear Forces Treaty, the KGB alleged that the CIA had exploited the opportunity to send a hundred agents into the USSR. He sounded an alarm about how foreign firms were taking advantage of the new cooperatives that were springing up in Moscow; he also warned about the threat to constitutional order in the Baltic republics.[52]

On 28 February Bush phoned Gorbachëv with a report on his talks with Kohl. The Americans and West Germans were of the opinion that the new Germany should belong to NATO. When Gorbachëv demurred, Bush tried to win him over by promising that East Germany would retain special separate status that would mollify the USSR's concerns; and he sensed a willingness on the Soviet side to continue to negotiate.[53] But Gorbachëv also expressed a deep worry. Kohl had still not declared his acceptance of the post-war frontiers in Europe, and Gorbachëv could see no possibility of progress until there was a change of attitude in Bonn.[54]

In March, as public criticisms of his policies grew in strength, Gorbachëv strove to boost his status by getting the Supreme Soviet to change his title from Chairman to President. This was done without reference to the electorate. The Supreme Soviet readily endorsed what he requested, but its obedience only papered over the cracks in the unity of the leadership. Meanwhile, Yeltsin continued his political comeback. After winning election from Sverdlovsk to the Congress of People's Deputies of Russia, he proceeded to be made Chairman of its Supreme Soviet despite Gorbachëv's efforts to deter the deputies from voting for him. Yeltsin was showing an ability to attract support from a wide range of people discontented with the Politburo. He saw his chance to use Russia, easily the biggest Soviet republic, as a base from which to undermine Gorbachëv. This would become manifest on 12 June, when the Russian Congress passed a declaration of sovereignty. Nobody could predict what would happen next, but obviously there was a possibility that Russia would soon start to follow its own internal policies and even to represent itself in international relations. Gorbachëv had reason for concern.

In Soviet republic after republic, national assertiveness was on the rise. The usual organized form was the 'popular front'. The common feature of the fronts was distrust of the Moscow political leadership. They brought together diverse trends of opinion and usually even attracted local communist party members. They first flourished in Lithuania, Latvia and Estonia, and soon they were emerging in nearly every republic outside Russia. Gorbachëv's reforms had enabled their creation. Now he had to contend with their challenge to his authority.

Baker and Shevardnadze talked again in March while attending the celebrations in Namibia for the country's independence. Shevardnadze affirmed that Soviet leaders agreed that it would be dangerous if the Germans adopted a neutral status in world politics: 'That would be a big problem.' He admitted: 'We don't know the answer to the problem. You and I will have to discuss this more and our Presidents will have to discuss this as well.' The Kremlin, Shevardnadze indicated, approved of American forces staying on in Germany after the USSR's military withdrawal. But although he had confidence in Kohl, he expressed a concern that a future government – perhaps one of the political far right – might close down the American military bases.[55] Shevardnadze ended on a downbeat note: 'Yes, we will manage the economy, as difficult as it is – but the nationalities are another matter.'[56] Baker gained a glimpse into the Soviet political crisis and reckoned that Gorbachëv and the reformers had yet to draw 'their bottom lines'.[57] When Shevardnadze spoke to Genscher in South Africa a couple of days later, he emphasized the Soviet objections to any scheme for the eastward expansion of NATO. The revolutions of the previous year had ended decades of strategic stability, and there was growing criticism in Moscow of the abandonment of communist traditions. Shevardnadze warned that *perestroika* was vulnerable to shocks. If it came to an end, a dictator could rise to power in the USSR. Genscher, only half-jokingly, replied that Shevardnadze was talking like a Western hawk.[58]

On 18 March, in line with Kohl's demands, elections were held in East Germany. The communists had campaigned as the Party of Democratic Socialism; like others in Europe, east and west, they recognized that the word 'communism' was toxic in the opinion of the electorate. Nevertheless, the Party of Democratic Socialism came only third in the contest; and groups of ex-dissidents who wanted to slow down the process of merging the two Germanies were trounced. Victory went by a large margin to the political coalition led by Christian Democrats under Lothar de Maizière – and de Maizière replaced Modrow as Prime Minister.[59]

Gorbachëv could not afford to become exclusively preoccupied with the German question. Politics in Moscow was hectic as never earlier. Chief of the General Staff Moiseev and Central Committee Secretary Baklanov felt that the USSR was offering to give up too many of its strategic nuclear forces. Why should the Soviet side destroy more missiles than America? At the Big Five meeting on 10 March, Moiseev had attacked Shevardnadze in his absence.[60] Baklanov wrote to Gorbachëv that the proposal for a fifty per cent reduction in strategic weapons was being mishandled; he regretted that military parity was no longer the leadership's official goal. Gorbachëv passed everything over to Zaikov's Politburo Commission. As ever, he wanted there to be collective responsibility. Zaikov took Baklanov's initiative as an attack on his recent work. Calm returned only on 30 March, when Zaikov reconvened the Big Five and, at Gorbachëv's suggestion, took note of Baklanov's points without agreeing to change policy. Stress was laid on the need for 'constructive approaches' in the talks with America.[61] Together with Moiseev, Baklanov criticized Gorbachëv himself for allowing a collapse in the country's defensive capacity. He asked for his opinion to be recorded separately from the rest of the Big Five.[62]

As a concession to the critics, Gorbachëv designated Akhromeev to lead the team to talk to the American working group in Washington. Akhromeev had recently expressed concern about the affects of *perestroika* by declaring: 'For seventy years the Americans have attempted to destroy our Union and they've finally achieved their end.' Deputy Foreign Affairs Minister Bessmertnykh added: 'It's not they who have destroyed it but we ourselves.'[63]

The Politburo nevertheless approved the Big Five's advice; it also highlighted the need to demand that the new Germany should stay out of NATO. Shevardnadze was to object to recent American statements, including the conditions being laid down for private companies to invest in the USSR.[64] Gorbachëv wrote a letter for Shevardnadze to hand over to Bush in preparation for a bilateral agreement to halve the number of strategic nuclear weapons.[65] Shevardnadze set off on his mission pleased that the general line of policy had been confirmed. But he felt the need to explain to Baker that the Soviet side felt a growing dislike of attempts to stampede it into decisions. The conversations were less amicable than in the recent past.[66] Baker repeated his objection to the USSR's involvement with Cuba and to Najibullah's retention of power in Afghanistan. Shevardnadze replied that foreign powers had no business in bringing down a country's rulers. These were routine exchanges. But when Baker mentioned that two or three members of the Warsaw Pact were in favour of the new Germany joining NATO, Shevardnadze grew agitated and demanded that the USSR should be centrally involved in any decision.[67]

Apparently he also indicated that the Kremlin's standpoint was not immutable.[68] Soviet critics of Shevardnadze and Gorbachëv worried that they were edging towards unacceptable compromises. The situation was aggravated by revelations about the USSR's past dealings with allies in Eastern Europe. Moscow had sold SS-23s to Bulgaria, East Germany and Czechoslovakia. Shevardnadze asked the Americans to have personal confidence in him and Gorbachëv. At a Washington press conference on 6 April he claimed that neither of them had known about the sale of those missiles; he added that the Soviet Union had scrupulously observed the terms of the Intermediate-Range Nuclear Forces Treaty.[69] Akhromeev took offence at Shevardnadze's words. He was to claim that Gorbachëv and Shevardnadze had known about the sale all along and to speculate that Shevardnadze improvised an answer which involved a blatant untruth because he had not mastered his ministerial brief. When Akhromeev's opportunity arose to set the record straight at the American Senate Armed Services Committee a month later, his speech removed the taint which, in his opinion, had attached itself to the reputation of the Soviet armed forces.[70]

On the return flight to Moscow, Akhromeev accentuated his

unease about trends in the negotiations. Shevardnadze sensed political danger after vain attempts to win him over. Akhromeev sat in his plane seat in stony silence.[71] Shevardnadze recognized that Akhromeev was right that the Americans were asking the USSR to scrap more strategic missiles than themselves.[72] Akhromeev was the most malleable of the leading military figures; Gorbachëv and Shevardnadze had the unenviable task of persuading the rest of the military lobby, who were far less flexible, that defensive sufficiency was a better criterion for strategic preparation – an argument they found easier to put to a visiting delegation of US Senators led by John Glenn than to make before their own General Staff.[73]

The one bright light in the situation was that the West Germans told the Americans that they would openly recognize Europe's existing frontiers.[74] Kohl had finally done what had been demanded of him, and Chernyaev and Shakhnazarov advised Gorbachëv to let Germany decide on its own constitutional and military future. Falin took the opposite approach. Recalling the year 1941, he cautioned that the new Germany might turn against Russia. On 18 April he sent a memorandum to Gorbachëv arguing for the need to compel the Germans to stay out of NATO.[75] Gorbachëv said that the safest way of handling Germany after reunification was to impose dual membership of NATO and the Warsaw Pact.[76] Shevardnadze warned Genscher against pushing too hard since it was no longer inconceivable that Gorbachëv would lose power as popular dissatisfaction with his economic management rose and political criticism increased in the Supreme Soviet and the media. A different government, he said, was unlikely to accommodate Chancellor Kohl's demands.[77] Baker at last appreciated the risks of upsetting the framework of cooperation that Reagan had established. Recognizing Shevardnadze as an indispensable collaborator, he asked his officials to pass on his 'deep gratitude' for the work that the Foreign Affairs Minister had accomplished.[78] Shevardnadze for his part assured Baker: 'I don't want a dispute about which of us is being the more generous in concessions.'[79]

The international situation, however, remained fraught. American and British authorities came to the Foreign Affairs Ministry with disturbing information about the USSR's illegal production of biological weapons. The Politburo's experts had assured it that their Soviet scientists restricted their research to defensive purposes.[80] America and the United Kingdom rejected the claim. On 14 May ambassadors Matlock and Braithwaite told Deputy Minister Bessmertnykh that Moscow must bring the programme quickly to a close. Braithwaite stressed that Zaikov knew all about what was going on.[81] Matlock added that Baker would want to discuss the matter with Shevardnadze at the next opportunity.[82]

Zaikov reported that a programme had indeed been under way in breach of the 1972 Biological Weapons Convention. He contended that the USSR had done this after discovering that NATO countries were circumventing their treaty obligations by basing facilities in third countries. The Soviet programme had been halted in 1989 when the scientist Vladimir Pasechnik defected to the United Kingdom and informed the British authorities about what was happening. Zaikov assured Gorbachëv and Shevardnadze that steps had been taken to open the research laboratories to inspection by 1990.[83] Under Western pressure, the decision was taken to end the programme. The production of chemical weapons was also to cease, and the Soviet and American administrations agreed on destroying their stockpiles by 2002. Chief of the General Staff Moiseev expostulated that the USSR lacked the necessary facilities.[84] The Big Five recommended that funds should be made available.[85]

The talks were kept under wraps since America and Britain wanted to avoid doing anything that might undermine Gorbachëv. Not that every Western politician behaved tactfully: US Defense Secretary Cheney rocked the boat by predicting that Gorbachëv would falter and probably be replaced by someone hostile to the West.[86] The Soviet military threat remained of deep concern for him.[87] He was saying what many in the Bush administration had always thought but felt it impolitic to express. Soviet leaders were aware of the growing scepticism and Shevardnadze pleaded with Genscher to recognize the acute problems that Gorbachëv was facing. The military victory over the Third Reich in 1945 had turned the USSR into a superpower, and its people were not going to forgive the current leadership if it were to lose that status.[88] When Shevardnadze met Baker on 1 May, he reminded him about the sacrifices made by Soviet citizens in defeating Nazi Germany. He stressed that the enemies of *perestroika* were capable of embarrassing Gorbachëv over the German question.[89] Western powers had a choice: either to deal gently with Gorbachëv or to take the risk of enabling his adversaries to get rid of him. The stakes could not be higher.

On 3 May Baker set out American purposes at a NATO Council meeting in Brussels. He stressed that the planned arms reductions did not mean that America would remove its entire nuclear stockpile and conventional forces from Europe. Their presence, he stressed, was crucial to 'long-term European stability'. Baker also announced that Bush, in a spirit of conciliation, would be cancelling several scheduled sectors of America's programme of strategic military modernization. He mentioned Washington's rising concern about the charged atmosphere in Moscow. He expressed regret that Gorbachëv was failing to push forward rapidly towards a market economy. He was perplexed about how to help Estonia, Latvia and Lithuania without boxing Gorbachëv into a corner. Baker voiced optimism about Gorbachëv's chances of political survival despite the growing public criticism in Moscow. His hope was that the Soviet leadership would accept that it was in everyone's interest that the new Germany should belong to NATO.[90] Much remained for America and the USSR to negotiate. There was no longer any disagreement about the German state's eastern frontier, but months of wrangling had produced no covenant on the geography of European military security. The campaign to end the Cold War stood at risk.

38. THE NEW GERMANY

The American administration had no plan for how to break the deadlock. Gorbachëv too was bereft of new ideas, and the cards in his hands for the next round of bidding were the weakest he had ever held. Being committed to military withdrawal from Eastern Europe, he could not recant without loss of political credit around the world. He also depended on America's cooperation in order to make savings through agreements on arms reduction. The Soviet Union was hurtling towards financial dissolution. The need for external assistance was no longer disguisable, and Gorbachëv projected an appeal to the capitalist powers. In early summer 1990 he sent out his officials on a mission to obtain emergency financial credits.[1]

The Americans wanted his assent to their ideas for Europe's political and territorial future. They oiled the diplomatic machinery that might bring Gorbachëv over to their view on the German question. The West Germans were delaying the process by omitting to promise that NATO forces would never operate on the territory of East Germany. Baker wrote to Genscher asking him to make a clear declaration that would assuage the USSR's objections. Washington and Bonn, he avowed, had to cooperate in lightening the atmosphere.[2] When Baker met Gorbachëv in Moscow on 11 May, the new Germany headed the agenda. They also discussed how to reduce the size of conventional forces. Gorbachëv's ideas were geared towards a gradual sequence of measures that might last nine whole years; he also thought it might take three years to achieve an agreement. He wanted numerical equality between NATO and the Warsaw Pact; he suggested that each side should retain no more than 1,350,000 troops and 20,000 tanks.[3] Kohl's aide Teltschik flew to Moscow for secret talks on 14 May. Ryzhkov made no attempt to disguise the economic disaster that was looming. He made a request for financial assistance in the form of credits that could be repaid over a period of fifteen years. Teltschik had brought along a couple of leading bankers.[4] The questions of German reunification and Soviet economic security were becoming entwined.

Nothing could happen until Gorbachëv and Kohl got together, and Teltschik recalled that the Soviet leader had once proposed a meeting in his native area around Stavropol and suggested that he needed credits to the value of DM5 billion.[5] Kohl used the opportunity of a trip to Washington, in a one-on-one conversation, to gauge Bush's opinion. Bush repeated that he could see no sense in offering direct financial aid to the USSR. This disconcerted Kohl, who asked: 'My question is do we want to help him or see someone else [in power in Moscow].' Bush lamely replied: 'Probably, but I can't say who would replace him or how the economy would go.'[6] Kohl was starting to think he needed to take the initiative. Teltschik heard from Scowcroft that Baker and Shevardnadze were making no progress on the German question.[7] The West Germans wished to break the deadlock and Kohl redoubled his endeavours with the bankers and laid plans to meet Gorbachëv in mid-July 1990.[8] Charm oozed from Genscher when he next encountered Shevardnadze. Sometimes he overdid it, as when he said: 'You're a superpower and we are a small, divided country!' Shevardnadze had a wry smile when replying: 'What modesty!'[9] But he and Gorbachëv could not fail to notice that while the Western powers were eager to talk about the new Germany, they were reluctant to help the economy of the old USSR.

It was with this in mind that Gorbachëv travelled to America for his summit meeting with Bush. He could be sure of a warm welcome from the President, who had confided to Kohl: 'The press says I am a Gorbachëv lover. That may be true. I have met the other kind. You've met Yazov. If you sent to central casting for the stereotype of a Soviet general, they would send you Yazov.'[10] Talks opened at the White House on 31 May 1990 before being transferred to Camp David. Bush wanted Gorbachëv to feel he was among friends. At Camp David, he asked whether he would like to drive a golf buggy. Gorbachëv jumped at the opportunity: 'Why ever not? I'm an old farm mechanic!' He applied his foot too hard on the accelerator and nearly crashed into a tree. He joked: 'I hope I'll not be accused of an attempt on the life of the President of the United States.' Gorbachëv also tried out the fitness treadmill. Not having exercised for years, he found this exhausting and transferred to an exercise bike. Bush nevertheless achieved his goal and the atmosphere was good-humoured from beginning to end.[11]

They went over many of the topics that had troubled them at the Malta summit: Lithuania, Cuba, Germany. Bush said he knew how hard it was for Soviet people, who had lost so many millions of lives in the war against the Third Reich, to look calmly upon the changed situation in Eastern Europe. He asked Gorbachëv to understand his own political difficulties over Lithuania. When Gorbachëv insisted that he intended to bring economic reform to the USSR, Bush pointed out that 'you've got to go all the way or it won't be effective'. He added that 'it's just like being pregnant – you can't be a little bit pregnant'. Quick as a flash, Gorbachëv replied: 'Well, you can't have a baby in the first month either – it takes nine months, and you want to be careful that you don't have an abortion along the way.' The point impressed Bush.[12] But he still could not give Gorbachëv the trade agreement that the Soviet leaders wanted. As he had said repeatedly, the Vanik-Jackson amendment had yet to be repealed. Gorbachëv became 'very agitated' at this and warned Bush that there was going to be a 'disaster' in the USSR unless external funds became available.[13] This was the first time that he talked this way. At Malta he had been the enabler of East European liberation; now he was a needy supplicant.

Gorbachëv turned to Falin for help in explaining to the Americans why East Germany stayed important to the USSR. A gap was opening between Gorbachëv and Shevardnadze. Falin later claimed that Gorbachëv told him: 'We were both right not to listen to Eduard. Of course, it's difficult to calculate what will concretely happen, but the Americans do have reserve variants or also variants about Germany's membership of NATO.'[14] Gorbachëv and Bush met without their advisers and agreed on an important compromise. They agreed that USSR would accept the new Germany's membership of NATO if the peoples of both Germanies endorsed the idea, and America would respect the decision if it went the other way.[15] The change of stance took Bush by surprise and he could imagine that Akhromeev and Falin were taking it badly. When he restated his understanding about what had been agreed, Gorbachëv repeated that he would respect the decision if the new Germany decided to stay outside NATO and adopt the status of a neutral power; and Bush confirmed his assent. Akhromeev and Falin began to mutter noisily. Shevardnadze tugged Gorbachëv by the sleeve and gesticulated frantically. Sensing suddenly that he had overstepped the mark, he recanted his earlier statement. The Soviet team fell apart before American eyes: there had never been a summit like it.[16]

Gorbachëv tried to unshoulder the negotiating duties to Shevardnadze and Baker. Usually Shevardnadze was cooperative, but not this time. Shevardnadze retorted that it was for the two Presidents to clarify policy. He relented only when he saw how distraught Gorbachëv had become. Shevardnadze and Baker agreed a verbal formula that answered the German question in ambiguous terms.[17] Nothing definite had been decided. Bush felt again that Gorbachëv was willing to be more flexible than in previous months, but as yet nothing was agreed on paper, and there were signs that Gorbachëv might face dangerous criticism in Moscow if he yielded ground.

On 7 June the Political Consultative Committee of the Warsaw Pact met in Moscow's Oktyabrskaya Hotel for Gorbachëv to explain Soviet policy. Czechoslovakia's Václav Havel exclaimed: 'This is the first time that I speak here, a place which always resounded to the dithyrambs of praise to the leaders of the Soviet Union and its politics.' Gorbachëv, defending the rationale of a renewed Pact, declared: 'We have said goodbye to the model that led our countries and people into a dead end and, on the basis of a sovereign choice made by each country, we have entered a new path of development.'[18] He welcomed the Eastern European revolutions: 'They are, for the most part, proceeding in a democratic and civilized manner, and we are not of the opinion that these changes are detrimental to fundamental Soviet interests.'[19] His big worry was about the German question. He proposed that Germany should stay outside the existing military blocs – at the most it should become an associate member of both the Warsaw Pact and NATO.[20] (Bush was confidentially calling this a 'screwy idea.')[21] Gorbachëv accepted that US forces were a stabilizing factor in Western Europe. He wanted to conserve the Warsaw Pact, primarily as a political organization that would contribute to the maintenance of security throughout Europe.[22] The final declaration placed an emphasis on fostering agreement among 'sovereign states with equal rights.'[23]

Later that month Kohl secured the assent of both German parliaments, in Bonn and East Berlin, recognizing the post-war border with Poland.[24] It had taken him months of persuasion to achieve this. He relieved the worries of East Europeans who thought that the new Germany could have expansionist pretensions. But he inadvertently weakened their need for Gorbachëv's support – and the rationale for the survival of the Warsaw Pact was put into question.

Gorbachëv in his earlier foreign policy had advanced in a straight line with only occasional zig-zags. Now he faced accusations of running around in ever-decreasing circles. In mid-June, Central Committee Secretary Baklanov could stand it no longer and spoke to the press about his concerns about the concessions being made in the arms talks.[25] Cracks were appearing in the leadership. Falin in the Party International Department had implored Gorbachëv in vain to be firm with Kohl, and now he felt disinclined to hold his tongue. On 19 July he told Ambassador Braithwaite that German politicians after Kohl's period in office could demand back the territory lost to Poland in 1945. Falin was in a frantic mood. He speculated that the Germans might seek to compensate the Poles at the expense of Belorussia and Ukraine, which by then might be independent states, by returning to Poland the eastern territories it had lost at the end of the war.[26] This showed that Falin had lost his grip on reality, but also that the new politics in the USSR enabled him and the other critics of Gorbachëv to air their opinions. It was urgent for the Soviet leadership to reach a firm and safe settlement about the new Germany and focus on its own political, economic and national problems.

NATO started a two-day summit in London on 5 July. America aimed to keep forces on the continent for as long as its allies wanted, but the active contingent was to be scaled down. Bush obtained assent to his proposals for the alliance to introduce 'a significantly reduced reliance on nuclear weapons, particularly those of the shortest range'. This was a much less ambitious objective of disarmament than Reagan had aimed at. But the final communiqué emphasized that NATO no longer needed to contemplate the use of its nuclear arsenal 'except as weapons of last resort'.[27]

Gorbachëv's appeal for financial credits was high on the agenda even before 10 July 1990, when the G7 summit started in Houston, Texas. Kohl and Bush kept in contact through the summer months. Gorbachëv was indicating an urgent need for assistance; he hoped for a multinational economic package that would enable him to buy much-needed consumer goods for Soviet consumers – and he asked Kohl for a direct loan of DM5 billion, implying that he would give something in return.[28] Kohl inferred that the Soviet leader was hinting at the possibility of concessions by the USSR if Deutschmarks were made available to the its stricken budget. He did not want to miss a momentous opportunity. On the eve of the summit he had a final pre-paratory talk with the American President at Houston's Manor Lodge and campaigned for an agreement to go to Gorbachëv's aid. Bush refused to budge. His opinion was that the USSR had yet to conduct the necessary economic reform and cease propping up Fidel Castro. But he could see why Kohl wanted to take a different stance and was determined to offer finance. He confirmed that he would not stand in his way. On Kohl's separate plans for a deal with Moscow, he said simply, 'That is a matter for the Chancellor of Germany.'[29]

Bush made no attempt to use the Jackson–Vanik amendment as an excuse, and some of his fellow leaders disliked his bluntness.[30] Thatcher, though, agreed with him. Opposing the provision of credits, she voiced a preference to limit assistance to advice and expertise. Mitterrand wanted some kind of action to help Gorbachëv without saying what he had in mind. The drift of the discussion alarmed Kohl, who warned that the world faced an immense challenge and said that the USSR deserved urgent assistance in opening up its economy. He accused the summit of treating Gorbachëv's message to the summit as if it came from the Congo. Kohl drew attention to Gorbachëv's achievements in removing abuses of human rights, whereas China had an awful record of oppression and yet was in receipt of Western assistance. Asked for an explanation of this discrepancy, Bush replied: 'China and the USSR aren't one and the same thing.' Although Mulroney added he wanted to assist, he omitted to say how; and Japan's Toshiki Kaifu shared in the opposition to credits.[31]

This left the Soviet leadership in a lamentable condition, and Gorbachëv was not alone in foreseeing calamity. Ryzhkov, who had primary responsibility for the economy, warned that bankruptcy was certain in the next six months unless external assistance was forthcoming.[32] Though he was no advocate of a comprehensive transition to market economics, he supported any move that might attract foreign credits. While the Council of Ministers despaired about the economy, the General Staff became despondent about international security. The East European revolutions deprived the Soviet Union of genuine allies. Only fears about the new Germany and political instability in Moscow stopped a mass exodus from the Warsaw Pact. When NATO Secretary General Wörner arrived in Moscow in the summer, Moiseev made no effort at hiding his judgement that the Pact was no longer of military value.[33]

Gorbachëv knew that he would take most of the blame for the growing military and economic trouble. He decided to take drastic action. Evidently he had some inkling about the unique standpoint that Kohl was taking and confirmed the invitation to visit Moscow and the Stavropol region for talks starting on 14 July. Kohl's entourage understood that something big was in the offing.[34] Excitement mounted on the West German side – and Finance Minister Waigel confirmed the government's guarantee for credits to the value of DM5 billion.[35] But what about German reunification in all this? Falin sent a memo to Gorbachëv urging firmness and repeated the idea of establishing German reunification on the basis of a confederal constitution so that East Germany could stay inside the Warsaw Pact.[36] Gorbachëv phoned him deep into the night of 9–10 July. When Falin implied that Kohl's actions were reminiscent of what Hitler did to Austria in 1938, Gorbachëv offered no cheer: 'I'll do what I can. Only that I'm afraid the train has already departed.'[37] Falin had been a witness to his confusion at Camp David and was known to believe that undue softness had been shown to Kohl. (If Gorbachëv knew the details of Falin's maladroit overture to Kohl's aide Teltschik, he overlooked them.) The danger was that Falin might become the standard-bearer for a revolt on the German question – and the potential consequences of such an outcome were deeply disturbing.

On 14 July Kohl arrived in Moscow. He got on splendidly with Gorbachëv, who thanked him for the DM5 billion in credits. He called it a 'chess move' that was pointed in the right direction. They agreed that world politics were entering a fresh stage. Ignoring the official temperance campaign, Gorbachëv offered a glass of vodka to his guest. (He recommended it as an ecologically sound product.) Curiously, this prompted Ryzhkov to propose the idea of joint German and Soviet breweries.[38] But Gorbachëv still declined to say yes to Germany, once reunified, belonging to NATO. Kohl said he would not go south to Arkhyz with Gorbachëv unless this was agreed, and he took the absence of an objection by Gorbachëv as a sign of compliance.[39] The Arkhyz trip was friendly and productive. Gorbachëv was copying the American technique of using familiar surroundings for informal discussions that could give momentum to a diplomatic breakthrough. Among those accompanying them were Shevardnadze and Genscher as well as economics ministers Theodor Waigel and Stepan Sitaryan. Raisa too joined them. Whereas Kohl brought along Teltschik, Chernyaev decided to stay in Moscow: he was feeling depressed and contemplating retirement, despite the historic moment that was at hand.[40] Gorbachëv and Kohl dined together and held friendly talks. This was the first time that they had enjoyed themselves like this, and Gorbachëv was pleased with the results.

The two leaders reached a momentous agreement. Gorbachëv yielded to Kohl's scheme for German reunification, including the new Germany's right to belong to NATO. Kohl was delighted. He in turn assured Gorbachëv that Poland need have no concern about its western frontier. The Chancellor hoped to sign a treaty with the Polish government very soon; he also promised that NATO forces would never operate on the territory of the soon-to-be-abolished German Democratic Republic. The West Germans strove to reinforce the growing confidence by offering to help with the cost of moving Soviet forces back to the USSR. Waigel undertook to allocate DM2 billion for this process in addition to the DM5 billion already promised.[41] Bonn would refrain from heavy pressure. Kohl agreed that the Soviet Army would not need to complete its withdrawal from East Germany for another three or four years. Germany would forgo the right to produce nuclear, chemical or biological weapons and reduce the size of its armed forces to 370,000 troops.[42] Kohl's financial grant was a crucial ingredient in the concordat: Gorbachëv knew of Ryzhkov's predictions of budgetary collapse if external assistance proved unobtainable.[43] The Houston proceedings had disappointed the Soviet leadership. Gorbachëv needed to do something drastic, and the deal he struck in southern Russia was the best option that he thought available.

Raisa had the feeling that her husband might not be obtaining the formal guarantees that he and the USSR needed. Taking Genscher aside and speaking in a sombre voice, she made him swear that everyone would stick to the commitments made in Arkhyz. Genscher held her hand and replied that both sides had 'learned the lessons of history'; he assured her that all would be well.[44]

Gorbachëv had consulted only Shevardnadze. They were the same two individuals who in 1979 had resented their exclusion from the Politburo decision to invade Afghanistan.[45] The Politburo had never set up a German Commission like its Afghan one. (There was even a Committee for South Yemen.)[46] Gorbachëv was never to offer an explanation for his volte-face. What Shevardnadze told his aides at the time was probably the nearest thing to the truth. He and Gorbachëv had already been considering their change of policy before Kohl's visit. The assurances they received from Wörner provided some basis for their confidence. Shevardnadze spoke about the vulnerability of Soviet forces on German soil. A single incident could set off an armed confrontation. Gorbachëv and Shevardnadze anyhow wanted to stick to the path of conciliation with the American administration; they could not afford to fall out with Bush. Shevardnadze was candid about the importance of the financial bail-out that Kohl had offered. But in a comment that showed the drastic depletion of Soviet authority, he also emphasized that the two Germanies could decide to come together regardless of Soviet wishes; short of a war, Moscow would be unable to do anything to prevent reunification. Kohl could tell them to 'go to the Devil' – and then there would be no chance of financial aid.[47]

On 17 July Bush called Kohl to hear about what had happened in Arkhyz. Kohl was ecstatic about Gorbachëv: 'He has burnt all his bridges behind him.'[48] He assured Bush that he had warned Gorbachëv that there would be no more money unless the USSR deepened its economic reform; he did not want to appear as having offered a blank cheque to Moscow.[49] On the same day, Bush called Gorbachëv to say that the Houston G7 summit was unanimously in favour of assisting the USSR.[50] Gorbachëv knew this did not amount to a row of beans. He argued against those Americans who thought that the provision of aid would have the effect of slowing down the USSR's advance towards becoming a market economy. But he kept his dignity and begged for nothing.[51]

Gorbachëv worried how Soviet people might react to the decisions. The changes in Europe were already enormous, but the projected answer to the German question would dwarf all of them. Generations of Soviet people had been brought up since 1945 to assume that the territorial settlement after the Third Reich's defeat was immutable. Even reformers were shaken about the prospect; Adamishin in the Foreign Affairs Ministry recorded that it seemed like 'the end of the world'.[52] The same Adamishin later accused Gorbachëv of making 'a real mess' and surrendering the German Democratic Republic too cheaply.[53] The DM5 billion grant was a small price for Kohl to pay. Yakovlev agreed that greater forethought should have been exercised, if only to avoid the humiliation of Soviet armed forces.[54] Primakov added that an elementary mistake had occurred when Gorbachëv allowed his understanding with Kohl to remain in oral form.[55] If Gorbachëv had been more professional about diplomacy, he would have insisted on getting everything written down in plain language. Nobody in Moscow thought that the Arkhyz encounter had seen Gorbachëv at his sharpest.

There was nothing in the Arkhyz understandings about the new Germany's eastern neighbours. Earlier in the year, Gorbachëv thought he had Baker's word that NATO would not expand eastward. Baker had indeed talked about America's 'considerations' on the matter. But nothing had been signed and sealed. Gorbachëv failed to corner Kohl about this in Arkhyz or later to get the Americans to include a guarantee in the treaty on German reunification. Even his supporters were to regret this omission in the 1990s when several ex-member states of the Warsaw Pact joined NATO.[56]

In the weeks after Arkhyz, Gorbachëv remained convinced that he had pulled off an historic deal. He had second thoughts only about the details. His concern was less about the Germans than about the Americans. He decided that if the Soviet Army was departing German soil, American armed forces should do the same. Shevardnadze flew to West Berlin for a meeting with Baker on 22 July. He referred the Secretary of State to the political difficulties facing Gorbachëv in Moscow. Shevardnadze pleaded with Baker to display some reciprocation. Baker was aware of the strains in *perestroika*. He was on good terms with Shevardnadze and enjoyed their work together. But politics was a harsh mistress. Baker contended that the American forces were in Germany by German consent: it was up to the Germans rather than foreigners to lay down what happened in their country.[57] Once Gorbachëv had made his deal with Kohl, he had to endure the consequences. The Bush administration had no intention of yielding on matters of importance to them. If the question of an American military presence had been a sticking point for Gorbachëv, he should have raised it in Arkhyz before shaking hands with the West German Chancellor.

Gorbachëv continued to liaise with Kohl by phone about the return of Soviet troops to the USSR. Kohl offered to pay more for their rehousing if a practical scheme could be agreed.[58] Gorbachëv's wider ambition was to persuade the Germans to involve themselves in rescuing the Soviet economy. Kohl responded encouragingly. On 10 September he suggested that he might be able to assemble interest-free credits over the next five years; he promised that Finance Minister Waigel would confirm the arrangements with Deputy Prime Minister Sitaryan.[59] By November Gorbachëv was asking President Richard von Weizsäcker for DM20 billion in credits.[60] Waigel informed him that he had already sanctioned DM24 billion in help for the USSR.[61]

There was commotion at the Congress of People's Deputies in Moscow when on 24 September the news broke that the German Democratic Republic was withdrawing from the Warsaw Pact. The Ministry of Foreign Affairs had to explain why there had been no prior warning. Kovalëv consulted with Falin, one of the critics of Gorbachëv's policy, before standing in for the absent Shevardnadze. The ministry had known in advance about the East German decision and had informed Gorbachëv's chief of staff, Valeri Boldin, who had inexplicably failed to pass on the message. It would have been indelicate for Kovalëv to state this baldly. Instead he confined himself to commenting that no one liked to advertise a forthcoming divorce.[62] The West German authorities meanwhile started legal proceedings against East Germany's former leaders. The Politburo at Falin's suggestion had sought to protect Honecker by giving sanctuary to him and his wife in a Soviet military hospital.[63] But Kohl followed this with moves to bring ex-Prime Minister Modrow to court. Modrow had been one of the communist reformers who ousted Honecker. Gorbachëv thought of him as a kindred spirit and told Kohl of his disquiet.[64] Kohl took no notice. At the moment of its reunification, Germany had ceased to be the Kremlin's supplicant and become its lender of last resort.

39. THE BALTIC TRIANGLE

Germany was not the only question of international politics to compli-cate Washington's dealings with Moscow. In summer 1989 Bush introduced a Baltic Freedom Day to the American official calendar, setting 14 June for an annual commemoration of Stalin's deportations of Lithuanian, Latvian and Estonian citizens. America had always asserted the right of the three Baltic Soviet republics to their indepen-dence. They fell victim to the Nazi–Soviet Pact in 1939 when Hitler and Stalin agreed – in secret protocols whose existence was always denied by the Kremlin – on spheres of interest in Eastern and East-Central Europe. Poland was divided between the USSR and the Third Reich, and Stalin annexed Lithuania, Latvia and Estonia in 1940. When Hitler invaded the USSR in mid-1941, the three countries fell under German occupation until the Red Army marched back into them in 1944 and enforced their reincorporation as Soviet republics. America and its NATO allies in the post-war years continually pro-tested against the brutality and illegality of this action. But they failed to match words with practical sanctions. The superpowers for decades preferred to deal with each other without treating the Baltic question as a sticking point. Bush's amendment of the calendar appeared to abandon this passive posture. To Gorbachëv's eyes, he was threatening the USSR's territorial integrity.

Gorbachëv told Mitterrand that the White House was playing with fire; he accused Bush and his officials of being motivated more by 'ideology than by realistic policy'. Mitterrand tried to soothe him by saying that Bush was only trying to mollify his conservative critics. As soon as Bush and Gorbachëv made close personal contact, he predicted, the obstacles to progress would disappear.[1]

Nearly all Soviet leaders, including Gorbachëv, started from the thought-curbing premise that it was only right and proper that Lithu-ania, Latvia and Estonia should remain as Soviet republics. They dismissed the fact that the three countries had been independent states between the world wars. They preferred to stress that the Baltic lands had belonged to the Russian Empire before 1917 even though this counted for nothing in international law. Gorbachëv himself visited Estonia and Latvia in February 1987 and expounded the benefits of belonging to the Soviet Union. He felt sure he was making progress: 'The political situation and the mood of people aren't bad in principle.' He told the Politburo that when he did hear complaints, they were chiefly about planning mechanisms and housing. Gorbachëv wanted party secretaries Karl Vaino of Estonia and Boris Pugo of Latvia to stay in post. He had set out to 'provoke frankness' among those whom he met on his visit. He declared that only one individual had become vituperative – a military veteran who had served three years in prison. He admitted that lower officials were hostile to criticism and that *perestroika* could not succeed until such an attitude disappeared. But he somehow persuaded himself that there were no 'oppositional moods' on any large scale.[2]

Being committed to harmonious understanding among the nations of the USSR, Gorbachëv found it shameful that very few items of Estonian and Latvian literature were being translated into Russian. He denounced the current restrictions on local-language teaching in the schools – the novelist Vasil Bykaŭ told him that the problem was common to the peoples of the region, including Belorussia. But Gorbachëv felt sure that reforms would put things right: 'How many nations has America put through the grinder? Total assimilation! Whereas we offer autonomy. And what's needed is a concrete approach to diverse nations, to diverse autonomies. Only sausage can be cut into equal bits.'[3]

Shevardnadze did not share this optimism. For years he had kept the lid on his disquiet about how the leadership was tackling the problem. When violent riots occurred in December 1986 over the appointment of the Russian Gennadi Kolbin to head the Communist Party of Kazakhstan, he exclaimed: 'What, didn't they know about Kazakh nationalism?'[4] The appointee himself was a political friend of Shevardnadze, but Shevardnadze looked on things objectively: Kazakhs felt deep resentment about the way they had suffered at communist hands in the 1930s. Gorbachëv's preference for Kolbin was staggeringly insensitive, but Shevardnadze made his comment to his entourage and not at the Politburo. He held back from intervening on the 'national question'. He was sensitive to the possibility that people would object to him as a Georgian if he spoke out. He kept his thoughts to himself.

Even his aides did not know how long he had dreamed of obtaining wide autonomy for his native Georgia and the other Soviet republics.[5] In February 1988 he was shocked by the Azeri massacre of Armenians in the coastal city of Sumgait in Azerbaijan.[6] Again he kept quiet. Gorbachëv's dominance of internal policy prevailed and, as a result, national resentments intensified.

The KGB sent him reports that supported the leadership's complacency by omitting to mention that the anticommunists had national opinion on their side.[7] The agency preferred to pinpoint specific difficulties. Radio Free Europe, which was no longer subject to jamming, called on Lithuanian adolescents to ignore their military call-up papers.[8] The Vatican was a constant irritation. Although it did not demand permission for a Papal visit to celebrate 600 years of Lithuanian Christianity in 1987, the Catholic clergy had not given up hope that John Paul II would make the trip – and the government in Moscow received petitions to this effect. Even bishoprics in West Germany raised the matter. Lithuania's parish priests encouraged people to place wooden crosses in their vegetable gardens. Believers no longer felt scared to object to the Soviet legal restrictions on the catechism and biblical teachings to the young.[9] Foreign intelligence services had opportunities for mischief after the opening of 'closed' cities made it possible for tourists – and secret agents – to penetrate most parts of the republic. The KGB expected America's special services to organize 'provocations'.[10]

The Lithuanians set up a popular front, Sąjūdis, to represent the nation's interests, and the Estonians and Latvians soon followed their example. Gorbachëv sent Yakovlev to Vilnius on an exploratory mission in August 1988. Sąjūdis sent activists including Vytautas Landsbergis to join in the public debate. Landsbergis told Yakovlev to put no trust in Lithuania's communist leaders, who really wanted a return to the policies of the Brezhnev era. Yakovlev took this calmly as even the nationalists applauded him, and Landsbergis expressed support for *perestroika*. The call went up to end the practice of appointing a Russian as Second Secretary of the Communist Party of Lithuania. Lithuanians disliked the current incumbent, Nikolai Mitkin. Yakovlev replied: 'Please correct me if I'm wrong, but I believe the Lithuanians are people of great culture. I ask whether it is fair of you to criticize Mitkin just because he is a Russian? If I were appointed Second Secretary for Lithuania, would you also want to get rid of me?' Some in the audience shouted that they would welcome Yakovlev's appointment.

Landsbergis exclaimed: 'There's only one flaw in the argument: *you* wouldn't allow yourself to be dropped into our lap like a Christmas present.'[11]

Yakovlev's performance gave rise to criticism in the leadership in Moscow. Filipp Bobkov of the KGB was later to claim that Yakovlev had a habit of saying one thing in the Kremlin and something different to anti-Soviet militants in Armenia, Azerbaijan and the USSR's other republics.[12]

Yakovlev claimed to be doing his duty on the Politburo's behalf.[13] His notes highlighted the worry that Baltic intellectuals were being drawn to leaders who made rowdy accusations against Moscow. But he also reported that nobody had spoken in an anti-Soviet fashion at the Vilnius meeting. According to Yakovlev, the main criticism had been about how the Moscow authorities monopolized industrial decisions, even telling Lithuanian food-processing enterprises how to cook their cocoa beans. The influx of Russians into the labour force incurred discontent. There was also a concern about Lithuania's Ignalina nuclear power station, which was built to the same design as the one which had exploded at Chernobyl. Yakovlev doubted that the communist leaderships in the Baltic republics recognized the scale of the problems; he called them apathetic, rigid and intolerant.[14] But he refused to be downcast. Sąjūdis, he emphasized, was a multi-layered organization with a diversity of viewpoints and the Lithuanian separatists did not yet have the upper hand in it. He offered no practical advice, except to suggest that Lithuanians and Latvians ought to be able to travel abroad more freely.[15]

Gorbachëv continued to insist that the region belonged legitimately to the USSR. His aide Chernyaev tried to persuade him otherwise, but to no effect. Gorbachëv was willing to make all manner of concessions short of secession. The Lithuanian, Latvian and Estonian Popular Fronts gathered ever more support for independence. In their view, they were trying to undo an illegal process of annexation rather than seeking to secede; and the Politburo's mixture of threats and promises served only to agitate opinion in the Baltic region.

The Lithuanian Communist Party leader Algirdas Brazauskas, who was livelier than Yakovlev had claimed, sympathized with the clamour for a declaration of national independence. Gorbachëv at last appreciated the scale of the threat. On 24 January 1989 he told the Politburo of his readiness to allow an experiment in 'national economics' and 'democracy' in Estonia, Latvia and Lithuania. He wanted this done in such a way as to avoid disrupting the rest of the USSR's economy, and he offered the consoling thought that the 'national surge' had achieved no impact on workers and peasants of the region. He banned Yakovlev from returning there.[16] This was more to protect himself from trouble with Ligachëv than to demote Yakovlev. What he now needed was a practical scheme for action. A group of Politburo members – including his allies Yakovlev, Medvedev and Lukyanov – drew up a draft. They argued for political methods and the avoidance of force. Only if persuasion failed to work, should the Politburo consider applying economic sanctions or raising the question of the Lithuanian frontiers (which had been drawn in Lithuania's favour when it became a Soviet republic at the end of the Second World War).[17]

The American administration called on the Kremlin and the Lithuanian government to settle their differences peacefully. America's willingness to negotiate with Gorbachëv was going to depend on the way he treated the Baltic peoples. Ambassador Matlock suggested the desirability of referendums on national independence – America would offer its services in facilitating the process. This was too much for Yakovlev, who knew that any referendum would produce a vote for independence. Yakovlev denied that Lithuania had been annexed in 1940 and 1944. He added that when Soviet Russia had recognized Lithuania's independence in 1920, the circumstances had been 'completely abnormal'. He pleaded with Matlock to recognize how difficult it was for Gorbachëv to have a dialogue with Landsbergis; he asked for this message to be relayed to the White House. He remarked that Soviet leaders had worked at lessening tensions with America despite their objections to American actions in Panama and the Philippines. They wanted the Americans to show the same restraint about Estonia, Latvia and Lithuania. Matlock repeated that if force were used on the Lithuanians, the Americans would refuse to 'continue the development of relations with the USSR'.[18]

Shevardnadze tried to assure Secretary Baker that the situation was becoming less troublesome in Lithuania; he was grateful for America's avoidance of anything that might inflame the situation.[19] The topic also arose when he met Bush, who reminded him about the criticism he was receiving from the Baltic diasporas. Bush repeated his request for the Soviet leadership to resolve the crisis without resort to armed repression.[20]

The April 1989 Tbilisi bloodshed proved that the Soviet order retained its capacity for ruthless brutality. As the commission of enquiry set about its business, fear spread in the leadership about the combustible political situation in the republics. The Politburo returned to Baltic matters on 11 May. Gorbachëv noted that the economic problems were acquiring a national dimension. He accused the Baltic communist leaders of being cut off from working people: 'You're using your opportunities poorly.'[21] He promised to keep Moscow's interference to a minimum: 'The interests of the Union – the Centre – aren't very large: the army, the state apparatus, science. All the rest is the business of the republics.' He wanted to see cooperation with the popular fronts. Wherever they united a nation, the task should be to establish communists as the front's left wing. Extremists should feel the full force of the law.[22] Ryzhkov demanded that the Baltic communist press should resume the publication of articles by Politburo members and cease depicting them as scoundrels.[23] Gorbachëv appreciated that he had underestimated the concerns of leading colleagues and asked Medvedev – not Yakovlev – to visit the Baltic Soviet republics. He too would make a trip: 'Action is needed.' He expressed sympathy for the Estonian, Latvian and Lithuanian communist leaders: 'Errors were committed at the stage when it was their predecessors who were ruling there. Let's start from the premise that all is not lost.' He concluded on an optimistic note: 'Lithuania won't leave us, I assure you.'[24]

Gorbachëv ignored the evidence: he really appeared to believe what he was saying. On 14 July he came to the Politburo with draft new policies on the 'national question'. This time Shevardnadze surprised everyone with the ferocity of his criticism as he warned the Politburo that *perestroika* would suffer unless the leadership revised its approach to the national question.[25]

Turning to Gorbachëv's specific proposals for a reform of the USSR's entire federal structure, Shevardnadze dismissed them for being too vague. He demanded a clear statement in favour of conserving the Soviet Union. He asked why nothing was being said about the right of secession as Lenin had conceived it. He remarked on the absence of a definition of nationalism. He described the draft as banal and inadequate at a time when events were running out of control.[26] Shevardnadze had never spoke so fiercely even about Afghanistan. Gorbachëv took this badly from his friend and ally. He asked whether it was worth the bother to hold a Central Committee plenum on the question. Ukraine's Shcherbitski sided with Shevardnadze – and everyone knew Shcherbitski as one of Brezhnev's veteran protégés. Shevardnadze stood his ground. Medvedev tried to calm things down by proposing to start a debate on a new Union treaty. He expressed concern that Russia might become a sovereign republic – and Gorbachëv agreed.[27] But Ryzhkov objected to Medvedev's wish to devolve powers to the republics: 'I have the feeling that you're ready to break everything up. That's why you can't be allowed into the Baltic region.' Chebrikov added: 'Among the people there's a negative attitude to the Baltic.'[28] The Politburo was a long way from reaching a consensus. But Gorbachëv's draft was the only one under consideration and, in the absence of an alternative, the decision was made to submit it to the Central Committee plenum in September.[29]

Gorbachëv had always believed in the benefits of Soviet federalism. He reminded everyone at the plenum that Latvia took ninety-six per cent of its fuel from other parts of the USSR. It produced only a half of its electricity and a fifth of its chemical materials. The Baltic region was unexceptional in its reliance on the other Soviet republics. At the same time he praised Lithuania for its computers, TVs and sound-recording equipment.[30]

On 9 November 1989, hours before the fall of the Berlin Wall, he reported to the Politburo on his recent meetings with Estonian and Latvian representatives. There had been no meeting of minds. They only wanted to talk about the mechanism for leaving the Soviet Union.[31] The Politburo was perplexed about how to handle the situation. Vorotnikov discouraged those who were in favour of an economic blockade. Any such action, he reasoned, would stir up hostility to the whole federal order.[32] But what was the Soviet leadership going to do? The revolutions in Eastern Europe were an additional complication. Talking with his aides on 18 November, Shevardnadze said that any 'destabilization' in East Germany would 'act as a catalyst for separatist tendencies in the Baltic region' and even in Ukraine.[33] He feared that people would say: 'Uncle Joe created a system and you have brought it to ruin.'[34] At the Malta summit on 3 December Bush expressed his concern lest Gorbachëv might lean towards tightening the screws on the Baltic republics. He repeated that the diasporas in America were raising the alarm about this possibility. Gorbachëv replied that he was expanding freedom in the USSR; he depicted separatism in Lithuania, Latvia and Estonia as a threat to *perestroika*. He asked Bush to take some account of the millions of ethnic Russians living in the non-Russian republics. American interference could damage relations with Moscow. Bush remarked: 'I've understood you, Mr President.'[35]

A Party Central Committee plenum was devoted to the Lithuanian question towards the end of the month after the Communist Party of Lithuania unequivocally advocated national independence. Gorbachëv spoke out angrily. The KGB's Kryuchkov declared that he 'subscribed to every word of Mikhail Sergeevich's report and the comments [sub-sequently] made by him'. He charged Brazauskas with having opened a 'second front' against the USSR by allowing the creation of rival political parties; he said that Lithuania would probably become the precedent for other Soviet republics to try to secede. This would not simply be a matter of territorial and constitutional disintegration. Socialism itself would come under attack, as was already happening in Hungary, Poland, East Germany and Czechoslovakia. He lamented that 'we' – the Soviet leadership – had a habit of putting up a struggle only when victory was beyond reach.[36]

On 11 January 1990 Gorbachëv visited Vilnius in a desperate attempt to appeal to Lithuanian popular opinion. Brazauskas, fearing to appear as a Moscow placeman, was less than cooperative – it was no longer in his interest to show deference. Gorbachëv lamented the years wasted under Brezhnev, when the Western powers reformed their economies. He pointed to the political and cultural changes he himself had introduced.[37] Lithuanian public affairs were reaching boiling point. Brazauskas announced the intention of the Communist Party of Lithuania to break away from the Communist Party of the Soviet Union. The situation in Armenia and Azerbaijan was moving in the same direction. The USSR was disintegrating before everybody's eyes, and Shevardnadze agreed with Yakovlev about the prospect of a 'domino effect'.[38] Lithuania was on the point of asserting its total independence.[39] Gorbachëv dismissed all pessimism. The Communist Party of the Soviet Union would hold together while he was leader, and he would refuse Baltic secessionist demands. He told the Politburo that Estonia had gained independence in 1920 only because Russia was weakened by civil war.[40]

This was accurate as military history but did nothing to answer Estonians, Latvians and Lithuanians who asked why he should now have any right to determine their fate. Sąjūdis had done handsomely in the national elections and on 11 March walked into the Lithuanian Supreme Soviet as victors. Landsbergis was chosen as head of state and Kazimira Prunskienė as Prime Minister. They quickly drew up legislation to declare national independence. The Sąjūdis leadership were throwing a stone into the river of Soviet politics – and disturbing the wider waters of Moscow's relations with Washington.

At the Politburo on 22 March Gorbachëv rejected Varennikov's call for a declaration of presidential rule. Gorbachëv rejected the idea but was open to using economic sanctions to squeeze Landsbergis and the nationalists. Something drastic had to be done after the Lithuanian government had cut off fuel deliveries to Soviet military units in Lithuania. Gorbachëv had a preference for dialogue but refused to discount the possibility of introducing martial law.[41] This failed to satisfy several Politburo members. Ligachëv argued for swift action. Ryzhkov suggested imposing a new parallel government, chosen by Moscow, just as Stalin had done when setting up a Finnish administration during the Winter War with Finland in 1939–1940.[42] Although Gorbachëv hoped to avoid extreme measures of this sort, he was less than clear about what might work instead. Yakovlev tried to help out by proposing to make overtures to Western governments; his idea was to inform them of latest events and to 'neutralize their provocational position'. Beyond that point, neither Gorbachëv nor Yakovlev had the slightest notion about how to cope with the political crisis by the Baltic.[43]

When on 6 April Bush received Shevardnadze at the White House, Shevardnadze asked the President to refrain from doing anything to encourage disturbance in the Baltic republics.[44] Bush warned against using force against Lithuania. Despite professing support for *perestroika*, he indicated that American leaders were watching Moscow warily.[45] Shevardnadze affected an air of confidence about Lithuania throughout his Washington visit. Baker confessed to being surprised at his composure.[46] Shevardnadze was only sticking to the instructions that Moscow had given him. His personal opinion was that Gorbachëv was listening too much to Varennikov and risking a breakdown in the arms talks with the Americans. Shevardnadze feared that this could restart an arms race which the USSR simply could not afford.[47] He told his ministry entourage about how nervous he felt at the growing hostility amidst the Soviet leadership to the official line of policy as the state began to break apart. Although Gorbachëv manoeuvred by offering tactical concessions to his critics, the reformers were nowhere near as secure as once they had been.[48]

Gorbachëv decided to teach the Lithuanians a lesson. On 19 April he announced a blockade of trade and fuel supplies from the rest of the USSR. He asked foreign leaders to recognize his duty to secure constitutional order. He assured British Foreign Secretary Douglas Hurd that, although Landsbergis and his friends were mere adventurers, he still aimed to behave with restraint in Vilnius.[49] Bush felt much sympathy. He could well imagine Akhromeev and others saying: 'Enough is enough!'[50] On 29 April he wrote confidentially to Gorbachëv along these lines, even stressing that he understood the Soviet official standpoint that the Baltic states belonged to the USSR.[51] When Baker came to Moscow in May, Gorbachëv asserted that 'Lithuania was always tied to Russia'. He hinted at the potential for trouble; he also noted that Stalin had set the Lithuanian border – and now the Belorussians wanted some of their territories back. Baker was accommodating and recalled how he had told the American Congress that Vilnius, the Lithuanian capital, had not even belonged to Lithuania but to Poland before 1940.[52] On 18 May Britain's Ambassador Braithwaite refused Lithuanian Prime Minister Kazimira Prunskienė's request for support for her government. Braithwaite urged dialogue and patience. The Lithuanian leadership, he affirmed, had an interest in Gorbachëv's *perestroika* remaining a success.[53]

When Gorbachëv flew to Washington later that month, Bush expressed sympathy for his Baltic predicament but asked him to understand the criticism he was attracting for failing to intervene on Lithuania's behalf. He mentioned his own reasons for disliking Landsbergis, who had compared him to Neville Chamberlain.[54] Bush made Gorbachëv an offer. In return for Moscow lifting restrictions on emigration and ending the Lithuanian economic blockade, the American President would ease the USSR's commercial difficulties: 'So, with this private understanding, I'm going to sign the trade agreement today, although my critics will give me hell.'[55] Senator Bob Dole was less gentle. He harangued Gorbachëv for denying independence to Estonia, Latvia and Lithuania. Gorbachëv angrily replied: 'Why did you let your administration intervene in Panama if you love freedom so much? . . . You have given Most Favoured Nation [status] to China after Tiananmen. What are we supposed to do, declare presidential rule in Lithuania?'[56] Richard Perle in the *New York Times* accused Bush and Baker of being too eager to please Gorbachëv. He reminded readers that the Lithuanians had a justified claim to independence.[57]

On 29 June, as the result of joint pressure from Washington and Moscow, the Lithuanian authorities suspended their declaration of independence. The Americans continued to ask the Kremlin for assurances about the Baltic region. Shevardnadze responded that the Estonian, Latvian and Lithuanian leaders were showing insufficient self-restraint.[58] There was no end to the public controversy in the USSR. Baltic politicians, including communists, chastised the Kremlin for refusing to acknowledge historic injustice. There was dispute about secret protocols in the Nazi–Soviet Pact of August 1939. Yakovlev was ordered to conduct an enquiry. The search for a full original copy of the treaty yielded no result. Apparently Molotov, just before losing his post as Foreign Affairs Minister in 1957, had requisitioned and hidden or destroyed the file.[59] In July Yakovlev stood by the idea that the Nazi–Soviet treaty was 'legitimate', but not the secret protocols.[60]

Gorbachëv's scheme was to offer the maximum of freedom to the Baltic Soviet republics but to keep them inside the USSR. He was a Soviet patriot and a proud Russian. Despite all his mental adaptiveness, he could barely understand why they refused to accept permanent association with Russia. The national movements in the republics started from opposite premises. In their opinion, they were not trying to secede since they had never consented to that original association. They had been forcibly and illegally annexed, and now they were re-asserting their right to independence. Concessions came from Gorbachëv, as they saw things, only at a time when Moscow was weak. They wanted to seize the moment, which might never happen again. If this meant falling out with Bush, too bad. Bush bore in mind that he had yet to complete agreements with the USSR on arms reduction; he also sought to maintain Soviet consent to the revolutionary changes in Germany and elsewhere. It was not in his interest to see Gorbachëv's authority undermined by the Baltic independence movement.

Bush and Gorbachëv wanted to end the Cold War with the minimum of fuss. The Lithuanian, Latvian and Estonian nationalists sought to make as much trouble as appeared necessary to prevent Moscow and Washington from ending their own hostilities without resolving Baltic grievances – and they were unwilling to yield to pleas on behalf of geopolitical convenience.

40. THE THIRD MAN BREAKS LOOSE

In getting out of Afghanistan and negotiating with America about other regional conflicts, Gorbachëv overturned the traditions of Soviet foreign policy. He dreamed of nothing less than a new world order resting on principles of peaceful change. Events in the Persian Gulf on 2 August 1990, when Saddam Hussein ordered Iraqi armed forces into Kuwait, called his thinking into question. This was a flagrant breach of international law; it alarmed every neighbouring country, and the Americans demanded immediate withdrawal. Bush issued an ultimatum that threatened dire consequences if Saddam refused to comply. Washington's bellicosity disappointed Gorbachëv, who still hoped to establish a global partnership with America that gave a commitment to non-violent methods. He feared that the Bush administration aspired to dominating the world as the single hyperpower. Gorbachëv had people around him who felt the same. Yevgeni Primakov, an academic who specialized in Middle Eastern affairs, argued that the USSR had an interest in preventing the defeat of its traditional allies in the region, including even Saddam's Baathist administration; Valentin Falin in the Party International Department lobbied Gorbachëv to ally with Europe's political left in opposing armed action against Iraq.[1]

On the other side of the debate were Shevardnadze and Cherny-aev, who wanted to align the USSR with American foreign policy.[2] They urged Gorbachëv to give Washington no cause for annoyance. A lot was at stake in international relations. The Middle East was important but should not take precedence over the big items of unfinished business between the superpowers. The Americans for their part wanted to bind the USSR into a partnership against Saddam. On 3 September, they made a request for the Soviet sea freighter *Magnitogorsk* to carry US forces to Saudi Arabia.[3] They continued to press for a favourable answer.[4]

At their next summit meeting in Helsinki on 9 September 1990, Gorbachëv complained to Bush about how the Americans had sent forces to the Middle East without prior consultation. Bush accepted this as 'constructive criticism'.[5] They agreed that Gorbachëv should make an overture to Saddam. His public stance aside, Bush expressed a preference to resolve the emergency by peaceful methods. When he added that he would welcome the sending of Soviet troops to the Gulf to strengthen the American contingent, Scowcroft winced at the thought.[6] Baker tried to win Gorbachëv over by signalling a readiness to bring American business leaders to Moscow. Gorbachëv welcomed any help in developing the Tengiz oilfields in western Siberia.[7] He and Shevardnadze also made a request for a $1.5 billion interest-free loan. Baker explained that this would be legally impossible for Bush in the light of outstanding financial grievances that the USSR had yet to settle with America, but he undertook to ask America's friends to advance the money. Gorbachëv warmed to this idea: 'What is one billion dollars to an Arab prince who has 104 or 105 billion dollars?'[8]

A rift opened between Shevardnadze and Gorbachëv after the summit when Gorbachëv chose Primakov as the man who went to Baghdad on his behalf. It was the first time that he overlooked Shevardnadze for an important mission, and Shevardnadze did not like it at all.

There had always been some tension in their partnership. As two strong-minded politicians who had to make judgements in times of momentous change, they would have hardly been human if they could agree on everything. In 1986 Shevardnadze had spoken against Gorbachëv's take-it-or-leave-it tactics for talks with the Americans; in 1988 he had opposed the refusal to leave a military contingent behind in Afghanistan. He disliked his leader's rhetoric – he cringed when Gorbachëv talked about 'our common home', regardless of where he might be in the world.[9] But he always accepted that, as a Georgian, he could never replace Gorbachëv at the helm: 'I'm . . . convinced that Mikhail Sergeevich is the only one who can lead the country.'[10] If *perestroika* met with failure, he added, the result would be 'anarchy and chaos' – and he predicted that those who were likely to replace Gorbachëv would suppress all dissent.[11] He believed that a dictator might come to power.[12] Gorbachëv and Shevardnadze, moreover, managed their disagreements without rancour or public disclosure. The partnership worked well enough for Gorbachëv to entrust Shevardnadze with a lot of freedom on weighty matters such as policy towards southern Africa. Shevardnadze's aides referred to him admiringly as the 'Vice-Misha'.[13] Foreign leaders regarded the two of them as the pillars of the USSR's new foreign policy.

By June 1989, when Soviet foreign policy first came in for public criticism in the USSR, Shevardnadze was the prime target at the Supreme Soviet's Committee on International Affairs in the Kremlin's Faceted Chamber. The questions would have riled even a very placid politician – and Shevardnadze had a fiery personality. Objection was made to the disproportionate number of women he had appointed to the ministry. The committee's chairman Valentin Falin opined that Shevardnadze had failed to recruit people with genuine professional expertise. Another member contended that Shevardnadze had proved too soft a negotiator and ought to 'show his teeth'. Only when Georgi Arbatov entered on Shevardnadze's side did the trouble subside; and the committee, in a throwback to the years before *perestroika*, confirmed him unanimously as Minister of Foreign Affairs.[14] This was not much more than a formality, but the session put Shevardnadze on alert about the growing peril faced by the leadership under conditions of widening freedom of expression; and although no one yet dared to criticize Gorbachëv, everyone understood that an arrow directed at Shevardnadze was meant to hit both of them.

Shevardnadze admitted to being a very 'emotional person'.[15] Georgian affairs always put him on edge. Whereas he saw himself as his nation's protector, his critics reminded him of his embarrassing statement in 1976 that the sun had risen not in the east but in the north.[16] Many Georgians rejected him as the 'deceiver of the people'.[17] The nationalist dissenter Zviad Gamsakhurdia accused him of being an 'agent of Moscow'.[18]

Communist traditionalists were equally combative, and Shevardnadze felt humiliated. On 24 December 1989 he asked to address the Congress of People's Deputies after a provocative statement by the Chief Military Procurator Alexander Katusev. The Georgian delegation had walked out. Shevardnadze thought that Katusev would not have dared to speak out without sanction by some higher authority.[19] Gorbachëv denied the microphone to Shevardnadze for fear that he might say something that both of them would regret.[20] Shevardnadze could stand it no longer. He told Gorbachëv that he was stepping down from office and left for his dacha. The Kremlin's politics were in chaos. Kryuchkov approached Shevardnadze's deputy Kovalëv and asked him to go out and reason with him. Gorbachëv seconded the request. Kovalëv took the precaution of ringing from his personal phone. Shevardnadze accepted the call. It became obvious that he retained a sense of duty for the ministry, which Kovalëv was running in his absence. When Shevardnadze demanded time for reflection, Kovalëv assured him of Gorbachëv's support; he added that if Shevardnadze stuck to his decision, he would jeopardize everything that he had achieved. Shevardnadze undertook to think things over again.[21]

Shevardnadze spoke to Gorbachëv that evening. Next day he was back at his desk in the ministry and rang Kovalëv: 'Come round to my office; I'm here.'[22] He left his letter of resignation locked in his safe. A few days later he told Stepanov-Mamaladze: 'The [Party Central Committee] plenum confirmed my very worst concerns. With only the rarest exceptions, everybody demanded severe measures. All this is directly linked to the demonstration of force on 24 December. It's a more cunning and dangerous blow aimed at *perestroika* than [the Tbilisi massacre of] 9 April.'[23] Gorbachëv reassured him somewhat by asking him to go to Lithuania and hold talks with those who were demanding independence.[24] Shevardnadze confided to Stepanov-Mamaladze: 'You know, I can walk out this very day. But I badly want – purely in a human way – to bring what has been started to completion . . . To bring it to a logical conclusion. This would make life worthwhile.'[25]

Opponents of Soviet foreign policy meanwhile continued to single out Shevardnadze for blame – it was dangerous for them to criticize Gorbachëv but everyone knew that they were really aiming their fire at both of them. Shevardnadze, furthermore, had undoubtedly pushed the reform of foreign policy with zest; and there had been no let-up in recent weeks. The critics were angry with him. Shevardnadze had yielded to Baker's terms for an 'open skies' agreement in September 1989 without any preliminary analysis of the military problems; he had consented to their proposals to reduce stockpiles of chemical weapons, ignoring the lack of decommissioning facilities in the USSR. On 23 October 1989, in breach of official policy, he told the Supreme Soviet that the Krasnoyarsk radar station was an infringement of the Anti-Ballistic Missile Treaty.[26] He implied that the whole Politburo had been deceived.[27] Kornienko later claimed to have briefed Shevardnadze fully about the history of the station in September 1985 before the minister flew to America.[28] The charge was also laid that Shevardnadze had failed to push for the agreed numbers in arms reduction the Ottawa talks in February 1990.[29]

What Shevardnadze suffered was mild in comparison with the attacks upon Yakovlev. KGB Chairman Kryuchkov regarded him as a traitor and, after liaising with Boldin, went to Gorbachëv with his agents' reports. The evidence for his allegation was decidedly paltry. Kryuchkov could only point to occasions when Yakovlev had had 'unsanctioned' conversations with Americans. Gorbachëv could see that this fell some distance short of hard proof, and he advised Kryuchkov to discuss the matter directly with Yakovlev.[30] It was a deft but unsatisfactory way of handling the matter. Kryuchkov had behaved badly and would have lost his job if Gorbachëv had not been committed to balancing the radicals and traditionalists in his administration. Gorbachëv would live to regret this calculation. Kryuchkov for the moment returned to a posture of loyalty to his leadership. He was a complicated figure inside the leadership. Sometime after being appointed as KGB Chairman, he had blurted out to Ambassador Matlock that some intelligence officials regarded the current Soviet leaders as being out of their minds. But he also acknowledged that the USSR had once been an evil regime, and he asked for advice on how to tackle ethnic problems in the light of the American experience.[31]

Shevardnadze considered whether to speak in his own defence at the Central Committee plenum that month after hearing that people held him culpable for the collapse of 'the socialist camp' in Eastern Europe.[32] In the event, he lost his temper on a separate matter. This happened when Ligachëv assured the plenum that the entire Politburo had approved the decision to use troops in Tbilisi in April 1989. Deeply offended, Shevardnadze interjected that the Politburo had approved the deployment of military units only with a view towards the maintenance of order. No permission was provided for the use of force. When Shevardnadze sat down, the economist Stanislav Shatalin was the only Central Committee member who voiced support. Nobody was more shocked than Shevardnadze: 'This was the first time that I met with *such* a reception from such an audience.'[33] He resolved to complete the tasks he had set himself in foreign policy on his own terms: 'I'm ready to take full responsibility upon myself; [but] if the people considers that this means the collapse of the system rather than democracy or that this is against our national interest, I'm ready to hand in my resignation.' He was proud of his part in the struggle against dictatorship.[34]

Presidential powers, according to Shevardnadze, needed strengthening if Gorbachëv was to overcome the resistance in the Politburo,

Central Committee and the Supreme Soviet.[35] In March and April 1990, Katusev and Rodionov raked over the coals of the Tbilisi massacre by claiming that Shevardnadze was tainted with Georgian nationalism.[36] To Shevardnadze's chagrin, Gorbachëv noticeably failed to defend him.[37] By July there was a chance Shevardnadze would fail to secure re-election to the Central Committee at the Party Congress. Not liking the idea of being 'dragged into the Central Committee by the ears', he asked Gorbachëv to withdraw his name from the candidates' list. Gorbachëv urged him to shoulder the load of political unpleasantness just as he himself did.[38] He ignored the plea from Shevardnadze, and Shevardnadze obtained a large majority.[39] In truth Gorbachëv had other things to worry about. Yeltsin came to the Congress but announced his resignation from the party when his radical proposals for democratization were rejected. He demonstratively walked out of the hall. Though Gorbachëv secured assent to most of his current policies, there was noisy criticism of the official party programme draft. But he could at least derive satisfaction from Ligachëv's failure to secure election as his deputy – and Ligachëv quickly departed from the Politburo.

But the tension grew inside the ascendant group in the leadership, and the rivalry between Shevardnadze and Yakovlev was an open secret.[40] Word spread that it suited Gorbachëv to have the two outstanding radicals competing for his favour. Shevardnadze in his brighter moods absolved Gorbachëv of making mischief: 'I don't think this comes from Gorbachëv. Ultimately he knows my moods. Rather this comes from others – from Alexander Nikolaevich [Yakovlev] and the International Department of the Central Committee.'[41] It was Yakovlev whom he suspected of unappetizing manoeuvres. He also resented his tendency to claim the paternity of *perestroika*. He himself disclaimed any ambition to replace Gorbachev. By implication he could not say the same about Yakovlev.[42] As for Yakovlev, he refused to share Shevardnadze's generous opinion of Gorbachëv, whom he said had never liked him and talked venomously about him.[43] He noticed that Gorbachëv declined to let him chair meetings of the Politburo or Secretariat in his absence. Yakovlev would love to have delivered one of the annual public speeches but Gorbachëv never invited him, whereas he granted that honour to Ligachëv. Yakovlev suspected that people around Gorbachëv had been muttering that 'Yakovlev had started his own game'.[44]

Since the end of 1989 Shevardnadze too had detected a decline in

Gorbachëv's confidence in him. He traced the change to something that Bush said to Gorbachëv at the Malta summit when he made the comment: 'I absolutely believe in Shevardnadze.'[45] Gorbachëv, he guessed, probably felt that he needed to be on his guard if the American President found ease in Shevardnadze's company.

Throughout the summer months, at Gorbachëv's request and with Yeltsin's agreement, a group of economists led by Stanislav Shatalin and Grigori Yavlinski worked on a plan to introduce a market economy to the USSR through a programme that would take 500 days to implement. The Party Central Committee met in mid-September 1990 to consider the proposals. The economy was in free fall, and Minister of Finance Valentin Pavlov reported that the USSR would go bankrupt without a massive inflow of foreign capital. He estimated that thirty-five per cent of enterprises were in the red. The gathering speed of collapse helped Ryzhkov to surmount his worries about social protests against the consequences of retail price reform. The need for firm action, he declared, was acute. At the same time he queried the recent decision to put Yakovlev in charge of the campaign against criminality – he said that Yakovlev was obviously out of his depth. Those who preferred the old economic system to the uncertainties of reform also came into the open. Yuri Prokofev dismissed the Shatalin draft programme as mere sloganeering, lacking any practical use. Oleg Baklanov asserted that the working class was on the point of taking to the streets.[46] The Central Committee was a house divided. The sole point of consensus was about the fact that the USSR faced an acute emergency.

Gorbachëv and Shevardnadze hoped to alleviate the situation with Western assistance. They grew worried when Yeltsin took a trip to America. Chernyaev recorded: 'And Bush and Co. are looking on him as an alternative.'[47] Gorbachëv had asked British Foreign Secretary Douglas Hurd to intercede for $2 billion of interest-free credit. He indicated that Moscow needed another $15–20 billion in credits, goods and expertise to overcome its difficulties. Hurd promised to relay the request to Thatcher, who alone could make the decision.[48]

The USSR's General Staff and Defence Ministry were less than helpful to their political leadership. On 18 September Shevardnadze alerted Gorbachëv about Western press coverage of the USSR's systematic infringement of arms agreements.[49] The story surfaced that the high command had removed tanks to the east of the Ural mountains instead of destroying them.[50] Shevardnadze felt he could not discharge

his duties effectively unless foreigners saw him as an honourable negotiator. The agreed idea had been for tanks to be converted into
bulldozers, fire engines and cranes. Instead they were being retained
for military use. Shevardnadze asked Gorbachëv to intervene so that a
general disarmament agreement might reach signature before the year
was out.[51] Grinevski wrote to Gorbachëv from Vienna along the same
lines. When Chernyaev joined the chorus, Gorbachëv ordered Yazov
and Zaikov to consult with Shevardnadze about how to resolve the
affair. Gorbachëv claimed to have cursed the offending commanders
in his message to Defence Minister Yazov.[52] The Conventional Armed
Forces in Europe Treaty was due for signature on 19 November 1990,
requiring the USSR to reduce its tanks, artillery pieces and armoured
combat vehicles by seventy per cent west of the Urals.[53]

While Shevardnadze was savouring his success in persuading Gorbachëv about the tanks, he suffered a shock on learning of Gorbachëv's
latest diplomatic move. Instead of sending him to Baghdad for talks
with Saddam Hussein, he chose Primakov. This infuriated Shevardnadze. When Gorbachëv rang him, Shevardnadze motioned to his
aide Tarasenko to stay in the room as a witness. Gorbachëv said that
no harm could come from Primakov's visit to Baghdad. If former British Prime Minister Edward Heath had gone on a peace mission, why
couldn't a Soviet public figure do the same?[54] According to Chernyaev's later account, Gorbachëv was merely sending the best man for
the job: Primakov spoke Arabic and was a veteran academic specialist
on the Middle East.[55] Such arguments failed to calm Shevardnadze,
who said to Tarasenko: 'Who is leading foreign policy? Me or Primakov? Who's responsible for it? I can't be the minister if various other
people are going to be involved in affairs that belong to my sphere.'[56]
Shevardnadze was quietly disruptive. The Soviet Ambassador to
Jordan told Karen Brutents in the Party International Department that
Shevardnadze ordered him to withhold active help from Primakov's
mission – apparently Shevardnadze indicated his concern that if the
USSR indulged Saddam, the Saudis would withdraw their promised
loans.[57]

Shevardnadze was faltering in his loyalty to Gorbachëv. He saw
the resolution of several urgent problems as requiring a deepened cooperation with America. These included further agreements on arms
reduction, pan-European military security, the composition of the
Warsaw Pact, Moscow's treatment of the Soviet Baltic and the collapse
of the USSR's economy. Whereas Shevardnadze considered the whole

range of tensions between America and the USSR, Primakov had only the Iraq emergency on his agenda; and Primakov was keener than Shevardnadze to find some way of accommodating Saddam.

Breaking with convention, Shevardnadze wrote confidentially to State Department official Dennis Ross to express disquiet about Gorbachëv's line of conduct. Tarasenko handed the letter to a trusted contact in the American embassy. Shevardnadze wanted Baker to know where he stood on the emergency in the Persian Gulf.[58] Shevardnadze himself met Bush and Baker in a sequence of meetings in New York between 22 September and 5 October. Bush wanted to place his 'bets on partnership'. If Saddam displayed 'irrational stubbornness', he said, the Soviet leadership would be able to act as mediator. It would seem that Baker apologized for publicly condemning Stalin's annexation of the Baltic states. While all this was encouraging for Soviet diplomacy, Shevardnadze asked Gorbachëv to avoid taking America's cooperation at the arms talks for granted. He reminded Gorbachëv about the current chances of getting financial credits to the value of $4 billion from the Saudis and $400 million from the Kuwaitis. Spain had offered $1 billion. On this 'delicate' question, Shevardnadze hinted, the credits were unlikely to arrive if Soviet foreign policy conflicted with American purposes in the Persian Gulf.[59]

The amount of aid being made available was changeable, and Gorbachëv strove to preserve the dignity of the USSR. Baker had striven to show good faith by travelling to Moscow in mid-September and taking a group of American business leaders with him representing Chevron, PepsiCo and other large corporations. The hope was to facilitate industrial and commercial investment. It was a timely intervention because Gorbachëv was introducing Shatalin's '500 Days Programme' to transform the Soviet economy.[60] The American businessmen felt unimpressed by the deals on offer, and they saw for themselves the chaotic conditions in society and the economy. Gorbachëv himself was under pressure from Prime Minister Ryzhkov to moderate Shatalin's radicalism. The 500 Days Programme was steadily emasculated. This pleased Ryzhkov and infuriated Yeltsin (and was to drive Gorbachëv's radical economics adviser Nikolai Petrakov to resign in December).[61]

Gorbachëv was striving to keep some elements of radicalism without annoying its bitter opponents. It was an impossible task. But he was not yet willing to concede defeat.

He did at least recognize the urgent need for direct financial aid and pleaded with Baker for an interest-free loan of $1.5 billion. Baker jotted down his impressions: 'Critical – help us now.'[62] The American administration continued to reject the Soviet request but encouraged allied powers to step into the breach. By the end of October, the Germans were offering $20 billion and the Saudis had advanced their $4 billion, the French $1.5 billion, the Spanish and Italians just a little more.[63] Not every Western power was consistent in its support. Deputy Prime Minister Sitaryan reproved the British for having withdrawn $7 billion that they had deposited with the USSR. Sitaryan expressed the hope that Prime Minister Major, who succeeded Thatcher on 28 November 1990, would reverse the policy.[64] Saudi Foreign Minister Saud al-Faisal had recently confirmed to Gorbachëv that King Fahad would guarantee the $4 billion of credits.[65] In trying to salvage his economy, Gorbachëv knew that foreign financial assistance came with strings attached. He continued to insist on the USSR's capacity to deal with its difficulties. The Soviet and American leaderships had drawn close despite – or perhaps because of – all the recent tensions. But a rift was opening between them over Kuwait that had implications for the kind of world over which they presided.

41. A NEW WORLD ORDER?

The American administration cast round for partners in a diplomatic offensive against Saddam. These were not hard to find inside NATO, but Bush also tried to attract support from elsewhere. He made clear that if the Iraqis refused to comply with the demands of the United Nations, military action would follow. Washington made plans to assemble an irresistible force of allies and friends in Saudi Arabia.

Primakov went to Baghdad for talks with the Iraqi leadership on 3–5 October. Shevardnadze had cabled him in Jordan to the effect that it would be immoral to meet Saddam – Primakov held the opposite viewpoint that it was immoral to overlook chances for a peaceful settlement. After telling the Iraqis that Gorbachëv demanded withdrawal from Kuwait, he formed the impression that Saddam was genuinely ready to make concessions. Gorbachëv welcomed Primakov's report on 6 October. Shevardnadze was present on the occasion and exchanged angry words with Primakov. Gorbachëv intervened only when Primakov said: 'How dare you, a graduate of a correspondence course from a teachers' college in Kutaisi, lecture me on the Middle East, the region I've studied since my student days!'[1] At Gorbachëv's behest, Primakov flew to London for consultations with Thatcher.[2] Shevardnadze wrote angrily to Gorbachëv: 'I've carefully acquainted myself with the packet of proposals from Yevgeni Maximovich [Primakov]. I've tried very hard to discover a grain of reason, but I just couldn't do it . . .'[3] Gorbachëv ignored him. On 30 October he told Mitterrand that Saddam was minded to withdraw from Kuwait. He asked for France's help in persuading the Americans.[4]

Shevardnadze's aide Tarasenko was in the minister's office during a phone call from Gorbachëv. The subject was Iraq. Whereas Shevardnadze favoured courting and cajoling the Americans, Gorbachëv aimed to steer a more independent line. It was a fiery exchange. Gorbachëv was sharply critical: 'So now let's take a look at what your friend Baker makes of you while you play up your friendship with him: the fact is that they're not coming clean about anything and are about to deliver a strike.' The Americans, he said, were playing him for a fool. Shevardnadze replied: 'I believe the Secretary of State. He promised to inform me if they take the decision to attack and that he'll keep me in the picture. They won't do that without having informed us of their plans. I believe that.' Gorbachëv told Shevardnadze that the Americans had fooled him into trusting everything they said.[5] It was a fiery conversation, and Gorbachëv used turns of phrase that gave personal offence to a man from the Caucasus.[6]

The Arabists in the Foreign Affairs Ministry disliked the idea of joining an invasion of Iraq. They shared Primakov's feeling that Saddam should not be abandoned, and they disapproved of Shevardnadze's whole approach after his aide Tarasenko reached a tentative under-standing with Dennis Ross in the State Department in favour of military action against Saddam. Shevardnadze stood by Tarasenko.[7] Chernyaev became convinced that he had secretly tipped the wink to Baker that the USSR would not obstruct an invasion. This could not have happened with Gorbachëv's knowledge or permission. Soviet policy was evidently no longer tightly coordinated.[8] Shevardnadze buried himself in his duties – and it cheered him for a while that the USSR, America and the European countries could at last sign the Con-ventional Armed Forces in Europe Treaty in Paris on 19 November. The situation in the Persian Gulf was less encouraging. Meeting Iraqi Foreign Affairs Minister Tariq Aziz on 26 November, Shevardnadze pointed out that Iraq had been at war for a whole decade. The Soviet Union had been its reliable supplier of military equipment and almost an ally. It had never been paid properly for its goods. Shevardnadze said this was intolerable and asked Aziz to discuss an agreeable sched-ule for payment.[9]

Evidence mounted in Moscow that influential people in the Soviet political elite were gunning for Shevardnadze. He and his wife Nanuli lived in some degree of fear. Information reached him that the KGB was up to something in Tbilisi. As Georgia's former Minister of Internal Affairs, Shevardnadze knew of the potential for skulduggery. The worry for him was that if anything like an emergency situation were to be declared, the intelligence agency might arrest his protégés. He felt the net tightening around him.[10] He assumed that if a coup occurred, his life would be in danger. He noted the boldness of the communist conservatives. When the new Vice President Gennadi Yanaev took a one-roomed apartment on the same floor as the large one occupied by the Shevardnadze family, Shevardnadze surmised that Yanaev's idea was to expand his living quarters at their expense.[11] At the same time he yearned to complete the work that had occupied him since the mid-1980s. He thought the Americans were becoming distracted from the tasks of completing a treaty on strategic nuclear forces.[12]

While all this was happening, Gorbachëv arranged to reorganize the structure of government. This would involve 'extraordinary measures' of a kind that his traditionalist critics had long demanded. There was a growth of separatist tendencies in the Baltic region and the south Caucasus, and practically every Soviet republic was asserting its right to sovereignty. Gorbachëv arranged to stabilize the situation by setting up a cabinet of ministers under his control. Law and order would be enforced. Shevardnadze saw dangers in the switch of policy and even unburdened himself of his worries in conversation with Chinese Foreign Affairs Minister Qian Qichen about it. He told him about the public demonstration on 7 November, when banners were brandished with the words 'Down with Gorbachëv!' and 'Down with the Gorbachëv–Shevardnadze–Yakovlev Clique'. Shevardnadze asked: 'What were we meant to do? Fire on them?'[13] This was a rhetorical question. His basic fear was that if Gorbachëv introduced any extraordinary measures, he might indeed soon find himself under pressure to use violence. He dreaded that the USSR would succumb to dictatorship. Next day, as he flew from Moscow to Paris, he talked to aides about whether he should resign.[14] He was reaching the limits of patience and endurance. He wanted to step down.

KGB Chairman Kryuchkov urged the Politburo to declare an emergency situation. He wanted the President to assume plenipotentiary powers.[15] This would have meant that Gorbachev put himself in the hands of the USSR's traditional agencies of coercion: the KGB, the Soviet armed forces and the communist party. Minister of Internal Affairs Vadim Bakatin – a reformer and one of Gorbachëv's close associates – rose up in fury. Although Gorbachëv defended him, Bakatin had spoken with a loose tongue.[16] Gorbachëv judged it prudent to mollify his communist-conservative critics – in October 1990 he had even given permission for the testing of a nuclear bomb on Novaya Zemlya between the Barents Sea and the Kara Sea. This was just before he was meant to go to Stockholm to receive the Nobel Peace Prize.[17] Bakatin was gone from office at his own request by 1 December 1990. As Gorbachëv manoeuvred to the side of his conservative critics, he dropped other prominent reformers from his entourage. Vadim Medvedev resigned from the Presidential Council with Gorbachëv's consent. Alexander Yakovlev removed himself from public view. In the Supreme Soviet, the enemies of reform were cock-a-hoop. Colonel Nikolai Petrushenko and the Soyuz group boasted that they would continue to achieve the removal of yet more reformers.[18]

On 11 December 1990 Bush announced a financial facility for the USSR to buy $1 billion worth of American wheat.[19] Shevardnadze visited him next day at the White House. Bush tried to dispel the Soviet reluctance to offer full support for military action in the Persian Gulf. He hoped that his offer of credits would show his Soviet friends that he appreciated that a hard winter lay ahead for them.[20] He also mentioned Lithuania and mentioned yet again that President Landsbergis had likened him to Prime Minister Neville Chamberlain before the Second World War – this was his way of reminding Shevardnadze that America was refraining from demanding immediate independence for the Lithuanians. Shevardnadze thanked Bush for the promise of economic assistance. Bush called for 'our beautiful coalition' to hold together.[21]

Unfortunately for Shevardnadze, Gorbachëv continued to yield ground to the critics of *perestroika* on internal policy, and Shevardnadze worried that the retreat might soon become a Gadarene rush that would trample all the gains of recent years. The rift between them in international relations was smaller because Shevardnadze knew that Gorbachëv wanted to remain on good terms with America; but they disagreed about how to achieve this. Shevardnadze recognized that Bush had resolved upon ejecting Saddam from Kuwait by force. He could see no point in obstructing the Americans in any serious fashion, especially if the Soviet leadership hoped to enlist their help with difficulties in the USSR, whereas Gorbachëv continued to aspire to a more independent line in international relations, giving priority to the solution of conflicts by peaceful methods. In mid-December the Soviet leadership informed the Americans that it could no longer agree to provide transport to the Persian Gulf for British helicopters.[22] At some point in the winter of 1990–1991 Gorbachëv received a menacing letter from a score of leaders of the armed forces. Akhromeev was to recall that they objected to a string of decisions that they felt had undermined the country's capacity to defend itself.[23] On 19 December 1990 Falin had criticized the German treaty at the Supreme Soviet's International Relations Committee.

Next day, Shevardnadze caused a political earthquake. The occasion was his own report to the full Supreme Soviet on what was happening in the Persian Gulf. He intended to quash all rumours that the leadership was going to send troops to the region. Speakers belonging to the Soyuz group denounced official foreign policy; they disliked what they saw as the USSR's capitulation to the West. Shevardnadze had heard such things before. He sat quietly in the third row on the right-hand side of the hall as he waited the call to speak.[24] As soon as he opened his mouth, it was obvious that he was in a passionate frame of mind. He noted that two Supreme Soviet deputies were boasting that they would follow up the removal of Internal Affairs Minister Vadim Bakatin with efforts to dismiss the Minister of Foreign Affairs. He recalled that when his name had been put forward at the Party Congress for election to the Central Committee, 800 votes had been recorded against him; he noted that the Supreme Soviet had begun to hold hearings on foreign policy in his absence. He highlighted the press campaigns against him.[25]

Then came the hammer blow:

> A dictatorship is on the way – I declare this with a full sense of responsibility. Nobody knows what kind of dictatorship it will be, who will come to power, what kind of dictator or what kind of order will be installed . . . I'm going into retirement. Don't react and don't curse me. Let this be my protest against the coming of dictatorship. I express my deep gratitude to Mikhail Sergeevich Gorbachëv; I am his friend and sympathizer; I always supported and to the end of my days will support the ideas of *perestroika*. But I cannot reconcile myself to events that are taking place in our country and to the trials that await our people. This is nevertheless what I believe: dictatorship will not succeed; the future belongs to democracy.[26]

One of the architects of *perestroika* was announcing his resignation. Half the audience rose to its feet in sorrow and admiration; the other half sat on their hands, pleased that Shevardnadze was departing. As Shevardnadze left the hall, Gorbachëv's face showed discomfort. Something very important had happened for the fate of reform in the USSR – and the worry was that it could have adverse consequences in Soviet foreign policy.

Gorbachëv asked him by phone: 'Why was I left out of this?' He speculated that the Georgian situation was Shevardnadze's real motive. Shevardnadze rebutted this. He stood by the rationale he had offered in the speech to the Supreme Soviet.[27] As he explained to his aides, he could not have alerted his president without giving him the chance to dissuade him: 'Not to leave, for me, would have meant political suicide.' Gorbachëv recognized that the decision was irreversible. He simply asked Shevardnadze to stay in post until arrangements could be made for a replacement.[28]

Shevardnadze wanted to remain on good terms with Gorbachëv; but he felt sure that his old partner would come under growing pressure from the reactionary elements. Gorbachëv would be 'forced to use tough measures (*deistvovat' zhestko*)'.[29] When they met on 30 December, Raisa was inconsolable: 'I fear, above all, for our friendship.'[30] Shevardnadze in the following days continued to defend his resignation. He told associates that a plot was under way and that the Soyuz organization was at the centre of it. He had predicted dictatorship, and hoped that Gorbachëv would wake up to the danger. He was not very optimistic about this. Furthermore, in Shevardnadze's opinion, Russians like Gorbachëv were less alert than people from other national groups – like himself – to the perils and nastiness of the current 'campaign of vilification'.[31] He never indicated his sources beyond claiming – many years later, in his last volume of memoirs – that they lay somewhere in the KGB and in certain Soviet embassies. He had taken his information to Gorbachëv, who seemed only to pretend to be listening.[32] The entire situation was deeply disturbing. And he could not believe that Gorbachëv was not in receipt of the same signals of alarm.[33]

Other factors also had an influence. Shevardnadze was worn out. Since 1985 he had lived like a nomad and failed to spend a single full month in the USSR. He told Stepanov-Mamaladze that he envied him the free time to take a trip to Tbilisi. He had not even been able to visit his elderly father when he needed to.[34] Stepanov-Mamaladze, who was as close to Shevardnadze as anyone, added that he had decided to jump before he was pushed. Gorbachëv had a proven capacity for ingratitude, having dropped so many of his loyal fellow reformers in autumn 1990.[35] Tarasenko put it somewhat differently. He surmised that Shevardnadze thought he had done most of the big things that he could as Foreign Affairs Minister. Soviet policy had changed beyond all recognition since 1985, and he had played an important part in the process. But the relationship with Gorbachëv was no longer what it had been. Shevardnadze was no longer one of Gorbachëv's intimates. Suspecting Gorbachëv would yield to pressure to use violence in the

Baltic republics, he wanted to free himself of any obligation to defend policies he did not believe in.[36]

Around the world there was concern that recent events could lead to renewed tensions in world politics. Gorbachëv had already dropped many of the prominent reformers; and he was continuing to baulk Bush's purposes in the Persian Gulf. The NATO powers deeply regretted Shevardnadze's departure. Baker told the American media: 'I am proud to call this man a friend . . . I would have to tell you that I'm going to miss him.'[37]

Gorbachëv spoke no ill of his departed friend and ally;[38] and Shevardnadze continued to accept that Gorbachëv, if possible, 'wanted to remain a democrat'.[39] Though they tried to stay on good terms, personal concerns had agitated Shevardnadze for some time. He mused that political leaders ought to retire on reaching the age of sixty-five – otherwise they begin to experience the old man's syndrome and think only about how to preserve their personal power.[40] Inside Gorbachëv's entourage there was talk that Shevardnadze had selfish motives for resignation. Chernyaev thought he wished to heap all the responsibility for the USSR's troubles on to Gorbachëv.[41] Falin made a more specific guess. He reckoned that Shevardnadze knew that people in Moscow knew that he had told Baker that he approved of the American military action and wanted the USSR to join the coalition. If called to account, he would not be able to talk himself out of trouble.[42]

Gorbachëv continued to canvass the NATO powers for a peaceful solution to the crisis in the Persian Gulf. He was under enormous internal pressure in the USSR as the feeling grew that he had been too willing to concede to Washington's demands in foreign policy and too complacent about the internal benefits of *perestroika*. Elites and people were troubled by the effects of economic and administrative dissolution. Gorbachëv sensed the need to be seen to hearken to what the critics and sceptics were saying even when he had no intention of acting on their advice. Sometimes he could hardly believe his ears, as when KGB Chairman Kryuchkov reported that the Americans were considering the use of nuclear weapons in Iraq. The Ministry of Foreign Affairs wrote to denounce this as nonsense. Chernyaev did the same.[43] Gorbachëv was able to consider both sides before tactfully ignoring the KGB. He himself was no sympathizer of Saddam. He had constantly urged him to pull out of Kuwait and believed that war was avoidable. He underestimated Saddam's intransigence and imprudence and, unlike Shevardnadze, failed to understand that a withdrawal of his forces by Saddam was the last thing that the White House wanted. Bush aimed to eject Saddam from the annexed territory by force.[44]

The Kremlin leadership overlooked the continued concern in the West about the transfer of the Soviet 'tank park' east of the Urals. Scowcroft wrote to Akhromeev to express disquiet about the situation. Akhromeev defended the high command. Gorbachëv asked Zaikov, Kryuchkov, Yazov, Baklanov and Shevardnadze to investigate and report. They denied any infringement of the Conventional Armed Forces in Europe Treaty since the transfer had occurred before the treaty's signature.[45] On 24 December 1990 British diplomat David Logan complained to Viktor Karpov. Karpov did not deny the undeniable but instead told Logan that the USSR was willing to show itself flexible on the matter.[46]

The question of Shevardnadze's successor caused lively debate. Gorbachëv's first preference was for the steady but unimaginative A. S. Dzasokhov. Shevardnadze's favoured candidate was the arms talks expert Kvitsinski.[47] The new cabinet was headed by Valentin Pavlov, whom Gorbachëv appointed as Prime Minister after Ryzhkov suffered a heart attack in December. Pavlov was no more enamoured of ideas for a market economy than Ryzhkov had been. On 15 January 1991 he gave an interview to the *Trud* newspaper claiming he had evidence that the Americans intended to flood the Soviet Union with 50- and 100-ruble notes so as to wreck its economy.[48] Gorbachëv in the end chose as Shevardnadze's successor Alexander Bessmertnykh, a diplomat known for his objections to radicalism in foreign policy. Shevardnadze vacated his ministry office no. 706 for the last time on 16 January.[49] He maintained contact with the Americans, including Baker and Matlock, and kept Soviet officials informed about what passed among them. He avoided saying anything that could embarrass the Kremlin. When Matlock expressed concern about the Soviet military build-up in Latvia, Shevardnadze replied that this was news to him. He badly wanted to see Baker signing a treaty in Moscow: 'History won't forgive a missed opportunity.'[50]

Gorbachëv worked to halt the offensive even after the start of bombing. On 18 January 1991 he phoned Mitterrand and proposed a joint political initiative. He also called Kohl and congratulated him on his election as Chancellor of a united Germany. Finally he phoned Bush. It was a frosty conversation as he tried to get him to order a pause in hostilities. Bush remained unmoved, and a hitch in the telephone linkage broke up the conversation.[51] Gorbachëv had received a sharp lesson about the latest shift in world politics. The Americans were the global hyperpower. Bush would have preferred to act in harness with Gorbachëv, but was now perfectly willing to gallop forward without him.

42. ENDINGS

Gorbachëv ruled according to his chosen political orientation; but he also lived by his wits, and now he drew deep on them for his survival. By early 1991 they were no longer of much help in the severe general crisis in the USSR. Communist party organizations were in chaos. The ministries were incapable of imposing central power and the armed forces were demoralized. Even the KGB's personnel no longer knew what they were meant to be doing. When Lev Shebarshin went on an investigative mission around the USSR on Kryuchkov's orders, he was shocked by the lost sense of purpose. He witnessed how seldom the phones were ringing in the Baltic capitals, Vladivostok and Krasnoyarsk.[1] On 2 January, Gorbachëv held consultations with his close associates, including even Shevardnadze, in a bid to prepare for the Central Committee plenum at the end of the month. For the moment he shifted the focus away from bilateral arms reduction, conflicts in the Third World, official ideology and even the Soviet economic collapse. His purpose was to work out a policy to deal with the proliferation of nationalism in every republic.

Among Azerbaijani politicians there were some who called for unification with northern Iran and its large Azeri population. Lithuania was in uproar. The media were engaged in constant criticism. There were reports that Soviet working-class opinion was beginning to favour the establishment of some kind of dictatorship. The solution, in Gorbachëv's opinion, was for Kremlin leaders to visit the trouble spots and calm the situation. He said that if there was to be constitutional reform, it had to occur inside a federal framework of some kind. Gorbachëv was determined to save the Union. The bastions of the old Soviet order were crumbling. This was a dangerous situation, and Gorbachëv urged the need to refrain from criticizing the armed forces. Georgi Razumovski, who had lost his place as a Politburo deputy member in mid-1990, spoke of the apathy he saw in the local party committees. Nikolai Slyunkov, until recently a Central Committee

Secretary, complained about the way that the new co-ops were paying themselves more than they received in income. Shevardnadze brought the discussion back to the Lithuanian question. He advised against precipitate measures and reasoned that inactivity was preferable to the kind of measures that the communist-conservatives and their military sympathizers had in mind.[2]

On 10 January Gorbachëv called on Landsbergis and the Lithuanian government to submit to Moscow's constitutional authority; he indicated that military intervention was a possibility – Shevardnadze's worst fears were coming to fulfilment. Soviet paratrooper units began to seize buildings next day. On 13 January there was violence at the Vilnius television tower, and thirteen Lithuanians were killed. The national response was angry and immediate. Crowds gathered in Lithuania's big cities.

Gorbachëv, supported by Defence Minister Yazov and Interior Minister Pugo, denied complicity in the bloodshed; but there was quickly a suspicion that even if he had not ordered it, he had chosen not to prevent it. He had always deliberately kept himself mysterious, and nobody in his entourage – not even Chernyaev, Yakovlev or Shakhnazarov – was sure what he thought he was doing when appointing obvious communist conservatives to high office. Shakhnazarov was to speculate that Gorbachëv was two people at once: a radical and an apparatchik.[3] Whatever part he might have played in the Vilnius massacre, the practical consequences were undeniably damaging for him and his cause. Nationalist agitation grew throughout Lithuania. Russia became a foreign country for the three self-declared independent Baltic states, and Boris Yeltsin recognized their status on 13 January at a meeting in Tallinn. Yeltsin was speaking as Chairman of Russia's Supreme Soviet when he condemned the Vilnius massacre. In Moscow the Russian democratic movement organized a demonstration protesting against the military violence.[4] Having omitted to enforce Yeltsin's retirement from politics in autumn 1987, Gorbachëv was having to confront a rival. Yeltsin called for more radical policies in politics and economics, and he was open to the idea of a Baltic secession.

Gorbachëv's international status was dipping. On 25 February, with his consent, the Warsaw Pact was dissolved at a Bucharest meeting of foreign affairs and defence ministers from the USSR, Bulgaria, Hungary, Poland, Czechoslovakia and Romania.[5] Comecon was wound up some months later.[6] Gorbachëv reluctantly recognized the inevitable:

countries of Eastern Europe had no wish for an alliance, military or economic, with the Soviet Union. They intended to strengthen their newly won freedom from Muscovite interference.

On 17 March the Soviet leadership tried to shore up its own position by holding a referendum on the preservation of the USSR. He received a resounding vote of approval across most of the republics. On a Moscow visit in March, British Foreign Secretary Douglas Hurd expressed hope for a 'renewed and voluntary Union'. He stated publicly that the USSR's disintegration would be bad for everyone, including the West. Behind the scenes, he added that Yeltsin was 'a dangerous man'.[7] The unequal status of the two superpowers became painfully obvious in the same month when Baker instructed the American embassy in Moscow to organize a Moscow meeting of the presidents of the fifteen Soviet Republics of the USSR. Gorbachëv angrily warned off the presidents from attending.[8] But the Western pressure continued. British Prime Minister John Major approached Gorbachëv with a repeated complaint about the Soviet biological weapons programme in April – Ambassador Braithwaite passed the letter to Chernyaev for delivery to the Soviet President.[9] The British continued to express their concern through to the end of the year.[10] They offered no prospect of economic assistance. Gorbachëv's triumph with his referendum meant nothing to a society whose households faced the prospect of ruin and even starvation.

Shevardnadze warned that the USSR might suddenly fall apart in civil war: 'I fear this more than anything else.' Gorbachëv, he added, should have encouraged the creation of a separate party of reform such as Shevardnadze and Yakovlev would have been eager to join. Yakovlev wrote to Gorbachëv advocating a two-party political system. Knowing that Gorbachëv suspected him of hoping to succeed him, he insisted that he was too old for any such bid.[11] Shevardnadze regretted the reluctance of Gorbachëv and Yeltsin to reconcile their differences; he was beginning to envisage Yeltsin as a desirable alternative to Gorbachëv. He admitted that whereas Gorbachëv would never want to be 'dictator', Yeltsin displayed 'authoritarian habits'. But as Gorbachëv lost control in Moscow, Yeltsin appeared the better guarantee of continued reform. Shevardnadze continued to speak in loyal terms about Gorbachëv. Nevertheless, his former deputy Adamishin sensed that Gorbachëv had let him down and even betrayed him.[12] Shevardnadze also felt that his old ministry no longer had any 'strategists' in high posts – he did not approve of Bessmertnykh's promotion.[13] When he claimed to have no regrets about his resignation, Adamishin thought that he was trying to persuade himself.[14]

Gorbachëv was exhausted. He could see that things might turn out badly for him: 'It always turns out that they crucify prophets. So that's why I wonder whether my time has come to be crucified.'[15] Although he hid his concerns, Raisa knew how ground-down he was. Quietly she told the man she loved: 'It's time, Mikhail Sergeevich, to leave, withdraw into private life and write your memoirs.' On another occasion she said: 'Mikhail Sergeevich, you've done your job.'[16] He rejected the advice. Outside the family and entourage, he behaved as if he expected to go on and on.

A secret Soviet estimate in April 1991 held out the prospect of saving 11.5 billion rubles from the state budget over the next six years by reducing the number of strategic offensive weapons.[17] Akhromeev admitted to British officials that the USSR could no longer hope to sustain military parity with the US. This was a comment that no Soviet commander would have risked making a few years earlier.[18] On 18 May Gorbachëv called together his Security Council to discuss the emergency. Nobody imagined that the USSR could cope much longer on its own. Western assistance was essential, and Gorbachëv had approached President Mitterrand for help in joining the International Monetary Fund – among the G7 countries, only Japan expressed dissent. His hope was to attain a five-year agreement for an annual loan of $15 billion. (The Harvard economist Jeffrey Sachs was touting the possibility that the USSR might receive double that amount, but Gorbachëv thought this unrealistic.)[19] He warned that the Soviet leadership would incur criticism by 'patriots' about the 'humiliation'. He urged the need for sober realism: 'Unfortunately we've fallen far behind the West and our science is correctly used only in the military sector . . . Cooperation with the West is in the country's interests, for its upturn – that too is patriotism. And what kind of cooperation should this be? Neither bilateral nor episodic but genuinely broad integration.'[20]

Baltic questions continued to complicate the political picture. Lithuania, Latvia and Estonia sent out their leaders to North America and Western Europe to stir up their diasporas. They wanted to counteract the idea that nothing should be done that might somehow undermine Gorbachëv. Landsbergis, Chairman of Lithuania's Supreme Council, addressed the American Congress's Commission for Human Rights, spelling out the continuing abuses of law and order on Lithuanian territory. He recounted how the USSR had annexed his country in 1944. He and the Latvian and Estonian prime ministers proceeded to a meeting with Bush.[21] They were also busy in Western Europe. Landsbergis lost patience with his French interlocutors: 'We are here in France and you are being very kind to us. However, you do not want to displease the Soviet Union, so you and the other countries are afraid to establish formal diplomatic relations with us. Now see what your friends, the Soviets, are up to while you hesitate!' This outburst had the desired effect, and Foreign Affairs Minister Roland Dumas let it be known that France would seriously consider how to put its links with Lithuania on a formal, separate basis.[22]

As the chaos grew in the USSR, Bush gave priority to finalizing agreements with Gorbachëv before anything could happen to him. Phoning Gorbachëv, he argued that they ought to crown their success with the Conventional Armed Forces in Europe Treaty with the long-discussed agreement on strategic nuclear weapons. In tactful language he nagged the Soviet President to give the topic his urgent attention. They easily concurred on the desirability of moving on to a fresh treaty that would cut the stockpiles of strategic weaponry by half. This would be a momentous achievement. On economics, Bush frankly explained his doubts about the likely effectiveness of Pavlov's policies; he could see no way of helping Gorbachëv until the Soviet authorities removed the barriers to a market economy.[23] On 5 June he wrote to Gorbachëv explaining American proposals to unblock the sticking points about definitions and numbers.[24] Gorbachëv confirmed his eagerness to reach rapid agreement.[25]

The conditions of disintegration spread throughout the country. On 17 June KGB Chairman Kryuchkov gave a report to the Supreme Soviet in closed session surmising that the USSR could cease to exist inside two to three months unless the authorities could restore order. He later claimed that one could hear a fly crossing the room.[26] While voicing support for market economics, he stressed the need for regulation. He ridiculed the idea that the West would supply vast financial credits. He claimed that the CIA was recruiting agents among Soviet citizens. The economy was in dire straits. Clashes between Soviet ethnic groups were bitter and violent. Organized crime was on the rise. The NATO countries rejected the post-war frontiers, often raising the case for the independence of the Baltic republics.[27] Nobody could listen to this and think that Kryuchkov was endorsing Gorbachëv's leadership. Kryuchkov was not alone. Prime Minister Pavlov asked for emergency powers, and admitted that he had not discussed this in advance with the President. Anti-reform deputies lined up to lambast Gorbachëv.[28]

This made fertile ground for rumours about a move to overthrow the President. There had been several scares in the previous year, and Gorbachëv had brushed them aside. He gave offence by telling a visitor from a foreign intelligence agency, in Kryuchkov's hearing, that he was fed up with the bias in the KGB's reports.[29] Pavlov complained about the reluctance of Western banks to advance financial credits.[30] Yazov questioned the original need for *perestroika*: 'So why did we generally need this?'[31] Boldin accused the radicals of searching for ways 'to surrender to Yeltsin'.[32] Baklanov continued to grumble about Gorbachëv's disarmament initiatives.[33] Akhromeev had come to believe that Gorbachëv had destroyed the USSR's defensive capacity.[34] The American administration worried on the Soviet President's behalf. On 23 June Bush rang him near midnight. Chernyaev gave an order for them to be put in contact with each other, but Gorbachëv was somewhere out of his apartment with Raisa. Next morning Gorbachëv told Kryuchkov and Boldin that the failure to find him was a gross dereliction of duty.[35] It was in the same frantic weeks that reports reached Gorbachëv from his own people that suspicious troop movements had been taking place outside Moscow – and Primakov counselled Gorbachëv to avoid putting too much faith in the KGB.[36]

Gorbachëv ignored the alert and focused on the agenda of political, national and economic problems. He and his supporters put up candidates against Yeltsin in elections for the presidency of the Russian republic in June 1991. Yeltsin won by a handsome majority. Gorbachëv recognized reality and held regular discussions with him. Priority was given to finding a way to build a new federal system for the USSR. Equally urgent for him was to alleviate difficulties in the economy. The shops were almost empty of goods for consumers. Popular discontent grew. The Supreme Soviet was increasingly raucous. Now, more than ever, he needed external assistance. Ambassador Braithwaite called on Gorbachëv and extended a formal invitation from Prime Minister Major to attend the G7 summit meeting in London. Braithwaite and Gorbachëv noted the fading euphoria about the end of the Cold War. Gorbachëv wanted the West to change its attitude and recognize that he would not be travelling to London like some small-time trader. He hoped for 'a big principled conversation'.[37] But he had no illusions. Braithwaite recorded: 'He knows there will be no money on the table in London, and agrees that there must be serious concrete work in advance.'[38]

Secretary Baker came before the Senate Foreign Relations Committee on 11 July to plead for Congress to ratify of the Conventional Armed Forces in Europe Treaty. He said it was crucial to guaranteeing an end to the USSR's massive preponderance of troops and weaponry and to consolidating democracy throughout the continent.[39]

On 17 July Bush and Gorbachëv had a preliminary discussion at the American embassy in London before the summit. Gorbachëv asked Bush directly what kind of USSR he wanted to work with. If billions of dollars could be found for the Gulf War, was it not sensible to assist the transformation of the Soviet Union? Bush replied that America wished for a democratic, dynamic USSR integrated into the world 'community' of nations; he denied taking pleasure from Gorbachëv's misfortunes. Gorbachëv stressed that he needed to be cautious in running down the military sector of his economy – armaments were the sector where the USSR's best inventors and engineers were to be found. Bush found it convenient to change the subject to Lubavich Jewish manuscripts and then to Yasser Arafat.[40] Gorbachëv had not expected total success, but Bush was offering even less than he had imagined. As he explained to his British hosts, the world's economic powers had to understand that his reforms would require many more years of effort. He protested about the continued embargo on technological transfer. His mood was bleak. He knew that if he returned to Moscow without some kind of deal, he could only expect the worst: 'Then [even] ten angels will not be able to save us.'[41]

When they lunched again on 23 July, Bush blushed and avoided eye contact with the Soviet President.[42] Disclaiming any wish to interfere in the USSR's affairs, he repeated that Gorbachëv could expect no foreign direct investment until the Kremlin introduced democracy and market economics and regularized its relations with the Soviet republics in a properly federal fashion.[43] Gorbachëv had come to London with cap in hand. He left without having obtained the offer of a single dollar. The London trip had proved to be a humiliation.

Less than a week passed before Bush arrived in Moscow to sign the Treaty on the Reduction and Limitation of Strategic Offensive Arms (or START in its usual acronym). Work by the expert teams on both sides had ironed out the remaining creases, and neither Gorbachëv nor Bush wished their own latest failure to achieve a financial entente to hold things up. On 31 July 1991 they put pen to paper. The

USSR and America accepted a restriction to deploy no more than 6,000 nuclear warheads. According to an agreed understanding, each superpower would reduce its military capacity to 1,600 missiles launched from land, sea or air. This would involve the largest and most complex process of arms reduction in history, and its final implementation in late 2001 was to result in the removal of about eighty per cent of all strategic nuclear weapons then in existence. What had begun in the middle of Reagan's second term was at last being realized. The missiles that could be fired from one continent to the heart of another had been discussed at every summit. Their very existence constituted the acute risks of the struggle between the superpowers. They were the symbol and reality of the Cold War.

Gorbachëv and Bush were conscious of the momentous importance of the treaty, and Bush wanted to do nothing to destabilize the Soviet administration. On 1 August he flew on to Ukraine. In his speech in Kiev he declined to espouse Ukrainian independence and condemned anyone who decided to 'promote a suicidal nationalism based on ethnic hatred'. He also warned Ukrainians to recognize that instant prosperity was not achievable. The reaction in America was a mixed one, and critics on the political right as well as in several national diasporas charged Bush with betraying the cause of the unfree peoples. Scowcroft sprang to the President's defence. He pointed out that Bush followed the traditional policy of refusing to recognize the incorporation of Estonia, Latvia and Lithuania in the USSR. At the same time, Scowcroft asserted, Americans should appreciate that a decent future for the Soviet population required a commitment to ethnic tolerance, respect for minorities and a truly open society. Political democracy alone was not enough. Building a better society would require wisdom and caution – and Bush had attempted to show favour neither to the central government in Moscow nor to its enemies in the republics.[44]

He had left Gorbachëv in Moscow finalizing a plan, which he co-ordinated with Yeltsin, to introduce a new Union Treaty on 20 August granting broad powers to republican administrations. Bush supported his constitutional reform and assured him by letter that he had not said anything untoward in Kiev.[45] Tired by his exertions, Gorbachëv took a vacation in Crimea and refreshed himself in time for the signing ceremony. He stayed in the Yuzhny sanatorium at Foros.[46] Pavlov and Yeltsin sent him some proposed amendments which Gorbachëv found no difficulty in embodying in the text that he was expecting to sign on returning to the Soviet capital.[47]

He chose to ignore the signs that discontent with his ideas for a looser federation were reaching fever pitch. In the previous month a Moscow newspaper had published 'A Word to the People'. Among the signatories were Varennikov and Gennadi Zyuganov, a Politburo of the Russian Communist Party. Its content bewailed the prospect for the USSR if Gorbachëv's constitutional project were ever to be realized: 'The Motherland, our country, the great state entrusted to us by history, by nature and by our glorious forebears is perishing, is being broken up, is being plunged into darkness and oblivion.' There was no mention of Lenin, the October Revolution or communism. The concern was patriotic: the Soviet Union, if something drastic was not done, would soon be in pieces.[48] KGB Chairman Kryuchkov quietly contacted like-minded fellow leaders with a view towards preventing the signature of the Union Treaty. On 18 August Varennikov and Gorbachëv's own personal assistant Boldin flew down to Crimea to seek presidential approval for the declaration of a state of emergency. Kryuchkov cut off the telephone links at Gorbachëv's villa. The idea was to present him with a fait accompli. Instead of complying with their demands, Gorbachëv threw them out before finding himself under house arrest. Kryuchkov and the hastily formed State Committee for the Emergency Situation on the same day announced that Gorbachëv was ill and that Vice President Gennadi Yanaev would assume his powers.

When the unwelcome visitors departed they took Vladimir Medvedev, Gorbachëv's chief bodyguard, with them. He too was betraying his President.[49] They also removed the apparatus with the 'nuclear button', intending to hand it over to Moiseev at the General Staff.[50] The telephone lines were down. No car was allowed to approach the Yuzhny sanatorium. A triple semicircle of guard cordons cut the building off from the world. The only route of escape from Yuzhny would have been by sea; the road between Yalta and Sevastopol was closed.[51]

The coup d'état shocked Western leaders even though something like it had been predicted for months. Bush was astounded. He wrote in his diary:

> The new President is Yanaev . . . He was the guy that met me at the Moscow airport. He was the guy that drove in with me. He was the guy who flew down on our plane to Kiev. He was the guy that

congratulated me after our speech in Ukraine about respect for the Union and the people choosing. I liked the guy. I sent him fishing lures. And, he was rather pleasant.[52]

Ex-Prime Minister Thatcher broke the news of the coup to Ambassador Leonid Zamyatin in London:

She called me at eight in the morning and said very angrily: 'Mister Ambassador, do you know what is happening in Russia?' 'I am sorry, madam, I don't.' 'Well, then turn on your TV set and see for yourself. I need permission for the flight of an English aircraft to Russia. You are flying with me. I will take a doctor along. Gorbachev must be sick. Maybe dying. I must be in Russia!'[53]

Her geography was shaky since Foros was not in Russia but in Ukraine, and perhaps her rhetoric owed something to Victorian melodrama; but her feelings for her Soviet friend were genuine.

The State Committee included Defence Minister Yazov and Interior Minister Pugo as well as Prime Minister Pavlov; its policies were guided behind the scenes by KGB Chairman Kryuchkov. When they appeared on television, it was obvious that Acting President Yanaev felt demoralized as his fingers involuntarily drummed a glass of water. To their surprise, a crowd of protesters gathered outside the Russian Supreme Soviet building. Kryuchkov omitted to take Yeltsin into custody. The shambles continued. Yeltsin appeared on top of a tank outside the same building and declared his defiance of the plotters. Army units refused to enforce the State Committee's orders. The coup quietly petered out on 20 August.

The State Committee sent a small party by plane to Foros, including Kryuchkov and Yazov. They were travelling to seek Gorbachëv's pardon and to argue that they had meant him no harm. Gorbachëv simply shunned them.[54] He was getting used to treating everyone cautiously – Yazov's treachery in particular had staggered him. With the phone system working again, he commanded the Kremlin to be cleared of the leading putschists. He spoke to George Bush and thanked him for his solidarity. Alexander Rutskoi, the Vice President of Russia, led a second group of travellers. After piloting his own plane south to Crimea, he appeared at Yuzhny with Russian Prime Minister Ivan Silaev. He had brought forty lieutenant-colonels in case of any trouble. Gorbachëv entrusted his family and aides to Rutskoi's care.[55] They took Kryuchkov on board as a guarantee against a mid-flight armed interception – he was searched for weapons before he took his seat.[56] One by one, the rescue party came to talk to Gorbachëv and his family; and it was then that they discovered that all was not well with Raisa. The experience at Yuzhny had caused a heart attack. Although she survived without medical attention, she found hand movement difficult. Gorbachëv himself suffered a relapse into the sciatica that had affected him since his younger days.[57]

His mood picked up as they neared the capital: 'We're flying into a new country.'[58] He never spoke a truer word. Yeltsin, the victor over the State Committee, was the master in Moscow and compelled Gorbachëv to purge all those who had supported or condoned the coup. Despite his experience at Foros, Gorbachëv was initially reluctant to acknowledge the sheer scale of betrayal. Yeltsin brusquely told him, in full public view, to read out the list of known traitors. Gorbachëv proceeded to proscribe the Communist Party of the Soviet Union and to replace the leaderships of most of the governmental agencies. He held the members of the State Committee in custody.

On 24 August there was a barrage of declarations of independence by Lithuania, Latvia and Estonia; and Yeltsin announced his approval of them. The Ukrainian leadership made a similar declaration.[59] Liberated from Crimean house arrest, Gorbachëv felt himself under political siege in Moscow and appealed to his former associates to return to his side. On 30 August Gorbachëv asked Shevardnadze: 'Come to the Kremlin immediately!' Shevardnadze no longer submitted to orders: 'Immediately is impossible. Things won't move so simply. We need to talk.' Gorbachëv exclaimed: 'But aren't we having a conversation at the moment?' Yakovlev was present at their ensuing meeting when Shevardnadze gave vent to his anger. Gorbachëv had destroyed his own life's cause, betrayed his allies and surrounded himself with mediocrities and flatterers: 'You became a person who – whether it was deliberately or involuntarily doesn't matter – provoked the coup, and I have every ground for supposing that you took part in the plot.'[60] When he refused to return as Foreign Affairs Minister, Gorbachëv asked why. Shevardnadze answered simply: 'I don't trust you.'[61] Yakovlev was equally harsh in his comments.[62] In past years Gorbachëv would have interrupted. Now he held his tongue. At the end of the conversation he told Shevardnadze and Yakovlev that he would forget everything and recognize his mistakes. What he was intending to forget, he did not say; and he never did fully explain the nature of his mistakes.[63]

Bush's loyalty to him was not what it had been, and on 2 September he gave official recognition to Lithuania, Latvia and Estonia as independent states.[64] But he stopped at this point and waited on events. Defense Secretary Cheney characteristically demanded a more active approach. He wanted to base American policy on objective calculation rather than continue to gamble on Gorbachëv and his survival; he raised an alarm about the spectre of civil war in the USSR. Cheney wished America to look after its national interests. He had never been in favour of accelerating the arms cuts as demanded by official policy. Now he felt able to say this publicly.[65] Scowcroft contradicted him. Whereas Cheney warned about the possible return of an authoritarian regime in Moscow, Scowcroft reasoned that it made little sense to undermine Gorbachëv any further – he rejected proposals to intervene directly in the Soviet republics and welcomed a report from Powell, Chairman of the Joint Chiefs of Staff since autumn 1989, that the 'centre' retained enough power to control the USSR's armed forces. Baker dourly added: 'The *peaceful* breakup of the Soviet Union is in our interests.' Bush declined to be hurried. He thought it prudent to see what happened with regard to the new Union Treaty.[66]

He made his own contribution to removing the last traces of tension with the USSR by announcing the decisions to cut down the American military budget and reduce the number of troops and weaponry. He reduced the state of alert of US forces around the world. He confirmed that America would eradicate tactical nuclear weapons from its stockpiles. He terminated funding for certain strategic missiles programmes. Speaking on television on 27 September, he assured the American people that no damage would occur to national security. He celebrated the benefits of a 'peace dividend'.[67] He phoned Gorbachëv to tell him all this on the same day;[68] and Gorbachëv set reciprocal measures in motion in Moscow.[69] By then Gorbachëv's preoccupation was with the economic and constitutional emergency across the USSR. He could not safely think of anything else. On 7 October an IMF delegation led by Michel Camdessus arrived in Moscow for talks with Gorbachëv, Yavlinski and others. Budgetary recovery was the sole topic, and Gorbachëv pressed Camdessus to avoid administering the medicine too harshly. He spoke as if he was still genuinely in charge.[70]

The truth was that the USSR was on the brink of dissolution. At the end of October Gorbachëv flew to Madrid for a long-planned conference on the Middle East. While he was there, he called Bush and pleaded for financial credits. Bush replied that he had to be able to assure Congress that any potential debtor was creditworthy – and he could not say this about the USSR. Gorbachëv stated that $10–15 billion could make all the difference to the Soviet economy without making a dent in the American budget and without much risk of a default. Bush demurred out of fear of criticism in America if he offered anything more than an advance of $1.5 billion for food imports. Baker supported Bush in taking this stand; he added that information had reached Washington that Yeltsin's Russian administration had plans to dissolve the USSR's Ministry of Foreign Affairs. Baker whispered informally to Gorbachëv's interpreter Pavel Palazhchenko, asking him to tell Gorbachëv to get a decision accepted on the food imports offer before the Americans changed their mind. Gorbachëv wanted more from the West and gave instructions for an overture to be made to Prime Minister John Major as that year's coordinator of the G7 countries.[71]

Yeltsin played along with the idea of sustaining the Union while obstructing Gorbachëv on a daily basis. He assured everyone that he wanted stability in relations with America. Russian Prime Minister Ivan Silaev appointed an arms deal team on the model of the old 'Big Five', as Vitali Kataev had helpfully suggested.[72] Yeltsin held his political fire until he heard the results of the Ukrainian referendum on independence on 1 December. The vote was overwhelmingly in favour of secession. Yeltsin seized his chance. Meeting with Ukraine's President Leonid Kravchuk and Belorussia's Stanislav Shushkevich at Belovezhskaya Pushcha a few days later, he resolved to bring the USSR to an end. He declined to consult the Russian electorate: his personal decision was final.

Gorbachëv accepted the inevitable. On 25 December he appeared on Soviet television and announced that he would step down from office at the stroke of midnight ushering in the New Year. The October Revolution of 1917 was tossed aside. Marxism-Leninism was discredited for ever in the country of its birth. Each of the fifteen Soviet republics became an independent state. The political and economic disintegration of one superpower – as well as the outcome of the personal duel between Gorbachëv and Yeltsin – diverted attention from the enormous achievements of the year. The Cold War's ragged ends were tidied away. A sequence of treaties had rendered a nuclear holocaust no longer a serious immediate likelihood even though both sides retained more than enough ballistic missiles to destroy each other. Gorbachëv bit by bit had conceded ground that his predecessors had considered sacred. He signed treaties with the Americans that reduced its global military power. The communist states of Eastern Europe were no more. The Warsaw Pact had been broken up and Soviet forces withdrawn from the region. Moscow no longer subsidized the Afghan communist government or acted like a first-rank power in Africa or the Middle East. America had prevailed, the Soviet Union was no more.

If anyone in the Kremlin or the White House had prophesied this even a few years earlier, they would have been thought off their heads. The impossible had turned into the probable and finally into the real. The world of 1945, held in aspic by the chemistry of struggle between two superpowers, dissolved before everyone's eyes. Nobody could be quite sure what would happen next.

POSTSCRIPT

The Cold War ended, just as it had begun, at no definable date. Though there was no clarity about the timing, no one could doubt the importance of the great thaw. Since the late 1940s, the struggle between America and the USSR often came terrifyingly close to turning into a global 'hot' war and always involved the nuclear arms race and regional military conflicts as well as clashes over political order, ideology, coalition maintenance, civil rights and the movement of people and information. A Third World War was a continuous possibility.

The thaw set in only after Soviet leaders concluded that they could no longer afford their geopolitical pretensions. Contrary to what is usually supposed, the Kremlin in the early 1980s was already starting to understand its difficulty. This was the crucial factor that enabled Gorbachëv to advance the cause of reform from 1985. The effects of chronic commercial embargoes and of a widening technological gap at last become too heavy to bear, and the Politburo reformers secured an agenda for change in foreign policy that might provide them with a breathing space in which to remodel socialism in their country. Reagan had a firm desire to eradicate the threat of nuclear war and hoped to come to terms with the Soviet leadership on matters of disarmament. At the same time he stuck to his programme of strategic military modernization, which under Gorbachëv served to increase Moscow's desire for a rapprochement with Washington. Reagan consistently pushed Gorbachëv further and faster than he had planned to move with regard to regional conflicts, to Soviet abuses in human rights, to disinformation campaigns and to contacts between East and West. The elites in the party, government, KGB and even the armed forces approved of much of the diagnosis and course of treatment that he recommended during his early years in power.

Meanwhile Gorbachëv and Reagan, with Shevardnadze and Shultz in support, developed a degree of confidence in each other; and lessons were accepted on both sides as the USSR deepened its commitment to self-reform and ceased to quarantine its politics and media from the rest of the world. Certainly the two leaderships continued to have sharp disputes.

The American bargaining position strengthened as the USSR's internal disintegration quickened. Where there were sticking points, Gorbachëv eventually had to give ground for fear of losing the opportunity of sealing a deal. He and Reagan genuinely aimed to reduce the danger of thermonuclear war, and together their achievement was magnificent. But Gorbachëv's other objective of renovating the Soviet economy turned into a nightmare as his own policies made a bad situation worse in industrial output and food supplies. Neither Reagan nor Bush was minded to bail him out – their priority was to secure international stability and America's global primacy and they could see no benefit in subsidizing Moscow's doomed economic reform. Behind the friendly facade at the summits the Americans insisted on tough terms for conciliation.

No Western or Soviet politician had expected the Cold War to end in their working lifetimes. Everything took place as if in a dream that unfolded with unexpected twists in the plot before people woke up to what had occurred. The military rivalry between Moscow and Washington, as everyone knew, was capable of producing a clash that would have exterminated human existence on earth. The peacemakers had diverse reasons to bring it to a close, but their cause was a noble one.

Though the superpowers' allies endorsed the need for peace, their influence, as I have had to conclude, was confined to the margins of grand policy. Gorbachëv warned the East European communist leaders that they would get no help from the Kremlin to repress their peoples – and Ceaușescu eventually paid a fatal penalty for his policies of violence and austerity. On entering the White House, Bush had appeared sceptical about the rationale for rapprochement with the USSR; but he was impressed by Gorbachëv's refusal to crush the East European revolutions of 1989 and reverted to the foreign-policy line marked out by Reagan and Shultz. It was a time of disorienting transformation, and the complexities of geopolitical management increased as the Baltic national movements rolled boulders in the path of agreements between America and the Soviet Union. In Western Europe, most leaders feared for their national security when Reagan set out to abolish nuclear weapons and advance his Strategic Defense Initiative. But though Thatcher, Mitterrand and Andreotti restrained him on some important matters, he never yielded to them on his broad strategy for disarmament. Only Kohl with his campaign for German reunification proved able to canalize the course of events; but even he needed Bush's connivance to bring this to fulfilment.

Europe's political map was redrawn in 1990 as the Cold War was brought towards closure and the USSR began to fall apart. The moribund 'world communist movement' passed into history and Marxism-Leninism was relegated to dusty library corners. World politics changed irreversibly. Through the rest of the decade, only one superpower survived. Russia, the largest of the Soviet Union's successor states, cut a weak figure in global diplomacy as its internal economic and political troubles continued and President Yeltsin had to play the role of supplicant in talks with the Western powers. Russia's stockpile of nuclear weapons, albeit a stockpile that had decreased through the treaties that Gorbachëv had signed, was the sole reason why meetings between Russian and American presidents were still ranked as summits. Washington grew used to lording it over Moscow. The situation started to change only at the turn of the century, when there was an abrupt rise in the world market price for oil and gas and the Kremlin benefited from a steep rise in revenues from Russian petrochemical exports. President Putin, who was elected in 2000, became more and more assertive on his country's behalf in international politics.

In the last decade of the twentieth century there had been talk in the West about the End of History. This was based on the idea that America's victory in the Cold War would soon lead to the worldwide introduction of liberal democracy and the market economy. Among many US commentators a triumphalist mood prevailed. America had become the single superpower. The crushing superiority of its weaponry was demonstrated when it led a military intervention in the former Yugoslavia in the 1990s; and no economy came anywhere near to American levels of inventiveness as the information technology revolution proceeded.

It steadily became evident, however, that the Cold War had acted as a brake on several chronic regional conflicts, and America's armed interventions in Afghanistan and the Middle East in the twenty-first century had untoward consequences that Washington had not anticipated. Islamic fundamentalism had harmed the USSR in Afghanistan. Now it was focused against America and its allies in other Moslem countries and beyond. International jihadist terrorism spread like a plague. At the same time, moreover, the US encountered a growing economic challenge around the world. China emerged as a great industrial power, and countries such as India, Brazil and Indonesia championed their own economic independence. The 'globalization' of financial operations, originally sponsored by US administrations, had the effect of weakening America's primacy even further.

Two states, China and Russia, were mentioned as potential enemies in a new Cold War with America. Deng's successors continued with his policy of collaborating with American corporations in pursuit of economic modernization. The priority for the Chinese leaders was to maintain the influx of investment capital and advanced technology. But as China's holdings of foreign financial bonds expanded and America's external debt increased, there arose concern that American policy had been nurturing a dangerous competitor. Scandals recurred as Chinese spying activities were exposed. China treated east Asia as its special zone of influence and pressed Vietnam and Japan to yield to its demands. At the start of his second presidential term in 2012, Barack Obama reset policy to focus on the maintenance of America's influence in the countries on both sides of the Pacific Ocean.

It was Russia that became the more overt challenger to US policy. At first Putin accommodated America's wishes by facilitating its armed intervention in Afghanistan in 2001. But he and the Russian ruling group felt that they received too little in return. America had pressed ahead with an expansion of NATO across the old Eastern Europe and into the former Baltic republics of the USSR. Gorbachëv claimed that this breached his understanding with Baker in 1990; Yeltsin added that American and other Western leaders were tearing up the assurances they gave after the USSR's collapse. Putin turned his back on compromise. In 2007 he objected to George W. Bush's plan for a missile shield in Poland. He frequently intimidated Ukraine by cutting off the gas supply. In 2008 he invaded Georgia and maintained an occupying force in South Ossetia. From 2011 he stood up for Baathist leader Bashar al-Assad in the Syrian civil war. In 2014 he intervened in the political tumult in Ukraine by annexing Crimea. The West reacted with economic sanctions as he proceeded to destabilize the situation in eastern Ukraine, where there is an ethnic Russian minority. The long truce between Russia and America was over, and Washington led the way in imposing sanctions against Russian economic interests.

Was this the beginning of another cold war? America and Russia beyond doubt retained ballistic nuclear missiles with the capacity at any moment to obliterate each other's main cities and set off a thermonuclear holocaust worldwide. As Putin reached into the Russian budget to modernize Russian conventional forces, his militarist posturings bore some similarities to Soviet traditions before Gorbachëv's ascent to power, and Russia became careless of foreign criticism. This was a bad turn in international relations. But there have always been some heavy constraints on Putin's freedom of action. Above all, the Russian economy continues to be over-reliant on the export of natural resources and has little prospect of matching American technological prowess. Although the Russian leadership desires to scare and bully its neighbours, it has only a limited capacity to confront America – and it is to be hoped that the Kremlin elite has the sense to recognize this.

The conflicts in eastern Ukraine give grounds for acute worry about the European future; but as yet they remain dwarfed by the dangers that prevailed throughout the Cold War. The trial of strength between USSR and America had touched every aspect of their military, ideological, economic, scientific and political resilience. Behind each superpower there stood a coalition of allies and friends. The danger of thermonuclear war was unvarying. In both Washington and Moscow, the routine assumption was that the rulers of the other superpower were wild enough to organize an all-out nuclear offensive. Such a scenario was never far from the concerns of the US President and the Soviet General Secretary. Even during the brief period of détente in the mid-1970s, there lingered the possibility of Armageddon. Although the ballistic missiles stayed in their silos, American and Soviet leaders continued to fire ideological salvos and to support those client states which shared their hostility to the other superpower. The USSR guarded the ramparts of its fortress state and minimized its people's contact with the capitalist West. Only a brittle peace was realizable in such conditions. Until the late 1980s, a global military cataclysm could all too easily have happened by accident, misjudgement or design.

Such an outcome is not yet unimaginable while international tension grows in Eastern Europe, the Middle East and East Asia and questions of nuclear proliferation remain unresolved. All of us living today owe a debt to the generation of leaders who ended the Cold War and made it less likely that their successors will go to thermonuclear war. Much was accomplished; more still urgently needs to be done.

Select Bibliography

The following sources were actively used in the chapters. An exhaustive list of archives, documentary publications, memoirs and secondary works on the end of the Cold War would call for a book in itself.

Archives

British Diplomatic Oral History Programme (abbreviated as BDOHP)

Sir Rodric Braithwaite, 'Moscow Diary'

George Bush Presidential Library

Central Intelligence Agency

Central Intelligence Agency Papers (abbreviated as CIA Papers)

Churchill College, Cambridge

Hoover Institution, Stanford University, CA (abbreviated as HIA)
  A. L. Adamishin Papers
  Richard V. Allen Papers
  William J. Casey Papers
  Committee on the Present Danger Records
  Deaver & Hannaford, Inc. Records
  John P. Dunlop Collection
  Eastern European Oral History Project interviews 1999–2001
  Eesti NSV Riikliku Julgeoleku Komitee records, 1920–1991
  Fond 89
  Charles Hill Papers
  Hoover Institution and Gorbachev Foundation Collection
    (abbreviated as HIGFC)
  Fred Charles Iklé Papers
  John O. Koehler Papers
  Vitali Korotych Papers
  Edward Landsdale Papers
  Lietuvos SSR Valstybes Saugumo Komitetas (Lithuanian SSR KGB)
  Selected Records

Lyn Nofziger Papers

George Vernon Orr Papers

Peter Robinson Papers

Scientists for Sakharov, Orlov and Shcharansky Records

T. G. Stepanov-Mamaladze Papers

Edward Teller Papers

Understanding the End of the Cold War: Reagan/Gorbachev Years: An Oral History Conference 7–10 May, 1998, Brown University: a compendium of declassified documents and chronology of events, comp. and ed. V. Zubok, C. Nielsen, G. Grant (Providence, RI : Watson Institute, Brown University, 1998)

Dmitri A. Volkogonov Papers

Zelikow-Rice Papers

National Security Archive, George Washington University, Washington DC

Ronald Reagan Presidential Papers (CD-Rom: BACM Research) (abbreviated as RRPP)

Ronald Reagan Presidential Library, Simi Valley, California (abbreviated as RRPL)

Rossiiskii Gosudarstvennyi Arkhiv Sotsial'no-Politicheskoi Istorii, Moscow (abbreviated as RGASPI)

Russian and Eurasian Studies Centre Archive, St Antony's College, Oxford University (abbreviated as RESCA)

Anatoli Chernyaev Papers

Online sources

CIA, *At Cold War's End: US Intelligence on the Soviet Union and Eastern Europe, 1989–1991,* www.cia.gov/library/center-for-the-study-of-intelligence/csi-publications/books-and-monographs/at-cold-wars-end-us-intelligence-on-the-soviet-union-and-eastern-europe-1989-1991/art-1.html

End of the Cold War Forum (abbreviated as ECWF)

B. B. Fischer, *A Cold War Conundrum: The 1983 Soviet War Scare* (Washington, DC: Center for the Study of Intelligence, 1997), retrieved online at www.cia.gov/library/center-for-the-study-of-intelligence/csi-publications/books-and-monographs/a-cold-war-conundrum

H. Kohl, 'Ten-Point Plan for German Unity', 28 November 1989, *German History in Documents and Images*: retrieved online at http://germanhistorydocs.ghi-dc.org/sub_document.cfm?document_id=223

Parallel History Project on Cooperative Security (abbreviated as PHPCS)

'Record of Conversation, M. S. Gorbachev and G. Bush, Washington DC', 31 May, Document 10, The Washington/Camp David Summit 1990: From the

Secret Soviet, American and German Files, National Security Archive, available at: www.gwu.edu/nsarchiv/NSAEBB/NSAEBB320/index.htm
Ronald Reagan Oral History Project, Miller Center of Public Affairs, Charlottesville, VA (abbreviated as RROHP)
Soviet Intentions 1965–1985, vol. 2: *Soviet Post-Cold War Testimonial Evidence*, ed. J. G. Hines, E. M. Mishulovich and J. F. Shull (BDF Federal Inc., 1995)
Margaret Thatcher Foundation Archive
US Department of State FOIA Documents

Newspapers and periodicals

Guardian
Kommersaut
New York Times
Pravda
The Times
Wall Street Journal

Books and articles

A. Adamishin, *Beloe solntse Angoly* (Moscow: Vagrius, 2001)
A. Adamishin and R. Schifter, *Human Rights, Perestroika, and the End of the Cold War* (Washington, DC: United States Institute of Peace, 2009)
H. Adomeit, *Imperial Overstretch: Germany in Soviet Policy from Stalin to Gorbachev* (Baden-Baden: Nomos Verlagsgesellshaft, 1998)
S. Akhromeev and G. Kornienko, *Glazami marshala i diplomata* (Moscow: Mezhdunarodnye otnosheniya, 1992)
R. Aldous, *Reagan and Thatcher: The Difficult Relationship* (London: Hutchinson, 2012)
A. M. Aleksandrov-Agentov, *Ot Kollontai do Gorbachëva: vospominaniya, sovetnika A. A. Gromyko, pomoshchnika L. I. Brezhneva, Yu. V. Andropova, K. U. Chernenko i M. S. Gorbachëva* (Moscow: Mezhdunarodnye otnosheniya, 1994)
M. Alexander, *Managing the Cold War: A View from the Front Line* (London: RUSI, 2005)
M. Anderson, *Revolution: The Reagan Legacy* (Stanford, CA: Hoover Institution Press, 1990)
M. Anderson and A. Anderson, *Reagan's Secret War: The Untold Story of His Fight to Save the World from Nuclear Disaster* (New York: Three Rivers Press, 2009)
G. Andreotti, *L'URSS vista da vicino: dalla guerra fredda a Gorbaciov* (Milan: Rizzoli, 1988)
C. Andrew, *For the President's Eyes Only: Secret Intelligence and the American Presidency from Washington to Bush* (New York: HarperPerennial, 1996)

C. Andrew and O. Gordievsky, *KGB: The Inside Story of Its Foreign Operations from Lenin to Gorbachev* (New York: HarperCollins, 1992)

C. Andrew and O. Gordievsky (eds), *Comrade Kryuchkov's Instructions: Top Secret Files on KGB Foreign Operations, 1975–1985* (Stanford, CA: Stanford University Press, 1993)

C. Andrew and V. Mitrokhin, *The Mitrokhin Archive: The KGB in Europe and the West* (London: Allen Lane, 1999)

S. Antohi and V. Tismaneanu (eds), *Between Past and Future: The Revolutions of 1989 and Their Aftermath* (Budapest: Central University Press, 2000)

G. Arbatov, *Chelovek sistemy: nablyudeniya i razmyshleniya ochevidtsa* (Moscow: Vagrius, 2002)

D. Arbel and Ran Edelist, *Western Intelligence and the Collapse of the Soviet Union: 1980–1990: Ten Years that Did Not Shake the World* (London: Cass, 2003)

G. Arrighi, *The Long Twentieth Century: Money, Power and the Origins of Our Time*, 2nd edn (London: Verso, 2009)

G. Arrighi, 'The World Economy and the Cold War, 1970–1990', in M. Leffler and O. A. Westad (eds), *The Cambridge History of the Cold War*, vol. 3 (Cambridge: Cambridge University Press, 2010)

A. Åslund, *How Russia Became a Market Economy* (Washington, DC: Brookings Institution, 1995)

J. Attali, *Verbatim*, vol. 1: *Chronique des années 1981–1986*; vol. 2: *Chronique des années 1986–1988*; vol. 3: *Chronique des années 1988–1991* (Paris: Fayard, 1995)

N. A. Bailey, *The Strategic Plan That Won the Cold War: National Security Decision Directive 75* (McLean, VA: Potomac Foundation, 1998)

V. Bakatin, *Izbavlenie ot KGB* (Moscow: Novosti, 1992)

J. Baker, 'The New Russian Revolution: Toward Democracy in the Soviet Union' (Washington, DC: US Department of State, March 1990)

J. Baker, 'Remarks before the International Affairs Committee of the USSR Supreme Soviet, 10 February 1990' (Washington, DC: US Department of State. 1990)

J. A. Baker III with T. M. DeFrank, *The Politics of Diplomacy: Revolution, War, and Peace, 1989–1992* (New York: G. P. Putnam's Sons, 1995)

J. R. Barletta, *Riding with Reagan from the White House to the Ranch* (New York: Citadel Press, 2005)

G. S. Barrass, *The Great Cold War: A Journey through the Hall of Mirrors* (Stanford, CA: Stanford University Press, 2009)

J. Baylis, S. Smith and P. Owens, *The Globalisation of World Politics*, 4th edn (Oxford: Oxford University Press, 2008)

M. Bearden and J. Risen, *The Main Enemy: The Inside Story of the CIA's Final Showdown with the KGB* (New York: Random House, 2003)

A. Belonogov, *MID: Kreml': kuveitskii krizis: zamministra inostrannykh del SSSR rasskazyvaet* (Moscow: Olma-Press, 2001)

I. Berend, *From the Soviet Bloc to the European Union* (Cambridge: Cambridge University Press, 2009)

D. M. Berkowitz, J. S. Berliner, P. R. Gregory, S. J. Linz and J. R. Millar, 'An Evaluation of the CIA's Analysis of Soviet Economic Performance, 1970–90', *Comparative Economic Studies*, no. 2 (1993)

M. S. Bernstam and S. M. Lipset, 'Punishing Russia', *The New Republic*, no. 3, 5 August 1985

M. R. Beschloss and S. Talbott, *At the Highest Levels: The Inside Account of the End of the Cold War* (Boston, MA: Little, Brown and Co., 1993)

V. Boldin, *Krushenie p'edestala: shtrikhi k portrete M. S. Gorbachëva* (Moscow: Respublika, 1995)

K. Booth and N. J. Wheeler, *The Security Dilemma: Fear, Cooperation, and Trust in World Politics* (Basingstoke: Palgrave Macmillan, 2008)

A. Bovin, *XX vek kak zhizn'. Vospominaniya* (Moscow: Zakharov, 2003)

F. Bozo, *Mitterrand, the End of the Cold War, and German Unification* (New York: Berghahn, 2009)

F. Bozo, M.-P. Rey, N. Ludlow and L. Nuti (eds), *Europe and the End of the Cold War: A Reappraisal* (London: Routledge, 2008)

R. Braithwaite, *Across the Moscow River: The World Turned Upside Down* (New Haven, CT: Yale University Press, 2002)

R. Braithwaite, *Afgantsy: The Russians in Afghanistan, 1979–1989* (London: Profile, 2011)

R. Braithwaite, 'Gorbachev and Thatcher', *Journal of European Integration History*, no. 1 (2010)

G. Breslauer, *Gorbachev and Yeltsin as Leaders* (Cambridge: Cambridge University Press, 2001)

A. Brown, *The Gorbachev Factor* (Oxford: Oxford University Press, 1996)

A. Brown, 'Margaret Thatcher and Perceptions of Change in the Soviet Union', *Journal of European Integration History*, no. 1 (2010)

A. Brown, *Seven Years that Changed the World: Perestroika in Perspective* (Oxford: Oxford University Press, 2007)

K. N. Brutents, *Nesbyvsheesya. Neravnodushnye zametki o perestroike* (Moscow: Mezhdunarodnye otnosheniya, 2005)

K. N. Brutents, *Tridtsat' let na Staroi ploshchadi* (Moscow: Mezhdunarodnye otnosheniya, 1998)

W. F. Buckley Jr, *The Reagan I Knew* (New York: Basic Books, 2008)

V. Bukovskii, *Moskovskii protsess* (Moscow: MIK, 1996)

G. Bush, *All the Best, George Bush: My Life in Letters and Other Writings* (New York: Simon and Schuster, 1999)

G. Bush and B. Scowcroft, *A World Transformed* (New York: Alfred A. Knopf, 1998)

L. Cannon, *President Reagan: The Role of a Lifetime* (New York: PublicAffairs, 2000)

A. Casaroli, *Il martirio della pazienza. La Santa Sede e i paesi comunisti (1963–1989)* (Turin: Einaudi, 2000)

G. Cervetti, *Zoloto Moskvy: svidetel'stvo uchastnika finansovykh operatsii KPSS* (Moscow: Mezhdunarodnye otnosheniya, 1995)

Chen Jian, 'China's Path Toward 1989', in J. A. Engel (ed.), *The Fall of the Berlin Wall: The Revolutionary Legacy of 1989* (Oxford: Oxford University Press, 2009)

Chen Jian, *Mao's China and the Cold War* (Chapel Hill, NC: University of North Carolina Press, 2001)

A. S. Chernyaev, *Beskonechnost' zhenshchiny* (Moscow: GOETAR Meditsiny, 2000)

A. S. Chernyaev, *Moya zhizn' i moë vremya* (Moscow: Mezhdunarodnye otnosheniya, 1995)

A. S. Chernyaev, *Shest' let s Gorbachëvym* (Moscow: Progress, 1993)

A. Chernyaev, *Sovmestnyi iskhod. Dnevnik dvukh epokh. 1971–1991 gody* (Moscow: Rosspen, 2010)

CIA and Defense Intelligence Agency, *Gorbachev's Economic Program: Problems Emerge* (n.p., 1988)

S. Coll, *Ghost Wars: The Secret History of the CIA, Afghanistan, and Bin Laden* (New York: Penguin, 2004)

Commission on Integrated Long-Term Strategy, *Discriminate Deterrence* (Washington, DC: US Government Printing House, 1988)

M. Cox (ed.), *Rethinking the Soviet Collapse: Sovietology, the Death of Communism and the New Russia* (London: Pinter, 1998)

P. Cradock, *In Pursuit of British Interests: Reflections on Foreign Policy under Margaret Thatcher and John Major* (London: Current Affairs, 1997)

B. Crawford, *Economic Vulnerability in International Relations: East–West Trade, Investment, and Finance* (New York: Columbia University Press, 1993)

W. Crowe, *In The Line of Fire: From Washington to the Gulf, the Politics and Battles of the New Military* (New York: Simon and Schuster, 1993)

B. Crozier, *Free Agent: The Unseen War, 1941–1991* (London: HarperCollins, 1993)

A. Dallin, *Black Box: KAL 007 and the Superpowers* (Berkeley: University of California Press, 1985)

K. Dawisha, *Eastern Europe, Gorbachev and Reform: The Great Challenge*, 2nd edn (Cambridge: Cambridge University Press, 1990)

M. K. Deaver, *Behind the Scenes* (New York: William Morrow, 1987)

M. K. Deaver, *A Different Drummer: My Thirty Years with Ronald Reagan* (New York: HarperCollins, 2001)

D. Deletant, *Ceaușescu and the Securitate: Coercion and Dissent in Romania, 1965–1989* (London: Hurst, 1995)

J. Delors, *Mémoires* (Paris: Plon, 2004)

M. Dennis, *The Rise and Fall of the German Democratic Republic, 1945–1990* (Harlow: Pearson Education, 2000)

Deutsche Einheit: Sonderedition aus den Akten des Bundeskanzleramtes 1989/90, ed. H. J. Kusters and D. Hofmann (Munich: Oldenbourg Verlag, 1998)

A. Dobrynin, *In Confidence: Moscow's Ambassador to America's Cold War Presidents* (New York: Times Books, 1995)

Documents of the National Security Council, 7th supplement, ed. P. Kesaris (Bethesda, MD: University Publications of America, 1996)

Documents of the National Security Council, 8th supplement, ed. D. Reynolds (Bethesda, MD: University Publications of America, 2000)

M. W. Doyle, *Liberal Peace: Selected Essays* (London: Routledge, 2012)

S. D. Drell, A. D. Sofaer and G. D. Wilson, *The New Terror: Facing the Threat of Biological and Chemical Weapons* (Stanford, CA: Hoover Institution Press, 1999)

J.-F. Drolet, *American Neo-Conservatism: The Politics and Culture of a Reactionary Idealism* (Oxford: Oxford University Press, 2013)

Dvadtsat' sed'moi s"ezd Kommunisticheskoi Partii Sovetskogo Soyuza, 25 fevralya – 6 marta 1986 goda, Stenograficheskii Otchët, vols. 1–3 (Moscow: Izdatel'stvo politicheskoi literatury, 1986)

L. Eden, *Whole World on Fire: Organizations, Knowledge, and Nuclear Weapons Devastation* (Ithaca, NY: Cornell University Press, 2006)

C. M. Ekedahl and M. A. Goodman, *The Wars of Eduard Shevardnadze* (University Park, PA: Pennsylvania State University Press, 1997)

D. C. Engerman, *Know Your Enemy. The Rise and Fall of America's Soviet Experts* (Oxford: Oxford University Press, 2009)

R. English, *Russia and the Idea of the West: Gorbachev, Intellectuals and the End of the Cold War* (New York: Columbia University Press, 2000)

C. Estier, *Dix ans qui ont changé le monde: Journal, 1989–2000* (Paris: B. Leprince, 2000)

A. B. Evans, *Soviet Marxism: The Decline of an Ideology* (London: Praeger, 1993)

V. Falin, *Bez skidok na obstoyatel'stva: politicheskie vospominaniya* (Moscow: Respublika, 1999)

V. Falin, *Konflikty v Kremle: sumerki bogov po-russki* (Moscow: Tsentrpoligraf, 1999)

F. Fejto, *La fine delle democrazie popolari. L'Europa orientale dopo la rivoluzione del 1989* (Milan: Mondadori, 1994)

B. A. Fischer, *The Reagan Reversal: Foreign Policy and the End of the Cold War* (Columbia, MO: University of Missouri Press, 1997)

F. Fitzgerald, *Way Out There in the Blue: Reagan, Star Wars and the End of the Cold War* (New York: Simon and Schuster, 2000)

D. S. Foglesong, *The American Mission and the 'Evil Empire': The Crusade for a Free Russia since 1881* (Cambridge: Cambridge University Press, 2007)

R. Foot, 'The Cold War and Human Rights', in M. Leffler and O. A. Westad (eds), *The Cambridge History of the Cold War*, vol. 3 (Cambridge: Cambridge University Press, 2010)

J. Lewis Gaddis, *The Cold War: A New History* (New York: Penguin Press, 2005)

Ye. Gaidar, *Gibel' imperii* (Moscow: Rosspen, 2006)

R. Garthoff, *Détente and Confrontation: American–Soviet Relations from Nixon to Reagan*, 2nd edn (Washington, DC: Brookings Institution, 1994)

R. Garthoff, *The Great Transition: American–Soviet Relations and the End of the Cold War* (Washington, DC: Brookings Institution, 1994)

T. Garton Ash, *In Europe's Name: Germany and the Divided Continent* (London: Cape, 1993)

T. Garton Ash, *The Magic Lantern: The Revolution of '89 Witnessed in Warsaw, Budapest, and Prague* (New York: Random House, 1990)

R. M. Gates, *From the Shadows: The Ultimate Insider's Story of Five Presidents and How They Won the Cold War* (New York: Simon and Schuster, 1996)

V. E. Genin, *The Anatomy of Russian Defense Conversion* (Walnut Creek, CA: Vega, 2001)

H.-D. Genscher, *Erinnerungen* (Berlin: Siedler, 1995)

H.-D. Genscher, *Rebuilding a House Divided: A Memoir by the Architect of Germany's Reunification* (New York: Broadway Books, 1998)

A. Giovanognoli, 'Karol Wojtila and the End of the Cold War', in S. Pons and F. Romero (eds), *Reinterpreting the End of the Cold War. Issues, Interpretations, Periodizations* (London: Frank Cass, 2005)

M. I. Goldman, *Petrostate: Putin, Power, and the New Russia* (Oxford: Oxford University Press, 2008)

M. S. Gorbachëv, *Gody trudnykh reshenii: izbrannoe, 1985–1992 gg.* (Moscow: Al'fa-Print, 1993)

M. Gorbachëv, *Naedine s soboi* (Moscow: Grin strit, 2012)

M. Gorbachëv, *Perestroika i novoe myshlenie dlya nashei strany i vsego mira* (Moscow: Izdatel'stvo politicheskoi literatury, 1987)

M. S. Gorbachëv, *Sobranie sochinenii*, vols 1– (Moscow: Ves' mir, 2008–)

M. S. Gorbachëv, *Zhizn' i reformy*, vols 1–2 (Moscow: Novosti, 1995)

M. Gorbachev and Z. Mlynar, *Conversations with Gorbachev on Perestroika, the Prague Spring, and the Crossroads of Socialism* (New York: Columbia University Press, 2002)

R. M. Gorbachëva, *Ya nadeyus'* (Moscow: Novosti, 1991)

A. Grachev, *Final Days: The Inside Story of the Collapse of the Soviet Union* (Boulder, CO: Westview, 1995)

A. Grachëv, *Gorbachëv* (Moscow: Vagrius, 2001)

A. Grachev, *Gorbachev's Gamble: Soviet Foreign Policy and the End of the Cold War* (Cambridge: Polity Press, 2008)

A. Grachev, 'Political and Personal: Thatcher and the End of the Cold War', *Journal of European Integration History*, no. 1 (2010)

N. A. Graebner, R. D. Burns and J. M. Siracusa, *Reagan, Bush, Gorbachev: Revisiting the End of the Cold War* (Westport, CT: Praeger, 2008)

O. Grinevsky, 'The Crisis that Didn't Erupt: the Soviet–American Relationship, 1980–1983', in K. Skinner, *Turning Points in the End of the Cold War* (Stanford, CA: Hoover Institution Press, 2007).

O. A. Grinevskii, 'Mister Net', in A. A. Gromyko (ed.), *'Luchshe desyat' let peregovorov, chem desyat' den' voiny': vospominaniya ob Andree Andreeviche Gromyko* (Moscow: Ves' mir, 2009)

O. Grinevskii, *Perelom: ot Brezhneva k Gorbachëvu* (Moscow: Olma-Press, 2004)

O. Grinevskii, *Tainy sovetskoi diplomatii* (Moscow: Vagrius, 2000)

O. Grinevsky and L. M. Hansen, *Making Peace: Confidence Building* (New York: Eloquent Books, 2009)

V. Grishin, *Ot Khrushchëva do Gorbachëva: politicheskie portrety pyati gensekov i A. N. Kosygina. Memuary* (Moscow: Aspol, 1996)

A. Gromyko, *Pamyatnoe*, vols 1–2 (Moscow: Politizdat, 1988)

B. A. Grushin, *Chetyre zhizni Rossii v zerkale oprosov obshchestvennogo mneniya: ocherki massovogo soznaniya rossiyan vremën Khrushchëva, Brezhneva, Gorbachëva i El'tsina v 4-kh knigakh* (Moscow: Progress – Traditsiya, 2001)

S. Guzzini, *Realism in International Relations and International Political Economy: The Continuing Story of a Death Foretold* (London: Routledge, 1998)

J. Harris, *Subverting the System: Gorbachev's Reform of the Party's Apparat, 1986–1991* (Lanham, MD: Rowman and Littlefield, 2005)

J. Haslam, *The Soviet Union and the Politics of Nuclear Weapons in Europe, 1969–87: The Problem of the SS-20* (Basingstoke: Palgrave Macmillan, 1989)

J. Haslam, *Russia's Cold War: From the October Revolution to the Fall of the Wall* (New Haven, CT: Yale University Press, 2011)

Hearings before the Subcommittee on National Security Economics of the Joint Economic Committee, Congress of the United States, April 13 and 21, 1988 (Washington DC: US Government Printing Office, 1989)

T. H. Hendriksen, *American Power after the Berlin Wall* (London: Palgrave Macmillan, 2007)

H.-H. Hertle, *Vom Ende der DDR-Wirtschaft zum Neubeginn in den ostdeutschen Bundesländern* (Hanover: Niedersächsischen Landeszentrale für politische Bildung, 1998)

C. Hill, *Grand Strategies: Literature, Statecraft, and World Order* (New Haven, CT: Yale University Press, 2010)

J. Hoffenaar and C. Findlay (eds), *Military Planning for European Theatre Conflict During the Cold War: An Oral History Roundtable, Stockholm, 24–25 April 2006* (Zurich: ETH Zurich 2007)

D. Hoffman, *Dead Hand: The Untold Story of the Cold War Arms Race and Its Dangerous Legacy* (New York: Random House, 2009)

S. Hoffman, *World Disorders: Troubled Peace in the Post-Cold War Era* (Lanham, MD: Rowman and Littlefield, 2000)

J. F. Hough, *Democratization and Revolution in the USSR, 1985–1991* (Washington, DC: Brookings Institution, 1997)

G. Howe, *Conflict of Loyalty* (London: Macmillan, 1994)

R. L. Hutchings, *American Diplomacy and the End of the Cold War: An Insider's Account of U.S. Policy in Europe, 1989–1992* (Baltimore, MD: Johns Hopkins University Press, 1997)

R. W. Johnson, *Shootdown: Flight 007 and the American Connection* (New York: Viking, 1986)

A. M. Kalinovsky, *A Long Goodbye: The Soviet Withdrawal from Afghanistan* (Cambridge, MA: Harvard University Press, 2011)

O. Kalugin with F. Montaigne, *The First Directorate: My 32 Years in Intelligence and Espionage against the West* (New York: St Martin's Press, 1994)

M. M. Kampelman, *Entering New Worlds: The Memoirs of a Private Man in Public Life* (London: HarperCollins, 1991)

A. Kemp-Welch, *Poland under Communism: A Cold War History* (Cambridge: Cambridge University Press, 2008)

P. Kengor, *The Crusader: Ronald Reagan and the Fall of Communism* (New York: HarperCollins, 2006)

P. Kengor, *The Judge: William P. Clarke, Ronald Reagan's Top Hand* (San Francisco: Ignatius Press, 2007)

P. Kenney, *A Carnival of Revolution: Central Europe 1989* (Princeton, NJ: Princeton University Press, 2003)

J. O. Koehler, *Spies in the Vatican: The Soviet Union's War against the Catholic Church* (New York: Pegasus Books, 2009)

J. O. Koehler, *Stasi: The Untold Story of the East German Secret Police* (Boulder, CO: Westview Press, 1999)

H. Kohl, *Erinnerungen*, vol. 3: *1990–1994* (Munich: Drömer, 2004)

I. Korchilov, *Translating History: Thirty Years on the Front Lines of Diplomacy with a Top Russian Interpreter* (New York: Lisa Drew/Scribner, 1997)

P. Kornbluh and M. Byrne (eds), *The Iran-Contra Scandal: The Declassified History* (New York: New Press, 1993)

G. M. Kornienko, *Kholodnaya voina: svidetel'stvo eë uchastnika* (Moscow: Mezhdunarodnye otnosheniya, 1994)

R. Koslowski and F. Kratochvil, 'Understanding Change in International Politics: The Soviet Empire's Demise and the International System', *International Organization*, no. 2 (1994)

S. Kotkin, *Armageddon Averted: The Soviet Collapse, 1970–2000* (New York: Oxford University Press, 2001)

S. Kotkin with J. Gross, *Uncivil Society: 1989 and the Implosion of the Communist Establishment* (New York: Modern Library, 2009)

M. Kramer, 'The Demise of the Soviet Bloc', *Journal of Modern History*, no. 4 (2011)

M. Kramer, 'The Warsaw Pact and the Polish Crises of 1980–1981', *Cold War International History Project*, no. 5 (1995)

M. Kramer, 'Gorbachev and the Demise of East European Communism', in S. Pons and F. Romero (eds), *Reinterpreting the End of the Cold War. Issues, Interpretations, Periodizations* (London: Frank Cass, 2005)

V. Kryuchkov, *Lichnoe delo*, vols. 1–2 (Moscow: Olimp, 1997)

Yu. Kvitsinskii, *Vremya i sluchai: zametki professionala* (Moscow: Olma-Press, 1999)

M. Laar, *The Power of Freedom: Central and Eastern Europe after 1945* (Brussels: Centre for European Studies, 2010)

V. Landsbergis, *Lithuania Independent Again: The Autobiography of Vytautas Landsbergis*, trans. and ed. A. Packer and E. Šova (Cardiff: University of Wales Press, 2000)

R. N. Lebow and T. Risse-Kappen, *International Relations Theory and the End of the Cold War* (New York: Columbia University Press, 1995)

M. P. Leffler, *For the Soul of Mankind: The United States, the Soviet Union, and the Cold War* (New York: Hill and Wang, 2007)

M. Leffler and O. A. Westad (eds), *The Cambridge History of the Cold War*, vols 1–3 (Cambridge: Cambridge University Press, 2010)

R. Legvold, 'Soviet Learning in the 1980s', in G. Breslauer and P. Tetlock (eds), *Learning in US and Soviet Foreign Policy* (Boulder, CO: Westview Press, 1991)

N. S. Leonov, *Likholet'e* (Moscow: Mezhdunarodnye otnosheniya, 1994)

P. Lettow, *Ronald Reagan and His Quest to Abolish Nuclear Weapons* (New York: Random House, 2005)

J. Lévesque, *The Enigma of 1989: The USSR and the Liberation of Eastern Europe* (Berkeley: University of California Press, 1997)

M. Lewin, *The Gorbachev Phenomenon: A Historical Interpretation* (London: Hutchinson Radius, 1988)

A. Lieven, *The Baltic Revolution* (New Haven, CT: Yale University Press, 1993)

Ye. Ligachev, *Kto predal SSSR?* (Moscow: Algoritm/Eksmo, 2009)

Ye. Ligachev with S. Cohen, *Inside Gorbachev's Kremlin: The Memoirs of Yegor Ligachev* (Boulder, CO: Westview Press, 1996)

B. Lo, *Axis of Convenience: Moscow, Beijing and the New Geopolitics* (London: Chatham House, 2008)

A. Luk'yanov, *Avgust 91-go: a byl li zagovor?* (Moscow: Algoritm/Eksmo, 2010)

R. Lyne, 'Making Waves: Mr Gorbachev's Public Diplomacy, 1985-6', *International Affairs*, no. 2 (1987)

D. J. MacEachin, *US Intelligence and the Polish Crisis, 1980–1981* (Washington, DC: Center for the Study of Intelligence, 2000)

C. Maier, *Dissolution: The Crisis of Communism and the End of East Germany* (Princeton, NJ: Princeton University Press, 1997)

J. Mann, *About Face: A History of America's Curious Relationship with China, from Nixon to Clinton* (New York: Alfred A. Knopf, 1999)

J. Mann, *The Rebellion of Ronald Reagan: A History of the End of the Cold War* (New York: Viking, 2009)

Z. Maoz and B. Russett, 'Normative and Structural Causes of the Democratic Peace, 1946-1986', *American Political Science Review*, no. 3 (1993)

S. Massie, *Land of the Firebird: The Beauty of Old Russia* (New York: Simon and Schuster, 1982)

S. Massie, *Trust But Verify: Reagan, Russia and Me* (Rockland, ME: Maine Authors Publishing, 2014)

M. Mastanduno, *Economic Containment: CoCom and the Politics of East–West Trade* (Ithaca, NY: Cornell University Press, 1992)

V. Mastny, 'How Able Was "Able Archer"? Nuclear Trigger and Intelligence in Perspective', *Journal of Cold War Studies*, no. 1 (2008)

V. Mastny and M. Byrne, *A Cardboard Castle? An Inside History of the Warsaw Pact, 1955–1991* (Budapest: Central European University Press, 2006)

Materialy plenuma Tsentral'nogo Komiteta KPSS, 27–28 yanvarya 1987 goda (Moscow: Politizdat, 1987)

J. F. Matlock, Jr, *Autopsy on an Empire: The American Ambassador's Account of the Collapse of the Soviet Union* (New York: Random House, 1995)

J. F. Matlock, Jr, *Reagan and Gorbachev: How the Cold War Ended* (New York: Random House, 2004)

J. F. Matlock, Jr, *Superpower Illusions* (New Haven, CT: Yale University Press, 2010)

R. C. McFarlane and Z. Smardz, *Special Trust* (New York: Cadell and Davies, 1994)

A. McGrew, 'Liberal Internationalism: Between Realism and Cosmopolitanism', in D. Held and A. McGrew (eds), *Governing Globalization: Power, Authority and Global Governance* (Cambridge: Polity Press, 2002)

J. Mearsheimer, *The Tragedy of Great Power Politics* (New York: W. W. Norton, 2001)

V. A. Medvedev, *Raspad: kak on nazreval v 'mirovoi sisteme sotsializma'* (Moscow: Mezhdunarodnye otnosheniya, 1994)

V. A. Medvedev, *V komande Gorbachëva: vzglyad izvnutri* (Moscow: Bylina, 1994)

E. Meese III, *With Reagan: The Inside Story* (Washington, DC: Regnery Gateway, 1992)

Mikhail Gorbachëv i germanskii vopros, ed. A. Galkin and A. Chernyaev (Moscow: Ves' mir, 2006)

L. Mlechin, *Ministry inostrannykh del* (Moscow: Tsentropoligraf, 2001)

National Security Directives of the Reagan and Bush Administrations: The Declassified History of U.S. Political and Military Policy, 1981–1991, ed. C. Simpson (Boulder, CO: Westview Press, 1995)

T. Naftali, *Blind Spot: The Secret History of American Counterterrorism* (New York: Basic Books, 2006)

J. Newton, 'Gorbachev, Mitterrand, and the Emergence of the Post-Cold War Order in Europe', *Europe-Asia*, no. 2 (2013)

J. Newton, *Russia, France and the Idea of Europe* (Basingstoke: Palgrave Macmillan, 2003)

P. Nitze, *From Hiroshima to Glasnost: At the Centre of Decision, A Memoir* (London: Weidenfeld and Nicolson, 1989)

A. Nove, 'Agriculture', in A. Brown and M. Kaser (eds), *Soviet Policy for the 1980s* (London: Macmillan, 1982)

A. Nove, *An Economic History of the USSR*, revised edn (London: Penguin, 1993)

D. Oberdorfer, *From the Cold War to a New Era: The United States and the Soviet Union, 1983–1991* (Baltimore, MD: Johns Hopkins University Press, 1998)

W. E. Odom, *The Collapse of the Soviet Military* (New Haven, CT: Yale University Press, 1998)

N. V. Ogarkov, 'Voennaya strategiya', *Sovetskaya voennaya entsiklopediya*, vol. 7 (Moscow: Voenizdat, 1979)

Otvechaya na vyzov vremeni: Vneshnyaya politika perestroiki: Dokumental'nye svidetel'stva (Moscow: Ves' mir, 2010)

P. J. Ognibene, *Scoop: The Life and Politics of Henry M. Jackson* (New York: Stein and Day, 1975)

T. O'Neill, *Man of the House: The Life and Times of Speaker Tip O'Neill* (London: Random House, 1987)

J. O'Sullivan, *The President, the Pope, and the Prime Minister: Three Who Changed the World* (Washington, DC: Regnery, 2006)

A. Paczkowski, *The Spring Will Be Ours: Poland and Poles from Occupation to Freedom* (University Park, PA: Pennsylvania State University Press, 2003)

P. Palazchenko, *My Years with Gorbachev and Shevardnadze: The Memoir of a Soviet Interpreter* (University Park, PA: Pennsylvania State University Press, 1997)

V. Pavlov, *Gorbachëv – putch* (Moscow: Delovoi mir, 1993)

R. Perle, *Hard Line: A Novel* (New York: Random House, 1992)

R. Pipes, *Communism: A History* (London: Weidenfeld and Nicolson, 2001)

R. Pipes, 'Misinterpreting the Cold War: The Hardliners Had It Right', *Foreign Affairs*, no. 1 (1995)

R. Pipes, *Vixi: Memoirs of a Non-Belonger* (New Haven, CT: Yale University Press, 2003)

S. Plokhy, *The Last Empire: The Final Days of the Soviet Union* (New York: Basic Books, 2014)

S. Pons, *Berlinguer e la fine del comunismo* (Turin: Einaudi, 2006)

S. Pons, *La rivoluzione globale: storia del comunismo internazionale 1917–1991* (Turin: Einaudi, 2012)

S. Pons and F. Romero (eds), *Reinterpreting the End of the Cold War. Issues, Interpretations, Periodizations* (London: Frank Cass, 2005)

R. E. Powaski, *Return to Armageddon: The United States and the Nuclear Arms Race* (New York: Oxford University Press US, 2003)

C. L. Powell and J. E. Persico, *My American Journey* (New York: Random House, 1995)

A. Pravda, 'Western Benevolence', *Cambridge History of the Cold War*, vol. 1 (Cambridge: Cambridge University Press, 2010)

Y. Primakov, *Russian Crossroads: Towards the New Millennium* (New Haven, CT: Yale University Press, 2004)

Yu. Prokof'ev, *Kak ubivali partiyu: pokazaniya pervogo sekretarya MGK KPSS* (Moscow: Algoritm Eksmo, 2011)

P. V. Pry, *War Scare: Russia and America on the Nuclear Brink* (Westport, CT: Greenwood Publishing Group, 1999)

Qian Qichen, *Ten Episodes in China's Diplomacy* (New York: HarperCollins, 2005)

R. Ratnesar, *Tear Down This Wall: A City, a President, and the Speech That Ended the Cold War* (New York: Simon and Schuster, 2009)

N. Reagan, *My Turn* (New York: Random House, 1989)

R. Reagan, *An American Life: The Autobiography* (New York: Simon and Schuster, 1990)

Reagan: A Life in Letters, ed. K. Skinner, A. Anderson and M. Anderson (New York: Free Press, 2003)

The Reagan Diaries (London: HarperCollins, 2007)

The Reagan Diaries Unabridged, vols 1–2 (New York: HarperCollins, 2009)

The Reagan Files: The Untold Story of Reagan's Top-Secret Efforts to Win the Cold War, ed. J. Saltoun-Ebin (privately published by the editor, 2010)

Reagan in His Own Hand, ed. K. Skinner, A. Anderson and M. Anderson (New York: Free Press, 2001)

R. Reagan, *Speaking My Mind* (New York: Simon and Schuster, 2004)

T. C. Reed, *At the Abyss* (New York: Ballantine Books, 2004)

R. Reeves, *President Reagan: The Triumph of Imagination* (New York: Simon and Schuster, 2005)

D. Regan, *For the Record: From Wall Street to Washington* (London: Hutchinson, 1988)

'Rencontre de Mikhail Gorbatchev avec la Délégation Française "Initiative-87"', *Actualités Soviétiques*, 7 October 1987

T. Risse-Kappen, *Bringing Transnational Relations Back In: Non-State Actors, Domestic Factors and International Institutions* (Cambridge: Cambridge University Press, 1995)

V. Riva, *Oro da Mosca: i finanziamenti sovietici al PCI dalla Rivoluzione d'ottobre al crollo dell' URSS. Con 240 documenti inediti degli archivi moscoviti* (Milan: Mondadori, 1994)

P. Robinson, *How Ronald Reagan Changed My Life* (New York: ReganBooks, 2003)

P. Robinson, *It's My Party: A Republican's Messy Love Affair with the GOP* (London: Warner, 2000)

P. W. Rodman, *Presidential Command: Power, Leadership, and the Making of Foreign Policy from Richard Nixon to George W. Bush* (New York: Alfred A. Knopf, 2009)

F. Romero, *Storia della guerra fredda. L'ultimo conflitto per l'Europa* (Turin: Einaudi, 2009)

D. Rothkopf, *Running the World: The Inside Story of the National Security Council and the Architects of American Power* (New York: PublicAffairs, 2004)

H. S. Rowen, 'Living with a Sick Bear', *National Interest*, no. 2 (Winter 1985–1986)

H. S. Rowen and C. Wolf, Jr (eds), *The Future of the Soviet Empire* (New York: St. Martin's Press, 1987)

H. S. Rowen and C. Wolf, Jr (eds), *The Impoverished Superpower: Perestroika and the Soviet Military Burden* (San Francisco, CA: Institute for Contemporary Studies, 1990)

E. L. Rowny, *It Takes Two To Tango* (London: Brassey's, 1992)

N. Ryzhkov, *Glavnyi svidetel'* (Moscow: Algoritm/Eksmo, 2010)

C. Sagan, 'Nuclear War and Climatic Catastrophe: Some Policy Implications', *Foreign Affairs*, no. 2 (Winter 1983–1984)

R. Z. Sagdeev, *The Making of a Soviet Scientist: My Adventures in Nuclear Fusion and Space from Stalin to Star Wars* (New York: John Wiley and Sons, 1994)

R. Z. Sagdeev and A. Kokoshkin, *Strategic Stability under the Conditions of Radical Nuclear Arms Reductions* (Moscow: Committee of Soviet Scientists for Peace, Against Nuclear War, 1987)

R. Sakwa, *Gorbachev and His Reforms, 1985–1990* (London: Philip Allan, 1990)

P. Salmon and K. A. Hamilton (eds), *Documents on British Policy Overseas Series III*, vol. 7 (London: Routledge, 2010)

R. Samuel, 'Conservative intellectuals and the Reagan–Gorbachev Summits', *Cold War History*, no. 1 (2012)

S. Sanders, *Living off the West: Gorbachëv's Secret Agenda and Why It Will Fail* (New York: Madison Books, 1990)

Ş. Săndulescu, *Decembrie '89: Lovitura de stat a confiscate revoluție română* (Bucharest: Omega Press, 1996)

M. E. Sarotte, *1989: The Struggle to Create Post-Cold War Europe* (Princeton, NJ: Princeton University Press, 2009)

A. G. Savel'yev and N. N. Detinov, *The Big Five: Arms Control Decision-Making in the Soviet Union* (Westport, CT: Praeger, 1995)

S. Savranskaya and T. Blanton, 'Preamble', The Washington/Camp David Summit 1990: From the Secret Soviet, American and German Files, National Security Archives, Electronic Briefing No. 320

S. Savranskaya, T. Blanton and V. Zubok, *Masterpieces of History: The Peaceful End of the Cold War in Europe* (Budapest: Central European University Press, 2010)

T. Schabert, *Mitterrand et la réunification allemande: Une histoire secrète, 1981–1995* (Paris: Grasset, 2002)

A. M. Schlesinger, Jr, *Journals, 1952–2000* (New York: Penguin, 2007)

P. Schweizer, *Victory* (New York: Atlantic Monthly Press, 1994)

V. Sebestyen, *Revolution 1989: The Fall of the Soviet Empire* (London: Weidenfeld and Nicolson, 2009)

Select Committee on Intelligence, United States Senate, *An Assessment of the Aldrich H. Ames Espionage Case and Its Implications for U.S. Intelligence: Report* (Washington, DC: US Government Printing Office, 1994)

M. J. Selverstone, *Constructing the Monolith. The United States, Great Britain, and International Communism, 1945–1950* (Cambridge, MA: Harvard University Press, 2009)

G. K. Shakhnazarov, *S vozdyami i bez nikh* (Moscow: Vagrius, 2001)

G. Shakhnazarov, *Tsena svobody: reformatsiya Gorbachëva glazami ego pomoschnika* (Moscow: Rossika, 1993)

L. V. Shebarshin, . . . *I zhizni melochnye sny* (Moscow: Mezhdunarodnye otnosheniya, 2000)

L. V. Shebarshin, *Ruka Moskvy: Zapiski nachal'nika sovetskoi razvedki* (Moscow: Tsentr-100, 1990)

E. Shevardnadze, *The Future Belongs to Freedom* (London: Sinclair-Stevenson, 1991)

E. Shevardnadze, *Kogda rukhnul zheleznyi zanaves: vstrechi i vospominaniya* (Moscow: Yevropa, 2009)

E. Shevardnadze, *Moi vybor: v zashchitu demokratii i svobody* (Moscow: Novosti, 1991)

E. Shlosser, *Command and Control: Nuclear Weapons, the Damascus Accident, and the Illusion of Safety* (New York: Penguin, 2013)

C. Shulgan, *The Soviet Ambassador: The Making of the Radical behind Perestroika* (Toronto: McClelland and Stewart, 2008)

G. P. Shultz, 'Managing the U.S.–Soviet Relationship over the Long Term', speech at Rand-UCLA, 18 October 1984 (Washington, DC: US Department of State, 1984)

G. P. Shultz, 'Nuclear Weapons, Arms Control, and the Future of Deterrence', address before the International House of the University of Chicago and the *Chicago Sun-Times*, 17 November 1986 (Washington, DC: US Department of State, 1986)

G. P. Shultz, 'The Shape, Scope, and Consequences of the Age of Information', address before the Stanford University Alumni Association, Paris, 21 March 1986 (Washington, DC: US Department of State, 1986)

G. Shultz, Statement to the Foreign Relations Committee, 31 January 1985 (Washington, DC: US Department of State, 1985)

G. Shultz, *Turmoil and Triumph: My Years as Secretary of State* (New York: Charles Scribner's Sons, 1993)

G. P. Shultz, S. D. Drell and J. E. Goodby (eds), *Reykjavik Revisited: Steps Towards a World Free of Nuclear Weapons* (Stanford, CA: Hoover Institution Press, 2008)

K. Skinner (ed.), *Turning Points in the End of the Cold War* (Stanford, CA: Hoover Institution Press, 2007)

S. Smith, 'Foreign Policy Is What States Make of It: Social Construction and International Relations Theory', in V. Kubálková (ed.), *Foreign Policy in a Constructed World* (Armonk, NY: M. E. Sharpe, 2001)

A. A. Snyder, *Warriors of Disinformation: American Propaganda, Soviet Lies, and the Winning of the Cold War: An Insider's Account* (New York: Arcade Publishing, 1995)

J. Snyder, 'One World, Rival Theories', *Foreign Policy*, no. 145 (2004)

Soviet Economy: Assessment of How Well the CIA Has Estimated the Size of the Economy (Washington, DC: US Government Accountability Office, 1991)

A. E. Stent, *The Limits of Partnership* (Princeton, NJ: Princeton University Press, 2014)

A. E. Stent, *Russia and Germany Reborn: Unification, the Soviet Collapse, and the New Europe* (Princeton, NJ: Princeton University Press, 1998)

C. Sterling, *The Terror Network: The Secret War of International Terrorism* (London: Weidenfeld and Nicolson, 1981)

N. Stone, *The Atlantic and Its Enemies: A Personal History of the Cold War* (London: Allen Lane, 2010)

P. Stroilov, *Behind the Desert Storm* (Chicago: Price World Publishing, 2011)

Tajne dokumenty Biura Politicznego i Sekretariatu KS: Ostatni rok władzy 1988–1989, ed. S. Perzkowski (Warsaw: Aneks, 1994)

W. Taubman and S. Savranskaya, 'If a Wall Fell in Berlin and Moscow Hardly Noticed, Would It Still Make a Noise?', in J. A. Engel (ed.), *The Fall of the Berlin Wall: The Revolutionary Legacy of 1989* (New York: Oxford University Press, 2009)

E. Teller, *Memoirs: A Twentieth-Century Journey in Science and Politics* (Cambridge, MA: Perseus Press, 2001)

H. Teltschik, *329 Tagen: Innenansichten der Einigung* (Berlin: Goldmann, 1993)

M. Thatcher, *The Downing Street Years* (London: HarperCollins, 1993)

D. C. Thomas, *The Helsinki Effect: International Norms, Human Rights, and the Demise of Communism* (Princeton, NJ: Princeton University Press, 2001)

K. Tōgō, *Japan's Foreign Policy, 1945–2009*, 3rd edn (Leiden: Brill, 2010)

J. Tower, *The Tower Report* (New York: Bantam, 1987)

P. E. Trudeau, *Memoirs* (Toronto: McClelland and Stewart, 1993)

V. N. Tsygichko, *Modeli v sisteme prinyatiya voennoi-strategicheskikh reshenii v SSSR* (Moscow: Imperium Press, 2005)

US Department of Defense, Trip Report. Visit of the United State Military Technology Delegation to the People's Republic of China. September 6–19, 1980

US Export Controls and Technology Transfer to China (New York: n.p., 1987)

USSR Ministry of Defense, *Whence the Threat to Peace*, 4th edn (Moscow: Military Publishing House, 1987)

C. Unger, *The Fall of the House of Bush* (New York: Simon and Schuster, 2007)

G. R. Urban, *Diplomacy and Disillusion at the Court of Margaret Thatcher* (London: I. B. Tauris, 1996)

J. Valenta and F. Cibulka (eds), *Gorbachev's New Thinking and Third World Conflicts* (London: Transaction Publishers, 1990)

V. I. Varennikov, *Nopovtorimoe*, vols 1–7 (Moscow: Sovetskii pisatel', 2001–2)

Ye. Velikhov, R. Sagdeev and A. Kokoshin (eds), *Weaponry in Space: The Dilemma of Security* (Moscow: Mir, 1986)

V. Vorotnikov, *A bylo eto tak . . . : iz dnevnika chlena Politbyuro TsK KPSS* (Moscow: Sovet Veteranov Knigoizdaniya, 1995)

V Politbyuro TsK KPSS. Po zapisyam Anatoliya Chernyaeva, Vadima Medvedeva, Georgiya Shakhnazarova, 1985–1991 (Moscow: Alpina Biznes Buks, 2006)

W. V. Wallace and R. A. Clarke, *Comecon, Trade and the West* (London: Pinter, 1986)

K. N. Waltz, *Realism and International Politics* (New York: Routledge, 2008)

K. Waltz, *Theory of International Politics* (New York: Random House, 1979)

C. Weber, *International Relations Theory: A Critical Introduction*, 2nd edn (London: Taylor and Francis, 2004)

G. Weigel, *Witness to Hope: The Biography of Pope John Paul II, 1920–2005* (New York: Harper, 2005)

C. Weinberger, *Annual Report to the Congress: Fiscal Year 1988* (Washington, DC: US Department of Defense, 12 January 1987)

C. W. Weinberger, *In the Arena: A Memoir of the Twentieth Century* (Washington, DC: Regnery, 2001)

B. Weiser, *A Secret Life: The Polish Officer, His Covert Mission, and the Price He Paid to Save His Country* (New York: PublicAffairs, 2004)

G. S. Weiss, *The Farewell Dossier: Duping the Soviets* (Washington, DC: Center for the Study of Intelligence); retrieved from www.cia.gov/library/center-for-the-study-of-intelligence/kent-csi/vol39no5/pdf/v39i5a14p.pdf

A. Wendt, *Social Theory of International Politics* (Cambridge: Cambridge University Press, 1999)

O. A. Westad, *The Global Cold War: Third World Interventions and the Making of Our Times* (Cambridge: Cambridge University Press, 2005)

S. White, *After Gorbachev* (Cambridge: Cambridge University Press, 1993)

S. White, *Political Culture and Soviet Politics* (London: Macmillan, 1979)

S. Whitefield, *Industrial Power and the Soviet State* (Oxford: Oxford University Press, 1993)

S. Wilentz, *The Age of Reagan: A History, 1974–2008* (New York: HarperCollins, 2008)

P. Willetts (ed.), *Pressure Groups in the Global System* (London: Pinter, 1982)

J. G. Wilson, *The Triumph of Improvisation: Gorbachev's Adaptability, Reagan's Engagement, and the End of the Cold War* (Ithaca, NY: Cornell University Press, 2014)

J. Winik, *On the Brink: The Dramatic Behind-the-Scenes Saga of the Reagan Era and the Men and Women Who Won the Cold War* (New York: Simon and Schuster, 1996)

W. C. Wohlforth, 'Revising Theories of International Politics in Response to the End of the Cold War', *World Politics*, No. 4 (1998)

W. C. Wohlforth (ed.), *Cold War Endgame: Oral History, Analysis, Debates* (University Park, PA: Pennsylvania State University Press, 2003)

W. Wohlforth (ed.), *Witnesses to the End of the Cold War* (Baltimore, MD: Johns Hopkins University Press, 1996)

P. Wolfowitz, 'Shaping the Future: Planning at the Pentagon, 1989–93', in M. P. Leffler and J. Legro (eds), *In Uncertain Times: American Foreign Policy after the Berlin Wall and 9/11* (Ithaca, NY: Cornell University Press, 2011)

M. Worthen, *The Man on Whom Nothing Was Lost: The Grand Strategy of Charles Hill* (New York: Houghton Mifflin Harcourt, 2006)

Aleksandr Yakovlev. Perestroika, 1985–1991. Neizdannoe, maloizvestnoe, zabytoe, ed. A. A. Yakovlev (Moscow: Mezhdunarodnyi fond 'Demokratiya', 2008)

A. Yakovlev, *Omut pamyati* (Moscow: Vagrius, 2001)

A. Yakovlev, *Sumerki* (Moscow: Materik, 2003)

D. Yergin, *The Prize: The Epic Quest for Oil, Money, and Power* (New York: Free Press, 1991)

P. Zelikow and C. Rice, *Germany Unified and Europe Transformed: A Study in Statecraft* (Cambridge, MA: Harvard University Press, 1995)

T. Zhivkov, *Memoary*, 2nd expanded edn (Sofia: Trud i pravo, 2006)

V. Zubok, *A Failed Empire: The Soviet Empire in the Cold War: From Stalin to Gorbachev* (Chapel Hill, NC: University of North Carolina Press, 2007)

NOTES

Preface

1. Central Committee plenum, 19 September 1989: RGASPI, f. 3, op. 5, d. 295, p. 32 (heavily corrected page of a minuted speech by Gorbachëv).
2. T. G. Stepanov (interview), Hoover Institution and Gorbachev Foundation Collection (hereafter HIGFC): Hoover Institution, Stanford University, CA (hereafter HIA), box 3, folder 1, pp. 40–1.

Introduction

1. See F. Romero, *Storia della guerra fredda. L'ultimo conflitto per l'Europa* (Turin: Einaudi, 2009); G. Arrighi, *The Long Twentieth Century: Money, Power and the Origins of Our Time*, 2nd edn (London: Verso, 2009); G. Arrighi, 'The World Economy and the Cold War, 1970–1990', in M. Leffler and O. A. Westad (eds), *The Cambridge History of the Cold War*, vol. 3 (Cambridge: Cambridge University Press, 2010).
2. See A. S. Chernyaev, *Shest' let s Gorbachëvym* (Moscow: Progress, 1993); see also R. Garthoff, *The Great Transition: American–Soviet Relations and the End of the Cold War* (Washington, DC: Brookings Institution Press, 1994); A. Brown, *The Gorbachev Factor* (Oxford: Oxford University Press, 1996); J. F. Hough, *Democratization and Revolution in the USSR, 1985-1991* (Washington, DC: Brookings Institution, 1997); J. Lévesque, *The Enigma of 1989: The USSR and the Liberation of Eastern Europe* (Berkeley: University of California Press, 1997); D. S. Foglesong, *The American Mission and the 'Evil Empire': The Crusade for a Free Russia since 1881* (Cambridge: Cambridge University Press, 2007); V. Zubok, *A Failed Empire: The Soviet Empire in the Cold War: From Stalin to Gorbachev* (Chapel Hill, NC: University of North Carolina Press, 2007).
3 See G. Shultz, *Turmoil and Triumph: My Years as Secretary of State* (New York: Charles Scribner's Sons, 1993). See also M. Anderson, *Revolution: The*

Reagan Legacy (Stanford, CA: Hoover Institution Press, 1990); M. Anderson and A. Anderson, *Reagan's Secret War: The Untold Story of His Fight to Save the World from Nuclear Disaster* (New York: Three Rivers Press, 2009); J. Mann, *The Rebellion of Ronald Reagan: A History of the End of the Cold War* (New York: Viking, 2009); J. Lewis Gaddis, *The Cold War: A New History* (New York: Penguin Press, 2005).

4. See J. F. Matlock Jr, *Autopsy on an Empire: The American Ambassador's Account of the Collapse of the Soviet Union* (New York: Random House, 1995); J. F. Matlock Jr, *Reagan and Gorbachev: How the Cold War Ended* (New York: Random House, 2004); M. P. Leffler, *For the Soul of Mankind: The United States, the Soviet Union, and the Cold War* (New York: Hill and Wang, 2007).

5. P. Zelikow and C. Rice, *Germany Unified and Europe Transformed: A Study in Statecraft* (Cambridge, MA: Harvard University Press, 1995); R. L. Hutchings, *American Diplomacy and the End of the Cold War: An Insider's Account of U.S. Policy in Europe, 1989–1992* (Baltimore, MD: Johns Hopkins University Press, 1997).

6. J. G. Wilson, *The Triumph of Improvisation: Gorbachev's Adaptability, Reagan's Engagement, and the End of the Cold War* (Ithaca, NY: Cornell University Press, 2014).

7. R. Pipes, 'Misinterpreting the Cold War: The Hardliners Had It Right', *Foreign Affairs*, no. 1 (1995).

8. R. English, *Russia and the Idea of the West: Gorbachev, Intellectuals and the End of the Cold War* (New York: Columbia University Press, 2000).

9. S. Whitefield, *Industrial Power and the Soviet State* (Oxford: Oxford University Press, 1993).

10. See A. Nove, *An Economic History of the USSR*, revised edn (London: Penguin, 1993); S. Kotkin, *Armageddon Averted: The Soviet Collapse, 1970–2000* (New York: Oxford University Press 2001); M. Lewin, *The Gorbachev Phenomenon: A Historical Interpretation* (London: Hutchinson Radius, 1988); S. G. Brooks and W. C. Wohlforth, 'Economic Constraints and the End of the Cold War', in W. C. Wohlforth (ed.), *Cold War Endgame: Oral History, Analysis, Debates* (University Park, PA: Pennsylvania State University Press, 2003).

11. R. Aldous, *Reagan and Thatcher: The Difficult Relationship* (London: Hutchinson, 2012).

12. S. Kotkin with J. Gross, *Uncivil Society: 1989 and the Implosion of the Communist Establishment* (New York: Modern Library, 2009).

13. T. Garton Ash, *The Magic Lantern: The Revolution of '89 Witnessed in Warsaw, Budapest, and Prague* (New York: Random House, 1990); T. Garton Ash, *In Europe's Name: Germany and the Divided Continent* (London: J. Cape, 1993); Lévesque, *The Enigma of 1989*; C. Maier, *Dissolution: The Crisis of Communism and the End of East Germany* (Princeton, NJ: Princeton University Press, 1997).

14. O. A. Westad, *The Global Cold War: Third World Interventions and the Making of Our Times* (Cambridge: Cambridge University Press, 2005);

S. Pons, *La rivoluzione globale: storia del comunismo internazionale 1917–1991* (Turin: Einaudi, 2012).

15. J. Haslam, *The Soviet Union and the Politics of Nuclear Weapons in Europe, 1969–87: The Problem of the SS-20* (Basingstoke: Palgrave Macmillan, 1989); Brooks and Wohlforth, 'Economic Constraints'. See also J. Haslam, *Russia's Cold War: From the October Revolution to the Fall of the Wall* (New Haven, CT: Yale University Press, 2011).

1: Ronald Reagan

1. A. F. Dobrynin to L. M. Zamyatin (International Information Department of the Secretariat), 27 January 1981: Rossiiskii Gosudarstvennyi Arkhiv Sotsial'no-Politicheskoi Istorii, Moscow (hereafter RGASPI), f. 89, op. 76, d. 70, p. 7.
2. Shultz later changed his mind: *The Reagan Diaries*, p. 113 (16 November 1982).
3. M. Deaver, HIGFC (HIA), box 1, folder 13, p. 37.
4. P. Hannaford, *ibid.*, box 2, folder 2, p. 4.
5. R. Reagan, *An American Life: The Autobiography*, pp. 257–8.
6. Richard V. Allen (interview), 28 May 2002: Ronald Reagan Oral History Project, Miller (hereafter RROHP), p. 71.
7. S. Massie, *Trust But Verify: Reagan, Russia and Me*, p. 121.
8. Kenneth Adelman, 30 September 2003: RROHP, p. 50.
9. M. Friedman, interview with P. Robinson, 21 March 2002: Peter Robinson Papers (HIA), box 29, p. 24.
10. M. Deaver, HIGFC (HIA), box 1, p. 23.
11. R. Reagan to Revd R. Rodgers, 12 November 1986: Ronald Reagan Presidential Library (hereafter RRPL), Presidential Handwriting File: Presidential Records, box 17, folder 263; Massie, *Trust But Verify*, p. 160.
12. F. Carlucci, HIGFC (HIA), box 1, folder 10, p. 6.
13. E. Meese, *ibid.*, box 2, folder 11, pp. 32–3.
14. *The Reagan Diaries*, p. 104 (1 October 1982). See also p. 190 (24 October 1983).
15. *Ibid.*, p. 331 (29 May 1985).
16. R. Conquest, letters page, *Washington Post*, 5 February 1981.
17. *Washington Post*, 5 February 1981; R. V. Allen to R. Reagan, 5 February 1981: Richard V. Allen Papers (HIA), box 45, folder: Memoranda for the President, 1981 Jan. – July.
18. R. Conquest, informal recollection, 14 August 2011.
19. M. Deaver, HIGFC (HIA), box 1, p. 20.
20. See, for example, the hand-edited draft of Presidential Address to National Association of Evangelicals (Orlando, FL), 8 March 1983, pp. 1–17: Ronald Reagan Presidential Papers; L. Nofziger, HIGFC (HIA), box 2, folder 12, p. 8.
21. Author's conversation with Peter Robinson, one of the President's speechwriters: 6 September 2013.

22. M. K. Deaver, *A Different Drummer: My Thirty Years with Ronald Reagan*, p. 14.
23. R. V. Allen to R. Reagan, talking points suggestion for telephone conversation with Paul Nitze, 25 November 1981: Richard V. Allen Papers (HIA), box 45, folder: Memoranda for the President, 1981 August – November.
24. C. Weinberger (interview), HIGFC (HIA), box 3, folder 4, pp. 35–6.
25. *The Reagan Diaries*, p. 100 (14 September 1982).
26. E. Meese III, *With Reagan: The Inside Story*, pp. 192–3.
27. Recollection by P. Robinson (about comment by William Buckley Jr) in his interview with M. Friedman, 21 March 2002, p. 8: Peter Robinson Papers (HIA), box 29.
28. *The Reagan Diaries*, p. 142 (6 April 1983).
29. See G. Arrighi, 'The World Economy and the Cold War, 1970–1990', in M. Leffler and O. A. Westad (eds), *The Cambridge History of the Cold War*, vol. 3, pp. 31–40; F. Romero, *Storia della guerra fredda. L'ultimo conflitto per l'Europa*, pp. 252–66.
30. *New York Times*, 31 March 1981.
31. V. A. Aleksandrov, HIGFC (HIA), box 1, folder 2, p. 15.
32. *The Reagan Diaries*, pp. 14–15 (23 April 1981).
33. *Ibid.*, p. 15: 24 April 1981; R. Harris (Reuters), 24 April 1981.
34. A. G. Savel'yev and N. N. Detinov, *The Big Five: Arms Control Decision-Making in the Soviet Union*, p. 62.
35. If Politburo deputy member Mikhail Gorbachëv already had such thoughts, he kept them to himself.
36. *The Reagan Diaries Unabridged*, vol. 1, pp. 92–3 (12–15 December 1981).
37. National Security Decision Directive no. 75, 17 January 1983, p. 1: Ronald Reagan Presidential Papers (hereafter RRPP).
38. *Ibid.*, pp. 2–3.
39. *Ibid.*, p. 4.
40. *Ibid.*, p. 5.
41. *Ibid.*, pp. 7–9.
42. *Ibid.*, p. 3.
43. Personal interview with Charles Hill, 22 July 2011.

2: Plans for Armageddon

1. N. V. Ogarkov, 'Voennaya strategiya', *Sovetskaya voennaya entsiklopediya*, vol. 7, p. 564.
2. *Soviet Intentions 1965–1985*, vol. 2: *Soviet Post-Cold War Testimonial Evidence* (eds J. G. Hines, E. M. Mishulovich and J. F. Shull): interview of Lt. Gen. G. V. Batenin, 6 August 1993, pp. 8–9; *ibid.*: interview of Col. Gen. A. A. Danilevich, 13 December 1992, p. 57.
3. *Ibid.*: interview of Lt. Gen. G. V. Batenin, 6 August 1993, pp. 8–9; *ibid.*: inter-

view of Col. Gen. A. A. Danilevich, 9 December 1994, pp. 68–9, and 13 December 1992, p. 57.

4. *Ibid.*: interview of Col. Gen. A. A. Danilevich, 21 September 1992, p. 28.

5. *Ibid.*: interview of V. M. Surikov, 11 September 1993, p. 135.

6. N. Creighton (testimony), in J. Hoffenaar and C. Findlay (eds), *Military Planning for European Theatre Conflict During the Cold War: An Oral History Roundtable, Stockholm, 24–25 April 2006*, pp. 48–9.

7. *Ibid.*, p. 54.

8. *Ibid.*, pp. 89 and 102.

9. *Ibid.*, testimonies of G. Johnson (p. 86) and M. Zachariáš (p. 91).

10. *Observer* (London), 17 April 1983.

11. Remarks by S. F. Akhromeev in O. Grinevsky and L. M. Hansen, *Making Peace: Confidence Building*, pp. 571–2. See also below, p. 204.

12. L. Chalupa (testimony), in *Military Planning for European Theatre Conflict During the Cold War*, pp. 107 and 112.

13. W. Odom (testimony), *ibid.*, p. 133.

14. A. L. Adamishin Papers (HIA), box 1: Diaries 1980, 9 December 1980.

15. *Soviet Intentions 1965–1985*, vol. 2: interview of Col. Gen. A. A. Danilevich, 21 September 1992, p. 27.

16. *Ibid.*: interview of Col. Gen. A. A. Danilevich, 21 September 1992, p. 28.

17. *Ibid.*: interview of Col. Gen. A. A. Danilevich, 9 December 1994, pp. 68–9.

18. *Ibid.*: interview of V. N. Tsygichko, 20 December 1990, p. 145.

19. 'Soviet Capabilities for Strategic Nuclear Conflict through the Mid-1990s: Key Judgements', p. 23: CIA National Intelligence Estimate, 25 April 1985: CIA Papers.

20. *Soviet Intentions 1965–1985*, vol. 2: interview of V. N. Tsygichko, 13 December 1990, pp. 136–40.

21. Rolf Ekéus's conversation with W. Jaruzelski in Sweden's Warsaw Embassy, 26 September 2002, p. 2 (Swedish report): Parallel History Project on Co-operative Security (hereafter PHPCS).

22. T. Pióro (testimony) in *Military Planning for European Theatre Conflict During the Cold War*, pp. 76–7 and 92.

23. Interview of Gen. T. Tuczapski, in conversation with other Polish commanders (n.d.), 'Nuclear Delusions: Soviet Weapons in Poland': PHPCS. I have reworked the translation into idiomatic English.

24. J. Attali, *Verbatim*, vol. 3: *Chronique des années 1988–1991*, p. 67 (F. Mitterrand, 20 July 1988); p. 95 (conversation between F. Mitterrand and R. Reagan, 29 September 1988).

25. V. N. Tsygichko (testimony), in *Military Planning for European Theatre Conflict During the Cold War*, pp. 65–6 and 139.

26. V. N. Tsygichko (testimony), *ibid.*, pp. 67, 79 and 81.

27. L. Chalupa (testimony), *ibid.*, p. 57.

28. R. Cirillo (testimony), *ibid.*, pp. 51–2.

29. *Ibid.*, pp. 53–4.

30. *Soviet Intentions 1965-1985*, vol. 2: *Soviet Post-Cold War Testimonial Evidence*: interview of H. C. Iklé, 11 December 1991, p. 78.
31. P. J. Crutzen and J. W. Birks, 'The Atmosphere after a Nuclear War: Twilight at Noon', *Ambio*, nos. 2-3 (1982), pp. 115-25.
32. L. Gouré, '"Nuclear Winter" in Soviet Mirrors', *Strategic Review*, 3 September 1985, p. 22.
33. C. Sagan, 'Nuclear War and Climatic Catastrophe: Some Policy Implications', *Foreign Affairs*, no. 2 (Winter 1983-1984), pp. 259-60 and 291.
34. C. Sagan to E. Teller, 23 February 1984: Edward Teller Papers (HIA), box 283, folder: Carl Sagan.
35. *Pravda*, 23 March 1980, p. 4.
36. Gouré, '"Nuclear Winter" in Soviet Mirrors', p. 25.
37. A. L. Adamishin Papers (HIA), box 1: Diaries 1987, 27 February 1987.
38. Yu. V. Andropov to the Central Committee, 21 February 1979, pp. 1-2: Dmitri A. Volkogonov Papers (HIA), reel 18.
39. Deputy Minister P. P. Falaleev, Ministry of Energy and Electrification, to the Central Committee, 16 March 1979: *ibid.*
40. Working lunch of R. Reagan and A. Casaroli (memcon), 15 December 1981: M. Anderson and A. Anderson, *Reagan's Secret War: The Untold Story of His Fight to Save the World from Nuclear Disaster*, p. 81.
41. G. P. Shultz to the American embassy (Rome), 16 January 1982: RRPL, Executive Secretariat, National Security Council (hereafter NSC), Head of State Files: USSR: The Vatican, Pope John Paul II: Cables, box 41.

3: The Reaganauts

1. Charles Hill, diary (8 December 1984): Molly Worthen's notes.
2. R. Pipes, *Vixi: Memoirs of a Non-Belonger*, pp. 134-4; W. R. Van Cleave (interview), *The Konzak Report*, January 1990, p. 1. See also C. Unger, *The Fall of the House of Bush*, pp. 48-50.
3. R. E. Pipes to R. V. Allen, 30 March 1981: Richard V. Allen Papers (HIA), box 46, folder 15.
4. R. V. Allen to R. E. Pipes, 6 April 1981: *ibid.*
5. I. Kristol, 'An Auto-Pilot Administration', *Wall Street Journal*, 14 December 1984.
6. E. Meese III, *With Reagan: The Inside Story*, pp. 64-5; interview with Martin Anderson, 11-12 December 2001, p. 105: RROHP.
7. A. L. Adamishin Papers (HIA), box 1: Diaries 1981, September 1981.
8. *The Reagan Diaries*, p. 88 (14 June 1982).
9. Interview with Martin Anderson, 11-12 December 2001, p. 105: RROHP.
10. *The Reagan Diaries Unabridged*, vol. 1, p. 139 (25 June 1982).
11. A. M. Schlesinger Jr, *Journals, 1952-2000*, p. 537.
12. Charles Hill, diary (3 January 1985): Molly Worthen's notes.

13. G. P. Shultz's interview with P. Robinson, 10 June 2002, p. 5: Peter Robinson Papers (HIA), box 21.
14. See the letters from M. Friedman to G. P. Shultz in Milton Friedman Papers (HIA), box 179, folder: Shultz, George P., 1969–2006.
15. M. Friedman to G. P. Shultz, 30 July 1982: *ibid.*
16. G. P. Shultz to M. Friedman, 26 November 1982: *ibid.*
17. Matlock Files, 'Saturday Group: late 83 – early 84' (RRPL): Jim Mann Papers (HIA), box 56, folder: Memoirs/Letters 1986–7.
18. Author's interview with Charles Hill, 20 July 2012.
19. C. W. Weinberger, *In the Arena: A Memoir of the Twentieth Century*, p. 259.
20. *Wall Street Journal*, 8 July 1982.
21. Author's interview with Charles Hill, 22 July 2011.
22. Profile by George C. Wilson, *Washington Post*, 25 August 1982.
23. *New York Times*, 24 August 1982.
24. C. P. Weinberger, Remarks to the California Chamber of Commerce, Los Angeles, 11 August 1982: News Release, p. 1: Committee on the Present Danger (HIA), box 136, folder: Weinberger: 1982.
25. C. W. Weinberger, Statement before the United States Senate Committee on Budget, 3 March 1982: *ibid.*
26. *New York Times*, 5 February 1985.
27. F. Hiatt, *Washington Post*, 1 February 1985.
28. K. Skinner, notes on conversation with H. Kissinger, 20 February 1992: Charles Hill Papers (HIA), box 60.
29. T. G. Stepanov-Mamaladze diary, 19 September 1986: T. G. Stepanov-Mamaladze Papers (HIA), box 5.
30. James Mann's interview with Jack Matlock, 27 April 1987, p. 14: Jim Mann Papers (HIA), box 58.
31. C. Weinberger (interview), HIGFC (HIA), box 3, folder 4, pp. 30–1.
32. *New York Times*, 10 August 1982; *Defense Daily*, 12 October 1982.
33. National Security Council, 6 July 1981, p. 3: CIA Papers.
34. *Ibid.*, pp. 4 and 8: CIA Papers.
35. *Soviet Support for International Terrorism and Revolutionary Violence*, Special National Intelligence Estimate, 27 May 1981.
36. W. J. Casey to R. Reagan, memo, 6 May 1981: CIA Papers.
37. National Security Council, 9 July 1981, p. 3: *ibid.*
38. W. J. Casey to R. Reagan, G. W. Bush and others, memo, 8 July 1981: CIA Papers; National Security Council, 9 July 1981, pp. 3–5: *ibid.*
39. National Security Council, 9 July 1981, pp. 11–12: *ibid.*
40. W. J. Casey to R. Reagan, National Security Council, 25 March 1982, p. 7: CIA Papers.
41. R. V. Allen to R. Reagan, 5 February 1981: talking points for the National Security Council meeting of 6 February 1981, p. 2: *ibid.*
42. E. Rostow to Ambassador W. J. Stoessel, 10 July 1981: Richard V. Allen Papers (HIA), box 46, folder 21.

43. E. Rowny to Joint Chiefs of Staff, 21 May 1979, pp. 1–3: Committee on the Present Danger (HIA), box 112, folder: SALT II.
44. C. Weinberger (interview), HIGFC (HIA), box 3, folder 4, pp. 32–3.

4: The American Challenge

1. Interview with Caspar Weinberger, 19 November 2002, p. 10: RROHP.
2. James Mann's interview with Jeane Kirkpatrick, 3 March 2005, p. 2: Jim Mann Papers (HIA), box 60.
3. DCI's notes for President-Elect's Foreign Policy Assessment Board, 21 November 1980: CIA Papers.
4. Remarks at the Annual Convention of the National Association of Evangelicals, Orlando, FL, 8 March 1983: R. Reagan, *Speaking My Mind*, pp. 178–9.
5. *Ibid.*, pp. 176–7.
6. *Ibid.*
7. C. Weinberger (interview), HIGFC (HIA), box 3, folder 4, p. 40.
8. P. Robinson in his interview with G. P. Shultz, 10 June 2002, p. 5: Peter Robinson Papers (HIA), box 21.
9. Author's interview with Charles Hill, 22 July 2011.
10. *Ibid.*
11. C. Weinberger, Report to Defense Department, 25 November 1983, pp. 1–4: RRPL, John Lenczowsky Files, box 1, Active Measures.
12. E. Teller to R. Reagan, 23 July 1983: Jim Mann Papers (HIA), box 55.
13. W. D. Suit to G. H. Bush, 5 March 1981, pp. 1–2: William J. Casey Papers (HIA), box 566, folder 10.
14. US Embassy (Islamabad) to Secretary of State, 4 October 1983: ISLAMA 17012: Digital National Security Archive.
15. Interview with A. G. Kovalëv: *Novaya gazeta*, July 1996.
16. V. N. Tsygichko (testimony), in *Military Planning for European Theatre Conflict During the Cold War: An Oral History Roundtable, Stockholm, 24–25 April 2006*, p. 184.
17. Y. Primakov, *Russian Crossroads: Towards the New Millennium*, pp. 124–5.
18. 'Problema protivosputnikovogo oruzhiya' (n.a., n.d.), p. 1: Vitalii Leonidovich Kataev Papers (HIA), disk 1, IS-M.
19. V. N. Tsygichko (testimony), in *Military Planning for European Theatre Conflict During the Cold War*, p. 115.
20. *Washington Post*, 11 July 1981: Jim Mann Papers (HIA), box 8.
21. Assistant Secretary of State P. Wolfowitz to Secretary of State G. Shultz, 27 January 1983 – briefing memo (RRPL): Jim Mann Papers (HIA), box 8.
22. Trip Report. Visit of the United States Military Technology Delegation to the People's Republic of China. September 6–19, 1980, p. 1: Jim Mann Papers (HIA), box 3.
23. U.S. Export Controls and Technology Transfer to China, p. 1: *ibid.*, box 19.

24. B. Crawford, *Economic Vulnerability in International Relations: East–West Trade, Investment, and Finance*, pp. 16, 139–44.
25. M. S. Bernstam and S. M. Lipset, 'Punishing Russia', *The New Republic*, no. 3, 5 August 1985.
26. Thomas H. Naylor, 'For More Trade With the Russians', *New York Times*, 17 December 1984.
27. *New York Times*, 2 August 1983.
28. *Ibid.*
29. *Ibid.*, 7 March 1984.
30. *Ibid.*
31. *Ibid.*, 17 May 1984.
32. T. C. Reed, *At the Abyss*, pp. 266–9.
33. G. S. Weiss, *The Farewell Dossier: Duping the Soviets* (CSI Publications: Studies in Intelligence); retrieved from www.cia.gov/library/center-for-the-study-of-intelligence/kent-csi/vol39no5/pdf/v39i5a14p.pdf, p. 125.
34. A. Dobrynin, *In Confidence: Moscow's Ambassador to America's Cold War Presidents*, p. 537.
35. G. M. Kornienko in S. F. Akhromeev and G. M. Kornienko, *Glazami marshala i diplomata*, pp. 49–50.
36. *Pravda*, 24 November 1983.
37. Interview with A. G. Kovalëv: *Novaya gazeta*, July 1996.
38. Dobrynin, *In Confidence*, p. 523.
39. *Soviet Intentions 1965–1985*, vol. 2: *Soviet Post-Cold War Testimonial Evidence*: interview of Lt. Gen. G. V. Batenin, 6 August 1993, p. 10.
40. *Ibid.*: interview of Col. Gen. A. A. Danilevich, 21 September 1992, p. 26.
41. *Ibid.*: comment by V. L. Kataev in interview of Col. Gen. V. V. Korobushin, 10 December 1992, p. 107.
42. *The Reagan Diaries*, p. 131 (15 February 1983).
43. Dobrynin, *In Confidence*, pp. 516–20.

5: Symptoms Recognized, Cures Rejected

1. A. G. Kovalëv (interview), HIGFC (HIA), box 2, folder 6, p. 17.
2. A. Dobrynin, *In Confidence: Moscow's Ambassador to America's Cold War Presidents*, p. 616.
3. *Ibid.*, p. 602.
4. *Ibid.*, pp. 615–16.
5. A. Chernyaev, *Sovmestnyi iskhod. Dnevnik dvukh epokh. 1971–1991 gody*, p. 758 (13 September 1988).
6. K. N. Brutents, *Nesbyvsheesya. Neravnodushnye zametki o perestroike*, p. 36.
7. V. A. Medvedev, *V komande Gorbachëva. Vzglyad izvnutri*, p. 34.
8. S. F. Akhromeev in S. F. Akhromeev and G. M. Kornienko, *Glazami marshala i diplomata*, p. 20.

9. *Ibid.*, p. 19.
10. Chernyaev, *Sovmestnyi iskhod*, p. 606 (8 March 1985).
11. E. Shevardnadze, *Moi vybor: v zashchitu demokratii i svobody*, p. 85.
12. RGASPI, f. 2, op. 3, d. 614, p. 32.
13. *Ibid.*
14. See A. Nove, 'Agriculture', in A. Brown and M. Kaser (eds), *Soviet Policy for the 1980s*, p. 171.
15. RGASPI, f. 2, op. 3, d. 614, p. 33.
16. *Ibid.*
17. *Ibid.*, p. 34.
18. *Ibid.*, pp. 41–2.
19. A. L. Adamishin Papers (HIA), box 1: Diaries 1981, 23 December 1981.
20. *Ibid.*: 25 December 1981.
21. RGASPI, f. 2, op. 3, d. 521, p. 12.
22. See R. Braithwaite, *Afgantsy: The Russians in Afghanistan, 1979–1989*, pp. 250–2; O. A. Westad, *The Global Cold War: Third World Interventions and the Making of Our Times*, p. 351.
23. On Vietnam, see A. L. Adamishin's account of USSR Ambassador to Vietnam, V. P. Chaplin: A. L. Adamishin Papers (HIA), box 1: Diaries 1982, 26 July 1982.
24. Central Committee plenum, 23 June 1980: RGASPI, f. 2, op. 3, d. 521, p. 70.
25. *Ibid.*, p. 77.
26. Working draft minutes of conference of CC Secretaries, 18 January 1983, p. 19: Dmitri A. Volkogonov Papers (HIA), reel 17.
27. M. S. Gorbachëv, *Zhizn' i reformy*, vol. 1, p. 233.
28. A. L. Adamishin Papers (HIA), box 1: Diaries 1986, 7 January 1986.
29. V. L. Kataev, untitled memoir notes filed as PAZNOGL, p. 2: Vitalii Leonidovich Kataev Papers (HIA), disk 3.
30. A. L. Adamishin Papers (HIA), box 1: Diaries 1981, 13 December 1983.
31. Chernyaev, *Sovmestnyi iskhod*, pp. 372–3 (4 August 1979).
32. *Ibid.*, pp. 396–7 (3 March 1980).
33. *Ibid.*
34. *Ibid.*, p. 480 (2 April 1982).
35. *Ibid.*
36. M. Gorbachëv, *Naedine s soboi*, pp. 337–8.
37. V. L. Kataev, 'Kakoi byla reaktsiya v SSSR na zayavleniya R. Reigana o razvër-tyvanii raboty v SShA po SOI', n.d., p. 5: Vitalii Leonidovich Kataev Papers (HIA), disk 3, SOI.
38. R. Z. Sagdeev, *The Making of a Soviet Scientist: My Adventures in Nuclear Fusion and Space from Stalin to Star Wars*, p. 261.
39. V. L. Kataev, 'Kakoi byla reaktsiya v SSSR na zayavleniya R. Reigana o razvër-tyvanii raboty v SShA po SOI', n.d., p. 5: Vitalii Leonidovich Kataev Papers (HIA), disk 3, SOI.
40. L. V. Shebarshin (interview), HIGFC (HIA), box 2, folder 19, p. 18.
41. Chernyaev, *Sovmestnyi iskhod*, p. 528 (13 March 1983).

42. *Ibid.*, p. 537 (6 September 1983). Sue S. Pons, *La rivoluzione globale*, chap. 6.
43. G. K. Shakhnazarov, *S vozdyami i bez nikh*, p. 263.
44. Chernyaev, *Sovmestnyi iskhod*, p. 523 (20 December 1982).
45. *Ibid.*, p. 546 (29 December 1983).
46. A. L. Adamishin Papers (HIA), box 1: Diaries 1985, 15 January 1985.
47. Excerpt from Politburo meeting minutes, 24 March 1983: Dmitri A. Volkogonov Papers (HIA), reel 18.
48. Politburo meeting, 24 March 1983, pp. 20–1: *ibid.*, reel 17.
49. Chernyaev, *Sovmestnyi iskhod*, p. 582 (16 October 1984).
50. See A. B. Evans, *Soviet Marxism: The Decline of an Ideology*, pp. 105–6; S. White, *Political Culture and Soviet Politics*, p. 133.
51. Shakhnazarov, *S vozdyami i bez nikh*, pp. 107–9.

6: Cracks in the Ice: Eastern Europe

1. *Poland: Its Renewal and a U.S. Strategy. A Report Prepared for the Committee on Foreign Relations, United States Senate. October 30, 1981*, p. 5.
2. *Ibid.*, p. 7.
3. *Ibid.*
4. *Ibid.*, pp. 8–9.
5. *Ibid.*, pp. 8–10.
6. A. Chernyaev, *Sovmestnyi iskhod. Dnevnik dvukh epokh. 1971–1991 gody*, p. 459 (10 August 1981).
7. Draft proposal for the Central Committee, 28 August 1980: Dmitri A. Volkogonov Papers (HIA), reel 18.
8. Politburo meeting, 9 September 1982: *ibid.*, reel 16.
9. RGASPI, f. 2, op. 3, d. 568, p. 128.
10. *Ibid.*, p. 129.
11. *Ibid.*, p. 130.
12. *Ibid.*, p. 131.
13. *Ibid.*, p. 136.
14. *Ibid.*, p. 137.
15. *Ibid.*, pp. 142–3.
16. *Ibid.*, p. 143.
17. Central Committee plenum, 16 November 1981: RGASPI, f. 2, op. 3, d. 569, p. 7.
18. Excerpt from Politburo meeting minutes, March 1981: V. Bukovskii (ed.), *Moskovskii protsess*, pp. 417–19.
19. Excerpt from Politburo meeting minutes, 10 December 1981: *ibid.*, pp. 408–12.
20. G. K. Shakhnazarov, *S vozdyami i bez nikh*, p. 150.
21. *Ibid.*, p. 250.
22. W. Jaruzelski to D. A. Volkogonov, 23 June 1994: Dmitri A. Volkogonov Papers (HIA), reel 7.

23. R. T. Davies to R. Reagan, 17 December 1981: Richard T. Davies Papers (HIA), box 15, folder: Polish Crisis, 1980–82.
24. R. T. Davies to A. Haig, 9 August 1981: *ibid.*
25. *The Reagan Diaries*, p. 57 (21 December 1981).
26. *Ibid.*, p. 58 (22 December 1981).
27. *Ibid.*, p. 65 (29 January 1982).
28. Working lunch of R. Reagan and A. Casaroli (memcon), 15 December 1981: M. Anderson and A. Anderson, *Reagan's Secret War: The Untold Story of His Fight to Save the World from Nuclear Disaster*, pp. 80–1.
29. A. L. Adamishin Papers (HIA), box 1: Diaries 1981, 30 March 1981.
30. G. H. Bush to R. Reagan via R. McFarlane (cable from Air Force 2), 15 February 1984: RRPL, Executive Secretariat, NSC, Head of State Files: USSR: The Vatican, Pope John Paul II: Cables, box 41.
31. A. L. Adamishin Papers (HIA), box 1: Diaries 1981, 23 December 1981.
32. *Ibid.*, 25 December 1981.
33. National Security Council, 5 January 1982, pp. 5–9: RRPL, box 91283, Executive Secretariat, NSC: National Security Council Meeting Files.
34. Politburo meeting, 19 August 1982, pp. 2–3: Dmitri A. Volkogonov Papers (HIA), reel 17.
35. Memo on financial assistance to Poland, September 1982: RGASPI, f. 89, op. 66, d. 8, pp. 1–2.
36. L. V. Shebarshin (interview), HIGFC (HIA), box 2, folder 19, p. 21.
37. Shakhnazarov, *S vozdyami i bez nikh*, pp. 242–4.
38. Politburo meeting, 9 September 1982, pp. 1–2: Dmitri A. Volkogonov Papers (HIA), reel 16.
39. Chernyaev, *Sovmestnyi iskhod*, p. 393 and 395 (9 February and 1 March 1980).
40. V. A. Andropov, Central Committee plenum, 15 June 1983: f. 2, op. 3, d. 631, pp. 19–20.
41. *Ibid.*, p. 21.
42. Chernyaev, *Sovmestnyi iskhod*, p. 368 (8 July 1979).
43. *Ibid.*, p. 537 (6 September 1983).
44. *Ibid.*, p. 318 (16 April 1978).
45. V. M. Falin (interview), HIGFC (HIA), box 1, folder 15, pp. 30–2.
46. A. S. Chernyaev (interview), *ibid.*, folder 16, pp. 29–30.
47. Chernyaev, *Sovmestnyi iskhod*, p. 383 (7 December 1979).
48. *Ibid.*, p. 391 (5 February 1980).
49. *Ibid.*, p. 368 (8 July 1979).
50. Shakhnazarov, *S vozdyami i bez nikh*, pp. 169–70.
51. Chernyaev, *Sovmestnyi iskhod*, p. 368 (8 July 1979).
52. D. Deletant, *Ceaușescu and the Securitate: Coercion and Dissent in Romania, 1965–1989*, pp. 69–76 and 327.
53. Chernyaev, *Sovmestnyi iskhod*, p. 251 (11 November 1976).
54. A. L. Adamishin Papers (HIA), box 1: Diaries 1982, 23 March 1982.
55. Interview with Sir Bryan Cartledge, 14 November 2007, pp. 44–5: BDOHP.

56. National Security Decision Directive no. 54, 9 September 1982, pp. 1–4: RRPL, Paula Dobriansky Files, RAC, box 7.

7: The Soviet Quarantine

1. See R. Service, *Russia: Experiment with a People. From 1991 to the Present*, pp. 312–13.

2. R. Z. Sagdeev, *The Making of a Soviet Scientist: My Adventures in Nuclear Fusion and Space from Stalin to Star Wars*, p. 292.

3. Author's observation, early 1974.

4. S. Voronitsyn in *Sovetskaya Rossiya* as reported in *Radio Liberty Research*, 5 July 1982.

5. See A. B. Evans, *Soviet Marxism: The Decline of an Ideology*, pp. 105–6.

6. Memorandum on 'hostile aspirations and anti-Soviet actions of the Lithuanian reactionary emigration against the Lithuanian SSR', 15 April 1985: Lithuanian SSR KGB (HIA), K-1/3/784, p. 4; P. Goble and A. Worobij to National Security Council, 'USSR: The Counterpropaganda Apparatus in the Ukraine' 12 October 1983, pp. 1–2: RRPL, John Lenczowsky Files, box 1, Active Measures. See also A. A. Snyder, *Warriors of Disinformation: American Propaganda, Soviet Lies, and the Winning of the Cold War: An Insider's Account*, pp. 26–7.

7. USPS booklet (1985), pp. 17–18: Center for International Civil Society (HIA), box 88, folder 1.

8. USSR KGB to Comrade Zvezdenkov, 7 January 1983: Lithuanian SSR KGB (HIA), K-1/3/775.

9. USSR KGB to the KGB leaderships in Tallinn, Vilnius, Riga, Grodno and Pskov, 9 March 1983: *ibid.*

10. Z. F. Osipov, Report of the 3rd Department of the Lithuanian SSR KGB, 7 December 1984: *ibid.*, K-1/3/782, p. 10.

11. Yu. V. Andropov to the Central Committee: 'Ob itogakh raboty po rozysku avtorov antisovetskikh anonimnykh dokumentakh za 1979 god', 31 January 1980: Dmitri A. Volkogonov Papers (HIA), reel 18.

12. V. M. Chebrikov to the Central Committee: 'Ob itogakh raboty po rozysku avtorov antisovetskikh anonimnykh dokumentakh za 1979 god', 9 February 1984: *ibid.*

13. Yu. V. Andropov, 'Otchët o rabote Komiteta gosudarstvennoi bezopasnosti SSSR za 1981 god', pp. 1–3 and 6–8: *ibid.* See also A. P. Rupshis, Report-memorandum on the results of the counter-intelligence activity of the 2nd Department of the Lithuanian SSR KGB for 1984, 14 January 1985: Lithuanian SSR KGB (HIA), K-1/3/783, pp. 1 and 4.

14. Memorandum on hostile aspirations and anti-Soviet actions of the Lithuanian reactionary emigration against the Lithuanian SSR, 15 April 1985: *ibid.*, K-1/3/784, pp. 2 and 5–8.

15. J. Petkevičius, Survey of operational information about the Lithuanian SSR KGB's service activity, 22 July 1983: *ibid.*, K-1/3/776, pp. 1–8.
16. Excerpt from Politburo meeting, 25 July 1980: Dmitri A. Volkogonov Papers (HIA), reel 18.
17. Z. F. Osipov, Report on agent-operational work and work with cadres of the 3rd Department of the Lithuanian SSR KGB (n.d.): *ibid.*, K-1/3/781, pp. 4–5 and 7.
18. Plan for agent network operational measures for 1982, signed by M. Misiukonis, 3 December 1981: *ibid.*, K-1/3/769.
19. J. Petkevičius: excerpt from plan to deal with Mossad's subversive activity, 18 August 1982: *ibid.*
20. Report: 'Mezhdunarodnye svyazi Litovskoi SSR v 1984 godu': *ibid.*, K-1/3/783.
21. Z. F. Osipov, Report on agent-operational work and work with cadres of the 3rd Department of the Lithuanian SSR KGB (n.d.): *ibid.*, K-1/3/781, p. 21.
22. A. P. Rupshis, Report-memorandum on the results of the counter-intelligence activity of the 2nd Department of the Lithuanian SSR KGB for 1983: *ibid.*, K-1/3/779, p. 5.
23. 'Mezhdunarodnye svyazi Litovskoi SSR v 1984 godu': *ibid.*, K-1/3/783, pp. 1–3 and table 1.
24. Z. F. Osipov, Report on agent-operational work and work with cadres of the 3rd Department of the Lithuanian SSR KGB (n.d.): *ibid.*, K-1/3/781, p. 10; Z. F. Osipov (3rd Department of 4th Administration of the Lithuanian KGB), report, 7 December 1984: *ibid.*, K-1/3/782.
25. Z. F. Osipov, Report on agent network operational work and work with cadres of the 3rd Department of the 2 Administration of the Lithuanian KGB, 21 January to 29 December 1984, p. 10: *ibid.*, K-1/3/781.
26. Yu. V. Andropov, 'Otchët o rabote Komiteta gosudarstvennoi bezopasnosti SSSR za 1981 god', pp. 2–3 and 6–8: Dmitri A. Volkogonov Papers (HIA), reel 18.
27. A. N. Gorbachëv of DOSAAF of the USSR, report on the planned 'Baltika' car rally, 11 April 1983: KGB Lithuanian SSR (HIA), K-1/3/775.
28. Z. F. Osipov, Report on agent-operational work and work with cadres of the 3rd Department of the Lithuanian SSR KGB (n.d.): *ibid.*, K-1/3/781, p. 18.
29. 'Basic Rules of Behaviour for Soviet Citizens Travelling to Capitalist and Developing Countries', July 1979: RGASPI, f. 89, op. 31, d. 7, pp. 1–8.

8: NATO and Its Friends

1 Internal FCO memo by Planning Staff, 'The Management of East–West Relations', 2 May 1980, p. 3. I am grateful to Sir Rodrick Lyne for sharing this document.
2. A. Dobrynin, *In Confidence: Moscow's Ambassador to America's Cold War Presidents*, p. 430.
3. *The Reagan Diaries Unabridged*, vol. 1, p. 277 (20 October 1983).

4. *Ibid.*, vol. 1, p. 41 (22 May 1981).
5. *Ibid.* (16 October 1981), p. 75.
6. *Ibid.* (15 November 1982), p. 172.
7. See S. F. Akhromeev's comments at meeting of F. C. Carlucci and D. Z. Yazov (Moscow), 30 May 1988, p. 3: RRPL, Fritz W. Ermath Files, Box 92084, US–Soviet Summit Intentions, May 26 – June 3, 1988.
8. V. L. Kataev, 1993 diary: Vitalii Leonidovich Kataev Papers (HIA), box 1, folder 3, pp. 66–7.
9. P. Cradock, *In Pursuit of British Interests: Reflections on Foreign Policy under Margaret Thatcher and John Major*, p. 56.
10. See C. Moore, *Margaret Thatcher: The Authorized Biography*, vol. 1: *Not For Turning* (Allen Lane: London, 2013), pp. 313–15.
11. Expanded meeting between R. Reagan and M. Thatcher, 22 December 1984: Margaret Thatcher Foundation from the Reagan Library: European and Soviet Affairs Directorate, NSC: Records (folder: Thatcher Visit – Dec. 1984 [1] Box 90902).
12. *The Reagan Diaries*, p. 22 (20–21 July 1981).
13. J. Attali, *Verbatim*, vol. 2: *Chronique des années 1986–1988*, p. 176 (13 October 1986).
14. Internal FCO memo by Planning Staff, 'The Management of East–West Relations', 2 May 1980, p. 8.

9: World Communism and the Peace Movement

1. A. L. Adamishin Papers (HIA), box 1: Diaries 1981, 23 December 1981.
2. Qian Qichen, *Ten Episodes in China's Diplomacy*, pp. 2–3.
3. Interview with Richard V. Allen, 28 May 2002, p. 70: RROHP.
4. *Ibid.*
5. National Security Archive Electronic Briefing Book no. 18, doc. 8: National Security Decision Directive no. 140, pp. 1–2.
6. *The Reagan Diaries Unabridged*, vol. 1, p. 341 (27 April 1984).
7. *Ibid.*, p. 342 (28 April 1984).
8. *Ibid.*, p. 343 (30 April 1984).
9. Excerpt from Politburo minutes, 7 July 1983: Dmitri A. Volkogonov Papers (HIA), reel 17.
10. V. A. Zagladin (Deputy Head, International Department) to Central Committee, 4 October 1979: RGASPI, f. 89, op. 32, d. 12.
11. A. L. Adamishin Papers (HIA), box 2: Diaries July and October–December 1991, 11 November 1991.
12. Politburo meeting, 8 January 1969: RGASPI, f. 89, op. 51, d. 28.
13. *Ibid.*
14. A. Chernyaev, *Sovmestnyi iskhod. Dnevnik dvukh epokh. 1971–1991 gody*, p. 379 (21 October 1979).

15. See S. Pons, *La rivoluzione globale. Storia del comunismo internazionale 1917-1991*, pp. 347-70.
16. RGASPI, f. 89, op. 38, d. 47; V. Riva, *Oro da Mosca: i finanziamenti sovietici al PCI dalla Rivoluzione d'ottobre al crollo dell' URSS. Con 240 documenti inediti degli archivi moscoviti*, p. 60.
17. Party Secretariat meeting, 5 January 1982: RGASPI, f. 89, op. 11, d. 47.
18. RGASPI, f. 89, op. 38, d. 47; Riva, *Oro da Mosca*, p. 60.
19. Chernyaev, *Sovmestnyi iskhod*, p. 371 (27 July 1979).
20. RGASPI, f. 89, op. 38, d. 47; Riva, *Oro da Mosca*, p. 60.
21. *Ibid.*
22. O. A. Westad, *The Global Cold War: Third World Interventions and the Making of Our Times*, pp. 215-16.
23. Draft letter of CPSU Secretariat, 18 February 1977: RGASPI, f. 89, op. 33, d. 15.
24. A. L. Adamishin Papers (HIA), box 1: Diaries 1982, 17 January 1982.
25. *Ibid.*, box 1: Diaries 1981, 25 December 1981.
26. Chernyaev, *Sovmestnyi iskhod*, p. 15 (8 April 1972).
27. Briefing paper on 'Military-Technical Collaboration' (n.d. but no earlier than 1992), p. 1: Vitalii Leonidovich Kataev Papers (HIA), box 12, folder 30.
28. A. L. Adamishin Papers (HIA), box 1: Diaries 1980, 9 December 1980.
29. V. I. Varennikov (interview), HIGFC (HIA), box 3, folder 3, pp. 20-1.
30. *Ibid.*, box 2, folder 4, p. 54.
31. *Congressional Record – House*, 24 March 1983, H1791-1793.
32. Chernyaev, *Sovmestnyi iskhod*, p. 461 (10 October 1979).
33. A. S. Chernyaev, *Moya zhizn' i moë vremya*, p. 416.
34. Chernyaev, *Sovmestnyi iskhod*, p. 585 (12 November 1984).
35. *Ibid.*, p. 588 (1 December 1984).
36. Report by Counsellor L. A. Parshin and First Secretary Yu. M. Mazur, 15 November 1984: Dmitri A. Volkogonov Papers (HIA), reel 19, pp. 139-42.

10: In the Soviet Waiting Room

1. R. Reagan, address to the nation, 16 January 1984: www.reagan.utexas.edu/archives/speeches/1984/11684a.htm
2. National Security Planning Group, 27 March 1984, p. 2: CIA Papers.
3. *Ibid.*, p. 5.
4. M. Gorbachëv, *Naedine s soboi*, p. 358.
5. *Ibid.*, pp. 358 and 395.
6. *Ibid.*, p. 355.
7. Politburo meeting, 10 February 1984, pp. 1-5: Dmitri A. Volkogonov Papers (HIA), reel 17; V. A. Medvedev, *V komande Gorbachëva. Vzglyad izvnutri*, p. 17; Gorbachëv, *Naedine s soboi*, p. 362.
8. A. Chernyaev, *Sovmestnyi iskhod. Dnevnik dvukh epokh. 1971-1991 gody*, p. 550 (14 February 1984).

9. *Ibid.*, pp. 550–1 (14 February 1984).
10. M. S. Gorbachëv, Central Committee plenum, 13 February 1984: RGASPI, f. 2, op. 3, d. 669, p. 30.
11. G. K. Shakhnazarov, *S vozdyami i bez nikh*, p. 250.
12. Chernyaev, *Sovmestnyi iskhod*, p. 588 (1 December 1984).
13. I. Korchilov, *Translating History: Thirty Years on the Front Lines of Diplomacy with a Top Russian Interpreter*, p. 274.
14. Chernyaev, *Sovmestnyi iskhod*, p. 571 (12 August 1984).
15. *Ibid.*, p. 572 (16 August 1984).
16. *Ibid.*, p. 566 (18 June 1984).
17. *Ibid.*, p. 582 (23 October 1984).
18. V. I. Varennikov (interview), HIGFC (HIA), box 3, folder 3, pp. 11–12.
19. A. L. Adamishin (interview), *ibid.*, box 1, folder 1, p. 5.
20. S. P. Tarasenko (interview), *ibid.*, box 3, folder 2, pp. 32–3.
21. A. L. Adamishin Papers (HIA), box 1: Diaries 1980, 13 January 1980.
22. Gorbachëv, *Naedine s soboi*, p. 362.
23. *Krasnaya Zvezda*, 9 May 1984.
24. *Soviet Intentions 1965–1985*, vol. 2: *Soviet Post-Cold War Testimonial Evidence*: interview of V. N. Tsygichko, 30 March 1991, p. 149.
25. *Ibid.*: interview of Maj. Gen. Yu. A. Kirshin, 9 January 1990, p. 102.
26. R. Braithwaite, 'Moscow Diary', 21 February 1990.
27. Chernyaev, *Sovmestnyi iskhod*, p. 567 (18 June 1984).
28. *Ibid.*, p. 571 (12 August 1984).
29. M. S. Gorbachëv to the Political Consultative Committee in Sofia (Soviet record), 22 October 1985, p. 14: PHPCS.
30. J. Attali, *Verbatim*, vol. 1: *Chronique des années 1981–1986*, p. 798 (18 April 1985).
31. See A. B. Evans, *Soviet Marxism: The Decline of an Ideology*, pp. 105–6.
32. K. U. Chernenko, Central Committee plenum, 23 October 1984: RGASPI, f. 2, op. 3, d. 685, p. 8.
33. A. Yakovlev, *Omut pamyati*, p. 165.
34. N. A. Tikhonov, Central Committee plenum, 23 October 1984: RGASPI, f. 2, op. 3, d. 685, pp. 26, 30, 40, 46 and 52.
35. A. L. Adamishin Papers (HIA), box 1: Diaries 1985, 23 February 1985.
36. A. A. Gromyko, Politburo meeting, 26 April 1984: RGASPI, f. 89, op. 42, d. 57, pp. 2–4.
37. D. F. Ustinov, *ibid.*, p. 5.
38. A. A. Gromyko, *ibid.*, p. 6.
39. L. Bezymenskii, 'Pod sen'yu amerikanskikh raket', *Pravda*, 27 July 1984.
40. James Mann's interview with E. Krenz, 17 November 2005, p. 5: Jim Mann Papers (HIA), box 60.
41. Chernyaev, *Sovmestnyi iskhod*, pp. 574–5 (25 August 1984).
42. *Pravda*, 30 June 1984. See also J. Haslam, *The Soviet Union and the Politics of Nuclear Weapons in Europe, 1969–87: The Problem of the SS-20*, pp. 143–4.
43. National Security Council, 18 September 1984, p. 9: CIA Papers.

44. Charles Hill, diary (7 December 1984): Molly Worthen's notes.
45. G. P. Shultz, 'Managing the U.S.–Soviet Relationship over the Long Term', speech at Rand-UCLA, 18 October 1984, p. 2.
46. A. Dobrynin, *In Confidence: Moscow's Ambassador to America's Cold War Presidents*, p. 555.
47. Haslam, *The Soviet Union and the Politics of Nuclear Weapons in Europe, 1969–87*, pp. 146–7.
48. P. Trudeau, *Memoirs*, p. 341; Yakovlev, *Omut pamyati*, p. 490.
49. Chernyaev, *Sovmestnyi iskhod*, p. 566 (14 June 1984).
50. *Ibid.*, p. 567 (18 June 1984).
51. Attali, *Verbatim*, vol. 1, p. 521 (20 October 1983).
52. Chernyaev, *Sovmestnyi iskhod*, p. 553 (18 February 1984).
53. Soviet record of Chernenko–Thatcher conversation, 14 February 1984, pp. 4–6: Dmitri A. Volkogonov Papers (HIA), reel 17.
54. Attali, *Verbatim*, vol. 1, pp. 655–6 (20 June 1984).
55. *Ibid.*, p. 681 (26 June 1984).
56. K. A. Bishop (interpreter), report on 3 July 1984 Moscow meeting, 4 July 1984, pp. 1–2: National Archives, PREM 19/1394.
57. Attali, *Verbatim*, vol. 1, p. 521 (20 October 1983); M. Thatcher, note on memo from C. D. Powell, 28 June 1984: National Archives, PREM 19/1394.
58. Trudeau, *Memoirs*, pp. 340–1; L. V. Appleyard (FCO) to C. D. Powell, 19 November 1984: National Archives, PREM 19/1394.
59. Note by M. Thatcher on memo from R. B. Bone (FCO) to A. J. Coles (PM's office), 4 June 1984: National Archives, PREM 19/1394; R. Thompson to R. B. Bone (DTI), 12 July 1984: *ibid.*; Moscow embassy to FCO, telegram 824, 3 July 1984: *ibid.*
60. Central Committee plenum, 10 April 1984: RGASPI, f. 2, op. 3, d. 674, p. 5a.
61. Interview with L. M. Zamyatin, *Kommersant*, 3 May 2005.
62. A. G. Kovalëv (interview), HIGFC (HIA), box 2, folder 6, p. 5.
63. R. Z. Sagdeev, *The Making of a Soviet Scientist: My Adventures in Nuclear Fusion and Space from Stalin to Star Wars*, p. 266.
64. A. G. Kovalëv (interview), HIGFC (HIA), box 2, folder 6, p. 5.
65. *Ibid.*
66. *Ibid.*, p. 24.
67. K. A. Bishop (interpreter), personal assessment of Gorbachëv during the December 1984 visit to the UK, 3 January 1985, p. 1: National Archives, PREM 19/1394.
68. C. D. Powell (10 Downing Street) to L. V. Appleyard (FCO), 17 December 1984: National Archives, PREM 19/1394.
69. Interview with L. M. Zamyatin, *Kommersant*, 3 May 2005; private meeting between R. Reagan and M. Thatcher, 22 December 1984: Margaret Thatcher Foundation from the Reagan Library: European and Soviet Affairs Directorate, NSC: Records (folder: Thatcher Visit – Dec. 1984 [1] Box 90902).
70. Notes on Chequers lunchtime discussion 16 December 1984, p. 3: National Archives, PREM 19/1394.

71. Interview with L. M. Zamyatin, *Kommersant*, 3 May 2005; private meeting between R. Reagan and M. Thatcher, 22 December 1984: Margaret Thatcher Foundation from the Reagan Library: European and Soviet Affairs Directorate, NSC: Records (folder: Thatcher Visit – Dec. 1984 [1] Box 90902).

72. Notes on Chequers lunchtime discussion 16 December 1984, p. 5: National Archives, PREM 19/1394.

73. *Ibid.*

74. Chernyaev, *Sovmestnyi iskhod*, p. 597 (26 January 1985).

75. Official record of Chequers lunchtime discussion 16 December 1984, p. 5: National Archives, PREM 19/1394.

76. *Ibid.*, p. 7.

77. Yakovlev, *Omut pamyati*, p. 236.

78. Braithwaite, 'Moscow Diary', 13 March 1992: entry on recollection by interpreter Tony Bishop.

79. K. A. Bishop (interpreter), personal assessment of Gorbachëv during the December 1984 visit to the UK, 3 January 1985, p. 3: National Archives, PREM 19/1394.

80. FCO to Hong Kong Embassy, 20 December 1984, p. 1: National Archives, PREM 19/1394.

81. M. Thatcher's notes before Camp David meeting (22 December 1984) with R. Reagan, pp. 1–2: National Archives, PREM 19/1394.

82. G. P. Shultz to R. Reagan, memo for meeting with M. Thatcher on 22 December 1984, p. 2: RRPL, Coordination Office, NSC: Records, box 4.

83. C. Hill, handwritten notes on 'Soviet: 1984, Oct. 1 to Oct. 31', p. 7: Charles Hill Papers (HIA), box 64.

84. C. Hill, notes on 'Soviet Union, Nov. 1 to Nov. 28', p. 8: *ibid.*, box 64, folder: G. P. Shultz – 'Turmoil' – Draft – Soviet Union.

85. Charles Hill, diary (8 December 1984): Molly Worthen's notes.

86. *Ibid.* (1 December 1984).

87. *Ibid.* (7 January 1985).

88. *Ibid.* (5 January 1985).

89. *Ibid.* (5 January 1985).

90. E. Shevardnadze, *Kogda rukhnul zheleznyi zanaves: vstrechi i vospominaniya*, p. 69.

91. A. L. Adamishin Papers (HIA), box 1: Diaries 1980, 5 May 1980 and Diaries 1982, 24 June 1982.

92. G. Shultz, *Turmoil and Triumph: My Years as Secretary of State*, p. 515; G. M. Kornienko in S. F. Akhromeev and G. M. Kornienko, *Glazami marshala i diplomata*, p. 89.

93. Charles Hill, diary (28 January 1985): Molly Worthen's notes.

94. G. Shultz, *Statement to the Foreign Relations Committee, 31 January 1985*, pp. 1–3: Committee on the Present Danger (HIA), box 113.

95. This exchange was reported weeks later in the *Wall Street Journal*, 21 March 1985.

96. *New York Times*, 5 February 1985.
97. *Washington Post*, 1 February 1985.

11: Mikhail Gorbachëv

1. Politburo meeting, 11 March 1985, p. 2: Dmitri A. Volkogonov Papers (HIA), reel 17.
2. A. Dobrynin, *In Confidence: Moscow's Ambassador to America's Cold War Presidents*, p. 571.
3. M. Gorbachëv, *Naedine s soboi*, p. 374.
4. A. Yakovlev, *Omut pamyati*, p. 442.
5. Gorbachëv, *Naedine s soboi*, p. 382.
6. *Ibid.*, pp. 383–4.
7. *Ibid.*, p. 385.
8. *Ibid.*, pp. 385–6.
9. Politburo meeting, 11 March 1985, pp. 2–4: Dmitri A. Volkogonov Papers (HIA), reel 17.
10. Yakovlev, *Omut pamyati*, p. 444.
11. A. Chernyaev, *Sovmestnyi iskhod. Dnevnik dvukh epokh. 1971–1991 gody*, p. 608 (11 March 1985).
12. Central Committee plenum, 11 March 1985: RGASPI, f. 2, op. 3, d. 697, pp. 5–6; *ibid.*, f. 2, op. 3, d. 700, p. 1.
13. Central Committee plenum, 21 October 1980: *ibid.*, f. 2, op. 3., d. 543, p. 2.
14. R. Braithwaite, 'Moscow Diary', 17 October 1990.
15. N. Ryzhkov, *Glavnyi svidetel'*, p. 63.
16. G. K. Shakhnazarov, *S vozdyami i bez nikh*, p. 284.
17. Chernyaev, *Sovmestnyi iskhod*, p. 699 (7 December 1986).
18. T. G. Stepanov-Mamaladze diary, 22 April 1986: T. G. Stepanov-Mamaladze Papers (HIA), box 5.
19. Gorbachëv, *Naedine s soboi*, pp. 44 and 113.
20. I. Korchilov, *Translating History: Thirty Years on the Front Lines of Diplomacy with a Top Russian Interpreter*, p. 302.
21. *Ibid.*, p. 39.
22. Gorbachëv, *Naedine s soboi*, p. 226; Chernyaev, *Sovmestnyi iskhod*, p. 434 (29 January 1981).
23. Dinner conversation at Geneva summit meeting between Reagan and Gorbachëv, 19 November 1985: National Security Archive Electronic Briefing Book no. 172, doc. 20 (US memorandum), p. 6.
24. *The Reagan Diaries*, p. 307 (11 March 1985). Because of the time-zone difference, Reagan heard the news at 4 a.m. on 11 March 1985, US Eastern time.
25. *Ibid.*, p. 310 (20 March 1985).
26. R. Reagan to M. S. Gorbachëv, 11 March 1985: RRPL, Executive Secretariat, NSC, Head of State Files: USSR: General Secretary Gorbachev, box 39.

27. *New York Times*, 12 March 1985.
28. J. Attali, *Verbatim*, vol. 1: *Chronique des années 1981–1986*, p. 780 (13 March 1985).
29. Conversation of M. S. Gorbachëv with B. Karmal, 14 March 1985: Dmitri A. Volkogonov Papers (HIA), reel 17.
30. Working notes of conference of Central Committee secretaries, 15 March 1985, p. 7: *ibid.*, reel 17.
31. *Ibid.*, p. 3.
32. Chernyaev, *Sovmestnyi iskhod*, p. 610 (14 March 1985).
33. G. Shultz: interview with R. Service and P. Robinson, Hoover Institution, 1 September 2009.
34. Working notes of conference of Central Committee secretaries, 15 March 1985, pp. 5–6: Dmitri A. Volkogonov Papers (HIA), reel 17.
35. *Ibid.*, pp. 4–5; Chernyaev, *Sovmestnyi iskhod*, p. 610 (14 March 1985).
36. Chernyaev, *Sovmestnyi iskhod*, p. 803 (23 September 1989).
37. *Ibid.*, p. 944 (28 May 1991).
38. *Ibid.*, p. 610 (14 March 1985); working notes of conference of Central Committee secretaries, 15 March 1985, pp. 4–5: Dmitri A. Volkogonov Papers (HIA), reel 17.
39. *Ibid.*, p. 6.
40. Gorbachëv, *Naedine s soboi*, pp. 393–4.
41. Working notes of conference of Central Committee secretaries, 15 March 1985, pp. 10–11: Dmitri A. Volkogonov Papers (HIA), reel 17.
42. Politburo meeting, 4 February 1988, p. 3: Anatoli Chernyaev Papers (Russian and Eurasian Studies Centre Archive, St Antony's College, Oxford University, hereafter RESCA), box 2, folder 3; Dobrynin, *In Confidence*, p. 616.
43. A. S. Chernyaev (interview), HIGFC (HIA), box 1, folder 12, p. 39.
44. Dobrynin, *In Confidence*, p. 616.
45. Chernyaev, *Sovmestnyi iskhod*, p. 613 (18 March 1985).
46. *Ibid.*, p. 619 (11 April 1985).
47. Working notes of conference of Central Committee secretaries, 15 March 1985, pp. 10–11: Dmitri A. Volkogonov Papers (HIA), reel 17.
48. Chernyaev, *Sovmestnyi iskhod*, p. 620 (11 April 1985).
49. Politburo meeting, 13 March 1988: Anatoli Chernyaev Papers (RESCA), box 1, p. 374.
50. 'Iz razmyshlenii v uzkom krugu po podgotovke 70-letiya Oktyabrya', 29 April 1987, p. 1: *ibid.*, box 2, folder 2.
51. T. G. Stepanov (interview), HIGFC (HIA), box 3, folder 1, p. 40.
52. Chernyaev, *Sovmestnyi iskhod*, p. 579 (2 October 1984).
53. M. S. Gorbachëv to R. Reagan, 24 March 1985, pp. 1–3: RRPL, Executive Secretariat, NSC, Head of State Files: USSR: General Secretary Gorbachev, box 39.
54. G. P. Shultz to R. Reagan, 25 March 1985: *ibid.*
55. *Guardian*, 18 April 1985.
56. *New York Times*, 11 April 1985; see also Reagan's reference to O'Neill's

testimony in R. Reagan to M. S. Gorbachëv, 30 April 1985, pp. 6–7: RRPL, Executive Secretariat, NSC, Head of State Files: USSR: General Secretary Gorbachev, box 39.

57. Central Committee plenum, 23 April 1985: RGASPI, f. 2, op. 3, d. 708, p. 34.
58. Ibid., pp. 34–5.
59. Ibid., p. 35.
60. Ibid., p. 38.
61. Ibid., p. 39.
62. Ibid., pp. 40–1.
63. Central Committee plenum report by M. S. Gorbachëv, 23 April 1985: V Politbyuro TsK KPSS. Po zapisyam Anatoliya Chernyaeva, Vadima Medvedeva, Georgiya Shakhnazarova, 1985–1991, p. 15.
64. Central Committee plenum, 23 April 1985: RGASPI, f. 2, op. 3, d. 708, p. 76.
65. S. F. Akhromeev in S. F. Akhromeev and G. M. Kornienko, Glazami marshala i diplomata, p. 35.
66. A. L. Adamishin Papers (HIA), box 1: Diaries 1986, 19 November 1986, p. 1.
67. Chernyaev, Sovmestnyi iskhod, p. 575 (16 September 1984).

12: The Moscow Reform Team

1. Ye. Ligachev with S. Cohen, Inside Gorbachev's Kremlin: The Memoirs of Yegor Ligachev, p. 21.
2. See above, p. 61.
3. Politburo meeting, 12 July 1984: V. Bukovskii (ed.), Moskovskii protsess, pp. 87–8.
4. A. L. Adamishin Papers (HIA), box 1: Diaries 1985, 10 April 1985.
5. V. A. Medvedev (interview), HIGFC (HIA), box 2, folder 10, p. 25.
6. Politburo meeting, 29 June 1985, p. 2: Dmitri A. Volkogonov Papers (HIA), reel 17.
7. T. G. Stepanov-Mamaladze diary, 26 April 1986: T. G. Stepanov-Mamaladze Papers (HIA), box 5; E. Shevardnadze, Kogda rukhnul zheleznyi zanaves: vstrechi i vospominaniya, pp. 67–8.
8. E. Shevardnadze, Moi vybor: v zashchitu demokratii i svobody, p. 80.
9. Politburo meeting, 29 June 1985, pp. 2–3: Dmitri A. Volkogonov Papers (HIA), reel 17.
10. Ibid., p. 3; confidential information given by B. N. Ponomarëv to A. S. Chernyaev: A. Chernyaev, Sovmestnyi iskhod. Dnevnik dvukh epokh. 1971–1991 gody, p. 637 (1 July 1985).
11. Shevardnadze, Moi vybor, p. 58.
12. Ibid., pp. 59–60; Shevardnadze, Kogda rukhnul zheleznyi zanaves, pp. 71–2.
13. Conference of Central Committee secretaries, n.d. but likely to be in January 1983: Dmitri A. Volkogonov Papers (HIA), reel 17.
14. Gorbachëv's second meeting with provincial party committee secretaries, 15 April 1988: Anatoli Chernyaev Papers (RESCA), box 2, folder 5.

15. T. G. Stepanov-Mamaladze diary, 20 April 1986: T. G. Stepanov-Mamaladze Papers (HIA), box 5.

16. *Ibid.*, 17 November 1985: box 5, folder 1; Shevardnadze, *Kogda rukhnul zheleznyi zanaves*, p. 91.

17. Shevardnadze, *Moi vybor*, p. 43.

18. *Ibid.*, p. 51.

19. R. Braithwaite, 'Moscow Diary', 29 March 1989.

20. T. G. Stepanov-Mamaladze working notes, 21 January 1986: T. G. Stepanov-Mamaladze Papers (HIA), box 1.

21. T. G. Stepanov-Mamaladze diary, 4–12 July 1990: *ibid.*, box 5. This was excised from the *Pravda* report of 10 July.

22. RGASPI, f. 2, op. 3, d. 521 p. 47.

23. A. L. Adamishin Papers (HIA), box 1: Diaries 1984, 22 February 1984.

24. T. G. Stepanov-Mamaladze working notes, 26 November 1985: T. G. Stepanov-Mamaladze Papers (HIA), box 1.

25. T. G. Stepanov-Mamaladze diary, 1 March 1986: *ibid.*, box 5.

26. *Ibid.*, 28 February 1986: box 5.

27. Politburo meeting, 23 January 1986: *V Politbyuro TsK KPSS. Po zapisyam Anatoliya Chernyaeva, Vadima Medvedeva, Georgiya Shakhnazarova, 1985–1991*, p. 25.

28. T. G. Stepanov-Mamaladze diary, 20 April 1986: T. G. Stepanov-Mamaladze Papers (HIA), box 5.

29. A. Yakovlev, *Omut pamyati*, pp. 190–1.

30. Chernyaev, *Sovmestnyi iskhod*, p. 376 (14 October 1979).

31. Yakovlev, *Omut pamyati*, p. 213.

32. *Ibid.*, p. 209.

33. A. N. Yakovlev (interview), HIGFC (HIA), box 3, folder 5, p. 8.

34. Yakovlev, *Omut pamyati*, p. 579.

35. A. N. Yakovlev (interview), HIGFC (HIA), box 3, folder 5, p. 17.

36. Braithwaite, 'Moscow Diary', 30 May 1990.

37. I. Korchilov, *Translating History: Thirty Years on the Front Lines of Diplomacy with a Top Russian Interpreter*, p. 197.

38. A. N. Yakovlev (interview), HIGFC (HIA), box 3, folder 5, p. 6.

39. O. D. Baklanov (interview), *ibid.*, box 1, folder 5, p. 29.

40. A. Luk'yanov, *Avgust 91-go: a byl li zagovor?*, p. 10.

41. Yakovlev, *Omut pamyati*, pp. 242–6.

42. V. A. Medvedev (interview), HIGFC (HIA), box 2, folder 10, p. 25.

43. V. L. Kataev (interview), *ibid.*, box 2, folder 4, p. 6.

44. Politburo meeting, 29 June 1985, p. 7: Dmitri A. Volkogonov Papers (HIA), reel 17.

45. *Ibid.*, p. 8.

46. L. N. Zaikov, proposal, August 1982: Vitalii Leonidovich Kataev Papers (HIA), box 13, folder 28.

47. Politburo meeting, 14 May 1987: Anatoli Chernyaev Papers (RESCA), box 1, p. 225.

48. V. L. Kataev, untitled memoir notes filed as PAZNOGL, p. 3: Vitalii Leonidovich Kataev Papers (HIA), disk 3.
49. V. L. Kataev, 'Struktura podgotovki i prinyatiya reshenii po voenno-politicheskim problemam v SSSR', pp. 4–5: *ibid.*, box 16.
50. A. S. Chernyaev to M. S. Gorbachëv, 13 November 1987: Anatoli Chernyaev Papers (RESCA), box 2, folder 2.
51. V. L. Kataev, 'Struktura podgotovki i prinyatiya reshenii po voenno-politicheskim problemam v SSSR', pp. 18–19: Vitalii Leonidovich Kataev Papers (HIA), box 16.; V. L. Kataev, 'Koordinatsiya v SSSR voprosov kontrolya nad vooruzheniyami do 1985', p. 2: *ibid.*, disk 2, PAB-GRUP; N. S. Leonov, *Likholet'e*, p. 323. Strictly speaking, the body was known as the Supreme (*Verkhnyaya*) Five.
52. V. L. Kataev, 'Struktura podgotovki i prinyatiya reshenii po voenno-politicheskim problemam v SSSR', pp. 10–11: Vitalii Leonidovich Kataev Papers (HIA), box 16; V. L. Kataev, untitled memoir notes filed as PAZNOGL, p. 6: *ibid.*, disk 3; V. L. Kataev (interview), HIGFC (HIA), box 2, folder 4, pp. 19–20.
53. V. L. Kataev in his untitled memoir notes filed as PAZNOGL, p. 8: Vitalii Leonidovich Kataev Papers (HIA), disk 3; V. L. Kataev, 'Struktura podgotovki i prinyatiya reshenii po voenno-politicheskim problemam v SSSR', p. 6: *ibid.*, box 16; V. L. Kataev, 'Koordinatsiya v SSSR voprosov kontrolya nad vooruzheniyami do 1985', p. 2: *ibid.*, disk 2, PAB-GRUP; S. F. Akhromeev, background briefing, 22 May 1988, pp. 1–2: *ibid.*, box 10, folder 14.
54. V. L. Kataev, 'Problemy voennoi politiki', p. 3: *ibid.*, box 16.
55. V. L. Kataev, diary for 15 February 1988: *ibid.*, box 1, folder 2; V. L. Kataev (interview), HIGFC (HIA), box 2, folder 4, p. 22.
56. V. L. Kataev, 'Koordinatsiya v SSSR voprosov kontrolya nad vooruzheniyami do 1985', p. 3: Vitalii Leonidovich Kataev Papers (HIA), disk 2 (PAB-GRUP); V. L. Kataev, 'Struktura podgotovki i prinyatiya reshenii po voenno-politicheskim problemam v SSSR', p. 17: *ibid.*, box 16.
57. O. D. Baklanov (interview), HIGFC (HIA), box 1, folder 5, pp. 7–8.
58. G. M. Kornienko in S. F. Akhromeev and G. M. Kornienko, *Glazami marshala i diplomata*, p. 91.
59. V. L. Kataev (interview), HIGFC (HIA), box 2, folder 4, pp. 18–19.
60. Leonov, *Likholet'e*, p. 328.
61. V. L. Kataev, diary for 1984–1986: 30 June 1986: Vitalii Leonidovich Kataev Papers (HIA), box 2, folder 3.
62. Notes on confidential conversation with E. A. Shevardnadze, 10 September 1985: T. G. Stepanov-Mamaladze Papers (HIA), box 5.
63. T. G. Stepanov-Mamaladze diary, 17 November 1985: *ibid.*
64. *Ibid.*, 25 February 1986: box 5, folder 2.
65. S. P. Tarasenko (interview), HIGFC (HIA), box 3, folder 2, p. 10.
66. Shevardnadze, *Moi vybor*, p. 42.
67. See the comment made to Anatoli Adamishin: A. L. Adamishin Papers (HIA), box 1: Diaries 1985, 7 October 1985, p. 1.

68. K. N. Brutents reports this comment to him by Ponomarëv in *Nesbyvsheesya. Neravnodushnye zametki o perestroike*, pp. 445–6.
69. T. G. Stepanov-Mamaladze diary, 1 December 1985: T. G. Stepanov-Mamaladze Papers (HIA), box 5.
70. *Ibid.*, 20 April 1986: box 5, folder 2.
71. Notes on confidential conversation with E. A. Shevardnadze, 10 September 1985: *ibid.*, box 5, folder 1.
72. T. G. Stepanov-Mamaladze diary, 18 November 1985: *ibid.*
73. T. G. Stepanov-Mamaladze working notes, 26 November 1985: *ibid.*, box 1, folder 3.
74. *Ibid.*, 2 September 1985: box 1.
75. T. G. Stepanov-Mamaladze diary, 30 June 1988: *ibid.*, box 5.
76. *Ibid.*, 17 November 1985; T. G. Stepanov-Mamaladze working notes, 15 February (miswritten as August) 1986: *ibid.*, box 1.
77. T. G. Stepanov-Mamaladze diary, 30 April 1986: *ibid.*, box 5.
78. Note on party conference (Ministry of Foreign Affairs), 30 November 1985: A. L. Adamishin Papers (HIA), box 1: Diaries 1985, 30 November 1985, pp. 42–5.
79. T. G. Stepanov-Mamaladze diary, 1 December 1985: *ibid.*, box 5.

13: One Foot on the Accelerator

1. G. Shultz: interview with R. Service and P. Robinson, Hoover Institution, 1 September 2009.
2. J. Attali, *Verbatim*, vol. 1: *Chronique des années 1981–1986*, p. 854 (28 September 1985).
3. R. Reagan to M. S. Gorbachëv, 30 April 1985, pp. 1–11: RRPL, Executive Secretariat, NSC, Head of State Files: USSR: General Secretary Gorbachev, box 39.
4. M. S. Gorbachëv to R. Reagan, 10 June 1985, pp. 3 and 7: *ibid.*, box 40.
5. M. S. Gorbachëv to R. Reagan, 22 June 1985, p. 3: *ibid.*
6. J. Matlock to R. McFarlane, 26 June 1985 (memo): *ibid.*
7. 'Soviet Strategic and Political Objectives in Arms Control in 1985', p. 6: Special National Intelligence Estimate (March 1985): CIA Papers.
8. 'Soviet Capabilities for Strategic Nuclear Conflict Through the Mid-1990s: Key Judgments', pp. 16–17: National Intelligence Estimate, 25 April 1985: *ibid.*
9. W. J. Casey to R. Reagan, 25 June 1985, report: 'Gorbachev, The New Broom', pp. 6–8 and 13: *ibid.*
10. 'Gorbachev's Economic Agenda: Promises, Potentials, and Pitfalls. An Intelligence Assessment', 6 September 1985: *ibid.*
11. E. Rowny, 'Gorbachev's First Hundred Days' (draft), 5 June 1985, pp. 1–4: RRPL, Jack Matlock Files, box 61, folder: USSR – Mikhail Sergeyevich Gorbachev – Gen. Secretary – March 11, 1985.

12. W. F. Buckley, 'Exit Chernenkoism?', *National Review*, 19 April 1985, p. 54.
13. R. Halloran, 'Export Ban Called Costly to Soviet', *New York Times*, 14 May 1985.
14. *Ibid.*
15. R. N. Perle, statement before House of Representatives Armed Services Committee Special Panel on Arms Control and Disarmament, pp. 1–6, 18 September 1985: Committee on the Present Danger (HIA), box 104.
16. *Washington Post*, 24 March 1985.
17. R. Perle, 'The Eastward Technology Flow: A Plan of Common Action', *Strategic Review*, spring 1984, p. 29.
18. *Washington Post*, 5 August 1986.
19. G. Andreotti, *L'URSS vista da vicino: dalla guerra fredda a Gorbaciov*, p. 233.
20. V. L. Kataev, untitled memoir notes filed as PAZNOGL, p. 4: Vitalii Leonidovich Kataev Papers (HIA), disk 3.
21. *Ibid.*, p. 4: Vitalii Leonidovich Kataev Papers (HIA), disk 3; V. L. Kataev (interview), HIGFC (HIA), box 2, folder 4, p. 12.
22. *Ibid.*, box 2, folder 4, pp. 12–13.
23. *Ibid.*
24. V. L. Kataev, 'Struktura podgotovki i prinyatiya reshenii po voenno-politicheskim problemam v SSSR', p. 8: Vitalii Leonidovich Kataev Papers (HIA), box 16.
25. *Ibid.*, pp. 8–9; V. L. Kataev, untitled memoir notes filed as PAZNOGL, p. 5: Vitalii Leonidovich Kataev Papers (HIA), disk 3.
26. V. L. Kataev, 'Struktura podgotovki i prinyatiya reshenii po voenno-politicheskim problemam v SSSR', pp. 8–9: Vitalii Leonidovich Kataev Papers (HIA), box 16.
27. *Ibid.*, pp. 9–10.
28. V. L. Kataev (interview), HIGFC (HIA), box 2, folder 4, pp. 16–17.
29. A. L. Adamishin Papers (HIA), box 1: Diaries 1985, 16 March 1985.
30. T. G. Stepanov-Mamaladze diary, 2 September 1985: T. G. Stepanov-Mamaladze Papers (HIA), box 5.
31. Meeting of G. P. Shultz and E. A. Shevardnadze (US Ambassador's Residence, memcon), 31 July 1985, pp. 2–20: National Security Archive, End of the Cold War series, box 1.
32. A. L. Adamishin Papers (HIA), box 1: Diaries 1986, 25 April 1985.
33. *Ibid.*, 29 July 1985, p. 2.
34. *Ibid.*, 20 August 1985, p. 1.
35. *Ibid.*, 11 August 1985, p. 1.
36. *Ibid.*, 15 October 1985.
37. *Ibid.*, 22 September 1985.
38. *Ibid.*, 20 August 1985.
39. *Ibid.*, 22 September 1985.
40. *Ibid.*, p. 2.
41. N. N. Detinov (interview), HIGFC (HIA), box 1, folder 14, p. 17.
42. W. J. Casey to R. Reagan, 9 September 1985, p. 1: CIA Papers.

43. C. Hill, notes (1 March 1991) on 'Terrorism', pp. 33–4: Charles Hill Papers (HIA), box 64.
44. *Ibid.*, p. 35.
45. *Ibid.*, p. 38.
46. C. Hill, diary (23 September 1985): Molly Worthen's notes.
47. C. Hill, notes (1 March 1991) on 'Terrorism', p. 42: Charles Hill Papers (HIA), box 64.
48. *Ibid.*, pp. 39–40.
49. National Security Council, 20 September 1985, p. 2 and 5–7: *The Reagan Files: The Untold Story of Reagan's Top-Secret Efforts to Win the Cold War* (ed. J. Saltoun-Ebin).
50. *Izvestiya*, 28 July 1985.
51. T. G. Stepanov-Mamaladze working notes, 3 September 1985: T. G. Stepanov-Mamaladze Papers (HIA), box 1.
52. T. G. Stepanov-Mamaladze diary, 23 September 1985: *ibid.*, box 5.
53. *Ibid.*, 24 September 1985.
54. *Ibid.*
55. T. G. Stepanov-Mamaladze diary, 28 September 1985: *ibid.*
56. *Ibid.*
57. *New York Times*, 28 September 1985.
58. R. M. Nixon to W. J. Casey, 5 November 1985, pp. 1–3: William J. Casey Papers (HIA), box 329, folder 8.
59. Qian Qichen, *Ten Episodes in China's Diplomacy*, pp. 17–18.
60. Attali, *Verbatim*, vol. 1, p. 803 (30 April 1985).
61. *Ibid.*, p. 853 (28 September 1985).
62. Flyposter: 'Gorbatchev à Paris: S.O.S. Droits de l'Homme. Appel'.
63. Spot commentary on Gorbachëv's Paris announcements, forwarded by D. Mahley and R. Linhard to R. McFarlane, 3 October 1985: CIA Papers.
64. Attali, *Verbatim*, vol. 1, p. 861 (2 October 1985).

14: To Geneva

1. A. Chernyaev, *Sovmestnyi iskhod. Dnevnik dvukh epokh. 1971–1991 gody*, p. 649 (16 October 1985).
2. *Ibid.*, p. 650 (17 October 1985).
3. M. S. Gorbachëv to the Political Consultative Committee in Sofia (Soviet record), 22 October 1985, p. 5: PHPCS.
4. *Ibid.*, pp. 7–8.
5. *Ibid.*, pp. 8–9.
6. *Ibid.*, p. 10.
7. *Ibid.*, pp. 5–7.
8. *Ibid.*, pp. 12–14.
9. *Ibid.*
10. Chernyaev, *Sovmestnyi iskhod*, p. 621 (16 March 1985).

11. Political Consultative Committee discussion, 23 October 1985 in Sofia (East German record, translated into English), p. 22: PHPCS.
12. *Ibid.*, p. 33.
13. *Ibid.*, pp. 39–40.
14. *Ibid.*, p. 47.
15. *Ibid.*, p. 50.
16. Meeting of R. Reagan and E. A. Shevardnadze, 24 October 1985 (memcon), pp. 3 and 5.
17. G. Andreotti, *L'URSS vista da vicino: dalla guerra fredda a Gorbaciov*, pp. 265–8.
18. R. Reagan to M. S. Gorbachëv, 31 October 1985, p. 1: RRPL, Executive Secretariat, NSC, Head of State Files: USSR: General Secretary Gorbachev, box 40.
19. J. Helms, S. Symms and J. MacClure to R. Reagan, 29 October 1985: Monique Garnier-Lançon Papers (HIA), box 27, folder 1.
20. *New York Times*, 3 November 1985.
21. T. G. Stepanov-Mamaladze working notes, 26 October 1985: T. G. Stepanov-Mamaladze Papers (HIA), box 1.
22. G. P. Shultz to R. Reagan, 12 November 1985, pp. 4, 6, 8 and 13–14: End of the Cold War Forum (hereafter ECWF), STY-1985-11-12.
23. R. C. McFarlane to R. Reagan, 8 November 1985, p. 1: National Security Archive, End of the Cold War series, box 2, folder 2.
24. G. P. Shultz to R. Reagan, memo, 7 November 1985, pp. 1–5: US Department of State FOIA Documents.
25. G. P. Shultz to R. Reagan, 12 November 1985, pp. 4, 6, 8–9 and 12–14: ECWF, STY-1985-11-12.
26. A. L. Adamishin Papers (HIA), box 1: Diaries 1985, 25 November 1985, pp. 35–6; note on E. A. Shevardnadze's report to the Foreign Affairs Ministry collegium, 25 November 1985: *ibid.*, p. 1.
27. *New York Times*, 15 November 1985.
28. A. L. Adamishin Papers (HIA), box 1: Diaries 1985, 24 November 1985, p. 1.
29. *Ibid.*, p. 2.
30. T. G. Stepanov-Mamaladze diary, 10 September 1985: T. G. Stepanov-Mamaladze Papers (HIA), box 5.
31. B. Kalb to G. P. Shultz, 31 October 1985: RRPL, Geneva: Reagan/Gorbachev, Sven F. Kraemer Files, box 941043.
32. Address by the President to the Nation, 14 November 1985 in Committee on the Present Danger Papers (HIA), box 140, folder: Reagan – 1985.
33. R. M. Nixon to R. W. Reagan: 14 November 1985: Jim Mann Papers (HIA), box 55.
34. M. Kampelman, J. Tower and M. Glitman to G. P. Shultz, '1985 Geneva Summit: Suggested Talking Points', 14 November 1985: National Security Archive, End of the Cold War series, box 2.
35. *New York Times*, 16 November 1985.
36. *The Reagan Diaries Unabridged*, vol. 1, p. 541 (17 November 1985).
37. A. L. Adamishin Papers (HIA), box 1: Diaries 1985, 24 November 1985, p. 4.

38. A. Dobrynin, *In Confidence: Moscow's Ambassador to America's Cold War Presidents*, p. 588.
39. *The Reagan Diaries*, p. 369 (19 November 1985).
40. First plenary session of Geneva summit meeting, 19 November 1985: National Security Archive Electronic Briefing Book no. 172, doc. 16 (US memorandum), p. 3.
41. *Ibid.*, pp. 7–8.
42. Second plenary session of Geneva summit meeting, 19 November 1985: *ibid.*, doc. 17 (US memorandum), p. 3.
43. *Ibid.*, p. 4.
44. *Ibid.*, pp. 7–8.
45. Second private session of Geneva summit meeting, 19 November 1985: *ibid.*, doc. 19 (US memorandum), p. 2.
46. See the full sentence in C. Hill, notes on Gorbachëv's January 1986 declaration, p. 5: Charles Hill Papers (HIA), box 64, folder: G. P. Shultz – 'Turmoil' – Draft – Soviet Union 1986.
47. Second private session of Geneva summit meeting, 19 November 1985: National Security Archive Electronic Briefing Book no. 172, doc. 19 (US memorandum), p. 2.
48. Third plenary session of Geneva summit meeting, 20 November 1985: *ibid.*, doc. 21 (US memorandum), p. 2.
49. *Ibid.*, pp. 3–4.
50. Dobrynin, *In Confidence*, pp. 589–90.
51. Third plenary session of Geneva summit meeting, 20 November 1985: National Security Archive Electronic Briefing Book no. 172, doc. 21 (US memorandum), p. 6.
52. *Ibid.*, pp. 6–7.
53. *Ibid.*, p. 10.
54. Fourth plenary session of Geneva summit meeting, 20 November 1985: *ibid.*, doc. 22 (US memorandum), p. 3.
55. *Ibid.*, pp. 3–4.
56. Dinner at Geneva summit meeting, 20 November 1985: *ibid.*, doc. 22 (US memorandum), p. 3.
57. Address to a joint session of the Congress, President's back-up copy, 21 November 1985, pp. 1–2: RRPP.
58. *Ibid.*, pp. 6–7.
59. W. Safire, 'The Fireside Summit', 21 November 1985; editorial *New York Times*, 22 November 1985. In general see R. Samuel, 'Conservative Intellectuals and the Reagan-Gorbachev Summits', *Cold War History*, no. 1 (2012), p. 144.
60. R. M. Smalley to the Acting Secretary of State, 29 November 1985: National Security Archive, End of the Cold War series, box 2.
61. Charles Z. Wick (Director of the American Information Agency) to G. P. Shultz, 'Highlight of European Public Opinion After the Geneva Summit', 18 December 1985, p. 1: *ibid.*

62. *Ibid.*, pp. 2–3.
63. Michael D. Schneider to Charles Z. Wick, Director of the American Information Agency, 12 December 1985: *ibid.*
64. R. Reagan to G. Murphy, 19 December 1985: Jim Mann Papers (HIA), box 51.
65. *The Reagan Diaries*, p. 371 (22 November 1985).
66. A. L. Adamishin Papers (HIA), box 1: Diaries 1985, 24 November 1985, p. 3.
67. *Ibid.*
68. Note on E. A. Shevardnadze's report to the Foreign Affairs Ministry collegium, *ibid.*, 25 November 1985, p. 38.
69. *Ibid.*, p. 40.
70. Discussion at the Foreign Affairs Ministry collegium, *ibid.*, 25 November 1985, p. 41.

15: Presenting the Soviet Package

1. R. Reagan to M. S. Gorbachëv (English translation), 28 November 1985, pp. 2–4: RRPL, Executive Secretariat, NSC, Head of State Files: USSR: General Secretary Gorbachev, box 40.
2. *Ibid.*, pp. 4–5.
3. M. S. Gorbachëv to R. Reagan, 24 December 1985, pp. 2–3: *ibid.*
4. A. Dobrynin, *In Confidence: Moscow's Ambassador to America's Cold War Presidents*, p. 596.
5. Meeting of R. Reagan and B. Aristov, 5 December 1985 (memcon), p. 2: RRPL, European and Soviet Affairs Directorate, RAC, box 14.
6. M. Baldrige, speech to US-USSR Trade and Economic Council (Moscow), 9 December 1985, pp. 1–12: RRPL, Stephen Danzansky Files (NSC): RAC, box 12.
7. *Washington Post*, 15 December 1985.
8. *Ibid.*, 16 December 1985.
9. *Ibid.*, 17 December 1985.
10. Politburo meeting, 26 November 1985: *V Politbyuro TsK KPSS. Po zapisyam Anatoliya Chernyaeva, Vadima Medvedeva, Georgiya Shakhnazarova, 1985–1991*, p. 19.
11. Meeting in the Central Committee with Secretaries and Department Heads, 10 March 1986: *ibid.*, p. 27.
12. V. A. Medvedev (interview), HIGFC (HIA), box 2, folder 10, p. 27.
13. O. Grinevsky in O. Grinevsky and L. M. Hansen, *Making Peace: Confidence Building*, pp. 425–6 and 430.
14. Gorbachëv's opening speech, quoted extensively by O. Grinevskii in *Perelom: ot Brezhneva k Gorbachëvu*, p. 314.
15. O. Grinevsky in Grinevsky and Hansen, *Making Peace: Confidence Building*, p. 434.
16. A. L. Adamishin Papers (HIA), box 1: Diaries 1986, 7 January 1986; O. Grinevsky in Grinevsky and Hansen, *Making Peace: Confidence Building*,

p. 432; O. A. Grinevskii (interview): HIGFC (HIA), box 2, folder 1, p. 20 (where it is suggested that the Politburo met on 2 January 1986).

17. *Ibid.*
18. Grinevsky and Hansen, *Making Peace: Confidence Building*, p. 434.
19. A. L. Adamishin Papers (HIA), box 1: Diaries 1986, 7 January 1986; O. Grinevsky in Grinevsky and Hansen, *Making Peace: Confidence Building*, pp. 432–3.
20. A. L. Adamishin Papers (HIA), box 1: Diaries 1986, 7 January 1986.
21. *Ibid.*, Diaries 1985, 24 November 1985.
22. *Ibid.*
23. *Ibid.*, Diaries 1986, 8 January 1986.
24. *Ibid.*
25. V. L. Kataev (interview), HIGFC (HIA), box 2, folder 4, p. 8; L. V. Shebarshin (interview), HIGFC (HIA), box 2, folder 19, p. 9; N. N. Detinov (interview), HIGFC (HIA), box 1, folder 14, pp. 19–20; O. A. Grinevskii (interview): HIGFC (HIA), box 2, folder 1, p. 21; Grinevsky and Hansen, *Making Peace: Confidence Building*, p. 436.
26. G. M. Kornienko in S. F. Akhromeev and G. M. Kornienko, *Glazami marshala i diplomata*, p. 89.
27. *Soviet Intentions 1965–1985*, vol. 2: *Soviet Post-Cold War Testimonial Evidence*: interview of Col. Gen. A. A. Danilevich, 21 September 1992, p. 29.
28. S. F. Akhromeev in Akhromeev and Kornienko, *Glazami marshala i diplomata*, 87–8.
29. A. L. Adamishin Papers (HIA), box 1: Diaries 1986, 8 January 1986; O. A. Grinevskii (interview): HIGFC (HIA), box 2, folder 1, p. 21; O. Grinevsky in Grinevsky and Hansen, *Making Peace: Confidence Building*, pp. 436–7.
30. O. A. Grinevskii (interview): HIGFC (HIA), box 2, folder 1, p. 22.
31. A. L. Adamishin Papers (HIA), box 1: Diaries 1986, 8 January 1986; N. N. Detinov (interview), HIGFC (HIA), box 1, folder 14, pp. 19–20; O. A. Grinevskii (interview): *ibid.*, box 2, folder 1, p. 21.
32. See the comments of Anatoli Adamishin in A. L. Adamishin Papers (HIA), box 1: Diaries 1986, 2 February 1986.
33. N. S. Leonov, *Likholet'e*, p. 319.
34. Grinevskii, *Perelom: ot Brezhneva k Gorbachëvu*, pp. 324–8; 'Zayavlenie General'nogo sekretarya TsK KPSS M. S. Gorbachëva', *Pravda*, 16 January 1986; 'Predlozhenie SSSR o programme polnoi likvidatsii yadernogo oruzhiya po vsemu mire k 2000 godu': Vitalii Leonidovich Kataev Papers (HIA), box 4, folder 8.
35. M. S. Gorbachëv to R. Reagan, 11 January 1986, p. 2: RRPL, Executive Secretariat, NSC, Head of State Files: USSR: General Secretary Gorbachev, box 40.
36. M. S. Gorbachëv to R. Reagan, 14 January 1986 (unofficial translation), pp. 1–5: *ibid.*, Robert E. Linhard Files, RAC, box 8, NSDD 214/NSDD 210.
37. 'Zayavlenie General'nogo sekretarya TsK KPSS M. S. Gorbachëva', *Pravda*, 16 January 1986.

38. *Ibid.*
39. T. G. Stepanov-Mamaladze working notes, 23 February 1986: T. G. Stepanov-Mamaladze Papers (HIA), box 1.
40. *Ibid.*, 15 March 1986.
41. A. L. Adamishin Papers (HIA), box 1: Diaries 1986, 2 February 1986.
42. T. G. Stepanov-Mamaladze working notes, 24 February 1986: T. G. Stepanov-Mamaladze Papers (HIA), box 1.
43. A. L. Adamishin Papers (HIA), box 1: Diaries 1986, 2 February 1986.

16: American Rejection

1. Charles Hill, diary (15 January 1986): Molly Worthen's notes.
2. C. Hill, notes on Gorbachëv's January 1986 declaration, pp. 4 and 7: Charles Hill Papers (HIA), box 64, folder: G. P. Shultz – 'Turmoil' – Draft – Soviet Union 1986.
3. G. Shultz, *Turmoil and Triumph: My Years as Secretary of State*, p. 700.
4. A. F. Dobrynin to G. P. Shultz, 15 January 1986: George Shultz Papers (RRPL), box 21a.
5. G. P. Shultz to R. Reagan, memo, 23 January 1986: *ibid.*, Jack Matlock Files, box 14, folder: Matlock Chron. January 1986.
6. Charles Hill, diary (15 January 1986): Molly Worthen's notes.
7. Shultz, *Turmoil and Triumph*, p. 700.
8. *Ibid.*, p. 699.
9. *New York Times*, 16 January 1986; *Washington Times*, 16 January 1986.
10. *New York Times*, 26 January 1986.
11. *Time Magazine*, 27 January 1986, p. 9.
12. A. Hartman to Secretary of State, telegram, 5 February 1986, pp. 1–5: RRPL, Jack Matlock Files, box 14, folder: Matlock Chron. February 1986.
13. C. Hill, notes on Gorbachëv's January 1986 declaration, p. 13: Charles Hill Papers (HIA), box 64, folder: G. P. Shultz – 'Turmoil' – Draft – Soviet Union 1986.
14. C. Weinberger to R. Reagan, 31 January 1986, pp. 1–3: RRPL, Robert Linhard Files, RAC, box 8, National Security Decision Directive no. 210.
15. W. J. Casey, 'Worldwide Briefing', 30 January 1986, pp. 1–16: *ibid.*, Jack Matlock Files, box 14, folder: Matlock Chron. February 1986.
16. C. Hill, notes on Gorbachëv's January 1986 declaration, pp. 8–9: Charles Hill Papers (HIA), box 64, folder: G. P. Shultz – 'Turmoil' – Draft – Soviet Union 1986.
17. Nitze's comment to M. Thatcher, 5 February 1986: US Embassy (London) to Secretary of State, 6 February 1986, pp. 2–3: RRPL, Robert E. Linhard Files, box 92083, folder: Mrs Thatcher on SDI/ABM.
18. National Security Planning Group, 3 February 1986, p. 2: *ibid.*, Executive Secretariat, NSC: NSPG, Records, box 91308.

19. *Ibid.*, pp. 3–4.
20. *Ibid.*, p. 4.
21. *Ibid.*
22. *Ibid.*, pp. 5–6.
23. National Security Decision Directive no. 210, 4 February 1986, pp. 1–3: RRPL, Robert Linhard Files, RAC, box 8.
24. R. Reagan to S. Massie, 10 February 1986: Jim Mann Papers (HIA), box 55.
25. M. S. Gorbachëv to R. Reagan, 16 February 1986, pp. 1–7: RRPL, Executive Secretariat, NSC, Head of State Files: USSR: General Secretary Gorbachev, box 40.
26. 'Soviet Forces and Capabilities for Strategic Nuclear Conflict Through the Mid-1990s', National Intelligence Estimate, April 1986, p. 7: CIA Papers; R. M. Gates, *From the Shadows: The Ultimate Insider's Story of Five Presidents and How They Won the Cold War*, p. 381.
27. E. Abrams to the National Security Council, memo, 11 March 1986, p. 1: RRPL, Jack Matlock Files, box 15, folder: Matlock Chron. March 1986.
28. O. Grinevsky and L. M. Hansen, *Making Peace: Confidence Building*, pp. 467–8; meeting of N. I. Ryzhkov and G. P. Shultz (Stockholm, memcon), 15 March 1986, pp. 4 and 6–7: RRPL, Jack Matlock Files, box 15, folder: Matlock Chron. March 1986.
29. Meeting of J. Matlock and T. Renton and others (London, memcon), 7 March 1986, p. 2: *ibid.*
30. G. P. Shultz to R. Reagan, memo, 19 February 1986, p. 1: RRPL, Robert E. Linhard Files, box 92168, folder: NSDD 214.
31. J. Matlock to R. Lehman, R. Linhard and S. Sestanovich, memo, 3 February 1986: RRPL, Jack Matlock Files, box 14, folder: Matlock Chron. February 1986.
32. A. Hartman to Secretary of State, telegram, 5 February 1986: *ibid.*
33. National Security Decision Directive, no. 214, 21 February 1986, pp. 1–2: RRPL, Robert E. Linhard Files, RAC, box 8.
34. R. Reagan to M. S. Gorbachëv, 22 February 1986, pp. 1–8: RRPL, Executive Secretariat, NSC, Head of State Files: USSR: General Secretary Gorbachev, box 40.
35. P. H. Nitze to R. Reagan, 14 February 1986: *ibid.*
36. E. L. Rowny to R. Reagan, 14 February 1986: *ibid.*
37. J. Attali, *Verbatim*, vol. 1: *Chronique des années 1981–1986*, pp. 930–1 (24 February 1986). See also the discussion by J. Newton, *Russia, France and the Idea of Europe*, p. 136.
38. M. Thatcher to R. Reagan, 11 February 1986, pp. 1–5: RRPL, Executive Secretariat, NSC, Head of State Files: USSR: General Secretary Gorbachev, box 40.
39. US Embassy (London) to Secretary of State, 7 March 1986, pp. 1–6: RRPL, Robert E. Linhard Files, box 92083, folder: Mrs Thatcher on SDI/ABM.
40. 'Gorbachev's Modernization Program: Implications for Defense. An Intelligence Assessment', 1 March 1986, p. 4: CIA Papers.

41. DCI talking points for National Security Planning Group, 16 April 1986, p. 1: *ibid.*
42. 'USSR: Facing the Dilemma of Hard Currency Shortages. A Research Paper': Office of Soviet Analysis, 1 May 1986, pp. 1–4 and 9–11; 'Implications of the Decline in Soviet Hard Currency Earnings: National Intelligence Estimate', September 1986, pp. 7 and 11: *ibid.*
43. A. Hartman (Moscow embassy) to G. P. Shultz (cable), 15 November 1986: RRPL, Stephen Danzansky Files (NSC): RAC, box 1.
44. H. S. Rowen, 'Living with a Sick Bear', *National Interest*, no. 2, winter 1985–1986, pp. 14–26.
45. Interview with Harry Rowen, 1 August 2013; S. I. Danzansky to J. M. Poindexter (preparatory memo), 9 April 1986: RRPL, Coordination Office, NSC Records, box 11; K. Lundberg, 'CIA and the Fall of the Soviet Empire: The Politics of "Getting It Right". A Case Study' (1994), p. 14: CIA Papers.
46. Personal communication from Harry Rowen, 3 August 2013.
47. W. J. Casey to National Intelligence Officer for the USSR, 22 April 1986: William J. Casey Papers (HIA), HIA-CASEY 3-A-5-26-2.
48. See the balanced verdict of the early post-Soviet enquiry by D. M. Berkowitz, J. S. Berliner, P. R. Gregory, S. J. Linz and J. R. Millar in 'An Evaluation of the CIA's Analysis of Soviet Economic Performance, 1970–90', *Comparative Economic Studies*, no. 2 (1993).
49. G. P. Shultz to R. Reagan, memo, 5 March 1986, pp. 1–3: RRPL, Jack Matlock Files, box 15, folder: Matlock Chron. March 1986.
50. Executive Secretary N. Platt to J. Poindexter, memo, n/e 5 March 1986, pp. 1–2: *ibid.*
51. C. Hill, notes (16 April 1991) on 'Soviet Union 3', p. 4: Charles Hill Papers (HIA), box 64, folder: G. P. Shultz – 'Turmoil' – Draft – Soviet Union.

17: The Stalled Interaction

1. V. M. Falin (interview), HIGFC (HIA), box 1, folder 15, p. 8.
2. A. G. Kovalëv (interview), *ibid.*, box 2, folder 6, p. 6.
3. E. Shevardnadze, *Kogda rukhnul zheleznyi zanaves: vstrechi i vospominaniya*, p. 92; T. G. Stepanov-Mamaladze working notes, 17 February 1991: T. G. Stepanov-Mamaladze Papers (HIA), box 3.
4. T. G. Stepanov-Mamaladze diary, 18 January 1986, *ibid.*, box 5.
5. *Ibid.*, 25 February 1986.
6. R. Z. Sagdeev, *The Making of a Soviet Scientist: My Adventures in Nuclear Fusion and Space from Stalin to Star Wars*, p. 272.
7. M. S. Gorbachëv, speech to the Party Congress, 25 February 1986: M. S. Gorbachëv, *Sobranie sochinenii*, vol. 3, pp. 305–6, 358 and 361.
8. See D. Yergin, *The Prize: The Epic Quest for Oil, Money, and Power*, pp. 727–31.
9. O. Grinevsky and L. M. Hansen, *Making Peace: Confidence Building*, p. 475.

10. M. S. Gorbachëv's comments on preparations for his speech in Tolyatti, 20 March 1986: Anatoli Chernyaev Papers (RESCA), box 2, folder 1, pp. 1–2; 'Zadaniya Gorbachëva pomoshchnikam po mezhdunarodnym voprosam', 20 March 1986: Anatoli Chernyaev Papers (RESCA), box 1, pp. 8–9.

11. See above, p. 204.

12. R. M. Gates, *From the Shadows: The Ultimate Insider's Story of Five Presidents and How They Won the Cold War*, p. 381.

13. Politburo meeting, 20 March 1986: *V Politbyuro TsK KPSS. Po zapisyam Anatoliya Chernyaeva, Vadima Medvedeva, Georgiya Shakhnazarova, 1985–1991*, p. 29.

14. M. S. Gorbachëv's consultation with small group, 24 March 1986, p. 11: Anatoli Chernyaev Papers (RESCA), box 1. The group consisted of V. M. Chebrikov, E. A. Shevardnadze, L. N. Zaikov, A. F. Dobrynin, A. N. Yakovlev and A. S. Chernyaev.

15. 'O prakticheskikh vyvodakh iz s"ezda dlya mezhdunarodnoi politiki', pp. 1–3: *ibid.*, box 2, folder 6.

16. Politburo meeting, 3 April 1986, p. 17: *ibid.*, box 1.

17. *Ibid.*

18. M. S. Gorbachëv to R. Reagan, 2 April 1986, pp. 1–3: RRPL, Executive Secretariat, NSC, Head of State Files: USSR: General Secretary Gorbachev, box 40.

19. M. S. Gorbachëv's instructions to his aides on international questions, 20 March 1986: Anatoli Chernyaev Papers (RESCA), box 1, p. 8.

20. 'O prakticheskikh vyvodakh iz s"ezda dlya mezhdunarodnoi politiki', pp. 5–7: *ibid.*, box 2, folder 6.

21. *Ibid.*

22. Politburo meeting, 28 March 1986, pp. 14–16: Anatoli Chernyaev Papers (RESCA), box 1.

23. 'Zadaniya Gorbachëva pomoshchnikam po mezhdunarodnym voprosam', 20 March 1986: *ibid.*, box 1, p. 8.

24. A. L. Adamishin Papers (HIA), box 1: Diaries 1986, 9 April 1986.

25. Politburo meeting, 24 April 1986, pp. 21 and 25: Anatoli Chernyaev Papers (RESCA), box 1.

26. Politburo meeting of 24 April 1986, quoted in Grinevsky and Hansen, *Making Peace: Confidence Building*, pp. 497–9.

27. A. L. Adamishin Papers (HIA), box 1: Diaries 1985, 21 April 1986, p. 4; Grinevsky and Hansen, *Making Peace: Confidence Building*, pp. 424–5.

28. A. L. Adamishin Papers (HIA), box 1: Diaries 1986, 25 April 1986; A. S. Chernyaev (interview), HIGFC (HIA), box 1, folder 12, p. 28.

29. A. L. Adamishin Papers (HIA), box 1: Diaries 1986, 21 April 1986.

30. *Ibid.*, Diaries 1986, 25 April 1986.

31. *Ibid.*, 21 and 22 April 1986.

32. K. N. Brutents, *Nesbyvsheesya. Neravnodushnye zametki o perestroike*, p. 210.

33. P. Cradock, *In Pursuit of British Interests Reflections on Foreign Policy under*

Margaret Thatcher and John Major, pp. 73–5.
34. T. G. Stepanov-Mamaladze diary, 20 April 1986: T. G. Stepanov-Mamaladze Papers (HIA), box 5.
35. Politburo meeting, 15 April 1986, p. 20: Anatoli Chernyaev Papers (RESCA), box 1.
36. *Ibid.*
37. T. G. Stepanov-Mamaladze diary, 30 April 1986: T. G. Stepanov-Mamaladze Papers (HIA), box 5.
38. See above, p. 32.
39. See his comments to George Bush (Soviet embassy, Washington), 10 December 1987: RRPL, Stephen Danzansky Files (NSC): RAC, box 12.
40. G. P. Shultz to R. Reagan, memo, 19 May 1986: RRPL, Jack Matlock Files, folder: Matlock Chron. May 1986, box 16.
41. C. Hill, notes on Gorbachëv's January 1986 declaration, pp. 41–2: Charles Hill Papers (HIA), box 64, folder: G. P. Shultz – 'Turmoil' – Draft – Soviet Union 1986.
42. G. P. Shultz to R. Reagan, memo, 19 May 1986: RRPL, Jack Matlock Files, folder: Matlock Chron. May 1986, box 16.
43. Politburo meeting, 29 May 1986: *Otvechaya na vyzov vremeni: Vneshnyaya politika perestroiki: Dokumental'nye svidetel'stva*, pp. 676–7.
44. T. G. Stepanov-Mamaladze working notes, probably 23 May 1986: T. G. Stepanov-Mamaladze Papers (HIA), box 1.
45. M. S. Gorbachëv, Political Consultative Committee meeting in Budapest (Soviet record, translated into English), 10 June 1986, pp. 2, 4, 6, 10 and 11: PHPCS.
46. Meeting of General and First Party Secretaries of the Warsaw Pact countries (East German report), 11 June 1986, pp. 3–10: PHPCS.
47. *Ibid.*, pp. 16–18.
48. *Ibid.*, pp. 19–21.
49. *Ibid.*, pp. 23–5.
50. *Ibid.*, p. 18.
51. *Ibid.*, pp. 33–4.
52. *Ibid.*, p. 37.
53. Communique of the Political Consultative Committee, 13 June 1986: PHPCS; meeting of General and First Party Secretaries of the Warsaw Pact countries (East German report), 11 June 1986, p. 39: *ibid.*
54. Gorbachëv's report to Central Committee plenum, 16 June 1986: RGASPI, f. 5, op. 3, d. 17, pp. 87–8 and 90; decree of Central Committee plenum, 16 June 1986: *ibid.*, f. 5, op. 3, d. 10, pp. 23–5.
55. Gorbachëv's report to Central Committee plenum, 16 June 1986: *ibid.*, f. 5, op. 3, d. 17, pp. 92–3 and 95.
56. M. S. Gorbachëv, written report to the Politburo, 26 June 1986: 'O nekotorykh aktual'nykh voprosakh sotrudnichestva s sotsstranami', pp. 1–6: Dmitri A. Volkogonov Papers (HIA), reel 17.
57. Politburo meeting, 3 July 1986: *V Politbyuro TsK KPSS*, p. 53.

58. National Security Planning Group, 6 June 1986, pp. 1–2: *The Reagan Files: The Untold Story of Reagan's Top-Secret Efforts to Win the Cold War.*

59. C. Hill, notes on Gorbachëv's January 1986 declaration, p. 44: Charles Hill Papers (HIA), box 64, folder: G. P. Shultz – 'Turmoil' – Draft – Soviet Union 1986.

60. National Security Planning Group, 12 June 1986, pp. 1–2: *The Reagan Files.*

61. *Ibid.*, pp. 2 and 4.

62. Discussion with George Bush at the Soviet embassy, Washington, 10 December 1987, p. 2: RRPL, Stephen Danzansky Files (NSC): RAC, box 12.

63. See V. Chernyshev on conventional-forces war in Europe, *Krasnaya Zvezda*, 29 March 1988.

64. R. Reagan, speech at Glassboro High School commencement ceremonies, 19 June 1986: www.reagan.utexas.edu/archives/speeches/1986/61986e.htm

65. C. Hill, diary (20 June 1986): Charles Hill Papers (HIA), box 64, folder: Soviet Union 1986.

66. *Ibid.*

67. Memcon of meeting between R. Reagan and Ambassador Dubinin, 23 June 1986, p. 2: ECWF, MTG-1986-6-23.

18: The Strategic Defense Initiative

1. C. Hill, notes on Gorbachëv's January 1986 declaration, p. 44: Charles Hill Papers (HIA), box 64, folder: G. P. Shultz – 'Turmoil' – Draft – Soviet Union 1986.

2. 'Gorbachev's Policy Toward the United States, 1986–88: Special National Intelligence Estimate', September 1986: CIA Papers.

3. C. Thomas Thorne (Directorate of Intelligence and Research to G. P. Shultz, 26 July 1985: National Security Archive, End of the Cold War series, box 1.

4. F. Carlucci (interview), HIGFC (HIA), box 1, folder 10, p. 38.

5. G. P. Shultz's interview with P. Robinson, 10 June 2002, p. 6: Peter Robinson Papers (HIA), box 21.

6. P. Robinson, notes on conversation with H. Kissinger, 14 November 2002, p. 1: *ibid.*, box 34.

7. J. Poindexter, on-the-record briefing on Air Force One, 12 October 1986: National Security Archive, End of the Cold War series, box 2, folder 3.

8. R. M. Gates to F. C. Carlucci, 15 January 1987, introducing report on 'Soviet and Other Foreign Reactions to a Zero-Ballistic Missile World' (see especially pp. 20–1): RRPL, Executive Secretariat, NSC: NSDD, Records, box 91297, NSDD 250.

9. P. Nitze, 'Presentation of SDI', 5 April 1985, pp. 2–7: RRPL, Robert E. Linhard Files, box 92083, folder: SDI – NSDD 172.

10. C. Weinberger (interview), HIGFC (HIA), box 3, folder 4, p. 33.

11. E. Teller to G. P. Shultz, 20 May 1986: Edward Teller Papers (HIA), box 283,

folder: George P. Shultz; C. Hill, handwritten notes on 'Soviet: 1984, Oct. 1 to Oct. 31', p. 7: Charles Hill Papers (HIA), box 64.

12. T. H. Johnson to J. Matlock, 20 December 1984, pp. 3–4: Thomas H. Johnson Papers (HIA), box 47, folder: Matlock Memos.

13. T. H. Johnson to J. Matlock, 23 September 1985: *ibid*.

14. T. H. Johnson to J. Matlock, 14 June 1986: *ibid*.

15. *Ballistic Missile Defense, NSIAD 94–219* (Washington, DC: General Accounting Office, July 1994), pp. 2–3 and 30.

16. *The Reagan Diaries*, p. 313 (3 April 1985).

17. T. G. Stepanov-Mamaladze diary, 2 October 1986: T. G. Stepanov-Mamaladze Papers (HIA), box 5.

18. C. Hill, notes on 'The Soviet Union, April 1 1985 to [*sic*]', pp. 69–70, Charles Hill Papers (HIA), box 64.

19. M. S. Gorbachëv's report to Politburo meeting, 2 December 1988, p. 507: Anatoli Chernyaev Papers (RESCA), box 1.

20. T. G. Stepanov-Mamaladze working notes, 13 July 1986: T. G. Stepanov-Mamaladze Papers (HIA), box 1.

21. Ye. Velikhov, R. Sagdeev and A. Kokoshin (eds), *Kosmicheskoe oruzhie: dilemma bezopasnosti* (Mir: Moscow, 1986), published in English as *Weaponry in Space: The Dilemma of Security* (Mir: Moscow, 1986).

22. R. Z. Sagdeev, *The Making of a Soviet Scientist: My Adventures in Nuclear Fusion and Space from Stalin to Star Wars*, p. 299.

23. V. L. Kataev, diary, 2 December 1985: Vitalii Leonidovich Kataev Papers (HIA), box 2, folder 3: Diary 1984–1985.

24. *Ibid*.

25. V. L. Kataev, untitled memoir notes filed as PAZNOGL, p. 18: Vitalii Leonidovich Kataev Papers (HIA), disk 3.

26. *Ibid*.

27. V. L. Kataev, 'Kakoi byla reaktsiya v SSSR na zayavleniya R. Reigana o razvërtyvanii raboty v SShA po SOI', n.d., pp. 6–7: Vitalii Leonidovich Kataev Papers (HIA), disk 3, SOI.

28. A. G. Kovalëv (interview), HIGFC (HIA), box 2, folder 6, p. 20.

29. V. A. Kryuchkov (interview), *ibid*., box 2, folder 7, p. 31.

30. O. D. Baklanov (interview), *ibid*., box 1, folder 5, p. 10.

31. V. L. Kataev, untitled memoir notes filed as PAZNOGL, pp. 19–20: Vitalii Leonidovich Kataev Papers (HIA), disk 3.

32. V. L. Kataev, 'Kakoi byla reaktsiya v SSSR na zayavleniya R. Reigana o razvërtyvanii raboty v SShA po SOI', n.d., pp. 3–4: *ibid*., disk 3, SOI.

33. T. G. Stepanov-Mamaladze working notes, 7 February 1986 (or a few days earlier): T. G. Stepanov-Mamaladze Papers (HIA), box 1.

34. V. L. Kataev, untitled memoir notes filed as PAZNOGL, pp. 18–19: Vitalii Leonidovich Kataev Papers (HIA), disk 3; V. L. Kataev, 'Kakoi byla reaktsiya v SSSR na zayavleniya R. Reigana o razvërtyvanii raboty v SShA po SOI', n.d., p. 8: *ibid*., disk 3 (SOI).

35. L. N. Zaikov, E. A. Shevardnadze, A. F. Dobrynin and A. N. Yakovlev to M. S. Gorbachëv, 21 July 1986: Vitalii Leonidovich Kataev Papers (HIA), box 4, folder 9.

19: The Lost Summer

1. C. Hill, notes on Gorbachëv's January 1986 declaration, p. 44: Charles Hill Papers (HIA), box 64, folder: G. P. Shultz – 'Turmoil' – Draft – Soviet Union 1986.
2. Interview with Frank Carlucci, 28 August 2001, p. 11: RROHP.
3. C. Hill, diary (20 June 1986): Charles Hill Papers (HIA), box 64, folder: Soviet Union 1986.
4. National Security Council, 1 July 1986, pp. 1–2: *The Reagan Files: The Untold Story of Reagan's Top-Secret Efforts to Win the Cold War.*
5. *Ibid.*, p. 3.
6. *Ibid.*, p. 4.
7. *Ibid.*, p. 5.
8. A. Hartman to Secretary of State, telegram, 14 July 1986, p. 6: RRPL, Jack Matlock Files, box 17, folder: Matlock Chron. June 1986.
9. Discussion with A. N. Yakovlev, A. S. Chernyaev, V. A. Medvedev and V. I. Boldin, 16 July 1986: Anatoli Chernyaev Papers (RESCA), box 1, pp. 49–52.
10. Politburo meeting, 22 May 1986: *V Politbyuro TsK KPSS. Po zapisyam Anatoliya Chernyaeva, Vadima Medvedeva, Georgiya Shakhnazarova, 1985–1991*, p. 40.
11. 'Vstrecha s sekretaryami TsK i zav. Otdelami', 23 June 1986: Anatoli Chernyaev Papers (RESCA), box 1, pp. 33–7 and 40.
12. *Ibid.*, p. 38.
13. N. I. Ryzhkov, Politburo meeting, 27 March 1986: *V Politbyuro TsK KPSS*, p. 32.
14. Gorbachëv's meeting with Politburo members, including Shevardnadze, and Gorbachëv's aides, 22 September 1986: Anatoli Chernyaev Papers (RESCA), box 1, p. 63.
15. N. I. Ryzhkov, Politburo meeting, 11 July 1986: *V Politbyuro TsK KPSS*, p. 58.
16. Politburo meeting, 14 August 1986: *ibid.*, p. 68.
17. J. Attali, *Verbatim*, vol. 2: *Chronique des années 1986–1988*, pp. 109–10 (4 July 1986).
18. *Ibid.* (7 July 1986).
19. *Ibid.*, p. 121 (F. Mitterrand to J. Attali, 10 July 1986).
20. Conversation between F. Mitterrand and M. S. Gorbachëv, 7 July 1986: *Otvechaya na vyzov vremeni: Vneshnyaya politika perestroiki: Dokumental'nye svidetel'stva*, p. 165.
21. National Security Decision Directive no. 233, pp. 1–2 and 5, 21 July 1986: www.fas.org/irp/offdocs/nsdd/index.html.

22. R. Reagan to M. S. Gorbachëv, 25 July 1986: *The Reagan Files*.

23. Memo to the Central Committee: 'O merakh po usileniyu nashego protivo-deistviya amerikanskoi politiki "neoglobalizma"', 31 July 1986, p. 1: Dmitri A. Volkogonov Papers (HIA), reel 17.

24. *Ibid.*, pp. 2–3.

25. *Ibid.*, p. 3.

26. *Ibid.*, pp. 4–5.

27. 'Central Committee' decree 'O merakh po usileniyu nashego protivodeistviya amerikanskoi politiki "neoglobalizma"': *ibid.*

28. A. L. Adamishin, African notes (1986, sometime after XXVII Party Congress), pp. 1 and 3: A. L. Adamishin Papers (HIA), box 1.

29. A. N. Yakovlev to M. S. Gorbachëv, 1 August 1986: *Aleksandr Yakovlev. Perestroika, 1985–1991. Neizdannoe, maloizvestnoe, zabytoe*, ed. A. A. Yakovlev, p. 55.

30. Meeting with Ye. K. Ligachëv, 1986: V. O. Korotych, 1986 diary: Vitalii Korotych Papers (HIA).

31. Politburo meeting, 30 January 1986, pp. 20–2: Dmitri A. Volkogonov Papers (HIA), reel 17; T. G. Stepanov-Mamaladze diary, 16, 20 and 23 January 1986: T. G. Stepanov-Mamaladze Papers (HIA), box 5.

32. M. S. Gorbachëv, speech in Vladivostok, 28 July 1986: M. S. Gorbachëv, *Sobranie sochinenii*, vol. 4, pp. 362, 366, 368, 370, 372, 374–6.

33. C. Hill, notes, pp. 62–4: Charles Hill Papers (HIA), box 64, folder: G. P. Shultz – 'Turmoil' – Draft – Soviet Union 1986.

34. National Security Decision Directive no. 232, pp. 1–3, 16 August 1986: www.fas.org/irp/offdocs/nsdd/index.html.

35. National Security Decision Directive no 238, 2 September 1986, pp. 2, 5, 6, 8 and 12–13: RRPL, Executive Secretariat, NSC: NSDD Records, box 91297.

36. O. Grinevsky and L. M. Hansen, *Making Peace: Confidence Building*, pp. 524–7.

37. *Ibid.*, p. 566.

38. *Ibid.*, pp. 568–71.

39. *Ibid.*, pp. 571–2.

40. *Ibid.*, pp. 575–9.

41. V. L. Kataev (interview), HIGFC (HIA), box 2, folder 4, p. 18.

42. Grinevsky and Hansen, *Making Peace: Confidence Building*, pp. 575–9.

43. O. A. Grinevskii (interview): HIGFC (HIA), box 2, folder 1, p. 29; Grinevsky and Hansen, *Making Peace: Confidence Building*, pp. 579–80 and 583.

44. L. M. Hansen's report quoted *ibid.*, pp. 602–3.

45. *Soviet Intentions 1965–1985*, vol. 2: *Soviet Post-Cold War Testimonial Evidence*: interview of S. F. Akhromeev, 5 March 1990, p. 6.

46. M. S. Gorbachëv to R. Reagan, 15 September 1986, pp. 1–3: RRPL, Executive Secretariat, NSC, Head of State Files: USSR: General Secretary Gorbachev, box 40.

47. T. G. Stepanov-Mamaladze diary, 20 September 1986: T. G. Stepanov-Mamaladze Papers (HIA), box 5.

48. *Ibid.*
49. *Ibid.*
50. A. L. Adamishin Papers (HIA), box 1: Diaries 1988, 21 September 1986, pp. 7–8. This diary entry is misdated by two years.
51. Charles Hill, diary (20 September 1986): Molly Worthen's notes.
52. Gorbachëv's meeting with Politburo members, including Shevardnadze, and Gorbachëv's aides, 22 September 1986, p. 64: Anatoli Chernyaev Papers (RESCA), box 1.
53. *Ibid.*, p. 65.
54. A. S. Chernyaev to M. S. Gorbachëv, 3 October 1986: *ibid.*, box 2, folder 7.
55. M. S. Gorbachëv to the Reykjavik planning group (V. M. Chebrikov, L. N. Zaikov, A. G. Kovalëv, A. S. Chernyaev and S. F. Akhromeev), 4 October 1986, p. 76: *ibid.*, box 1.
56. *Ibid.*, pp. 73–4 and 76–7.
57. *Ibid.*, pp. 74–5.
58. *Ibid.*, p. 77.
59. *Ibid.*, p. 78.
60. *Ibid.*, p. 77.
61. *Ibid.*, pp. 76–7.
62. Gorbachëv at the Reykjavik preparatory group (this time consisting of V. M. Chebrikov, L. N. Zaikov, A. G. Kovalëv, A. S. Chernyaev and S. F. Akhromeev), 4 October 1986: *V Politbyuro TsK KPSS*, pp. 72–4.
63. 'Zapis' besedy A. N. Yakovleva s direktorom instituta mezhdunarodnykh izmenenii Kolumbiiskogo Universiteta (SShA) S. Bialerom', 20 May 1986: *Aleksandr Yakovlev. Perestroika, 1985–1991*, p. 48. See also later conversations, *ibid.*, pp. 159–63, 166–71 and 307–12.
64. T. G. Stepanov-Mamaladze diary, 2 October 1986: T. G. Stepanov-Mamaladze Papers (HIA), box 5.
65. Politburo meeting, 6 October 1986, pp. 1–8: Dmitri A. Volkogonov Papers (HIA), reel 18.
66. Memo of preparatory group (L. N. Zaikov, V. M. Chebrikov, S. L. Sokolov, A. F. Dobrynin and A. G. Kovalëv) to the Central Committee, October 1986: Vitalii Leonidovich Kataev Papers (HIA), box 4, folder 11.
67. Politburo meeting, 6 October 1986, p. 8: Dmitri A. Volkogonov Papers (HIA), reel 18.
68. Politburo meeting, 8 October 1986: *V Politbyuro TsK KPSS*, p. 75.
69. Comments to British Foreign Secretary Sir Geoffrey Howe: T. G. Stepanov-Mamaladze working notes, 4 October 1986: T. G. Stepanov-Mamaladze Papers (HIA), box 1; A. L. Adamishin Papers (HIA), box 1: Diaries 1986, 19 November 1986 and 5 December 1986.
70. *Ibid.*

20: Summit in Reykjavik

1. S. Massie, *Trust But Verify: Reagan, Russia and Me*, p. 230.
2. National Security Decision Directive no. 244, 3 October 1986: www.fas.org/irp/offdocs/nsdd/index.html.
3. E. A. Shultz to R. R. Reagan, 2 October 1986: National Security Archive, End of the Cold War series, box 2, folder 3.
4. B. Oldfield to R. Reagan, 30 September 1986 and R. Reagan to B. Oldfield, 6 October 1986: RRPL, Presidential Handwriting File: Presidential Records, box 16, folder 259.
5. C. Heston to R. Reagan, 6 October 1986: *ibid.*, folder 266.
6. L. Nofziger (interview), HIGFC (HIA), box 2, folder 12, pp. 27–8.
7. J. Courter, J. Kemp and E. Teller to R. Reagan, 1 October 1986: Albert J. Wohlstetter Papers (HIA), box 26, folder 1.
8. S. A. Gecys, Lithuanian–American Community of the USA to R. Reagan, 6 October 1986: National Security Archive, End of the Cold War series, box 2, folder 3.
9. G. Will, 'Downhill to a Summit', *Newsweek*, 29 September 1986; President's talking points, 25 September 1986: RRPL, Jack Matlock Files, box 18, folder: Matlock Chron. September 1986.
10. 'The Secretary's Pre-Reykjavik Congressional Briefing and Media Events. October 7–8, 1986': National Security Archive, End of the Cold War series, box 2, folder 3.
11. Charles Hill, diary (23 September 1986): Molly Worthen's notes.
12. Conversation with B. Mulroney: T. G. Stepanov-Mamaladze diary, 2 October 1986: T. G. Stepanov-Mamaladze Papers (HIA), box 5.
13. J. Poindexter to E. A. Shultz, 4 October 1986, pp. 1–2: National Security Archive, End of the Cold War series, box 2, folder 3; S. Sestanovich, briefing memo for R. Reagan, no later than 5 October 1986: RRPL, Jack Matlock Files, box 18, folder: Matlock Chron. October 1986; J. Matlock to J. Poindexter, 21 September 1986, p. 2: RRPL, Jack Matlock Files, box 17, folder: Matlock Chron. September 1986.
14. Gorbachëv's consultation with E. A. Shevardnadze, A. F. Dobrynin, S. F. Akhromeev and A. S. Chernyaev, 26 May 1986: *V Politbyuro TsK KPSS. Po zapisyam Anatoliya Chernyaeva, Vadima Medvedeva, Georgiya Shakhnazarova, 1985–1991*, p. 40.
15. National Security Planning Group list of participants, 7 October 1986: RRPL, Executive Secretariat, NSC: NSPG, Records, box 91308.
16. National Security Decision Directive no. 245, 7 October 1986: www.fas.org/irp/offdocs/nsdd/index.html.
17. A. G. Kovalëv (interview), HIGFC (HIA), box 2, folder 6, p. 17; N. S. Leonov, *Likholet'e*, p. 321; 'The Iceland Summit: Lost in the Shuffle; Protest Thwarted', *New York Times*, 13 October 1986.

18. 'Iceland Chronology', 18 October 1986, p. 1: RRPL, Sven Kraemer Files, box 91171.

19. James Mann's interviews with Kenneth Adelman, 10 August 1987 (pp. 2 and 5) and 24 August 1987 (p. 11): Jim Mann Papers (HIA), box 58.

20. C. Hill, notes, p. 7: Charles Hill Papers (HIA), box 63, folder: G. P. Shultz – 'Turmoil' – Draft – Reykjavik.

21. *Ibid.*, pp. 7–8.

22. 'Iceland Chronology', 18 October 1986, pp. 2–3: RRPL, Sven Kraemer Files, box 91171.

23. M. Gorbachëv, *Naedine s soboi*, p. 473.

24. N. Reagan, *My Turn*, p. 344.

25. 'Iceland Chronology', 18 October 1986, p. 3: RRPL, Sven Kraemer Files, box 91171; first session of Reykjavik summit meeting between Reagan and Gorbachëv, 11 October 1986: National Security Archive Electronic Briefing Book no. 303, doc. 9 (US memorandum), pp. 1–6.

26. C. Hill, notes: Charles Hill Papers (HIA), box 63, folder: G. P. Shultz – 'Turmoil' – Draft – Reykjavik, p. 10.

27. First session of Reykjavik summit meeting, 11 October 1986: National Security Archive Electronic Briefing Book no. 303, doc. 9 (US memorandum), pp. 6–7.

28. *Ibid.*, pp. 7–8.

29. C. Hill, notes: Charles Hill Papers (HIA), box 63, folder: G. P. Shultz – 'Turmoil' – Draft – Reykjavik, pp. 10–11.

30. Second session of Reykjavik summit meeting, 11 October 1986: National Security Archive Electronic Briefing Book no. 303, doc. 11 (US memorandum), pp. 8–9.

31. *Ibid.*, pp. 11–13.

32. *Ibid.*, pp. 14–15.

33. Charles Hill, diary (11 October 1986): Molly Worthen's notes.

34. 'Iceland Chronology', 18 October 1986, p. 2: RRPL, Sven Kraemer Files, box 91171; Brook Lapping interview with summit note taker Tom Simons, 13 August 1987, p. 5: Jim Mann Papers (HIA), box 58.

35. Exchange between Roz Ridgeway and George Shultz: 'Reykjavik Summit Anniversary', Fora TV: Hoover Institution, 11 October 2006; G. Shultz to Jacalyn Stein, 13 October 1986: George Shultz Papers (RRPL), box 56b, Official Memoranda.

36. James Mann's interview with Paul Nitze, 12 August 1987, p. 5: Jim Mann Papers (HIA), box 58.

37. Interview with Kenneth Adelman, 10 August 1987: *ibid.*

38. C. Hill, notes: Charles Hill Papers (HIA), box 63, folder: G. P. Shultz – 'Turmoil' – Draft – Reykjavik, pp. 14–15.

39. Soviet Transcript of Talks in the Working Group on Military Issues, 11–12 October 1986, pp. 30–52: ECWF.

40. Third session of Reykjavik summit meeting, 12 October 1986: National

Security Archive Electronic Briefing Book no. 303, doc. 13 (US memorandum), p. 1.

41. *Ibid.*, pp. 4–5 and 7.
42. *Ibid.*, pp. 7–8.
43. *Ibid.*, pp. 10–11.
44. *Ibid.*, p. 13.
45. *Ibid.*, pp. 13–17.
46. *Ibid.*, pp. 17–20.
47. Fourth session of Reykjavik summit meeting, 12 October 1986: *ibid.*, doc. 15 (US memorandum), p. 2.
48. *Ibid.*, p. 3.
49. *Ibid.*, pp. 4–5.
50. *Ibid.*, p. 8.
51. *Ibid.*, p. 11.
52. *Ibid.*, pp. 12–14; E. Meese III, *With Reagan: The Inside Story*, 1992), p. 197; G. Shultz (interview), HIGFC (HIA), box 2, folder 20, p. 5.
53. Fourth session of Reykjavik summit meeting, 12 October 1986: National Security Archive Electronic Briefing Book no. 303, doc. 15 (Soviet memorandum), p. 8.
54. *Ibid.*
55. G. Shultz, *Turmoil and Triumph: My Years as Secretary of State*, pp. 773–4.
56. *The Reagan Diaries Unabridged*, vol. 2, p. 647 (12 October 1986).
57. Press conference (Reykjavik), 12 October 1986: M. S. Gorbachëv, *Sobranie sochinenii*, vol. 5, pp. 46–56.
58. G. P. Shultz, Press Briefing, pp. 1–4, 12 October 1986 (Loftleidir Hotel: Reykjavik): Committee on the Present Danger (HIA), box 112, folder: Shultz 1986.

21: The Month of Muffled Drums

1. Gorbachëv's comments on the aeroplane, 12 October 1986: Anatoli Chernyaev Papers (RESCA), box 1, pp. 80–1.
2. Presidential Address to the Nation, 13 October 1986, p. 6: Ronald Reagan Presidential Papers.
3. *Ibid.*, pp. 6–8.
4. Peter Robinson's account of email exchange with N. Podhoretz: see his interview with G. P. Shultz, 10 June 2002, p. 7: Peter Robinson Papers (HIA), box 21.
5. *Newsweek*, 13 October 1986.
6. W. F. Buckley to R. Reagan, 13 October 1986: RRPL, Presidential Handwriting File: Presidential Records, box 17, folder 268; W. F. Buckley, 'Saved from the Brink', *National Review*, 21 November 1986, p. 68.
7. J. Attali, *Verbatim*, vol. 2: *Chronique des années 1986–1988*, p. 184 (18 October 1986).
8. Memcon of telephone conversation between R. Reagan and M. Thatcher, 13

October 1986, p. 3: RRPL, Jack Matlock Files, box 18, folder: Matlock Chron. October 1986; J. M. Poindexter to R. Reagan, 6 November 1986 (memo): *ibid.*, Coordination Office of NSC, Records, box 15, 'Thatcher Visit, 11/15/1986'; G. P. Shultz: interview with P. Robinson, 10 June 2002, pp. 7–8: Peter Robinson Papers (HIA), box 21; P. R. Sommer to J. M. Poindexter, 1 October 1986 (memo), p. 1: RRPL, Coordination Office of NSC, Records, box 13, Thatcher Visit.

9. Attali, *Verbatim*, vol. 2, pp. 180–2 (16 October 1986).

10. P. R. Sommer to J. M. Poindexter, 1 October 1986 (memo): RRPL, Coordination Office of NSC, Records, box 13, 'Thatcher Visit'.

11. P. R. Sommer to J. M. Poindexter, 6 November 1986 (memo): *ibid.*, box 13, 'Thatcher Visit, 11/15/1986'; R. Reagan, note (n.d.): RRPL, Presidential Handwriting File: Presidential Records, box 16, folder 260.

12. P. Cradock, *In Pursuit of British Interests Reflections on Foreign Policy under Margaret Thatcher and John Major*, pp. 68–9.

13. *New York Times*, 16 November 1986.

14. Attali, *Verbatim*, vol. 2, pp. 205–6 (conversation of M. Thatcher and F. Mitterrand, 20 November 1986).

15. *Ibid.*, p. 271 (4 March 1987).

16. G. P. Shultz to R. Reagan, aircraft cable, 13 October 1986: RRPL, Jack Matlock Files, box 18, folder: Matlock Chron. October 1986.

17. G. P. Shultz to R. Reagan, aircraft cable (2), 13 October 1986: *ibid.*

18. C. Hill, talking points for G. P. Shultz's meeting with R. Reagan, no earlier than 13 October 1986: Charles Hill Papers (HIA), box 63, folder: G. P. Shultz – 'Turmoil' – Draft – Reykjavik.

19. C. Hill, notes, p. 33: *ibid.*

20. 'The Secretary's Post-Reykjavik Media Events. October 17 and 19, 1986': National Security Archive, End of the Cold War series, box 2, folder 3.

21. Secretary Shultz, Address before the Commonwealth Club, 'Reykjavik: A Watershed in U.S.–Soviet Relations', pp. 1–3, 31 October 1986 (Washington DC: US Department of State, 1986): Committee on the Present Danger (HIA), box 112, folder: Shultz 1986; Secretary Shultz, Address before the Los Angeles World Affairs Council, 'Human Rights and Soviet–American Relations', pp. 1–4, 31 October 1986 (Washington DC: US Department of State, 1986): *ibid.*, box 112, folder: Shultz 1986.

22. Secretary Shultz, Address at the University of Chicago, 'Nuclear Weapons, Arms Control, and the Future of Deterrence', 17 November 1986: Committee on the Present Danger (HIA), box 112, folder: Shultz 1986.

23. C. Hill, notes, p. 33: Charles Hill Papers (HIA), box 63, folder: G. P. Shultz – 'Turmoil' – Draft – Reykjavik.

24. Politburo meeting, 14 October 1986, pp. 1–4: Dmitri A. Volkogonov Papers (HIA), reel 17; Politburo meeting, 14 October 1986: *V Politbyuro TsK KPSS. Po zapisyam Anatoliya Chernyaeva, Vadima Medvedeva, Georgiya Shakhnazarova, 1985–1991*, p. 77; S. K. Sokolov to the Central Committee, 17 May 1987: Vitalii Leonidovich Kataev Papers (HIA), box 7, folder 25.

25. Politburo meeting, 14 October 1986, pp. 4–11: Dmitri A. Volkogonov Papers (HIA), reel 17.
26. S. P. Tarasenko (interview), HIGFC (HIA), box 3, folder 2, p. 46.
27. T. G. Stepanov-Mamaladze working notes, 19 August 1987: T. G. Stepanov-Mamaladze Papers (HIA), box 1; S. P. Tarasenko (interview), HIGFC (HIA), box 3, folder 2, pp. 48–9.
28. T. G. Stepanov-Mamaladze working notes, 18 October 1986: T. G. Stepanov-Mamaladze Papers (HIA), box 1.
29. A. L. Adamishin Papers (HIA), box 1: Diaries 1987, 25 January 1987, p. 2.
30. Charles Hill, diary (15 October 1986): Molly Worthen's notes.
31. Conversation between M. S. Gorbachëv and G. Hart (Moscow), 15 December 1986: *Otvechaya na vyzov vremeni: Vneshnyaya politika perestroiki: Dokumental'nye svidetel'stva*, p. 180.
32. M. S. Gorbachëv's conversation with A. S. Chernyaev, 17 November 1986: Anatoli Chernyaev Papers (RESCA), box 1, pp. 92–3.
33. T. G. Stepanov-Mamaladze working notes, 4 November (miswritten as October) 1986: T. G. Stepanov-Mamaladze Papers (HIA), box 1.
34. *Ibid.*, n.d. but earlier than 8 November 1986 and after the Reykjavik summit.
35. S. F. Akhromeev in S. F. Akhromeev and G. M. Kornienko, *Glazami marshala i diplomata*, p. 125.
36. *Ibid.*, pp. 124–7.
37. Gorbachev's meeting with the USSR government deputy premiers, 30 October 1986, p. 89: Anatoli Chernyaev Papers (RESCA), box 1.
38. *Ibid.*, pp. 89–90.
39. *Ibid.*, p. 88.
40. *Ibid.*
41. J. Poindexter to R. Reagan, memo, 22 October 1986, p. 1: RRPL, Jack Matlock Files, box 18, folder: Matlock Chron. October 1986.
42. National Security Decision Directive no. 250, pp. 9–10 and 14, 3 November 1986: *ibid.*, Executive Secretariat, NSC: NSDD, box 91297.
43. National Security Decision Directive no. 249, 29 October 1986: www.fas.org/irp/offdocs/nsdd/index.html.
44. J. M. Poindexter to R. Reagan, earlier than the NSPG meeting of 27 October 1986 (memo): RRPL, Executive Secretariat, NSC: NSPG, Records, box 91308.
45. C. Weinberger to J. M. Poindexter, 31 October 1986 (memo), pp. 1 and 3: *ibid.*, Executive Secretariat, NSC: NSDD 250, Records, box 91297.
46. W. J. Casey to A. G. Keel, 31 October 1986 (notes to memo), pp. 1–3: *ibid.*
47. G. P. Shultz to R. Reagan, 14 November 1986, p. 1: RRPL, Jack Matlock Files, box 19, folder: Matlock Chron. December 1986.
48. G. P. Shultz to R. Reagan, 14 November 1986, memo, p. 4 and 'Notional Plan for Elimination of Nuclear Weapons', pp. 1–3: *ibid.*
49. G. P. Shultz to R. Reagan, 14 November 1986, pp. 2–3: *ibid.*
50. C. Hill, notes (19 September 1991) for G. Shultz, *Turmoil and Triumph*, folder: Soviet Union, 1986–1987, pp. 1–2, Charles Hill Papers (HIA), box 64.
51. Memo from Alton G. Keel on President's forthcoming meeting (19 December

1986) with Joint Chiefs of Staff, 18 December 1986: Jim Mann Papers (HIA), box 58.

52. G. P. Shultz to R. Reagan, memo 'One Eye Only', n.d., pp. 1–3: folder: Soviet Union, 1986–1987, Charles Hill Papers (HIA), box 64.

53. C. Hill, notes (19 September 1991) for G. Shultz, *Turmoil and Triumph*, folder: Soviet Union, 1986–1987, p. 7, Charles Hill Papers (HIA), box 64.

22: The Soviet Package Untied

1. Briefing for White House Senior Staff, 5 November 1986, pp. 9–10: Peter Robinson Papers (HIA), box 24.

2. V. L. Kataev, 'Kakoi byla reaktsiya v SSSR na zayavleniya R. Reigana ob otkaze SShA soblyudat' kolichestvennye dogovornye ogranicheniya SNV', n.d., pp. 10–11: Vitalii Leonidovich Kataev Papers (HIA), disk 3 (SOI).

3. *Ibid.*, pp. 11–12.

4. Meeting with Politburo members and Central Committee secretaries, 1 December 1986: Anatoli Chernyaev Papers (RESCA), box 1, pp. 94–6, 100 and 102.

5. A. L. Adamishin Papers (HIA), box 1: Diaries 1986, December 1986 summary.

6. Politburo meeting, 13 November 1986: Anatoli Chernyaev Papers (RESCA), box 1, pp. 91–2.

7. A. L. Adamishin Papers (HIA), box 1: Diaries 1986, 19 and 21 November 1986.

8. T. G. Stepanov-Mamaladze working notes, 19 December 1986: T. G. Stepanov-Mamaladze Papers (HIA), box 1.

9. Conversation of M. S. Gorbachëv and G. Hart, 15 December 1986: M. S. Gorbachëv, *Sobranie sochinenii*, vol. 5, pp. 306–23.

10. T. G. Stepanov-Mamaladze working notes, 19 December 1986: T. G. Stepanov-Mamaladze Papers (HIA), box 1.

11. Notes taken by O. Grinevskii, *Perelom: ot Brezhneva k Gorbachëvu*, p. 522.

12. V. L. Kataev to L. N. Zaikov, c. 18 December 1986, pp. 1–10: Vitalii Leonidovich Kataev Papers (HIA), box 4, folder 15.

13. Grinevskii, *Perelom: ot Brezhneva k Gorbachëvu*, p. 507.

14. P. J. Wallison to R. Reagan, 22 December 1986: RRPL, Frank C. Carlucci Files, box 92462, folder: Chronology – Official (12/31/1986 – 01/24/1986); P. J. Wallison to D. Regan and F. Carlucci, 7 January 1987: RRPL, Frank C. Carlucci Files, box 92462, folder: Chronology – Official (12/31/1986 – 01/24/1986).

15. V. L. Kataev, 'Sovetskii voenno-promyshlennyi kompleks', p. 31: Vitalii Leonidovich Kataev Papers (HIA), box 16.

16. *Materialy plenuma Tsentral'nogo Komiteta KPSS, 27–28 yanvarya 1987 goda* (Moscow: Politizdat, 1987).

17. 'Reagan May Pick an SDI System Soon', *Washington Post*, 14 January 1987.

18. C. Hill, notes (24 September 1991) for G. Shultz, *Turmoil and Triumph*, folder: Soviet Union, 1986–1987, pp. 4–5, Charles Hill Papers (HIA), box 64.

19. *Ibid.*, p. 4.
20. *Ibid.*, p. 6.
21. Meeting of the Senior Presidential Advisers, 3 February 1987, pp. 11–12: RRPL, Executive Secretariat, NSC, NSPG, box 91306.
22. *Washington Times*, 5 February 1987.
23. C. Weinberger, *Annual Report to the Congress: Fiscal Year 1988*, pp. 302–3.
24. C. Hill, notes (24 September 1991) on 'Soviet Union 1987', pp. 8–10, for G. Shultz, *Turmoil and Triumph*, folder: Soviet Union, 1986–1987, Charles Hill Papers (HIA), box 64.
25. *New York Times*, 9 February 1987.
26. P. Dobriansky to F. C. Carlucci, 6 January 1986 (draft memo): RRPL, Paula Dobriansky Files, RAC, box 7, Whitehead Visit to Eastern Europe; C. Hill, notes (24 September 1991) on 'Soviet Union 1987', pp. 10–11, for G. Shultz, *Turmoil and Triumph*, folder: Soviet Union, 1986–1987, Charles Hill Papers (HIA), box 64.
27. J. Attali, *Verbatim*, vol. 1: *Chronique des années 1981–1986*, p. 788 (25 March 1985).
28. *Washington Times*, 12 January 1987.
29. *Wall Street Journal*, 12 January 1987.
30. *New York Times*, 23 January 1987.
31. *Washington Times*, 18 February 1987.
32. *New York Times*, 25 February 1987.
33. T. H. Johnson to J. Matlock, 23 February 1987 (memo): Thomas H. Johnson Papers (HIA), box 47, folder: Matlock Memos.
34. 'O nashei takticheskoi linii v otnoshenii peregovorov s SShA po voprosam yadernykh i kosmicheskikh vooruzheniyakh', 20 February 1987: Vitalii Leonidovich Kataev Papers (HIA), box 5, folder 24, pp. 1–5.
35. Politburo meeting, 26 February 1987, p. 156: Anatoli Chernyaev Papers (RESCA), box 1.
36. *Ibid.*, pp. 156–7.
37. *Ibid.*, p. 157.
38. A. N. Yakovlev to M. S. Gorbachëv. 25 February 1987: *Aleksandr Yakovlev. Perestroika, 1985–1991. Neizdannoe, maloizvestnoe, zabytoe* (ed. A. A. Yakovlev), pp. 77–89.
39. Politburo meeting, 26 February 1987, pp. 157–8: Anatoli Chernyaev Papers (RESCA), box 1.
40. *Pravda*, 1 March 1987; Attali, *Verbatim*, vol. 2: *Chronique des années 1986–1988*, p. 165 (28 February 1987); M. M. Kampelman, *Entering New Worlds: The Memoirs of a Private Man in Public Life*, pp. 319–20. Kampelman received an advance alert about the contents that day.
41. T. G. Stepanov-Mamaladze diary, 1 March 1987: T. G. Stepanov-Mamaladze Papers (HIA), box 5.
42. *The Reagan Diaries Unabridged*, vol. 2, p. 696 (6 March 1987).
43. R. W. Reagan, RRPL, Presidential Handwriting File, Series II, Presidential Records, box 18, folders 280–5.

44. V. L. Kataev, 'O programme SOI', p. 1 in 'SOI-A': Vitalii Leonidovich Kataev Papers (HIA), disk 5.
45. Note on C. Weinberger's behalf to C. Powell, 9 April 1987: RRPL, Executive Secretariat, NSC, Head of State Files: USSR: General Secretary Gorbachev, box 41.
46. National Security Decision Directive no. 267, pp. 1–4, 9 April 1987: www.fas. org/irp/offdocs/nsdd/index.html. p. 2.
47. C. Weinberger, 'Toward Real Reductions in Weapons', *New York Times*, 14 April 1987.
48. F. C. Carlucci to M. Baldrige, 27 March 1987: RRPL, Stephen Danzansky Files (NSC): RAC, box 2.
49. R. L. Lesher (President, US Chamber of Commerce) and A. B. Trowbridge (President, National Association of Manufacturers) to R. Reagan, 6 October 1986: *ibid.*, box 8; Senator L. Bentsen to M. Baldrige, 15 December 1986: *ibid.*
50. Talking points for Reagan's meeting with USSR Foreign Trade Minister B. I. Aristov, 5 December 1986: *ibid.*, box 2.
51. *New York Times*, 24 February 1987.
52. Press release of US Department of Commerce (n.d.) for session of the US–USSR Commercial Commission, 4–5 December 1986: RRPL, Stephen Danzansky Files (NSC): RAC, box 2.
53. R. Reagan to M. S. Gorbachëv, 10 April 1987, p. 1: *The Reagan Files: The Untold Story of Reagan's Top-Secret Efforts to Win the Cold War.*
54. Soviet transcript (excerpted) of conversation between M. S. Gorbachëv and G. P. Shultz, 14 April 1987, pp. 1–2 and 5–7: ECWF (translated for the National Security Archive by S. Savranskaya).
55. *Ibid.*
56. Politburo meeting, 16 April 1987: Anatoli Chernyaev Papers (RESCA), box 1, pp. 189–90.
57. Politburo meeting, 16 April 1987: *V Politbyuro TsK KPSS. Po zapisyam Anatoliya Chernyaeva, Vadima Medvedeva, Georgiya Shakhnazarova, 1985–1991*, pp. 145–6.
58. T. G. Stepanov-Mamaladze diary, 2–3 May 1987: T. G. Stepanov-Mamaladze Papers (HIA), box 5.
59. From discussion led by E. A. Shevardnadze: T. G. Stepanov-Mamaladze working notes, 13 June 1987: *ibid.*, box 1.
60. *Ibid.*, 29 May 1987; M. S. Gorbachëv to the Political Consultative Committee in East Berlin (East German report), 29 May 1987, pp. 2–3: PHPCS.
61. *Ibid.*, p. 5.
62. T. G. Stepanov-Mamaladze working notes, 29 May 1987: T. G. Stepanov-Mamaladze Papers (HIA), box 1.
63. Politburo meeting, 30 May 1987, pp. 493–502: Dmitri A. Volkogonov Papers (HIA), reel 17.
64. Politburo meeting, 9 July 1987: Anatoli Chernyaev Papers (RESCA), box 1, pp. 261–2.
65. From discussion led by E. A. Shevardnadze: T. G. Stepanov-Mamaladze

working notes, 13 June 1987: T. G. Stepanov-Mamaladze Papers (HIA), box 1.

66. *Ibid.*, 9 November 1987: box 2.
67. Politburo meeting, 9 July 1987: Anatoli Chernyaev Papers (RESCA), box 1, p. 261.
68. National Security Decision Directive no. 278, 13 June 1987: www.fas.org/irp/offdocs/nsdd/index.html. p. 2.
69. T. G. Stepanov-Mamaladze diary, 13 June 1987: T. G. Stepanov-Mamaladze Papers (HIA), box 1.
70. T. G. Stepanov-Mamaladze diary, 23 July 1987: *ibid.*, box 5.

23: The Big Four

1. Yakovlev was important for Soviet foreign policy but had always been much more influential on internal policy.
2. Memcon of meeting between R. Reagan and M. Koivisto: RRPL, Fritz W. Ermath Files, box 98084, 1988 US–USSR Memcons, May 26 – June 3, 1988.
3. M. K. Deaver, *A Different Drummer: My Thirty Years with Ronald Reagan*, p. 31.
4. Gorbachev's meeting with the USSR government deputy premiers, 30 October 1986, p. 89: Anatoli Chernyaev Papers (RESCA), box 1.
5. Meeting with Politburo members and Central Committee secretaries, 1 December 1986: *ibid.*, p. 99.
6. T. G. Stepanov-Mamaladze working notes, 24 October 1985: T. G. Stepanov-Mamaladze Papers (HIA), box 1.
7. A. Chernyaev, *Sovmestnyi iskhod. Dnevnik dvukh epokh. 1971–1991 gody*, p. 710 (15 June 1987).
8. T. G. Stepanov-Mamaladze working notes, 11 December 1987: T. G. Stepanov-Mamaladze Papers (HIA), box 2.
9. Chernyaev, *Sovmestnyi iskhod*, p. 754 (26 April 1988).
10. T. G. Stepanov-Mamaladze working notes, 16 October 1987: T. G. Stepanov-Mamaladze Papers (HIA), box 1.
11. T. G. Stepanov-Mamaladze diary, 19 September 1986: *ibid.*, box 5.
12. Chernyaev, *Sovmestnyi iskhod*, p. 734 (17 December 1987).
13. T. G. Stepanov-Mamaladze working notes, 15 September 1987: T. G. Stepanov-Mamaladze Papers (HIA), box 2.
14. *Ibid.*, 16 October 1987.
15. *Ibid.*, 4 December 1989; 3 December 1989: *ibid.*, box 5.
16. C. Hill, handwritten notes on 1986–1987, p. 68: Charles Hill Papers (HIA), box 64.
17. Chernyaev, *Sovmestnyi iskhod*, p. 736 (17 December 1987).
18. T. G. Stepanov-Mamaladze working notes, 30 October 1987: T. G. Stepanov-Mamaladze Papers (HIA), box 2.
19. Interview with Kenneth Adelman, 30 September 2003, p. 58: RROHP.

20. See the analysis offered to J. M. Poindexter by J. Matlock, 15 February 1986, p. 2: RRPL, Executive Secretariat, NSC, Head of State Files: USSR: General Secretary Gorbachev, box 40.
21. S. Massie, *Trust But Verify: Reagan, Russia and Me*, p. 230.
22. T. G. Stepanov-Mamaladze diary, 25 September 1985: T. G. Stepanov-Mamaladze Papers (HIA), box 5.
23. *Ibid.*, 28 September 1985.
24. *Ibid.*, 23 March 1988.
25. *Ibid.*, 17 September 1987.
26. *Ibid.*, 15 September 1987.
27. I. Korchilov, *Translating History: Thirty Years on the Front Lines of Diplomacy with a Top Russian Interpreter*, p. 80.
28. Interview with Caspar Weinberger, 19 November 2002, p. 34: RROHP.
29. Interview with Richard V. Allen, 28 May 2002, p. 68: *ibid.*
30. Interview with Martin Anderson, 11–12 December 2001, p. 88: *ibid.*
31. D. Regan (interview), HIGFC (HIA), box 2, folder 15, p. 7.
32. T. G. Stepanov-Mamaladze diary, 15 September 1987: T. G. Stepanov-Mamaladze Papers (HIA), box 5.
33. T. G. Stepanov-Mamaladze working notes, 15 September 1987: *ibid.*, box 2; T. G. Stepanov-Mamaladze diary, 15 September 1987: *ibid.*, box 5.
34. Shevardnadze's report to the Ministry of Foreign Affairs collegium, 16 October 1987: T. G. Stepanov-Mamaladze working notes: *ibid.*, box 1.
35. T. G. Stepanov-Mamaladze diary, 23 March 1988: *ibid.*, box 5.
36. E. Shevardnadze, *Kogda rukhnul zheleznyi zanaves: vstrechi i vospominaniya*, p. 78.
37. T. G. Stepanov-Mamaladze diary, 2 June 1988: T. G. Stepanov-Mamaladze Papers (HIA), box 5.
38. A. S. Chernyaev (interview), HIGFC (HIA), box 1, folder 12, p. 17.
39. T. G. Stepanov-Mamaladze diary, 2 June 1988: T. G. Stepanov-Mamaladze Papers (HIA), box 5.
40. R. Braithwaite, 'Moscow Diary', 6 April 1989 and 7 November 1989.
41. C. Hill, notes (19 December 1991), p. 9: Charles Hill Papers (HIA), box 67, folder: Soviet Union, Late 1987: The Cold War is Over.
42. D. Regan (interview), HIGFC (HIA), box 2, folder 15, p. 51.
43. T. G. Stepanov-Mamaladze working notes, 27 November 1986: T. G. Stepanov-Mamaladze Papers (HIA), box 1.
44. T. G. Stepanov-Mamaladze diary, 6 December 1988: *ibid.*, box 5.
45. Braithwaite, 'Moscow Diary', 6 April 1989.
46. Korchilov, *Translating History*, p. 216.
47. A. L. Adamishin Papers (HIA), box 1: Diaries 1988, 15 May 1988.
48. Braithwaite, 'Moscow Diary', 29 March 1989.
49. T. G. Stepanov-Mamaladze working notes, 9 November 1985: T. G. Stepanov-Mamaladze Papers (HIA), box 1.
50. T. G. Stepanov-Mamaladze diary, 25 September 1985: *ibid.*, box 5.

51. T. G. Stepanov-Mamaladze working notes, 9 November 1986: *ibid.*, box 1.
52. G. Shultz: interview with R. Service and P. Robinson, Hoover Institution, 1 September 2009.
53. *Ibid.*
54. T. G. Stepanov-Mamaladze diary, 13 April 1987: T. G. Stepanov-Mamaladze Papers (HIA), box 5. Stepanov-Mamaladze's informant about this was S. P. Tarasenko.
55. E. Shevardnadze, *Moi vybor: v zashchitu demokratii i svobody*, pp. 131–2.
56. T. G. Stepanov-Mamaladze diary, 24 October 1987: T. G. Stepanov-Mamaladze Papers (HIA), box 5.
57. *Ibid.*, 24 October 1987.
58. *Ibid.*, 15 March 1988.
59. C. Hill, notes (19 December 1991), p. 10: Charles Hill Papers (HIA), box 67, folder: Soviet Union, Late 1987: The Cold War is Over.
60. Politburo meeting, 16 April 1987: *V Politbyuro TsK KPSS. Po zapisyam Anatoliya Chernyaeva, Vadima Medvedeva, Georgiya Shakhnazarova, 1985–1991*, p. 145.
61. Personal interview with Charles Hill, 22 July 2011.
62. C. Hill, notes (24 September 1991) on 'Soviet Union 1987', p. 69, for G. Shultz, *Turmoil and Triumph*, folder: Soviet Union, 1986–1987, Charles Hill Papers (HIA), box 64.
63. T. G. Stepanov-Mamaladze working notes, 14 March 1988: T. G. Stepanov-Mamaladze Papers (HIA), box 2.
64. G. P. Shultz, 'The Shape, Scope, and Consequences of the Age of Information', address before the Stanford University Alumni Association, Paris, 21 March 1986, pp. 1 and 3.
65. C. Hill, notes (27 January 1992), p. 16: Charles Hill Papers (HIA), box 66, folder: The Last of the Superpower Summits.
66. T. G. Stepanov-Mamaladze working notes, 5 November 1987: T. G. Stepanov-Mamaladze Papers (HIA), box 2.
67. G. Shultz: interview with R. Service and P. Robinson, Hoover Institution, 1 September 2009.
68. Chernyaev, *Sovmestnyi iskhod*, p. 754 (26 April 1988).

24: Getting to Know the Enemy

1. J. Matlock to J. Poindexter, 11 June 1986: RRPL, Jack Matlock Files, box 16, folder: Matlock Chron. June 1986.
2. R. Reagan to J. M. Poindexter, no earlier than 16 June 1986, pp. 2–6: *ibid.*
3. See J. Haslam, *Russia's Cold War: From the October Revolution to the Fall of the Wall*, p. 329.
4. The exception was the leading biological weapons programme scientist Vladimir Pasechnik: see below, pp. 372 and 439.
5. W. J. Casey, Speech to US–USSR Trade Council and New York CEOs (hand-

written notes), New York City, 29 July 1985, p. 1: William J. Casey Papers (HIA), box 310, folder 10.

6. T. G. Stepanov-Mamaladze diary, 28 October 1985: T. G. Stepanov-Mamaladze Papers (HIA), box 5.

7. N. S. Leonov, *Likholet'e*, pp. 283–5.

8. Select Committee on Intelligence, United States Senate, *An Assessment of the Aldrich H. Ames Espionage Case and Its Implications for U.S. Intelligence: Report*, pp. 2, 11, 19, 26, 53 and 62–3.

9. W. J. Casey, Remarks before World Affairs Council (draft notes), Pittsburgh, PA, 29 April 1985, p. 5: William J. Casey Papers (HIA), box 310, folder 1.

10. F. Ermath, draft speech written for W. J. Casey, 16 May 1986, pp. 3 and 12: *ibid.*, box 311, folder 11.

11. 'Gorbachev: Steering the USSR Into the 1990s', pp. v–ix: CIA Papers.

12. R. M. Gates to F. C. Carlucci, 15 January 1987, introducing National Intelligence Council report on 'Soviet and Other Foreign Reactions to a Zero-Ballistic Missile World' (see especially p. 32): RRPL, Executive Secretariat, NSC: NSDD, Records, box 91297, NSDD 250.

13. 'Whither Gorbachev? Soviet Policy and Politics in the 1990s: National Intelligence Estimate', November 1987, pp. 6, 8, 12 and 17: CIA Papers.

14. National Security Archive Electronic Briefing Book No. 238: R. M. Gates, 'Gorbachev's Endgame: The Long View', 24 November 1987, pp. 2–5.

15. M. Gorbachëv, *Perestroika i novoe myshlenie dlya nashei strany i vsego mira*.

16. Hearings before the Subcommittee on National Security Economics of the Joints Economic Committee, Congress of the United States, April 13 and 21, 1988, pp. 71–2 and 78: National Security Archive, End of Cold War series, box A1.

17. Intelligence Research Report, no. 183, 9 September 1988, p. 1 and appendices 1 and 2: National Security Archive, Soviet Flashpoints series, box 37.

18. Memorandum of dinner conversation, 18 September 1987, p. 5: RRPL, Nelson Ledsky Files, RAC, box 8.

19. CIA and Defense Intelligence Agency, *Gorbachev's Economic Program: Problems Emerge* (n.p., 1988), p. 12 and table 9: National Security Archive, Soviet Flashpoints series, box 37.

20. D. MacEachin to R. Kerr, memo, 27 September 1988: CIA Papers.

21. W. J. Casey, draft speech to CSIS International Councillors on Soviet Political Developments, 16 May 1986, p. 11: William J. Casey Papers (HIA), box 311, folder 11.

22. See for example V. M. Chebrikov, 'O rezul'tatakh raboty po preduprezhdeniyu terroristicheskikh proyavlenii na territorii SSSR', 11 January 1988, pp. 1–5: Dmitri A. Volkogonov Papers (HIA), reel 18.

23. R. M. Gates, *From the Shadows: The Ultimate Insider's Story of Five Presidents and How They Won the Cold War*, pp. 410–11.

24. C. Hill, notes on '1987: Shultz–Gates meeting after Gates became acting DCI', pp. 12–13, for G. Shultz, *Turmoil and Triumph*, folder: Soviet Union, 1986–1987, Charles Hill Papers (HIA), box 67.

25. Interview with George Shultz, 18 December 2002, p. 27: RROHP.
26. C. Hill, notes on '1987: Shultz-Gates meeting after Gates became acting DCI', pp. 14–15 and 16, for G. Shultz, *Turmoil and Triumph*, folder: Soviet Union, 1986–1987, Charles Hill Papers (HIA), box 67.
27. *Ibid.*, p. 17.
28. *Whence the Threat to Peace*, pp. 3, 29, 68, 70 and 74.
29. R. Z. Sagdeev and A. Kokoshkin, *Strategic Stability under the Conditions of Radical Nuclear Arms Reductions*, p. 21.
30. *Congressional Record – House*, 17 July 1985, pp. 5866–5883.
31. W. J. Casey, speech to Dallas World Affairs Council, 18 September 1985, pp. 1–17: RRPL, John Lenczowsky Files, box 1, Active Measures.
32. A. A. Snyder, *Warriors of Disinformation: American Propaganda, Soviet Lies, and the Winning of the Cold War: An Insider's Account*, p. xiii.
33. Chapter and verse was supplied in a USIA memo, 'Soviet Disinformation Campaigns in 1987', n.d., pp. 1–4: John O. Koehler Papers (HIA), box 16, folder: Eastern Europe, 1974–1995. See also 'The USSR's Disinformation Campaign': Foreign Affairs Note, State Department, July 1987: Citizens for International Civil Society (HIA), box 89, folder 1. The Pravda cartoon appeared on 31 October 1986.
34. Snyder, *Warriors of Disinformation*, pp. 93–4.
35. *Ibid.*, pp. 94–5.
36. *New York Times*, 22 January 1983.
37. P. J. Buchanan to R. Arledge (President, ABC News), 27 February 1987: RRPL, Presidential Handwriting File: Presidential Records, folder 230.
38. C. Wick to F. Carlucci, 7 March 1987: RRPL, Frank C. Carlucci Files, box 92463, Official Correspondence.
39. F. C. Carlucci to C. Z. Wick, 12 August 1987: *ibid.*, Fritz W. Ermath Files, box 92244, Soviet Active Measures.
40. V. L. Kataev (interview), HIGFC (HIA), box 2, folder 4, p. 53.
41. A. L. Adamishin Papers (HIA), box 1: Diaries 1987, 25 July 1987.
42. R. Reagan to R. C. McFarlane, no earlier than 28 July 1985: RRPL, Co-ordination Office, NSC: Records, box 9, folder: Meeting with Suzanne Massie, 9/3/85; S. Massie, *Trust But Verify: Reagan, Russia and Me*, pp. 90 and 97–101.
43. *The Reagan Diaries*, p. 412 (20 May 1986).
44. S. Massie to R. Reagan, 10 August 1985, pp. 2–3: RRPL, Coordination Committee, NSC, box 9, folder: Meeting with Suzanne Massie, 9/3/85.
45. S. Massie to R. Reagan, 27 October 1985: Jim Mann Papers (HIA), box 55.
46. S. Massie to R. Reagan, 12 March 1986: RRPL, Coordination Office, NSC: Records, box 12, folder: Meeting with Suzanne Massie, May 20, 1986.
47. Charles Hill, diary (24 September 1986): Molly Worthen's notes.
48. F. Carlucci (interview), HIGFC (HIA), box 1, folder 10, p. 14.
49. F. Carlucci to R. Reagan, 25 February 1987 (RRPL): Jim Mann Papers (HIA), box 56.

50. S. Massie to R. Reagan, 14 October 1986: RRPL, Presidential Handwriting File, box 16, folder 261.
51. C. Hill, notes (24 September 1991) for G. P. Shultz, *Turmoil and Triumph*, folder: Soviet Union, 1986–1987, pp. 6–7, Charles Hill Papers (HIA), box 64.
52. R. Reagan to S. Massie, 13 January 1987: Jim Mann Papers (HIA), box 55.
53. S. Massie to R. Reagan, 6 February 1987: *ibid.*
54. Politburo meeting, 17 December 1987: Anatoli Chernyaev Papers (RESCA), box 1, p. 321.
55. Discussion with George Bush at the Soviet embassy, Washington, 10 December 1987, p. 5: RRPL, Stephen Danzansky Files (NSC): RAC, box 12.
56. Politburo meeting, 27–28 December 1988: *V Politbyuro TsK KPSS. Po zapisyam Anatoliya Chernyaeva, Vadima Medvedeva, Georgiya Shakhnazarova, 1985–1991*, p. 366.
57. T. G. Stepanov-Mamaladze diary, 22 March 1986: T. G. Stepanov-Mamaladze Papers (HIA), box 5.
58. M. Gorbachëv, *Naedine s soboi*, pp. 343–4.
59. Gorbachëv at Politburo meeting, 26 October 1986: *Otvechaya na vyzov vremeni: Vneshnyaya politika perestroiki: Dokumental'nye svidetel'stva*, p. 122.
60. V. L. Kataev to the Central Committee (memo, n.d., on the consequences of the intermediate-range nuclear weapons treaty), p. 2: Vitalii Leonidovich Kataev Papers (HIA), disk 2, RSMD-2.
61. Politburo meeting, 26 February 1987, p. 159: Anatoli Chernyaev Papers (RESCA), box 1.
62. V. Bakatin, *Izbavlenie ot KGB*, pp. 44–6.
63. Meeting of Politburo members and Central Committee secretaries, 1 December 1986: Anatoli Chernyaev Papers (RESCA), box 1, p. 99.
64. Politburo meeting, 26 March 1987: *ibid.*, p. 172.
65. Politburo meeting, 21 January 1987: *ibid.*, p. 129.
66. Politburo meeting, 16 April 1987: *ibid.*, p. 185.
67. Politburo meeting, 23 April 1987: *ibid.*, p. 196.
68. Politburo meeting, 30 April 1987: *ibid.*, p. 203.
69. Politburo meeting, 26 March 1987: *ibid.*, pp. 172 and 174.
70. T. G. Stepanov-Mamaladze working notes, 12 December 1987: T. G. Stepanov-Mamaladze Papers (HIA), box 2.
71. F. Carlucci (interview), HIGFC (HIA), box 1, folder 10, pp. 17–18.
72. M. S. Gorbachëv's second meeting with obkom secretaries, 15 April 1988, p. 6: Anatoli Chernyaev Papers (RESCA), box 2, folder 5.
73. T. G. Stepanov-Mamaladze diary, 22 January 1988: T. G. Stepanov-Mamaladze Papers (HIA), box 5.
74. *Ibid.*, 28 April 1988.
75. T. G. Stepanov-Mamaladze working notes, 26 April 1988: *ibid.*, box 2.
76. *Ibid.*, 20 December 1988.
77. T. G. Stepanov-Mamaladze diary, 15 January 1986: *ibid.*, box 5.
78. *Ibid.*, 17 January 1986.

79. Meeting with newspaper editors, writers and ideological personnel, 7 May 1988: Anatoli Chernyaev Papers (RESCA), box 1, p. 417.
80. T. G. Stepanov-Mamaladze diary, 13 July 1986: T. G. Stepanov-Mamaladze Papers (HIA), box 5.
81. *Ibid.*, 19 September 1986.
82. *The Reagan Diaries*, p. 557 (10 December 1987).
83. V. A. Alexandrov (interview), HIGFC (HIA), box 1, folder 2, p. 23.
84. I. Korchilov, *Translating History: Thirty Years on the Front Lines of Diplomacy with a Top Russian Interpreter*, p. 44.
85. T. G. Stepanov-Mamaladze diary, 14 September 1987: T. G. Stepanov-Mamaladze Papers (HIA), box 5.
86. Korchilov, *Translating History*, pp. 121–3.
87. *Ibid.*, p. 101.
88. *Ibid.*, pp. 82–7.
89. E. Teller to G. P. Shultz, 20 May 1986: Edward Teller Papers (HIA), box 283, folder: George P. Shultz.
90. *Washington Post*, 11 July 1987.
91. Notes on meetings with American officials in 1987, pp. 2, 4 and 6: A. L. Adamishin Papers (HIA), box 1: Diaries 1987.
92. *Dvadtsat' sed'moi s'ezd Kommunisticheskoi Partii Sovetskogo Soyuza, 25 fevralya – 6 marta 1986 goda, Stenograficheskii Otchët*, vol. 1, pp. 347–9.
93. Ye. K. Ligachëv and V. M. Chebrikov to the Central Committee, 26 September 1986: RGASPI, f. 89, op. 18, d. 105, pp. 1–2.
94. N. Ryzhkov, *Glavnyi svidetel'*, p. 33.
95. T. G. Stepanov-Mamaladze diary, 22 January 1988: T. G. Stepanov-Mamaladze Papers (HIA), box 5.
96. V. L. Kataev, 'Kartina kontsa 80-x', filed as 80–90, p. 3: Vitalii Leonidovich Kataev Papers (HIA), disk 3.
97. ITAR-TASS, 5 September 2012; Interview with Sir Roderic Lyne, 6 June 2006, p. 42: BDOHP.
98. Politburo meeting minutes, 23 July 1987: RGASPI, f. 89, op. 42, d. 17, p. 1.
99. *Ibid.*, p. 2.
100. *New York Times*, 23 March 1988.

25: Sticking Points

1. Joint letter (L. N. Zaikov, E. A. Shevardnadze and V. M. Chebrikov) to the Central Committee, 13 January 1987, pp. 1–3: Vitalii Leonidovich Kataev Papers (HIA), box 14, folder 24.
2. R. Z. Sagdeev, *The Making of a Soviet Scientist: My Adventures in Nuclear Fusion and Space from Stalin to Star Wars*, pp. 299–300.
3. Discussion with George Bush at the Soviet embassy, Washington, 10 December 1987, pp. 8–9: RRPL, Stephen Danzansky Files (NSC): RAC, box 12.

4. Sagdeev, *The Making of a Soviet Scientist*, pp. 301–2.

5. Politburo meeting, 30 July 1987: *V Politbyuro TsK KPSS. Po zapisyam Anatoliya Chernyaeva, Vadima Medvedeva, Georgiya Shakhnazarova, 1985–1991*, pp. 183–4.

6. Politburo meeting, 3 March 1988: *ibid.*, pp. 257–8.

7. S. K. Sokolov to the Central Committee, 17 May 1987: Vitalii Leonidovich Kataev Papers (HIA), box 7, folder 25.

8. Excerpt from Politburo minutes, 19 May 1987: *ibid.*

9. T. G. Stepanov-Mamaladze working notes, 10 July 1987: T. G. Stepanov-Mamaladze Papers (HIA), box 2.

10. T. G. Stepanov-Mamaladze working notes, 19 August 1987: *ibid.*, box 1.

11. Central Committee decree, 12 February 1987: Vitalii Leonidovich Kataev Papers (HIA), box 10, folder 32.

12. E. Teller to F. Seitz, 14 February 1987: Edward Teller Papers (HIA), box 283, folder: Frederick Seitz.

13. Sagdeev, *The Making of a Soviet Scientist*, p. 303.

14. Politburo meeting, 8 May 1987: Anatoli Chernyaev Papers (RESCA), box 1, p. 218.

15. M. S. Gorbachëv to R. Reagan, 22 September 1987: RRPL, Executive Secretariat, NSC, Head of State Files: USSR: General Secretary Gorbachev, box 41.

16. G. P. Shultz to R. Reagan, 30 October 1987: *ibid.*

17. J. Attali, *Verbatim*, vol. 3: *Chronique des années 1988–1991*, p. 134 (conversation between F. Mitterrand and M. Gorbachëv, 25 November 1988).

18. Soviet transcript of talks at the Pentagon between S. F. Akhromeev and F. Carlucci, 9 December 1987, pp. 1–3: ECWF.

19. V. L. Kataev, diary notes on questions of military-technical collaboration and meetings in Zaikov's office, 1988–1990, 2 March 1988: Vitalii Leonidovich Kataev Papers (HIA), box 2, folder 6.

20. *Ibid.*

21. Meeting of C. L. Powell and Yu. Dubinin (Washington, memcon), 29 April 1988, p. 7: RRPL, Fritz W. Ermath Files, box 92084, 1988 US–Soviet Summit Memcons, May 26 – June 3, 1988.

22. Background briefing (n.d.) on 17 November 1986 speech by R. Gates: Vitalii Leonidovich Kataev Papers (HIA), box 7, folder 26; V. I. Stepanov, background briefing, 24 December 1986, pp. 1–5: *ibid.*, folder 27.

23. G. M. Kornienko in S. F. Akhromeev and G. M. Kornienko, *Glazami marshala i diplomata*, p. 256.

24. N. N. Detinov (interview), HIGFC (HIA), box 1, folder 14, pp. 32–4.

25. *Ibid.*, p. 34.

26. T. G. Stepanov-Mamaladze working notes, 24 February 1987: T. G. Stepanov-Mamaladze Papers (HIA), box 1.

27. N. N. Detinov (interview), HIGFC (HIA), box 1, folder 14, p. 35.

28. T. G. Stepanov-Mamaladze diary, 15 September 1987: T. G. Stepanov-Mamaladze Papers (HIA), box 5.

29. T. G. Stepanov-Mamaladze working notes, 15 September 1987: *ibid.*, box 1.

30. O. Belyakov, G. Kornienko, S. Akhromeev and A. Kovalëv: memo to Central Committee, September 1987 (sent on 3 October 1987?): Vitalii Leonidovich Kataev Papers (HIA), box 7, folder 24.
31. N. N. Detinov (interview), HIGFC (HIA), box 1, folder 14, p. 35.
32. 'O direktivakh dlya besed s gosudarstvennym sekretarëm SShA Dzh. Shul'tsem', 17 February 1988, pp. 1–2 (signed by Zaikov, Shevardnadze, Chebrikov, Yazov, Dobrynin, Belousov): Vitalii Leonidovich Kataev Papers (HIA), box 4, folder 20.
33. R. Reagan to M. S. Gorbachëv, 12 August 1988: *ibid.*, box 7, folder 20.
34. M. S. Gorbachëv to R. Reagan, 13 September 1988: RRPL, Executive Secretariat, NSC, Head of State Files: USSR: General Secretary Gorbachev, box 41.
35. G. P. Shultz to R. Reagan, 16 September 1988: *ibid.*; 'Soviet Policy Toward the West and the Gorbachev Challenge', National Intelligence Estimate, April 1989, p. 9: CIA Papers.
36. T. G. Stepanov-Mamaladze working notes, 22 September 1988: T. G. Stepanov-Mamaladze Papers (HIA), box 2.
37. N. N. Detinov (interview), HIGFC (HIA), box 1, folder 14, p. 35.
38. V. L. Kataev, untitled memoir notes filed as PAZNOGL, p. 11: Vitalii Leonidovich Kataev Papers (HIA), disk 3.
39. L. Zaikov, V. Kryuchkov, E. Shevardnadze, D. Yazov, O. Baklanov and I. Belousov, draft to Central Committee: 'O likvidatsii krasnoyarskoi RLS', n.d.: *ibid.*, box 7, folder 24.
40. O. Belyakov to the Central Committee (draft memo), November 1986: *ibid.*, box 12, folder 13.
41. Politburo meeting, 5 March 1987: Anatoli Chernyaev Papers (RESCA), box 1, p. 161.
42. O. D. Belyakov to the Central Committee (draft memo), April 1987: Vitalii Leonidovich Kataev Papers (HIA), box 12, folder 13.
43. Politburo meeting, 8 May 1987: Anatoli Chernyaev Papers (RESCA), box 1, p. 217.
44. Politburo minutes, 8 May 1987: *Otvechaya na vyzov vremeni: Vneshnyaya politika perestroiki: Dokumental'nye svidetel'stva*, p. 186.
45. Politburo meeting, 8 May 1987: Anatoli Chernyaev Papers (RESCA), box 1, pp. 217–19.
46. Report to Central Committee, 20 July 1987, pp. 1–3, signed by N. I. Ryzhkov, L. N. Zaikov, E. A. Shevardnadze, A. S. Yakovlev, A. F. Dobrynin, F. D. Bobkov: Vitalii Leonidovich Kataev Papers (HIA), box 12, folder 13.
47. *Ibid.*
48. 'Spravka' (n.d.), pp. 1–2: *ibid.*, box 11, folder 31.
49. L. N. Zaikov to Yu. D. Maslyukov, S. F. Akhromeev and others, 13 August 1987: *ibid.*, box 12, folder 13.
50. A. N. Yakovlev (interview), HIGFC (HIA), box 3, folder 5, p. 15.
51. V. L. Kataev (interview), *ibid.*, box 2, folder 4, p. 42.
52. Memo to the Central Committee, 16 February 1988, 'Ob itogakh oznakomitel'nykh poezdok sovetskikh i amerikanskikh spetsialistov na yadernye

ispytatel'nye poligony SSSR i SShA' (signed by L. N. Zaikov, V. M. Chebrikov, E. A. Shevardnadze, D. T. Yazov, Yu. D. Maslyukov and L. D. Ryabev), pp. 1–2 and 6: Vitalii Leonidovich Kataev Papers (HIA), box 6, folder 6.

53. V. A. Medvedev (interview), HIGFC (HIA), box 2, folder 10, pp. 23–4.
54. T. G. Stepanov-Mamaladze working notes, 11 November 1987: T. G. Stepanov-Mamaladze Papers (HIA), box 2.
55. T. G. Stepanov-Mamaladze diary, 24 November 1987: *ibid.*, box 5.
56. V. L. Kataev, diary notes on arms reduction and 'Five' work, 1988–1990, 11 February 1990: Vitalii Leonidovich Kataev Papers (HIA), box 2, folder 5.
57. T. G. Stepanov-Mamaladze diary, 10 May 1988: T. G. Stepanov-Mamaladze Papers (HIA), box 5.
58. V. L. Kataev, untitled memoir notes filed as PAZNOGL, p. 9: Vitalii Leonidovich Kataev Papers (HIA), disk 3.
59. *Ibid.*, pp. 1–2.
60. V. L. Kataev, untitled memoir notes filed as PAZNOGL, p. 13: Vitalii Leonidovich Kataev Papers (HIA), disk 3; G. M. Kornienko, *Kholodnaya voina: svidetel'stvo eë uchastnika*, pp. 253–4.
61. V. I. Varennikov (interview), HIGFC (HIA), box 3, folder 3, p. 10.
62. S. F. Akhromeev in Akhromeev and Kornienko, *Glazami marshala i diplomata*, p. 133.
63. V. L. Kataev (interview), HIGFC (HIA), box 2, folder 4, p. 30.
64. *Ibid.*, p. 31.
65. N. N. Detinov (interview), *ibid.*, box 1, folder 14, p. 28; V. L. Kataev (interview), *ibid.*, box 2, folder 4, p. 31.

26: Grinding Out the Treaty

1. Talking points for National Security Planning Group, 8 September 1987, p. 1: Jim Mann, box, 58.
2. National Security Planning Group, 8 September 1987, pp. 2–3: CIA Papers.
3. *Ibid.*, pp. 3–4.
4. *Ibid.*, pp. 4–7.
5. *Ibid.*, p. 8.
6. *Ibid.*
7. *Ibid.*, pp. 8–9.
8. *Ibid.*, p. 9.
9. *Ibid.*, pp. 9–10.
10. *Ibid.*, pp. 10–11.
11. *Ibid.*, pp. 11–12.
12. T. G. Stepanov-Mamaladze working notes, 13 September 1987: T. G. Stepanov-Mamaladze Papers (HIA), box 1.
13. *Ibid.* (15 September 1987?).
14. T. G. Stepanov-Mamaladze diary, 15 September 1987: *ibid.*, box 5.
15. T. G. Stepanov-Mamaladze working notes (15 September 1987?): *ibid.*, box 1.

16. T. G. Stepanov-Mamaladze diary, 17 September 1987: *ibid.*, box 5.
17. *Ibid.*, 15 September 1987.
18. *Ibid.*, 17 September 1987.
19. T. G. Stepanov-Mamaladze working notes, 16 October 1987: *ibid.*, box 1.
20. 'Puti razvitiya vooruzhënnykh sil SShA i NATO' (unidentified official paper), 24 September 1987, pp. 1–7: Vitalii Leonidovich Kataev Papers (HIA), box 16.
21. National Security Planning Group, 14 October 1987, p. 2: *The Reagan Files: The Untold Story of Reagan's Top-Secret Efforts to Win the Cold War.*
22. *Ibid.*, p. 3.
23. *Ibid.*, p. 8.
24. *Ibid.*, pp. 8–9.
25. T. G. Stepanov-Mamaladze diary, 22–23 October 1987: T. G. Stepanov-Mamaladze Papers (HIA), box 5.
26. *Ibid.*, 24 October 1987.
27. Soviet record of meeting of M. S. Gorbachëv and G. P. Shultz, 23 October 1987: *Mirovaya ekonomika i mezhdunarodnye otnosheniya*, 1993, nos. 10, pp. 69–81 and 11, pp. 73–84.
28. G. P. Shultz to R. Reagan, 1 December 1987 (memo), p. 2: RRPL, Briefing book for meeting between President Reagan and General Secretary Gorbachev, 12/1987, Stephen Danzansky Files (NSC): RAC, box 19.
29. V. O. Korotych, 'Otrazhenie' (typescript memoir, n.d.), p. 190: Vitalii Korotych Papers (HIA).
30. C. Hill, notes (19 December 1991), p. 7: Charles Hill Papers (HIA), box 67, folder: Soviet Union, Late 1987: The Cold War is Over.
31. *The Reagan Diaries Unabridged*, vol. 2, p. 810 (9 December 1987); I. Korchilov, *Translating History: Thirty Years on the Front Lines of Diplomacy with a Top Russian Interpreter*, p. 103.
32. C. Hill, notes (19 December 1991), p. 8: Charles Hill Papers (HIA), box 67, folder: Soviet Union, Late 1987: The Cold War is Over.
33. *The Reagan Diaries*, p. 557 (10 December 1987).
34. *Ibid.*
35. C. Hill, notes (19 December 1991), p. 10: Charles Hill Papers (HIA), box 67, folder: Soviet Union, Late 1987: The Cold War is Over.
36. Secretary of State to all diplomatic and consular posts, 12 December 1987, p. 11: ECWF.
37. C. Hill, notes (19 December 1991), p. 10: Charles Hill Papers (HIA), box 67, folder: Soviet Union, Late 1987: The Cold War is Over.
38. G. P. Shultz, statement before the Senate Foreign Relations Committee, 25 January 1988, pp. 1–10: United States Department of State, Washington, February 1988.
39. G. P. Shultz to R. Byrd, 4 February 1988: Charles Hill Papers (HIA), box 66, folder: The Last of the Superpower Summits.
40. G. P. Shultz to R. Byrd and S. Nunn, 8 February 1988: *ibid.*
41. C. Hill, notes (27 January 1922), p. 10: *ibid.*
42. National Security Planning Group, 9 February 1988, p. 2: *The Reagan Files.*

43. *Ibid.*, p. 3.
44. *Ibid.*, p. 4.
45. *Ibid.*, p. 5.
46. *Ibid.*, p. 7.
47. *Ibid.*, p. 9.
48. Politburo meeting, 25 February 1988: *V Politbyuro TsK KPSS. Po zapisyam Anatoliya Chernyaeva, Vadima Medvedeva, Georgiya Shakhnazarova, 1985–1991*, p. 253.
49. *Ibid.*
50. H. Kissinger, 'The Dangers Ahead', *Newsweek*, 21 December 1987.
51. *Wall Street Journal*, 8 February 1988.
52. *Washington Post*, 15 March 1988.
53. V. L. Kataev, diary notes on questions of military-technical collaboration and meetings in Zaikov's office, 1988–1990, 11 March 1988: Vitalii Leonidovich Kataev Papers (HIA), box 2, folder 6.
54. T. G. Stepanov-Mamaladze diary, 22 March 1988: T. G. Stepanov-Mamaladze Papers (HIA), box 5.
55. *Ibid.*, 22 and 23 March 1988.
56. C. Hill, notes on 'April 1988: Noriega', pp. 5–7: Charles Hill Papers (HIA), box 79, folder: April 1988: Noriega.
57. Remarks to the World Affairs Council of Western Massachusetts, 21 April 1988: www.reagan.utexas.edu/archives/speeches/1988/042188c.htm
58. C. Hill, notes (27 January 1992), pp. 14–15: Charles Hill Papers (HIA), box 66, folder: The Last of the Superpower Summits.
59. *Ibid.*, pp. 15–16.
60. C. Hill, notes on 'April 1988: Noriega', p. 9: *ibid.*, box 79, folder: April 1988: Noriega.
61. *Ibid.*, p. 16.
62. T. G. Stepanov-Mamaladze diary, 10 May 1988: T. G. Stepanov-Mamaladze Papers (HIA), box 5.
63. National Security Planning Group, 23 May 1988, pp. 1–2: *The Reagan Files*.
64. *Ibid.*, p. 8.
65. *Ibid.*, p. 9.
66. *Ibid.*, pp. 10–11.
67. Memo to the Central Committee, 24 May 1988: 'O kontseptsii sovetsko-amerikanskoi vstrechi na vysshem urovne v Moskve', pp. 11–15 (signed by L. N. Zaikov, E. A. Shevardnadze, V. M. Chebrikov, D. T. Yazov, O. D. Baklanov, A. F. Dobrynin and I. S. Belousov): Vitalii Leonidovich Kataev Papers (HIA), box 4, folder 22.
68. A. Chernyaev, *Sovmestnyi iskhod. Dnevnik dvukh epokh. 1971–1991 gody*, p. 755 (19 June 1988).
69. Korchilov, *Translating History*, pp. 145–6.
70. Meeting of G. P. Shultz and E. A. Shevardnadze, 29 May 1988 (memcon), p. 2: RRPL, Fritz W. Ermath Files, box 92084, 1988 US–Soviet Memcons, May 26 – June 3, 1988.

71. *Ibid.*, p. 6.
72. *Ibid.*, p. 9.
73. *Ibid.*, p. 10.
74. First meeting (led by C. Crocker and A. L. Adamishin), 29 May 1988 (memcon), p. 5: RRPL, Fritz W. Ermath Files, box 92084, 1988 US–Soviet Memcons, May 26 – June 3, 1988.
75. *Ibid.*, p. 2.
76. Second meeting (led by P. Solomon and V. Polyakov), 29 May 1988 (memcon), pp. 4 and 6: *ibid.*
77. C. Crocker, first meeting (led by C. Crocker and A. L. Adamishin), 30 May 1988 (memcon), p. 3: *ibid.*
78. Second meeting (led by P. Solomon and V. Polyakov), 30 May 1988 (memcon), pp. 4–14: *ibid.*
79. Third meeting (led by P. Solomon and V. Polyakov), 30 May 1988 (memcon), p. 4: *ibid.*; meeting between C. L. Powell and Yu. Dubinin (Washington, memcon), 29 April 1988, p. 8: *ibid.*
80. Yu. Alekseev and P. Solomon, third meeting (led by P. Solomon and V. Polyakov), 30 May 1988 (memcon), pp. 5–6: *ibid.*
81. *Ibid.*
82. See S. F. Akhromeev's comments at meeting of F. C. Carlucci and D. Z. Yazov (Moscow), 30 May 1988, p. 3: *ibid.*
83. *The Reagan Diaries*, p. 613 (29 May 1988).
84. *Ibid.*, p. 614 (31 May 1988).
85. First private meeting of R. Reagan and M. S. Gorbachëv, 29 May 1988 (memcon), pp. 6 and 8: RRPL, Fritz W. Ermath Files, box 92084, 1988 US–Soviet Memcons, May 26 – June 3, 1988.
86. Second private meeting of R. Reagan and M. S. Gorbachëv, 31 May 1988 (memcon), pp. 4–5: *ibid.*
87. The question was put by Sam Donaldson of ABC: see J. Mann, *The Rebellion of Ronald Reagan: A History of the End of the Cold War*, p. 304. I. Korchilov offers a slightly different wording in *Translating History*, pp. 168–9.
88. G. P. Shultz, interview with T. Brokaw, Moscow, 31 May 1988: Committee on the Present Danger (HIA), box 112, folder: Shultz 1987–1989.
89. T. G. Stepanov-Mamaladze diary, 1 June 1988: T. G. Stepanov-Mamaladze Papers (HIA), box 5; *The Reagan Diaries*, p. 614 (1 June 1988).

27: Calls to Western Europe

1. J. Attali, *Verbatim*, vol. 3: *Chronique des années 1988–1991*, p. 43 (conversation between R. Reagan and F. Mitterrand, 19 June 1988).
2. *Ibid.*, pp. 67–8 (20 July 1988).
3. Attali, *Verbatim*, vol. 2: *Chronique des années 1986–1988*, p. 103 (conversation of H. Kohl and F. Mitterrand, 27 June 1986).
4. See above, p. 193.

5. Attali, *Verbatim*, vol. 2, p. 103 (conversation of H. Kohl and F. Mitterrand, 27 June 1986).

6. E. Meese (interview), HIGFC (HIA), box 2, folder 11, p. 59.

7. Memorandum on hostile aspirations and anti-Soviet actions of the Lithuanian reactionary emigration against the Lithuanian SSR, 15 April 1985: Lithuanian SSR KGB (HIA), K-1/3/784, p. 6.

8. Conversation between V. A. Medvedev and W. Jaruzelski, 3 July 1987: *Aleksandr Yakovlev. Perestroika, 1985–1991. Neizdannoe, maloizvestnoe, zabytoe*, ed. A. A. Yakovlev, pp. 114 and 116–17.

9. *New York Times*, 12 June 1987.

10. E. Meese (interview), HIGFC (HIA), box 2, folder 11, p. 59.

11. Attali, *Verbatim*, vol. 1: *Chronique des années 1981–1986*, p. 839 (1 August 1985).

12. See the reference to this in the President's draft response to her letter to him of 7 March 1987: RRPL, Nelson Ledsky Files, RAC, box 9, United Kingdom – 1987 – Memos, Letters.

13. P. Cradock, *In Pursuit of British Interests Reflections on Foreign Policy under Margaret Thatcher and John Major*, p. 95.

14. A. Chernyaev, *Sovmestnyi iskhod. Dnevnik dvukh epokh. 1971–1991 gody*, p. 806 (5 October 1989).

15. *Ibid.*, p. 653 (3 November 1985).

16. G. Shultz: interview with R. Service and P. Robinson, Hoover Institution, 1 September 2009.

17. Politburo meeting, 21–22 May 1987: Anatoli Chernyaev Papers (RESCA), box 1, p. 231.

18. *Los Angeles Times*, 25 October 1986.

19. Politburo meeting, 4 June 1987: Anatoli Chernyaev Papers (RESCA), box 1, p. 238.

20. House of Commons Debates, 29 January 1987, vol. 109, cc. 341–2.

21. Cradock, *In Pursuit of British Interests*, p. 100.

22. T. G. Stepanov-Mamaladze diary, 1 April 1987: T. G. Stepanov-Mamaladze Papers (HIA), box 5.

23. Interview with Sir Bryan Cartledge, 14 November 2007, p. 56: BDOHP.

24. Personal recollection about a Moscow trip in October 1987.

25. Gorbachëv's meeting with E. A. Shevardnadze, A. F. Dobrynin, A. N. Yakovlev, V. A. Medvedev and A. S. Chernyaev, 1 April 1987: Anatoli Chernyaev Papers (RESCA), box 1, pp. 175–6.

26. Politburo meeting, 2 April 1987: *ibid.*, p. 183.

27. *Ibid.*, pp. 180–2.

28. Interview with Sir Bryan Cartledge, 14 November 2007, p. 57: BDOHP.

29. House of Commons Debates, 26 June 1987, vol. 118, cols. 158–68.

30. Interview with L. M. Zamyatin, *Kommersant*, 3 May 2005; M. Thatcher, press conference, 7 December: Margaret Thatcher Foundation: www.margaret-thatcher.org/document/106982.

31. A. S. Chernyaev to M. S. Gorbachëv, 10 November 1987: Anatoli Chernyaev Papers (RESCA), box 2, folder 8.
32. M. Thatcher, press conference, 7 December: Margaret Thatcher Foundation: www.margaretthatcher.org/document/106982
33. Interview with L. M. Zamyatin, *Kommersant*, 3 May 2005.
34. Cradock, *In Pursuit of British Interests*, p. 100.
35. *Ibid.*, p. 101.
36. R. Braithwaite, 'Moscow Diary', 6 April 1989.
37. They addressed each other with the equivalent of the Russian familiar 'you': T. G. Stepanov-Mamaladze working notes, 14 July 1987: T. G. Stepanov-Mamaladze Papers (HIA), box 2.
38. G. Shultz: interview with R. Service and P. Robinson, Hoover Institution, 1 September 2009.
39. Record of conversation with M. Thatcher: Braithwaite, 'Moscow Diary', 13 September 1988.
40. Politburo meeting 10 March 1988: Anatoli Chernyaev Papers (RESCA), box 1, p. 371.
41. Polish Central Committee meeting, 10 December 1988: Poland, 1986–1989: The End of the System (HIA), box 1, folder 2, item 8, pp. 26–7.
42. Braithwaite, 'Moscow Diary', 13 September 1988.
43. T. G. Stepanov-Mamaladze working notes, 18 January 1988: T. G. Stepanov-Mamaladze Papers (HIA), box 1.
44. Attali, *Verbatim*, vol. 2, p. 287 (28 March 1987).
45. T. G. Stepanov-Mamaladze diary, 19 January 1988: T. G. Stepanov-Mamaladze Papers (HIA), box 5.
46. *Ibid.*
47. H. Kohl's interview with G. Palkot (n.d.): Peter Robinson Papers (HIA), box 21.
48. *Ibid.*
49. A. S. Chernyaev (interview), HIGFC (HIA), box 1, folder 12, p. 17.
50. I. Korchilov, *Translating History: Thirty Years on the Front Lines of Diplomacy with a Top Russian Interpreter*, p. 201.
51. Attali, *Verbatim*, vol. 3, p. 132 (conversation between F. Mitterrand and M. Gorbachëv, 25 November 1988).
52. Politburo meeting, 2 December 1988: Anatoli Chernyaev Papers (RESCA), box 1, p. 509; Politburo meeting, 2 December 1988: *V Politbyuro TsK KPSS. Po zapisyam Anatoliya Chernyaeva, Vadima Medvedeva, Georgiya Shakhnazarova, 1985–1991*, pp. 365–6.
53. Chernyaev, *Sovmestnyi iskhod*, p. 788 (16 April 1989).
54. Korchilov, *Translating History*, p. 209.
55. Politburo meeting, 13 April 1989: Anatoli Chernyaev Papers (RESCA), box 1, p. 38.
56. Korchilov, *Translating History*, p. 213.
57. Chernyaev, *Sovmestnyi iskhod*, p. 788 (16 April 1989).

58. Politburo meeting, 13 April 1989: Anatoli Chernyaev Papers (RESCA), box 1, p. 37.
59. *Ibid.*, pp. 37–8.
60. Braithwaite, 'Moscow Diary', 19 May 1989.

28: Eastern Europe: Perplexity and Protest

1. General Department of the Secretariat, 'Nekotorye dannye o deyatel'nosti Politbyuro i Sekretariata TsK KPSS v 1985' (n.d.), pp. 13–14: Dmitri A. Volkogonov Papers (HIA), reel 17.
2. T. G. Stepanov-Mamaladze working notes, 19 March 1986: T. G. Stepanov-Mamaladze Papers (HIA), box 1.
3. Gorbachëv's conversation with his aides, 29 September 1986: Anatoli Chernyaev Papers (RESCA), box 1, pp. 70–1 and *V Politbyuro TsK KPSS. Po zapisyam Anatoliya Chernyaeva, Vadima Medvedeva, Georgiya Shakhnazarova, 1985–1991*, p. 71.
4. T. G. Stepanov-Mamaladze working notes, 30 June 1986: T. G. Stepanov-Mamaladze Papers (HIA), box 1.
5. Politburo meeting, 23 October 1986: *Otvechaya na vyzov vremeni: Vneshnyaya politika perestroiki: Dokumental'nye svidetel'stva*, pp. 524–5.
6. V. M. Falin (interview), HIGFC (HIA), box 1, folder 15, p. 29.
7. A. S. Grachëv's interview with V. Musatov, 20 December 1997: A. Grachev, *Gorbachev's Gamble: Soviet Foreign Policy and the End of the Cold War*, p. 119.
8. Gorbachëv's report to Politburo meeting, 13 November 1986: *V Politbyuro TsK KPSS*, pp. 92–3.
9. Politburo meeting, 13 November 1986: RGASPI, f. 89, op. 42, d. 16, p. 1.
10. J. Attali, *Verbatim*, vol. 2: *Chronique des années 1986–1988*, p. 189 (27 October 1986).
11. 'Ob itogakh Varshavskogo soveshchaniya sekretarei TsK stran SEV', Politburo meeting, 29 January 1987: Anatoli Chernyaev Papers (RESCA), box 1, pp. 140–1.
12. Gorbachëv's résumé, Politburo meeting, 29 January 1987: *V Politbyuro TsK KPSS*, p. 122.
13. Gorbachëv's conversation with his aides, 29 September 1986: Anatoli Chernyaev Papers (RESCA), box 1, pp. 70–1 and *V Politbyuro TsK KPSS*, p. 71.
14. Gorbachëv's résumé, Politburo meeting, 29 January 1987: *V Politbyuro TsK KPSS*, pp. 122–3.
15. 'Eduard Ambrosevich's Impressions from Poland' (n.d.), pp. 9–10: A. L. Adamishin Papers (HIA), box 1: Diaries 1987.
16. Politburo meeting, 23 April 1987: Anatoli Chernyaev Papers (RESCA), box 1, p. 197.
17. Politburo meeting, 1 July 1987: *ibid.*, pp. 256–7; record of conversation between M. S. Gorbachëv and E. Krenz, 1 November 1989: *Mikhail Gorbachëv*

i germanskii vopros (eds A. Galkin and A. Chernyaev), pp. 235–6; interview with L. M. Zamyatin, *Kommersant*, 3 May 2005.

18. V. M. Falin (interview), HIGFC (HIA), box 1, folder 15, p. 29.
19. V. Falin, *Konflikty v Kremle: sumerki bogov po-russki*, p. 148.
20. T. G. Stepanov (interview), HIGFC (HIA), box 3, folder 1, p. 25.
21. *Ibid.*
22. Politburo meeting, 2 April 1987: Anatoli Chernyaev Papers (RESCA), box 1, p. 188; Politburo meeting, 16 April 1987: *V Politbyuro TsK KPSS*, pp. 143–4.
23. 'Iz razmyshlenii v uzkom krugu po podgotovke 70-letiya Oktyabrya', 29 April 1987, p. 1: Anatoli Chernyaev Papers (RESCA), box 2, folder 2.
24. Politburo meeting, 4 June 1987: *V Politbyuro TsK KPSS*, p. 168.
25. T. G. Stepanov-Mamaladze, 'K besede s nemtsami iz Nut'ingena' (retrospective notes: n.d.), p. 1: T. G. Stepanov-Mamaladze Papers (HIA), box 2; T. G. Stepanov (interview), HIGFC (HIA), box 3, folder 1, pp. 25–6.
26. Attali, *Verbatim*, vol. 2, p. 279 (17 March 1987).
27. V. A. Kryuchkov (interview), HIGFC (HIA), box 2, folder 7, p. 39.
28. S. P. Tarasenko (interview), *ibid.*, box 3, folder 2, p. 56.
29. T. G. Stepanov-Mamaladze working notes, 30 May 1987: T. G. Stepanov-Mamaladze Papers (HIA), box 2.
30. National Security Committee annotations on Robinson's 29 May 1987 draft: Jim Mann Papers (HIA), box 55.
31. C. L. Powell to T. Griscom, 1 June 1987: *ibid.*
32. A. R. Dolan to R. Reagan, who had asked him to thank Robinson, 15 June 1987: *ibid.*
33. R. Reagan, speech at the Brandenburg Gate, 12 June 1987: www.reagan.utexas.edu/archives/speeches/1987/061287d.htm.
34. A. Bovin, *Izvestiya*, 18 June 1986.
35. *New York Times*, 12 June 1987.
36. *Chicago Tribune*, 27 September 1987.
37. Conversation between G. H. W. Bush and M. S. Gorbachëv (Washington), 10 December 1987: *Otvechaya na vyzov vremeni*, pp. 190–1.
38. 'K vystupleniyu na rabochei vstreche 10 noyabrya 1987 goda', pp. 7, 9, 10 and 14–15: Anatoli Chernyaev Papers (RESCA), box 2, folder 6.
39. Politburo meeting, 19 November 1987: *ibid.*, box 1, p. 306.
40. A. S. Chernyaev (interview), HIGFC (HIA), box 1, folder 12, pp. 69–70.
41. V. A. Medvedev (interview), *ibid.*, box 2, folder 10, pp. 47–8.
42. Quoting an article in *Baricada*; V. A. Medvedev (interview), HIGFC (HIA), box 2, folder 10, p. 35.
43. T. G. Stepanov-Mamaladze diary, 11 December 1987: T. G. Stepanov-Mamaladze Papers (HIA), box 5; S. P. Tarasenko (interview), HIGFC (HIA), box 3, folder 2, p. 56.
44. S. P. Tarasenko (interview), HIGFC (HIA), box 3, folder 2, pp. 56–7.
45. T. G. Stepanov-Mamaladze working notes, 11 December 1987: T. G. Stepanov-Mamaladze Papers (HIA), box 2.
46. T. G. Stepanov-Mamaladze diary, 11 December 1987: *ibid.*, box 5.

47. Conversation between M. S. Gorbachëv and M. Jakes (Moscow), 11 January 1988: *Otvechaya na vyzov vremeni*, p. 542.
48. Conversation between M. S. Gorbachëv and M. Jakes (Moscow), 18 April 1989: *ibid.*, p. 566.
49. Politburo meeting, 10 March 1988: Anatoli Chernyaev Papers (RESCA), box 1, p. 369.
50. Politburo meeting, 3 March 1988: *ibid.*, p. 365.
51. Politburo meeting, 10 March 1988: *ibid.*, pp. 368–70.
52. Joint Soviet-Yugoslav declaration, *Pravda*, 19 March 1988, p. 1.
53. A. N. Yakovlev, 'Ob itogakh soveshchaniya sekretarei TsK bratskikh partii sotsialisticheskikh stran po ideologicheskim voprosam (Ulan-Bator, 16–17 marta 1988 g.)': memorandum to the Central Committee, 21 March 1988: *Aleksandr Yakovlev. Perestroika, 1985–1991. Neizdannoe, maloizvestnoe, zabytoe* (ed. A. A. Yakovlev), pp. 187–91.
54. T. G. Stepanov-Mamaladze working notes, 29 March 1988: T. G. Stepanov-Mamaladze Papers (HIA), box 2.
55. T. G. Stepanov-Mamaladze diary, 30 March 1988: *ibid.*, box 5.
56. T. G. Stepanov-Mamaladze working notes, 26 April 1988: *ibid.*, box 2, folder 7; T. G. Stepanov-Mamaladze diary, 28 April 1988: *ibid.*, box 5; T. G. Stepanov-Mamaladze, 'K besede s nemtsami iz Nut'ingena' (retrospective notes: n.d.), p. 1: *ibid.*, box 2.
57. Directorate of Intelligence report, 22 July 1988, pp. 1 and 8: RRPL, Nelson Ledsky Files, RAC, box 8.
58. *Tajne dokumenty Biura Politicznego i Sekretariatu KS: Ostatni rok władzy 1988–1989* (ed. S. Perzkowski), pp. 32–3: Polish Politburo, 23 August 1989.
59. Politburo meeting, 21 July 1988: Anatoli Chernyaev Papers (RESCA), box 1, p. 437.
60. Polish Politburo meeting, 21 August 1988: Poland, 1986–1989: The End of the System (HIA), box 1, folder 2, item 4, p. 10.
61. Polish Central Committee secretariat meeting, 4 October 1988: *ibid.*, box 1, folder 2, item 6, pp. 40–1.
62. *Ibid.*, p. 52.
63. V. A. Medvedev, *Raspad: kak on nazreval v 'mirovoi sisteme sotsializma'*, pp. 89–91. See also M. Kramer, 'Gorbachev and the Demise of East European Communism', in S. Pons and F. Romero (eds), *Reinterpreting the End of the Cold War. Issues, Interpretations, Periodizations*, p. 188.
64. G. Shakhnazarov, *Tsena svobody: reformatsiya Gorbachëva glazami ego pomoschnika*, pp. 367–9.
65. T. G. Stepanov-Mamaladze working notes, 29 October 1988: T. G. Stepanov-Mamaladze Papers (HIA), box 2.
66. 'Zapis' besedy A. N. Yakovleva s General'nym sekretarëm TsK KPCh M. Yakeshem', 14 November 1988: *Aleksandr Yakovlev. Perestroika, 1985–1991*, p. 273.
67. T. G. Stepanov-Mamaladze diary, 29 October 1988: T. G. Stepanov-Mamaladze Papers (HIA), box 5.

68. V. L. Kataev, diary 1987–1992: 10 November 1988: Vitalii Leonidovich Kataev Papers (HIA), box 2, folder 4.
69. J. Sasser to F. C. Carlucci, 21 June 1988: RRPL, Stephen Danzansky Files (NSC): RAC, box 12.
70. 'Soviet Policy During the Next Phase of Arms Control in Europe', Special National Intelligence Estimate: November 1988, p. 12: CIA Papers.
71. 'Soviet Policy Toward Eastern Europe Under Gorbachev: National Intelligence Estimate', May 1988, pp. 16–17 and 19: *ibid.*
72. 'Soviet Policy During the Next Phase of Arms Control in Europe', Special National Intelligence Estimate: November 1988, p. 12: *ibid.*

29: The Leaving of Afghanistan

1. A. L. Adamishin, conspectus of notes on the year 1986, p. 6 (comments by E. A. Shevardnadze): A. L. Adamishin Papers (HIA), box 1: Diaries 1986.
2. Politburo meeting, 23 February 1987: Anatoli Chernyaev Papers (RESCA), box 1, p. 153; Politburo meeting, 23 February 1987: *V Politbyuro TsK KPSS. Po zapisyam Anatoliya Chernyaeva, Vadima Medvedeva, Georgiya Shakhnazarova, 1985–1991*, p. 129.
3. E. A. Shevardnadze in a comment to T. G. Stepanov-Mamaladze: T. G. Stepanov-Mamaladze diary, 17 November 1985: T. G. Stepanov-Mamaladze Papers (HIA), box 5.
4. A. J. Kuperman, 'The Stinger Missile and the U.S. Intervention in Afghanistan', *Political Science Quarterly*, no. 2 (1999), p. 235.
5. *The Pentagon's Spies* (National Security Archive Electronic Briefing Book), doc. 13: report of Commander of 500th Military Intelligence Group (INSCOM), 1987, p. 1.
6. Interview with Caspar Weinberger, 19 November 2002, p. 31: RROHP.
7. 'Afghanistan', briefing paper prepared for M. S. Gorbachëv on the history of the decisions on the Soviet military withdrawal from the war in Afghanistan, no earlier than 23 August 1990, p. 1: Anatoli Chernyaev Papers (RESCA), box 2, folder 4.
8. M.S. Gorbachëv at Politburo meeting, 26 June 1986: *V Politbyuro TsK KPSS*, p. 52.
9. Aide-memoire, 'Afghanistan', prepared for M. S. Gorbachëv on the history of the decisions on the Soviet military withdrawal from the war in Afghanistan, no earlier than 23 August 1990, pp. 1–2: Anatoli Chernyaev Papers (RESCA), box 2, folder 4.
10. *Ibid.*, p. 2.
11. Politburo meeting, 13 November 1986: RGASPI, f. 89, op. 42, d. 16, pp. 8–9; Politburo meeting, 13 November 1986: *V Politbyuro TsK KPSS*, pp. 94–5.
12. T. G. Stepanov-Mamaladze working notes, 5 January 1987: T. G. Stepanov-Mamaladze Papers (HIA), box 2.

13. *Ibid.*, 8 January 1987.
14. *Ibid.*, 13 January 1987.
15. Politburo meeting, 21 January 1987, pp. 129–30: Anatoli Chernyaev Papers (RESCA), box 1.
16. Politburo meeting, 21 January 1987, pp. 130–1: *ibid.*; Politburo meeting, 21–22 January 1987: *V Politbyuro TsK KPSS*, pp. 118–20.
17. Politburo meeting, 21 January 1987, p. 131: Anatoli Chernyaev Papers (RESCA), box 1.
18. Politburo meeting, 23–26 February 1987, p. 153: *ibid.*; Politburo meeting, 23 February 1987: *V Politbyuro TsK KPSS*, p. 129.
19. Politburo meeting, 23–26 February 1987, p. 153: Anatoli Chernyaev Papers (RESCA), box 1; Politburo meeting, 23 February 1987: *V Politbyuro TsK KPSS*, p. 129.
20. Politburo meeting, 26 February 1987, p. 156: Anatoli Chernyaev Papers (RESCA), box 1.
21. Politburo meeting, 21–22 May 1987, pp. 232–3: *ibid.*; *V Politbyuro TsK KPSS*, pp. 164–6.
22. Politburo meeting, 21–22 May 1987, pp. 234–5: Anatoli Chernyaev Papers (RESCA), box 1.
23. Politburo meeting, 11 June 1987, p. 248: *ibid.*
24. T. G. Stepanov-Mamaladze working notes, 15 July 1987: T. G. Stepanov-Mamaladze Papers (HIA), box 2.
25. I. Korchilov, *Translating History: Thirty Years on the Front Lines of Diplomacy with a Top Russian Interpreter*, p. 41.
26. Secretary of State to all diplomatic and consular posts, 12 December 1987, p. 4: ECWF.
27. T. G. Stepanov-Mamaladze working notes, 2 January 1988: T. G. Stepanov-Mamaladze Papers (HIA), box 2.
28. *Ibid.*
29. USSR Kabul Embassy meeting: T. G. Stepanov-Mamaladze working notes, 4 January 1988: T. G. Stepanov-Mamaladze Papers (HIA), box 2.
30. T. G. Stepanov-Mamaladze working notes, 11 March 1988: *ibid.*
31. T. G. Stepanov-Mamaladze diary, 23 March 1988: *ibid.*, box 5.
32. A. Chernyaev, *Sovmestnyi iskhod. Dnevnik dvukh epokh. 1971–1991 gody*, p. 749 (2 April 1988); T. G. Stepanov-Mamaladze working notes, 3 April 1988: T. G. Stepanov-Mamaladze Papers (HIA), box 2.
33. Chernyaev, *Sovmestnyi iskhod*, p. 749 (2 April 1988).
34. *Ibid.*, p. 749 (2 April 1988); T. G. Stepanov-Mamaladze working notes, 3 April 1988: T. G. Stepanov-Mamaladze Papers (HIA), box 2.
35. *Ibid.*, 4 April 1988.
36. Politburo meeting, 14 April 1988: *V Politbyuro TsK KPSS*, pp. 288–9; T. G. Stepanov (interview), HIGFC (HIA), box 3, folder 1, p. 8.
37. Politburo meeting, 14 April 1988: *V Politbyuro TsK KPSS*, pp. 288–9; T. G. Stepanov (interview), HIGFC (HIA), box 3, folder 1, p. 8.

38. Politburo meeting, 18 April 1988: *V Politbyuro TsK KPSS*, pp. 290–1.
39. T. G. Stepanov-Mamaladze diary, 4 August 1988: T. G. Stepanov-Mamaladze Papers (HIA), box 5.
40. T. G. Stepanov-Mamaladze working notes, 16 July 1990: *ibid.*, box 3; T. G. Stepanov-Mamaladze diary, 16 July 1990: *ibid.*, box 5.
41. T. G. Stepanov-Mamaladze working notes, 8 January 1987: *ibid.*, box 1, folder 14.
42. Politburo meeting, 18 April 1988: *V Politbyuro TsK KPSS*, p. 291.
43. G. P. Shultz to R. Reagan, 23 June 1988: RRPL, Executive Secretariat, NSC, Head of State Files: USSR: General Secretary Gorbachev, box 41.
44. P. Solomon: third meeting (led by P. Solomon and V. Polyakov), 30 May 1988 (memcon), pp. 5–6: RRPL, Fritz W. Ermath Files, box 92084, 1988 US–Soviet Memcons, May 26 – June 3, 1988.
45. T. G. Stepanov-Mamaladze diary, 4 August 1988: T. G. Stepanov-Mamaladze Papers (HIA), box 5.
46. Chernyaev, *Sovmestnyi iskhod*, p. 769 (28 October 1988).
47. T. G. Stepanov-Mamaladze diary, 16 January 1989: T. G. Stepanov-Mamaladze Papers (HIA), box 5.
48. *Ibid.*, 23 January 1989.
49. T. G. Stepanov-Mamaladze working notes, 23 January 1989: T. G. Stepanov-Mamaladze Papers (HIA), box 2.
50. Chernyaev, *Sovmestnyi iskhod*, pp. 782–3 (20 January 1989).
51. E. A. Shevardnadze in a comment to T. G. Stepanov-Mamaladze: T. G. Stepanov-Mamaladze diary, 11 March 1989: T. G. Stepanov-Mamaladze Papers (HIA), box 5.
52. Chernyaev, *Sovmestnyi iskhod*, p. 786 (11 March 1989).

30: Spokes in the Wheel

1. Directorate of Central Intelligence, 'Soviet Dependence on Imports from the West: Why the Numbers Belie the Rhetoric', November 1988, pp. 2, 5, 7 and 9: CIA Papers.
2. 'Soviet Policy Toward the West and the Gorbachev Challenge', National Intelligence Estimate, April 1989, pp. 11–12 and 17: *ibid.*
3. *Washington Post*, 17 April 1987.
4. C. W. Weinberger, 'It's Time to Get S.D.I. Off the Ground', *New York Times*, 21 August 1987.
5. C. Weinberger (interview), HIGFC (HIA), box 3, folder 4, pp. 18 and 54.
6. C. Weinberger to R. Reagan, 15 May 1987: RRPL, Frank C. Carlucci Files, box 92463, Secretary Weinberger (Meetings with President).
7. C. Weinberger, *Annual Report to the Congress: Fiscal Year 1988*, pp. 13, 23–4, 52–5.
8. *Ibid.*, p. 213.
9. *Ibid.*, p. 215.

10. *Wall Street Journal*, 15 May 1987.
11. *Washington Post*, 6 November 1987.
12. T. G. Stepanov-Mamaladze diary, 9 November 1987: T. G. Stepanov-Mamaladze Papers (HIA), box 5.
13. Maureen Dowd, *New York Times*, 12 December 1987.
14. C. P. Weinberger, statement before the Senate Foreign Relations Committee, 2 February 1988, pp. 1–8: Committee on the Present Danger Papers (HIA), box 68.
15. R. Perle, *New York Times*, 1 August 1988.
16. Personal interview with Charles Hill, 22 July 2011.
17. R. B. Dawson to H. H. Baker, memo on conversation with Perle, 19 November 1987: RRPL, H. H. Baker Files, box 2, folder: INF.
18. R. Perle, statement before the Senate Foreign Relations Committee, 16 February 1988, pp. 1–9: Committee on the Present Danger Papers (HIA), box 68.
19. J. J. Kirkpatrick, testimony before the Senate Armed Services Committee, 29 January 1988, pp. 1–6: *ibid*.
20. F. W. Ermath to C. L. Powell, 12 November 1987 (memo): RRPL, Fritz W. Ermath Files, box 92244, Policy Review Group – Summit Planning.
21. Notes on meeting with conference of presidents of major Jewish organizations (Washington), 12 August 1987, p. 5: *ibid*., Max Green Files, box 39.
22. J. Attali, *Verbatim*, vol. 2: *Chronique des années 1986–1988*, p. 278 (17 March 1987).
23. Interview of G. P. Shultz by D. Brinkley, ABC News, 6 December 1987: Committee on the Present Danger (HIA), box 112, folder: Shultz 1987–1989.
24. *National Review*, 22 January 1987, p. 72.
25. R. Reagan to W. F. Buckley, 5 May 1987: W. F. Buckley Jr, *The Reagan I Knew*, p. 201.
26. R. Nixon and H. Kissinger, 'A Real Peace', *National Review*, 22 May 1987, p. 32.
27. W. F. Buckley to R. Reagan, 18 October 1987: Buckley, *The Reagan I Knew*, p. 205.
28. W. F. Buckley, 'Thank God He's Gone', *National Review*, 22 January 1988.
29. G. Will, 'Reagan's Disarmament': *Newsweek*, 14 December 1987.
30. Interview with Frank Carlucci, 28 August 2001, p. 24: RROHP.
31. *New York Times*, 18 December 1986.
32. F. Carlucci (interview), HIGFC (HIA), box 1, folder 10, pp. 26–7; G. Shultz (interview), *ibid*., box 2, folder 20, p. 46; Interview with Frank Carlucci, 28 August 2001, pp. 22–3: RROHP.
33. *Washington Post*, 13 November 1987.
34. F. Carlucci (interview), HIGFC (HIA), box 1, folder 10, pp. 5–6.
35. T. G. Stepanov-Mamaladze diary, 22 March 1988: T. G. Stepanov-Mamaladze Papers (HIA), box 5.
36. Notes for the Politburo, 28 September 1987, p. 6: Anatoli Chernyaev Papers (RESCA), box 2, folder 2.

37. D. Andreas (Chairman, Archer-Daniels-Midland Company) to R. Reagan, 11 July 1988 (memo on meeting with N. I. Ryzhkov): RRPL, Stephen Danzansky Files (NSC): RAC, box 12.

38. Commission on Integrated Long-Term Strategy, *Discriminate Deterrence*, pp. 2, 3, 7 and 28.

39. P. Kennedy, 'Not So Grand Strategy', *New York Review of Books*, 12 May 1988.

40. A. Chernyaev, *Sovmestnyi iskhod. Dnevnik dvukh epokh. 1971–1991 gody*, p. 745 (28 March 1988).

41. *Ibid.*, pp. 747–8 (1 April 1988).

42. A. S. Chernyaev (interview), HIGFC (HIA), box 1, folder 12, pp. 26–7.

43. K. N. Brutents, *Nesbyvsheesya. Neravnodushnye zametki o perestroike*, p. 210.

44. Chernyaev, *Sovmestnyi iskhod*, p. 753 (24 April 1988).

45. *Ibid.*, p. 814 (29 October 1989).

46. V. L. Kataev, diary for 1988, p. 158 (no date): Vitalii Leonidovich Kataev Papers (HIA), box 1, folder 2.

47. L. N. Zaikov, speech, n.d., p. 2: *ibid.*, disk 1, LEW-28.

48. L. N. Zaikov, Theses (some time in 1987), p. 6: *ibid.*, box 13, folder 28.

49. V. L. Kataev, 'Struktura podgotovki i prinyatiya reshenii po voenno-politicheskim problemam v SSSR', p. 17: *ibid.*, box 16.

50. V. L. Kataev (interview), HIGFC (HIA), box 2, folder 4, p. 21.

51. R. Z. Sagdeev, *The Making of a Soviet Scientist: My Adventures in Nuclear Fusion and Space from Stalin to Star Wars*, pp. 257 and 260.

52. Politburo meeting, 3 March 1988, p. 5: Anatoli Chernyaev Papers (RESCA), box 2, folder 3.

53. Central Committee plenum, 23 May 1988: *V Politbyuro TsK KPSS. Po zapisyam Anatoliya Chernyaeva, Vadima Medvedeva, Georgiya Shakhnazarova, 1985–1991*, pp. 318–19 and 320.

54. T. G. Stepanov-Mamaladze diary, 23 May 1988: T. G. Stepanov-Mamaladze Papers (HIA), box 5.

55. Politburo meeting, 20 June 1988: *V Politbyuro TsK KPSS*, pp. 327–8.

56. T. G. Stepanov (interview), HIGFC (HIA), box 3, folder 1, p. 7.

57. T. G. Stepanov-Mamaladze diary, 13 September 1987: T. G. Stepanov-Mamaladze Papers (HIA), box 5.

58. *Ibid.*, 23 May 1988.

59. Central Committee plenum, 30 September 1988: *V Politbyuro TsK KPSS*, p. 351.

60. *Ibid.*, p. 351.

61. Central Committee plenum, 28 November 1988: RGASPI, f. 3, op. 5, d. 178, pp. 33 and 35.

62. Central Committee plenum, 30 September 1988: *V Politbyuro TsK KPSS*, pp. 351–2.

63. V. M. Chebrikov, 'O rezul'tatakh raboty po preduprezhdeniyu terroristicheskikh proyavlenii na territorii SSSR', 11 January 1988, pp. 1–5: Dmitri A. Volkogonov Papers (HIA), reel 18.

64. *Ibid.*, p. 772 (9 November 1988).
65. S. F. Akhromeev in S. F. Akhromeev and G. M. Kornienko, *Glazami marshala i diplomata*, p. 216.
66. A. L. Adamishin Papers (HIA), box 1: Diaries 1987, 25 July 1987.
67. *Soviet Intentions 1965–1985*, vol. 2: *Soviet Post-Cold War Testimonial Evidence*: interview of Col. Gen. A. A. Danilevich, 9 December 1994, pp. 67–8.
68. Shevardnadze in conversation with Baker: T. G. Stepanov-Mamaladze working notes, 12 September 1991: T. G. Stepanov-Mamaladze Papers (HIA), box 3.
69. *Soviet Intentions 1965–1985*, vol. 2: interview of Lt. Gen. G. V. Batenin, 6 August 1993, p. 8.
70. R. Braithwaite, 'Moscow Diary', 21 February 1990.
71. T. G. Stepanov-Mamaladze working notes, 25 March 1988: T. G. Stepanov-Mamaladze Papers (HIA), box 2.
72. A. L. Adamishin Papers (HIA), box 1: Diaries 1987, 25 July 1987; V. L. Kataev (interview), HIGFC (HIA), box 2, folder 4, pp. 52–4.
73. S. P. Tarasenko (interview), HIGFC (HIA), box 3, folder 2, p. 27.
74. This was V. L. Kataev's judgement in his untitled memoir notes filed as PAZNOGL, p. 8: Vitalii Leonidovich Kataev Papers (HIA), disk 3.
75. *Ibid.*, p. 8.
76. *Soviet Intentions 1965–1985*, vol. 2: interview of Col. Gen. A. A. Danilevich, 9 December 1994, p. 68.
77. *Ibid.*: interview of Col. Gen. A. A. Danilevich, 24 September 1992, p. 43.
78. V. L. Kataev, untitled memoir notes filed as PAZNOGL, p. 3: Vitalii Leonidovich Kataev Papers (HIA), disk 3.
79. V. N. Chernavin (interview), HIGFC (HIA), box 1, folder 11, p. 8.

31: Reagan's Window of Departure

1. Politburo meeting, 6 June 1988: Anatoli Chernyaev Papers (RESCA), box 1, p. 423.
2. M. S. Gorbachëv to the Political Consultative Committee in Warsaw (Soviet record), 15 July 1988, p. 2: PHPCS.
3. *Ibid.*, pp. 3–4.
4. *Ibid.*, p. 8.
5. *Ibid.*, p. 16.
6. V. L. Kataev, 'Struktura podgotovki i prinyatiya reshenii po voenno-politicheskim problemam v SSSR', p. 21: Vitalii Leonidovich Kataev Papers (HIA), box 16.
7. M. S. Gorbachëv to R. Reagan, 20 September 1988: RRPL, Executive Secretariat, NSC, Head of State Files: USSR: General Secretary Gorbachev, box 41.
8. T. G. Stepanov-Mamaladze diary, 23 September 1988: T. G. Stepanov-Mamaladze Papers (HIA), box 5.

9. *Ibid.*
10. G. Shultz: interview with R. Service and P. Robinson, Hoover Institution, 1 September 2009.
11. *New York Times*, 15 October 1988.
12. C. Hill, diary (17 October 1988): Charles Hill Papers (HIA), box 66, folder: Miscellany.
13. Gorbachëv's meeting with E. A. Shevardnadze, A. N. Yakovlev, A. F. Dobrynin, V. M. Falin and A. S. Chernyaev, 31 October 1988: Anatoli Chernyaev Papers (RESCA), box 1, pp. 499–500.
14. Politburo meeting, 24 November 1988: *V Politbyuro TsK KPSS. Po zapisyam Anatoliya Chernyaeva, Vadima Medvedeva, Georgiya Shakhnazarova, 1985–1991*, p. 361.
15. *Ibid.*
16. Gorbachëv's meeting with E. A. Shevardnadze, A. N. Yakovlev, A. F. Dobrynin, V. M. Falin and A. S. Chernyaev, 31 October 1988: Anatoli Chernyaev Papers (RESCA), box 1, p. 500.
17. Politburo meeting, 20 June 1988: *V Politbyuro TsK KPSS*, pp. 327–8.
18. T. G. Stepanov-Mamaladze diary, 7 December 1988 (afterthoughts written a day later, pp. 109–11): T. G. Stepanov-Mamaladze Papers (HIA), box 5; V. L. Kataev, 'Kartina kontsa 80-x', filed as 80–90, p. 3: Vitalii Leonidovich Kataev Papers (HIA), disk 3.
19. T. G. Stepanov-Mamaladze diary, 6 December 1988: T. G. Stepanov-Mamaladze Papers (HIA), box 5.
20. *Ibid.*, 7 December 1988.
21. M. S. Gorbachëv, *Sobranie sochinenii*, vol. 13, pp. 20, 22, 23–4, 31–2, 33–4 and 36.
22. T. G. Stepanov-Mamaladze diary, 7 December 1988: T. G. Stepanov-Mamaladze Papers (HIA), box 5.
23. Meeting on Governors Island, 7 December 1988 (memcon): National Security Archive Electronic Briefing Book no. 261, doc. 8, p. 2.
24. *Ibid.*, pp. 2–6.
25. Phone conversation (New York) between G. H. W. Bush and M. S. Gorbachëv, 8 December 1988: *Otvechaya na vyzov vremeni: Vneshnyaya politika perestroiki: Dokumental'nye svidetel'stva*, p. 221.
26. T. G. Stepanov-Mamaladze diary, 7 December 1988: T. G. Stepanov-Mamaladze Papers (HIA), box 5; T. G. Stepanov-Mamaladze working notes, 7 December 1988: T. G. Stepanov-Mamaladze Papers (HIA), box 2.
27. A. Adamishin and R. Schifter, *Human Rights, Perestroika, and the End of the Cold War*, pp. 175–6 (R. Schifter).
28. *Ibid.*, p. 179.
29. *Ibid.*, p. 180.
30. Politburo meeting, 27–8 December 1988: RGASPI, f. 89, op. 42, d. 24, pp. 1–2.
31. *Ibid.*, p. 3.
32. *Ibid.*, pp. 4–6 and 8–10.

33. *Ibid.*, pp. 6 and 12.
34. Politburo meeting minutes, 27–28 December 1988: *ibid.*, f. 89, op. 17, d. 42, p. 13.
35. Politburo meeting, 27–28 December 1988: *ibid.*, f. 89, op. 42, d. 24, pp. 8–9.
36. Politburo meeting minutes, 27–28 December 1988: *ibid.*, f. 89, op. 17, d. 42, pp. 13–19.
37. *Ibid.*, pp. 22–4.
38. *Ibid.*, pp. 24–5.
39. *Ibid.*, p. 25.
40. *Ibid.*, pp. 25–6.
41. Politburo meeting, 27–8 December 1988: *ibid.*, f. 89, op. 42, d. 24, pp. 16–17.
42. *Ibid.*, pp. 13–14.
43. Politburo meeting minutes, 27–28 December 1988: *ibid.*, f. 89, op. 17, d. 42, pp. 26–8.
44. *Ibid.*, pp. 32–4.
45. *Ibid.*, p. 34.

32: The Fifth Man

1. *New York Times*, 3 November 1989.
2. *Ibid.*
3. G. H. W. Bush to M. S. Gorbachëv, letter handed over by H. Kissinger in Moscow, 17 January 1989: *Otvechaya na vyzov vremeni: Vneshnyaya politika perestroiki: Dokumental'nye svidetel'stva*, p. 223.
4. Telephone conversation between G. H. W. Bush and M. S. Gorbachëv, 23 January 1989, p. 2: http://bushlibrary.tamu.edu/research/pdfs/memcons_telcons/1989-01-23--Gorbachev.pdf
5. T. G. Stepanov-Mamaladze diary, 8 January 1989: T. G. Stepanov-Mamaladze Papers (HIA), box 5.
6. *New York Times*, 25 January 1989.
7. C. Hill, notes (5 March 1992) on 'Transition', p. 1: Charles Hill Papers (HIA), box 67.
8. J. Attali, *Verbatim*, vol. 3: *Chronique des années 1988–1991*, p. 271 (F. Mitterrand, 28 June 1989).
9. First AAASS Conference on Science, Arms Control and National Security, 4–5 December 1986, p. 44: Thomas H. Johnson Papers (HIA), box 52.
10. G. H. W. Bush, 'Address on Administration Goals', 9 February 1989: http://bushlibrary.tamu.edu/research/public_papers.php?id=51&year=1989&month=2.
11. Attali, *Verbatim*, vol. 3, p. 202 (31 March 1989).
12. Central Committee plenum, 10 January 1989: RGASPI, f. 3, op. 5, d. 195, p. 20.
13. Briefing paper for Big Five (Politburo commission) meeting of 16 January 1989, pp. 1–3: Vitalii Leonidovich Kataev Papers (HIA), box 13, folder 29.

14. 'Iz besedy s G. Kissindzherom, 17 yanvarya 1989 goda', *Otvechaya na vyzov vremeni*, pp. 221–3.

15. Recollection in T. G. Stepanov-Mamaladze diary, 6 February 1989: T. G. Stepanov-Mamaladze Papers (HIA), box 5.

16. Politburo meeting, 24 January 1989, p. 6: Anatoli Chernyaev Papers (RESCA), box 1b. I have translated *balovalis'* as 'did not play up' – with its notion of childish naughtiness.

17. Politburo meeting, 24 January 1989, p. 5: *ibid.*

18. 'Zapis' besedy A. N. Yakovleva c politologom i gosudarstvennym deyatelem SShA G. Kissindzherom', 16 January 1989: *Aleksandr Yakovlev. Perestroika, 1985–1991. Neizdannoe, maloizvestnoe, zabytoe*, pp. 305–6.

19. Notes for Politburo meeting, 24 January 1989, p. 4: Anatoli Chernyaev Papers (RESCA), box 1b, folder 4.

20. V. Falin, *Bez skidok na obstoyatel'stva: politicheskie vospominaniya*, p. 437.

21. Politburo meeting, 24 January 1989: Anatoli Chernyaev Papers (RESCA), box 1, p. 6.

22. Falin, *Bez skidok na obstoyatel'stva*, p. 436.

23. Politburo meeting, 24 January 1989: *V Politbyuro TsK KPSS. Po zapisyam Anatoliya Chernyaeva, Vadima Medvedeva, Georgiya Shakhnazarova, 1985–1991*, pp. 375–6.

24. Politburo meeting, 24 January 1989: Anatoli Chernyaev Papers (RESCA), box 1b, pp. 4–5.

25. *Ibid.*, p. 4.

26. *Ibid.*, p. 5.

27. Excerpt from Politburo decree, 1 February 1989, pp. 1–3: Vitalii Leonidovich Kataev Papers (HIA), box 4, folder 31.

28. V. L. Kataev, untitled memoir notes filed as PAZNOGL, p. 10: *ibid.*, disk 3.

29. V. L. Kataev, 'Sovetskii voenno-promyshlennyi kompleks', p. 30: *ibid.*, box 16.

30. *Ibid.*, p. 33.

31. O. D. Baklanov and I. S. Belousov's commentary on V. A. Kryuchkov's analysis of the socio-economic consequences of 'conversion', 4 March 1989: *ibid.*, box 11, folder 30, pp. 1–2.

32. *Ibid.*, pp. 3–4.

33. J. Abrahamson to Deputy Secretary of Defense, 9 February 1989: Albert J. Wohlstetter Papers (HIA), box 24, folder 4.

34. See the report on progress in laser-beam uniformity in Laboratory for *Laser Energetics Review: Quarterly Report* (Laboratory for Laser Energetics, University of Rochester), July–September 1989, pp. 185–202.

35. G. H. W. Bush, memo on National Security Review no. 12, 3 March 1989, pp. 1–10: National Security Archive, End of the Cold War series, box A1, folder 1.

36. T. G. Stepanov-Mamaladze diary, 5–7 March 1989: T. G. Stepanov-Mamaladze Papers (HIA), box 5; T. G. Stepanov-Mamaladze working notes, 7 March 1989: T. G. Stepanov-Mamaladze Papers (HIA), box 2.

37. *Ibid.*, 6 March 1989.
38. T. G. Stepanov-Mamaladze diary, 5–7 March 1989: *ibid.*, box 5.
39. *Ibid.*
40. *Ibid.*; T. G. Stepanov-Mamaladze working notes, 6 March 1989: *ibid.*, box 2.
41. G. E. Brown to V. A. Medvedev, no earlier than 9 March 1989: Vitalii Leonidovich Kataev Papers, box 14, folder 26.
42. See S. White, *After Gorbachev*, pp. 52–3.
43. T. G. Stepanov-Mamaladze diary, 9–18 April 1989, p. 1: T. G. Stepanov-Mamaladze Papers (HIA), box 5.
44. *Ibid.*, p. 36.
45. T. G. Stepanov(-Mamaladze) (interview), HIGFC (HIA), box 3, folder 1, p. 33.
46. *Guardian*, 19 April 1989.
47. 'Besedy N. I. v Lyuksemburge. 18.04.1989 g.', pp. 1–3: A. L. Adamishin Papers (HIA), box 1: Diaries 1989.
48. *Ibid.*, pp. 6–7.
49. *Ibid.*, pp. 8–9.
50. *Ibid.*, p. 13.
51. *Ibid.*, pp. 11–12.
52. Response to National Security Review no. 12 – Review of US Defense Strategy, part 1, 16 March 1989, pp. 7–12: National Security Archive, End of the Cold War series, box A1, folder 1.
53. Response to National Security Review no. 12 – Review of US Defense Strategy, part 2, US Defense Objectives and Strategies for the 1990s and Beyond, 3 April 1989, pp. 3, 5 and 10: *ibid.*
54. *Ibid.*
55. *Washington Post*, 5 April 1989.
56. *New York Times*, 2 April 1989.
57. *Ibid.*, 2 May 1989, p. 1.
58. R. Braithwaite, 'Moscow Diary', 25 April 1989.
59. L. N. Zaikov's report to M. S. Gorbachëv, 15 May 1990, pp. 1–3: Vitalii Leonidovich Kataev Papers (HIA), box 10, folder 2.
60. Excerpt from Politburo minutes, 25 April 1990 and accompanying 'Informat-sionnyi material ob ob"ekte v Sverdlovske': Dmitri A. Volkogonov Papers (HIA), reel 17.
61. Politburo Commission on Arms Reduction Talks (minutes), 27 July 1989, pp. 1–4: Vitalii Leonidovich Kataev Papers (HIA), box 13, folder 29.
62. Aide-memoire on chemical and biological weapons (no earlier than 16 March 1990), pp. 1–2: *ibid.*, box 10, folder 4.
63. Conversation between M. S. Gorbachëv and J. A. Baker (Moscow), 11 May 1989: *Otvechaya na vyzov vremeni*, pp. 227–30.
64. *Ibid.*, p. 231.
65. Response to National Security Review no. 12 – Review of US Defense Strategy. Executive Summary, 13 May 1989, pp. 1–10: National Security Archive, End of the Cold War series, box A1, folder 1.

66. *Ibid.*, pp. 22–4.
67. G. H. W. Bush to M. S. Gorbachëv, 29 May 1989, pp. 1–2: Vitalii Leonidovich Kataev Papers (HIA), box 8, folder 20.
68. Associated Press, 13 June 1989.
69. Conversation M. S. Gorbachëv and F. Mitterrand, 4 July 1989: Gorbachëv Foundation Archive, fond 1, op. 1, reproduced in P. Stroilov, *Behind the Desert Storm*, p. 130; conversation between M. S. Gorbachëv and F. Mitterrand conversation, 5 July 1989: *ibid.*
70. G. H. W. Bush to M. S. Gorbachëv, 21 July 1989: G. Bush, *All the Best, George Bush: My Life in Letters and Other Writings*, pp. 433–4.
71. A. Chernyaev, *Sovmestnyi iskhod. Dnevnik dvukh epokh. 1971–1991 gody*, p. 818 (10 December 1989).
72. Central Committee plenum, 28 May 1989: Anatoli Chernyaev Papers (RESCA), box 1, pp. 71–2.
73. O. S. Belyakov to O. D. Baklanov, 6 June 1989: Vitalii Leonidovich Kataev Papers (HIA), box 13, folder 29.
74. T. G. Stepanov-Mamaladze working notes, 28 July 1989: T. G. Stepanov-Mamaladze Papers (HIA), box 2.
75. J. A. Baker III with T. M. DeFrank, *The Politics of Diplomacy: Revolution, War, and Peace, 1989–1992*, p. 139.
76. T. G. Stepanov-Mamaladze working notes, 21 September 1989: T. G. Stepanov-Mamaladze Papers (HIA), box 2.
77. T. G. Stepanov-Mamaladze diary, 21 August 1989: *ibid.*, box 5.
78. Memcon, meeting of G. H. W. Bush and E. A. Shevardnadze, 21 September 1989, p. 6: http://bushlibrary.tamu.edu/research/pdfs/memcons_telcons/1989 -09-21-Shevardnadze.pdf
79. T. G. Stepanov-Mamaladze working notes, 21 September 1989: T. G. Stepanov-Mamaladze Papers (HIA), box 2.
80. *Ibid.*, 22 September 1989.
81. Chernyaev, *Sovmestnyi iskhod*, pp. 809–10 (15 October 1989).
82. T. G. Stepanov-Mamaladze working notes, 22 September 1989: T. G. Stepanov-Mamaladze Papers (HIA), box 2.
83. Baker with DeFrank, *The Politics of Diplomacy*, pp. 145–50.
84. Thomas Friedman, 'Baker Bars Expert's Speech About Gorbachev's Chances', *New York Times*, 27 October 1989.

33: The Other Continent: Asia

1. Politburo meeting, 4 December 1986, p. 102: Anatoli Chernyaev Papers (RESCA), box 1a; see also the conversation between M. S. Gorbachëv and T. Zhivkov (Moscow), 11 May 1987: *Otvechaya na vyzov vremeni: Vneshnyaya politika perestroiki: Dokumental'nye svidetel'stva*, p. 531.
2. T. G. Stepanov-Mamaladze diary, 23 July 1987: T. G. Stepanov-Mamaladze Papers (HIA), box 5.

3. Politburo meeting, 8 May 1987: Anatoli Chernyaev Papers (RESCA), box 1, p. 220.
4. Shevardnadze's analysis in T. G. Stepanov-Mamaladze working notes, 11 May 1987: T. G. Stepanov-Mamaladze Papers (HIA), box 1.
5. *Ibid.*, 1–3 December 1988: box 2; Qian Qichen, *Ten Episodes in China's Diplomacy*, pp. 23–6.
6. Politburo meeting, 22 May 1987: *Otvechaya na vyzov vremeni*, p. 830.
7. K. Tōgō, *Japan's Foreign Policy, 1945–2009*, p. 244.
8. Meeting with newspaper editors, writers and ideological personnel, 7 May 1988: Anatoli Chernyaev Papers (RESCA), box 1, p. 411.
9. T. G. Stepanov-Mamaladze diary, 19 December 1988: T. G. Stepanov-Mamaladze Papers (HIA), box 5.
10. *Ibid.*, 20 December 1988.
11. *Ibid.*, 8 January 1989.
12. James Mann's interview with James Lilley, 10 September 1996, p. 5: Jim Mann Papers (HIA), box 60.
13. *Ibid.*, 3 February 1989.
14. Czechoslovak record of Li Peng's trip to Moscow, pp. 1–4, 22–23 December 1985: PHPCS.
15. *Ibid.*, pp. 5–6.
16. A. L. Adamishin Papers (HIA), box 1: Notes on Ministry of Foreign Affairs collegium meetings, 25 April 1987, p. 8.
17. *Ibid.*, p. 7.
18. *Ibid.*, p. 8.
19. Politburo meeting, 8 May 1987: Anatoli Chernyaev Papers (RESCA), box 1, p. 220.
20. T. G. Stepanov-Mamaladze diary, 3 February 1989: T. G. Stepanov-Mamaladze Papers (HIA), box 5.
21. *Ibid.*, 4 February 1989.
22. T. G. Stepanov-Mamaladze working notes, 4 February 1989: *ibid.*, box 2.
23. T. G. Stepanov-Mamaladze diary, 4 February 1989: *ibid.*, box 5.
24. T. G. Stepanov-Mamaladze working notes, 4 February 1989: *ibid.*, box 2.
25. *Ibid.*
26. T. G. Stepanov-Mamaladze diary, 4 February 1989: *ibid.*, box 5; T. G. Stepanov-Mamaladze working notes, 4 February 1989: *ibid.*, box 2.
27. E. Shevardnadze, *Kogda rukhnul zheleznyi zanaves: vstrechi i vospominaniya*, p. 115.
28. T. G. Stepanov-Mamaladze diary, 4 February 1989: T. G. Stepanov-Mamaladze Papers (HIA), box 5.
29. *Ibid.*, 5 February 1989.
30. *Ibid.*, 16 February 1989; E. A. Shevardnadze and M. S. Gorbachëv, Politburo meeting, 16 February 1989: Central Committee plenum report by M. S. Gorbachëv, 23 April 1985: *V Politbyuro TsK KPSS*, p. 388.
31. Conversation between M. S. Gorbachëv and H. Assad, 24 April 1987:

Gorbachëv Foundation Archive, fond 1, op. 1, reproduced in P. Stroilov, *Behind the Desert Storm*, p. 73.

32. T. G. Stepanov-Mamaladze diary, 17–27 February 1989: T. G. Stepanov-Mamaladze Papers (HIA), box 5.

33. *Ibid.*, n.d. but after 17–27 February 1989.

34. *Ibid.*

35. A. S. Chernyaev's notes on conversation between M. S. Gorbachëv and K. K. Katushev (3 March 1989), reproduced in Stroilov, *Behind the Desert Storm*, p. 64.

36. US embassy (Beijing) to Secretary of State, 18 April 1989: BEIJIN 10518: Jim Mann Papers (HIA), box 8.

37. State Department memo for B. Scowcroft, 13 May 1989, pp. 2–3: *ibid.*

38. Politburo meeting, 8 May 1987: Anatoli Chernyaev Papers (RESCA), box 1, p. 220.

39. Gorbachëv's conversation with his aides, 29 September 1986: Anatoli Chernyaev Papers (RESCA), box 1, p. 71.

40. Conversation with A. S. Chernyaev, 5 August 1988: *ibid.*, box 2, folder 2.

41. Gorbachëv frequently cast doubt on the effectiveness of Deng's path of reforms. In May 1987, when Todor Zhivkov returned from a visit to China full of admiration for the profusion of goods on sale, Gorbachëv interrupted with sceptical remarks. Two months later Gorbachëv told Rajiv Gandhi that China was running out of foreign currency and that sales of its industrial output were restricted to its elites: Karen Brutents reports these conversations, without documentary references, in *Nesbyvsheesya. Neravnodushnye zametki o perestroike*, pp. 228–9.

42. Qichen, *Ten Episodes in China's Diplomacy*, pp. 29–30.

43. T. G. Stepanov-Mamaladze working notes, 16 May 1989: T. G. Stepanov-Mamaladze Papers (HIA), box 2.

44. Discussion in Shevardnadze's entourage: *ibid.*, 19 May 1989: T. G. Stepanov-Mamaladze Papers (HIA), box 2.

45. *Ibid.*, 16 May 1989.

46. *Ibid.*

47. *Ibid.*

48. *Ibid.*

49. M. S. Gorbachëv, speech, 17 May 1989: M. S. Gorbachëv, *Sobranie sochinenii*, vol. 14, pp. 207–20.

50. T. G. Stepanov-Mamaladze diary, 17 May 1989: T. G. Stepanov-Mamaladze Papers (HIA), box 5.

51. *Ibid.*

52. T. G. Stepanov-Mamaladze working notes, 18 May 1989: *ibid.*, box 2.

53. Karen Brutents reports the conversation, without documentary reference, in *Nesbyvsheesya. Neravnodushnye zametki o perestroike*, pp. 228–9.

54. M. S. Gorbachëv to the Political Consultative Committee in Bucharest (Soviet record), 7 July 1989, p. 30: PHPCS.

55. J. A. Baker to G. H. Bush, memo, not later than 5 June 1989: US Department of State FOIA Documents.
56. *Los Angeles Times*, 6 June 1989.
57. *Ibid.*, 9 April 1989.
58. Background briefing on Sino-Soviet arms reduction talks (n.d.): Vitalii Leonidovich Kataev Papers (HIA), box 10, folder 16. For the background see B. Lo, *Axis of Convenience: Moscow, Beijing and the New Geopolitics*, pp. 28–9.
59. Karen Brutents reports the conversation, without documentary reference, in *Nesbyvshcheesya. Neravnodushnye zametki o perestroika*, pp. 228–9. See also above, note 53.

34: Epitaph for World Communism

1. V. O. Korotych, diary no. 1, 22 February 1988 (misdated as 1987): Vitalii Korotych Papers (HIA).
2. A. N. Yakovlev, 'Ob itogakh soveshchaniya sekretarei TsK bratskikh partii sotsialisticheskikh stran po ideologicheskim voprosam (Ulan-Bator, 16–17 marta 1988 g.': memorandum to the Central Committee, 21 March 1988: *Aleksandr Yakovlev. Perestroika, 1985–1991. Neizdannoe, maloizvestnoe, zabytoe*, pp. 187–91.
3. Report to Central Committee plenum, 26 June 1969: RGASPI, f. 2, op. 3, d. 161, pp. 5–6 and 8–14. See also S. Pons, *Berlinguer e la fine del comunismo*, p. 10.
4. See O. A. Westad, *The Global Cold War: Third World Interventions and the Making of Our Times*, pp. 378–95.
5. RGASPI, f. 89, op. 2, d. 2: decree of Party Secretariat, 6 May 1988.
6. V. Zagladin, Deputy Head of the International Department, to the Central Committee secretariat, 15 May 1987: *ibid.*, f. 89, op. 11, d. 41.
7. Excerpt from Secretariat meeting minutes, 18 January 1988: *ibid.*, f. 89, op. 13, d. 17.
8. Memo of K. N. Brutents, 6 January 1989: *ibid.*, f. 89, op. 13, d. 34.
9. Memo from V. M. Falin to the Central Committee, 5 December 1989; excerpt from Politburo meeting minutes, 11 December 1989: Dmitri A. Volkogonov Papers (HIA), reel 18.
10. Excerpt from Secretariat meeting, 22 February, and accompanying note from the International and Ideological Departments, pp. 1–3: *ibid.*, reel 1.
11. A. Adamishin, *Beloe solntse Angoly*, pp. 183–4.
12. A. L. Adamishin Papers (HIA), box 1: Diaries 1988, 16 April 1988; Adamishin, *Beloe solntse Angoly*, p. 104.
13. T. G. Stepanov-Mamaladze working notes, 10 May 1988: T. G. Stepanov-Mamaladze Papers (HIA), box 2.
14. A. L. Adamishin Papers (HIA), box 1: Diaries 1988, 25 August 1988.
15. Adamishin, *Beloe solntse Angoly*, pp. 59, 175–7 and 181.
16. A. S. Chernyaev to A. N. Yakovlev, 30 September 1988: A. S. Chernyaev,

Shest' let s Gorbachëvym, pp. 259-60; A. S. Chernyaev to A. N. Yakovlev, 10 October 1988: Anatoli Chernyaev Papers (RESCA), box 2, folder 3.

17. Excerpt from Politburo meeting minutes, 19 September 1989: RGASPI, f. 89, op. 10, d. 43.

18. Excerpt from Politburo minutes, 20 December 1989 plus N. I. Ryzhkov's proposal: *ibid.*, f. 89, op. 9, d. 66, pp. 1–2.

19. G. Kh. Shakhnazarov and A. S. Chernyaev to M. S. Gorbachëv, 10 October 1989: Anatoli Chernyaev Papers (RESCA), box 2, folder 4.

20. Briefing paper on 'Military-Technical Collaboration' (n.d. but no earlier than 1992), p. 4: Vitalii Leonidovich Kataev Papers (HIA), box 12, folder 30.

21. T. G. Stepanov-Mamaladze diary, 8 January 1989: T. G. Stepanov-Mamaladze Papers (HIA), box 5.

22. *Ibid.*, 27 October 1985.

23. *Ibid.*, 17 November 1985.

24. *Ibid.*, 7 October 1987.

25. T. G. Stepanov-Mamaladze working notes, 8 October 1987: *ibid.*, box 1.

26. A. L. Adamishin Papers (HIA), box 1: Diaries 1988, 30 March 1988, pp. 1–3.

27. A. Chernyaev, *Sovmestnyi iskhod. Dnevnik dvukh epokh. 1971–1991 gody*, p. 781 (15 January 1989).

28. Politburo meeting, 28 March 1989: Anatoli Chernyaev Papers (RESCA), box 1, p. 5; Politburo meeting, 28 March 1989: *V Politbyuro TsK KPSS. Po zapisyam Anatoliya Chernyaeva, Vadima Medvedeva, Georgiya Shakhnazarova, 1985–1991*, p. 397.

29. Politburo meeting, 13 April 1989: Anatoli Chernyaev Papers (RESCA), box 1, pp. 35–7.

30. Excerpt from Politburo meeting minutes, 17 February 1990 plus proposal from E. A. Shevardnadze and A. N. Yakovlev: RGASPI, f. 89, op. 9, d. 80, pp. 1–6.

31. Briefing paper on 'Military-Technical Collaboration' (n.d. but no earlier than 1992), p. 1: Vitalii Leonidovich Kataev Papers (HIA), box 12, folder 30.

32. M. Moiseev to L. N. Zaikov, 21 March 1990: RGASPI, f. 89, op. 2, d. 10, pp. 1–2.

33. Aide-memoire, 'Afghanistan', prepared for M. S. Gorbachëv on the history of the decisions on the Soviet military withdrawal from the war in Afghanistan, no earlier than 23 August 1990, p. 17: Anatoli Chernyaev Papers (RESCA), box 2, folder 4.

34. Excerpt from Politburo meeting minutes, 13 April 1990, including memo from Shevardnadze, Yakovlev and Kryuchkov: RGASPI, f. 89, op. 9, d. 177.

35. J. F. Matlock to J. A. Baker, telegram, 23 June 1989: US Department of State FOIA Documents.

36. Proposal by V. Ryvin (Deputy Chief of the International Department), 13 May 1991: RGASPI, f. 89, op. 4, d. 29, p. 1.

37. Draft letter, prepared on the International Department's advice, from M. S. Gorbachëv, May 1990: Dmitri A. Volkogonov Papers (HIA), reel 1.

35: Revolution in Eastern Europe

1. Party International Department to A. N. Yakovlev, February 1989: National Security Archive, End of the Cold War series, Box A8.
2. Politburo meeting, 12 March 1989: Anatoli Chernyaev Papers (RESCA), box 1, p. 31.
3. A. Chernyaev, *Sovmestnyi iskhod. Dnevnik dvukh epokh. 1971–1991 gody*, p. 787 (3 April 1989).
4. See M. Kramer, 'Gorbachev and the Demise of East European Communism', in S. Pons and F. Romero (eds), *Reinterpreting the End of the Cold War. Issues, Interpretations, Periodizations*, p. 188.
5. T. G. Stepanov-Mamaladze diary, 20 May 1989: T. G. Stepanov-Mamaladze Papers (HIA), box 5.
6. J. Attali, *Verbatim*, vol. 3: *Chronique des années 1988–1991*, p. 241 (conversation between F. Mitterrand and G. H. W. Bush, 20 May 1989).
7. See A. Paczkowski, *The Spring Will Be Ours: Poland and the Poles from Occupation to Freedom*, pp. 507–8.
8. The first serious reference is made on 16 August; and what is more, no mention appears in that entry to Shevardnadze's personal reaction: T. G. Stepanov-Mamaladze working notes in T. G. Stepanov-Mamaladze Papers (HIA), box 2.
9. Andrei Kozyrev's testimony: R. Braithwaite, 'Moscow Diary', 12 April 1991.
10. T. G. Stepanov-Mamaladze diary, 9 June 1989: T. G. Stepanov-Mamaladze Papers (HIA), box 5.
11. M. S. Gorbachëv to the Political Consultative Committee in Bucharest (Soviet record), 7 July 1989, p. 2: PHPCS.
12. *Ibid.*, pp. 7–8.
13. *Ibid.*, pp. 11–13.
14. *Ibid.*, p. 22.
15. Conversation between M. S. Gorbachëv and F. Mitterrand (Moscow), 25 November 1988: *Otvechaya na vyzov vremeni: Vneshnyaya politika perestroiki: Dokumental'nye svidetel'stva*, p. 400.
16. M. S. Gorbachëv to the Political Consultative Committee in Bucharest (Soviet record), 7 July 1989, p. 25: PHPCS.
17. W. Jaruzelski to the Political Consultative Committee in Bucharest (East German record, translated into English), 7 July 1989, pp. 1–5: *ibid.*
18. Memcon, meeting of G. H. W. Bush and W. Jaruzelski, 10 July 1989, pp. 1–3: http://bushlibrary.tamu.edu/research/pdfs/memcons_telcons/1989-07-10--Jaruzelski.pdf
19. Memcon, meeting of G. H. W. Bush and M. Rakowski, 10 July 1989, p. 3: *ibid.*
20. Memcon, meeting of G. H. W. Bush and M. Németh, 12 July 1989, p. 3: http://bushlibrary.tamu.edu/research/pdfs/memcons_telcons/1989-07-12--Nemeth.pdf
21. Memcon, meeting of G. H. W. Bush and I. Poszgay, 12 July 1989, p. 2: http://

bushlibrary.tamu.edu/research/pdfs/memcons_telcons/1989-07-12-- Poszgay.pdf

22. Braithwaite, 'Moscow Diary', 12 July 1989.

23. 'Zapis' besedy A. N. Yakovleva s poslom v SSSR Dzh. Metlokom', 20 July 1989: *Aleksandr Yakovlev. Perestroika, 1985–1991. Neizdannoe, maloizvestnoe, zabytoe*, pp. 340–2.

24. See Kramer, 'Gorbachev and the Demise of East European Communism', p. 189.

25. See also *ibid.*, p. 190.

26. T. G. Stepanov-Mamaladze diary, 16 August 1989: T. G. Stepanov-Mamaladze Papers (HIA), box 5.

27. *Ibid.*

28. *Gazeta Wyborcza*, 29 September – 1 October 1989, p. 6.

29. GDR Ambassador Plashke to G. Wittag, telegram, 20 August 1989: Poland, 1986–1989: The End of the System (HIA), box 1, folder 2, item 22, pp. 1–2; official GDR response to Foreign Affairs Minister Totu, 29 August 1989, box 1, folder 2, item 29, p. 1.

30. *Gazeta Wyborcza*, 29 September – 1 October 1989, p. 6.

31. See Kramer, 'Gorbachev and the Demise of East European Communism', p. 190.

32. See M. Kramer, 'The Demise of the Soviet Bloc', pp. 788–854, citing especially 'Vstrechi v Varshave', *Izvestiya*, 27 August 1988, p. 3.

33. See Paczkowski, *The Spring Will Be Ours*, pp. 508–9.

34. L. V. Shebarshin (interview), HIGFC (HIA), box 2, folder 19, p. 21.

35. *Ibid.*, pp. 22–3.

36. V. A. Medvedev (interview), *ibid.*, box 2, folder 10, p. 46.

37. Braithwaite, 'Moscow Diary', 13 September 1989.

38. Central Committee plenum, 19 September 1989: RGASPI, f. 3, op. 5, d. 318, p. 8.

39. Central Committee plenum, 19 September 1989: *ibid.*, f. 3, op. 5, d. 323, p. 182; for Bush's speech on 7 September 1989 see http://bushlibrary.tamu.edu/research/public_papers.php?id=872&year=1989&month=9.

40. Proposal to the Central Committee by E. A. Shevardnadze, A. N. Yakovlev, D. T. Yazov and V. M. Kryuchkov, 20 September 1989, pp. 8–12: Zelikow–Rice Papers (HIA), box 3.

41. Excerpt from minute on Politburo meeting, 28 September 1989 and accompanying proposal: RGASPI, f. 89, op. 9, d. 33, pp. 1–5.

42. Attali, *Verbatim*, vol. 3, p. 297 (conversation between F. Mitterrand and M. Thatcher, 1 September 1989).

43. Chernyaev, *Sovmestnyi iskhod*, p. 808 (9 October 1989).

44. National Security Archive Electronic Briefing Book no. 293, doc. 3: A. S. Chernyaev's notes on conversation between M. S. Gorbachëv and M. Thatcher, 23 September 1989, p. 4.

45. *Ibid.*

46. Chernyaev, *Sovmestnyi iskhod*, p. 808 (9 October 1989).

47. V. Falin, *Bez skidok na obstoyatel'stva: politicheskie vospominaniya*, p. 440.

48. *Ibid.*, p. 442.

49. East German Politburo, 7 October 1989: *Mikhail Gorbachëv i germanskii vopros*, pp. 209–12.

50. Chernyaev, *Sovmestnyi iskhod*, pp. 805–6 (5 October 1989).

51. Conversation between M. S, Gorbachëv and E. Honecker, 7 October 1989: *Mikhail Gorbachëv i germanskii vopros*, pp. 206–7.

52. Chernyaev, *Sovmestnyi iskhod*, pp. 805–6 (5 and 8 October 1989).

53. *Ibid.*, p. 808 (11 October 1989).

54. DPA report (18 August 1991) on Tisch's article in *Kurier am Sonntag*: John Koehler Papers (HIA), box 52, folder: End of the DDR, 1990–1997.

55. V. I. Varennikov (interview), HIGFC (HIA), box 3, folder 3, p. 23.

56. Braithwaite, 'Moscow Diary', 23 October 1989; T. G. Stepanov-Mamaladze diary, 21–29 October 1989: T. G. Stepanov-Mamaladze Papers (HIA), box 5; E. A. Shevardnadze, speech to USSR Supreme Soviet, 23 October 1989: *Pravda*, 24 October 1989.

57. V. A. Aleksandrov (interview), HIGFC (HIA), box 1, folder 2, p. 42.

58. Politburo meeting, 12 October 1989: *V Politbyuro TsK KPSS. Po zapisyam Anatoliya Chernyaeva, Vadima Medvedeva, Georgiya Shakhnazarova, 1985–1991*, p. 443.

59. Joint memorandum of the Hungarian Foreign Affairs Ministry and the Ministry of National Defence on the future of the Warsaw Treaty (translated into English), pp. 4–5, 6 March 1989: PHPCS.

60. E. A. Shevardnadze to the Warsaw Pact's Foreign Ministers' meeting in Warsaw (East German report), 26 October 1989, pp. 6, 14, 24 and 28: *ibid.*

61. Record of conversation between M. S. Gorbachëv and W. Brandt, 17 October 1989: *Mikhail Gorbachëv i germanskii vopros*, pp. 229–30.

62. Record of conversation between Alexander Yakovlev and Zbigniew Brzezinski, 31 October 1989, pp. 4–5: ECWF, MTG-1989-10-31-AY-ZB.

63. 'Memorandum of Krenz-Gorbachëv Conversation, 1 November 1989', *Cold War International History Project Bulletin*, no. 12/13 (2001), p. 19.

64. Conversation between M. S. Gorbachëv and E. Krenz, 1 November 1989: *Mikhail Gorbachëv i germanskii vopros*, pp. 238–9.

65. Excerpt from record of conversation between M. S. Gorbachëv and E. Krenz, 1 November 1989: Poland, 1986–1989: The End of the System (HIA), box 1, folder 2, item 32, pp. 26–7 from A. S. Chernyaev Archive.

66. Politburo meeting, 3 November 1989: *V Politbyuro TsK KPSS*, p. 450.

67. *Ibid.*, p. 451.

68. T. G. Stepanov-Mamaladze working notes, 19 November 1989: T. G. Stepanov-Mamaladze Papers (HIA), box 2.

69. *Deutsche Einheit: Sonderedition aus den Akten des Bundeskanzleramtes 1989/90*, pp. 492–6.

70. T. Stepanov-Mamaladze working notes, 9 November 1989: T. G. Stepanov-Mamaladze Papers (HIA), box 2.

71. Telephone conversation of G. H. W. Bush and H. Kohl, 10 November 1989, p. 1: http://bushlibrary.tamu.edu/research/pdfs/memcons_telcons/1989-11-10--Kohl.pdf

72. Conversation between M. S. Gorbachëv and H. Kohl, 11 November 1989: *Mikhail Gorbachëv i germanskii vopros*, p. 249.

73. Attali, *Verbatim*, vol. 3, p. 339 (14 November 1989).

74. T. G. Stepanov-Mamaladze working notes, 18 November 1989: T. G. Stepanov-Mamaladze Papers (HIA), box 2.

75. V. M. Falin (interview), HIGFC (HIA), box 1, folder 15, p. 33.

76. *Ibid.*, p. 34.

77. H. Teltschik, *329 Tagen: Innenansichten der Einigung*, pp. 44–6 (21 November 1989). See also A. Grachev, *Gorbachev's Gamble: Soviet Foreign Policy and the End of the Cold War*, pp. 144–5; M. E. Sarotte, *1989: The Struggle to Create Post-Cold War Europe*, pp. 71–2.

78. H. Kohl, speech to the Bundestag, 28 November 1989: German History in Documents and Images (http://ghdi.ghi-dc.org/sub_document.cfm?document_id=223&language=german).

79. Conversation of G. H. W. Bush and H. Kohl, 29 November 1989 (telcon), p. 4: http://bushlibrary.tamu.edu/research/pdfs/memcons_telcons/1989-11-29--Kohl.pdf

80. Attali, *Verbatim*, vol. 3, p. 350 (28 November 1989).

81. Braithwaite, 'Moscow Diary', 7 December 1989 (conversation with V. M. Falin); A. G. Kovalëv (interview), HIGFC (HIA), box 2, folder 6, p. 16.

36: The Malta Summit

1. *New York Times*, 15 November 1989.

2. CIA National Intelligence Estimate: 'The Soviet System in Crisis: Prospects for the Next Two Years', 18 November 1989, pp. vi–vii: ECWF, INT-1989-11-18.

3. E. Rowny to J. A. Baker, 17 November 1989, p. 1: *ibid.*, STY-1989-11-17-Rowny.

4. B. Scowcroft to G. H. Bush, 30 November 1989, pp. 3–4: *ibid.*

5. J. F. Matlock to Secretary of State, 14 November 1989, pp. 1–3: *ibid.*, STY-1989-11-14.

6. Telephone conversation between G. H. W. Bush and H. Kohl, 29 November 1989, p. 5: http://bushlibrary.tamu.edu/research/pdfs/memcons_telcons/1989-11-29--Kohl.pdf.

7. G. H. W. Bush to M. S. Gorbachëv, 22 November 1989: G. Bush, *All the Best, George Bush: My Life in Letters and Other Writings*, p. 444.

8. J. A. Baker to G. H. W. Bush, 29 November 1989, pp. 1–4: ECWF, STY-1989-11-29.

9. A. Chernyaev, *Sovmestnyi iskhod. Dnevnik dvukh epokh. 1971–1991 gody*, p. 802 (16 September 1989).

10. *Ibid.*, pp. 812–13 (23 October 1989).

11. 'Primernyi perechen' voprosov k vstreche c Dzh. Bushem, 2–3 dekabrya 1989 goda', pp. 1–7: Vitalii Leonidovich Kataev Papers (HIA), box 4, folder 27.

12. Politburo meeting, 22 September 1988: Anatoli Chernyaev Papers (RESCA), box 2, folder 3.

13. T. G. Stepanov-Mamaladze working notes, 29 November 1989: T. G. Stepanov-Mamaladze Papers (HIA), box 3.

14. Conversation between M. S. Gorbachëv and A. Casaroli (Moscow), 13 June 1988: *Otvechaya na vyzov vremeni: Vneshnyaya politika perestroiki: Dokumental'nye svidetel'stva*, pp. 494–6.

15. Conversation between John Paul II and M. S. Gorbachëv (Vatican), 1 December 1989: *ibid.*, pp. 501–2; T. G. Stepanov-Mamaladze diary, 1 December 1989: T. G. Stepanov-Mamaladze Papers (HIA), box 5; Gorbachëv's report to the leaders of Warsaw Pact countries: T. G. Stepanov-Mamaladze working notes, 1 and 4 December 1989: *ibid.*, box 2.

16. Chernyaev, *Sovmestnyi iskhod*, p. 819 (10 December 1989).

17. One-on-one conversation between G. H. Bush and M. S. Gorbachëv (Malta), 2 December 1989: *Otvechaya na vyzov vremeni*, pp. 234–6.

18. Chernyaev, *Sovmestnyi iskhod*, p. 822 (10 December 1989); Malta talks between G. H. Bush and M. S. Gorbachëv (Malta), 2 December 1989: *Otvechaya na vyzov vremeni*, pp. 237–9.

19. Chernyaev, *Sovmestnyi iskhod*, p. 822 (10 December 1989).

20. *Ibid.*, p. 824 (10 December 1989); Malta talks between G. H. Bush and M. S. Gorbachëv (Malta), 2 December 1989: *Otvechaya na vyzov vremeni*, p. 240.

21. Chernyaev, *Sovmestnyi iskhod*, pp. 823–4 (10 December 1989); Malta summit talks between G. H. Bush and M. S. Gorbachëv (Malta), 2 December 1989: *Otvechaya na vyzov vremeni*, pp. 236–7.

22. Lunchtime summit talks between G. H. Bush, J. A. Baker and M. S. Gorbachëv (Malta), 2 December 1989: *ibid.*, p. 243; Chernyaev, *Sovmestnyi iskhod*, pp. 824–5 (10 December 1989).

23. Chernyaev, *Sovmestnyi iskhod*, p. 825 (10 December 1989).

24. Malta summit talks between G. H. Bush and M. S. Gorbachëv, 3 December 1989: *Otvechaya na vyzov vremeni*, pp. 243–4.

25. *Ibid.*, p. 246.

26. Chernyaev, *Sovmestnyi iskhod*, pp. 826–7 (10 December 1989).

27. *Ibid.*, pp. 827–8.

28. Malta summit talks between G. H. Bush and M. S. Gorbachëv, 3 December 1989: *Otvechaya na vyzov vremeni*, p. 247.

29. *Ibid.*

30. One-on-one conversation between G. H. Bush and M. S. Gorbachëv (Malta), 3 December 1989: *ibid.*, pp. 248–9.

31. T. G. Stepanov-Mamaladze diary, 3 December 1989: T. G. Stepanov-Mamaladze Papers (HIA), box 5.

32. Secretary of State to Tokyo and Beijing embassies, 8 December 1989: STATE 391698: Jim Mann Papers (HIA), box 8.

33. Meeting of G. H. W. Bush and H. Kohl, 3 December 1989 (memcon), pp. 1–4: George Bush Presidential Library, http://bushlibrary.tamu.edu/research/pdfs/memcons_telcons/1989-12-03--Kohl.pdf.
34. B. Scowcroft to G. H. W. Bush (memo), 5 December 1989: STY-1989-12-05.
35. T. G. Stepanov-Mamaladze diary, 4 December 1989: T. G. Stepanov-Mamaladze Papers (HIA), box 5.
36. T. G. Stepanov-Mamaladze working notes, 4 December 1989: *ibid.*, box 2.
37. T. G. Stepanov-Mamaladze diary, 4 December 1989: *ibid.*, box 5.
38. T. G. Stepanov-Mamaladze working notes, 4 December 1989: *ibid.*, box 2.
39. T. G. Stepanov-Mamaladze diary, 4 December 1989: *ibid.*, box 5.
40. T. G. Stepanov-Mamaladze working notes, 4 December 1989: *ibid.*, box 2.
41. T. G. Stepanov-Mamaladze diary, 4 December 1989: *ibid.*, box 5.
42. *Ibid.*; T. G. Stepanov-Mamaladze working notes, 4 December 1989: *ibid.*, box 2.
43. T. G. Stepanov-Mamaladze diary, 4 December 1989: *ibid.*, box 5.
44. 'Initsiativy prezidenta Busha, vydvinutye v khode vstrechi na Mal'te' (unsigned, n.d.), p. 1: Vitalii Leonidovich Kataev Papers (HIA), box 4, folder 3.
45. 'Plenum TsK KPSS – 9 dekabrya 1989 goda. Stenograficheskii otchët', *Izvestiya TsK KPSS*, no. 4 (1990), pp. 58 and 61.
46. *Ibid.*, pp. 61–2.
47. *Ibid.*, pp. 27–9.
48. *Ibid.*, pp. 76–9.

37: Redrawing the Map of Europe

1. 'Zapis' besedy M. S. Gorbachëva s ministrom inostrannykh del FRG G.-D. Gensherom', 5 December 1989, pp. 33–6: Zelikow–Rice Papers (HIA), box 3.
2. Conversation between M. S. Gorbachëv and H.-D. Genscher, 5 December 1989: *Mikhail Gorbachëv i germanskii vopros*, pp. 276–7.
3. 'Zapis' besedy M. S. Gorbachëva s prezidentom Frantsii F. Mitteranom', 5 December 1989, pp. 38–9: Zelikow–Rice Papers (HIA), box 3.
4. 'Beseda [V. Zagladina] s Zhakom Attali v Kiev', 6 December 1989, p. 37: *ibid.*
5. J. Attali, *Verbatim*, vol. 3: *Chronique des années 1988–1991*, p. 371 (conversation between F. Mitterrand and M. Thatcher, 8 December 1989).
6. *Ibid.*, pp. 369–70.
7. *Ibid.*, p. 371.
8. T. G. Stepanov-Mamaladze diary, 21 December 1989: T. G. Stepanov-Mamaladze Papers (HIA), box 5.
9. *Ibid.*, 17 December 1989.
10. R. Braithwaite, 'Moscow Diary', 4 November 1989.
11. T. G. Stepanov-Mamaladze diary, 17 December 1989: T. G. Stepanov-Mamaladze Papers (HIA), box 5.
12. V. A. Medvedev (interview), HIGFC (HIA), box 2, folder 10, p. 35.

13. Meeting of M. S. Gorbachëv, N. I. Ryzhkov, N. Ceauşescu and C. Dadalescu, 4 December 1989: Ş. Săndulescu, *Decembrie '89: Lovitura de stat a confiscate revoluţie română*, pp. 289–93.

14. T. G. Stepanov-Mamaladze diary, 17 December 1989: T. G. Stepanov-Mamaladze Papers (HIA), box 5.

15. Politburo meeting, 23 December 1989: RGASPI, f. 89, op. 9, d. 67.

16. T. G. Stepanov-Mamaladze diary, 3 January 1990: T. G. Stepanov-Mamaladze Papers (HIA), box 5.

17. *Ibid.*, 6 January 1990.

18. *Ibid.*

19. See M. E. Sarotte, *1989: The Struggle to Create Post-Cold War Europe*, p. 99.

20. G. K. Shakhnazarov, *S vozdyami i bez nikh*, p. 173.

21. Politburo meeting, 26 January 1990: *V Politbyuro TsK KPSS. Po zapisyam Anatoliya Chernyaeva, Vadima Medvedeva, Georgiya Shakhnazarova, 1985–1991*, p. 474.

22. Shakhnazarov, *S vozdyami i bez nikh*, p. 173.

23. V. L. Kataev, diary notes on arms reduction and 'Five' work, 1988–1990, 29 January 1990: Vitalii Leonidovich Kataev Papers (HIA), box 2, folder 5.

24. T. G. Stepanov-Mamaladze diary, 1 February 1990: T. G. Stepanov-Mamaladze Papers (HIA), box 5.

25. T. G. Stepanov-Mamaladze diary, 11 February 1990: *ibid.*, box 5.

26. Politburo minute, 9 March 1990: RGASPI, f. 89, op. 8, d. 78, p. 1.

27. See also M. Kramer, 'Gorbachev and the Demise of East European Communism', in S. Pons and F. Romero (eds), *Reinterpreting the End of the Cold War. Issues, Interpretations, Periodizations*, p. 193.

28. Central Committee plenum, 5 February 1990: RGASPI, f. 3, op. 5, d. 420, p. 11.

29. *Ibid.*, f. 3, op. 5, d. 421, pp. 20–1.

30. *Ibid.*, p. 113.

31. *Ibid.*, f. 3, op. 5, d. 422, pp. 27–8.

32. Politburo meeting, 29 January 1990: *V Politbyuro TsK KPSS*, p. 481.

33. J. A. Baker to E. A. Shevardnadze, 3 February 1990: Vitalii Leonidovich Kataev Papers (HIA), box 4, folder 35.

34. Meeting of J. A. Baker and E. A. Shevardnadze, 9 February 1990 (memcon), p. 3: National Security Archive, Soviet Flashpoints, box 38.

35. 'O peregovorakh c Dzh. Beikerom, 7–8 fevralya 1990, pp. 1–5: Vitalii Leonidovich Kataev Papers (HIA), box 4, folder 36.

36. J. A. Baker to all diplomatic posts, 13 February 1990, pp. 3–4: US Department of State FOIA Documents.

37. First telephone conversation of G. H. W. Bush and H. Kohl, 13 February 1990, pp. 1–2: http://bushlibrary.tamu.edu/research/pdfs/memcons_tel-cons/1990-02-13--Kohl%20%5B1%5D.pdf. See also P. Zelikow and C. Rice, *Germany Unified and Europe Transformed: A Study in Statecraft*, p. 184.

38. Official Soviet note on Baker's position in the Moscow talks: Vitalii Leonidovich Kataev Papers (HIA), box 4, folder 36; memcon: J. A. Baker, M. S.

Gorbachëv and E. A. Shevardnadze, 9 February 1990, pp. 6 and 9–11: National Security Archive, Soviet Flashpoints, box 38.

39. Excerpt from Soviet record of conversation between M. S. Gorbachëv and J. A. Baker, 9 February 1990: *Otvechaya na vyzov vremeni: Vneshnyaya politika perestroiki: Dokumental'nye svidetel'stva*, p. 379.

40. Official Soviet note on Baker's position in the Moscow talks: Vitalii Leonidovich Kataev Papers (HIA), box 4, folder 36; meeting of J. A. Baker, M. S. Gorbachëv and E. A. Shevardnadze, 9 February 1990 (memcon), pp. 6 and 9–11: National Security Archive, Soviet Flashpoints, box 38.

41. J. Baker, 'Remarks before the International Affairs Committee of the USSR Supreme Soviet, 10 February 1990', pp. 1–3: Committee on the Present Danger, box 115.

42. J. Baker, 'The New Russian Revolution: Toward Democracy in the Soviet Union' (Washington, DC: US Department of State, March 1990), pp. 1–2 and 7; meeting of J. A. Baker, M. S. Gorbachëv and E. A. Shevardnadze, 9 February 1990 (memcon), pp. 4 and 11: National Security Archive, Soviet Flashpoints, box 38.

43. Baker, 'The New Russian Revolution', pp. 4–9.

44. Record of conversation between M. S. Gorbachëv and H. Kohl, 10 February 1990: *Mikhail Gorbachëv i germanskii vopros*, pp. 341–53.

45. T. G. Stepanov-Mamaladze diary, 14 February 1990: T. G. Stepanov-Mamaladze Papers (HIA), box 5.

46. *Ibid.*, 13 February 1990.

47. *Ibid.*

48. *Ibid.*, 14 February 1990.

49. *Ibid.*, 24 February 1990.

50. V. A. Kryuchkov to M. S. Gorbachëv and the Supreme Soviet, 14 February 1990: RGASPI, f. 89, op. 51, d. 16, p. 2.

51. *Ibid.*

52. *Ibid.*, pp. 4–6.

53. Excerpt from phone conversation between G. H. Bush and M. S. Gorbachëv, 28 February 1990: Vitalii Leonidovich Kataev Papers (HIA), disk 2, TEL-GERM.

54. Telephone conversation of G. H. W. Bush and M. S. Gorbachëv, 28 February 1990, p. 3: http://bushlibrary.tamu.edu/research/pdfs/memcons_telcons/1990-02-28--Gorbachev.pdf

55. J. A. Baker to G. H. Bush, cabled memo, 20 March 1990, section 2, pp. 1–2: US Department of State FOIA Documents.

56. *Ibid.*, section 3, p. 1.

57. *Ibid.*, p. 4.

58. T. G. Stepanov-Mamaladze diary, 22 March 1990: T. G. Stepanov-Mamaladze Papers (HIA), box 5.

59. See M. Dennis, *The Rise and Fall of the German Democratic Republic, 1945–1990*, pp. 279–83 and 296–97.

60. N. S. Leonov, *Likholet'e*, p. 328.

61. Politburo Commission on Arms Reduction Talks (minutes), 30–31 March

1990, p. 2: Vitalii Leonidovich Kataev Papers (HIA), box 13, folder 29; V. L. Kataev (interview), HIGFC (HIA), box 2, folder 4, p. 58; V. L. Kataev, untitled memoir notes filed as PAZNOGL, p. 10: Vitalii Leonidovich Kataev Papers (HIA), disk 3.

62. Aide-memoir, based on report from Yu. K. Nazarkin: T. G. Stepanov-Mamaladze working notes, 6 April 1990: T. G. Stepanov-Mamaladze Papers (HIA), box 3; V. L. Kataev, 'Problemy voennoi politiki', p. 9: Vitalii Leonidovich Kataev Papers (HIA), box 16; V. L. Kataev, untitled memoir notes filed as PAZNOGL, pp. 9–10: *ibid.*, disk 3.

63. T. G. Stepanov-Mamaladze diary, 6 April 1990: T. G. Stepanov-Mamaladze Papers (HIA), box 5. Stepanov-Mamaladze's information came from Yu. K. Nazarkin, who attended the Big Five.

64. 'Direktivy dlya peregovorov ministra inostrannykh del SSSR s Prezidentom SShA Dzh. Bushem i gosudarstvennym sekretarëm Dzh. Beikerom, 4–6 aprelya 1990 goda', pp. 44–6: RGASPI, f. 89, op. 9, d. 100.

65. Letter of M. S. Gorbachëv to G. W. Bush, to be delivered by E. A. Shevardnadze on 4–6 April 1990, pp. 1–6: RGASPI, f. 89, op. 9, d. 101.

66. T. G. Stepanov-Mamaladze diary, 3 April 1990: T. G. Stepanov-Mamaladze Papers (HIA), box 5.

67. T. G. Stepanov-Mamaladze working notes, 5 April 1990: *ibid.*, box 3.

68. Attali, *Verbatim*, vol. 3, p. 460 (6 April 1990).

69. S. F. Akhromeev in S. F. Akhromeev and G. M. Kornienko, *Glazami marshala i diplomata*, p. 232.

70. *Ibid.*

71. T. G. Stepanov-Mamaladze working notes, 6 April 1990: T. G. Stepanov-Mamaladze Papers (HIA), box 3. Stepanov-Mamaladze's information came from Yu. K. Nazarkin, who attended the Big Five.

72. *Ibid.*, 13 April 1990 (?): T. G. Stepanov-Mamaladze Papers (HIA), box 3.

73. *Ibid.*, 12 April 1990.

74. Attali, *Verbatim*, vol. 3, p. 468 (19 April 1990).

75. V. Falin, *Konflikty v Kremle: sumerki bogov po-russki*, pp. 163–4 and 168; the memorandum is reproduced *ibid.*, pp. 368–85.

76. Shevardnadze in conversation with US Senate delegation led by John Glenn: T. G. Stepanov-Mamaladze working notes, 12 April 1990: T. G. Stepanov-Mamaladze Papers (HIA), box 3.

77. *Ibid.*, 4 May 1990.

78. Notes on conversation between J. A. Baker and V. P. Karpov, 20 April 1990: Vitalii Leonidovich Kataev Papers (HIA), box 4, folder 37.

79. T. G. Stepanov-Mamaladze working notes, 5 May 1990 : T. G. Stepanov-Mamaladze Papers (HIA), box 3.

80. Excerpt from Politburo minutes, 25 April 1990 and accompanying 'Informatsionnyi material ob ob"ekte v Sverdlovske': Dmitri A. Volkogonov Papers (HIA), reel 17.

81. Braithwaite, 'Moscow Diary', 14 May 1990; Soviet minute on A. A. Bessmert-

nykh's meeting with J. F. Matlock and R. Braithwaite, 14 May 1990, pp. 1–3: Vitalii Leonidovich Kataev Papers (HIA), box 10, folder 1.

82. *Ibid.*, p. 4.
83. L. N. Zaikov's report to M. S. Gorbachëv, 15 May 1990, pp. 1–3: *ibid.*, box 10, folder 2.
84. M. Moiseev to L. N. Zaikov, 13 June 1990, pp. 1–3: *ibid.*, box 10, folder 4.
85. L. N. Zaikov, V. Kryuchkov, E. A. Shevardnadze, D. Yazov, O. Baklanov and I. Belousov to M. S. Gorbachëv, June 1990: *ibid.*
86. *Washington Post*, 30 April 1990.
87. *Ibid.*, 29 June 1990.
88. T. G. Stepanov-Mamaladze diary, 30 April 1990: T. G. Stepanov-Mamaladze Papers (HIA), box 5.
89. *Ibid.*, 1 May 1990.
90. Memcon of J. A. Baker's intervention at NATO Council meeting, 3 May 1990, pp. 2–5: US NATO Mission to Secretary of State, 10 May 1990, US Department of State FOIA Documents.

38: The New Germany

1. J. Attali, *Verbatim*, vol. 3: *Chronique des années 1988–1991*, pp. 506–7 (1 June 1990).
2. J. A. Baker to H.-D. Genscher via US Embassy (Bonn), 4 May 1990 (sent from Bonn a day later): US Department of State FOIA Documents.
3. Excerpt from Soviet minute on M. S. Gorbachëv's meeting with J. A. Baker, 11 May 1990: Vitalii Leonidovich Kataev Papers (HIA), box 4, folder 38.
4. H. Teltschik, *329 Tagen: Innenansichten der Einigung*, pp. 230–2 (14 May 1990).
5. *Ibid.*, pp. 234 and 235 (14 and 15 May 1990).
6. One-on-one meeting between G. H. W. Bush and H. Kohl, 17 May 1990, p. 3: http://bushlibrary.tamu.edu/research/pdfs/memcons_telcons/1990-05-17--Kohl%20%5B1%5D.pdf
7. Teltschik, *329 Tagen*, p. 243 (21 and 22 May 1990).
8. *Ibid.*, p. 269 (12 June 1990).
9. T. G. Stepanov-Mamaladze working notes, 23 May 1990 : T. G. Stepanov-Mamaladze Papers (HIA), box 3.
10. Second meeting of G. H. W. Bush and H. Kohl, 17 May 1990, memcon, p. 5: http://bushlibrary.tamu.edu/research/pdfs/memcons_telcons/1990-05-17--Kohl%20%5B2%5D.pdf
11. I. Korchilov, *Translating History: Thirty Years on the Front Lines of Diplomacy with a Top Russian Interpreter*, p. 278.
12. G. Bush, diary entry, 31 May 1990: G. Bush, *All the Best, George Bush: My Life in Letters and Other Writings*, p. 471.
13. *Ibid.*, 1 June 1990, p. 472.
14. V. Falin, *Konflikty v Kremle: sumerki bogov po-russki*, p. 172. In an interview,

Falin remembered the comment differently: 'Eduard is not right.': V. M. Falin (interview), HIGFC (HIA), box 1, folder 15, p. 40.

15. V. M. Falin (interview), HIGFC (HIA), box 1, folder 15, p. 41.

16. G. Bush in G. Bush and B. Scowcroft, *A World Transformed*, pp. 282–3.

17. *Ibid.*, p. 283.

18. M. S. Gorbachëv to the Political Consultative Committee in Moscow (East German record, translated into English), 7 June 1990, p. 3: PHPCS; T. G. Stepanov-Mamaladze diary, 9 June 1990: T. G. Stepanov-Mamaladze Papers (HIA), box 5. Stepanov-Mamaladze recorded the events of 7 June 1990 two days later.

19. M. S. Gorbachëv to the Political Consultative Committee in Moscow (East German record, translated into English), 7 June 1990, p. 3: PHPCS.

20. *Ibid.*, p. 6.

21. Telephone conversation of G. H. W. Bush and H. Kohl, 1 June 1990, p. 1: http://bushlibrary.tamu.edu/research/pdfs/memcons_telcons/1990-06-01--Kohl.pdf

22. M. S. Gorbachëv to the Political Consultative Committee in Moscow (East German record, translated into English), 7 June 1990, pp. 8–10: PHPCS.

23. Warsaw Pact States' Declaration at Political Consultative Committee in Moscow: *Pravda*, 8 June 1990.

24. See M. E. Sarotte, *1989: The Struggle to Create Post-Cold War Europe*, p. 171.

25. Interview in *Rabochaya tribuna*, 12 June 1990; V. L. Kataev, untitled memoir notes filed as PAZNOGL, p. 10: Vitalii Leonidovich Kataev Papers (HIA), disk 3.

26. R. Braithwaite, 'Moscow Diary', 19 July 1990.

27. US State Department's Briefing Book on the NATO Summit in London, 5–6 July 1990, pp. 3–4: PHPCS.

28. Meeting of G. H. W. Bush and H. Kohl, 8 June 1990 (Washington, memcon), p. 3: http://bushlibrary.tamu.edu/research/pdfs/memcons_telcons/1990-06-08--Kohl.pdf

29. Meeting of G. H. W. Bush and H. Kohl, 9 July 1990 (Houston, memcon), pp. 1–2: http://bushlibrary.tamu.edu/research/pdfs/memcons_telcons/1990-07-09--Kohl.pdf; Teltschik, *329 Tagen*, p. 305 (9 July 1990).

30. Attali, *Verbatim*, vol. 3, p. 533 (sherpas' discussion, 9 July 1990).

31. Opening session of the Economic Summit of Industrialized Nations (Houston, memcon), 9 July 1990, pp. 2 and 6–7; first plenary session of the Economic Summit of Industrialised Nations (Houston), 10 July 1990, memcon, pp. 4–6; Teltschik, *329 Tagen*, pp. 306–10 (10–11 July 1990); Attali, *Verbatim*, vol. 3, pp. 533–4 (10 July 1990).

32. T. G. Stepanov-Mamaladze working notes, 16 July 1990: T. G. Stepanov-Mamaladze Papers (HIA), box 3.

33. Braithwaite, 'Moscow Diary', 16 July 1990.

34. Teltschik, *329 Tagen*, p. 310 (11 July 1990); Attali, *Verbatim*, vol. 3, pp. 533–4 (10 July 1990).

35. Teltschik, *329 Tagen*, p. 316 (13 July 1990).

36. V. M. Falin to M. S. Gorbachëv, 9 July 1990 (appendix 19): Falin, *Konflikty v Kremle*, pp. 386–92.
37. *Ibid.*, pp. 185–7.
38. Teltschik, *329 Tagen*, p. 325 (15 July 1990).
39. H. Kohl, *Erinnerungen*, vol. 3: *1990–1994*, pp. 169–70.
40. *Ibid.*, p. 332; T. G. Stepanov-Mamaladze diary, 16 July 1990: T. G. Stepanov-Mamaladze Papers (HIA), box 5; record of conversation between M. S. Gorbachëv and H. Kohl, 16 July 1990: *Mikhail Gorbachëv i germanskii vopros*, p. 507; A. Chernyaev, *Sovmestnyi iskhod. Dnevnik dvukh epokh. 1971–1991 gody*, p. 865 (15 July 1990).
41. Record of conversation between M. S. Gorbachëv and H. Kohl, 16 July 1990: *Mikhail Gorbachëv i germanskii vopros*, p. 509, 511–13, 517 and 519.
42. T. G. Stepanov-Mamaladze diary, 17 July 1990: T. G. Stepanov-Mamaladze Papers (HIA), box 5.
43. T. G. Stepanov-Mamaladze working notes, 16 July 1990: T. G. Stepanov-Mamaladze Papers (HIA), box 3.
44. H.-D. Genscher, *Erinnerungen*, p. 837.
45. Falin, *Konflikty v Kremle*, pp. 156–7, 180 and 187.
46. Ye. K. Ligachëv (interview), HIGFC (HIA), box 2, folder 9, p. 32.
47. T. G. Stepanov-Mamaladze diary, 16 July 1990: T. G. Stepanov-Mamaladze Papers (HIA), box 5; T. G. Stepanov-Mamaladze working notes, 16 July 1990: *ibid.*, box 3.
48. G. Bush in Bush and Scowcroft, *A World Transformed*, pp. 296–7.
49. Telephone conversation of G. H. W. Bush and H. Kohl, 17 July 1990, p. 2: http://bushlibrary.tamu.edu/research/pdfs/memcons_telcons/1990-07-17--Kohl.pdf
50. Phone conversation between M. S. Gorbachëv and G. H. W. Bush, 17 July 1990: *Otvechaya na vyzov vremeni: Vneshnyaya politika perestroiki: Dokumental'nye svidetel'stva*, p. 266.
51. Phone conversation between M. S. Gorbachëv and G. H. W. Bush, 17 July 1990: M. S. Gorbachëv, *Sobranie sochinenii*, vol. 21, pp. 277–8.
52. A. L. Adamishin Papers (HIA), box 1: Diaries 1990, March 1990.
53. A. L. Adamishin (interview), HIGFC (HIA), box 1, folder 1, p. 23.
54. A. N. Yakovlev (interview), *ibid.*, box 3, folder 5, p. 17.
55. E. I. Primakov (interview), *ibid.*, box 2, folder 14, p. 6.
56. See above, p. 432; and excerpt from Soviet record of conversation between M. S. Gorbachëv and J. A. Baker, 9 February 1990: *Otvechaya na vyzov vremeni*, p. 379. A. E. Stent gives an excellent account of the Gorbachëv–Baker conversation, albeit one that is more definite about the implications of the contents than I have adopted, in *Russia and Germany Reborn: Unification, the Soviet Collapse, and the New Europe*, pp. 113–14 and 225.
57. J. A. Baker and E. A. Shevardnadze (West Berlin, memcon), 22 July 1990, pp. 4–5 and 12–14: National Security Archive, Soviet Flashpoints, box 38.
58. Record of conversation between M. S. Gorbachëv and H. Kohl, 7 September 1990: *Mikhail Gorbachëv i germanskii vopros*, pp. 555–6.

59. Record of conversation between M. S. Gorbachëv and H. Kohl, 10 September 1990: *ibid.*, p. 565.
60. Record of conversation between M. S. Gorbachëv and R. von Weizsäcker, 9 November 1990: *ibid.*, p. 597.
61. Record of conversation between M. S. Gorbachëv and T. Waigel, 10 November 1990: *ibid.*, p. 622.
62. A. G. Kovalëv (interview), HIGFC (HIA), box 2, folder 6, p. 36.
63. Politburo vote, 4 April 1990: Dmitri A. Volkogonov Papers (HIA), reel 1.
64. Coded telegram to Soviet embassy, 16 October 1990: *ibid.*

39: The Baltic Triangle

1. J. Attali, *Verbatim*, vol. 3: *Chronique des années 1988–1991*, p. 275 (conversation between F. Mitterrand and M. S. Gorbachëv, 5 July 1989).
2. Politburo meeting, 23 February 1987: *V Politbyuro TsK KPSS. Po zapisyam Anatoliya Chernyaeva, Vadima Medvedeva, Georgiya Shakhnazarova, 1985–1991*, pp. 127–9.
3. Politburo meeting, 23 February 1987, p. 152: Anatoli Chernyaev Papers (RESCA), box 1.
4. T. G. Stepanov-Mamaladze diary, 15 and 23 December 1986: T. G. Stepanov-Mamaladze Papers (HIA), box 5.
5. E. Shevardnadze, *Kogda rukhnul zheleznyi zanaves: vstrechi i vospominaniya*, p. 199.
6. T. G. Stepanov-Mamaladze working notes, 26 April 1988: T. G. Stepanov-Mamaladze Papers (HIA), box 2, folder 7; T. G. Stepanov-Mamaladze diary, 28 April 1988: *ibid.*, box 5; T. G. Stepanov-Mamaladze, 'K besede s nemtsami iz Nut'ingena' (retrospective notes: n.d.), p. 1: *ibid.*, box 2.
7. V. Bakatin, *Izbavlenie ot KGB*, p. 45.
8. Survey of operational information of the Lithuanian SSR KGB, 22 April 1987 (p. 2): Lithuanian SSR KGB (HIA), K-1/10/712.
9. Survey of operational information of the Lithuanian SSR KGB, 6 March 1987 (pp. 1–6): *ibid.*
10. Survey of operational information of the Lithuanian SSR KGB, 10 June 1987 (pp. 2–3): *ibid.*
11. V. Landsbergis, *Lithuania Independent Again: The Autobiography of Vytautas Landsbergis*, pp. 113–14.
12. F. D. Bobkov (interview), HIGFC (HIA), box 1, folder 6, p. 28.
13. *Ibid.*, p. 28 and 32.
14. A. N. Yakovlev, theses for speech at the Politburo, 18 August 1988: *Aleksandr Yakovlev. Perestroika, 1985–1991. Neizdannoe, maloizvestnoe, zabytoe*, pp. 218–22.
15. *Ibid.*, pp. 221 and 223.
16. Politburo meeting, 24 January 1989: Anatoli Chernyaev Papers (RESCA),

box 1, p. 6; Politburo meeting, 24 January 1989: *V Politbyuro TsK KPSS*, p. 376.

17. Draft policy document (signed by V. A. Medvedev, Yu. D. Maslyukov, N. Slyunkov, A. N. Yakovlev, A. I. Lukyanov and G. Razumovski), 1 February 1990, pp. 1–5: Dmitri A. Volkogonov Papers (HIA), reel 1.

18. 'Zapis' besedy A. N. Yakovleva s poslom SShA v SSSR Dzh. Metlokom', 30 March 1990: *Aleksandr Yakovlev. Perestroika*, pp. 437–42.

19. J. A. Baker and G. H. Bush, 20 March 1990 (memo), section 2, p. 3: US Department of State FOIA Documents.

20. T. G. Stepanov-Mamaladze working notes, 5 April 1990: T. G. Stepanov-Mamaladze Papers (HIA), box 3.

21. Politburo meeting, 11 May 1989: Anatoli Chernyaev Papers (RESCA), box 1, pp. 62–3.

22. *Ibid.*, p. 64.

23. *Ibid.*, p. 65.

24. *Ibid.*

25. Politburo meeting, 14 July 1989: *V Politbyuro TsK KPSS*, pp. 427–8.

26. Politburo meeting, 14 July 1989: Anatoli Chernyaev Papers (RESCA), box 1, pp. 73–4.

27. *Ibid.*, 75–6.

28. *Ibid.*, pp. 78–9.

29. *Ibid.*, p. 82.

30. Central Committee plenum, 19 September 1989: RGASPI, f. 3, op. 5, d. 295, pp. 31–2.

31. Politburo meeting, 9 November 1989: Anatoli Chernyaev Papers (RESCA), box 1, p. 99.

32. *Ibid.*, p. 100.

33. T. G. Stepanov-Mamaladze working notes, 19 November 1989: T. G. Stepanov-Mamaladze Papers (HIA), box 2.

34. *Ibid.*, 18 November 1989.

35. One-on-one conversation between G. H. Bush and M. S. Gorbachëv (Malta), 3 October 1989: *Otvechaya na vyzov vremeni: Vneshnyaya politika perestroiki: Dokumental'nye svidetel'stva*, pp. 248–9.

36. Central Committee plenum, 25 December 1989: RGASPI, f. 3, op. 5, d. 374, pp. 194–5.

37. M. S. Gorbachëv, speech in the House of Culture (Vilnius), 11 January 1990: M. S. Gorbachëv, *Sobranie sochinenii*, vol. 18, pp. 73–85.

38. T. G. Stepanov-Mamaladze diary, 12 January 1990: T. G. Stepanov-Mamaladze Papers (HIA), box 5.

39. *Ibid.*, 16 January 1990.

40. Politburo meeting, 13 February 1990: Anatoli Chernyaev Papers (RESCA), box 1b, p. 48.

41. Politburo meeting, 22 March 1990: *ibid.*, pp. 59–60.

42. *Ibid.*, p. 60.

43. *Ibid.*, pp. 60–1.

44. 'Ukazaniya dlya besedy ministra inostrannykh del SSSR s Prezidentom SShA Dzh. Bushem (Vashington, 6 aprelya 1990 goda)', pp. 2–46: RGASPI, f. 89, op. 9, d. 100.

45. T. G. Stepanov-Mamaladze diary, 6 April 1990: T. G. Stepanov-Mamaladze Papers (HIA), box 5.

46. J. A. Baker to G. H. Bush, 9 May 1990, memo: US Department of State FOIA Documents.

47. T. G. Stepanov-Mamaladze working notes, 6 April 1990: T. G. Stepanov-Mamaladze Papers (HIA), box 3.

48. *Ibid.*

49. R. Braithwaite, 'Moscow Diary', 10 April 1990.

50. Attali, *Verbatim*, vol. 3, pp. 469–70 (19 April 1990).

51. G. H. W. Bush to M. S. Gorbachëv, 29 April 1990: G. Bush, *All the Best, George Bush: My Life in Letters and Other Writings*, p. 468.

52. Conversation between M. S. Gorbachëv and J. A. Baker (Moscow), 18 May 1990: *Otvechaya na vyzov vremeni*, p. 259.

53. Braithwaite, 'Moscow Diary', 18 May 1990.

54. Conversation between G. H. W. Bush and M. S. Gorbachëv (Washington), 31 May 1990: *Otvechaya na vyzov vremeni*, p. 263.

55. I. Korchilov, *Translating History: Thirty Years on the Front Lines of Diplomacy with a Top Russian Interpreter*, p. 263.

56. *Ibid.*, p. 255.

57. *New York Times*, 6 June 1990.

58. Meeting of J. A. Baker and E. A. Shevardnadze (West Berlin, memcon), 22 July 1990, pp. 4–5 and 12–14: National Security Archive, Soviet Flashpoints, box 38.

59. Shevardnadze, *Kogda rukhnul zheleznyi zanaves*, p. 182.

60. A. N. Yakovlev, Question-and-answer session at the XXVIII Party Congress, 7 July 1990: *Aleksandr Yakovlev. Perestroika*, p. 511.

40: The Third Man Breaks Loose

1. A. Chernyaev, *Sovmestnyi iskhod. Dnevnik dvukh epokh. 1971–1991 gody*, p. 872 (13 September 1990).

2. *Ibid.*

3. Meeting of A. A. Obukhov and J. Matlock, 3 September 1990: Vitalii Leonidovich Kataev Papers (HIA), box 4, folder 48.

4. Message from official to E. A. Shevardnadze, 19 September 1990: *ibid.*, box 4, folder 49.

5. Helsinki Summit, 9 September 1990: *Otvechaya na vyzov vremeni: Vneshnyaya politika perestroiki: Dokumental'nye svidetel'stva*, p. 726.

6. Conversation between M. S. Gorbachëv and G. H. W. Bush, 9 September 1990: Gorbachëv Foundation Archive, fond 1, op. 1, reproduced in P. Stroilov,

Behind the Desert Storm, p. 149; B. Scowcroft in G. Bush and B. Scowcroft, *A World Transformed*, p. 364.

7. Helsinki summit transcript (Soviet), 9 September 1990: Gorbachëv Foundation Archive, fond 1, op. 1, reproduced in Stroilov, *Behind the Desert Storm*, p. 182.

8. *Ibid.*, pp. 184–6.

9. T. G. Stepanov-Mamaladze diary, 28 April 1988: T. G. Stepanov-Mamaladze Papers (HIA), box 5.

10. T. G. Stepanov-Mamaladze working notes, 1 February 1990: *ibid.*, box 3.

11. *Ibid.*

12. *Ibid.*, 22 March 1990.

13. T. G. Stepanov-Mamaladze diary, 5–9 February 1990: *ibid.*, box 5.

14. *Ibid.*, 23 June 1989.

15. T. G. Stepanov-Mamaladze working notes, 1 June 1990 : *ibid.*, box 3.

16. T. G. Stepanov-Mamaladze diary, 30 June 1988: *ibid.*, box 5.

17. *Ibid.*, 28 December 1989.

18. T. G. Stepanov (interview), HIGFC (HIA), box 3, folder 1, p. 38.

19. T. G. Stepanov-Mamaladze diary, 28 December 1989: T. G. Stepanov-Mamaladze Papers (HIA), box 5.

20. *Ibid.*, 25 December 1989; S. P. Tarasenko (interview), HIGFC (HIA), box 3, folder 2, p. 57.

21. A. G. Kovalëv (interview), *ibid.*, box 2, folder 6, p. 38; S. P. Tarasenko (interview), *ibid.*, box 3, folder 2, pp. 58 and 99–100.

22. A. G. Kovalëv (interview), *ibid.*, box 2, folder 6, p. 39; S. P. Tarasenko (interview), *ibid.*, box 3, folder 2, pp. 58 and 99–100.

23. T. G. Stepanov-Mamaladze diary, 28 December 1989: T. G. Stepanov-Mamaladze Papers (HIA), box 5.

24. *Ibid.*, 30 December 1989.

25. *Ibid.*, 1 February 1990. The Russian phrase is: 'Radi etogo stoilo by eshchë pozhit.'

26. 'O nekotorykh aspektakh polozheniya del na peregovorakh po sokrashcheniyu vooruzhenii', 23 March 1990 (n.a.), pp. 1–5: Vitalii Leonidovich Kataev Papers (HIA), box 13, folder 28.

27. G. M. Kornienko in S. F. Akhromeev and G. M. Kornienko, *Glazami marshala i diplomata*, p. 255.

28. *Ibid.*, p. 256.

29. 'O nekotorykh aspektakh polozheniya del na peregovorakh po sokrashcheniyu vooruzhenii', 23 March 1990 (n.a.), pp. 1–5: Vitalii Leonidovich Kataev Papers (HIA), box 13, folder 28.

30. V. Kryuchkov, *Lichnoe delo*, vol. 1, pp. 296–8 and 301.

31. R. Braithwaite, 'Moscow Diary', 4 January 1989.

32. T. G. Stepanov-Mamaladze diary, 1 February 1990: T. G. Stepanov-Mamaladze Papers (HIA), box 5.

33. *Ibid.*, 5–9 February 1990.

34. T. G. Stepanov-Mamaladze working notes, 27 February 1990: T. G. Stepanov-Mamaladze Papers (HIA), box 3.

35. A. L. Adamishin Papers (HIA), box 1: Diaries 1990, March 1990.

36. Lt. Gen. A. F. Katusev, 'Proshu opublikovat', *Sovetskaya Rossiya*, 25 March 1990; Col. Gen. I. Rodionov, 'Lish' polnaya pravda mozhet ubedit', *Literaturnaya Rossiya*, 20 April 1990; T. G. Stepanov-Mamaladze diary, 17–25 April 1990: T. G. Stepanov-Mamaladze Papers (HIA), box 5.

37. T. G. Stepanov-Mamaladze working notes, 13 April 1990: T. G. Stepanov-Mamaladze Papers (HIA), box 3.

38. A. S. Chernyaev (interview), HIGFC (HIA), box 1, folder 16, p. 89.

39. In fact over a thousand out of 4,459 delegates rejected Defence Minister Yazov whereas only 872 spurned Shevardnadze: T. G. Stepanov-Mamaladze diary, 13 July 1990: T. G. Stepanov-Mamaladze Papers (HIA), box 5.

40. A. N. Yakovlev (interview), HIGFC (HIA), box 3, folder 4, p. 17.

41. T. G. Stepanov-Mamaladze diary, 12 January 1990: T. G. Stepanov-Mamaladze Papers (HIA), box 5.

42. T. G. Stepanov-Mamaladze working notes, 2 July 1990: *ibid.*, box 3.

43. A. S. Chernyaev (interview), HIGFC (HIA), box 1, folder 12, p. 90.

44. A. Yakovlev, *Omut pamyati*, p. 484.

45. T. G. Stepanov-Mamaladze working notes, 1 February 1990: T. G. Stepanov-Mamaladze Papers (HIA), box 3. The Russian phrase is: 'Ya absolyutno veryu v Shevardnadze.'

46. V. L. Kataev, 'Kartina kontsa 80-x', filed as 80–90, p. 3: Vitalii Leonidovich Kataev Papers (HIA), disk 3.

47. Chernyaev, *Sovmestnyi iskhod*, p. 802 (16 September 1989).

48. Braithwaite, 'Moscow Diary', 14 September 1990.

49. E. A. Shevardnadze to M. S. Gorbachëv, 18 September 1990, p. 5: Vitalii Leonidovich Kataev Papers (HIA), box 4, folder 50.

50. E. Shevardnadze, *Moi vybor: v zashchitu demokratii i svobody*, p. 20.

51. E. A. Shevardnadze to M. S. Gorbachëv, item 2 (October 1990?), pp. 6–8: Vitalii Leonidovich Kataev Papers (HIA), box 4, folder 53; T. G. Stepanov-Mamaladze working notes, 17 February 1991: T. G. Stepanov-Mamaladze Papers (HIA), box 3.

52. Chernyaev, *Sovmestnyi iskhod*, p. 883 (23 October 1990).

53. P. Cradock, *In Pursuit of British Interests Reflections on Foreign Policy under Margaret Thatcher and John Major*, p. 115.

54. S. P. Tarasenko (interview), HIGFC (HIA), box 3, folder 2, p. 80.

55. A. S. Chernyaev (interview), *ibid.*, box 1, folder 12, p. 88.

56. S. P. Tarasenko (interview), *ibid.*, box 3, folder 2, p. 58.

57. K. N. Brutents, *Nesbyvsheesya. Neravnodushnye zametki o perestroike*, p. 534.

58. S. P. Tarasenko (interview), HIGFC (HIA), box 3, folder 2, p. 81.

59. E. A. Shevardnadze to M. S. Gorbachëv (n.d.), 'Ob itogakh peregovorov v N'yu-Iorke, 22 sentyabrya – 5 oktyabrya 1990 goda', pp. 2–7 and 17: Vitalii Leonidovich Kataev Papers (HIA), box 4, folder 53.

60. See J. G. Wilson, *The Triumph of Improvisation: Gorbachev's Adaptability, Reagan's Engagement, and the End of the Cold War*, p. 191.
61. See A. Brown, *The Gorbachev Factor*, pp. 152–3.
62. See Wilson, *The Triumph of Improvisation*, p. 192.
63. Chernyaev, *Sovmestnyi iskhod*, p. 884 (31 October 1990).
64. Braithwaite, 'Moscow Diary', 4 December 1990; Y. Primakov, *Russian Cross-roads: Towards the New Millennium*, p. 48.
65. Meeting of M. S. Gorbachëv and S. Al-Feisal (Moscow), 27 November 1990: *Otvechaya na vyzov vremeni*, p. 740.

41: A New World Order?

1. Y. Primakov, *Russian Crossroads: Towards the New Millennium*, p. 51.
2. S. P. Tarasenko (interview), HIGFC (HIA), box 3, folder 2, p. 81.
3. T. G. Stepanov-Mamaladze diary, 19 October 1990: T. G. Stepanov-Mamaladze Papers (HIA), box 5.
4. J. Attali, *Verbatim*, vol. 3: *Chronique des années 1988–1991*, pp. 620–1 (conversation between F. Mitterrand and M. Gorbachëv, 30 October 1990).
5. S. P. Tarasenko (interview), HIGFC (HIA), box 3, folder 2, pp. 84–5.
6. *Ibid.*, pp. 84–6.
7. T. G. Stepanov (interview), *ibid.*, box 3, folder 1, p. 8.
8. A. S. Chernyaev (interview), *ibid.*, box 1, folder 12, p. 88.
9. T. G. Stepanov-Mamaladze working notes, 26 November 1990: T. G. Stepanov-Mamaladze Papers (HIA), box 3.
10. *Ibid.*, 27 November 1990.
11. E. Shevardnadze, *Kogda rukhnul zheleznyi zanaves: vstrechi i vospominaniya*, pp. 191–2; conversation between N. Shevardnadze and J. Braithwaite: R. Braithwaite, 'Moscow Diary', 10 September 1991.
12. T. G. Stepanov-Mamaladze working notes, 9 December 1990: T. G. Stepanov-Mamaladze Papers (HIA), box 3.
13. *Ibid.*, 23 November 1990.
14. *Ibid.*, 24 November 1990.
15. V. V. Bakatin (interview), HIGFC (HIA), box 1, p. 6.
16. *Ibid.*, p. 7.
17. A. Chernyaev, *Sovmestnyi iskhod. Dnevnik dvukh epokh. 1971–1991 gody*, p. 883 (23 October 1990).
18. T. G. Stepanov-Mamaladze working notes, 4 December 1990: T. G. Stepanov-Mamaladze Papers (HIA), box 3.
19. Attali, *Verbatim*, vol. 3, p. 657 (11 December 1990).
20. T. G. Stepanov-Mamaladze working notes, 12 December 1990: T. G. Stepanov-Mamaladze Papers (HIA), box 3.
21. *Ibid.*
22. Braithwaite, 'Moscow Diary', 14 December 1990.
23. Letter from Zh. A. Medvedev to the British authorities, 11 July 1991 about

information collected by Roy Medvedev from S. F. Akhromeev: Braithwaite, 'Moscow Diary', 18 July 1991.

24. T. G. Stepanov-Mamaladze working notes, 20 December 1990: T. G. Stepanov-Mamaladze Papers (HIA), box 3.

25. *Pravda*, 21 December 1990; Chernyaev, *Sovmestnyi iskhod*, p. 890 (19 December 1990).

26. *Pravda*, 21 December 1990.

27. T. G. Stepanov-Mamaladze working notes, 20 and 21 December 1990: T. G. Stepanov-Mamaladze Papers (HIA), box 3.

28. *Ibid.*, 21 December 1990.

29. *Ibid.*

30. *Ibid.*, 30 December 1990.

31. *Ibid.*, 2 January 1991.

32. Shevardnadze, *Kogda rukhnul zheleznyi zanaves*, pp. 191–2.

33. *Ibid.*, p. 193.

34. T. G. Stepanov-Mamaladze diary, 28 April 1988: T. G. Stepanov-Mamaladze Papers (HIA), box 5.

35. V. M. Falin (interview), HIGFC (HIA), box 1, folder 15, pp. 20–1.

36. S. P. Tarasenko (interview), *ibid.*, box 3, folder 2, pp. 59–60.

37. *New York Times*, 21 December 1990.

38. A. S. Chernyaev (interview), HIGFC (HIA), box 1, folder 16, p. 90.

39. T. G. Stepanov-Mamaladze working notes, 18 March 1991: T. G. Stepanov-Mamaladze Papers (HIA), box 3.

40. T. G. Stepanov-Mamaladze diary, 30 June 1988: *ibid.*, box 5.

41. Chernyaev, *Sovmestnyi iskhod*, p. 934 (31 March 1991).

42. V. M. Falin (interview), HIGFC (HIA), box 1, folder 15, pp. 20–1.

43. Chernyaev, *Sovmestnyi iskhod*, p. 912 (29 January 1991).

44. *Ibid.*, p. 921 (25 February 1991).

45. L. N. Zaikov, V. M. Kryuchkov, E. A. Shevardnadze, D. T. Yazov, O. D. Baklanov and I. S. Belousov to M. S. Gorbachëv (draft memo), December 1990: Vitalii Leonidovich Kataev Papers (HIA), disk 1, AKHROMEEV, pp. 1–2. I have no idea whether this memo went to Gorbachëv as drafted.

46. Soviet record of conversation between D. Logan and V. P. Karpov, 24 December 1990: *ibid.*, box 11, folder 12.

47. A. L. Adamishin Papers (HIA), box 2, folder 1: Diaries 1991, 17 February 1991.

48. Chernyaev, *Sovmestnyi iskhod*, p. 917 (15 January 1991).

49. E. Shevardnadze, *Moi vybor: v zashchitu demokratii i svobody*, p. 85.

50. E. A. Shevardnadze to J. A. Baker, January 1991: Vitalii Leonidovich Kataev Papers (HIA), box 4, folder 54; and record of conversation with J. Matlock, 1 February 1991: *ibid.*, folder 55.

51. Chernyaev, *Sovmestnyi iskhod*, p. 908 (18 January 1991).

42: Endings

1. L. V. Shebarshin, *Ruka Moskvy: Zapiski nachal'nika sovetskoi razvedki*, p. 274.
2. V. L. Kataev, 'Sovetskii voenno-promyshlennyi kompleks', p. 41: Vitalii Leonidovich Kataev Papers (HIA), box 16.
3. R. Braithwaite, 'Moscow Diary', 25 September 1991.
4. V. Landsbergis, *Lithuania Independent Again: The Autobiography of Vytautas Landsbergis*, pp. 259–60.
5. Protocol on the cessation of the Warsaw Pact's military agreements and the elimination of its organs and structures, 25 February 1991 (Soviet record): PHPCS.
6. See also M. Kramer, 'Gorbachev and the Demise of East European Communism', in S. Pons and F. Romero (eds), *Reinterpreting the End of the Cold War. Issues, Interpretations, Periodizations*, p. 194.
7. Braithwaite, 'Moscow Diary', 21 March 1991.
8. A. Chernyaev, *Sovmestnyi iskhod. Dnevnik dvukh epokh. 1971–1991 gody*, p. 928 (14 March 1991).
9. J. Major to M. S. Gorbachëv, 5 April 1991: Vitalii Leonidovich Kataev Papers (HIA), box 4, folder 57; Braithwaite, 'Moscow Diary', 5 April 1991.
10. *Ibid.*, 5 December 1991.
11. A. N. Yakovlev (interview), HIGFC (HIA), box 3, folder 4, pp. 11–12.
12. A. L. Adamishin Papers (HIA), box 2, folder 1: Diaries 1991, 14 March 1991.
13. *Ibid.*, 15 March 1991.
14. *Ibid.*, 14 March 1991.
15. G. K. Shakhnazarov, *S vozdyami i bez nikh*, p. 472.
16. Chernyaev, *Sovmestnyi iskhod*, p. 815 (29 October 1989).
17. 'Spravka' on the expected savings from the fulfilment of the strategic offensive weapons treaty, probably April 1991: Vitalii Leonidovich Kataev Papers (HIA), box 11, folder 33.
18. Braithwaite, 'Moscow Diary', 6 May 1991.
19. Security Council meeting, 18 May 1991: *V Politbyuro TsK KPSS. Po zapisyam Anatoliya Chernyaeva, Vadima Medvedeva, Georgiya Shakhnazarova, 1985–1991*, p. 573.
20. *Ibid.*, p. 574.
21. Landsbergis, *Lithuania Independent Again*, pp. 261–2.
22. *Ibid.*, pp. 263–4.
23. Telephone conversation of G. H. W. Bush and M. S. Gorbachëv, 11 May 1991, pp. 3–4: http://bushlibrary.tamu.edu/research/pdfs/memcons_telcons/1991-05-11--Gorbachev.pdf
24. G. H. W. Bush to M. S. Gorbachëv, 5 June 1991: Vitalii Leonidovich Kataev Papers (HIA), box 4, folder 58.
25. M. S. Gorbachëv to G. H. W. Bush, 13 June 1991: *ibid.*, box 4, folder 59.
26. V. A. Kryuchkov (interview), HIGFC (HIA), box 2, folder 7, pp. 47–8.

27. V. Kryuchkov, *Lichnoe delo*, vol. 2, pp. 389–92.
28. A. L. Adamishin Papers (HIA), box 2, folder 1: Diaries 1991, 26 June 1991; Braithwaite, 'Moscow Diary', 17 June 1991.
29. L. V. Shebarshin (interview), HIGFC (HIA), box 2, folder 19, p. 39.
30. Braithwaite, 'Moscow Diary', 6 June 1991.
31. V. Kryuchkov, *Lichnoe delo*, vol. 1, p. 261.
32. Presidential Council, 16 October 1990: Anatoli Chernyaev Papers (RESCA), box 1, p. 61.
33. V. L. Kataev, untitled memoir notes filed as PAZNOGL, p. 10: Vitalii Leonidovich Kataev Papers (HIA), disk 3.
34. V. M. Falin (interview), HIGFC (HIA), box 1, folder 15, p. 17.
35. Chernyaev, *Sovmestnyi iskhod*, p. 954 (23 June 1991).
36. *Ibid.*
37. Meeting of Gorbachëv and Rodric Braithwaite, 15 June 1991: *V Politbyuro TsK KPSS*, p. 579.
38. Braithwaite, 'Moscow Diary', 15 June 1991.
39. J. A. Baker, 'CFE: Foundation for Enduring European Security', statement before Senate Foreign Relations Committee, 11 July 1991, p. 1: Committee on the Present Danger, box 126, folder: CFE.
40. Gorbachëv and Bush 17 July 1991 (London): *V Politbyuro TsK KPSS*, pp. 594–6.
41. Braithwaite, 'Moscow Diary', 18 July 1991.
42. Chernyaev, *Sovmestnyi iskhod*, p. 966 (23 July 1991).
43. *Ibid.*, pp. 966–7.
44. B. Scowcroft, 'Bush Got It Right in the Soviet Union', *New York Times*, 18 August 1991.
45. G. Bush, *All the Best, George Bush: My Life in Letters and Other Writings*, p. 530.
46. Chernyaev, *Sovmestnyi iskhod*, p. 970.
47. G. I. Revenko (interview), HIGFC (HIA), box 2, folder 16, p. 33.
48. *Sovetskaya Rossiya*, 23 July 1991.
49. Chernyaev, *Sovmestnyi iskhod*, p. 971 (21 August 1991).
50. *Ibid.*, p. 975.
51. *Ibid.*, p. 972.
52. Bush, *All the Best, George Bush*, p. 533 (diary: 19 August 1991).
53. Interview with L. M. Zamyatin, *Kommersant*, 3 May 2005.
54. Chernyaev, *Sovmestnyi iskhod*, p. 982 (21 August 1991).
55. *Ibid.*
56. V. A. Medvedev, *V komande Gorbachëva. Vzglyad izvnutri*, p. 198.
57. Chernyaev, *Sovmestnyi iskhod*, p. 973 (21 August 1991).
58. *Ibid.*, p. 984 (21 August 1991).
59. S. Plokhy, *The Last Empire: The Final Days of the Soviet Empire*, p. 174.
60. T. G. Stepanov-Mamaladze working notes, 30 August 1991: T. G. Stepanov-Mamaladze Papers (HIA), box 3; E. Shevardnadze, *Kogda rukhnul zheleznyi zanaves: vstrechi i vospominaniya*, pp. 211–12.

61. A. Yakovlev, *Omut pamyati*, p. 469. Yakovlev did not specify that Gorbachëv made the offer at that meeting, but the balance of probability is that it was then and there.
62. Shevardnadze, *Kogda rukhnul zheleznyi zanaves*, pp. 211–12. On 30 November 1991, Shevardnadze was to ask Yeltsin whether he thought that Gorbachëv had been involved in the August coup. Apparently Yeltsin had replied: 'I don't exclude [the possibility].': T. G. Stepanov-Mamaladze working notes, 30 November 1991: T. G. Stepanov-Mamaladze Papers (HIA), box 3.
63. Shevardnadze, *Kogda rukhnul zheleznyi zanaves*, pp. 211–12.
64. G. Bush and B. Scowcroft, *A World Transformed*, p. 539.
65. *Washington Post*, 30 August 1991.
66. Bush and Scowcroft, *A World Transformed*, pp. 541–2.
67. G. H. W. Bush, Address to the Nation on Reducing United States and Soviet Nuclear Weapons, 27 September 1991: www.presidency.ucsb.edu/ws/?pid=20035
68. Bush and Scowcroft, *A World Transformed*, p. 546.
69. *Ibid.*, p. 547.
70. Braithwaite, 'Moscow Diary', 7 October 1991.
71. Chernyaev, *Sovmestnyi iskhod*, p. 1016 (3 November 1991).
72. V. L. Kataev, diary: 15 November 1991: Vitalii Leonidovich Kataev Papers (HIA), box 3, folder 5.

Index